D0056464

Webster's

COMPACT
RHYMING
DICTIONARY

A Merriam-Webster®

MERRIAM-WEBSTER INC.

Springfield, Massachusetts

A GENUINE MERRIAM-WEBSTER

The name *Webster* alone is no guarantee of excellence. It is used by a number of publishers and may serve mainly to mislead an unwary buyer.

A Merriam-Webster® is the registered trademark you should look for when you consider the purchase of dictionaries or other fine reference books. It carries the reputation of a company that has been publishing since 1831 and is your assurance of quality and authority.

Copyright © 1987 by Merriam-Webster Inc.

Philippines Copyright 1987 by Merriam-Webster Inc.

Library of Congress Cataloging in Publication
Main entry under title:

Webster's compact rhyming dictionary.

    1. English language—Rhyme—Dictionaries.
I. Merriam-Webster Inc. II. Title: Compact rhyming
dictionary.
PE1519.W43   1987   423′.1   86-33165
ISBN 0-87779-185-6

MADE IN THE UNITED STATES OF AMERICA

161718H/R999897

CONTENTS

PREFACE

Webster's Compact Rhyming Dictionary is a listing of words arranged into groups according to the way they rhyme. All of the words included in this book are drawn from *Webster's Ninth New Collegiate Dictionary,* and decisions about which words rhyme with which other words are based on pronunciations given in that dictionary. In selecting words for entry in this book, the editors have focused on words that are most likely to be used in poetry; highly technical or otherwise obscure words are generally not included. However, some words that are restricted in their usage (such as slang or archaic words) as well as many words that are likely to be unfamiliar to many users have been included. Thus, not every word listed in this book will be appropriate in every context. In a similar way, the editors have assigned words to rhyming groups only on the basis of pronunciations that are in standard and widespread use. However, many words in this book have more than one standard pronunciation, and these alternate pronunciations often produce alternate rhyming sounds, so some words may appear on more than one list. For this reason, not every word on every list will rhyme for every person. Users of this book who are uncertain about any aspect of the meaning, usage status, or pronunciation of any word listed here should consult the entry for that word in *Webster's Ninth New Collegiate Dictionary.*

The rhyming sound Words in this book are gathered into entries on the basis of their rhyming sound. The rhyming sound is the terminal part of the word, from the vowel sound in the last stressed syllable to the end of the word. In this

book, the rhyming sound may have one, two, or three syllables. One-syllable rhyming sounds are found in one-syllable
words and in words in which primary or secondary stress
falls on the final syllable. For example, *fox* \\'fäks\\, *delight*
\\di-'līt\\, *homespun* \\'hom-ˌspən\\, and *handlebar* \\'han-dᵊl-
ˌbär\\ all have one-syllable rhyming sounds. For *fox,* the
rhyming sound is \\äks\\, as in *boondocks* and *orthodox.* For
delight, it is \\īt\\, as in *fight* and *appetite.* For *homespun,* it
is \\ən\\, as in *gun* and *megaton.* For *handlebar,* it is \\är\\, as
in *car* and *ajar.*

Two-syllable rhyming sounds are found in words in which
the last syllable with primary or secondary stress is the next-
to-last syllable in the word (often called the penultimate syllable or penult). For example, *varnish* \\'vär-nish\\ and
maneuver \\mə-'nü-vər\\ have two-syllable rhyming sounds.
For *varnish,* the rhyming sound is \\är-nish\\, as in *garnish*
and *tarnish.* For *maneuver,* it is \\ü-vər\\, as in *louver* and
remover.

Three-syllable rhyming sounds are found in words in
which the last syllable with primary or secondary stress is the
syllable before the next-to-last syllable (often called the ante-
penultimate syllable or antepenult). For example, *mutable*
\\'müt-ə-bəl\\ and *frivolity* \\friv-'äl-ət-ē\\ have three-syllable
rhyming sounds. For *mutable,* the rhyming sound is \\üt-ə-
bəl\\, as in *suitable* and *inscrutable.* For *frivolity,* it is \\äl-ət-
ē\\, as in *jollity* and *equality.*

Using this book *Webster's Compact Rhyming Dictionary* is
designed to be used easily with a minimum of instruction. In
order to use this book successfully, the reader needs to understand the following four points:

1. All of the words in the book are gathered into main entries
   on the basis of their rhyming sounds.

2. All of the main entries in the book are arranged according to the way the rhyming sound is most often spelled. This spelling is the boldface form that begins each main entry.

3. All of the alternate spellings of the rhyming sound are entered in the book as cross-reference entries that direct the user to the appropriate main entry. The alternate spelling is the boldface form that begins each cross-reference entry.

4. All main entries and cross-reference entries, whether for one-, two-, or three-syllable rhyming sounds, are alphabetized by the boldface form in a single sequence.

To find a rhyme for a given word, then, you need to know only the spelling of the word and its rhyming sound. If, for instance, you wanted to find a word to rhyme with *deep*, you would look up *eep*, because that is the way the rhyming sound is spelled in your word. When you look up *eep*, you will find the following entry:

> **eep** \ēp\ beep, bleep, cheap,
> cheep, clepe, creep, deep,
> heap, jeep, keep, . . .

If the word you wanted to find a rhyme for had been *cheap*, you might have looked up *eap*, because that is how the rhyming sound is spelled in that word. If you had done so, you would have found the following cross-reference entry:

> **eap** \ēp\ see EEP

In some cases, for reasons that will be explained in more detail later in this Preface, you may find two entries for the same spelling. If, for instance, you wanted a rhyme for *give*,

and you looked up *ive,* you would have found the following
entries:

> ¹**ive** \īv\ chive, dive, drive,
>   five, gyve, hive, I've, jive,
>   . . .
> ²**ive** \iv\ give, live, sheave,
>   shiv, sieve, spiv, forgive,
>   . . .
> ³**ive** \ēv\ see ¹EAVE

In cases like this, you can look at the pronunciation given in
the entry. The rhyming sound in *give* is \iv\, and the pronunciation given at ²**ive** is \iv\; therefore, the entry ²**ive** is the
appropriate one.
   The following sections of this Preface discuss in detail the
major features of this book. A careful reading of these sections will ensure that the user gets the maximum benefit
from this book when seeking words that rhyme.

Main entries The bulk of this book is made up of main
entries. Main entries consist of three principal elements: an
entry form, a pronunciation, and a list of words that rhyme:

> **orum** \ōr-əm\ foram,
>   forum, jorum, quorum,
>   decorum, ad valorem,
>   cockalorum, indecorum,
>   variorum, pons asino-
>   rum, sanctum sanctorum,
>   schola cantorum

The entry form in this entry is **orum.** It represents the way
the rhyming sound is most often spelled in the words in this

list. When two or more spellings are used with virtually equal frequency, the editors have chosen one arbitrarily to be the entry form.

The rhyming sound itself is \ōr-əm\, and it is shown in the pronunciation that appears in reversed virgules following the entry form. In the pronunciation, the rhyming sound is represented through the use of pronunciation symbols. These symbols are listed and explained beginning on page xvi. The pronunciations include no stress marks; the reader is meant to understand that the first syllable in the pronunciation is the stressed syllable. The pronunciation is given for identification purposes only; that is, it is meant to help the user confirm that the entry includes the words with the desired rhyming sound. Each entry includes only one pronunciation even though there may be more than one way to pronounce the entry form. Users who wish to know the alternate ways to pronounce a word in the list can consult the entry for that word in *Webster's Ninth New Collegiate Dictionary*.

Following the pronunciation is the list of words that share the rhyming sound. The words are arranged by number of syllables: the words with the fewest syllables are listed first, followed by groups of words with successively more syllables. Within a group of words having the same number of syllables, words are arranged alphabetically. In the list in the sample entry shown above, *foram, forum, jorum,* and *quorum,* each with two syllables, come first. They are followed by *decorum,* with three syllables; *ad valorem, cockalorum, indecorum,* and *variorum,* with four syllables; and *pons asinorum, sanctum sactorum,* and *schola cantorum,* with five syllables.

Cross-reference entries The main entries in this book are supplemented by thousands of cross-reference entries. Like main entries, cross-reference entries have an entry form and a pronunciation, but in place of a list of rhyming words, cross-reference entries provide a note that directs users to a main entry where the list of rhyming words can be found. The following cross-reference entries, for instance, send users to the entry **orum** shown as a sample earlier:

> **oram** \ōr-əm\ see ORUM
> **orem** \ōr-əm\ see ORUM

The entry form in a cross-reference entry represents an alternate way in which a rhyming sound can be spelled. In the sample entries above, the cross-reference entries **oram** and **orem** have been included because the spellings *-oram* and *-orem* are represented by the words *foram* and *ad valorem,* respectively, in the list of rhyming words at the main entry **orum**. In this book, a cross-reference entry has been included for every spelling of a rhyming sound that is represented by one or more words in the list at a main entry.

The pronunciation in the cross-reference entry is that of the rhyming sound of the words in the main entry being referred to and matches the pronunciation shown at the main entry. The pronunciation is provided to help the user confirm that the cross-reference leads to a main entry that includes words with the desired rhyming sound. The entry that is being cross-referred to is shown in small capital letters.

Identification numbers In some cases, the same spelling may be used to represent more than one rhyme and will therefore be used as entry form for more than one entry.

> **¹age** \äj\ dodge, lodge, raj,
> stodge, barrage, corsage,
> dislodge, garage, hodge-

> podge, massage, swaraj,
> camouflage, espionage,
> counterespionage
>
> ²**age** \äzh\ plage, assuage,
> barrage, collage, corsage,
> dressage, frottage, gavage,
> lavage, massage, ménage,
> mirage, montage, mou-
> lage, . . .
>
> ³**age** \āj\ age, cage, gage,
> gauge, mage, page, rage,
> sage, stage, swage, wage,
> assuage, backstage,
> downstage
>
> ⁴**age** \āg\ see ¹EG
>
> ⁵**age** \āzh\ see ¹EIGE
>
> ⁶**age** \äg-ə\ see ¹AGA

In order to alert users whenever this situation occurs, identification numbers have been added to all identically spelled
entry forms. Identification numbers appear as small raised
numerals that precede the entry form. In order to assist read-
ers in following cross-references, identification numbers also
appear as part of the cross-reference when necessary.

> **aj** \äj\ see ¹AGE
> **iv** \iv\ see ²IVE

Inflected and derived forms In order to save space in this
book, most regular inflected forms of words have not been
included in the lists of rhymes. For example; there is no entry
eaks to cover words such as *beaks, cheeks, cliques,* and
antiques. In order to find a rhyme for these words, you need

to go to the entry for the base word (in this case ¹**eak** \ēk\) and look for words on the list that will take the inflection that creates the desired rhyming sound.

In some cases, both inflected and noninflected forms share the same rhyming sounds. For example, the uninflected forms *lox* and *paradox* share the same rhyming sound with the inflected forms *docks* and *socks*. In such cases, there is an entry for the rhyming sound, and all of the uninflected forms are listed. At the end of the list, an italicized note appears, telling the user that additional rhymes exist and directing the user to the entry where the base words can be found:

> **ox** \äks\ box, cox, fox,
> . . .—*also plurals and*
> *possessives of nouns and*
> *third singular presents of*
> *verbs listed at* ¹OCK

Notes such as this have been added whenever two or more rhyming words could be created by adding inflections to the base words at the other entry. If only one such rhyme could be created, it has simply been added to the list of words that rhyme with the inflected form.

The particular inflected forms that are covered by such notes are plurals and possessives of nouns, comparatives and superlatives of adjectives, and past tense and third person singular present tense forms of verbs. In addition, present participles of verbs are covered at entries where the spelling of the entry form (after the *-ing* ending has been removed and any elided *e* or doubled consonant taken into account) does not match the spelling of the entry form of the entry for the base words:

> **aining** \ā-niŋ\ veining,
>   complaining, sustaining,
>   . . .—*see also present par-*
>   *ticiples of verbs listed at*
>   [1]ANE

The treatment of words derived by adding a suffix to
another word is somewhat similar. There is no entry for a
rhyming sound if all of the words that would be on the list
are regular derived words formed by adding a suffix to words
drawn from another list. This treatment applies mostly to
adverbs ending in *-ly,* nouns ending in *-ness* or *-ment,* and
adjectives ending in *-less.* For instance, there is no entry for
arkly \ärk-lē\, because the only words on the list would be
darkly and *starkly,* and they are both formed by adding an
-ly ending to adjectives found at the entry **ark** \ärk\. If, however, any of the words on the list are not derived forms, a
complete list is entered. There is an entry [1]**eanly** \ēn-lē\, for
instance, because among the adverbs at the entry there is also
the adjective *queenly;* and, for the purposes of this book,
adjectives ending in *-ly* are not treated as regular derived
forms.

Editorial acknowledgements Like other Merriam-Webster®
publications, *Webster's Compact Rhyming Dictionary* is the
product of a collective effort. William A. Llewellyn, President, and Frederick C. Mish, Editorial Director, helped to
develop the plan for this book; and Thomas L. Coopee, Treasurer, devised the computer programs that made the creation
of this book possible. Editing of the text was the responsibility of Julie A. Collier and David B. Justice, Associate Editors.
Cross-reference of the book was done by Eileen M. Haraty,
Assistant Editor, with the assistance of Peter D. Haraty,

Assistant Editor, and Kelly L. Tierney, Editorial Assistant.
Data-entry work was accomplished by Georgette B. Boucher
and Barbara A. Winkler, under the supervision of Gloria J.
Afflitto, Head of the Typing Room. Clerical assistance was
provided by Ruth W. Gaines, Senior General Clerk; additional manuscript typing was done by Valerie L. Jackson.
Madeline L. Novak, Associate Editor, Eileen M. Haraty,
Peter D. Haraty, and Daniel J. Hopkins, Assistant Editors,
were responsible for proofreading. Overall project coordination was provided by John M. Morse, Manager of Editorial
Operations and Planning.

PRONUNCIATION SYMBOLS

ə ..... h**u**mdr**u**m, c**o**llide, **a**but

ᵊ ..... immediately preceding \l\ and \n\, as in batt**le**,
mitt**en**, and eat**en**; immediately following \l\,
\m\, \r\, as often in French tab**le**, pris**me**, tit**re**

ər ..... furth**er**, m**er**ger, b**ir**d

a ..... m**a**t, m**a**p, m**a**d, g**a**g, sn**a**p, p**a**tch

ā ..... d**ay**, f**a**de, d**a**te, **ao**rta, dr**a**pe, c**a**pe

ä ..... b**o**ther, c**o**t

au̇ ..... n**ow**, l**ou**d, **ou**t

b ..... **b**a**b**y, ri**b**

ch ..... **ch**in, nature \'nā-chər\ (actually, this sound is
\t\ + \sh\)

d ..... **d**i**d**, a**dd**er

e ..... b**e**t, b**e**d, p**e**ck

ē ..... b**ea**t, nosebl**ee**d, **ea**sy

f ..... **f**i**f**ty, cu**ff**

g ..... **g**o, bi**g**, **g**ift

h ..... **h**at, a**h**ead

i ..... t**i**p, ban**i**sh, act**i**ve

ī ..... site, side, buy, tripe (actually, this sound is \ä\ + \i\)

j ..... job, gem, edge, join, judge (actually, this sound is \d\ + \zh\)

k ..... kin, cook, ache

k̲ ..... German ich, Buch; one pronunciation of loch

l ..... lily, pool

m ..... murmur, dim, nymph

n ..... no, own

ⁿ ..... indicates that a preceding vowel or diphthong is pronounced with the nasal passages open, as in French *un bon vin blanc* \œⁿ-bōⁿ-vaⁿ-bläⁿ\

ŋ ..... sing \'siŋ\, singer \'siŋ-ər\, finger \'fiŋ-gər\, ink \'iŋk\

ō ..... bone, know, beau

o̊ ..... saw, all, gnaw, caught

o̊i ..... coin, destroy

p ..... pepper, lip

r ..... red, car, rarity

s ..... source, less

sh ..... as in shy, mission, machine, special (actually, this is a single sound, not two); with a hyphen between, two sounds as in *grasshopper* \'gras-ˌhäp-ər\

t . . . . . tie, attack, late, later, latter

th . . . . . as in thin, ether (actually, this is a single sound, not two); with a hyphen between, two sounds as in *knighthood* \\'nīt-ˌhůd\\

<u>th</u> . . . . . then, either, this (actually, this is a single sound, not two)

ü . . . . . rule, youth, union \\'yün-yən\\, few \\'fyü\\

ů . . . . . pull, wood, book, lurid, curable \\'kyůr-ə-bəl\\,

v . . . . . vivid, give

w . . . . . we, away

y . . . . . yard, young, cue \\'kyü\\, mute \\'myüt\\, union \\'yün-yən\\

z . . . . . zone, raise

zh . . . . . as in vision, azure \\'azhər\\ (actually, this is a single sound, not two); with a hyphen between, two sounds as in *hogshead* \\'hȯgz-ˌhed, 'hägz-\\

\\ . . . . . slant line used in pairs to mark the beginning and end of a transcription: \\'pen\\

ˈ . . . . . mark preceding a syllable with primary (strongest) stress: \\'pen-mən-ˌship\\

ˌ . . . . . mark preceding a syllable with secondary (medium) stress: \\'pen-mən-ˌship\\

- . . . . . mark of syllable division

a

¹**a** \ä\ aah, ah, baa, bah, blah,
bra, dah, droit, fa, Fra, ha,
Kwa, la, ma, na, nah, pa,
pas, qua, rah, schwa, shah,
spa, à bas, aba, aha, Allah,
blah-blah, bourgeois, brava,
Casbah, chamois, éclat, fa la,
faux pas, fellah, fetah, foie
gras, galah, grandma,
grandpa, ha-ha, halvah, hoo-
ha, hoopla, Hsia, hurrah,
huzzah, isba, Issa, markka,
mudra, opah, orgeat, pai-hua,
paisa, pasha, patois, pooh-
bah, prutah, pya, sangfroid,
selah, Shema, sola, supra,
tola, Valois, Vaudois, viva,
voilà, whoopla, abaca, agora,
ahimsa, aloha, assignat,
Aymara, baccarat, baklava,
brouhaha, cervelat,
Chippewa, coup d'état,
entrechat, feria, habdalah,
haftarah, koruna, la-di-da,
Libera, ma-and-pa, Malinois,
Mardi Gras, moussaka,
Omaha, Ottawa, padishah,
panama, parashah, pas de
trois, persona, picara, pietà,
podesta, polenta, polynya,
port de bras, Quebecois,
reseda, Shangri-la, tempura,
ulema, usquebaugh,
ayatollah, Baha' Allah,
caracara, con anima, coureur
de bois, hispanidad, hors de
combat, je ne sais quoi,
ménage à trois, res publica,
sursum corda, tamandua,
Katharevusa, mousseline de
soie, pâté de foie gras,
exempli gratia

²**a** \ā\ see ¹AY

³**a** \ȯ\ see ¹AW

aa \a\ see ³AH

¹**aal** \äl\ see AIL

²**aal** \ȯl\ see ALL

aam \äm\ see ¹OM

aan \an\ see ⁵AN

¹**aans** \äns\ see ²ANCE

²**aans** \änz\ see ONZE

aaron \ar-ən\ see ²ARON

¹**ab** \äb\ see ¹OB

²**ab** \äv\ see ²OLVE

³**ab** \ab\ blab, cab, crab, dab,
drab, flab, gab, grab, jab,
lab, Mab, nab, scab, slab,
stab, tab, baobab, Cantab,
confab, prefab, Rajab, rehab,
smack-dab, astrolabe,
pedicab, taxicab

aba \äb-ə\ Kaaba, casaba,
djellaba, indaba, Ali Baba,
jaboticaba

abala \ab-ə-lə\ cabala, parabola

abalist \ab-ə-ləst\ cabalist,
  diabolist

abard \ab-ərd\ clapboard,
  scabbard, tabard—*also pasts
  of verbs listed at* ²ABBER

abatis \ab-ət-əs\ abatis, habitus

abbard \ab-ərd\ see ABARD

abbas \ab-əs\ see ABBESS

abbat \ab-ət\ see ABIT

abbed \ab-əd\ crabbed, rabid

¹**abber** \äb-ər\ see OBBER

²**abber** \ab-ər\ blabber, clabber,
  crabber, dabber, drabber,
  gabber, grabber, jabber,
  slabber, stabber, yabber,
  rehabber, bonnyclabber

abbess \ab-əs\ abbess, Barabbas

abbet \ab-ət\ see ABIT

abbey \ab-ē\ see ABBY

abbie \äb-ē\ see OBBY

abbin \ab-ən\ see ABIN

abbit \ab-ət\ see ABIT

abbitry \ab-ə-trē\ see ABBITTRY

abbitt \ab-ət\ see ABIT

abbittry \ab-ə-trē\ Babbittry,
  rabbitry

¹**abble** \äb-əl\ bauble, bobble,
  cobble, gobble, hobble,
  nobble, obol, squabble,
  wabble, wobble

²**abble** \ab-əl\ Babel, babble,
  brabble, dabble, drabble,
  gabble, grabble, habile,
  rabble, scrabble, bedabble,
  hardscrabble

abblement \ab-əl-mənt\
  babblement, rabblement

abbler \ab-lər\ babbler,
  dabbler, gabbler, grabbler,
  rabbler, scrabbler

abbly \ab-lē\ see ABLY

abbot \ab-ət\ see ABIT

abby \ab-ē\ abbey, blabby,
  cabbie, crabby, flabby,
  gabby, grabby, scabby,
  shabby, tabby, kohlrabi,
  Panjabi, Punjabi

¹**abe** \āb\ babe, mabe, nabe,
  astrolabe

²**abe** \ab\ see AB

abel \ā-bəl\ see ABLE

aben \äb-ən\ see OBIN

¹**aber** \ā-bər\ see ABOR

²**aber** \äb-ər\ see OBBER

abes \ā-bēz\ see ABIES

¹**abi** \äb-ē\ see OBBY

²**abi** \əb-ē\ see UBBY

³**abi** \ab-ē\ see ABBY

abian \ā-bē-ən\ Fabian, gabion

abid \ab-əd\ see ABBED

abies \ā-bēz\ rabies, scabies,
  tabes—*also plurals and
  possessives of nouns listed at*
  ABY

abile \ab-əl\ see ²ABBLE

abilis \äb-ə-ləs\ obelus, annus
  mirabilis

abin \ab-ən\ cabin, rabbin

abion \ā-bē-ən\ see ABIAN

abit \ab-ət\ abbot, babbitt,
  Babbitt, habit, rabbet, rabbit,

rebate, sabbat, cohabit, inhabit, jackrabbit

abitant \ ab-ət-ənt \ cohabitant, inhabitant

abitus \ ab-ət-əs \ see ABATIS

able \ ā-bəl \ Abel, able, Babel, cable, fable, Froebel, gable, label, sable, stable, table, disable, enable, instable, retable, round table, timetable, turntable, unable, unstable, worktable

abled \ ā-bəld \ fabled, gabled— *also pasts of verbs listed at* ABLE

ablis \ ab-lē \ see ABLY

ably \ ab-lē \ chablis, drably, scrabbly

abo \ ab-ō \ abo, sabot

abola \ ab-ə-lə \ see ABALA

abolist \ ab-ə-ləst \ see ABALIST

abor \ ā-bər \ caber, labor, neighbor, saber, tabor, belabor, zeitgeber

aborer \ ā-bər-ər \ laborer, taborer

abot \ ab-ō \ see ABO

¹abra \ äb-rə \ sabra, candelabra

²abra \ ab-rə \ candelabra, abracadabra

abre \ äb \ see ¹OB

abular \ ab-yə-lər \ fabular, tabular, vocabular, acetabular

abulous \ ab-yə-ləs \ fabulous, fantabulous

abulum \ ab-yə-ləm \ pabulum, acetabulum, incunabulum

aby \ ā-bē \ baby, gaby, maybe, crybaby, grandbaby

ac \ ak \ see ²ACK

¹aca \ äk-ə \ see ¹AKA

²aca \ ak-ə \ paca, alpaca, malacca, sifaka, tobacco, portulaca

acable \ ak-ə-bəl \ see ACKABLE

acao \ ō-kō \ see OCO

acas \ ak-əs \ Bacchus, fracas

acca \ ak-ə \ see ACA

accent \ ak-sənt \ accent, relaxant

acchanal \ ak-ən-ᵊl \ see ACONAL

acchic \ ak-ik \ bacchic, halakic, stomachic, tribrachic, amphibrachic

acchus \ ak-əs \ see ACAS

accid \ as-əd \ see ACID

accio \ äch-ō \ see ACHO

¹acco \ ak-ə \ see ACA

²acco \ ak-ō \ see ²AKO

acculus \ ak-yə-ləs \ sacculus, miraculous

¹ace \ ās \ ace, base, bass, beth, brace, case, chase, dace, face, grace, lace, mace, Mace, pace, place, plaice, prase, race, res, space, teth, trace, vase, abase, airspace, ambsace, apace, backspace, biface, birthplace, blackface, boldface, bookcase, bootlace, braincase, briefcase,

crankcase, debase, deface,
disgrace, displace, dogface,
doughface, efface, embrace,
emplace, encase, enchase,
enlace, erase, fireplace,
footpace, footrace, foreface,
grimace, half-space, hard
case, headspace, lightface,
manes, millrace, milreis,
misplace, notecase, null-
space, outface, outpace,
outrace, paleface, plebes,
postface, replace, retrace,
scapegrace, shoelace,
showcase, showplace,
slipcase, smearcase,
someplace, staircase, subbase,
subspace, suitcase, surbase,
tailrace, tenace, typeface,
ukase, unbrace, unlace,
watchcase, wheelbase, whey-
face, whiteface, workplace,
about-face, aerospace,
anyplace, boniface,
bouillabaisse, carapace,
commonplace, contrabass,
double-space, everyplace,
interface, interlace, lemures,
lowercase, marketplace,
pillowcase, single-space,
steeplechase, thoroughbass,
thoroughbrace, triple-space,
uppercase, rarae aves, in
medias res, litterae
humaniores

²**ace** \ā-sē\ see ACY

³**ace** \äs\ see ¹OS

⁴**ace** \as\ see ³ASS

⁵**ace** \äch-ē\ see OTCHY

⁶**ace** \äs-ə\ see ¹ASA

aceable \ā-sə-bəl\ placeable,
traceable, displaceable,
effaceable, embraceable,
erasable, persuasible,
replaceable, ineffaceable,
irreplaceable

acean \ā-shən\ see ¹ATION

aced \āst\ based, baste, chaste,
geest, haste, laced, mayest,
paste, taste, waist, waste,
bald-faced, barefaced, bold-
faced, distaste, dough-faced,
foretaste, impaste, lambaste,
lightfaced, pie-faced, po-
faced, posthaste, self-paced,
shamefaced, shirtwaist, snail-
paced, slipcased, straight-
faced, straitlaced, toothpaste,
two-faced, unchaste, white-
faced, aftertaste, brazen-
faced, double-faced, Janus-
faced, hatchet-faced,
pantywaist, poker-faced,
thorough-paced—*also pasts of
verbs listed at* ¹ACE

aceless \ā-sləs\ baseless,
faceless, graceless, laceless,
placeless, spaceless, traceless

aceman \ā-smən\ baseman,
placeman, spaceman

acement \ā-smənt\ basement,
casement, placement,

abasement, debasement, defacement, displacement, effacement, embracement, emplacement, encasement, enlacement, misplacement, outplacement, replacement, self-effacement

acence \ās-ᵊns\ see ¹ASCENCE

acency \ās-ᵊn-sē\ adjacency, complacency, subjacency

acent \ās-ᵊnt\ nascent, adjacent, complacent, complaisant, subjacent, circumjacent, superjacent

aceor \ā-sər\ see ¹ACER

aceous \ā-shəs\ see ACIOUS

¹**acer** \ā-sər\ baser, bracer, chaser, facer, pacer, placer, racer, spacer, tracer, defacer, disgracer, effacer, embraceor, embracer, eraser, replacer, subchaser, steeplechaser

²**acer** \as-ər\ see ASSER

acery \ās-rē\ tracery, embracery

¹**acet** \ā-sət\ hic jacet, non placet

²**acet** \as-ət\ asset, facet, tacet, tacit

acey \ā-sē\ see ACY

¹**ach** \äk̲\ saugh, Pesach, pibroch

²**ach** \äk\ see ¹OCK

³**ach** \ak\ see ²ACK

⁴**ach** \ach\ see ⁴ATCH

acha \äch-ə\ cha-cha, dacha, kwacha, viscacha

¹**ache** \āk\ see ¹AKE

²**ache** \ash\ see ³ASH

³**ache** \äch-ē\ see OTCHY

⁴**ache** \ach-ē\ see ATCHY

ached \acht\ attached, detached, unattached, semidetached— *also pasts of verbs listed at* ⁴ATCH

acher \ā-kər\ see ¹AKER

achet \ach-ət\ see ATCHET

achi \äch-ē\ see OTCHY

achian \ā-shən\ see ¹ATION

achic \ak-ik\ see ACCHIC

aching \ā-kiŋ\ see ¹AKING

achio \ash-ō\ mustachio, pistachio

achm \am\ see ²AM

achment \ach-mənt\ see ATCHMENT

acho \äch-ō\ muchacho, quebracho, bocaccio, carpaccio

achou \ash-ü\ see ASHEW

acht \ät\ see ¹OT

achtsman \ät-smən\ see OTSMAN

achy \ā-kē\ see AKY

acia \ā-shə\ fascia, geisha, acacia, ex gratia, prima facie, exempli gratia

acial \ā-shəl\ facial, glacial, racial, spatial, abbatial, bifacial, biracial, englacial, palatial, primatial, subglacial, interfacial, interglacial, interracial

acian \ ā-shən \ see ¹ATION

acias \ ā-shəs \ see ACIOUS

acid \ as-əd \ acid, Chasid, flaccid, Hasid, jassid, placid, Abbasid, antacid

acie \ ā-shə \ see ACIA

acient \ ā-shənt \ see ATIENT

¹acier \ ā-shər \ see ¹ASURE

²acier \ ā-zhər \ see AZIER

acile \ as-əl \ see ²ASSEL

acing \ ā-siŋ \ bracing, casing, facing, lacing, racing, spacing, tracing, catfacing, effacing, all-embracing, letterspacing, self-effacing

acious \ ā-shəs \ gracious, spacious, audacious, bodacious, capacious, ceraceous, cretaceous, crustaceous, curvaceous, edacious, fallacious, flirtatious, fugacious, herbaceous, Horatius, loquacious, mendacious, mordacious, pomaceous, predaceous, pugnacious, rapacious, sagacious, salacious, sebaceous, sequacious, setaceous, tenacious, testaceous, ungracious, veracious, vexacious, vinaceous, vivacious, voracious, alliaceous, arenaceous, argillaceous, carbonaceous, contumacious, coriaceous, disputatious, efficacious, farinaceous, foliaceous, ostentatious, pectinaceous, perspicacious, pertinacious, saponaceous, scire facias, stercoraceous, violaceous, inefficacious, fieri facias

acis \ as-ē \ see ASSY

acist \ ā-səst \ see ASSIST

acit \ as-ət \ see ²ACET

¹acity \ as-tē \ see ²ASTY

²acity \ as-ət-ē \ audacity, capacity, loquacity, mendacity, opacity, rapacity, sagacity, tenacity, veracity, vivacity, voracity, efficacity, incapacity, overcapacity

acive \ ā-siv \ see ASIVE

¹ack \ äk \ see ¹OCK

²ack \ ak \ back, black, clack, claque, crack, flack, flak, hack, jack, knack, lac, lack, mac, Mac, pack, plaque, quack, rack, sac, sack, sacque, shack, slack, slake, smack, snack, stack, tach, tack, thwack, track, Wac, whack, wrack, yak, aback, ack-ack, alack, amtrac, Anzac, attack, backpack, backtrack, bareback, blackjack, blue-black, bootblack, bootjack, brushback, bushwhack, callback, calpac, champac, cheapjack, Coalsack, coatrack, cognac, come back, comeback, cookshack, cossack, crackback, crookback, cut back, cutback, Dayak, dieback, draw back, drawback, fall back, fallback, fastback, fatback, feedback, finback, flapjack, flareback, flashback, fullback, gimcrack, graywacke, greenback, gripsack, guaiac, halfback, half-track, hardback, hardhack, hardtack, hatchback, hayrack, haystack, hijack, hogback, hold back, holdback, hopsack, horseback, humpback, hunchback, jam-pack, kayak, kickback, knapsack, knickknack, Kodak, kulak, kyack, laid-back, lampblack, linac, macaque, man jack, manpack, Micmac, mossback, muntjac, Muzak, notchback, offtrack, outback, packsack, payback, pitch-black, play back, playback, plow back, plowback, Polack, pullback, quillback, racetrack, ransack, rickrack, roll back, rollback, roorback, rucksack, runback, scatback, serac, set back, setback, shellac, shellback, shoeblack, shoepac, sidetrack, six-pack, skewback, skipjack, skyjack, slapjack, slotback,

Slovak, smokejack, smokestack, snap back, snapback, snowpack, softback, sumac, swayback, sweepback, swept-back, switchback, tailback, tarmac, thornback, throw back, throwback, thumbtack, ticktack, tieback, tie tack, tombac, touchback, tow sack, trictrac, tripack, unpack, Welsbach, wetback, whaleback, wingback, wisecrack, woolpack, woolsack, yashmak, Yurak, zwieback, almanac, amberjack, anorak, antiblack, applejack, Arawak, Armagnac, birdyback, bivouac, bric-a brac, camelback, canvasback, cardiac, carryback, celiac, coeliac, cornerback, Cousin Jack, crackerjack, cul-de-sac, diamondback, fiddleback, fishyback, gunnysack, hackmatack, haversack, high-low-jack, huckaback, hydrocrack, iliac, ipecac, ladder-back, leatherback, lumberjack, maniac, minitrack, nunatak, otomac, paperback, pickaback, piggyback, portapak, quarterback, razorback, retropack, sandarac, Sazerac,

single-track, snapper-back,
solonchak, steeplejack,
stickleback, supplejack,
Syriac, tamarack, theriac,
tokamak, turtleback, umiak,
zodiac, ammoniac, amnesiac,
biofeedback, celeriac,
counterattack, demoniac,
elegiac, insomniac, Monterey
Jack, paranoiac, simoniac,
tacamahac, aphrodisiac,
coprophiliac, Dionysiac,
dipsomaniac, egomaniac,
hemophiliac, hypochondriac,
intracardiac, kleptomaniac,
melancholiac, monomaniac,
mythomaniac, necrophiliac,
neophiliac, nymphomaniac,
pedophiliac, pyromaniac,
Rhodesian Ridgeback,
sacroiliac, sal ammoniac,
megalomaniac

ackable \ak-ə-bəl\ packable,
placable, stackable,
implacable

ackage \ak-ij\ package,
trackage, prepackage,
repackage

ackal \ak-əl\ see ACKLE

acked \akt\ see ACT

acken \ak-ən\ blacken, bracken,
flacon, slacken, Arawakan

acker \ak-ər\ backer, clacker,
cracker, hacker, jacker,
knacker, lacquer, packer,
sacker, slacker, smacker,
stacker, tacker, tracker,
whacker, attacker,
backpacker, bushwacker,
firecracker, hijacker, kayaker,
linebacker, nutcracker,
racetracker, ransacker,
safecracker, shellcracker,
skyjacker, unpacker,
wisecracker, simulacre,
counterattacker

ackerel \ak-rəl\ see ACRAL

ackery \ak-rē\ flackery,
quackery, gimcrackery

acket \ak-ət\ bracket, jacket,
packet, placket, racket,
bluejacket, straitjacket

ackey \ak-ē\ see ACKY

ackguard \ag-ərd\ see AGGARD

ackie \ak-ē\ see ACKY

acking \ak-iŋ\ backing,
blacking, cracking, packing,
sacking, smacking, tracking,
whacking, bushwacking,
kayaking, linebacking, nerve-
racking, safecracking,
skyjacking

ackish \ak-ish\ blackish,
brackish, quackish

ackle \ak-əl\ cackle, crackle,
grackle, hackle, jackal,
macle, rackle, shackle,
spackle, tackle, debacle,
ramshackle, unshackle,
tabernacle

ackly \ak-lē\ blackly, crackly,

hackly, abstractly, compactly, exactly, inexactly

ackman \ak-mən\ hackman, packman, trackman

ackney \ak-nē\ see ACNE

ackneyed \ak-nēd\ see ACNED

acko \ak-ō\ see ²AKO

acksman \ak-smən\ see AXMAN

acky \ak-ē\ hackie, khaki, lackey, tacky, wacky, ticky-tacky

¹acle \ik-əl\ see ICKLE

²acle \äk\ see ¹OCK

³acle \äk-əl\ see OCKLE

⁴acle \ak-əl\ see ACKLE

acne \ak-nē\ acne, hackney

acned \ak-nēd\ acned, hackneyed

aco \äk-ō\ see OCCO

¹acon \ā-kən\ see ¹AKEN

²acon \ak-ən\ see ACKEN

aconal \ak-ən-ᵊl\ bacchanal, diaconal, archidiaconal

acque \ak\ see ²ACK

acquer \ak-ər\ see ACKER

acral \ak-rəl\ mackerel, sacral

¹acre \ā-kər\ see ¹AKER

²acre \ak-ər\ see ACKER

acrum \ak-rəm\ sacrum, simulacrum

act \akt\ act, backed, bract, cracked, fact, packed, pact, stacked, tact, tracked, tract, abstract, attract, coact, compact, contact, contract, crookbacked, detract, didact, diffract, distract, enact, entr'acte, epact, exact, extract, half-tracked, humpbacked, hunchbacked, impact, infract, intact, mossbacked, playact, protract, react, redact, refract, subtract, swaybacked, transact, unbacked, abreact, artifact, cataract, chain-react, counteract, cross-react, inexact, interact, overact, paperbacked, razor-backed, reenact, subcompact, subcontract, underact, vacuum-packed, ventifact, autodidact, matter-of-fact, semiabstract, underreact—*also pasts of verbs listed at* ²ACK

actable \ak-tə-bəl\ actable, tractable, abstractable, attractable, compactible, contractible, distractable, extractable, intractable

actance \ak-təns\ attractance, reactance

actant \ak-tənt\ attractant, reactant, surfactant, interactant

¹acte \äkt\ see OCKED

²acte \akt\ see ACT

acted \ak-təd\ fracted, abstracted, impacted—*also pasts of verbs listed at* ACT

acter \ak-tər\ see ACTOR

actery\ak-trē\see ACTORY

actible\ak-tə-bəl\see ACTABLE

actic\ak-tik\lactic, tactic, climactic, didactic, galactic, syntactic, ataractic, chiropractic, parallactic, paratactic, prophylactic, anaphylactic, anticlimactic, autodidactic, extragalactic, intergalactic, intragalactic, stereotactic

actical\ak-ti-kəl\practical, tactical, didactical, impractical, syntactical

actice\ak-təs\cactus, practice, malpractice, cataractous

actics\ak-tiks\tactics, didactics, syntactics—*also plurals and possessives of nouns listed at* ACTIC

actile\ak-tᵊl\dactyl, tactile, contractile, protractile, refractile, retractile, polydactyl, pterodactyl

acting\ak-tiŋ\acting, exacting, self-acting

action\ak-shən\action, faction, fraction, taction, traction, abstraction, attraction, bolt-action, coaction, compaction, contraction, detraction, diffraction, distraction, exaction, extraction, impaction, inaction, infraction, olfaction, protraction, reaction,

redaction, refraction, retraction, subtraction, transaction, benefaction, counteraction, interaction, liquefaction, malefaction, overaction, petrifaction, putrefaction, rarefaction, retroaction, satisfaction, single-action, stupefaction, tumefaction, dissatisfaction, photoreaction, self-satisfaction

actional\ak-shnəl\factional, fractional, tractional, abstractional, contractional, redactional, transactional, interactional, rarefactional

actious\ak-shəs\factious, fractious

active\ak-tiv\active, tractive, abstractive, attractive, coactive, contractive, detractive, distractive, extractive, impactive, inactive, proactive, reactive, refractive, subtractive, counteractive, hyperactive, interactive, overactive, psychoactive, putrefactive, retroactive, unattractive, radioactive

actly\ak-lē\see ACKLY

actor\ak-tər\actor, factor, tractor, abstractor, attractor, cofactor, compactor, contractor, detractor, enactor, exactor, extractor, impactor,

infractor, protractor, reactor,
redactor, refractor, retractor,
subtracter, transactor,
benefactor, chiropractor,
malefactor, subcontractor

actory \ak-trē\ factory,
olfactory, phylactery,
refractory, calefactory,
manufactory, satisfactory,
dissatisfactory, unsatisfactory

actous \ak-təs\ see ACTICE

actress \ak-trəs\ actress,
benefactress

actual \ak-chəl\ actual, factual,
tactual, artifactual

acture \ak-chər\ facture,
fracture, contracture,
manufacture, remanufacture

actus \ak-təs\ see ACTICE

actyl \ak-tᵊl\ see ACTILE

acular \ak-yə-lər\ macular,
oracular, spectacular,
spiracular, tentacular,
vernacular, tabernacular

aculate \ak-yə-lət\ maculate,
ejaculate, immaculate

aculous \ak-yə-ləs\ see
  ACCULUS

acy \ā-sē\ lacy, pace, précis,
racy, spacey, prima facie

acyl \as-əl\ see ²ASSEL

¹ad \ä\ see ¹A

²ad \äd\ see ¹OD

³ad \ad\ ad, add, bad, bade,
brad, cad, chad, Chad, clad,
dad, fad, gad, Gad, glad,

grad, had, lad, mad, pad,
plaid, rad, sad, scad, shad,
tad, trad, aoudad, caudad,
comrade, crawdad, doodad,
dorsad, dryad, dyad, egad,
farad, footpad, forbade,
gonad, granddad, heptad,
hexad, horn-mad, ironclad,
keypad, launchpad, maenad,
monad, naiad, nomad,
notepad, pentad, pleiad,
Sindbad, tetrad, thinclad,
triad, triclad, armor-clad,
cephalad, chiliad, ennead,
Galahad, hebdomad, helipad,
laterad, mediad, oread,
overplaid, Pythiad,
bromeliad, hamadryad,
olympiad, seminomad,
Upanishad

¹ada \äd-ä\ Dada, Dhu'l-
Qa'dah, aficionada

²ada \äd-ə\ sadhe, tsade,
Agada, armada, Haggadah,
Jumada, panada, posada,
tostada, autostrada,
empanada, enchilada,
Theravada, aficionada,
cascara sagrada

³ada \ād-ə\ Veda, armada,
cicada, alameda

adable \ād-ə-bəl\ gradable,
tradable, wadable, abradable,
degradable, evadable,
persuadable, biodegradable

a'dah \äd-ä\ see ¹ADA

adah \ äd-ə \ see ²ADA

adal \ ad-ᵊl \ see ADDLE

adam \ ad-əm \ Adam, madam, macadam, tarmacadam

adant \ ād-ᵊnt \ cadent, abradant, decadent

add \ ad \ see ³AD

adden \ ad-ᵊn \ gladden, madden, sadden, Aladdin

adder \ ad-ər \ adder, bladder, gadder, ladder, madder, stepladder—*also comparatives of adjectives listed at* ³AD

addie \ ad-ē \ see ADDY

addik \ äd-ik \ see ODIC

addin \ ad-ᵊn \ see ADDEN

adding \ ad-iŋ \ cladding, padding

¹addish \ äd-ish \ see ODDISH

²addish \ ad-ish \ see ADISH

addle \ ad-ᵊl \ addle, paddle, raddle, saddle, staddle, straddle, astraddle, foresaddle, gonadal, packsaddle, sidesaddle, skedaddle, unsaddle, fiddle-faddle

¹addler \ äd-lər \ see ODDLER

²addler \ ad-lər \ saddler, paddler, straddler, skedaddler

addo \ ad-ō \ see ADOW

¹addock \ ad-ik \ see ²ADIC

²addock \ ad-ək \ haddock, paddock, shaddock

addy \ ad-ē \ baddie, caddie, caddy, daddy, faddy, laddie, paddy, forecaddie, granddaddy, finnan haddie

¹ade \ ād \ aid, aide, bade, blade, braid, cade, fade, glade, grade, jade, lade, laid, made, maid, paid, raid, rayed, shade, spade, stade, staid, suede, they'd, trade, wade, abrade, afraid, aggrade, arcade, Band-Aid, barmaid, blockade, bondmaid, bridesmaid, brigade, brocade, cascade, charade, clichéd, cockade, corrade, cross-trade, crusade, decade, degrade, dissuade, downgrade, evade, eyeshade, fair-trade, forebade, gainsaid, glissade, grenade, handmade, handmaid, homemade, housemaid, inlaid, invade, limeade, low-grade, man-made, mermaid, milkmaid, navaid, nightshade, nursemaid, outlaid, parade, persuade, pervade, plain-laid, pomade, postpaid, repaid, sacheted, scalade, sea-maid, self-made, shroud-laid, souffléed, stockade, sunshade, switchblade, tirade, torsade, twayblade, twice-laid, unbraid, unlade, unmade, unpaid, upbraid, upgrade, waylaid, accolade, ambuscade, aquacade,

autocade, balustrade, barricade, bastinade, cable-laid, cannonade, carronade, cavalcade, centigrade, chambermaid, colonnade, custom-made, dairymaid, defilade, enfilade, escalade, escapade, esplanade, everglade, fusillade, gallopade, gasconade, grant-in-aid, hawser-laid, intergrade, lemonade, marinade, marmalade, masquerade, medicaid, motorcade, orangeade, orthograde, overtrade, palisade, pasquinade, plantigrade, promenade, ready-made, renegade, retrograde, serenade, stock-in-trade, tailor-made, underlaid, fanfaronade, harlequinade, overpersuade, rodomontade

²**ade** \ ād \ see ¹OD

³**ade** \ ad \ see ³AD

⁴**ade** \ äd-ə \ see ²ADA

aded \ ād-əd \ bladed, arcaded, brocaded, cockaded, colonnaded—*also pasts of verbs listed at* ¹ADE

adeless \ ād-ləs \ fadeless, gradeless, shadeless

adely \ ad-lē \ see ADLY

aden \ ād-ᵊn \ laden, maiden, handmaiden, menhaden

adent \ ād-ᵊnt \ see ADANT

ader \ ād-ər \ aider, braider, cheder, fader, grader, heder, nadir, raider, seder, shader, spader, trader, wader, blockader, crusader, dissuader, evader, persuder, masquerader, serenader

adery \ ad-rē \ cadre, comradery

¹**ades** \ ād-ēz \ ladies, Hades, quaker-ladies

²**ades** \ ādz \ AIDS, antitrades, jack-of-all-trades—*also plurals and possessives of nouns and third singular presents of verbs listed at* ¹ADE

adge \ aj \ badge, cadge, hajj

adger \ aj-ər \ badger, cadger

¹**adhe** \ äd-ə \ see ²ADA

²**adhe** \ äd-ē \ see ¹ODY

adia \ ād-ē-ə \ stadia, arcadia, palladia

adial \ ād-ē-əl \ radial, biradial, interstadial

adian \ ād-ē-ən \ Acadian, Akkadian, Arcadian, Canadian, circadian, Orcadian, Palladian

adiant \ ād-ē-ənt \ gradient, radiant

¹**adic** \ ād-ik \ Vedic, tornadic

²**adic** \ ad-ik \ haddock, paddock, balladic, dyadic, faradic, haggadic, hexadic, maenadic, monadic, nomadic, sporadic,

tetradic, tornadic, triadic,
Iliadic, seminomadic

adient\ād-ē-ənt\see ADIANT

adies\ād-ēz\see ¹ADES

ading\ād-iŋ\braiding, lading,
shading, arcading, degrading,
downgrading, unfading

adir\ād-ər\see ADER

adish\ad-ish\caddish, faddish,
radish, horseradish

¹**adist**\ȯd-əst\broadest,
sawdust, haggadist

²**adist**\ād-əst\see ODEST

adium\ād-ē-əm\radium,
stadium, caladium, palladium,
vanadium

adle\ād-ȧ\cradle, dreidel,
ladle, wedel

adly\ad-lē\badly, gladly,
madly, sadly, comradely

adness\ad-nəs\badness,
gladness, madness, sadness

¹**ado**\äd-ō\bravado, camisado,
carbonado, cruzado, mikado,
passado, stoccado, strappado,
avocado, bastinado,
desperado, El Dorado,
hacendado, amontillado,
zapateado, aficionado,
incommunicado

²**ado**\ād-ō\dado, credo,
crusado, gambado, strappado,
teredo, tornado, barricado,
bastinado, camisado,
carbonado, desperado, El
Dorado, fettuccine Alfredo

adow\ad-ō\Caddo, shadow,
foreshadow, overshadow

adrate\äd-rət\see ODERATE

¹**adre**\äd-rē\see AWDRY

²**adre**\ad-rē\see ADERY

adual\aj-əl\see AGILE

ady\ād-ē\cedi, glady, lady,
shady, forelady, landlady,
milady, saleslady

¹**ae**\ä\see ¹AY

²**ae**\ē\see ¹EE

³**ae**\ī\see ¹Y

aea\ē-ə\see ¹IA

aean\ē-ən\see ¹EAN

aedal\ēd-ᵊl\see EEDLE

aedile\ēd-ᵊl\see EEDLE

aedra\ē-drə\see EDRA

¹**aegis**\ā-jəs\see AGEOUS

ael\āl\see AIL

aeli\ā-lē\see AILY

¹**aelic**\äl-ik\see ¹OLIC

²**aelic**\al-ik\see ALLIC

¹**aena**\ā-nä\scena, faena

²**aena**\ē-nə\see ²INA

¹**aenia**\ē-nē-ə\see ¹ENIA

²**aenia**\ē-nyə\see ²ENIA

aeon\ē-ən\see ¹EAN

aera\ir-ə\see ²ERA

¹**aere**\er-ē\see ¹ARY

²**aere**\ir-ē\see EARY

¹**aerial**\er-ē-əl\see ARIAL

²**aerial**\ir-ē-əl\see ERIAL

¹**aerie**\ā-rē\aerie, aery, faerie

²**aerie**\er-ē\see ¹ARY

³**aerie**\ir-ē\see EARY

¹**aero** \er-ō \see ²ERO

²**aero** \ar-ō \see ²ARROW

¹**aery** \ā-rē \see ¹AERIE

²**aery** \er-ē \see ¹ARY

aesar \ē-zər \see ²EASER

aese \ā-zə \see ²ESA

aestor \ē-stər \see EASTER

aestus \es-təs \see ESTIS

aet \āt \see ¹ATE

aetor \ēt-ər \see ¹EATER

aeum \ē-əm \see ¹EUM

aeus \ē-əs \see ¹EUS

af \af \see APH

¹**afe** \āf \chafe, safe, strafe, waif, fail-safe, vouchsafe, bathyscaphe

²**afe** \af \see APH

afel \äf-əl \offal, waffle, falafel, pantofle

afer \ā-fər \chafer, safer, wafer, cockchafer

aff \af \see APH

affable \af-ə-bəl \affable, laughable

affe \af \see APH

affed \aft \see ²AFT

¹**affer** \äf-ər \see ¹OFFER

²**affer** \af-ər \chaffer, gaffer, Kaffir, kafir, Kafir, staffer, zaffer, paragrapher, polygrapher

affia \af-ē-ə \raffia, agraphia

affic \af-ik \see APHIC

affick \af-ik \see APHIC

affir \af-ər \see ²AFFER

affish \af-ish \raffish, giraffish

¹**affle** \äf-əl \see AFEL

²**affle** \af-əl \baffle, raffle, snaffle

affron \af-rən \saffron, Biafran

affy \af-ē \chaffy, daffy, taffy

afic \af-ik \see APHIC

afir \af-ər \see ²AFFER

afran \af-rən \see AFFRON

¹**aft** \äft \tośt, waft, gemeinschaft, gesellschaft— *also pasts of verbs listed at* ¹OFF

²**aft** \aft \aft, craft, daft, draft, graft, haft, kraft, raft, shaft, waft, abaft, aircraft, campcraft, camshaft, crankshaft, engraft, handcraft, indraft, kingcraft, rockshaft, scoutcraft, seacraft, spacecraft, stagecraft, statecraft, updraft, witchcraft, woodcraft, countershaft, fore-and-aft, handicraft, Hovercraft, overdraft, rotorcraft, turboshaft, understaffed, watercraft, antiaircraft

aftage \af-tij \graftage, waftage

after \af-tər \after, dafter, drafter, grafter, laughter, rafter, hereafter, thereafter, fore-and-after, handicrafter, hereinafter, thereinafter

aftness \af-nəs \daftness, Daphnis, halfness

aftsman \af-smən \craftsman,

draftsman, raftsman,
handcraftsman,
handicraftsman
afty \af-tē \crafty, drafty
ag \ag \bag, brag, crag, dag,
  drag, fag, flag, gag, hag, jag,
  lag, mag, nag, quag, rag,
  sag, scag, scrag, shag, slag,
  snag, sprag, stag, swag, tag,
  wag, YAG, zag, beanbag,
  black-flag, chin-wag, dishrag,
  fleabag, gasbag, greylag,
  handbag, hangtag, mailbag,
  postbag, ragbag, ragtag,
  sandbag, schoolbag, seabag,
  washrag, wigwag, windbag,
  workbag, zigzag, ballyrag,
  bullyrag, carpetbag, litterbag,
  lollygag, saddlebag,
  scalawag, tucker-bag
¹aga \äg-ə \quagga, raga, saga,
  anlage, vorlage
²aga \ä-gə \Vega, bodega,
  omega, rutabaga
³aga \eg-ə \see ¹EGA
⁴aga \ȯ-gə \see AUGA
agan \ä-gən \see AGIN
¹agar \ä-gər \Hagar, jaeger
²agar \äg-ər \see ¹OGGER
agary \ag-ə-rē \see AGGERY
agate \ag-ət \see AGGOT
¹age \äj \dodge, lodge, raj,
  stodge, barrage, corsage,
  dislodge, garage,
  hodgepodge, massage,

swaraj, camouflage,
espionage, counterespionage
²age \äzh \plage, assuage,
  barrage, collage, corsage,
  dressage, frottage, gavage,
  lavage, massage, ménage,
  mirage, montage, moulage,
  portage, potage, treillage,
  triage, arbitrage, assemblage,
  badinage, bon voyage,
  bricolage, cabotage,
  camouflage, colportage,
  curettage, decoupage,
  empennage, enfleurage,
  entourage, fuselage,
  Hermitage, maquillage,
  persiflage, repechage,
  sabotage, vernissage,
  décolletage, espionage,
  photomontage, rite de
  passage, counterespionage
³age \āj \age, cage, gage,
  gauge, mage, page, rage,
  sage, stage, swage, wage,
  assuage, backstage,
  downstage, encage, engage,
  enrage, forestage, front-page,
  greengage, offstage, onstage,
  Osage, outrage, presage,
  rampage, restage, soundstage,
  space-age, substage, teenage,
  uncage, upstage, disengage,
  multistage, ossifrage,
  overage, saxifrage, underage
⁴age \ȧg \see ¹EG
⁵age \äzh \see ¹EIGE

⁶age \äg-ə\ see ¹AGA

ageable \ā-jə-bəl\ gaugeable,
stageable, unassuageable

aged \ājd\ aged, engaged,
unpaged, middle-aged—*also
pasts of verbs listed at* ³AGE

agel \ā-gəl\ bagel, plagal,
finagle, inveigle, wallydraigle

ageless \āj-ləs\ ageless,
wageless

agenous \aj-ə-nəs\ see AGINOUS

ageous \ā-jəs\ aegis,
ambagious, courageous,
contagious, outrageous,
rampageous, umbrageous,
advantageous,
disadvantageous

¹ager \ā-jər\ gauger, major,
pager, stager, wager,
teenager, Canis Major,
golden-ager, middle-ager,
Ursa Major

²ager \äg-ər\ see ¹OGGER

agey \ā-jē\ see AGY

agga \äg-ə\ see ¹AGA

aggard \ag-ərd\ blackguard,
haggard, laggard

agged \ag-əd\ cragged, jagged,
ragged

agger \ag-ər\ bagger, bragger,
dagger, dragger, gagger,
jagger, lagger, nagger,
sagger, stagger, swagger,
wagger, four-bagger, one-
bagger, sandbagger, three-
bagger, two-bagger,
carpetbagger

aggery \ag-ə-rē\ jaggery,
staggery, vagary, waggery,
carpetbaggery

aggie \ag-ē\ see ²AGGY

agging \ag-iŋ\ bagging,
flagging, lagging, nagging,
brown bagging, foot-
dragging, unflagging,
carpetbagging

aggish \ag-ish\ haggish,
waggish

aggle \ag-əl\ draggle, gaggle,
haggle, raggle, straggle,
waggle, bedraggle, raggle-
taggle

aggly \ag-lē\ scraggly, straggly,
waggly

aggot \ag-ət\ agate, faggot,
fagot, maggot

¹aggy \äg-ē\ see ¹OGGY

²aggy \ag-ē\ aggie, baggy,
braggy, craggy, draggy,
jaggy, quaggy, ragi, scraggy,
shaggy, snaggy, staggy

¹agi \äg-ē\ see ¹OGGY

²agi \ag-ē\ see ²AGGY

agian \ā-jən\ see AJUN

agic \aj-ik\ magic, tragic,
choragic, pelagic

agile \aj-əl\ agile, fragile,
gradual, vagile

agin \ā-gən\ fagin, pagan

aginal \aj-ən-ᵊl\ paginal,
vaginal, imaginal

aging \ā-jiŋ\ aging, raging, staging, unaging

aginous \aj-ə-nəs\ collagenous, farraginous, plumbaginous, viraginous, cartilaginous, mucilaginous, oleaginous

agion \ā-jən\ see AJUN

agious \ā-jəs\ see AGEOUS

¹**aglia** \äl-yə\ see ¹AHLIA

²**aglia** \al-yə\ see ALUE

aglio \al-yō\ intaglio, seraglio

agm \am\ see ²AM

agma \ag-mə\ magma, syntagma

agman \ag-mən\ bagman, flagman, swagman

agna \än-yə\ see ¹ANIA

agne \ān\ see ¹ANE

agnum \ag-nəm\ magnum, sphagnum

¹**ago** \äg-ō\ farrago, galago, Iago, virago, Asiago, Calinago, solidago

²**ago** \ā-gō\ dago, sago, farrago, galago, imago, lumbago, plumbago, sapsago, virago, solidago

agon \ag-ən\ dragon, flagon, lagan, wagon, bandwagon, jolt-wagon, snapdragon, battlewagon

agonal \ag-ən-ᵊl\ agonal, diagonal, heptagonal, hexagonal, octagonal, pentagonal, tetragonal

agora \ag-ə-rə\ agora, mandragora

agot \ag-ət\ see AGGOT

agrance \ā-grəns\ flagrance, fragrance

agrancy \ā-grən-sē\ flagrancy, fragrancy, vagrancy

agrant \ā-grənt\ flagrant, fragrant, vagrant, conflagrant

agster \ag-stər\ dragster, gagster

agua \äg-wə\ majagua, piragua

¹**ague** \āg\ see ¹EG

²**ague** \āg\ see ¹OG

aguey \eg-ē\ see EGGY

agus \ā-gəs\ magus, choragus, Simon Magus

agy \ā-jē\ cagey, Meiji, stagy

¹**ah** \ä\ see ¹A

²**ah** \ȯ\ see ¹AW

³**ah** \a\ baa, eh, nah

ahdi \äd-ē\ see ¹ODY

ahdom \äd-əm\ see ODOM

ahib \äb\ see ¹OB

¹**ahlia** \äl-yə\ dahlia, passacaglia

²**ahlia** \al-yə\ see ALUE

³**ahlia** \ä-lē-ə\ see ¹ALIA

¹**ahma** \ä-mə\ see ³AMA

²**ahma** \äm-ə\ see ²AMA

³**ahma** \am-ə\ see ⁴AMA

¹**ahman** \äm-ən\ see OMMON

²**ahman** \am-ən\ see AMMON

ahn \än\ see ¹ON

ahnda \än-də\ see ONDA

aht \ät\ see ¹OT

ahum \ ā-əm \ mayhem, Nahum, Te Deum

ahveh \ ä-vä \ see ¹AVE

¹ai \ ā \ see ¹AY

²ai \ ē \ see ¹EE

³ai \ ī \ see ¹Y

⁴ai \ ȯi \ see OY

a'i \ ī \ see ¹Y

¹aia \ ā-ə \ Freya, Aglaia, cattleya, Hosea, Isaiah

²aia \ ī-ə \ see ¹IAH

¹aiad \ ā-əd \ naiad, pleiad

²aiad \ ī-əd \ see YAD

aiah \ ā-ə \ see AIA

aias \ ā-əs \ see ¹AIS

aic \ ā-ik \ laic, alcaic, Altaic, archaic, Chaldaic, deltaic, Hebraic, Incaic, Judaic, Mishnaic, Mithraic, mosaic, Mosaic, prosaic, Romaic, spondaic, stanzaic, trochaic, voltaic, algebraic, Aramaic, Cyrenaic, faradaic, formulaic, pharisaic, Ptolemaic, apotropaic, paradisaic, Ural-Altaic

aical \ ā-ə-kəl \ laical, pharisaical, paradisaical

aice \ ās \ see ¹ACE

aich \ āk̲ \ see AIGH

¹aid \ ād \ see ¹ADE

²aid \ ed \ see ¹EAD

³aid \ ad \ see ³AD

¹aide \ ād \ see ¹ADE

²aide \ īd-ē \ see IDAY

aiden \ ād-ᵊn \ see ADEN

aider \ ād-ər \ see ADER

aiding \ ād-iŋ \ see ADING

aids \ ādz \ see ²ADES

aiety \ ā-ət-ē \ see AITY

aif \ āf \ see ¹AFE

aiga \ ī-gə \ taiga, Auriga

aigh \ āk̲ \ laigh, quaich

aight \ āt \ see ¹ATE

aighten \ āt-ᵊn \ see ¹ATEN

aightly \ āt-lē \ see ¹ATELY

aign \ ān \ see ¹ANE

aigne \ ān \ see ¹ANE

aignment \ ān-mənt \ see AINMENT

aiian \ ä-yən \ zayin, Hawaiian

aik \ īk \ see ²IKE

aika \ ī-kə \ see ¹ICA

ail \ āl \ ail, ale, baal, bail, bale, brail, braille, dale, drail, fail, flail, frail, Gael, gale, grail, hail, hale, jail, kale, mail, male, nail, pail, pale, quail, rail, sail, sale, scale, shale, snail, stale, swale, tael, tail, taille, tale, they'll, trail, vail, vale, veil, wail, wale, whale, airmail, assail, avail, bangtail, bewail, blackmail, blacktail, bobtail, broadtail, bucktail, canaille, cattail, Clydesdale, coattail, cocktail, contrail, curtail, derail, detail, doornail, dovetail, ducktail, entail, exhale, fantail, female, fishtail, folktale, foresail, foxtail, full-scale, guardrail,

Hallel, handrail, hangnail, headsail, hightail, hobnail, horntail, horsetail, impale, inhale, lugsail, mainsail, oxtail, pass-fail, percale, pigtail, pintail, pinwale, portrayal, prevail, rattail, regale, resale, rescale, retail, ringtail, Sangreal, shavetail, shirttail, skysail, small-scale, springtail, spritsail, staysail, surveil, swordtail, taffrail, telltale, thumbnail, toenail, topsail, travail, treenail, trysail, unnail, unveil, upscale, ventail, wagtail, wassail, whitetail, wholesale, abigail, aventail, betrayal, bristletail, Chippendale, Corriedale, cottontail, countervail, defrayal, disentail, draggle-tail, farthingale, fingernail, flickertail, forestaysail, gaff-topsail, galingale, martingale, monorail, montadale, nightingale, ponytail, romeldale, scissortail, swallowtail, tattletale, tripletail, trundle-tail, yellowtail, self-betrayal

ailable \ā-lə-bəl\ bailable, mailable, sailable, salable, scalable, assailable, available, resalable, unassailable

ailant \ā-lənt\ see ALANT

aile \ī-lē\ see YLY

ailed \āld\ mailed, nailed, sailed, scaled, tailed, veiled, detailed, engrailed, hobnailed, pigtailed, ring-tailed, unveiled, ponytailed, swallow-tailed—*also pasts of verbs listed at* AIL

ailer \ā-lər\ alar, bailer, bailor, baler, hailer, jailer, mailer, malar, nailer, sailer, sailor, scalar, scaler, tailer, tailor, trailer, wailer, waler, whaler, blackmailer, curtailer, derailleur, detailer, entailer, inhaler, retailer, wassailer, wholesaler, semitrailer—*also comparatives of adjectives listed at* AIL

ailey \ā-lē\ see AILY

ailful \āl-fəl\ see ALEFUL

ailie \ā-lē\ see AILY

ailiff \ā-ləf\ bailiff, caliph

ailing \ā-liŋ\ failing, grayling, mailing, paling, railing, sailing, tailing, veiling, whaling, prevailing, retailing, self-mailing, unfailing, unavailing

¹aille \āl\ see AIL

²aille \ī\ see ¹Y

³aille \īl\ see ¹ILE

⁴aille \ä-yə\ see ¹AYA

ailleur \ā-lər\ see AILER

ailment \āl-mənt\ ailment, bailment, curtailment,

derailment, entailment, impalement

ailor \ā-lər\ see AILER

ails \ālz\ see ALES

ailsman \ālz-mən\ see ALESMAN

aily \ā-lē\ bailey, bailie, daily, gaily, grayly, paly, scaly, shaley, wally, Israeli, shillelagh, triticale, ukulele

aim \ām\ see ¹AME

aima \ī-mə\ see YMA

aimable \ā-mə-bəl\ see AMABLE

aiman \ā-mən\ see ¹AMEN

aimant \ā-mənt\ see AYMENT

aiment \ā-mənt\ see AYMENT

aimer \ā-mər\ blamer, claimer, framer, tamer, declaimer, defamer, disclaimer, exclaimer—*also comparatives of adjectives listed at* ¹AME

aimless \ām-ləs\ see AMELESS

¹ain \ā-ən\ see ¹AYAN

²ain \ān\ see ¹ANE

³ain \en\ see ¹EN

⁴ain \in\ see ¹IN

⁵ain \īn\ see ¹INE

⁶ain \aⁿ\ see ⁴IN

aina \ī-nə\ see ¹INA

ainable \ā-nə-bəl\ stainable, attainable, containable, explainable, maintainable, restrainable, retrainable, sustainable, inexplainable

ainder \ān-dər\ attainder, remainder

aine \ān\ see ¹ANE

ained \ānd\ grained, maned, pained, paned, stained, vaned, strained, veined, birdbrained, bloodstained, close-grained, coarse-grained, crackbrained, cross-grained, edge-grained, harebrained, ingrained, lamebrained, mad-brained, membraned, restrained, tearstained, unfeigned, featherbrained, rattlebrained, scatterbrained, self-contained, unrestrained— *also pasts of verbs listed at* ¹ANE

ainer \ā-nər\ caner, drainer, feigner, gainer, planar, planer, seiner, stainer, strainer, trainer, veiner, campaigner, complainer, container, coplanar, cordwainer, detainer, lupanar, maintainer, ordainer, profaner, restrainer, retainer, sustainer, entertainer—*also comparatives of adjectives listed at* ¹ANE

ainful \ān-fəl\ baneful, gainful, painful, disdainful

aininess \ā-nē-nəs\ braininess, graininess

aining \ā-niŋ\ veining, complaining, sustaining, self-sustaining, uncomplaining— *also present participles of verbs listed at* ¹ANE

ainish \ā-nish\ brainish, Danish, swainish

ainless \ān-ləs\ brainless, painless, stainless

ainly \ān-lē\ mainly, plainly, thegnly, vainly, humanely, insanely, profanely, ungainly, inhumanely

ainment \ān-mənt\ arraignment, attainment, containment, detainment, detrainment, enchainment, entrainment, ordainment, refrainment, entertainment, preordainment, self-containment

aino \ī-nō\ see ¹INO

ains \ānz\ Plains, reins, cremains, remains—*also plurals and possessives of verbs listed at* ¹ANE

ainsman \ānz-mən\ plainsman, reinsman

aint \ānt\ ain't, faint, feint, mayn't, paint, plaint, quaint, saint, taint, 'tain't, acquaint, attaint, bepaint, complaint, constraint, distraint, greasepaint, impaint, restraint, unconstraint, unrestraint

ain't \ānt\ see AINT

aintly \ānt-lē\ faintly, quaintly, saintly

ainy \ā-nē\ brainy, grainy, meiny, rainy, veiny, zany

aipse \āps\ see APES

¹air \er\ see ⁴ARE

²air \ir\ see ¹IRE

aira \ī-rə\ see YRA

aird \erd\ see AIRED

¹aire \er\ see ⁴ARE

²aire \ir\ see ²EER

³aire \ir\ see ¹IRE

aired \erd\ caird, haired, laird, merde, long-haired, misleared, prepared, shorthaired, unpaired, wirehaired, multilayered, underprepared—*also pasts of verbs listed at* ⁴ARE

airer \er-ər\ see ³EARER

aires \er\ see ⁴ARE

¹airess \er-əs\ see ERROUS

²airess \ar-əs\ see ²ARIS

airie \er-ē\ see ¹ARY

airing \er-iŋ\ see ¹ARING

airish \er-ish\ see ¹ARISH

airist \er-əst\ see ARIST

airly \er-lē\ fairly, ferlie, rarely, squarely

airn \ern\ see ¹ERN

airs \erz\ theirs, backstairs, downstairs, nowheres, somewheres, upstairs, unawares—*also plurals and possessives of verbs listed at* ⁴ARE

airy \er-ē\ see ¹ARY

¹ais \ā-əs\ dais, Laius, Isaias, chaparajos, Menelaus

²ais \ā\ see ¹AY

¹aisal \ā-zəl\ see ²ASAL

²aisal \ī-səl\ see ¹ISAL

aisance \ās-ᵊns\ see ¹ASCENCE

aisant \ās-ᵊnt\ see ACENT

aise \āz\ see ¹AZE

aisement \āz-mənt\ see AZEMENT

¹aiser \ā-zər\ see AZER

²aiser \ī-zər\ see IZER

aisian \ā-zhən\ see ASION

aisin \āz-ᵊn\ see AZON

aising \ā-ziŋ\ glazing, hazing, phrasing, appraising, fund-raising, hair-raising, hell-raising, house-raising, stargazing, trailblazing—*also present participles of verbs listed at* ¹AZE

aisle \īl\ see ¹ILE

aisley \āz-lē\ paisley, nasally

aisse \ās\ see ¹ACE

aisson \ās-ᵊn\ see ¹ASON

¹aist \ā-əst\ see AYEST

²aist \āst\ see ACED

³aist \āst\ see ¹OST

aisy \ā-zē\ see AZY

¹ait \ā\ see ¹AY

²ait \āt\ see ¹ATE

³ait \īt\ see ¹ITE

⁴ait \at\ see ⁵AT

aite \īt\ see ¹ITE

aited \āt-əd\ see ATED

aiten \āt-ᵊn\ see ¹ATEN

aiter \āt-ər\ see ATOR

aith \āth\ eighth, faith, saithe, scathe, wraith, unfaith, interfaith

aithe \āth\ see AITH

aithless \āth-ləs\ faithless, natheless

aitian \ā-shən\ see ¹ATION

aiting \āt-iŋ\ see ATING

aitly \āt-lē\ see ¹ATELY

aitor \āt-ər\ see ATOR

aitorous \āt-ə-rəs\ see ATERESS

aitour \āt-ər\ see ATOR

aitress \ā-trəs\ traitress, traitorous, waitress, aviatress

aity \ā-ət-ē\ deity, gaiety, laity, corporeity, spontaneity, synchroneity, diaphaneity, contemporaneity, extemporaneity

aius \ā-əs\ see ¹AIS

aiva \ī-və\ see ¹IVA

aive \āv\ see ²AVE

aize \āz\ see ¹AZE

aj \äj\ see ¹AGE

ajj \aj\ see ADGE

ajor \ā-jər\ see ¹AGER

ajos \ā-əs\ see ¹AIS

ajun \ā-jən\ Cajun, contagion, Pelagian, reagin

¹ak \äk\ see ¹OCK

²ak \ak\ see ²ACK

¹aka \äk-ə\ kaka, paca, taka, maraca, medaka, pataca, saltimbocca

²aka \ak-ə\ see ²ACA

akable \ā-kə-bəl\ breakable, makable, shakable, mistakable, unmistakable

¹akan \äk-ən\ see ²AKEN

²akan \ak-ən\ see ACKEN
akar \äk-ər\ see OCKER
¹ake \āk\ ache, bake, brake,
 break, cake, crake, drake,
 fake, flake, hake, lake, make,
 quake, rake, sake, shake,
 sheikh, slake, snake, spake,
 stake, steak, strake, take,
 wake, awake, backache,
 beefcake, beefsteak, betake,
 blacksnake, canebrake,
 caretake, cheesecake,
 clambake, corncrake,
 cupcake, daybreak, earache,
 earthquake, firebreak,
 firedrake, forsake, friedcake,
 fruitcake, grubstake,
 handshake, headache,
 heartache, heartbreak,
 hoecake, hotcake,
 housebreak, intake, jailbreak.
 keepsake, lapstrake,
 mandrake, Marsquake,
 mistake, moonquake,
 muckrake, namesake,
 newsbreak, oatcake, opaque,
 outbreak, outtake, Pan-Cake,
 pancake, partake, remake,
 retake, rewake, seaquake,
 seedcake, sheldrake,
 shortcake, snowflake,
 swoopstake, toothache,
 unmake, uptake, windbreak,
 youthquake, bellyache, give-
 and-take, halterbreak,
 johnnycake, kittiwake, make-

or-break, microquake,
 overtake, put-and-take,
 rattlesnake, stomachache,
 undertake, wapentake,
 wideawake, semiopaque
²ake \ak\ see ²ACK
³ake \äk-ē\ see OCKY
aked \ākt\ awaked, half-baked,
 ringstraked, sunbaked—*also
 pasts of verbs listed at* ¹AKE
akeless \ā-kləs\ brakeless,
 wakeless
¹aken \ā-kən\ bacon, waken,
 shaken, taken, awaken,
 partaken, retaken, betaken,
 forsaken, mistaken, rewaken,
 well-taken, godforsaken,
 overtaken, undertaken
²aken \äk-ən\ kraken,
 Arawakan
¹aker \ā-kər\ acre, baker,
 breaker, faker, laker, maker,
 nacre, quaker, Quaker, raker,
 saker, shaker, taker, waker,
 backbreaker, bookmaker,
 caretaker, carmaker, comaker,
 dressmaker, drugmaker,
 earthshaker, filmmaker,
 glassmaker, grubstaker,
 hatmaker, haymaker,
 heartbreaker, homemaker,
 housebreaker, icebreaker,
 jawbreaker, kingmaker,
 lawbreaker, lawmaker,
 mapmaker, matchmaker,
 mistaker, muckraker,

mythmaker, noisemaker,
pacemaker, peacemaker,
phrasemaker, platemaker,
playmaker, printmaker,
rainmaker, saltshaker,
shirtmaker, shoemaker,
snowmaker, stavesacre,
strikebreaker, tastemaker,
ticbreaker, toolmaker,
trailbreaker, watchmaker,
windbreaker, wiseacre,
automaker, bellyacher,
boilermaker, merrymaker,
money-maker, moviemaker,
papermaker, simulacre,
troublemaker, undertaker,
cabinetmaker, holidaymaker,
policymaker

²aker \ak-ər\ see ACKER

akery \ā-krē\ bakery, fakery

akes \āks\ jakes, cornflakes,
sweepstakes—*also plurals
and possessives of verbs listed
at* ¹AKE

akey \ā-kē\ see AKY

akh \äk\ see ¹OCK

¹aki \äk-ē\ see OCKY

²aki \ak-ē\ see ACKY

akian \äk-ē-ən\ see OCKIAN

akic \ak-ik\ see ACCHIC

¹aking \ā-kiŋ\ aching, making,
waking, bookmaking,
breathtaking, caretaking,
dressmaking, earthshaking,
filmmaking, glassmaking,
heartbreaking, housebreaking,

lawbreaking, lawmaking,
leave-taking, lovemaking,
mapmaking, matchmaking,
mythmaking, noisemaking,
pacemaking, painstaking,
peacemaking, phrasemaking,
printmaking, rainmaking,
snowmaking, stocktaking,
strikebreaking, toolmaking,
watchmaking, world-shaking,
merrymaking, moneymaking,
moviemaking, papermaking,
undertaking, cabinetmaking,
policymaking

²aking \ak-iŋ\ see ACKING

¹ako \äk-ō\ see OCCO

²ako \ak-ō\ shako, wacko,
tobacco

aku \äk-ü\ Bunraku, nunchaku

akum \ā-kəm\ vade mecum,
shalom aleichem

aky \ā-kē\ achy, braky, cakey,
flaky, laky, shaky, snaky,
headachy

¹al \äl\ col, doll, loll, moll, nal,
pol, sol, Sol, Taal, toile,
Algol, atoll, austral, cabal,
chorale, grand mal, gun moll,
hamal, jacal, mistral,
narwhal, nopal, petrol,
quetzal, real, rial, riyal,
Shawwal, tical, timbale, à
cheval, aerosol, Emmenthal,
falderal, femme fatale,
folderol, parasol, pastoral,
pastorale, protocol,

Provençal, Simmental, urial,
entente cordiale, Neanderthal,
procès-verbal, sublittoral,
succès de scandale

²**al** \ el \ see ¹EL

³**al** \ òl \ see ALL

⁴**al** \ al \ gal, pal, rale, sal, banal,
cabal, canal, chorale, copal,
corral, decal, fal-lal, grand
mal, joual, locale, mescal,
moral, morale, nopal, pall-
mall, pascal, percale, quetzal,
salal, serval, vinal,
bacchanal, caracal, chaparral,
femme fatale, musicale,
pastoral, pastorale, pedocal,
rationale, retinal, Seconal,
sublittoral

¹**ala** \ äl-ä \ à la, Allah, gala

²**ala** \ äl-ə \ Allah, follow, olla,
swallow, tala, wallah,
wallow, cabala, cantala,
chuckwalla, cicala, corolla,
halala, koala, Lingala,
marsala, nyala, tambala,
Valhalla, Walhalla, ayotollah

³**ala** \ ā-lə \ ala, gala, zarzuela

⁴**ala** \ al-ə \ see ALLOW

alaam \ ä-ləm \ Balaam, golem

alable \ ā-lə-bəl \ see AILABLE

alace \ al-əs \ see ²ALIS

alad \ al-əd \ see ²ALID

alam \ äl-əm \ see OLUMN

alamine \ al-ə-mən \ allemande,
calamine

alance \ al-əns \ balance,

valance, imbalance,
outbalance, unbalance,
counterbalance, overbalance

alant \ ā-lənt \ assailant,
inhalant, surveillant

alap \ al-əp \ see ²ALLOP

alar \ ā-lər \ see AILER

alary \ al-rē \ see ALLERY

alas \ al-əs \ see ²ALIS

alate \ al-ət \ see ²ALLET

¹**alcon** \ ò-kən \ see ¹ALKIN

²**alcon** \ al-kən \ falcon,
gyrfalcon, grimalkin

ald \ òld \ bald, scald, skald,
walled, close-hauled, kobold,
piebald, ribald, skewbald, so-
called, sunscald, coveralled,
overalled—*also pasts of verbs
listed at* ALL

alder \ òl-dər \ alder, balder,
Balder

aldron \ òl-drən \ aldron,
caldron, chaldron

¹**ale** \ ā-lē \ see AILY

²**ale** \ āl \ see AIL

³**ale** \ äl \ see ¹AL

⁴**ale** \ al \ see ⁴AL

⁵**ale** \ äl-ē \ see ¹OLLY

⁶**ale** \ al-ē \ see ⁴ALLY

alea \ ā-lē-ə \ see ¹ALIA

¹**aleck** \ el-ik \ see ²ELIC

²**aleck** \ al-ik \ see ALLIC

aled \ āld \ see AILED

aleful \ āl-fəl \ baleful, wailful

alement \ āl-mənt \ see AILMENT

alence\ā-ləns\valence, surveillance
alends\al-ənz\see ALLANS
alent\al-ənt\see ALLANT
alep\al-əp\see ²ALLOP
¹**aler**\ā-lər\see AILER
²**aler**\äl-ər\see OLLAR
ales\ālz\sales, entrails, Marseilles, Prince of Wales, cat-o'-nine-tails—*also plurals and possessives of verbs listed at* AIL
alesman\ālz-mən\bailsman, dalesman, salesman, talesman
alet\al-ət\see ²ALLET
alette\al-ət\see ²ALLET
aley\ā-lē\see AILY
alf\af\see APH
alfa\al-fə\see ALPHA
alfness\af-nəs\see AFTNESS
algia\al-jə\neuralgia, nostalgia
¹**ali**\äl-ē\see ¹OLLY
²**ali**\al-ē\see ⁴ALLY
³**ali**\ȯ-lē\see AWLY
¹**alia**\ā-lē-ə\dahlia, azalea, battalia, realia, regalia, vedalia, bacchanalia, genitalia, glossolalia, inter alia, Lupercalia, marginalia, paraphernalia, penetralia, saturnalia
²**alia**\al-yə\see ALUE
¹**alian**\ā-lē-ən\alien, Australian, Daedalian, Deucalion, Hegelian, mammalian, Pygmalion,

Uralian, bacchanalian, Lupercalian, saturnalian, Episcopalian, sesquipedalian, tatterdemalion
²**alian**\al-yən\see ALLION
alic\al-ik\see ALLIC
alice\al-əs\see ²ALIS
¹**alid**\äl-əd\see OLID
²**alid**\al-əd\ballad, hallowed, pallid, salad, valid, invalid, unhallowed
alien\ā-lē-ən\see ¹ALIAN
aling\ā-liŋ\see AILING
alinist\äl-ə-nəst\see OLONIST
¹**alion**\ā-lē-ən\see ¹ALIAN
²**alion**\al-yən\see ALLION
aliph\ā-ləf\see AILIFF
¹**alis**\ā-ləs\see AYLESS
²**alis**\al-əs\balas, callous, callus, chalice, gallus, malice, palace, Pallas, phallus, talus, thallous, thallus, oxalis, digitalis, hemerocallis, aurora borealis, Corona Borealis
alish\ā-lish\palish, Salish
alist\al-əst\ballast, callused, gallused, cabalist, sodalist
¹**ality**\äl-ət-ē\jollity, polity, quality, equality, frivolity, coequality, inequality
²**ality**\al-ət-ē\anality, banality, brutality, carnality, causality, centrality, duality, extrality, fatality, feudality, finality, formality, frontality,

frugality, legality, locality,
mentality, modality, morality,
mortality, nasality, natality,
neutrality, nodality, orality,
plurality, primality, rascality,
reality, regality, rurality,
sodality, tonality, totality,
venality, vitality, vocality,
abnormality, actuality,
amorality, animality,
atonality, axiality, bestiality,
bimodality, cardinality,
classicality, coevality,
comicality, commonality,
communality, conjugality,
cordiality, corporality,
criminality, criticality,
ethicality, externality,
factuality, farcicality,
fictionality, functionality,
generality, geniality,
hospitality, ideality, illegality,
immorality, immortality,
informality, integrality,
internality, irreality,
lexicality, liberality, lineality,
literality, logicality,
musicality, mutuality,
nationality, notionality,
nuptiality, optimality,
partiality, personality,
physicality, principality,
punctuality, rationality,
seasonality, sexuality,
sociality, spaciality,
speciality, subnormality,

technicality, temporality,
topicality, triviality,
unmorality, unreality,
verticality, virtuality,
whimsicality, asexuality,
atypicality, bisexuality,
collaterality, collegiality,
colloquiality, commerciality,
conceptuality, conditionality,
congeniality, connaturality,
conventionality, conviviality,
corporeality, dimensionality,
directionality, effectuality,
emotionality, ephemerality,
equivocality, essentiality,
ethereality, eventuality,
exceptionality, extensionality,
fantasticality, grammaticality,
illiberality, illogicality,
impersonality, impracticality,
inhospitality, instrumentality,
irrationality, materiality,
microtonality, monumentality,
municipality, originality,
orthogonality, pansexuality,
paranormality, polytonality,
potentiality, provinciality,
self-partiality, sentimentality,
spirituality, substantiality,
theatricality, transexuality,
triaxiality, universality,
veridicality, ambisexuality,
artificiality, circumstantiality,
confidentiality,
consequentiality,
constitutionality,

homosexuality,
hypersexuality, immateriality,
individuality, ineffectuality,
insubstantiality,
intellectuality,
internationality,
intersexuality, paradoxicality,
psychosexuality,
referentiality, superficiality,
supranationality, territoriality,
tridimensionality, two-
dimensionality,
uncongeniality,
unconventionality,
ungrammaticality,
unisexuality, unsubstantiality,
exterritoriality,
heterosexuality,
inconsequentiality,
unconstitutionality,
unidimonsionality,
extraterritoriality

alium \ al-ē-əm \ see ALLIUM

alk \ ȯk \ auk, balk, calk, caulk,
chalk, gawk, hawk, squawk,
stalk, talk, walk, baroque,
bemock, boardwalk,
cakewalk, catwalk, cornstalk,
crosswalk, eyestalk, fast-talk,
goshawk, jaywalk, langue
d'oc, leafstalk, Mohawk,
nighthawk, outtalk, ropewalk,
shoptalk, sidewalk, skywalk,
sleepwalk, Suffolk, sweet-
talk, catafalque, double-talk,
tomahawk

alker \ ȯ-kər \ balker, caulker,
gawker, hawker, squawker,
stalker, walker, cakewalker,
deerstalker, floorwalker,
jayhawker, jaywalker,
nightwalker, ropewalker,
sleepwalker, spacewalker,
streetwalker, trackwalker,
double-talker

alkie \ ȯ-kē \ balky, chalky,
gawky, pawky, stalky, talkie,
talky, Handie-Talkie, walkie-
talkie

¹alkin \ ȯ-kən \ falcon, malkin,
gyrfalcon, grimalkin

²alkin \ al-kən \ see ²ALCON

alking \ ȯ-kiŋ \ caulking,
walking, spacewalking,
streetwalking

alky \ ȯ-kē \ see ALKIE

all \ ȯl \ all, awl, ball, bawl,
brawl, call, caul, crawl, doll,
drawl, fall, Gaul, hall, haul,
kraal, mall, maul, moll, pall,
Paul, pawl, Saul, scall,
scrawl, shawl, small, spall,
sprawl, squall, stall, tall,
thrall, trawl, wall, y'all,
yauld, yawl, Algol, ALGOL,
appall, argol, at all, atoll,
AWOL, baseball, beanball,
befall, best-ball, birdcall,
blackball, Bokmål, bookstall,
boxhaul, bradawl, broomball,
catcall, catchall, COBOL,
cornball, cure-all, curveball,

deadfall, dewfall, dodgeball,
downfall, downhaul, drywall,
enthrall, eyeball, fastball,
fireball, floodwall, football,
footfall, footstall, footwall,
forestall, four-ball, free-fall,
gadwall, goofball, googol,
guildhall, handball, hardball,
headstall, heelball, highball,
holdall, icefall, install,
keelhaul, landfall, Landsmål,
line-haul, lowball, meatball,
menthol, Metol, miscall,
mothball, naphthol, nightfall,
nutgall, oddball, outfall,
outhaul, pitfall, plimsoll,
pratfall, pub-crawl, puffball,
punchball, pushball, rainfall,
rainsquall, recall, rial,
Riksmål, riyal, rockfall,
rorqual, save-all, screwball,
seawall, short-haul, shortfall,
sidewall, snowball, snowfall,
softball, speedball, spitball,
stickball, stonewall,
stoopball, three-ball,
waterfall, Whitehall,
whitewall, windfall, windgall,
withal, withdrawal, you-all,
aerosol, alcohol, barbital,
basketball, butterball,
buttonball, cannonball,
carryall, caterwaul, cover-all,
coverall, Demerol, disenthrol,
entresol, evenfall, free-for-all,
gasohol, girasole, Grand

Guignol, haute école, know-
it-all, knuckleball,
Komsomol, methanol, minié
ball, Nembutal, overall,
overcall, overhaul,
paddleball, parasol, Pentothal,
protocol, racquetball,
Seconal, tattersall, tetherball,
therewithal, volleyball,
wherewithal, cholesterol,
Neanderthal, be-all and end-
all
¹alla \äl-ə\ see ²ALA
²alla \al-ə\ see ⁴ALLOW
allable \ȯ-lə-bəl\ callable,
    spallable
allacy \al-ə-sē\ fallacy, jalousie
allad \al-əd\ see ²ALID
¹allah \äl-ä\ see ¹ALA
²allah \äl-ə\ see ²ALA
³allah \al-ə\ see ⁴ALLOW
allan \al-ən\ see ALLON
allans \al-ənz\ calends,
    Lallans—*also plurals and*
    possessives of nouns listed at
    ALLON
allant \al-ənt\ callant, gallant,
    talent, topgallant, fore-
    topgallant
allas \al-əs\ see ²ALIS
allast \al-əst\ see ALIST
alle \al-ē\ see ⁴ALLY
alled \ȯld\ see ALD
alleé \al-ē\ see ⁴ALLY
allemande \al-ə-mən\ see
    ALAMINE

allen \ȯ-lən\ fallen, stollen, befallen, chapfallen, chopfallen, crestfallen, downfallen, tarpaulin

¹**aller** \ȯ-lər\ bawler, brawler, caller, drawler, faller, hauler, mauler, scrawler, squaller, trawler, footballer, forestaller, installer, stonewaller, knuckleballer

²**aller** \al-ər\ caller, pallor, valor, high yaller

allery \al-rē\ gallery, calorie, salary, kilocalorie

¹**allet** \äl-ət\ see OLLET

²**allet** \al-ət\ ballot, callet, mallet, palate, palette, pallet, sallet, shallot, valet

alley \al-ē\ see ⁴ALLY

alli \ȯl-ē\ see ⁴ALLY

alliard \al-yərd\ galliard, halyard

allic \al-ik\ Gaelic, Gallic, malic, phallic, salic, Salic, thallic, cephalic, italic, mandalic, medallic, metallic, smart aleck, Uralic, Vandalic, vocalic, genitalic, intervallic, ithyphallic, nonmetallic, postvocalic, prevocalic

allid \al-əd\ see ²ALID

alling \ȯ-liŋ\ calling, galling, name-calling

allion \al-yən\ scallion, stallion, battalion, Italian, medallion, rapscallion, tatterdemalion

¹**allis** \al-əs\ see ²ALIS

²**allis** \al-ē\ see ⁴ALLY

allish \ȯ-lish\ Gaulish, smallish

¹**allith** \äl-əs\ see OLIS

²**allith** \äl-ət\ see OLLET

allium \al-ē-əm\ allium, gallium, pallium, thallium, Valium

allment \ȯl-mənt\ enthrallment, forestallment, installment

allon \al-ən\ gallon, lallan, talon

¹**allop** \äl-əp\ see OLLOP

²**allop** \al-əp\ gallop, galop, jalap, salep, scallop, shallop, escallop

allor \al-ər\ see ²ALLER

allot \al-ət\ see ²ALLET

allous \al-əs\ see ²ALIS

¹**allow** \el-ō\ see ELLO

²**allow** \äl-ə\ see ²ALA

³**allow** \äl-ō\ see ¹OLLOW

⁴**allow** \al-ə\ Allah, callow, fallow, gala, Galla, hallow, sallow, shallow, tallow, cavalla, impala, unhallow, Valhalla

⁵**allow** \al-ō\ aloe, callow, fallow, hallow, mallow, sallow, shallow, tallow, unhallow

allowed \al-əd\ see ²ALID

allows \al-ōz\ gallows, Allhallows—*also plurals and possessives of nouns listed at* ⁴ALLOW

allsy \ ȯl-zē \ see ALSY

allus \ al-əs \ see ²ALIS

allused \ al-əst \ see ALIST

¹ally \ ā-lē \ see AILY

²ally \ äl-ē \ see ¹OLLY

³ally \ ȯ-lē \ see AWLY

⁴ally \ al-ē \ alley, challis, dally,
galley, gally, mallee, pally,
rally, sally, tally, valley,
Aunt Sally, bialy, crevalle,
finale, Nepali, tomalley,
dillydally, shilly-shally,
teocalli

alm \ äm \ see ¹OM

almar \ äm-ər \ see ¹OMBER

almer \ äm-ər \ see ¹OMBER

almily \ äm-ə-lē \ see OMALY

almish \ äm-ish \ see ¹AMISH

almist \ äm-əst \ palmist,
psalmist, Islamist

almody \ äm-əd-ē \ see OMEDY

almon \ am-ən \ see AMMON

almoner \ äm-ə-nər \ see
OMMONER

alms \ ämz \ alms, Psalms—*also
plurals and possessives of
nouns and third singular
presents of verbs listed at* ¹OM

almy \ äm-ē \ see ¹AMI

alo \ äl-ō \ see ¹OLLOW

aloe \ al-ō \ see ⁵ALLOW

¹alogist \ äl-ə-jəst \ see OLOGIST

²alogist \ al-ə-jəst \ analogist,
dialogist, mammalogist,
genealogist

¹alogy \ äl-ə-jē \ see OLOGY

²alogy \ al-ə-jē \ analogy,
mammalogy, tetralogy,
mineralogy

alom \ äl-əm \ see OLUMN

alon \ al-ən \ see ALLON

alop \ al-əp \ see ²ALLOP

¹alor \ al-ər \ see OLLAR

²alor \ al-ər \ see ²ALLER

alorie \ al-rē \ see ALLERY

alousie \ al-ə-sē \ see ALLACY

alp \ alp \ alp, scalp

alpa \ al-pə \ salpa, catalpa

alpal \ al-pəl \ palpal, scalpel

alpel \ al-pəl \ see ALPAL

alpha \ al-fə \ alpha, alfalfa

¹alque \ ȯk \ see ALK

²alque \ alk \ calque, talc,
catafalque

alsa \ ȯl-sə \ balsa, salsa

alse \ ȯls \ false, waltz

alsy \ ȯl-zē \ ballsy, palsy

alt \ ȯlt \ fault, gault, halt, malt,
salt, smalt, vault, volt,
asphalt, assault, basalt,
cobalt, default, desalt, exalt,
footfault, gestalt, stringhalt,
double-fault, somersault,
pepper-and-salt

altar \ ȯl-tər \ see ALTER

alter \ ȯl-tər \ altar, alter, falter,
halter, palter, Psalter, salter,
vaulter, defaulter, desalter,
exalter, Gibraltar, pole-vaulter

altery \ ȯl-trē \ see ALTRY

¹alti \ əl-tē \ Balti, difficulty

²alti \ ȯl-tē \ see ALTY

altic\ȯl-tik\Baltic, asphaltic, cobaltic, systaltic, peristaltic

alting\ȯl-tiŋ\halting, salting, vaulting

altless\ȯlt-ləs\faultless, saltless

alto\al-tō\alto, contralto, rialto

altry\ȯl-trē\paltry, psaltery, psaltry

alty\ȯl-tē\Balti, faulty, malty, salty, vaulty

altz\ȯls\see ALSE

alue\al-yə\dahlia, value, battalia, devalue, disvalue, misvalue, revalue, transvalue, overvalue, passacaglia, undervalue

¹alus\ā-ləs\see AYLESS

²alus\al-əs\see ²ALIS

¹alve\äv\see ²OLVE

²alve\alv\salve, valve, bivalve, univalve, inequivalve

³alve\av\calve, halve, have, salve

alver\al-vər\salver, salvor, quacksalver

alvor\al-vər\see ALVER

aly\al-ē\see ⁴ALLY

alyard\al-yərd\see ALLIARD

alysis\al-ə-səs\analysis, dialysis, paralysis, cryptanalysis, self-analysis

¹am\äm\see ¹OM

²am\am\am, cam, cham, clam, cram, dam, damn, damned, drachm, dram, Edam, flam, gam, gram, ham, Ham, jam, jamb, lam, lamb, ma'am, pram, ram, SAM, scam, scram, sham, slam, swam, tam, tram, wham, yam, ashram, dirham, engram, exam, flimflam, goddamn, grandam, iamb, logjam, madame, milldam, nizam, Priam, program, quondam, tam-tam, thiram, trigram, whim-wham, ziram, Abraham, aerogram, anagram, cablegram, centigram, Christogram, chronogram, cofferdam, cryptogram, decagram, diagram, diaphragm, dithyramb, epigram, hexagram, histogram, hologram, kilogram, logogram, milligram, Minicam, monogram, nomogram, oriflamme, pentagram, phonogram, pictogram, reprogram, scattergram, skiagram, subprogram, telegram, tetradrachm, thank-you-ma'am, Uncle Sam, ad nauseam, cardiogram, heliogram, ideogram, in personam, microprogram, parallelogram

¹ama\äm-ä\ama, amah

²ama\äm-ə\Brahma, comma, drama, Kama, lama, llama,

mama, momma, squama,
Rama, pajama, cyclorama,
Dalai Lama, diorama,
docudrama, melodrama,
monodrama, panorama,
photodrama, psychodrama
³**ama** \ā-mə\ Brahma, squama
⁴**ama** \am-ə\ Brahma, drama,
gamma, grama, mamma,
Miami, pajama, cyclorama,
diorama, docudrama,
melodrama, monodrama,
panorama, photodrama,
psychodrama
amable \ā-mə-bəl\ blamable,
claimable, framable,
nameable, tamable,
irreclaimable
amah \äm-ä\ see ¹AMA
¹**aman** \ā-mən\ see AMEN
²**aman** \äm-ən\ see OMMON
¹**amant** \ā-mənt\ see AYMENT
²**amant** \am-ənt\ see ²AMENT
amas \am-əs\ see AMICE
amash \äm-ish\ see ¹AMISH
amateur \am-ət-ər\ see AMETER
amatist \am-ət-əst\ dramatist,
epigrammatist, melodramatist
amba \äm-bə\ gamba, mamba,
samba, viola da gamba
¹**ambar** \äm-bər\ see ²OMBER
²**ambar** \am-bər\ camber,
sambar, timbre, liquidambar
ambe \am-bē\ see AMBY
ambeau \am-bō\ see AMBO
¹**amber** \am-bər\ see ²AMBAR

²**amber** \am-ər\ see AMMER
ambit \am-bət\ ambit, gambit
¹**amble** \äm-bəl\ see ¹EMBLE
²**amble** \am-bəl\ amble,
bramble, gamble, gambol,
ramble, scramble, shamble,
preamble, unscramble,
skimble-skamble
ambler \am-blər\ ambler,
gambler, rambler, scrambler,
unscrambler
ambo \am-bō\ crambo,
jambeau, sambo
ambol \am-bəl\ see ²AMBLE
ambray \am-brē\ see AMBRY
ambrel \am-brəl\ gambrel,
timbral
ambry \am-brē\ ambry,
chambray
ambulant \am-byə-lənt\
ambulant, somnambulant
amby \am-bē\ crambe, namby-
pamby
¹**ame** \ām\ aim, blame, came,
claim, dame, fame, flame,
frame, game, hame, kame,
lame, maim, name, same,
shame, tame, wame, A-
frame, acclaim, aflame,
airframe, became, byname,
declaim, defame, disclaim,
endgame, exclaim, forename,
freeze-frame, grandame,
inflame, mainframe,
misname, nickname, place-
name, prename, proclaim,

quitclaim, reclaim, selfsame, surname, counterclaim, overcame, Niflheim

²ame \ äm \ see ¹OM

³ame \ am \ see ²AM

ameable \ ā-mə-bəl \ see AMABLE

amed \ āmd \ famed, named, ashamed, forenamed, unashamed—*also pasts of verbs listed at* ¹AME

ameful \ ām-fəl \ blameful, shameful

amel \ am-əl \ see AMMEL

ameless \ ām-ləs \ aimless, blameless, nameless, shameless, tameless

amely \ ām-lē \ gamely, lamely, namely, tamely

¹amen \ ā-mən \ caiman, Damon, drayman, flamen, Haman, layman, shaman, stamen, examen, gravamen, highwayman

²amen \ äm-ən \ see OMMON

ameness \ ām-nəs \ gameness, lameness, sameness, tameness

¹ament \ ā-mənt \ see AYMENT

²ament \ am-ənt \ ament, clamant

amer \ ā-mər \ see AIMER

ameter \ am-ət-ər \ amateur, decameter, diameter, heptameter, hexameter, octameter, parameter, pentameter, tetrameter

¹amfer \ am-pər \ see ²AMPER

²amfer \ am-fər \ camphor, chamfer

¹ami \ äm-ē \ balmy, commie, mommy, palmy, pommy, qualmy, swami, Tommy, pastrami, salami, tatami, tsunami, origami

²ami \ am-ə \ see ⁴AMA

³ami \ am-ē \ see AMMY

amia \ ā-mē-ə \ lamia, zamia

¹amic \ ō-mik \ see ²OMIC

²amic \ am-ik \ gamic, Adamic, agamic, balsamic, ceramic, dynamic, adynamic, cleistogamic, cryptogrammic, cycloramic, dioramic, exogamic, panoramic, phonogrammic, polygamic, aerodynamic, hydrodynamic, hypothalamic, ideogramic, thermodynamic

amice \ am-əs \ amice, camas, chlamys, Lammas

amics \ äm-iks \ see OMICS

¹amie \ ā-mē \ ramie, cockamamy

²amie \ am-ē \ see AMMY

¹amil \ äm-əl \ see ¹OMMEL

²amil \ am-əl \ see AMMEL

amin \ am-ən \ see AMMON

amina \ am-ə-nə \ lamina, stamina

aminal \ am-ən-ᵊl \ laminal, foraminal

aminant \ am-ə-nənt \ contaminant, examinant

aminar \am-ə-nər\ see ²AMINER

amine \am-ən\ see AMMON

¹**aminer** \äm-ə-nər\ see
OMMONER

²**aminer** \am-ə-nər\ laminar,
gewurztraminer

aming \ā-miŋ\ flaming,
framing, gaming

¹**amish** \äm-ish\ Amish,
qualmish, quamash,
schoolmarmish

²**amish** \am-ish\ Amish, famish

amist \äm-əst\ see ALMIST

amity \am-ət-ē\ amity, calamity

amlet \am-lət\ camlet, hamlet,
Hamlet, samlet

amma \am-ə\ see ⁴AMA

ammable \am-ə-bəl\
flammable, programmable,
diagrammable

ammal \am-əl\ see AMMEL

ammany \am-ə-nē\ see
AMMONY

ammar \am-ər\ see AMMER

ammas \am-əs\ see AMICE

ammatist \am-ət-əst\ see
AMATIST

amme \am\ see ²AM

ammel \am-əl\ camel,
mammal, stammel, Tamil,
trammel, enamel

ammer \am-ər\ clamber,
clammer, clamor, clamour,
crammer, dammar, gammer,
glamour, grammar, hammer,
jammer, lamber, rammer,

shammer, slammer, stammer,
yammer, clawhammer,
enamor, flimflammer,
jackhammer, programmer,
sledgehammer, trip-hammer,
windjammer, katzenjammer,
monogrammer, ninnyhammer,
yellowhammer

ammes \äm-əs\ see OMISE

amming \am-iŋ\ damning,
programming

ammock \am-ək\ drammock,
hammock, mammock

ammon \am-ən\ Brahman,
famine, gamin, gammon,
mammon, salmon,
backgammon, examine, cross-
examine

ammony \am-ə-nē\ scammony,
Tammany

ammy \am-ē\ chamois,
clammy, Grammy, hammy,
mammy, ramie, shammy,
whammy, Miami

amn \am\ see ²AM

amned \am\ see ²AM

amning \am-iŋ\ see AMMING

amois \am-ē\ see AMMY

amon \ā-mən\ see ¹AMEN

amor \am-ər\ see AMMER

amorous \am-rəs\ amorous,
clamorous, glamorous

amos \ā-məs\ see AMOUS

amour \am-ər\ see AMMER

amous \ā-məs\ Amos, famous,

shamus, squamous, biramous,
mandamus, ignoramus

¹**amp** \ämp\ see ¹OMP

²**amp** \äⁿ\ see ¹ANT

³**amp** \amp\ amp, camp,
champ, clamp, cramp, damp,
gamp, gramp, guimpe, lamp,
ramp, samp, scamp, stamp,
tamp, tramp, vamp,
blackdamp, chokedamp,
decamp, encamp, firedamp,
headlamp, preamp, revamp,
sunlamp, unclamp,
afterdamp, aide-de-camp

¹**ampean** \äm-pē-ən\ pampean,
tampion

²**ampean** \am-pē-ən\ see
²AMPION

¹**amper** \äm-pər\ see OMPER

²**amper** \am-pər\ camper,
chamfer, damper, hamper,
pamper, scamper, stamper,
tamper

amphor \am-fər\ see ²AMFER

¹**ampi** \äm-pē\ see OMPY

²**ampi** \am-pē\ see AMPY

¹**ampion** \äm-pē-ən\ see
¹AMPEAN

²**ampion** \am-pē-ən\ campion,
champion, pampean,
rampion, tampion

ample \am-pəl\ ample, sample,
trample, ensample, example,
subsample, counterexample

ampler \am-plər\ sampler,
trampler

ampo \äm-pō\ see OMPO

ampus \am-pəs\ campus,
grampus, hippocampus

ampy \am-pē\ campy, scampi

amster \am-stər\ hamster,
lamster

amulus \am-yə-ləs\ famulus,
hamulus

¹**amus** \ā-məs\ see AMOUS

²**amus** \äm-əs\ see OMISE

amy \ā-mē\ see ¹AMIE

amys \am-əs\ see AMICE

¹**an** \äⁿ\ see ¹ANT

²**an** \än\ see ¹ON

³**an** \ən\ see UN

⁴**an** \aŋ\ see ²ANG

⁵**an** \an\ an, ban, bran, can,
clan, crayon, Dan, fan, flan,
Klan, man, pan, Pan, panne,
plan, ran, scan, Shan, span,
tan, van, adman, Afghan,
aidman, ape-man, ashcan,
bedpan, began, birdman,
boardman, brainpan, brogan,
caftan, caiman, cancan,
capstan, captan, caveman,
Cheyenne, chlordan, claypan,
cooncan, corban, cowman,
Cruzan, cyan, deadpan,
deskman, dishpan, divan,
doorman, dustpan, fan-tan,
fibranne, flyman, foreran,
FORTRAN, freedman,
freeman, frogman, G-man,
gagman, Gosplan, hardpan,
he-man, iceman, inspan,

japan, jazzman, kneepan,
Koran, leadman, legman,
liftman, loran, madman,
mailman, merman, milkman,
newsman, oilcan, oilman,
outran, pavane, pecan,
plowman, postman, preman,
pressman, propman, Queen
Anne, Qur'an, ragman,
rattan, reedman, reman,
rodman, routeman, sampan,
sandman, Saran, saucepan,
scalepan, schoolman, sedan,
sideman, snowman, soutane,
spaceman, stewpan, stickman,
stockman, strongman,
stuntman, suntan, T-man,
taipan, Tarzan, tisane,
toucan, trainman, trashman,
trepan, Tristan, unman,
vegan, wingspan, yardman,
yes-man, Alcoran, allemande,
also-ran, Ameslan,
anchorman, astrakhan,
ataman, attackman, automan,
balmacaan, Bantustan,
bartizan, black-and-tan,
bogeyman, boogeyman,
businessman, Caliban,
cameraman, caravan, catalan,
cattleman, Civitan,
cornerman, counterman,
counterplan, countryman,
courtesan, dairyman,
defenseman, everyman,
exciseman, expressman,

fellowman, funnyman,
gamelan, garageman,
garbageman, handyman,
harmattan, hotelman, jerrican,
Ku Klux Klan, Kurdistan,
man-for-man, man-to-man,
middleman, minuteman,
ombudsman, overman,
overran, Parmesan, partisan,
Peter Pan, pivotman,
plainclothesman, Ramadan,
repairman, rewrite man,
safetyman, selectman,
serviceman, shandrydan,
Shantyman, shovelman,
signalman, spick-and-span,
superman, tallyman, tamarin,
teleman, teleran, triggerman,
trimaran, turbofan,
weatherman, workingman,
yataghan, arrière-ban,
bipartisan, catamaran, catch-
as-catch-can, cavalryman,
committeeman, deliveryman,
newspaperman, orangutan,
radioman

¹**ana** \ än-ə \ ana, anna, bwana,
donna, fauna, mana, chicana,
gymkhana, iguana, jacana,
lantana, liana, Madonna,
mañana, nagana, nirvana,
piranha, Purana, ruana,
zenana, Africana, belladonna,
epifauna, Hinayana, ikebana,
Mahayana, marijuana,
parmigiana, pozzolana, prima

donna, Rosh Hashanah,
Americana, fata morgana,
Lincolniana, nicotiana,
Shakespeareana, Victoriana

²ana\ä-nə\ana, Africana,
cantilena, nicotiana,
Shakespeareana

³ana\an-ə\ana, canna, manna,
nana, banana, bandanna,
cabana, Diana, goanna,
gymkhana, Havana, hosanna,
savanna, sultana, Africana,
poinciana, Pollyanna, Santa
Ana, Americana, fata
morgana, nicotiana,
Shakespeareana, Victoriana

anacle\an-i-kəl\see ANICAL

anage\an-ij\manage, tannage,
stage-manage

¹anah\ō-nə\see ¹ONA

²anah\än-ə\see ¹ANA

anal\ān-ᵊl\anal, banal

analyst\an-ᵊl-əst\analyst,
annalist, panelist,
cryptanalyst, psychoanalyst

anape\an-ə-pē\see ANOPY

¹anary\ān-rē\see ANERY

²anary\an-rē\see ²ANNERY

anate\an-ət\see ANNET

anative\an-ət-iv\sanative,
explanative

¹anc\aⁿ\see ¹ANT

²anc\aŋ\see ²ANG

³anc\aŋk\see ANK

anca\aŋ-kə\barranca, lingua
franca

¹ance\äⁿs\nuance, outrance,
séance, à outrance, diligence,
ordonnance, renaissance,
mésalliance, par excellence,
concours d'elegance, pièce de
résistance

²ance\äns\nonce, ponce,
sconce, brisance, ensconce,
faience, nuance, response,
seance, Afrikaans,
complaisance, fer-de-lance,
nonchalance, provenance,
renaissance, pièce de
résistance

³ance\ans\chance, dance,
glance, lance, manse, nance,
prance, stance, trance, trans,
advance, askance, bechance,
enhance, entrance, expanse,
finance, mischance,
perchance, romance,
Romance, side-glance,
sweatpants, circumstance,
complaisance, contredanse,
country-dance, fer-de-lance,
happenchance, happenstance,
Liederkranz, refinance,
smarty-pants, underpants—
*also plurals and possessives
of verbs listed at* ⁵ANT

anceable\an-sə-bəl\see
ANSIBLE

anced\anst\canst,
circumstanced,
underfinanced—*also pasts of
verbs listed at* ³ANCE

ancel \ an-səl \ cancel, chancel, handsel, expansile, precancel

anceler \ an-slər \ canceler, chancellor, vice-chancellor

ancellor \ an-slər \ see ANCELER

ancement \ an-smənt \ advancement, enhancement

ancer \ an-sər \ answer, cancer, dancer, glancer, lancer, prancer, advancer, enhancer, free-lancer, merganser, romancer, ropedancer, anticancer, geomancer, necromancer, rhabdomancer

ancet \ an-sət \ lancet, Narraganset

¹anch \ änch \ see ¹AUNCH

²anch \ önch \ see ²AUNCH

³anch \ anch \ blanch, branch, ranch, rebranch, avalanche

¹anche \ ä^nsh \ tranche, carte blanche, revanche

²anche \ anch \ see ³ANCH

³anche \ an-chē \ see ANCHY

¹ancher \ òn-chər \ see AUNCHER

²ancher \ an-chər \ ceinture, rancher

anchion \ an-chən \ see ANSION

anchor \ aŋ-kər \ see ANKER

anchoress \ aŋ-krəs \ see ANKEROUS

anchy \ an-chē \ branchy, Comanche

ancial \ an-chəl \ see ANTIAL

ancolin \ aŋ-klən \ see ANKLIN

ancor \ aŋ-kər \ see ANKER

ancorous \ aŋ-krəs \ see ANKEROUS

ancre \ aŋ-kər \ see ANKER

ancrous \ aŋ-krəs \ see ANKEROUS

anct \ aŋt \ see ANKED

ancy \ an-sē \ chancy, fancy, unchancy, chiromancy, geomancy, hydromancy, necromancy, pyromancy, rhabdomancy, sycophancy, oneiromancy

¹and \ ä^n \ see ¹ANT

²and \ änd \ see ¹OND

³and \ and \ and, band, bland, brand, canned, gland, grand, hand, land, manned, NAND, rand, sand, stand, strand, backhand, badland, bandstand, blackland, broadband, brushland, cabstand, cloudland, coastland, command, cowhand, crash-land, cropland, deckhand, demand, disband, dockhand, dockland, dreamland, dryland, duneland, expand, farmhand, farmland, firebrand, firsthand, flatland, forehand, four-hand, free hand, freehand, gangland, glad-hand, grandstand, grassland, handstand, hardstand, hatband, headband, headstand, heartland,

homeland, inkstand, inland,
kickstand, left-hand,
longhand, mainland,
marshland, misbrand,
newsstand, nightstand,
northland, noseband, offhand,
outland, outstand, parkland,
pineland, playland, proband,
quicksand, rangeland,
remand, repand, ribband,
right-hand, rimland, roband,
scabland, screenland,
scrubland, seastrand,
shorthand, sideband, softland,
southland, spaceband,
stagehand, summand,
swampland, sweatband,
thirdhand, tideland, trainband,
unhand, unmanned,
waistband, washstand,
wasteland, watchband,
wetland, wildland, withstand,
wristband, ampersand,
beforehand, behindhand,
bellyband, belly-land,
borderland, bottomland,
contraband, countermand,
Dixieland, fairyland,
fatherland, forestland, four-in-
hand, graduand, hand-to-
hand, hand to hand,
hinterland, Krugerrand,
lotusland, meadowland,
motherland, no-man's-land,
operand, ordinand, overhand,
overland, pastureland,

reprimand, saraband,
secondhand, tableland,
timberland, underhand,
undermanned, understand,
wonderland, analysand,
cloud-cuckoo-land,
fantasyland, misunderstand,
multiplicand, vacationland,
videoland, Alice-in-
Wonderland—*also pasts of
verbs listed at* ⁵AN

anda \an-də\ Ganda, panda,
   veranda, jacaranda,
   memoranda, nomina
   conservanda, propaganda

andable \an-də-bəl\ mandible,
   commandable, demandable,
   expandable, understandable

andaed \an-dəd\ see ANDED

andal \an-dᵊl\ see ANDLE

andaled \an-dᵊld\ handled,
   sandaled, well-handled—*also
   pasts of verbs listed at* ANDLE

andalous \an-dləs\ see ²ANDLESS

andam \an-dəm\ see ANDUM

andant \an-dənt\ see ANDENT

andarin \an-drən\ mandarin,
   alexandrine, salamandrine

¹**ande** \ən\ see UN

²**ande** \an\ see ⁵AN

anded \an-dəd\ banded, candid,
   handed, landed, stranded,
   backhanded, bare-handed,
   cleanhanded, forehanded,
   four-handed, freehanded,
   ham-handed, hardhanded,

high-handed, ironhanded, left-handed, light-handed, offhanded, one-handed, red-handed, right-handed, shorthanded, sure-handed, three-handed, two-handed, unbranded, verandaed, empty-handed, evenhanded, heavy-handed, openhanded, overhanded, singlehanded, underhanded—*also pasts of verbs listed at* ³AND

andel \ an-dᵊl \ see ANDLE

andem \ an-dəm \ see ANDUM

andent \ an-dənt \ candent, scandent, demandant

¹**ander** \ en-dər \ see ENDER

²**ander** \ än-dər \ see ¹ONDER

³**ander** \ an-dər \ bander, brander, candor, dander, gander, grandeur, lander, pander, sander, slander, strander, zander, auslander, blackhander, bystander, commander, demander, expander, flatlander, germander, glad-hander, goosander, grandstander, inlander, Leander, left-hander, mainlander, meander, outlander, philander, pomander, right-hander, scrimshander, soft-lander, Uitlander, Africander, alexander, calamander, coriander, gerrymander, oleander, salamander, single-hander—*also comparatives of adjectives listed at* ³AND

anderous \ an-drəs \ see ANDROUS

anders \ an-dərz \ Bouvier des Flandres, golden alexanders—*also plurals and possessives of verbs listed at* ³ANDER

andery \ an-drē \ see ANDRY

¹**andeur** \ an-dər \ see ³ANDER

²**andeur** \ an-jər \ see ⁴ANGER

andhi \ an-dē \ see ANDY

andi \ an-dē \ see ANDY

andible \ an-də-bəl \ see ANDABLE

andid \ an-dəd \ see ANDED

anding \ an-diŋ \ standing, commanding, freestanding, hardstanding, long-standing, outstanding, upstanding, mind-expanding, notwithstanding, understanding

andish \ an-dish \ blandish, brandish, standish, outlandish

andist \ an-dəst \ contrabandist, propagandist—*also superlatives of adjectives listed at* ³AND

andit \ an-dət \ bandit, pandit

andle \ an-dᵊl \ candle, dandle, handle, sandal, scandal, vandal, footcandle, manhandle, mishandle,

panhandle, stickhandle,
coromandel

andler \ an-lər \ candler,
chandler, handler,
panhandler, stickhandler

¹andless \ an-ləs \ see ANLESS

²andless \ an-dləs \ landless,
scandalous

andly \ an-lē \ see ²ANLY

andment \ an-mənt \
commandment, disbandment

andom \ an-dəm \ see ANDUM

andor \ an-dər \ see ³ANDER

andra \ an-drə \ Cassandra,
pachysandra

andrel \ an-drəl \ mandrel,
mandrill, spandrel

andres \ an-dərz \ see ANDERS

andrill \ an-drəl \ see ANDREL

andrine \ an-drən \ see ANDARIN

androus \ an-drəs \ slanderous,
gynandrous, meandrous,
polyandrous

andry \ an-drē \ commandery,
monandry, polyandry

andsel \ an-səl \ see ANCEL

andsman \ anz-mən \ bandsman,
clansman, Klansman,
landsman

andsome \ an-səm \ see ANSOM

andum \ an-dəm \ fandom,
grandam, random, tandem,
memorandum, nomen
conservandum, subpoena ad
testificandum

andy \ an-dē \ bandy, brandy,
candy, dandy, handy, pandy,
randy, sandhi, sandy, shandy,
jim-dandy, unhandy, modus
operandi

¹ane \ ān \ ain, ane, bane, blain,
brain, Cain, cane, chain,
crane, Dane, deign, drain,
fain, fane, feign, gain, grain,
lane, main, mane, pain, pane,
plain, plane, quean, rain,
reign, rein, sain, sane, seine,
skein, slain, sprain, stain,
stane, strain, swain, thane,
thegn, train, twain, vain,
vane, vein, wain, wane,
abstain, again, airplane,
amain, arcane, arraign, attain,
biplane, birdbrain, bloodstain,
bugbane, campaign,
champagne, champaign,
checkrein, chicane, chilblain,
chow mein, cinquain,
cocaine, Cockaigne,
coxswain, complain,
constrain, contain, cordwain,
cowbane, crackbrain,
demesne, deplane, destain,
detain, detrain, disdain,
distain, distrain, dogbane,
domain, drivetrain, edge-
grain, Elaine, emplane,
enchain, engrain, enplane,
entrain, explain, eyestrain,
fleabane, floatplane,
floodplain, Gawain, germane,

grosgrain, henbane, house-
train, humane, Igraine,
immane, inane, ingrain,
insane, lamebrain, lightplane,
maintain, marchpane,
membrane, migraine,
montane, moraine, mortmain,
mundane, neck-rein, obtain,
octane, ordain, pertain, plain-
Jane, profane, ptomaine,
purslane, quatrain, refrain,
remain, restrain, retain,
retrain, romaine, sailplane,
sea-lane, seaplane, seatrain,
sustain, tearstain, terrain,
terrane, triplane, unchain,
urbane, vervain, vicereine,
villein, volplane, warplane,
wolfsbane, aeroplane,
appertain, aquaplane,
ascertain, avellane,
cellophane, Charles's Wain,
chatelain, chatelaine,
counterpane, entertain,
featherbrain, foreordain,
frangipane, gyroplane,
hurricane, hydroplane,
hyperplane, inhumane, Mary
Jane, mise-en-scène,
monoplane, Novocain,
neutercane, novocaine,
overlain, paravane, peneplain,
preordain, rattlebrain,
scatterbrain, shaggymane,
sugarcane, suzerain,

terreplein, tramontane,
transmontane, windowpane,
auf Wiedersehen,
balletomane, convertiplane,
demimondaine, elecampane,
extramundane, intermontane,
legerdemain, ultramontane
²**ane** \an\ see ⁵AN
anea \ä-nē-ə\ see ²ANIA
anean \ä-nē-ən\ see ²ANIAN
aned \änd\ see AINED
anee \an-ē\ see ANNY
aneful \ān-fəl\ see AINFUL
anel \an-ᵊl\ see ANNEL
anelist \an-ᵊl-əst\ see ANALYST
aneous \ā-nē-əs\ cutaneous,
extraneous, spontaneous,
coetaneous, consentaneous,
instantaneous, miscellaneous,
porcelaneous, simultaneous,
succedaneous,
contemporaneous,
extemporaneous
¹**aner** \ā-nər\ see AINER
²**aner** \än-ər\ see ¹ONOR
anery \än-rē\ granary,
chicanery
anet \an-ət\ see ANNET
aneum \ā-nē-əm\ see ANIUM
¹**ang** \äŋ\ see ¹ONG
²**ang** \aŋ\ bang, bhang, clang,
dang, fang, gang, gangue,
hang, pang, prang, rang,
sang, slang, spang, sprang,
stang, tang, twang, whang,

yang, cliff-hang, defang,
ginseng, harangue, linsang,
meringue, mustang, orang,
parang, press-gang, probang,
shebang, slam-bang,
straphang, trepang, whizbang,
boomerang, charabanc,
overhang, parasang, siamang,
interrobang, orangutan

anga \ äŋ-gə \ see ONGA

angar \ aŋ-ər \ see ²ANGER

¹**ange** \ äⁿzh \ blancmange,
mélange

²**ange** \ ānj \ change, grange,
mange, range, strange,
arrange, derange, downrange,
estrange, exchange, long-
range, outrange, short-range,
shortchange, counterchange,
disarrange, interchange,
onmirange

³**ange** \ anj \ flange, phalange

angel \ aŋ-gəl \ see ANGLE

angement \ ānj-mənt \
arrangement, derangement,
estrangement, disarrangement

angency \ an-jən-sē \ plangency,
tangency

angent \ an-jənt \ plangent,
tangent

¹**anger** \ ān-jər \ changer, danger,
granger, manger, ranger,
stranger, bushranger,
endanger, estranger,
exchanger, shortchanger,
interchanger

²**anger** \ aŋ-ər \ banger, clangor,
clangour, ganger, hangar,
hanger, languor, twanger,
cliff-hanger, straphanger,
haranguer, paperhanger

³**anger** \ aŋ-gər \ anger, clangor

⁴**anger** \ an-jər \ flanger,
grandeur, phalanger

angi \ aŋ-ē \ see ²ANGY

angible \ an-jə-bəl \ frangible,
tangible, infrangible,
intangible, refrangible

angie \ aŋ-ē \ see ²ANGY

¹**anging** \ ān-jiŋ \ bushranging,
unchanging, wide-ranging

²**anging** \ aŋ-iŋ \ hanging, cliff-
hanging, paperhanging

angle \ aŋ-gəl \ angle, bangle,
dangle, jangle, mangel,
mangle, spangle, strangle,
tangle, wangle, wrangle,
embrangle, entangle,
pentangle, quadrangle,
rectangle, triangle, untangle,
wide-angle, disentangle

angled \ aŋ-gəld \ angled,
tangled, newfangled,
oldfangled, right-angled, star-
spangled—*also pasts of verbs
listed at* ANGLE

anglement \ aŋ-gəl-mənt \
tanglement, embranglement,
entanglement,
disentanglement

angler \ aŋ-glər \ angler,
dangler, jangler, mangler,

strangler, wangler, wrangler,
entangler

angles \aŋ-gəlz \ Angles,
strangles—*also plurals and
possessives of nouns and third
singular presents of verbs
listed at* ANGLE

anglian \aŋ-glē-ən \ Anglian,
ganglion

angling \aŋ-gliŋ \ angling,
gangling

anglion \aŋ-glē-ən \ *see*
ANGLIAN

angly \aŋ-glē \ gangly, tangly

ango \aŋ-gō \ mango, tango,
fandango

¹angor \aŋ-ər \ *see* ²ANGER

²angor \aŋ-gər \ *see* ³ANGER

angorous \aŋ-ə-rəs \ clangorous,
languorous

angour \aŋ-ər \ *see* ²ANGER

angster \aŋ-stər \ gangster,
prankster

anguage \aŋ-gwij \ language,
slanguage, metalanguage,
paralanguage, protolanguage

angue \aŋ \ *see* ²ANG

anguer \aŋ-ər \ *see* ²ANGER

anguish \aŋ-gwish \ anguish,
languish

anguor \aŋ-ər \ *see* ²ANGER

anguorous \aŋ-ə-rəs \ *see*
ANGOROUS

¹angy \än-jē \ mangy, rangy

²angy \aŋ-ē \ tangy, twangy,
Ubangi, collieshangie

anha \än-ə \ *see* ¹ANA

anhope \an-əp \ *see* ANNUP

¹ani \än-ē \ bonny, fawny,
johnny, tawny, afghani,
Fulani, chalcedony, maharani,
quadriphony, Rajasthani,
mulligatawny

²ani \an-ē \ *see* ANNY

¹ania \än-yə \ lasagna, Titania

²ania \ā-nē-ə \ mania, titania,
Urania, Anglomania,
collectanea, dipsomania,
egomania, hypomania,
kleptomania, miscellanea,
monomania, mythomania,
nymphomania, pyromania,
balletomania, bibliomania,
decalcomania,
megalomania—*see also* ³ANIA

³ania \än-yə \ Titania,
malaguena—*also words listed
at* ²ANIA

¹anian \än-ē-ən \ Kiwanian,
Araucanian, Turanian

²anian \ā-nē-ən \ Albanian,
Dardanian, Iranian,
Romanian, Rumanian,
Sassanian, Turanian,
Ukrainian, Uranian,
vulcanian, Lithuanian,
Pennsylvanian, Pomeranian,
Ruritanian, subterranean,
Indo-Iranian, Mediterranean

aniard \an-yərd \ lanyard,
Spaniard

anic \an-ik \ manic, panic,

tannic, Brahmanic, Britannic, cyanic, galvanic, Germanic, Hispanic, Koranic, mechanic, melanic, organic, Romanic, satanic, shamanic, Sudanic, titanic, tympanic, volcanic, aldermanic, Alemannic, councilmanic, epiphanic, inorganic, messianic, oceanic, Ossianic, talismanic, theophanic, Indo-Germanic, megalomanic, Rhaeto-Romanic, suboceanic, transoceanic

anical \ an-i-kəl \ manacle, panicle, sanicle, botanical, mechanical, tyrannical, puritanical

anicle \ an-i-kəl \ see ANICAL

anics \ an-iks \ annex, mechanics—*also plurals and possessives of nouns listed at* ANIC

¹**anid** \ ā-nəd \ ranid, tabanid

²**anid** \ an-əd \ canid, ranid, Sassanid

¹**aniel** \ an-ᵊl \ see ANNEL

²**aniel** \ an-yəl \ see ANUAL

anigan \ an-i-gən \ see ANNIGAN

anikin \ an-i-kən \ see ANNIKIN

animous \ an-ə-məs \ animus, magnanimous, unanimous, pusillanimous

animus \ an-ə-məs \ see ANIMOUS

¹**anion** \ än-yən \ see ¹ONYON

²**anion** \ an-yən \ banyan, canon, canyon, fanion, companion

anise \ an-əs \ anise, stannous, johannes, pandanus, titanous

¹**anish** \ ā-nish \ see AINISH

²**anish** \ an-ish \ banish, clannish, mannish, planish, Spanish, tannish, vanish, Pollyannish, Judeo-Spanish

anist \ än-əst \ see ONEST

anister \ an-ə-stər \ canister, ganister

anite \ an-ət \ see ANNET

anity \ an-ət-ē \ sanity, vanity, humanity, inanity, insanity, profanity, urbanity, Christianity, churchianity, inhumanity, superhumanity

anium \ ā-nē-əm \ cranium, geranium, uranium, succedaneum

ank \ aŋk \ bank, blank, brank, clank, crank, dank, drank, flank, franc, frank, Frank, hank, lank, plank, prank, rank, sank, shank, shrank, spank, stank, swank, tank, thank, yank, Yank, claybank, embank, foreshank, gangplank, greenshank, nonbank, outflank, outrank, pickthank, point-blank, redshank, sandbank, sheepshank, snowbank, mountebank, riverbank, clinkety-clank

anka\äŋ-kə\concha, tanka

ankable\aŋ-kə-bəl\bankable, frankable

anked\aŋt\shanked, tanked, spindle-shanked, sacrosanct— *also pasts of verbs listed at* ANK

ankee\an-kē\see ANKY

anken\aŋ-kən\flanken, Rankine

anker\aŋ-kər\anchor, banker, canker, chancre, flanker, franker, hanker, rancor, ranker, spanker, tanker, thanker, co-anchor, unanchor—*also comparatives of adjectives listed at* ANK

ankerous\aŋ-krəs\anchoress, cankerous, chancrous, rancorous, cantankerous

ankh\äŋk\see [1]ONK

ankie\an-kē\see ANKY

ankine\aŋ-kən\see ANKEN

ankish\aŋ-kish\Frankish, prankish

ankle\aŋ-kəl\ankle, crankle, rankle

anklin\aŋ-klən\franklin, francolin

ankly\aŋ-klē\blankly, dankly, frankly

anks\aŋs\see ANX

ankster\aŋ-stər\see ANGSTER

anky\aŋ-kē\cranky, hankie, lanky, swanky, Yankee, hanky-panky

anless\an-ləs\handless, manless, planless

anli\an-lē\see [2]ANLY

[1]anly\än-lē\fondly, thrawnly, wanly

[2]anly\an-lē\blandly, grandly, manly, Osmanli, unmanly

[1]anna\än-ə\see [1]ANA

[2]anna\an-ə\see [3]ANA

annage\an-ij\see ANAGE

annalist\an-ᵊl-əst\see ANALYST

anne\an\see [5]AN

anned\and\see [3]AND

annel\an-ᵊl\channel, Daniel, flannel, panel, scrannel, spaniel, impanel

annequin\an-i-kən\see ANNIKIN

anner\an-ər\banner, canner, fanner, lanner, manner, manor, planner, scanner, spanner, tanner, vanner, deadpanner, japanner, caravanner

[1]annery\än-rē\ornery, swannery

[2]annery\an-rē\cannery, granary, tannery

annes\an-əs\see ANISE

anness\än-nəs\fondness, wanness

annet\an-ət\gannet, granite, planet, pomegranate

annexe\an-iks\see ANICS

annic\an-ik\see ANIC

annigan \an-i-gən\ brannigan, shenanigan

annikin \an-i-kən\ cannikin, manikin, mannequin, pannikin

annin \an-ən\ see ANNON

annish \an-ish\ see ²ANISH

annon \an-ən\ cannon, canon, tannin, colcannon

annous \an-əs\ see ANISE

anns \anz\ see ⁴ANS

annual \an-yəl\ see ANUAL

annular \an-yə-lər\ annular, cannular, granular

annulate \an-yə-lət\ annulate, annulet, campanulate

annulet \an-yə-lət\ see ANNULATE

annum \an-əm\ see ²ANUM

annup \an-əp\ sannup, stanhope

anny \an-ē\ canny, cranny, fanny, granny, nanny, afghani, ca'canny, kokanee, uncanny, frangipani, Hindustani, hootenanny

¹ano \än-ō\ guano, llano, mano, mono, Chicano, Marrano, piano, Romano, soprano, altiplano, boliviano, forte-piano, messo piano, mezzo-soprano

²ano \ä-nō\ ripieno, volcano

³ano \an-ō\ Hispano, piano, soprano, mezzo-soprano

¹anon \an-ən\ see ANNON

²anon \an-yən\ see ²ANION

anopy \an-ə-pē\ canape, canopy

anor \an-ər\ see ANNER

anous \an-əs\ see ANISE

anqui \än-kē\ see ONKY

¹ans \äns\ see ²ANCE

²ans \änz\ see ONZE

³ans \ans\ see ³ANCE

⁴ans \anz\ banns, sans, trans, Sextans—*also plurals and possessives of nouns and third singular presents of verbs listed at* ⁵AN

anse \ans\ see ³ANCE

anser \an-sər\ see ANCER

anset \an-sət\ see ANCET

ansible \an-sə-bəl\ danceable, expansible

ansile \an-səl\ see ANCEL

ansion \an-chən\ mansion, scansion, stanchion, expansion

ansman \anz-mən\ see ANDSMAN

ansom \an-səm\ handsome, hansom, ransom, transom, unhandsome

anst \anst\ see ANCED

answer \an-sər\ see ANCER

ansy \an-zē\ pansy, tansy, chimpanzee

¹ant \äⁿ\ arpent, beurre blanc, croissant, riant, roman, savant, versant, accouchement, aide-de-camp, au courant, battement, ci-devant, contretemps,

debridement, denouement, en
passant, rapprochement,
revenant, se tenant, soi-
disant, vol-au-vent,
arrondissement,
chateaubriand, idiot savant,
ressentiment, sauvignon blanc

²**ant** \änt \aunt, can't, daunt,
flaunt, font, fount, gaunt,
taunt, vaunt, want, wont,
avaunt, bacchant, bacchante,
Balante, bouffant, brisant,
courante, entente, gallant,
grandaunt, piedmont, piquant,
romaunt, savant, sirvente,
bon vivant, commandant,
complaisant, confidant,
debridement, debutant,
debutante, dilettante,
intrigant, nonchalant, poste
restante, restaurant, symbiont,
subdebutante, sinfonia
concertante

³**ant** \ənt \see ¹ONT

⁴**ant** \ȯnt \see ¹AUNT

⁵**ant** \ant \ant, aunt, brant, cant,
can't, chant, grant, hant,
pant, plant, rant, scant,
shan't, slant, aslant,
bacchant, bacchante, bezant,
courante, decant, descant,
discant, displant, eggplant,
enceinte, enchant, explant,
extant, formant, gallant,
grandaunt, houseplant,
implant, incant, leadplant,

levant, pieplant, plainchant,
pourpoint, preplant, rampant,
recant, replant, savant,
supplant, transplant, adamant,
commandant, complaisant,
confidant, cormorant,
corposant, Corybant,
covenant, dilettante,
disenchant, gallivant,
hierophant, interplant,
sycophant

anta \ant-ə \anta, manta,
infanta, vedanta, Atalanta

antage \ant-ij \vantage,
advantage, coign of vantage,
disadvantage

antain \ant-ᵊn \see ²ANTON

¹**antal** \änt-ᵊl \see ¹ONTAL

²**antal** \ant-ᵊl \see ANTLE

antam \ant-əm \bantam,
phantom

antar \ant-ər \see ²ANTER

antasist \ant-ə-səst \see
ANTICIST

¹**ante** \än-tä \andante, volante

²**ante** \änt \see ²ANT

³**ante** \ant \see ⁵ANT

⁴**ante** \änt-ē \see ¹ANTI

⁵**ante** \ant-ē \ante, canty,
chantey, pantie, scanty,
shanty, slanty, andanti,
Ashanti, Chianti, infante, non
obstante, penny-ante,
vigilante, pococurante, status
quo ante

antean \ ant-ē-ən \ Dantean,
  Atlantean, post-Kantian
anteau \ an-tō \ see ²ANTO
antel \ ant-ᵊl \ see ANTLE
antelet \ ant-lət \ mantelet,
  plantlet
¹**anter** \ änt-ər \ see ¹AUNTER
²**anter** \ ant-ər \ antre, banter,
  canter, cantor, chanter,
  granter, grantor, planter,
  planter, ranter, scanter,
  decanter, implanter, instanter,
  levanter, transplanter,
  trochanter, covenanter,
  covenantor, disenchanter
antey \ ant-ē \ see ⁵ANTE
anth \ anth \ amaranth,
  coelacanth, perianth,
  tragacanth
antha \ an-thə \ polyantha,
  pyracantha
anthemum \ an-thə-məm \
  chrysanthemum,
  mesembryanthemum
anther \ an-thər \ anther, panther
anthropy \ an-thrə-pē \
  lycanthropy, misanthropy,
  philanthropy
anthus \ an-thəs \ acanthus,
  ailanthus, dianthus,
  agapanthus, amianthus,
  polyanthus, Rhadamanthus
¹**anti** \ änt-ē \ jaunty, monte,
  vaunty, andante, Ashanti,
  Chianti
²**anti** \ ant-ē \ see ⁵ANTE

antial \ an-chəl \ financial,
  substantial, circumstantial,
  consubstantial, insubstantial,
  transsubstantial, unsubstantial,
  supersubstantial
¹**antian** \ änt-ē-ən \ see ONTIAN
²**antian** \ ant-ē-ən \ see ANTEAN
¹**antic** \ änt-ik \ see ONTIC
²**antic** \ ant-ik \ antic, frantic,
  mantic, Atlantic, bacchantic,
  gigantic, pedantic, romantic,
  semantic, Vedantic,
  corybantic, geomantic,
  hierophantic, necromantic,
  sycophantic, transatlantic
anticist \ ant-ə-səst \ fantasist,
  Atlanticist, romanticist,
  semanticist
antid \ ant-əd \ mantid,
  Quadrantid—*also pasts of
  verbs listed at* ⁵ANT
antie \ ant-ē \ see ⁵ANTE
antine \ ant-ᵊn \ see ²ANTON
¹**anting** \ ant-iŋ \ anting, canting,
  disenchanting
²**anting** \ ənt-iŋ \ see UNTING
antis \ ant-əs \ cantus, mantis,
  Atlantis
antish \ ant-ish \ dilettantish,
  sycophantish
antle \ ant-ᵊl \ cantle, mantel,
  mantle, quintal, dismantle,
  quadrantal, consonantal,
  covenantal, overmantel,
  determinantal
antlet \ ant-lət \ see ANTELET

antling \ant-liŋ\ bantling, scantling

¹**anto** \än-tō\ Esperanto, bel canto

²**anto** \an-tō\ canto, coranto, portmanteau, Esperanto

antom \ant-əm\ see ANTAM

¹**anton** \änt-ᵊn\ see ONTON

²**anton** \ant-ᵊn\ canton, plantain, adamantine

antor \ant-ər\ see ²ANTER

antra \ən-trə\ tantra, yantra

antre \ant-ər\ see ²ANTER

antry \an-trē\ chantry, gantry, pantry

ants \ans\ see ³ANCE

antua \anch-wə\ mantua, Gargantua

antus \ant-əs\ see ANTIS

anty \ant-ē\ see ⁵ANTE

anual \an-yəl\ Daniel, spaniel, annual, manual, biannual, bimanual, Immanuel, semiannual

anuel \an-yəl\ see ANUAL

anular \an-yə-lər\ see ANNULAR

anulate \an-yə-lət\ see ANNULATE

¹**anum** \ā-nəm\ paynim, arcanum

²**anum** \an-əm\ per annum, solanum

¹**anus** \ā-nəs\ see AYNESS

²**anus** \an-əs\ see ANISE

anx \aŋs\ Manx, thanks, phalanx—*also plurals and possessives of nouns and third singular presents of verbs listed at* ANK

¹**any** \ā-nē\ see AINY

²**any** \en-ē\ see ENNY

anyan \an-yən\ see ²ANION

anyard \an-yərd\ see ANIARD

anyon \an-yən\ see ²ANION

anz \ans\ see ³ANCE

¹**anza** \än-zə\ Kwanza, Sancho Panza

²**anza** \an-zə\ stanza, zanza, bonanza, organza, Sancho Panza, extravaganza

anzee \an-zē\ see ANSY

anzer \än-sər\ see ONSOR

anzo \än-zō\ gonzo, garbanzo

anzy \än-zē\ bronzy, Ponzi

¹**ao** \ä-ō\ see ¹EO

²**ao** \ō\ see ¹OW

³**ao** \aů\ see ²OW

aoedic \ēd-ik\ see ¹EDIC

aole \aů-lē\ see ²OWLY

aori \aůr-ē\ see OWERY

aotian \ō-shən\ see OTION

aow \aů\ see ²OW

¹**ap** \äp\ see ¹OP

²**ap** \əp\ see UP

³**ap** \ap\ cap, chap, clap, crap, flap, frap, gap, gape, hap, Jap, knap, lap, Lapp, map, nap, nape, nappe, pap, rap, sap, scrap, slap, snap, strap, tap, trap, wrap, yap, zap, backslap, backwrap, blackcap, bootstrap, burlap,

catnap, claptrap, dewlap,
dognap, earflap, entrap,
enwrap, firetrap, flatcap,
foolscap, giddap, heeltap,
hubcap, jockstrap, kidnap,
kneecap, lagniappe, livetrap,
madcap, mantrap, mayhap,
mishap, mobcap, mousetrap,
nightcap, pinesap, rattrap,
recap, redcap, remap, riprap,
satrap, shiplap, shrink-wrap,
skullcap, skycap, snowcap,
steel-trap, stopgap, unsnap,
unstrap, unwrap, verb sap,
whitecap, wiretap, afterclap,
gingersnap, handicap,
overlap, rattletrap,
thunderclap, verbum sap,
wentletrap, Venus's-flytrap

¹apa \ äp-ə \ grappa, papa,
poppa, tapa, jinijapa

²apa \ ap-ə \ kappa, tapa, Phi
Beta Kappa

apable \ ā-pə-bəl \ capable,
drapable, shapable,
escapable, incapable,
inescapable

apal \ ā-pəl \ see APLE

apboard \ ab-ərd \ see ABARD

¹ape \ āp \ ape, cape, chape,
crape, crepe, drape, gape,
grape, jape, nape, rape,
scape, scrape, shape, tape,
agape, broomrape, escape,
landscape, moonscape,
reshape, seascape, shipshape,

snowscape, townscape,
transshape, undrape,
waveshape, cityscape,
waterscape, audiotape,
stereotape, videotape

²ape \ ap \ see ³AP

³ape \ äp-ē \ see OPPY

⁴ape \ ap-ē \ see APPY

apel \ ap-əl \ sec APPLE

apelin \ ap-lən \ see APLAIN

apen \ ā-pən \ capon, shapen,
unshapen

aper \ ā-pər \ caper, draper,
gaper, paper, scraper, shaper,
taper, tapir, vapor, vapour,
curlpaper, endpaper, flypaper,
landscaper, newspaper,
notepaper, sandpaper,
skyscraper, wallpaper,
wastepaper, run-of-paper

aperer \ ā-pər-ər \ paperer,
taperer, vaporer

apery \ ā-prē \ drapery, japery,
napery, papery, vapory,
sandpapery

apes \ āps \ traipse, jackanapes—
*also plurals and possessives
of nouns and third singular
presents of verbs listed at*
¹APE

apey \ ā-pē \ crepey, drapy,
grapey, kepi, scrapie

aph \ af \ calf, chaff, daff, gaff,
gaffe, graph, half, laugh,
quaff, raff, sclaff, staff,
staph, Waf, waff, agrafe,

behalf, carafe, chiffchaff,
cowlstaff, digraph, distaff,
Falstaff, flagstaff, giraffe,
half-staff, horselaugh, kenaf,
mooncalf, paraph, pikestaff,
riffraff, tipstaff, autograph,
barograph, bathyscaphe,
cenotaph, chronograph,
cryptograph, epigraph,
epitaph, half-and-half,
hectograph, holograph,
homograph, hygrograph,
kymograph, lithograph,
logograph, micrograph,
monograph, pantograph,
paragraph, phonograph,
photograph, pictograph,
polygraph, quarterstaff,
seismograph, serigraph,
shadowgraph, shandygaff,
spectrograph, sphygmograph,
telegraph, thermograph,
typograph, cardiograph,
choreograph, heliograph,
ideograph, mimeograph,
oscillograph, pseudepigraph,
radiograph, chromolithograph,
cinematograph,
encephalograph,
photomicrograph,
radiotelegraph,
electrocardiograph,
electroencephalograph

aphael\af-ē-əl\see APHIAL

¹aphe\äf\see ¹AFE

²aphe\af\see APH

apher\af-ər\see ²AFFER

aphia\af-ē-ə\see AFFIA

aphial\af-ē-əl\Raphael,
epitaphial

aphic\af-ik\graphic, maffick,
sapphic, traffic, digraphic,
edaphic, serafic, triaphic,
allographic, autographic,
barographic, biographic,
calligraphic, cartographic,
cosmographic, cryptographic,
demographic, epigraphic,
epitaphic, ethnographic,
geographic, hectographic,
homographic, lithographic,
logographic, mammographic,
monographic, orthographic,
pantographic, paragraphic,
petrographic, phonographic,
photographic, pictographic,
polygraphic, pornographic,
reprographic, stenographic,
stratigraphic, telegraphic,
tomographic, topographic,
typographic, xerographic,
bibliographic, choreographic,
crystallographic,
hagiographic, homolographic,
iconographic, ideographic,
lexicographic, oceanographic,
autobiographic,
cinematographic,
echocardiographic,
historiographic,
electroencephalographic

aphical\af-i-kəl\graphical,

biographical, cartographical, cosmographical, cryptographical, epigraphical, ethnographical, geographical, orthographical, petrographical, topographical, typographical, bibliographical, choreographical, hagiographical, iconographical, lexicographical, oceanographical, autobiographical, historiographical

aphics \af-iks\ graphics, demographics, micrographics, supergraphics

aphnis \af-nəs\ see AFTNESS

api \äp-ē\ see OPPY

apid \ap-əd\ rapid, sapid, vapid

apie \ā-pē\ see APEY

apin \ap-ən\ see APPEN

apine \ap-ən\ see APPEN

apir \ā-pər\ see APER

apis \ā-pəs\ Apis, Priapus, Serapis

apist \ā-pəst\ papist, rapist, escapist, landscapist

aplain \ap-lən\ chaplain, capelin, sapling

aple \ā-pəl\ maple, papal, staple

apless \ap-ləs\ hapless, napless, sapless, strapless

aply \ap-lē\ see APTLY

apnel \ap-nᵊl\ grapnel, shrapnel

apo \äp-ō\ capo, da capo, gestapo

apon \ā-pən\ see APEN

apor \ā-pər\ see APER

aporer \ā-pər-ər\ see APERER

apory \ā-prē\ see APERY

apour \ā-pər\ see APER

app \ap\ see ³AP

¹appa \äp-ə\ see ¹APA

²appa \ap-ə\ see ²APA

appable \ap-ə-bəl\ flappable, mappable, recappable, unflappable, recappable

appe \ap\ see ³AP

apped \apt\ see APT

appen \ap-ən\ happen, lapin, rapine

¹apper \äp-ər\ see OPPER

²apper \ap-ər\ capper, clapper, crapper, dapper, flapper, knapper, rapper, sapper, scrapper, snapper, strapper, tapper, wrapper, backslapper, catnapper, didapper, kidnapper, petnapper, wiretapper, handicapper, snippersnapper, understrapper, whippersnapper

appet \ap-ət\ lappet, tappet

apphic \af-ik\ see APHIC

appie \äp-ē\ see OPPY

appily \ap-ə-lē\ happily, scrappily, snappily, unhappily

appiness \ap-ē-nəs\ sappiness,

scrappiness, snappiness, unhappiness

apping \ap-iŋ\ capping, mapping, strapping, trapping, wrapping, petnapping

apple \ap-əl\ apple, chapel, dapple, grapple, scrapple, mayapple, pineapple

apps \aps\ see APSE

appy \ap-ē\ crappy, flappy, gappy, happy, nappy, pappy, sappy, scrappy, snappy, zappy, satrapy, serape, slaphappy, unhappy, triggerhappy

aps \aps\ see APSE

apse \aps\ apse, chaps, craps, lapse, schnapps, taps, traps, collapse, elapse, perhaps, prolapse, relapse, synapse, time-lapse—*also plurals and possessives of nouns and third singular presents of verbs listed at* ³AP

apt \apt\ apt, napped, rapt, adapt, black-capped, coapt, dewlapped, enrapt, inapt, snowcapped, unapt, untapped, periapt—*also pasts of verbs listed at* ³AP

apter \ap-tər\ captor, chapter, raptor, adapter

aption \ap-shən\ caption, adaption, contraption

aptive \ap-tiv\ captive,

adaptive, maladaptive, preadaptive

aptly \ap-lē\ aptly, haply, raptly, inaptly, unaptly

aptor \ap-tər\ see APTER

apture \ap-chər\ rapture, enrapture, recapture

apular \ap-yə-lər\ papular, scapular

apus \ā-pəs\ see APIS

¹**apy** \ā-pē\ see APEY

²**apy** \ap-ē\ see APPY

aqi \äk-ē\ see OCKY

¹**aque** \āk\ see ¹AKE

²**aque** \ak\ see ²ACK

aqui \äk-ē\ see OCKY

¹**ar** \er\ see ⁴ARE

²**ar** \or\ see ¹OR

³**ar** \är\ ar, are, bar, barre, car, char, charr, czar, far, gar, gnar, guar, jar, Lar, mar, moire, our, par, parr, R, quare, scar, spar, SPAR, star, tar, tsar, tzar, yare, Adar, afar, ajar, all-star, armoire, attar, bazaar, beaux arts, bizarre, boudoir, boxcar, boyar, briard, bulbar, Bulgar, bursar, canard, catarrh, Cathar, cigar, clochard, cougar, couloir, crossbar, crowbar, daystar, debar, decare, devoir, dinar, disbar, drawbar, durbar, earthstar, eschar, feldspar, five-star, flatcar, four-star, fulmar,

guitar, Gunnar, Hagar,
handcar, horsecar, hussar,
Invar, Iyar, jack-tar, jowar,
Khowar, lahar, lekvar,
lodestar, Magyar, memoir,
Mizar, nightjar, paillard,
peignoir, petard, pissoir,
planar, plantar, polestar,
pourboire, pulsar, qintar,
quasar, radar, railcar, Safar,
sandbar, scalar, shikar,
shofar, sidebar, sidecar,
sirdar, sitar, sofar, solar,
sonar, streetcar, tramcar,
trocar, unbar, volar, voussoir,
abattoir, acinar, aide-
memoire, au revoir, avatar,
bete noire, beurre noir,
bolivar, caviar, cinnabar,
commissar, communard,
coplanar, cultivar, deciare,
deodar, Dreyfusard, escolar,
escritoire, exemplar,
fluorspar, handlebar, insofar,
isobar, Issachar, jacamar,
jaguar, kilobar, megabar,
millibar, minicar,
montagnard, motorcar,
Mudejar, muscle car, objet
d'art, registrar, rent-a-car,
repertoire, reservoir, samovar,
scimitar, seminar, simular,
steak tartare, subahdar,
superstar, tutelar, turbocar,
VCR, Veadar, zamindar,
budgerigar, café noir,

conservatoire, kala-azar,
proseminar

¹ara \ är-ə \ borrow, morrow,
  para, sorrow, vara, Bambara,
  begorra, Camorra, Gemarara,
  saguaro, samsara, tantara,
  tiara, tomorrow, capybara,
  carbonara, deodara, solfatara,
  tuatara

²ara \ er-ə \ see ¹ERA

³ara \ ar-ə \ see ¹ARROW

⁴ara \ òr-ə \ see ²ORA

arab \ ar-əb \ Arab, Carib,
  carob, scarab

arable \ ar-ə-bəl \ arable,
  bearable, parable, shareable,
  spareable, wearable,
  declarable, unbearable,
  inenarrable

aracen \ ar-ə-sən \ see ARISON

aracin \ ar-ə-sən \ see ARISON

arad \ ar-əd \ see ARID

araday \ ar-əd-ē \ faraday,
  parody

arage \ ar-ij \ see ARRIAGE

aragon \ ar-ə-gən \ paragon,
  tarragon

¹arah \ er-ə \ see ¹ERA

²arah \ ar-ə \ see ¹ARROW

¹aran \ er-ən \ see ¹ARON

²aran \ ar-ən \ see ²ARON

¹arant \ er-ənt \ see ¹ARENT

²arant \ ar-ənt \ see ²ARENT

¹araoh \ er-ō \ see ²ERO

²araoh \ ar-ō \ see ²ARROW

araph \ ar-əf \ see ARIFF

aras \ är-əs \ see ¹ORRIS

arat \ ar-ət \ carat, caret, carrot, claret, garret, karat, parrot, disparate

arate \ ar-ət \ see ARAT

¹arative \ er-ət-iv \ declarative, imperative

²arative \ ar-ət-iv \ narrative, comparative, declarative, preparative, reparative

arator \ ar-ət-ər \ barrator, apparitor, comparator, preparator

arb \ ärb \ barb, barbe, carb, darb, garb, rhubarb

arbel \ är-bəl \ see ¹ARBLE

arber \ är-bər \ see ARBOR

arbered \ är-bərd \ see ARBOARD

¹arble \ är-bəl \ barbel, garble, marble

²arble \ ȯr-bəl \ see ORBEL

arboard \ är-bərd \ barbered, larboard, starboard, astarboard, unbarbered

arbor \ är-bər \ arbor, barber, harbor

¹arc \ äk \ see ¹OCK

²arc \ ärk \ see ¹ARK

arca \ är-kə \ see ¹ARKA

¹arce \ ers \ scarce, Nez Percé

²arce \ ärs \ see ¹ARSE

arcel \ är-səl \ see ARSAL

arcener \ ärs-nər \ larcener, parcener, coparcener

arch \ ärch \ arch, larch, march, March, parch, starch, cornstarch, countermarch

archal \ är-kəl \ darkle, sparkle, exarchal, monarchal, hierarchal, matriarchal, patriarchal

archate \ är-kət \ see ARKET

arche \ ärsh \ see ARSH

arched \ ärcht \ arched, parched—also pasts of verbs listed at ARCH

archer \ är-chər \ archer, marcher, departure

archic \ är-kik \ anarchic, autarchic, autarkic, monarchic, tetrarchic, hierarchic, oligarchic

archical \ är-ki-kəl \ autarchical, autarkical, monarchical, oligarchical

archon \ är-kən \ see ARKEN

archy \ är-kē \ barky, charqui, darky, larky, anarchy, autarchy, autarky, dyarchy, eparchy, exarchy, heptarchy, malarkey, menarche, monarchy, pentarchy, squirearchy, tetrarchy, triarchy, trierarchy, hierarchy, matriarchy, patriarchy, oligarchy

arco \ är-kō \ arco, narco

arct \ ärkt \ see ARKED

¹arctic \ ärk-tik \ arctic, antarctic, Holarctic, Nearctic,

subarctic, Palearctic, subantarctic

²arctic \ ärt-ik \ see ¹ARTIC

arcy \ är-sē \ farcy, Parsi

¹ard \ ärd \ bard, barred, card, chard, Dard, fard, guard, hard, lard, nard, pard, sard, shard, yard, Asgard, backyard, bankcard, barnyard, blackguard, blowhard, bombard, boneyard, brassard, brickyard, canard, churchyard, courtyard, deeryard, die-hard, diehard, discard, dockyard, dooryard, farmyard, filmcard, fireguard, foreyard, foulard, graveyard, ill-starred, jacquard, junkyard, lifeguard, Lombard, mansard, Midgard, milliard, mudguard, petard, placard, postcard, poularde, rear guard, rearguard, regard, retard, ritard, safeguard, scorecard, shipyard, spikenard, steelyard, stockyard, switchyard, tabard, tanyard, tiltyard, unbarred, unguard, vanguard, vizard, avant-garde, bodyguard, boulevard, disregard, goliard, interlard, Langobard, leotard, Longobard, no-holds-barred, lumberyard, Saint Bernard, Savoyard, Scotland Yard,

self-regard, camelopard—*also pasts of verbs listed at* ³AR

²ard \ är \ see ³AR

³ard \ órd \ see ²OARD

ardant \ ärd-°nt \ ardent, guardant, regardant, retardant

arde \ ärd \ see ¹ARD

¹arded \ ärd-əd \ guarded, mansarded, retarded, unguarded—*also pasts of verbs listed at* ¹ARD

²arded \ órd-əd \ corded, sordid, swarded, warded—*also pasts of verbs listed at* ²OARD

ardee \ órd-ē \ see ¹ORDY

¹arden \ ärd-°n \ Dardan, garden, harden, pardon, bombardon, caseharden, face-harden

²arden \ órd-°n \ cordon, warden, churchwarden

ardener \ ärd-nər \ gardener, hardener, pardner, pardoner, partner

ardent \ ärd-°nt \ see ARDANT

¹arder \ ärd-ər \ ardor, carder, guarder, harder, larder, discarder, green-carder

²arder \ órd-ər \ see ORDER

ardi \ ärd-ē \ see ARDY

¹ardian \ ärd-ē-ən \ guardian, Edwardian, Lombardian

²ardian \ órd-ē-ən \ see ORDION

ardic \ ärd-ik \ bardic, Dardic, Lombardic, Sephardic, goliardic, Longobardic

arding \ órd-iŋ \ see ¹ORDING

ardingly \ òrd-iŋ-lē \ see
ORDINGLY
ardom \ ärd-əm \ czardom,
stardom, superstardom
ardon \ ärd-ᵊn \ see ¹ARDEN
ardoner \ ärd-nər \ see ARDENER
ardor \ ärd-ər \ see ¹ARDER
ardy \ ärd-ē \ hardy, lardy,
tardy, foolhardy, Sephardi
¹**are** \ er-ē \ see ¹ARY
²**are** \ är \ see ³AR
³**are** \ är-ē \ see ¹ARI
⁴**are** \ er \ air, bare, bear, blare,
chair, chare, dare, e'er, ere,
err, eyre, fair, fare, flair,
flare, glair, glare, hair, hare,
Herr, heir, lair, mare, ne'er,
pair, pare, pear, prayer,
quare, rare, rear, scare, share,
snare, spare, square, stair,
stare, swear, tare, tear, their,
there, they're, vair, ware,
wear, weir, where, yare,
affair, aglare, airfare, Altair,
armchair, au pair, aware,
barware, beachwear, beware,
bricklayer, bugbear,
caneware, carfare, clayware,
cochair, coheir, compare,
compere, confrere, cookware,
corsair, cudbear, day-care,
daymare, decare, declare,
delftware, despair, dishware,
éclair, elsewhere, ensnare,
fanfare, fieldfare, firmware,
flatware, footwear, forbear,

forebear, forswear,
foursquare, funfair, galère,
giftware, glassware, Gruyère,
hardware, hectare, horsehair,
impair, infare, Khmer,
knitwear, longhair,
loungewear, menswear,
meunière, midair, mohair,
nightmare, outstare, outwear,
playwear, plein air,
plowshare, Poor Clare,
portiere, premiere, prepare,
pushchair, rainwear, redware,
repair, shorthair, skiwear,
sleepwear, slipware, software,
somewhere, spongeware,
sportswear, stemware,
stoneware, threadbare,
tinware, tracklayer, trouvère,
tuyere, unfair, unhair,
unswear, warfare, welfare,
wheelchair, wirehair,
workfare, aftercare, air-to-air,
anywhere, bayadere, bêche-
de-mer, billionaire,
boutonniere, Camembert,
chinaware, crackleware,
cultivar, debonair, deciare,
derriere, Delaware,
dinnerware, disrepair,
doctrinaire, earthenware,
étagère, everywhere,
fourragère, Frigidaire,
graniteware, hollowware,
ironware, jasperware,
kitchenware, laissez-faire,

legionnaire, luminaire, lusterware, maidenhair, mal de mer, medicare, metalware, millionaire, minaudière, minelayer, Mon-Khmer, Mousquetaire, nom de guerre, otherwhere, outerwear, overbear, overwear, potty-chair, porte cochere, questionnaire, rivière, savoir faire, self-aware, self-despair, silverware, solitaire, tableware, thoroughfare, unaware, underwear, Venushair, vivandière, willowware, woodenware, chargé d'affaires, chemin de fer, commissionaire, concessionaire, couturiere, Croix de guerre, devil-may-care, enamelware, memoriter, pied-à-terre, ready-to-wear, son et lumière, vin ordinaire

area \er-ē-ə\ see ARIA
¹areable \er-ə-bəl\ see ¹EARABLE
²areable \ar-ə-bəl\ see ARABLE
areal \er-ē-əl\ see ARIAL
¹arean \er-ē-ən\ see ¹ARIAN
²arean \ar-ē-ən\ see ²ARIAN
ared \erd\ see AIRED
aredness \ar-əd-nəs\ see ARIDNESS
arel \ar-əl\ see ²ARREL
¹arely \er-lē\ see AIRLY
²arely \är-lē\ see ARLIE
arem \er-əm\ see ²ARUM

arence \er-əns\ clarence, forbearance, transparence
¹arent \er-ənt\ daren't, errant, parent, aberrant, afferent, apparent, declarant, deferent, efferent, godparent, grandparent, inapparent, inerrant, knight-errant, sederunt, stepparent, transparent, semitransparent
²arent \ar-ənt\ arrant, daren't, parent, apparent, declarant, godparent, grandparent, stepparent, transparent, inapparent, semitransparent
¹aren't \er-ənt\ see ¹ARENT
²aren't \ar-ənt\ see ²ARENT
¹arer \er-ər\ see ¹EARER
²arer \ar-ər\ see ³EARER
¹ares \erz\ see AIRS
²ares \ar-ēz\ Ares, caries, nares, Antares, primus inter pares—*also plurals and possessives of nouns and third singular presents of verbs listed at* ³ARRY
aret \ar-ət\ see ARAT
areve \är-və\ see ARVA
¹arf \ärf\ barf, scarf
²arf \orf\ see ORPH
argain \är-gən\ bargain, jargon, plea-bargain
arge \ärj\ barge, charge, large, marge, parge, sarge, sparge, targe, discharge, enlarge, litharge, recharge, surcharge,

uncharge, by and large,
hypercharge, overcharge,
supercharge, undercharge
argent \är-jənt \argent,
    margent, sergeant
arger \är-jər \charger,
    discharger, enlarger,
    recharger, supercharger,
    turbocharger,
    turbosupercharger
arget \är-gət \argot, garget,
    target, nontarget
argle \är-gəl \gargle, argle-
    bargle
argo \är-gō \Argo, argot, cargo,
    largo, embargo, supercargo
argon \är-gən \see ARGAIN
¹argot \är-gət \see ARGET
²argot \är-gō \see ARGO
¹ari \er-ē \corrie, gharry,
    quarry, sari, scarry, sorry,
    starry, tarry, Bihari, curare,
    Imari, safari, scalare, shikari,
    calamari, Stradivari,
    zamindari, certiorari
²ari \er-ē \see ¹ARY
³ari \är-ē \see ³ARRY
aria \er-ē-ə \area, Beria, feria,
    kerria, varia, hysteria,
    malaria, planaria, adularia,
    cineraria, fritillaria, laminaria,
    luminaria, militaria,
    sanguinaria, opera seria,
    acetabularia
arial \er-ē-əl \aerial, areal,
    Ariel, burial, glossarial,

notarial, subaerial, vicarial,
    actuarial, adversarial,
    estuarial, secretarial,
    prothonotarial
¹arian \er-ē-ən \Arian, Aryan,
    Marian, parian, Parian,
    agrarian, Aquarian, barbarian,
    Bavarian, Bulgarian,
    cesarean, Caesarian,
    grammarian, Hungarian,
    Khymerian, librarian, Maid
    Marian, ovarian, Pierian,
    riparian, rosarian, Rotarian,
    sectarian, Sumerian,
    Tartarean, Tartarian,
    Tocharian, Tractarian,
    Vulgarian, Wagnerian,
    antiquarian, apiarian,
    centenarian, Indo-Aryan,
    jubilarian, lapidarian,
    libertarian, millenarian,
    nonsectarian, prelapsarian,
    proletarian, Rastafarian,
    Ripuarian, Sabbatarian,
    Sagittarian, sanitarian,
    seminarian, trinitarian,
    unitarian, vegetarian,
    abecedarian, authoritarian,
    communitarian, disciplinarian,
    documentarian, egalitarian,
    equalitarian, futilitarian,
    hereditarian, humanitarian,
    majoritarian, necessitarian,
    nonagenarian, octogenarian,
    parliamentarian,
    postmillinarian,

premillinarian, predestinarian,
radiolarian, Sacramentarian,
sexagenarian, totalitarian,
utilitarian, veterinarian,
establishmentarian,
inegalitarian, latitudinarian,
platitudinarian,
septuagenarian, solitudinarian,
uniformitarian, valetudinarian,
disestablishmentarian

²**arian** \ ar-ē-ən \ Arian, Aryan,
carrion, clarion, parian,
Parian, agrarian, Aquarian,
barbarian, Bavarian,
Bulgarian, caesarean,
Caesarian, cesarean,
Megarian, ovarian, rosarian,
Tartarean, Tartarian,
Tocharian, vulgarian, Indo-
Aryan, Rastafarian

ariance \ ar-ē-əns \ tarriance,
variance, covariance

¹**ariat** \ er-ē-ət \ heriot, lariat,
variate, bivariate, salariat,
vicariate, commissariat,
multivariate, proletariat,
secretariat, undersecretariat

²**ariat** \ är-ē-ət \ see ¹AUREATE

³**ariat** \ ar-ē-ət \ chariot, lariat,
bivariate, salariat,
commissariat, proletariat,
Judas Iscariot

ariate \ er-ē-ət \ see ¹ARIAT

arib \ ar-əb \ see ARAB

aric \ ar-ik \ barrack, carrack,

Amharic, barbaric, Megaric,
Pindaric

arid \ ar-əd \ arid, farad,
semiarid

aridness \ ar-əd-nəs \ aridness,
preparedness

¹**aried** \ er-ēd \ see ERRIED

²**aried** \ ar-ēd \ see ARRIED

ariel \ er-e-əl \ see ARIAL

¹**arier** \ er-ē-ər \ see ERRIER

²**arier** \ ar-ē-ər \ see ²ARRIER

aries \ ar-ēz \ see ²ARES

ariff \ ar-əf \ paraph, tariff

aril \ ar-əl \ see ²ARREL

arily \ ar-ə-lē \ merrily, scarily,
sterily, verily, contrarily,
primarily, arbitrarily,
customarily, dietarily,
exemplarily, fragmentarily,
honorarily, literarily,
mercenarily, militarily,
momentarily, necessarily,
salutarily, sanguinarily,
sanitarily, secondarily,
temporarily, unitarily,
voluntarily, contemporarily,
elementarily, extemporarily,
extraordinarily, hereditarily,
imaginarily, involuntarily,
preliminarily, rudimentarily,
subsidiarily, unnecessarily,
documentarily, evolutionarily,
revolutionarily

arin \ är-ən \ see ¹ORIN

arinate \ ar-ə-nət \ see ARONET

arinet \ ar-ə-nət \ see ARONET

¹**aring** \er-iŋ\ airing, fairing,
flaring, glaring, herring,
paring, raring, sparing,
tearing, wearing,
cheeseparing, childbearing,
seafaring, time-sharing,
unerring, unsparing,
wayfaring

²**aring** \er-ən\ see ¹ARON

arion \ar-ē-ən\ see ²ARIAN

ariot \ar-ē-ət\ see ³ARIAT

arious \er-ē-əs\ carious,
scarious, various, Aquarius,
burglarious, calcareous,
contrarious, denarius,
gregarious, guarnerius,
hilarious, nefarious,
precarious, senarius,
vagarious, vicarious,
multifarious, omnifarious,
septenarius, Stradivarius,
Sagittarius, temerarious

¹**aris** \är-əs\ see ¹ORRIS

²**aris** \ar-əs\ arras, arris,
heiress, Paris, parous, varus,
coheiress, embarrass, Polaris,
disembarrass, millionairess,
plaster of paris

¹**arish** \er-ish\ bearish, cherish,
fairish, garish, perish,
squarish, nightmarish

²**arish** \ar-ish\ garish, marish,
parish

arison \ar-ə-sən\ characin,
garrison, Saracen, warison,
caparison, comparison

arist \er-əst\ Marist, querist,
aquarist, pleinairist, scenarist,
apiarist—*also superlatives of
adjectives listed at* ⁴ARE

aritan \er-ət-ⁿn\ see ERATIN

aritor \er-ət-ər\ see ARATOR

¹**arity** \er-ət-ē\ see ERITY

²**arity** \ar-ət-ē\ carroty, charity,
clarity, parity, rarity,
barbarity, disparity, hilarity,
imparity, polarity, unclarity,
vulgarity, angularity,
familiarity, insularity,
peculiarity, popularity,
regularity, similarity,
singularity, solidarity,
complementarity,
dissimilarity, irregularity,
particularity, unfamiliarity,
unpopularity

arium \er-ē-əm\ barium,
aquarium, herbarium,
sacrarium, samarium,
solarium, terrarium, velarium,
vivarium, cinerarium,
columbarium, honorarium,
leprosarium, oceanarium,
planetarium, sanitarium,
syllabarium, termitarium,
armamentarium

arius \er-ē-əs\ see ARIOUS

¹**ark** \ärk\ arc, ark, bark, dark,
hark, lark, marc, mark,
Mark, marque, narc, nark,
park, quark, sark, shark,
spark, stark, aardvark,

airpark, anarch, ballpark, birchbark, birthmark, bookmark, debark, demark, earmark, embark, endarch, exarch, footmark, futhark, Graustark, hallmark, landmark, monarch, ostmark, pitch-dark, pockmark, postmark, pressmark, pugmark, reichsmark, remark, remarque, ringbark, seamark, shagbark, sitzmark, skylark, soapbark, tanbark, tetrarch, tidemark, titlark, touchmark, trademark, cutty sark, deutsche mark, disembark, double-park, hierarch, matriarch, meadowlark, metalmark, minipark, oligarch, patriarch, stringybark, telemark, trierarch, watermark, heresiarch, symposiarch

²ark\órk\see ²ORK

¹arka\är-kə\charka, parka, anasarca

²arka\ər-kə\see ¹URKA

arked\ärkt\marked, chop-marked, infarct, ripple-marked, unremarked—*also pasts of verbs listed at* ¹ARK

arken\är-kən\archon, darken, hearken

arker\är-kər\barker, larker, marker, parker, sparker, bookmarker, skylarker, nosey

parker—*also comparatives of adjectives listed at* ¹ARK

arket\är-kət\market, newmarket, upmarket, aftermarket, hypermarket, matriarchate, patriarchate, supermarket

arkey\är-kē\see ARCHY

arkian\är-kē-ən\Graustarkian, Lamarckian, Monarchian

arkic\är-kik\see ARCHIC

arking\är-kiŋ\carking, parking, loan-sharking

arkle\är-kəl\see ARCHAL

arky\är-kē\see ARCHY

arl\ärl\farl, gnarl, jarl, marl, parle, quarrel, snarl, ensnarl, housecarl, unsnarl

arlatan\är-lət-ᵊn\charlatan, tarlatan

arlay\är-lē\see ARLIE

arler\är-lər\see ARLOR

arless\är-ləs\parlous, scarless, starless

arlet\är-lət\charlotte, harlot, scarlet, starlet, varlet

arley\är-lē\see ARLIE

arlic\är-lik\garlic, pilgarlic

arlie\är-lē\barley, charlie, Charlie, gnarly, marly, parlay, parley, snarly, yarely, bizarrely, Mr. Charlie

arlin\är-lən\see ARLINE

arline\är-lən\carline, marlin, marline

arling \ är-liŋ \ carling, darling, starling

arlor \ är-lər \ parlor, quarreler, snarler

arlot \ är-lət \ see ARLET

arlotte \ är-lət \ see ARLET

arlous \ är-ləs \ see ARLESS

arly \ är-lē \ see ARLIE

¹**arm** \ ärm \ arm, barm, charm, farm, harm, alarm, disarm, firearm, forearm, gendarme, gisarme, poor farm, rearm, sidearm, stiff-arm, straight-arm, strong-arm, tonearm, unarm, yardarm, overarm, underarm

²**arm** \ äm \ see ¹OM

³**arm** \ órm \ see ²ORM

¹**arma** \ är-mə \ dharma, karma

²**arma** \ ər-mə \ see ERMA

arman \ är-mən \ barman, carmine

armed \ ärmd \ armed, charmed, unarmed—also pasts of verbs listed at ¹ARM

arment \ är-mənt \ garment, varmint, debarment, disbarment, undergarment, overgarment

¹**armer** \ är-mər \ armoir, armor, charmer, farmer, harmer, disarmer

²**armer** \ ór-mər \ see ¹ORMER

armic \ ər-mik \ see ERMIC

armine \ är-mən \ see ARMAN

¹**arming** \ är-miŋ \ charming, farming, alarming, disarming

²**arming** \ ór-miŋ \ see ORMING

armint \ är-mənt \ see ARMENT

armless \ ärm-ləs \ armless, charmless, harmless

armoir \ är-mər \ see ¹ARMER

army \ är-mē \ army, barmy, smarmy

¹**arn** \ ärn \ barn, darn, tarn, yarn, carbarn, lucarne

²**arn** \ órn \ see ²ORN

arna \ ər-nə \ see ERNA

arnal \ ärn-ᵊl \ see ARNEL

arnate \ är-nət \ garnet, discarnate, incarnate

¹**arne** \ ärn \ see ¹ARN

²**arne** \ är-nē \ see ARNY

arnel \ ärn-ᵊl \ carnal, charnel, darnel

¹**arner** \ är-nər \ darner, garner, yarner

²**arner** \ ór-nər \ see ORNER

arness \ är-nəs \ harness, bizarreness

arnet \ är-nət \ see ARNATE

arney \ är-nē \ see ARNY

arning \ ór-niŋ \ see ORNING

arnish \ är-nish \ garnish, tarnish, varnish

arny \ är-nē \ barny, blarney, carny, chili con carne

¹**aro** \ er-ō \ see ²ERO

²**aro** \ ar-ō \ see ²ARROW

³**aro** \ är-ə \ see ¹ARA

⁴**aro** \ är-ō \ see ¹ORROW

arob \ ar-əb \ see ARAB

arody \ ar-əd-ē \ see ARADAY

arol \ ar-əl \ see ²ARREL

arom \ er-əm \ see ²ARUM

¹aron \ er-ən \ Aaron, Charon, garron, heron, perron, raring, sierran, rose of Sharon, sub-Saharan

²aron \ ar-ən \ Aaron, baron, barren, Charon, garron, rose of Sharon, sub-Saharan

aronet \ ar-ə-nət \ baronet, carinate, clarinet

¹arous \ er-əs \ see ERROUS

²arous \ ar-əs \ see ²ARIS

¹arp \ ärp \ carp, harp, scarp, sharp, tarp, cardsharp, escarp, Jews harp, Autoharp, vibraharp

²arp \ órp \ see ORP

arpen \ är-pən \ sharpen, tarpon

arper \ är-pər \ carper, harper, scarper, sharper, cardsharper

arpie \ är-pē \ see ARPY

arpon \ är-pən \ see ARPEN

arpy \ är-pē \ harpy, sharpie

arque \ ärk \ see ¹ARK

arquetry \ är-kə-trē \ marquetry, parquetry

arqui \ är-kē \ see ARCHY

arrable \ ar-ə-bəl \ see ARABLE

¹arrack \ ar-ik \ see ARIC

²arrack \ ar-ək \ arrack, barrack, carrack

arragon \ ar-ə-gən \ see ARAGON

arral \ ar-əl \ see ²ARREL

arram \ ar-əm \ see ²ARUM

¹arrant \ ar-ənt \ see ²ARENT

²arrant \ ór-ənt \ see ORRENT

arras \ ar-əs \ see ²ARIS

arrass \ ar-əs \ see ²ARIS

arrative \ ar-ət-iv \ see ²ARATIVE

arrator \ ar-ət-ər \ see ARATOR

arre \ är \ see ³AR

arred \ ärd \ see ¹ARD

¹arrel \ órl \ see ³ORAL

²arrel \ ar-əl \ aril, barrel, carol, carrel, parol, parral, parrel, apparel, cracker-barrel, double-barrel

arreler \ är-lər \ see ARLOR

arrely \ är-lē \ see ARLIE

¹arren \ ar-ən \ see ²ARON

²arren \ ór-ən \ see ²ORIN

³arren \ ór-ən \ see ¹ORIN

arrener \ ór-ə-nər \ see ORONER

arreness \ är-nəs \ see ARNESS

arret \ ar-ət \ see ARAT

arrh \ är \ see ³AR

arriage \ ar-ij \ carriage, marriage, disparage, miscarriage, intermarriage, undercarriage

arriance \ ar-ē-əns \ see ARIANCE

arried \ ar-ēd \ harried, married, varied, unmarried

¹arrier \ ór-ē-ər \ see ARRIOR

²arrier \ ar-ē-ər \ barrier, carrier, farrier, harrier, varier, ballcarrier, spear-carrier

arrion \ ar-ē-ən \ see ²ARIAN

arrior \ȯr-ē-ər \ quarrier, sorrier, warrior

arris \ar-əs \ see ²ARIS

arrison \ar-ə-sən \ see ARISON

arron \ar-ən \ see ²ARON

arrot \ar-ət \ see ARAT

arroty \ar-ət-ē \ see ²ARITY

¹**arrow** \ar-ə \ arrow, barrow, farrow, jarrah, narrow, Sarah, sparrow, yarrow, cascara, handbarrow, mascara, samara, straight-arrow, tantara, tiara, wheelbarrow, capybara, caracara, marinara

²**arrow** \ar-ō \ aero, arrow, barrow, faro, farrow, harrow, marrow, narrow, pharaoh, sparrow, taro, tarot, yarrow, handbarrow, wheelbarrow

arrowy \ar-ə-wē \ arrowy, marrowy

¹**arry** \är-ē \ see ¹ARI

²**arry** \ȯr-ē \ see ORY

³**arry** \ar-ē \ carry, chary, gharry, harry, marry, nary, parry, tarry, glengarry, miscarry, safari, shikari, cash-and-carry, hari-kari, intermarry, Stradivari; Tom, Dick, and Harry

ars \ärz \ Mars, ours, parse— *also plurals and possessives of nouns and third singular presents of verbs listed at ³AR*

arsal \är-səl \ parcel, versal, tarsal, metatarsal

¹**arse** \ärs \ farce, marse, parse, sparse

²**arse** \ärz \ see ARS

arsh \ärsh \ harsh, marsh, demarche

arshal \är-shəl \ see ARTIAL

arshen \är-shən \ harshen, martian

arsi \är-sē \ see ARCY

arsis \är-səs \ see ARSUS

arsle \äs-əl \ see OSSAL

arson \ärs-ᵊn \ arson, parson

arsus \är-səs \ arsis, tarsus, catharsis, metatarsus

¹**art** \ärt \ art, cart, chart, dart, fart, hart, heart, kart, mart, part, scart, smart, start, tart, apart, blackheart, compart, depart, dispart, dogcart, flowchart, forepart, go-cart, greenheart, handcart, impart, mouthpart, outsmart, oxheart, pushcart, rampart, redstart, restart, sweetheart, tipcart, upstart, à la carte, anti-art, applecart, counterpart, heart-to-heart, underpart, upperpart

²**art** \ȯrt \ see ¹ORT

artable \ärt-ə-bəl \ see ARTIBLE

¹**artan** \ärt-ᵊn \ see ARTEN

²**artan** \ȯrt-ᵊn \ see ORTEN

artar \ärt-ər \ see ¹ARTER

arte \ärt-ē \ see ¹ARTY

¹**arted** \ärt-əd \ see EARTED

²**arted** \ òrt-əd \ see ORTED
arten \ ärt-ᵊn \ carton, hearten, marten, martin, smarten, Spartan, tartan, dishearten, freemartin, kindergarten
¹**arter** \ ärt-ər \ barter, carter, charter, darter, garter, martyr, starter, tartar, nonstarter, self-starter, protomartyr—*also comparatives of adjectives listed at* ¹ART
²**arter** \ òt-ər \ see ¹ATER
artern \ òt-ərn \ see AUTERNE
artery \ ärt-ə-rē \ artery, martyry
arth \ ärth \ garth, hearth
arti \ ärt-ē \ see ¹ARTY
artial \ är-shəl \ marshal, martial, partial, court-martial, impartial
artian \ är-shən \ see ARSHEN
artible \ ärt-ə-bəl \ partible, impartible, restartable
¹**artic** \ ärt-ik \ arctic, antarctic, cathartic, Nearctic, Palearctic
²**artic** \ òrt-ik \ quartic, aortic
article \ ärt-i-kəl \ article, particle
artile \ òrt-ᵊl \ see ORTAL
artily \ ärt-ᵊl-ē \ artily, heartily
artin \ ärt-ᵊn \ see ARTEN
arting \ ärt-iŋ \ karting, parting, flowcharting, self-starting
artisan \ ärt-ə-zən \ artisan, bartizan, partisan, bipartisan, nonpartisan

artist \ ärt-əst \ artist, chartist, Chartist, Bonapartist
artizan \ ärt-ə-zən \ see ARTISAN
artless \ ärt-ləs \ artless, heartless
artlet \ ärt-lət \ martlet, partlet, tartlet
¹**artly** \ ärt-lē \ partly, smartly
²**artly** \ òrt-lē \ see ²ORTLY
artment \ ärt-mənt \ apartment, compartment, department
artner \ ärt-nər \ partner, kindergartner
arton \ ärt-ᵊn \ see ARTEN
artridge \ är-trij \ cartridge, partridge
arts \ är \ see ³AR
arture \ är-chər \ see ARCHER
¹**arty** \ ärt-ē \ arty, hearty, party, smarty, Astarte, ex parte, Havarti, commedia del l'arte
²**arty** \ òrt-ē \ see ORTY
artyr \ ärt-ər \ see ¹ARTER
artyry \ ärt-ə-rē \ see ARTERY
artz \ òrts \ see ORTS
¹**arum** \ är-əm \ larum, alarum
²**arum** \ er-əm \ arum, carom, harem, Sarum, Muharram, harum-scarum, arbiter elegantiarum
arus \ ar-əs \ see ²ARIS
arva \ är-və \ larva, parve, pareve
arval \ är-vəl \ see ARVEL
¹**arve** \ ärv \ carve, starve, varve
²**arve** \ är-və \ see ARVA

arvel\är-vəl\carvel, larval,
  marvel
¹**ary**\er-ē\aerie, aery, airy,
  berry, bury, cherry, chary,
  clary, dairy, fairy, ferry,
  glairy, glary, hairy, Jerry,
  kerry, Mary, marry, merry,
  nary, perry, prairie, quaere,
  query, scary, serry, sherry,
  skerry, terry, vary, very,
  wary, wherry, baneberry,
  barberry, bayberry, bearberry,
  bilberry, blackberry,
  blueberry, bunchberry,
  Burberry, canary, chokeberry,
  chokecherry, cloudberry,
  contrary, coralberry,
  costmary, cowberry,
  cranberry, crowberry,
  deerberry, dewberry, equerry,
  February, gooseberry,
  ground-cherry, hackberry,
  hegari, inkberry, Juneberry,
  knobkerrie, library, mulberry,
  nondairy, pokeberry, primary,
  raspberry, rosemary, scalare,
  shadberry, sheepberry,
  snowberry, soapberry,
  strawberry, summary,
  teaberry, tilbury, twinberry,
  unwary, vagary, wolfberry,
  youngberry, actuary,
  adversary, airy-fairy,
  ancillary, antiquary, apiary,
  arbitrary, aviary, axillary,
  beriberi, bestiary, biliary,
  boysenberry, breviary,
  budgetary, calamari,
  calamary, candleberry,
  capillary, cartulary,
  cassowary, catenary,
  cautionary, cavitary,
  cemetery, centenary,
  certiorari, chartulary,
  checkerberry, chinaberry,
  ciliary, cinerary, cometary,
  commentary, commissary,
  condottiere, corollary,
  coronary, culinary,
  customary, dictionary,
  dietary, dignitary,
  dingleberry, dromedary,
  dysentery, elderberry,
  farkleberry, formicary,
  formulary, fragmentary,
  fritillary, functionary,
  funerary, honorary,
  huckleberry, intermarry,
  janissary, January, lamasery,
  lapidary, lectionary,
  legendary, legionary,
  limitary, lingonberry, literary,
  loganberry, luminary,
  mammillary, mandatary,
  maxillary, medullary,
  mercenary, miliary, military,
  millenary, milliary, millinery,
  miserere, missionary,
  momentary, monastery,
  monetary, mortuary,
  necessary, ordinary, ossuary,

papillary, parcenary,
partridgeberry, pensionary,
phalanstery, pigmentary,
plagiary, planetary,
prebendary, presbytery,
pulmonary, pupillary,
quaternary, questionary,
reliquary, rowanberry,
salivary, salmonberry,
salutary, sanctuary,
sanguinary, sanitary,
secondary, secretary,
sedentary, seminary,
serviceberry, silverberry,
solitary, stationary,
stationery, statuary,
Stradivari, subcontrary,
sublunary, sugarberry,
sumptuary, syllabary,
temporary, termitary, tertiary,
textuary, thimbleberry, Tom
and Jerry, topiary, tributary,
tutelary, unitary, urinary,
vestiary, visionary, voluntary,
vulnerary, whortleberry,
winterberry, ablutionary,
accretionary, antiphonary,
apothecary, bicentenary,
bilmillenary, concessionary,
concretionary, confectionary,
confectionery, constabulary,
contemporary, convulsionary,
coparcenary, depositary,
delusionary, digressionary,
disciplinary, discretionary,
distributary, diversionary,
electuary, epistolary,
exclusionary, expansionary,
expeditionary, extemporary,
extortionary, extraordinary,
fiduciary, hereditary,
illusionary, imaginary,
incendiary, inflationary,
insanitary, intercalary,
involuntary, itinerary,
judiciary, libationary,
obituary, officiary, pecuniary,
petitionary, precautionary,
preliminary, presidiary,
previsionary, probationary,
proprietary, provisionary,
reactionary, recessionary,
reflationary, residuary,
reversionary, revisionary,
stagflationary, stipendiary,
subliterary, subsidiary,
subversionary, tercentenary,
traditionary, tumultuary,
unnecessary, veterinary,
vocabulary, voluptuary,
abolitionary, beneficiary,
consuetudinary, deflationary,
devolutionary, disinflationary,
domiciliary, eleemosynary,
elocutionary, evidentiary,
evolutionary, extraliterary,
intermediary, paramilitary,
penitentiary, quatercentenary,
revolutionary, semicentenary,
semilegendary,
sesquicentenary, superciliary,
supernumerary,

tintinnabulary, usufructuary,
valetudinary,
interdisciplinary,
plenipotentiary,
counterrevolutionary
²ary \ ar-ē \ see ³ARRY
¹aryan \ er-ē-ən \ see ¹ARIAN
²aryan \ ar-ē-ən \ see ²ARIAN
¹as \ ash \ see ³ASH
²as \ as \ see ³ASS
³as \ az \ see AZZ
⁴as \ ä \ see ¹A
⁵as \ äsh \ see ¹ASH
⁶as \ äz \ see ¹OISE
⁷as \ əz \ see ¹EUSE
¹asa \ äs-ə \ casa, fossa, glossa,
kielbasa, Landrace, tabula
rasa
²asa \ äz-ə \ see ¹AZA
¹asable \ ā-zə-bəl \ grazeable,
persuasible, paraphrasable
²asable \ ā-sə-bəl \ see ACEABLE
¹asal \ ā-səl \ basal, stay sail,
forestay sail
²asal \ ā-zəl \ basal, hazel, nasal,
phrasal, appraisal, Azazel
asally \ āz-lē \ see AISLEY
ascal \ as-kəl \ paschal, rascal
ascar \ as-kər \ see ASKER
¹ascence \ ās-ᵊns \ nascence,
complacence, complaisance,
renascence
²ascence \ as-ᵊns \ nascence,
renascence
¹ascent \ as-ᵊnt \ nascent,
passant, renascent

²ascent \ ās-ᵊnt \ see ACENT
asch \ ask \ see ASK
aschal \ as-kəl \ see ASCAL
¹ascia \ ā-shə \ see ACIA
²ascia \ ash-ə \ see ²ASHA
ascible \ as-ə-bəl \ see ASSABLE
ascicle \ as-i-kəl \ see ASSICAL
¹asco \ äs-kō \ see OSCOE
²asco \ as-kō \ fiasco, Tabasco
ascon \ as-kən \ see ASKIN
ascot \ as-kət \ see ASKET
¹ase \ ās \ see ¹ACE
²ase \ āz \ see ¹AZE
³ase \ äz \ see ¹OISE
ased \ āst \ see ACED
aseless \ ā-sləs \ see ACELESS
aseman \ ā-smən \ see ACEMAN
¹aser \ ā-sər \ see ¹ACER
²aser \ ā-zər \ see AZER
¹ash \ ash \ bosh, cosh, frosh,
gosh, gouache, josh, nosh,
posh, quash, slosh, squash,
swash, tosh, wash, awash,
backwash, blackwash,
cohosh, czardas, eyewash,
galosh, goulash, kibosh,
midrash, mishmash,
mouthwash, musquash,
panache, rainwash, Siwash,
whitewash, wish-wash,
mackintosh, McIntosh
²ash \ ȯsh \ gosh, grosz, quash,
slosh, squash, swash, wash,
awash, backwash,
blackwash, brainwash,
brioche, eyewash, hogwash,

mouthwash, rainwash, Siwash, whitewash, wish-wash

³ash \ ash \ ash, bash, brash, cache, cash, clash, crash, dash, fash, flash, gash, gnash, hash, lash, mash, pash, plash, rash, sash, slash, smash, splash, stash, thrash, thresh, trash, abash, backlash, calash, czardas, encash, eyelash, goulash, mishmash, moustache, mustache, panache, potash, rehash, slapdash, soutache, stramash, tongue-lash, unlash, whiplash, balderdash, calabash, succotash

¹asha \ äsh-ə \ kasha, pasha, quassia, Falasha

²asha \ ash-ə \ cassia, fascia, pasha

ashan \ ash-ən \ see ASSION

¹ashed \ òsht \ sloshed, unwashed—*also pasts of verbs listed at* ²ASH

²ashed \ asht \ dashed, smashed, unabashed—*also pasts of verbs listed at* ³ASH

ashen \ ash-ən \ see ASSION

¹asher \ äsh-ər \ josher, nosher, squasher, swasher, washer, dishwasher

²asher \ òsh-ər \ swasher, washer, brainwasher, dishwasher, whitewasher

³asher \ ash-ər \ Asher, basher, brasher, clasher, crasher, dasher, flasher, masher, rasher, slasher, smasher, splasher, thrasher, gate-crasher, haberdasher

ashew \ ash-ü \ cachou, cashew

ashi \ äsh-ē \ see ¹ASHY

ashing \ ash-iŋ \ crashing, flashing, slashing, smashing

ashion \ ash-ən \ see ASSION

¹ashy \ äsh-ē \ dashi, squashy, washy, wishy-washy

²ashy \ ash-ē \ ashy, flashy, splashy, trashy

¹asi \ äs-ē \ see ¹OSSY

²asi \ äz-ē \ see ¹AZI

asia \ ā-zhə \ aphasia, fantasia, euthanasia

¹asian \ ā-shən \ see ¹ATION

²asian \ ā-zhən \ see ASION

asible \ ā-zə-bəl \ see ¹ASABLE

asic \ ā-zik \ basic, phasic, diphasic, multiphasic, polyphasic

asid \ as-əd \ see ACID

¹asil \ as-əl \ see ²ASSEL

²asil \ az-əl \ see AZZLE

asin \ äs-ᵊn \ see ¹ASON

¹asing \ ā-siŋ \ see ACING

²asing \ ā-ziŋ \ see AISING

asion \ ā-zhən \ Asian, suasion, abrasion, Caucasian, corrasion, dissuasion, equation, Eurasian, evasion, invasion, occasion,

persuasion, pervasion,
Amerasian, Athanasian,
dermabrasion, Rabelaisian,
overpersuasion
asional \ āzh-nəl \ equational,
occasional
¹**asis** \ ā-səs \ basis, stasis, oasis
²**asis** \ as-əs \ see ²ASSIS
asium \ ā-zē-əm \ dichasium,
gymnasium
asive \ ā-siv \ suasive, abrasive,
assuasive, corrasive,
dissuasive, embracive,
evasive, invasive, persuasive,
pervasive, noninvasive
ask \ ask \ ask, bask, Basque,
cask, casque, flask, mask,
masque, Pasch, task, unmask
askan \ as-kən \ see ASKIN
asked \ ast \ see ²AST
asker \ as-kər \ lascar, masker,
masquer
asket \ as-kət \ ascot, basket,
casket, gasket, breadbasket,
wastebasket, workbasket
askin \ as-kən \ gascon, gaskin,
Athapaskan
asm \ az-əm \ chasm, plasm,
spasm, chiasm, orgasm,
phantasm, sarcasm, chiliasm,
ectoplasm, pleonasm,
enthusiasm, iconoclasm
asma \ az-mə \ asthma, plasma,
chiasma, miasma, phantasma
asn't \ əz-ᵊnt \ doesn't, wasn't
¹**ason** \ ās-ᵊn \ basin, caisson,

chasten, hasten, Jason,
mason, Freemason,
stonemason, washbasin,
diapason
²**ason** \ āz-ᵊn \ see AZON
asp \ asp \ asp, clasp, gasp,
grasp, hasp, rasp, enclasp,
handclasp, unclasp
asper \ as-pər \ clasper, jasper
asperate \ as-prət \ aspirate,
exasperate
aspirate \ as-prət \ see ASPERATE
asque \ ask \ see ASK
asquer \ as-kər \ see ASKER
¹**ass** \ ās \ see ¹ACE
²**ass** \ äs \ see ¹OS
³**ass** \ as \ as, ass, bass, brass,
class, crass, gas, glass, grass,
has, lass, mass, pass, sass,
sauce, strass, tace, tasse,
trass, vas, wrasse, admass,
alas, amass, avgas, badass,
bagasse, bluegrass,
bromegrass, bunchgrass,
bypass, crabgrass, crevasse,
cuirass, cut-grass, declass,
degas, eelgrass, en masse,
eyeglass, groundmass, harass,
high-class, hourglass,
impasse, jackass, knotgrass,
landmass, morass, outclass,
outgas, palliasse, repass,
ribgrass, rubasse, ryegrass,
sandglass, shortgrass,
spyglass, subclass, sunglass,
surpass, switchgrass, teargas,

trespass, wineglass, wiseass, witchgrass, biomass, demitasse, fiberglass, gallowglass, Hallowmas, hardinggrass, hippocras, isinglass, lemongrass, lower-class, middle-class, overpass, peppergrass, Plexiglas, sassafras, superclass, underclass, underpass, weatherglass

assa \ as-ə \ massa, Manasseh

assable \ as-ə-bəl \ chasuble, passable, passible, impassable, impassible, irascible

assail \ äs-əl \ see OSSAL

assailer \ äs-ə-lər \ see OSSULAR

assal \ as-əl \ see ²ASSEL

assant \ as-ᵊnt \ see ¹ASCENT

assar \ as-ər \ see ASSER

¹asse \ as \ see ³ASS

²asse \ äs \ see ¹OS

assed \ ast \ see ²AST

asseh \ as-ə \ see ASSA

¹assel \ äs-əl \ see OSSAL

²assel \ as-əl \ acyl, basil, castle, facile, gracile, hassle, passel, tassel, vassal, wrestle, forecastle

asser \ as-ər \ crasser, gasser, placer, harasser, antimacassar

asset \ as-ət \ see ²ACET

¹assia \ ash-ə \ see ²ASHA

²assia \ äsh-ə \ see ¹ASHA

assian \ ash-ən \ see ASSION

assible \ as-ə-bəl \ see ASSABLE

assic \ as-ik \ classic, Jurassic, Liassic, thalassic, Triassic, neoclassic, pseudoclassic, semiclassic

assical \ as-i-kəl \ classical, fascicle, postclassical, unclassical, semiclassical

assid \ as-əd \ see ACID

¹assie \ as-ē \ see ASSY

²assie \ äs-ē \ see ¹OSSY

¹assim \ äs-əm \ see OSSUM

²assim \ as-əm \ passim, sargassum

assin \ as-ᵊn \ see ²ASTEN

assion \ ash-ən \ ashen, fashion, passion, ration, Circassian, compassion, dispassion, impassion, refashion, Wakashan

assional \ ash-nəl \ see ³ATIONAL

¹assis \ as-ē \ see ASSY

²assis \ as-əs \ chassis, classis, stasis

assist \ ā-səst \ bassist, racist, contrabassist

assive \ as-iv \ massive, passive, impassive

assle \ as-əl \ see ²ASSEL

assless \ as-ləs \ classless, glassless, massless

assment \ as-mənt \ blastment, amassment, harassment

assness \ as-nəs \ see ASTNESS

asso \ as-ō \ basso, lasso, sargasso

assock \as-ək\ cassock, hassock

assum \as-əm\ see ²ASSIM

assy \as-ē\ brassy, chassis, classy, gassy, glacis, glassie, glassy, grassy, lassie, massy, sassy, saucy, Malagasy

¹**ast** \əst\ see ¹UST

²**ast** \ast\ bast, blast, cast, caste, clast, fast, gast, ghast, hast, last, mast, past, vast, aghast, avast, bedfast, bombast, broadcast, bypast, contrast, dicast, dismast, downcast, dynast, fantast, flypast, forecast, foremast, forepassed, gymnast, half-assed, half-caste, half-mast, handfast, holdfast, lightfast, mainmast, makefast, march-past, miscast, newscast, oblast, offcast, outcast, outcaste, precast, recast, repast, roughcast, sandblast, sand-cast, shamefast, soothfast, sportscast, steadfast, sunfast, topmast, trade-last, typecast, unasked, upcast, windblast, acid-fast, chiliast, cineast, colorcast, colorfast, flabbergast, fore-topmast, hard-and-fast, main-topmast, mizzenmast, narrowcast, overcast, pederast, rebroadcast, scholiast, simulcast, telecast, ecdysiast, encomiast,

enthusiast, iconoclast, radiocast, symposiast, radiobroadcast—*also pasts of verbs listed at* ³ASS

¹**asta** \äs-tə\ see OSTA

²**asta** \as-tə\ Rasta, canasta, Jocasta

astable \at-ə-bəl\ see ATIBLE

astard \as-tərd\ bastard, dastard, mastered, plastered

¹**aste** \āst\ see ACED

²**aste** \ast\ see ²AST

asted \as-təd\ blasted, masted, plastid—*also pasts of verbs listed at* ²AST

asteful \āst-fəl\ tasteful, wasteful, distasteful

¹**asten** \ās-ᵊn\ see ¹ASON

²**asten** \as-ᵊn\ fasten, assassin, unfasten

¹**aster** \ā-stər\ taster, waster

²**aster** \as-tər\ aster, caster, castor, Castor, faster, gaster, master, pastor, plaster, raster, bandmaster, bushmaster, cadastre, choirmaster, disaster, drillmaster, headmaster, linecaster, loadmaster, paymaster, piaster, pilaster, postmaster, quizmaster, remaster, ringmaster, schoolmaster, scoutmaster, shinplaster, shipmaster, taskmaster, three-master, toastmaster, truckmaster, wharfmaster,

whoremaster, yardmaster,
alabaster, burgomaster,
concertmaster, criticaster,
ironmaster, oleaster,
overmaster, poetaster,
quartermaster, rallymaster,
stationmaster, cotoneaster

astered \ as-tərd \ see ASTARD

astes \ as-tēz \ cerastes,
Ecclesiastes—*also plurals and
possessives of nouns listed at*
²ASTY

asthma \ az-mə \ see ASMA

astian \ as-chən \ see ASTION

astic \ as-tik \ drastic, mastic,
plastic, spastic, bombastic,
dynastic, elastic, fantastic,
gymnastic, monastic,
sarcastic, scholastic,
stochastic, anelastic,
Hudibrastic, inelastic,
onomastic, orgiastic,
paraphrastic, pederastic,
periphrastic, superplastic,
ecclesiastic, enthusiastic,
iconoclastic, interscholastic,
semimonastic

astid \ as-təd \ see ASTED

astie \ as-tē \ see ²ASTY

astiness \ ā-stē-nəs \ hastiness,
pastiness

¹asting \ ā-stiŋ \ basting,
wasting—*also present
participles of verbs listed at*
ACED

²asting \ as-tiŋ \ everlasting,
overcasting

astion \ as-chən \ bastion,
Erastian

astle \ as-əl \ see ²ASSEL

astly \ ast-lē \ ghastly, lastly

astment \ as-mənt \ see ASSMENT

astness \ as-nəs \ crassness,
fastness, gastness, pastness

asto \ as-tō \ impasto, antipasto

astor \ as-tər \ see ²ASTER

astoral \ as-trəl \ see ASTRAL

astral \ as-trəl \ astral, gastral,
pastoral, plastral, cadastral

astre \ as-tər \ see ²ASTER

astrophe \ as-trə-fē \ anastrophe,
catastrophe

¹asty \ ā-stē \ hasty, pasty, tasty

²asty \ as-tē \ blastie, nasty,
pasty, vasty, capacity,
contrasty, pederasty,
overcapacity

asuble \ as-ə-bəl \ see ASSABLE

¹asure \ ā-shər \ glacier, rasure,
erasure

²asure \ ā-zhər \ see AZIER

asy \ as-ē \ see ASSY

¹at \ ä \ see ¹A

²at \ ät \ see ¹OT

³at \ ət \ see ¹UT

⁴at \ ȯt \ see ¹OUGHT

⁵at \ at \ bat, batt, blat, brat, cat,
Cat, chat, chert, drat, fat,
flat, frat, gat, gnat, hat, mat,
matt, matte, pat, plait, plat,
rat, sat, scat, scatt, skat, slat,

spat, splat, sprat, stat, tat, that, vat, all that, at bat, begat, bobcat, brickbat, bullbat, chitchat, combat, comsat, cowpat, cravat, Croat, defat, dingbat, doormat, fiat, format, Hallstatt, hellcat, hepcat, high-hat, jurat, muscat, muskrat, nonfat, polecat, savate, Sno-Cat, stand pat, standpat, stonechat, strawhat, thereat, tipcat, tomcat, whereat, whinchat, wildcat, wombat, acrobat, apparat, assignat, autocrat, Automat, bureaucrat, butterfat, caveat, cervelat, concordat, copycat, democrat, diplomat, Dixiecrat, Eurocrat, habitat, Laundromat, marrowfat, mobocrat, monocrat, ochlocrat, pas de quatre, photostat, pit-a-pat, plutocrat, pussycat, rat-a-tat, scaredy-cat, semimatte, technocrat, theocrat, thermostat, tit for tat, Uniate, ziggurat, aristocrat, gerontocrat, heliostat, Jehoshaphat, magnificat, Physiocrat, requiescat, thalassocrat, proletoriat, professoriat, secretariat

¹ata \ ät-ə \ cotta, balata, cantata, data, errata, fermata, frittata, Maratha, non grata, pinata, pro rata, reata, riata, regatta, sonata, toccata, caponata, serenata, terracotta, desiderata, inamorata, medulla oblongata, missa cantata, persona grata, res judicata, persona non grata, res adjudicata

²ata \ āt-ə \ beta, data, eta, strata, theta, zeta, muleta, peseta, potato, pro rata, substrata, tomato, viewdata, corona radiata

³ata \ at-ə \ data, errata, mulatto, non grata, pro rata, reata, regatta, riata, viewdata, paramatta, persona grata, persona non grata

¹atable \ āt-ə-bəl \ datable, ratable, statable, debatable, dilatable, inflatable, locatable, rotatable, translatable, allocatable, circulatable, confiscatable, correlatable, detonatable, undebatable

²atable \ at-ə-bəl \ see ATIBLE

atal \ āt-ᵊl \ fatal, natal, ratel, shtetl, hiatal, postnatal, prenatal, antenatal, neonatal, perinatal

atally \ āt-ᵊl-ē \ fatally, postnatally, prenatally, antenatally, neonatally, perinatally

atalyst \ at-⁹l-əst \ catalyst, philatelist

¹atan \ āt-ən \ see ¹ATEN

²atan \ at-ⁿn \ see ²ATIN

atancy \ āt-ⁿn-sē \ blatancy, latency, patency, dilatancy

¹atant \ āt-ⁿnt \ blatant, latent, natant, patent, statant

²atant \ at-ⁿnt \ patent, combatant, noncombatant

atany \ at-ⁿn-ē \ atony, rhatany

¹atch \ ech \ see ETCH

²atch \ äch \ see OTCH

³atch \ óch \ see ¹AUCH

⁴atch \ ach \ bach, batch, catch, cratch, hatch, klatch, latch, match, natch, patch, ratch, scratch, snatch, thatch, attach, book-match, crosshatch, crosspatch, despatch, detach, dispatch, nuthatch, outmatch, potlatch, rematch, Sasquatch, throatlatch, unlatch, coffee klatch, kaffeeklatsch, overmatch

¹atcher \ äch-ər \ botcher, watcher, bird-watcher, clock-watcher, debaucher, topnotcher

²atcher \ ach-ər \ batcher, catcher, hatcher, matcher, scratcher, stature, thatcher, cowcatcher, dispatcher, dogcatcher, eye-catcher,

flycatcher, gnatcatcher, oyster catcher

atchet \ ach-ət \ hatchet, latchet, rachet, ratchet, statute

atchily \ ach-ə-lē \ patchily, patchouli

atching \ ach-iŋ \ cross-hatching, eye-catching, nonmatching

atchman \ äch-mən \ see OTCHMAN

atchment \ ach-mənt \ catchment, hatchment, attachment, detachment

atchouli \ ach-ə-lē \ see ATCHILY

atchy \ ach-ē \ catchy, patchy, scratchy, Apache

¹ate \ āt \ ait, ate, bait, bate, beth, blate, cate, crate, date, eight, fate, fete, freight, gait, gate, grate, great, haet, hate, heth, late, mate, pate, plait, plate, prate, quoit, rate, sate, skate, slate, spate, state, straight, strait, teth, trait, wait, weight, abate, ablate, adnate, aerate, age-mate, agnate, airdate, airfreight, alate, arête, await, baldpate, bedmate, bedplate, berate, birthrate, bistate, bookplate, breastplate, casemate, castrate, caudate, cerate, cheapskate, checkmate, chordate, classmate, clavate, cognate, collate, comate, conflate, connate, cordate,

create, cremate, crenate,
curate, cut-rate, deadweight,
debate, deflate, delate,
dentate, dictate, dilate,
disrate, donate, doorplate,
downstate, drawplate, elate,
equate, estate, faceplate,
falcate, fellate, filtrate, first-
rate, fishplate, fixate,
floodgate, flyweight, formate,
frustrate, gelate, gestate,
gyrate, hamate, hastate,
headgate, helpmate,
housemate, hydrate, ice-skate,
inflate, ingrate, inmate,
innate, instate, irate, jailbait,
jugate, khanate, lactate,
legate, liftgate, ligate,
lightweight, liquate, lobate,
locate, lunate, lustrate, lych-
gate, lyrate, magnate,
makebate, makeweight,
mandate, messmate, migrate,
misstate, mutate, nameplate,
narrate, negate, Newgate,
notate, nutate, oblate, orate,
ornate, ovate, palmate,
palpate, peltate, phonate,
pinnate, placate, playmate,
plicate, portrait, postdate,
predate, primate, probate,
prolate, prorate, prostate,
prostrate, pulsate, punctate,
pupate, quadrate, ramate,
rebate, red-bait, relate,
restate, roommate, rostrate,

rotate, saccate, schoolmate,
seatmate, sedate, sensate,
septate, serrate, shipmate,
short weight, soleplate,
spectate, spicate, squamate,
stagnate, stalemate, stellate,
striate, sublate, substrate,
sulcate, summate, tailgate,
teammate, Tebet, tenth-rate,
ternate, terneplate, testate,
third-rate, tinplate, toeplate,
tollgate, tractate, translate,
truncate, unweight, update,
upstate, V-8, vacate, vallate,
valvate, vibrate, virgate,
vulgate, whitebait, workmate,
zonate, abdicate, abnegate,
abrogate, absorbate,
acclimate, acerbate, acetate,
activate, actuate, adsorbate,
advocate, adulate, adumbrate,
aggravate, aggregate, agitate,
allocate, altercate, alternate,
ambulate, amputate, animate,
annotate, annulate, antedate,
antiquate, apartheid, apostate,
approbate, approximate,
arbitrate, arcuate, arrogate,
aspirate, automate, aviate,
bantamweight, bifurcate,
billingsgate, bipinnate,
boilerplate, bombinate,
brachiate, cachinnate,
calculate, calibrate, caliphate,
candidate, cantillate, capitate,
captivate, carbonate, carbon-

date, carinate, castigate, catenate, cavitate, celebrate, cerebrate, circinate, circulate, city-state, cogitate, collimate, collocate, commentate, commutate, compensate, complicate, concentrate, condensate, confiscate, conglobate, conjugate, consecrate, constellate, consternate, constipate, consummate, contemplate, copperplate, copulate, correlate, corrugate, coruscate, counterweight, crenulate, crepitate, criminate, cruciate, cucullate, culminate, cultivate, cumulate, cuneate, cupulate, cuspidate, cyclamate, decimate, decollate, decorate, decussate, dedicate, defalcate, defecate, delegate, demarcate, demonstrate, denigrate, deviate, deprecate, depredate, derivate, derogate, desecrate, desiccate, designate, desolate, detonate, devastate, deviate, digitate, diplomate, discarnate, dislocate, dissertate, dissipate, distillate, divagate, dominate, duplicate, edentate, educate, elevate, elongate, eluate, emanate, emigrate, emirate, emulate, enervate, ephorate, escalate,

estimate, estivate, excavate, exculpate, execrate, expiate, explicate, expurgate, exsiccate, extirpate, extricate, exudate, fabricate, fascinate, featherweight, fecundate, federate, fenestrate, festinate, fibrillate, flabellate, flagellate, flocculate, fluctuate, fluoridate, foliate, formulate, fornicate, fractionate, fragmentate, fulminate, fumigate, fustigate, geminate, generate, germinate, glaciate, graduate, granulate, gratulate, gravitate, heavyweight, hebetate, herniate, hesitate, hibernate, hundredweight, hyphenate, ideate, illustrate, imamate, imbricate, imitate, immigrate, immolate, impetrate, implicate, imprecate, impregnate, incarnate, increate, incubate, inculcate, inculpate, incurvate, indagate, indicate, indurate, infiltrate, innervate, innovate, insensate, insolate, inspissate, instigate, insulate, interstate, intestate, intimate, intonate, inundate, invocate, iodate, irrigate, irritate, isolate, iterate, jubilate, juniorate, lacerate, laminate, Latinate, laureate, legislate, levigate, levitate,

liberate, liquidate, litigate,
littermate, lubricate,
macerate, machinate,
magistrate, marginate,
margravate, marinate,
masticate, masturbate,
maturate, mediate, medicate,
meditate, meliorate,
menstruate, microstate,
micturate, middleweight,
militate, ministrate,
miscreate, mithridate,
mitigate, moderate, modulate,
motivate, multistate, mutilate,
nation-state, nauseate,
navigate, neonate, nictitate,
nominate, numerate,
obfuscate, objurgate, obligate,
obovate, obviate, operate,
opiate, orchestrate, ordinate,
oscillate, osculate, out-of-
date, overstate, overweight,
ovulate, paginate, palliate,
palpitate, paperweight,
patinate, peculate, penetrate,
pennyweight, percolate,
perennate, perforate,
permeate, perorate,
perpetrate, personate,
pollinate, populate, postulate,
potentate, predicate,
procreate, profligate,
promulgate, propagate,
prorogate, pullulate,
pulmonate, punctuate,
quantitate, rabbinate, radiate,

re-create, reclinate, recreate,
regulate, reinstate, relegate,
relocate, reluctate,
remonstrate, renovate,
replicate, reprobate, resonate,
retardate, retranslate, roseate,
rubricate, ruminate, runagate,
rusticate, sagittate, salivate,
sanitate, satiate, saturate,
scintillate, second-rate,
segregate, separate,
sequestrate, seriate, sibilate,
simulate, sinuate, situate,
speculate, spoliate,
stablemate, stimulate,
stipulate, strangulate,
stridulate, stylobate,
subjugate, sublimate,
subrogate, subulate,
suffocate, sultanate,
supplicate, surrogate,
syncopate, syndicate,
tablemate, tabulate, terminate,
tessellate, tête-à-tête, thirty-
eight, titillate, titivate,
tolerate, transmigrate,
transudate, tribulate,
tribunate, trifurcate, trilobate,
tripinnate, triplicate, tunicate,
turbinate, ulcerate, ululate,
umbellate, uncinate,
underrate, understate,
underweight, undulate,
ungulate, urinate, vaccinate,
vacillate, validate, valuate,
variate, vaticinate, vegetate,

venerate, ventilate, vertebrate,
vicarate, vindicate, violate,
vitiate, Watergate,
welterweight, abbreviate,
abominate, accelerate,
accentuate, accommodate,
acculturate, accumulate,
acidulate, adjudicate,
administrate, adulterate,
affiliate, agglomerate,
agglutinate, alienate,
alleviate, alliterate,
amalgamate, ameliorate,
annihilate, annunciate,
anticipate, apostolate,
appreciate, appropriate,
articulate, asphyxiate,
assassinate, asseverate,
assimilate, associate,
attenuate, authenticate,
barbiturate, bicarbonate,
calumniate, campanulate,
capacitate, capitulate,
catholicate, certificate,
circumvallate, coagulate,
coelenterate, collaborate,
commemorate, commiserate,
communicate, compassionate,
concatenate, concelebrate,
conciliate, confabulate,
confederate, conglomerate,
congratulate, consociate,
consolidate, contaminate,
cooperate, coordinate,
corroborate, de-escalate,
deaerate, debilitate,

decapitate, decerebrate,
deconcentrate, deconsecrate,
decrepitate, defibrinate,
defribrillate, degenerate,
deliberate, delineate,
demodulate, denominate,
depopulate, depreciate,
deregulate, desegregate,
desiderate, devaluate,
diaconate, dilapidate,
discriminate, disintegrate,
disseminate, dissimilate,
dissimulate, dissociate,
divaricate, domesticate,
edulcorate, effectuate,
ejaculate, elaborate,
electroplate, eliminate,
elucidate, elucubrate,
elutriate, emaciate,
emancipate, emarginate,
emasculate, encapsulate,
enumerate, enunciate,
episcopate, equilibrate,
equivocate, eradicate,
etiolate, evacuate, evaluate,
evaporate, eventuate,
eviscerate, exacerbate,
exaggerate, exasperate,
excogitate, excoriate,
excruciate, exfoliate,
exhilarate, exonerate,
expatiate, expatriate,
expectorate, expostulate,
expropriate, extenuate,
exterminate, extrapolate,
extravagate, exuberate,

facilitate, fantasticate,
felicitate, gesticulate,
habilitate, habituate,
hallucinate, homologate,
humiliate, hypothecate,
illuminate, impersonate,
inactivate, inaugurate,
incarcerate, incinerate,
incorporate, incriminate,
indoctrinate, inebriate,
infatuate, infuriate, ingratiate,
ingurgitate, initiate, inoculate,
inosculate, inseminate,
insinuate, instantiate,
intenerate, intercalate,
interpellate, interpolate,
interrelate, interrogate,
intimidate, intoxicate,
invaginate, invalidate,
investigate, invigorate,
irradiate, italianate, itinerate,
lanceolate, legitimate,
luxuriate, machicolate,
mandarinate, manipulate,
matriarchate, matriculate,
Merthiolate, necessitate,
negotiate, noncandidate,
obliterate, obnubilate,
officiate, orientate, originate,
oxygenate, participate,
particulate, patriarchate,
patriciate, penicillate,
perambulate, peregrinate,
perpetuate, pontificate,
potentiate, precipitate,
predestinate, predominate,

prefabricate, premeditate,
prenominate, preponderate,
prevaricate, procrastinate,
prognosticate, proliferate,
propitiate, proportionate,
quadruplicate, quintuplicate,
reciprocate, recriminate,
recuperate, redecorate,
redintegrate, reduplicate,
reeducate, refrigerate,
regenerate, regurgitate,
reincarnate, reintegrate,
reiterate, rejuvenate,
remunerate, renominate,
repatriate, repristinate,
repudiate, resupinate,
resuscitate, retaliate,
reticulate, revaluate,
revegetate, reverberate,
scholasticate, self-portrait,
seventy-eight, sextuplicate,
somnambulate, sophisticate,
stereobate, subordinate,
substantiate, syllabicate,
tergiversate, transliterate,
transvaluate, triangulate,
variegate, vituperate,
vociferate, beneficiate,
circumambulate,
circumnavigate,
circumstantiate,
contraindicate, decontaminate,
deteriorate, differentiate,
disaffiliate, disambiguate,
disarticulate, disassociate,
discombobulate, disintoxicate,

disorientate, disproportionate,
domiciliate, excommunicate,
free-associate, hyperventilate,
incapacitate, individuate,
intermediate, interpenetrate,
microencapsulate,
misappropriate, multivariate,
ratiocinate, recapitulate,
rehabilitate, renegotiate,
superannuate, superelevate,
superordinate, supersaturate,
transilluminate,
transubstantiate,
underestimate,
intercommunicate,
phosphoenolpyruvate

²ate \ at \ see ⁵AT

³ate \ ät \ see ¹OT

⁴ate \ ät-ē \ see ATI

ated \ āt-əd \ gaited, lated,
pated, stated, belated, ill-
fated, outdated, pustulated,
related, striated, three-gaited,
truncated, unbated, aberrated,
addlepated, animated,
asteriated, calculated,
capsulated, castellated,
complicated, crenellated,
disrelated, elevated,
fenestrated, fimbriated,
floriated, foliated, inspissated,
intoxicated, laminated,
marginated, mentholated,
perforated, pileated, pixilated,
saturated, tessellated,
trabeated, unabated,

uncreated, understated,
variegated, affiliated,
configurated, coordinated,
decaffeinated, domesticated,
incorporated, inebriated,
interrelated, intoxicated,
opinionated, sophisticated,
uncalculated, uncelebrated,
uncomplicated, underinflated,
unmitigated, unsaturated,
unsegregated, unadulterated,
unanticipated, unarticulated,
unconsolidated,
undereducated,
underpopulated,
undissociated,
unsophisticated,
polyunsaturated,
underappreciated—*also pasts
of verbs listed at* ¹ATE

ateful \ āt-fəl \ fateful, grateful,
hateful, ungrateful

¹atel \ ət-ʰl \ see OTTLE

²atel \ āt-ʰl \ see ATAL

ateless \ āt-ləs \ dateless,
stateless, weightless

atelist \ at-ʰl-əst \ see ATALYST

¹ately \ āt-lē \ greatly, lately,
stately, straightly, straitly,
innately, irately, ornately, up-
to-dately, Johnny-come-lately

²ately \ at-ʰl-ē \ see ATTILY

atem \ ät-əm \ see ¹ATUM

atement \ āt-mənt \ statement,
abatement, debatement,
misstatement, restatement,

overstatement, reinstatement, understatement

¹**aten** \āt-ᵊn \greaten, laten, Satan, straighten, straiten

²**aten** \at-ᵊn \see ²ATIN

³**aten** \āt-ᵊn \see OTTEN

¹**atent** \at-ᵊnt \see ¹ATANT

²**atent** \at-ᵊnt \see ²ATANT

¹**ater** \ot-ər \daughter, quarter, slaughter, tauter, water, backwater, bathwater, blackwater, breakwater, cutwater, dewater, dishwater, firewater, floodwater, forequarter, freshwater, goddaughter, granddaughter, groundwater, headquarter, headwater, hindquarter, jerkwater, lamb's-quarter, limewater, manslaughter, meltwater, rainwater, rosewater, saltwater, seawater, self-slaughter, shearwater, springwater, stepdaughter, tailwater, tidewater, wastewater, milk-and-water, polywater, underwater

²**ater** \āt-ər \see ATOR

ateral \at-ə-rəl \lateral, bilateral, collateral, trilateral, contralateral, dorsolateral, equilateral, ipsilateral, multilateral, quadrilateral, unilateral, ventrolateral, posterolateral

aterer \ot-ər-ər \slaughterer, waterer, dewaterer

ateress \āt-ə-rəs \cateress, traitorous

atery \ot-ə-rē \cautery, watery

ates \āt-ēz \Achates, nates, Penates—*also plurals and possessives of nouns listed at* ATY

atest \āt-əst \latest, statist—*also superlatives of adjectives listed at* ¹ATE

atey \āt-ē \see ATY

¹**ath** \āth \see ¹OTH

²**ath** \oth \see ²OTH

³**ath** \ath \bath, hath, lath, math, path, rathe, snath, strath, wrath, birdbath, bloodbath, bypath, footbath, footpath, sunbath, towpath, warpath, aftermath, polymath, psychopath, naturopath, osteopath, sociopath

atha \ät-ə \see ¹ATA

¹**athe** \āth \swathe, enswathe, unswathe

²**athe** \āth \bathe, lathe, rathe, saithe, scathe, spathe, swathe, sunbathe, unswathe

³**athe** \ath \see ³ATH

atheless \āth-ləs \see AITHLESS

¹**ather** \äth-ər \bother, father, pother, rather, forefather, godfather, grandfather, housefather, stepfather

²**ather** \oth-ər \see ¹OTHER

³**ather** \ ath-ər \ blather, gather,
lather, rather, slather,
forgather, ingather, wool-
gather

athering \ ath-riŋ \ ingathering,
woolgathering

athi \ ät-ē \ see ATI

athic \ ath-ik \ empathic,
psychopathic, telepathic,
homeopathic, idiopathic,
sociopathic

athlon \ ath-lən \ biathlon,
decathlon, pentathlon,
triathlon

athy \ ath-ē \ wrathy, allelopathy

ati \ ät-ē \ Ate, dotty, knotty,
naughty, plotty, potty,
Scottie, snotty, spotty,
squatty, Amati, coati, flokati,
karate, Marathi, metate,
glitterati, Gujarati, literati,
manicotti, illuminati

atia \ ā-shə \ see ACIA

atial \ ā-shəl \ see ACIAL

atian \ ā-shən \ see ¹ATION

atians \ ā-shənz \ see ATIONS

atible \ at-ə-bəl \ compatible,
getatable, incompatible, self-
compatible, self-incompatible

¹**atic** \ ät-ik \ see ¹OTIC

²**atic** \ at-ik \ attic, Attic, batik,
phatic, static, vatic, agnatic,
aquatic, astatic, asthmatic,
chromatic, climatic, comatic,
dalmatic, dogmatic, dramatic,
ecstatic, emphatic, erratic,

fanatic, hepatic, judgmatic,
komatik, lymphatic,
magmatic, neumatic,
phlegmatic, plasmatic,
pneumatic, pragmatic,
prismatic, protatic, quadratic,
rheumatic, schematic,
schismatic, sciatic, sematic,
Socratic, somatic, spermatic,
stigmatic, sylvatic, thematic,
traumatic, villatic,
achromatic, acrobatic,
aerobatic, anabatic, antistatic,
aromatic, Asiatic, astigmatic,
autocratic, automatic,
bureaucratic, charismatic,
cinematic, democratic,
dilemmatic, diplomatic,
Dixiecratic, Eleatic,
emblematic, enigmatic,
enzymatic, Hanseatic,
hieratic, Hippocratic,
kerygmatic, leviratic,
melismatic, miasmatic,
mobocratic, monocratic,
morganatic, numismatic,
ochlocratic, operatic,
phonematic, plutocratic, pre-
Socratic, problematic,
programmatic, symptomatic,
syntagmatic, systematic,
technocratic, theocratic,
timocratic, undogmatic,
undramatic, anagrammatic,
apothegmatic, aristocratic,
asymptomatic, axiomatic,

atic

conglomeratic, diagrammatic,
diaphragmatic, epigrammatic,
gerontocratic, gynecocratic,
homeostatic, idiomatic,
logogrammatic,
melodramatic, meritocratic,
monochromatic,
monodramatic,
monogrammatic,
pantisocratic, paradigmatic,
physiocratic, psychodramatic,
psychosomatic, semiaquatic,
theorematic, undemocratic,
undiplomatic, antidemocratic,
Austroasiatic, biosystematic,
ideogrammatic, semiautomatic

atica \at-i-kə \ hepatica, sciatica,
viatica

atical \at-i-kəl \ statical,
dogmatical, erratical,
fanatical, grammatical,
piratical, pragmatical,
sabbatical, schismatical,
autocratical, emblematical,
enigmatical, magistratical,
mathematical, ochlocratical,
problematical, systematical,
theocratical, timocratical,
ungrammatical,
anagrammatical,
diagrammatical,
epigrammatical,
pantisocratical

atics \at-iks \ statics, chromatics,
dogmatics, dramatics,
pneumatics, pragmatics,

acrobatics, mathematics,
numismatics, systematics,
melodramatics,
psychosomatics—*also plurals
and possessives of nouns
listed at* ²ATIC

atiens \ā-shənz \ see ATIONS

atient \ā-shənt \ patient,
impatient, inpatient,
outpatient, rubefacient,
somnifacient

atik \at-ik \ see ²ATIC

atile \at-ᵊl-ē \ see ATTILY

atim \ät-əm \ see ²ATUM

¹atin \ät-ᵊn \ see OTTEN

²atin \at-ᵊn \ baton, batten,
fatten, flatten, gratin, Latin,
latten, matin, paten, patten,
platan, platen, ratton, satin,
manhattan, Neo-Latin

ating \āt-iŋ \ bating, grating,
plating, rating, skating,
slating, bearbaiting,
bullbaiting, frustrating, self-
rating, calculating,
lancinating, maid-in-waiting,
nauseating, operating,
titillating, humiliating, lady-
in-waiting, nonterminating,
self-liquidating, self-
regulating, self-replicating,
subordinating, uncalculating,
undeviating, unhesitating,
indiscriminating, self-
incriminating

atinous \at-nəs \ see ATNESS

¹ation \ā-shən\ Asian, Haitian, nation, ration, station, Thracian, ablation, agnation, Alsatian, carnation, castration, causation, cessation, cetacean, citation, cognation, collation, conation, conflation, creation, cremation, crenation, Croatian, crustacean, cunctation, dalmatian, damnation, deflation, dictation, dilation, donation, duration, elation, enation, equation, Eurasian, filtration, fixation, flotation, formation, foundation, frustration, furcation, gestation, gradation, gustation, gyration, hydration, illation, inflation, lactation, laudation, lavation, legation, libation, libration, ligation, location, lustration, mentation, migration, mutation, narration, natation, negation, notation, novation, nutation, oblation, oration, outstation, ovation, phonation, planation, plantation, plication, potation, predation, privation, probation, pronation, proration, prostration, pulsation, purgation, quotation, reflation, relation, rogation, rotation, saltation, salvation, sedation, sensation, serration, slumpflation, squamation, stagflation, stagnation, starvation, striation, stylization, sublation, substation, summation, taxation, temptation, translation, truncation, vacation, venation, vexation, vibration, vocation, workstation, zonation, abdication, aberration, abjuration, abnegation, acceptation, acclamation, acclimation, accusation, activation, actuation, adaptation, adjuration, admiration, adoration, adulation, adumbration, advocation, affectation, affirmation, aggravation, aggregation, allegation, allocation, amputation, alteration, altercation, alternation, Amerasian, angulation, animation, annexation, annotation, annulation, antiquation, Appalachian, appellation, application, approbation, arbitration, aspiration, assentation, assignation, attestation, augmentation, Aurignacian, automation, aviation, avocation, botheration,

brachiation, cachinnation,
calculation, calibration,
cancellation, capitation,
captivation, carbonation,
castigation, celebration,
cementation, cerebration,
circulation, claudication,
cogitation, collocation,
coloration, combination,
commendation, commination,
commutation, compellation,
compensation, compilation,
complication, compurgation,
computation, concentration,
condemnation, condensation,
condonation, confirmation,
confiscation, conflagration,
conformation, confrontation,
confutation, congelation,
congregation, conjugation,
conjuration, connotation,
consecration, conservation,
consolation, conspiration,
constellation, consternation,
constipation, consultation,
consummation,
contemplation, contestation,
conurbation, conversation,
convocation, copulation,
coronation, corporation,
correlation, corrugation,
coruscation, crenellation,
culmination, cupellation,
cuspidation, cybernation,
decimation, declamation,
declaration, declination,

decoration, dedication,
defalcation, defamation,
defecation, defloration,
deformation, degradation,
degustation, dehydration,
delectation, delegation,
demarcation, demonstration,
denegation, denigration,
denotation, depilation,
deportation, depravation,
depredation, deprivation,
deputation, derivation,
derogation, desecration,
desiccation, designation,
desolation, desperation,
destination, detestation,
detonation, devastation,
devastation, deviation,
dilatation, disclamation,
disinflation, dislocation,
dispensation, disputation,
disrelation, dissertation,
dissipation, distillation,
divination, domination,
dubitation, duplication,
education, elevation,
elongation, emanation,
embarkation, embrocation,
emendation, emigration,
emulation, encrustation,
enervation, epilation,
equitation, eructation,
escalation, estimation,
estivation, evocation,
exaltation, excavation,
excitation, exclamation,

exculpation, execration,
exhalation, exhortation,
expectation, expiation,
expiration, explanation,
explication, exploitation,
exploration, exportation,
expurgation, extirpation,
extrication, exudation,
exultation, fabrication,
fascination, federation,
fenestration, fermentation,
fibrillation, figuration,
filiation, flagellation,
fluoridation, fluctuation,
foliation, fomentation,
formulation, fornication,
fragmentation, fulguration,
fulmination, fumigation,
gemination, generation,
germination, glaciation,
graduation, granulation,
gravitation, habitation,
hesitation, hibernation,
hyphenation, ideation,
illustration, imbrication,
imitation, immigration,
immolation, implantation,
implication, importation,
imprecation, imputation,
incantation, incarnation,
incitation, inclination,
incrustation, incubation,
inculcation, indentation,
indexation, indication,
indignation, infestation,
infiltration, inflammation,

information, inhalation,
innovation, insolation,
inspiration, installation,
instauration, insufflation,
insulation, intonation,
inundation, invitation,
invocation, irrigation,
irritation, isolation, iteration,
jactitation, jubilation,
laceration, lacrimation,
lamentation, lamination,
legislation, levitation,
liberation, limitation,
lineation, liquidation,
literation, litigation,
lubrication, lucubration,
maceration, machination,
maculation, malformation,
malversation, margination,
mastication, masturbation,
maturation, mediation,
medication, meditation,
melioration, menstruation,
mensuration, metrication,
ministration, moderation,
modulation, molestation,
motivation, navigation,
nomination, numeration,
obfuscation, obligation,
observation, obturation,
occultation, occupation,
operation, orchestration,
ordination, oscillation,
osculation, ostentation,
ovulation, oxidation,
pagination, palliation,

palpitation, patination,
penetration, perforation,
permeation, permutation,
peroration, perpetration,
perspiration, perturbation,
pigmentation, pixilation,
pollination, population,
postulation, predication,
preformation, prelibation,
preparation, presentation,
proclamation, procreation,
procuration, profanation,
prolongation, propagation,
prorogation, protestation,
provocation, publication,
punctuation, radiation,
recitation, reclamation,
recordation, re-creation,
recreation, reformation,
refutation, registration,
regulation, relaxation,
relocation, reparation,
replantation, replication,
reprobation, reputation,
reservation, resignation,
respiration, restoration,
retardation, revelation,
revocation, ruination,
salivation, salutation,
sanitation, satiation,
saturation, scatteration,
scintillation, segmentation,
segregation, separation,
sequestration, sexploitation,
simulation, situation,
solmization, speciation,

speculation, spoliation,
sternutation, stimulation,
stipulation, strangulation,
subjugation, sublimation,
subrogation, suffocation,
suspiration, susurration,
sustentation, syncopation,
syndication, tabulation,
termination, tessellation,
titillation, titivation,
toleration, transformation,
translocation, transmigration,
transmutation, transpiration,
transplantation, transportation,
trepidation, tribulation,
trituration, ulceration,
ululation, undulation,
urination, usurpation,
vaccination, vacillation,
validation, valuation,
variation, vegetation,
veneration, ventilation,
vindication, violation,
visitation, abbreviation,
abomination, acceleration,
accentuation, accommodation,
accreditation, acculturation,
accumulation, actualization,
adjudication, administration,
adulteration, affiliation,
afforestation, agglomeration,
agglutination, alienation,
alleviation, alliteration,
amalgamation, amelioration,
amortization, amplification,
analyzation, anglicization,

annihilation, annunciation,
anticipation, appreciation,
appropriation, approximation,
argumentation, articulation,
asphyxiation, assassination,
asseveration, assimilation,
association, attenuation,
authorization, barbarization,
bastardization, beautification,
bowdlerization, brutalization,
canalization, canonization,
capacitation, capitulation,
centralization, certification,
cicatrization, civilization,
clarification, classification,
coagulation, coeducation,
cohabitation, colonization,
collaboration, columniation,
commemoration,
commiseration,
communication,
communization,
compartmentation,
complementation,
concatenation, conciliation,
confabulation, confederation,
configuration,
conglomeration,
congratulation, consideration,
consociation, consolidation,
contamination, continuation,
cooperation, coordination,
corroboration, crustification,
crystallization, deactivation,
debilitation, decapitation,
decompensation,

defenestration, deforestation,
degeneration, deification,
deliberation, delineation,
denomination, denunciation,
depopulation, depreciation,
deregulation, desegregation,
despoliation, determination,
devaluation, dilapidation,
diphthongization,
disapprobation, discoloration,
discrimination,
disembarkation,
disinclination, disinformation,
disintegration, dissemination,
dissimilation, dissimulation,
dissociation, divarication,
documentation,
domestication, dramatization,
echolocation, edification,
ejaculation, elaboration,
elicitation, elimination,
elucidation, emaciation,
emancipation, emasculation,
enumeration, enunciation,
equalization, equivocation,
eradication, evacuation,
evagination, evaluation,
evaporation, evisceration,
exacerbation, exaggeration,
examination, exasperation,
excoriation, excruciation,
exercitation, exhilaration,
exoneration, expostulation,
expropriation, extenuation,
extermination, extrapolation,
facilitation, factorization,

falsification, fantastication,
feminization, fertilization,
Finlandization, formalization,
formulization, fortification,
fossilization, fructification,
gentrification, gesticulation,
glamorization, globalization,
glorification, gratification,
habituation, hallucination,
harmonization, hellenization,
humanization, idolization,
illumination, imagination,
immunization, impersonation,
implementation,
improvisation, inauguration,
incarceration, incardination,
incineration, incorporation,
incrimination, indoctrination,
inebriation, infatuation,
ingratiation, inhabitation,
initiation, inoculation,
insemination, insinuation,
instrumentation,
internalization, interpretation,
interrelation, intimidation,
intoxication, invagination,
investigation, invigoration,
irradiation, itemization,
jollification, justification,
laicization, latinization,
legalization, lionization,
localization, machicolation,
magnetization, magnification,
maladaptation, manifestation,
masculinization,
matriculation, maximization,

mechanization,
miscegenation, mobilization,
modernization, modification,
mollification, mongrelization,
monopolization, moralization,
mortification, multiplication,
mystification, nationalization,
naturalization, necessitation,
negotiation, neutralization,
normalization, notarization,
notification, novelization,
nullification, optimization,
organization, orientation,
ornamentation, ossification,
pacification, paralyzation,
participation, pasteurization,
patronization, penalization,
perambulation, perpetuation,
perseveration, personalization,
plasticization, pluralization,
petrification, polarization,
pontification, preadaptation,
precipitation, predestination,
prefiguration, premeditation,
preoccupation, preregistration,
prettification, procrastination,
prognostication, proliferation,
pronunciation, propitiation,
pulverization, purification,
qualification, quantification,
ramification, randomization,
ratification, ratiocination,
realization, reciprocation,
recombination,
recommendation,
recrimination, recuperation,

redecoration, reduplication, reforestation, refrigeration, regeneration, regimentation, regurgitation, reification, reincarnation, reintegration, remediation, remuneration, renunciation, representation, republication, repudiation, reticulation, retrogradation, reverberation, robotization, romanization, sanctification, sanitization, scarification, secularization, sedimentation, sensitization, Serbo-Croatian, signification, simplification, socialization, solemnization, solicitation, solidification, sophistication, specialization, specification, stabilization, standardization, sterilization, stratification, stultification, subalternation, subinfeudation, subordination, subpopulation, subsidization, summarization, supplementation, syllabication, symbolization, synchronization, systemization, teleportation, tergiversation, terrorization, theorization, transfiguration, transliteration, transvaluation, traumatization, triangulation, trivialization, uglification, unification, unionization, urbanization, vandalization,

vaporization, variegation, vaticination, velarization, verbalization, verification, versification, victimization, vilification, vinification, vitalization, vituperation, vocalization, vociferation, vulgarization, westernization, x-radiation, acclimatization, allegorization, alphabetization, automatization, capitalization, characterization, circumnavigation, codetermination, commercialization, conceptualization, consubstantiation, containerization, counterreformation, criminalization, cross-examination, de-Stalinization, decasualization, decentralization, declassification, decontamination, dehumanization, delegitimation, demystification, derealization, deterioration, differentiation, disassociation, discombobulation, disorientation, disorganization, disproportionation, disqualification,

diversification, electrification,
excommunication,
exemplification,
experimentation,
extemporization,
externalization,
familiarization, federalization,
generalization,
homogenization,
hospitalization,
hyperventilation, idealization,
identification, immobilization,
immortalization,
incapacitation,
inconsideration,
incoordination,
indemnification,
indetermination,
indiscrimination,
individuation,
institutionalization,
insubordination,
intensification,
intermediation,
intrapopulation, italicization,
legitimization,
maladministration,
mathematization,
militarization, miniaturization,
misappropriation,
miscommunication,
misinterpretation,
mispronunciation,
misrepresentation,
noncooperation,
nonproliferation,

overcompensation,
overpopulation, palatalization,
periodization, personification,
popularization,
predetermination,
prestidigitation,
proselytization, radicalization,
ratiocination, rationalization,
reafforestation, recapitulation,
reconciliation,
reconsideration, rehabilitation,
reinterpretation, renegotiation,
reorganization, revitalization,
ritualization, subvocalization,
supererogation,
syllabification,
tintinnabulation,
transubstantiation,
unappreciation,
underestimation,
undervaluation,
unsophistication,
visualization,
Americanization,
automanipulation,
decriminalization,
depersonalization,
intercommunication,
industrialization,
materialization,
oversimplification,
particularization,
pictorialization,
pseudosophistication,
recapitalization,
spiritualization,

telecommunication,
universalization,
deinstitutionalization,
intellectualization,
internationalization

²**ation** \ā-zhən\ see ASION

³**ation** \ash-ən\ see ASSION

¹**ational** \ā-shnəl\ stational,
citational, formational,
gestational, gradational,
migrational, narrational,
notational, relational,
sensational, vocational,
aberrational, adaptational,
compensational,
computational,
conformational,
confrontational,
congregational, conjugational,
connotational, conservational,
conversational, convocational,
derivational, educational,
fluctuational, generational,
gravitational, ideational,
informational, innovational,
inspirational, invitational,
irrotational, limitational,
navigational, observational,
operational, orchestrational,
postranslational,
prevocational, progestational,
recreational, reformational,
situational, transformational,
communicational,
coeducational,
denominational,

improvisational,
interpretational,
investigational,
organizational,
representational,
nonrepresentational,
reorganizational,
interdenominational

²**ational** \āzh-nəl\ see ASIONAL

³**ational** \ash-nəl\ national,
passional, rational, binational,
cross-national, irrational,
transnational, international,
multinational, supranational,
suprarational

ationist \ā-shnəst\ salvationist,
vacationist, annexationist,
confrontationist,
conservationist, educationist,
integrationist, isolationist,
liberationist, operationist,
preservationist, recreationist,
segregationist, separationist,
preservationist,
accomodationist,
administrationist,
assimilationist, associationist,
collaborationist,
emancipationist

ations \ā-shənz\ Galatians,
impatiens, Lamentations,
Revelations

atious \ā-shəs\ see ACIOUS

¹**atis** \at-əs\ see ³ATUS

²**atis** \ät-əs\ see OTTIS

atist \ät-əst\ see ATEST

atium \ā-shē-əm\ pancratium, solatium

atius \ā-shəs\ see ACIOUS

ative \āt-iv\ dative, native, stative, ablative, creative, dilative, mutative, rotative, summative, translative, aggregative, agitative, alterative, applicative, carminative, cogitative, combinative, commutative, connotative, consecrative, consultative, contemplative, copulative, corporative, cumulative, decorative, denotative, dissipative, educative, explicative, facultative, federative, generative, germinative, imitative, implicative, innovative, integrative, irritative, iterative, legislative, limitative, meditative, meliorative, motivative, nominative, nuncupative, operative, palliative, pejorative, penetrative, procreative, propagative, qualitative, quantitative, recreative, regulative, replicative, separative, speculative, terminative, vegetative, accelerative, accumulative, administrative, agglutinative, alliterative, appreciative, assimilative, associative, authoritative, collaborative, commemorative, commiserative, communicative, contaminative, continuative, cooperative, corroborative, degenerative, deliberative, delineative, determinative, discriminative, evaporative, exhilarative, exonerative, illuminative, interpretative, investigative, justificative, multiplicative, obliterative, opinionative, originative, postoperative, premeditative, preoperative, proliferative, reciprocative, recuperative, regenerative, remunerative, reverberative, significative, vituperative, excommunicative, incommunicative, noncooperative, quasi-legislative, semiquantitative, uncommunicative

atl \ät-ᵊl\ see OTTLE

atlas \at-ləs\ atlas, hatless

atless \at-ləs\ see ATLAS

atli \ät-lē\ see OTLY

atling \at-liŋ\ fatling, flatling, rattling

atly \at-lē\ flatly, rattly

atness \at-nəs\ fatness, flatness, platinous, gelatinous

¹ato \ät-ō\ auto, blotto, grotto,

lotto, motto, otto, potto,
annatto, castrato, legato,
marcato, mulatto, rabato,
rebato, ridotto, rubato,
sfumato, spiccato, staccato,
agitato, animato, ben trovato,
moderato, obbligato, ostinato,
pizzicato

²ato \ āt-ō \ Orvieto, potato,
tomato

atomist \ at-ə-məst \ atomist,
anatomist

atomy \ at-ə-mē \ atomy,
anatomy

aton \ at-ᵊn \ see ²ATIN

atony \ at-ᵊn-ē \ see ATANY

ator \ āt-ər \ baiter, cater, crater,
dater, faitour, freighter,
gaiter, gator, grater, hater,
krater, mater, plater, rater,
satyr, skater, slater, stater,
stator, tater, traitor, waiter,
aerator, collator, Bay Stater,
creator, curator, debater,
dictator, donator,
dumbwaiter, equator, first-
rater, glossator, headwaiter,
levator, locator, mandator,
Mercator, narrator, pronator,
pulsator, rotator, spectator,
tailgater, testator, theater,
third-rater, translator,
upstater, vibrator, actuator,
abdicator, activator, adulator,
advocator, agitator, alligator,
allocator, alternator,

animator, annotator,
applicator, arbitrator,
aspirator, aviator, calculator,
captivator, carburetor,
celebrator, circulator,
commentator, commutator,
compensator, compurgator,
concentrator, confiscator,
congregator, consecrator,
consummator, contemplator,
corporator, correlator,
depredator, desecrater,
desecrator, designator,
cultivator, decorator,
delegator, demonstrator,
detonator, deviator,
dissipater, dominator,
duplicator, dura mater,
educator, elevator, emulator,
escalator, estimator,
excavator, explicator,
expurgator, extirpator,
fascinator, formulator,
fornicator, generator,
gladiator, hibernator,
illustrator, incubator,
indicator, infiltrator,
innovator, inhalator,
inspirator, insulator,
integrator, lacrimator,
liquidator, literator, mediator,
moderator, motivator,
navigator, nomenclator,
nominator, numerator,
obturator, operator,
orchestrator, oscillator,

percolator, perpetrator, pia mater, pollinator, postulator, procreator, procurator, propagator, radiator, regulator, resonator, respirator, revelator, second-rater, selling-plater, separator, simulator, subjugator, syndicator, tabulator, terminator, valuator, ventilator, violator, accelerator, accommodator, accumulator, administrator, adulterator, alienator, alleviator, annihilator, annunciator, anticipator, appreciator, appropriator, assassinator, attenuator, continuator, calumniator, collaborator, commemorator, communicator, conciliator, congratulator, consolidator, contaminator, cooperator, coordinator, corroborator, delineator, denominator, depreciator, determinator, discriminator, disseminator, dissimulator, ejaculator, eliminator, emancipator, enumerator, equivocator, eradicator, evaluator, evaporator, exterminator, extrapolator, impersonator, improvisator, incinerator, inseminator, interrogator, intimidator, investigator,

negotiator, oxygenator, pacificator, perambulator, predestinator, procrastinator, purificator, redecorator, refrigerator, regenerator, resuscitator, totalizator, subordinator, excommunicator, rehabilitator—*also comparatives of adjectives listed at* ¹ATE

¹atre \ ätrᵊ \ coup de theatre, pas de quatre

²atre \ at \ see ⁵AT

atric \ a-trik \ sympatric, theatric, allopatric, geriatric, pediatric, podiatric, psychiatric

atrics \ a-triks \ theatrics, pediatrics

atrist \ a-trəst \ geriatrist, physiatrist

atrix \ ā-triks \ matrix, cicatrix, testatrix, aviatrix, mediatrix, administratrix

atron \ ā-trən \ matron, natron, patron

¹ats \ äts \ see OTS

²ats \ ats \ bats, ersatz—*also plurals and possessives of nouns and third singular presents of verbs listed at* ⁵AT

atsch \ ach \ see ⁴ATCH

atsy \ at-sē \ see ³AZI

¹att \ at \ see ⁵AT

²att \ ät \ see ¹OT

atta\ät-ə\see ¹ATA

attage\ät-ij\see OTTAGE

attan\at-ᵊn\see ²ATIN

atte\at\see ⁵AT

attel\at-ᵊl\see ATTLE

atten\at-ᵊn\see ²ATIN

atter\at-ər\attar, batter, blatter, chatter, clatter, fatter, flatter, hatter, latter, matter, natter, patter, platter, ratter, satyr, scatter, shatter, smatter, spatter, splatter, tatter, backscatter, bespatter, flat-hatter, standpatter, wildcatter, antimatter, pitter-patter

attering\at-ə-riŋ\smattering, backscattering, earth-shattering, self-flattering, unflattering

attern\at-ərn\pattern, Saturn, slattern

attery\at-ə-rē\battery, cattery, clattery, flattery, mattery, self-flattery

attic\at-ik\see ²ATIC

¹attice\at-əs\see ³ATUS

²attice\at-ish\see ATTISH

attily\at-ᵊl-ē\cattily, chattily, nattily, rattly, philately, sal volatile

atting\at-iŋ\batting, matting, tatting

attish\at-ish\brattice, brattish, fattish, flattish

attle\at-ᵊl\battle, brattle, cattle, chattel, prattle, rattle, tattle, embattle, tittle-tattle

attler\at-lər\battler, prattler, rattler, tattler

attling\at-liŋ\see ATLING

¹attly\at-ᵊl-ē\see ATTILY

²attly\at-lē\see ATLY

¹atto\at-ə\see ³ATA

²atto\ät-ō\see ¹ATO

atton\at-ᵊn\see ²ATIN

atty\at-ē\batty, catty, bratty, chatty, fatty, natty, patty, platy, ratty, scatty, tatty

¹atum\ät-əm\bottom, datum, satem, erratum, pomatum, desideratum

²atum\āt-əm\datum, pomatum, substratum, verbatim, ageratum, literatim, seriatim, ultimatum, corpus allatum, desideratum

³atum\at-əm\atom, datum, erratum, substratum, seriatim

atuous\ach-wəs\fatuous, ignis fatuus

atural\ach-rəl\natural, connatural, transnatural, unnatural, preternatural, seminatural, supernatural

¹ature\ā-chər\nature, denature, 4-H'er, magistrature, nomenclature, supernature

²ature\ach-ər\see ²ATCHER

aturn\at-ərn\see ATTERN

¹atus\āt-əs\flatus, gratis,

status, stratus, afflatus,
hiatus, meatus, apparatus,
coitus reservatus

²**atus** \ät-əs \see OTTIS

³**atus** \at-əs \brattice, gratis,
lattice, status, stratus,
clematis, altostratus,
apparatus, cirrostratus,
nimbostratus

atute \ach-ət \see ATCHET

atuus \ach-wəs \see ATUOUS

aty \āt-ē \eighty, matey, platy,
slaty, weighty, yeti, 1080

atyr \āt-ər \see ATOR

¹**atz** \ats \see ²ATS

²**atz** \äts \see OTS

¹**atzo** \ät-sə \matzo, tazza

²**atzo** \ät-sō \see ¹AZZO

¹**au** \ō \see ¹OW

²**au** \ü \see ¹EW

³**au** \au̇ \see ²OW

⁴**au** \ȯ \see ¹AW

aub \äb \see ¹OB

auba \ȯ-bə \carnauba, Catawba

aube \ōb \see ¹OBE

auber \ȯb-ər \dauber,
Micawber

auble \äb-əl \see ¹ABBLE

¹**auce** \as \see ³ASS

²**auce** \ȯs \see ¹OSS

aucer \ȯ-sər \see OSSER

aucet \äs-ət \see OSSET

¹**auch** \ȯch \nautch, watch,
debauch

²**auch** \äch \see OTCH

auche \ōsh \see ²OCHE

auchely \ōsh-lē \see OCIALLY

aucous \ȯ-kəs \caucus,
glaucous, raucous

aucus \ȯ-kəs \see AUCOUS

aucy \as-ē \see ASSY

¹**aud** \ȯd \awed, baud, bawd,
broad, clawed, fraud, gaud,
god, jawed, laud, yod,
abroad, applaud, belaud,
defraud, dewclawed, maraud,
whipsawed, eisteddfod,
lantern-jawed, quartersawed—
also pasts of verbs listed at
¹AW

²**aud** \äd \see ¹OD

audable \ȯd-ə-bəl \audible,
laudable, applaudable,
illaudable, inaudible

audal \ȯd-°l \caudal, caudle,
dawdle

audative \ȯd-ət-iv \see
AUDITIVE

¹**aude** \au̇d-ē \see OWDY

²**aude** \ȯd-ē \see AWDY

³**aude** \au̇d-ə \howdah, cum
laude, magna cum laude,
summa cum laude

audible \ȯd-ə-bəl \see AUDABLE

auding \ȯd-iŋ \auding, self-
applauding

audit \ȯd-ət \audit, plaudit

auditive \ȯd-ət-iv \auditive,
laudative

audle \ȯd-°l \see AUDAL

¹**audy** \äd-ē \see ¹ODY

²**audy** \ȯd-ē \see AWDY

auf \aúf\ see OWFF

auffeur \ō-fər\ see OFER

auga \o-gə\ massasauga, Onondaga

auge \āj\ see ³AGE

augeable \ā-jə-bəl\ see AGEABLE

¹**auger** \o-gər\ see ²OGGER

²**auger** \ā-jər\ see ¹AGER

¹**augh** \af\ see APH

²**augh** \ä\ see ¹A

³**augh** \äk\ see ¹ACH

⁴**augh** \o\ see ¹AW

aughable \af-ə-bəl\ see AFFABLE

¹**aught** \ät\ see ¹OT

²**aught** \ot\ see ¹OUGHT

¹**aughter** \af-tər\ see AFTER

²**aughter** \ot-ər\ see ¹ATER

aughterer \ot-ər-ər\ see ATERER

¹**aughty** \ot-ē\ haughty, naughty, zloty

²**aughty** \ät-ē\ see ATI

augre \og-ər\ see ²OGGER

augur \og-ər\ see ²OGGER

augury \o-gə-rē\ see ²OGGERY

auk \ok\ see ALK

aul \ol\ see ALL

auld \ol\ see ALL

auled \old\ see ALD

auler \o-lər\ see ¹ALLER

aulin \o-lən\ see ALLEN

aulish \o-lish\ see ALLISH

aulk \ok\ see ALK

aulker \o-kər\ see ALKER

aulking \o-kiŋ\ see ALKING

aulm \om\ see ¹AUM

ault \olt\ see ALT

aulter \ol-tər\ see ALTER

aulting \ol-tiŋ\ see ALTING

aultless \olt-ləs\ see ALTLESS

aulty \ol-tē\ see ALTY

¹**aum** \om\ gaum, haulm, poem, qualm, shawm, meerschaum

²**aum** \äm\ see ¹OM

¹**aun** \än\ see ¹ON

²**aun** \ən\ see UN

³**aun** \on\ see ³ON

¹**auna** \än-ə\ see ¹ANA

²**auna** \on-ə\ see ¹ONNA

aunce \ons\ jaunce, launce

¹**aunch** \änch\ conch, cranch, craunch, paunch, raunch, stanch, Romansh

²**aunch** \onch\ craunch, haunch, launch, paunch, raunch, stanch, staunch

auncher \on-chər\ launcher, stancher, stauncher

aunchy \on-chē\ paunchy, raunchy

aund \ond\ awned, maund— *also pasts of verbs listed at* ³ON

¹**aunder** \on-dər\ launder, maunder

²**aunder** \än-dər\ see ¹ONDER

aunish \än-ish\ see ONISH

¹**aunt** \ont\ daunt, flaunt, gaunt, haunt, jaunt, taunt, vaunt, want, wont, avaunt, keeshond, romaunt

²**aunt** \ant\ see ⁵ANT

¹**aunt** \änt\ see ²ANT

aunted \ȯnt-əd\ see ONTED

¹**aunter** \änt-ər\ saunter, mishanter, rencontre

²**aunter** \ȯnt-ər\ gaunter, haunter, saunter

¹**aunty** \ȯnt-ē\ flaunty, jaunty, vaunty

²**aunty** \änt-ē\ see ¹ANTI

aunus \än-əs\ see ¹ONUS

aup \ȯp\ scaup, whaup, yawp

aupe \ōp\ see OPE

auphin \ȯ-fən\ see OFFIN

¹**aur** \au̇r\ see ²OWER

²**aur** \ȯr\ see ¹OR

aura \ȯr-ə\ see ²ORA

aural \ȯr-əl\ see ²ORAL

¹**aure** \ȯr\ see ¹ORE

²**aure** \ȯr\ see ¹OR

aurea \ȯr-ē-ə\ see ORIA

aurean \ȯr-ē-ən\ see ORIAN

¹**aureate** \är-ē-ət\ baccalaureate, commisariat

²**aureate** \ȯr-ē-ət\ aureate, laureate, baccalaureate, professoriat

aurel \ȯr-əl\ see ²ORAL

aureus \ȯr-ē-əs\ see ORIOUS

auri \au̇r-ē\ see OWERY

aurian \ȯr-ē-ən\ see ORIAN

auric \ȯr-ik\ see ORIC

auricle \ȯr-i-kəl\ see ORICAL

aurous \ȯr-əs\ see AURUS

aurus \ȯr-əs\ aurous, chorus, morris, orris, porous, sorus, torus, Taurus, canorous, Centaurus, clitoris, decorous, pelorus, phosphorous, sonorous, thesaurus, brontosaurus, stegosaurus, tyrannosaurus

aury \ȯr-ē\ see ORY

¹**aus** \ā-əs\ see ¹AIS

²**aus** \au̇s\ see ²OUSE

³**aus** \ȯz\ see ¹AUSE

ausal \ȯ-zəl\ causal, clausal, menopausal, postmenopausal

¹**ause** \ȯz\ cause, clause, gauze, hawse, pause, tawse, yaws, applause, because, kolkhoz, sovkhoz, aeropause, diapause, menopause, Santa Claus— *also plurals and possessives of nouns and third singular presents of verbs listed at* ¹AW

²**ause** \az\ see ¹EUSE

auseous \ȯ-shəs\ see AUTIOUS

auser \ȯ-zər\ causer, hawser

ausey \ȯ-zē\ causey, gauzy

auss \au̇s\ see ¹OUSE

¹**aussie** \äs-ē\ see ¹OSSY

²**aussie** \ȯ-sē\ see ²OSSY

aust \au̇st\ see OUST

²**aust** \ȯst\ see ³OST

austless \ȯst-ləs\ costless, exhaustless

¹**austral** \äs-trəl\ see OSTREL

²**austral** \ȯs-trəl\ see ¹OSTRAL

¹**aut** \ō\ see ¹OW

²**aut** \au̇t\ see ³OUT

³**aut** \ät\ see ¹OT

⁴**aut** \ȯt\ see ¹OUGHT

autch \ och \ see ¹AUCH

aute \ ōt \ see OAT

auten \ òt-ᵊn \ boughten, tauten

auterne \ òt-ᵊrn \ quartern, sauterne, sauternes

auternes \ òt-ᵊrn \ see AUTERNE

autery \ òt-ə-rē \ see ATERY

autic \ òt-ik \ orthotic, aeronautic, astronautic

autical \ òt-i-kəl \ nautical, aeronautical, astronautical

autics \ ät-iks \ see OTICS

aution \ ò-shən \ caution, groschen, incaution, precaution

autious \ ò-shəs \ cautious, nauseous, incautious

¹auto \ òt-ō \ auto, risotto

²auto \ ät-ō \ see ¹ATO

auve \ ōv \ see ²OVE

auze \ òz \ see ¹AUSE

auzer \ au̇-zər \ see OUSER

auzy \ ò-zē \ see AUSEY

¹av \ äv \ see ²OLVE

²av \ av \ see ²ALVE

¹ava \ äv-ə \ brava, guava, kava, lava, cassava, ottava, balaclava, lavalava, piassava

²ava \ av-ə \ java, balaclava

avage \ av-ij \ ravage, savage

avant \ av-ənt \ haven't, savant

avarice \ av-rəs \ see AVEROUS

¹ave \ äv-ä \ ave, clave, grave, Jahveh, soave

²ave \ āv \ brave, clave, cave, crave, gave, glaive, grave,

knave, lave, nave, pave, rave, save, shave, slave, stave, they've, trave, waive, wave, Wave, airwave, behave, concave, conclave, depravc, dissave, drawshave, enclave, engrave, enslave, exclave, forgave, margrave, octave, outbrave, palsgrave, shortwave, spokeshave, aftershave, architrave, biconcave, microwave, contraoctave, photoengrave

³ave \ av \ see ³ALVE

⁴ave \ äv \ see ²OLVE

aved \ āvd \ waved, depraved, unsaved—*also pasts of verbs listed at* ²AVE

avel \ av-əl \ cavil, gavel, gravel, ravel, travel, unravel

aveless \ āv-ləs \ graveless, waveless

aveling \ av-liŋ \ raveling, traveling

avement \ āv-mənt \ pavement, depravement, enslavement

¹aven \ ā-vən \ craven, graven, haven, maven, raven, shaven, riboflavin

²aven \ av-ən \ see AVIN

aven't \ av-ənt \ see AVANT

¹aver \ äv-ər \ slaver, palaver, windhover

²aver \ ā-vər \ caver, claver, favor, flavor, graver, haver, laver, laver, quaver, raver,

saver, savor, shaver, slaver,
waiver, waver, disfavor,
enslaver, face-saver, flag-
waver, lifesaver, semiquaver,
demisemiquaver,
hemidemisemiquaver—*also
comparatives of adjectives
listed at* ²AVE

³**aver** \av-ər\ slaver, cadaver,
palaver

avern \av-ərn\ cavern, klavern,
tavern

averous \av-rəs\ avarice,
cadaverous

avery \āv-rē\ bravery, knavery,
quavery, savory, slavery,
wavery, unsavory

avey \ā-vē\ see AVY

avial \ā-vē-əl\ gavial,
margravial

avian \ā-vē-ən\ avian, Shavian,
Moravian, Scandinavian

avid \av-əd\ avid, gravid, pavid

avie \ā-vē\ see AVY

avil \av-əl\ see AVEL

avin \av-ən\ raven, ravin,
savin, spavin

aving \ā-viŋ\ caving, craving,
paving, raving, saving,
shaving, flagwaving,
lifesaving, timesaving,
laborsaving

avis \ā-vəs\ favus, mavis, rara
avis

¹**avish** \ā-vish\ knavish, slavish

²**avish** \av-ish\ lavish, ravish

avist \āv-əst\ provost, Slavist,
suavest, Pan-Slavist

avity \av-ət-ē\ cavity, gravity,
concavity, depravity,
antigravity

¹**avo** \äv-ō\ bravo, Bravo,
centavo, octavo

²**avo** \ä-vō\ octavo, relievo,
mezzo relievo

avor \ā-vər\ see ²AVER

avored \ā-vərd\ favored,
flavored, ill-favored, well-
favored—*also pasts of verbs
listed at* ²AVER

avory \āv-rē\ see AVERY

avus \ā-vəs\ see AVIS

avvy \av-ē\ navvy, savvy

avy \ā-vē\ cavy, gravy, navy,
shavie, slavey, wavy

¹**aw** \ȯ\ aw, awe, blaw, braw,
ca, caw, chaw, claw, craw,
daw, draw, faugh, flaw,
gnaw, haugh, haw, jaw, la,
law, maw, pa, paw, pshaw,
Ra, rah, raw, saw, shah,
shaw, slaw, spa, squaw,
straw, tau, taw, thaw, yaw,
backsaw, bashaw, bedstraw,
bucksaw, bylaw, cat's-paw,
coleslaw, cumshaw, cushaw,
Danelaw, dewclaw, forepaw,
fretsaw, grandma, grandpa,
guffaw, hacksaw, handsaw,
hawkshaw, hee-haw, hurrah,
in-law, jackdaw, jackstraw,
jigsaw, kickshaw, lockjaw,

macaw, old-squaw, outdraw, outlaw, pasha, pooh-bah, ricksha, ringtaw, ripsaw, scofflaw, scrimshaw, seesaw, southpaw, tussah, undraw, vizsla, whipsaw, windflaw, wiredraw, withdraw, Chickasaw, Chippewa, clapperclaw, decree-law, foofaraw, jinrikisha, Kiowa, mackinaw, Omaha, Ottawa, overawe, overdraw, oversaw, overslaugh, padishah, panama, son-in-law, usquebaugh, williwaw, windlestraw, Yakima, brother-in-law, daughter-in-law, father-in-law, mother-in-law, pipsissewa, serjeant-at-law, sister-in-law

²aw \ äv \ see ²OLVE

³aw \ óf \ see ²OFF

⁴aw \ äf \ see ¹OFF

awain \ aú-ən \ see ²OWAN

awba \ ó-bə \ see AUBA

¹awber \ äb-ər \ see OBBER

²awber \ ób-ər \ see AUBER

awd \ ód \ see ¹AUD

awddle \ äd-ᵊl \ see ODDLE

awdle \ ód-ᵊl \ see AUDAL

awdry \ äd-rē \ doddery, padre, tawdry

awdust \ ód-əst \ see ¹ADIST

awdy \ ód-ē \ bawdy, gaudy, summa cum laude

awe \ ó \ see ¹AW

awed \ ód \ see ¹AUD

aweless \ ò-ləs \ see AWLESS

awer \ ór \ see ¹OR

awers \ órz \ see ²OORS

awful \ ó-fəl \ awful, coffle, lawful, offal, god-awful, unlawful

awing \ óiŋ \ cloying, drawing, wappenschawing

awk \ ók \ see ALK

awker \ ò-kər \ see ALKER

awkish \ ó-kish \ gawkish, hawkish, mawkish

awky \ ó-kē \ see ALKIE

awl \ ól \ see ALL

awler \ ò-lər \ see ¹ALLER

awless \ ò-ləs \ aweless, flawless, lawless

awly \ ó-lē \ brawly, crawly, dolly, drawly, scrawly, squally, Bengali

awm \ óm \ see ¹AUM

¹awn \ än \ see ¹ON

²awn \ ón \ see ³ON

awned \ ónd \ see AUND

¹awner \ òn-ər \ fawner, goner, pawner, prawner, spawner

²awner \ än-ər \ see ¹ONOR

awney \ ó-nē \ see ¹AWNY

awning \ än-iŋ \ see ¹ONING

awnly \ än-lē \ see ¹ANLY

¹awny \ ò-nē \ brawny, fawny, lawny, sawney, scrawny, tawny, mulligatawny

²awny \ än-ē \ see ¹ANI

awp \ óp \ see AUP

awry \ȯr-ē \ see ORY

aws \ȯz \ see ¹AUSE

awse \ȯz \ see ¹AUSE

awser \ȯ-zər \ see AUSER

awsi \aủ-sē \ see ²OUSY

awy \ȯi \ see OY

awyer \ȯ-yər \ lawyer, sawyer

¹ax \äks \ see OX

²ax \aks \ ax, fax, flax, lax,
pax, rax, sax, tax, wax,
addax, Ajax, anthrax,
beeswax, borax, broadax,
climax, coax, earwax, galax,
hyrax, meat-ax, panchax,
pickax, poleax, pretax, relax,
smilax, storax, styrax, surtax,
syntax, thorax, toadflax,
aftertax, battle-ax, minimax,
overtax, parallax, supertax,
anticlimax, Astyanax—*also
plurals and possessives of
nouns and third singular
presents of verbs listed at*
²ACK

axant \ak-sənt \ see ACCENT

axen \ak-sən \ see AXON

axi \ak-sē \ see AXY

axic \ak-sik \ ataraxic,
stereotaxic

axis \ak-səs \ axis, praxis

axman \ak-smən \ axman,
cracksman

axon \ak-sən \ flaxen, Klaxon,
Saxon, waxen, Anglo-Saxon

axy \ak-sē \ flaxy, maxi, taxi,
waxy

¹ay \ā \ a , ae, aye, bay, bey,
blae, brae, bray, chez, clay,
day, dey, dray, eh, fay, fey,
flay, fley, frae, fray, Frey,
gay, gey, gley, gray, greige,
hae, hay, he, hey, j, jay, k,
kay, Kay, lay, lei, may,
May, nay, né, née, neigh,
pay, pe, play, pray, prey,
qua, quai, quay, ray, re, say,
sei, shay, slay, sleigh, spae,
spay, splay, spray, stay,
stray, sway, they, tray, trey,
way, weigh, whey, yea,
abbé, affray, agley, airplay,
airway, all-day, allay,
archway, array, ashtray,
assay, astray, away, aweigh,
backstay, ballet, belay,
beltway, benday, bèret,
betray, bewray, bidet,
bikeway, birthday, blasé,
bobstay, bouchée, bouclé,
boule, bouquet, bourrée,
breezeway, Broadway, buffet,
byplay, byway, cachet, café,
cahier, causeway, chaîné,
chalet, chambray, chassé,
ciré, cliché, cloqué, congé,
convey, corvée, coudé,
coupé, crawlway, crochet,
croquet, crossway, cube,
curé, cy pres, DA, daresay,
decay, deejay, defray, delay,
dengue, dismay, display,
distrait, donnée, doomsday,

doorway, dossier, downplay,
dragée, driveway, duvet,
embay, entrée, épée, essay,
estray, Ewe, fairway, filé,
filet, fillet, fireclay, fishway,
flambé, floodway, flyway,
folkway, footway, foray,
forebay, foreplay, forestay,
formée, forte, four-way,
fourchée, foyer, franglais,
frappé, freeway, frieze, frisé,
gainsay, gamay, gangway,
gateway, gelée, glacé,
gourmet, guideway, gunplay,
halfway, hallway, hatchway,
headway, hearsay, heyday,
highway, homestay, hooray,
horseplay, in re, inlay,
inveigh, issei, jackstay, jeté,
keyway, koine, lamé, leeway,
lifeway, lwei, lycée, M-day,
maguey, mainstay, Malay,
malgré, man-day, Mande,
manqué, margay, massé,
maté, May Day, Mayday,
melee, metier, midday,
mislay, misplay, moiré,
moray, nevé, nisei, noonday,
nosegay, obey, ofay, OK,
olé, ombré, osprey, outlay,
outré, outstay, outweigh,
oyez, parfait, parkway,
parlay, parquet, partway,
passé, pâté, pathway, pavé,
payday, per se, pince-nez,
piqué, piquet, PK, plié,

plissé, pommée, portray,
prepay, projet, pulque, puree,
purvey, quale, raceway,
railway, rappee, recamier,
relay, repay, replay, risqué,
roadway, role-play, ropeway,
rosé, rosebay, roué,
routeway, runway, sachet,
sansei, sashay, sauté,
screenplay, seaway, semé,
shipway, short-day, sideway,
skyway, slideway, slipway,
sluiceway, soigné, soiree,
someday, someway, soothsay,
soufflé, speedway, spillway,
stairway, sternway, stingray,
straightway, strathspey,
subway, survey, swordplay,
tempeh, thoughtway,
thruway, tideway, Tigré,
today, Tokay, tollway,
touché, toupee, trackway,
tramway, unlay, unsay, valet,
V-day, vide, visé, walkway,
waylay, weekday, windway,
wireway, wordplay, workday,
X ray, x-ray, A-OK,
alleyway, anyway, appliqué,
arrivé, atelier, attaché,
ballonet, Beaujolais, beurre
manié, BHA, botonée,
braciole, breakaway, cabaret,
cableway, canapé, cap-a-pie,
caraway, carriageway,
cassoulet, castaway,
champlevé, chansonnier,

chardonnay, Charolais,
chevalier, Chippewa,
cloisonné, consommé,
coryphée, croupier, crudités,
cutaway, day-to-day,
debauchee, déclassé, dégagé,
degree-day, démodé, devotee,
disarray, disobey, distingué,
divorcé, divorcée, émigré,
engagé, entranceway,
entremets, entryway, espalier,
everyday, exposé,
expressway, fadeaway,
faraday, faraway, fiancé,
fiancée, flageolet, flyaway,
foldaway, Galloway,
getaway, giveaway, gratiné,
haulageway, hereaway,
hideaway, Hogmanay,
holiday, inter se, interplay,
intraday, IPA, kyrie,
lackaday, latter-day, layaway,
lingerie, macramé, matinee,
MIA, motorway, muscadet,
negligee, overlay, overplay,
overstay, overweigh,
passageway, photoplay,
pikake, piolet, pis aller, play-
by-play, popinjay, pourparler,
pousse-café, present-day,
protégé, protégée,
rambouillet, ratiné, rechauffé,
recherché, reconvey, repartee,
repoussé, résumé, retroussé,
ricochet, right-of-way,
rockaway, rondelet,

roundelay, runaway,
semplice, sobriquet,
sommelier, steerageway,
standaway, stowaway,
straightaway, taboret, tarsier,
taxiway, teleplay, Tenebrae,
throwaway, underlay,
underpay, underplay,
underway, Venite, vérité,
vertebra, virelay, walkaway,
waterway, wellaway,
Whitsunday, workaday,
Agnus Dei, areaway, auto-da-
fé, bichon frisé, boulevardier,
cabriolet, café au lait,
cantabile, communiqué,
costumier, couturier,
décolleté, diamanté, Dies
Irae, felo-de-se, garde-
manger, habitué, Jubilate,
laissez-passer, marrons glacé,
mezzo forte, Morgan le Fay,
objet trouvé, out-of-the-way,
papier collé, papier-mâché,
pas de bourrée, pouilly-fuissé,
prêt-à-porter, roche
moutonnée, roman à clef,
roturier, sine die, sub judice,
superhighway, ukiyo-e, yerba
maté, arrière pensée, lettre de
cachet, catalogue raisonné,
cinema verité, vers de
société, video verité, sinfonia
concertante
²ay \ē\see ¹EE
³ay \ī\see ¹Y

¹**aya** \ä-yə\ ayah, maya, taille

²**aya** \ī-ə\ see ¹IAH

ayable \ā-ə-bəl\ payable, playable, sayable, defrayable, displayable, unsayable

ayah \ī-ə\ see ¹IAH

ayal \āl\ see AIL

¹**ayan** \ā-ən\ crayon, Malayan, ouabain, papain, Galilean, Himalayan

²**ayan** \ī-ən\ see ¹ION

¹**aybe** \ā-bē\ see ABY

²**aybe** \eb-ē\ see EBBY

¹**aye** \ā\ see ¹AY

²**aye** \ī\ see ¹Y

ayed \ād\ see ¹ADE

¹**ayer** \ā-ər\ brayer, layer, mayor, payer, player, prayer, preyer, sayer, sprayer, stayer, strayer, betrayer, bilayer, bricklayer, cardplayer, conveyer, crocheter, decayer, delayer, doomsayer, doomsdayer, gainsayer, horseplayer, inlayer, essayer, forayer, inveigher, obeyer, manslayer, minelayer, portrayer, purveyor, ratepayer, soothsayer, swordplayer, surveyor, taxpayer, tracklayer, yea-sayer, disobeyer, holidayer— *also comparatives of adjectives listed at* ¹AY

²**ayer** \er\ see ⁴ARE

ayered \erd\ see AIRED

ayest \ā-əst\ mayest, sayest, épéeist, essayist, fideist, Hebraist, Mithraist—*also superlatives of adjectives listed at* ¹AY

¹**ayin** \ī-ən\ see ¹ION

²**ayin** \īn\ see ¹INE

³**ayin** \ā-yən\ see AIIAN

aying \ā-iŋ\ maying, playing, saying, delaying, long-playing, soothsaying, surveying, taxpaying, tracklaying

ayish \ā-ish\ clayish, grayish

ayist \ā-əst\ see AYEST

ayless \ā-ləs\ rayless, talus, wayless, aurora australis, Corona Australis

ayling \ā-liŋ\ see AILING

ayly \ā-lē\ see AILY

ayman \ā-mən\ see ¹AMEN

ayment \ā-mənt\ ament, claimant, clamant, payment, raiment, embayment, prepayment, underlayment, underpayment

ayness \ā-nəs\ anus, feyness, gayness, grayness, awayness, Uranus, everydayness, heinous, Janus, manus, uranous

aynim \ā-nəm\ see ¹ANUM

ayn't \ā-ənt\ see EYANT

ayo \ī-ō\ see ¹IO

¹**ayon** \an\ see ⁵AN

²**ayon** \ā-ən\ see ¹AYAN

ayor \ā-ər\ see ¹AYER

¹**ayou** \ī-ə\ see ¹IAH

²**ayou** \ī-ō\ see ¹IO

¹**ays** \ez\ fez, Geez, says, gainsays, unsays, Louis Seize, Louis Treize

²**ays** \āz\ see ¹AZE

ay-so \ā-sō\ see ¹ESO

¹**ayyid** \ī-əd\ see YAD

²**ayyid** \ēd-ē\ see EEDY

az \az\ see AZZ

¹**aza** \äz-ə\ plaza, piazza, tabula rasa

²**aza** \az-ə\ plaza, piazza

¹**azar** \äz-ər\ see OZZER

²**azar** \az-ər\ lazar, alcazar, Belshazzar

azard \az-ərd\ hazard, mazard, mazzard, haphazard

¹**aze** \āz\ baize, blaze, braise, braze, chaise, craze, days, daze, faze, feaze, fraise, gaze, glaze, graze, haze, lase, laze, maize, maze, phase, phrase, praise, raise, rase, raze, smaze, vase, ways, ablaze, agaze, amaze, appraise, breadthways, catchphrase, crossways, deglaze, dispraise, edgeways, emblaze, endways, flatways, gainsays, hereways, leastways, lengthways, liaise, malaise, mores, pj's, sideways, slantways, stargaze, ukase, upraise, weekdays, anyways, chrysoprase, cornerways, holidays, Louis Seize, Louis Treize, lyonnaise, mayonnaise, multiphase, nowadays, overglaze, overgraze, paraphrase, polonaise, polyphase, single-phase, underglaze—*also plurals and possessives of nouns and third singular presents of verbs listed at* ¹AY

²**aze** \äz\ see ¹OISE

³**aze** \äz-ē\ see ¹AZI

azeable \ā-zə-bəl\ see ¹ASABLE

azel \ā-zəl\ see ²ASAL

azement \āz-mənt\ amazement, appraisement

azen \āz-ᵊn\ see AZON

azer \ā-zər\ blazer, brazer, gazer, glazer, grazer, hazer, laser, maser, mazer, appraiser, razor, praiser, razer, fund-raiser, hair-raiser, hell-raiser, stargazer, trailblazer, paraphraser

¹**azi** \äz-ē\ quasi, Swazi, Anasazi, kamikaze

²**azi** \az-ē\ see AZZY

³**azi** \at-sē\ Nazi, patsy, neo-Nazi

azier \ā-zhər\ brazier, glacier, glazier, grazier, leisure, measure, pleasure, rasure, treasure, admeasure, embrasure, erasure

azing \ā-ziŋ\ see AISING
azo \az-ō\ diazo, terrazzo
azon \āz-ᵊn\ blazon, brazen, raisin, emblazon, Marquesan, diapason, hexenbesen
azor \ā-zər\ see AZER
azy \ā-zē\ crazy, daisy, hazy, lazy, mazy, stir-crazy, witch of Agnesi
azz \az\ as, has, jazz, razz, pizzazz, topaz, whenas, whereas, razzmatazz
¹azza \az-ə\ see ²AZA

²azza \äz-ə\ see ¹AZA
³azza \ät-sə\ see ¹ATZO
azzar \az-ər\ see ²AZAR
azzard \az-ərd\ see AZARD
azzle \az-əl\ basil, dazzle, frazzle, bedazzle, razzle-dazzle
¹azzo \ät-sō\ matzo, palazzo, terrazzo, paparazzo
²azzo \az-ō\ see AZO
azzy \az-ē\ jazzy, snazzy, Ashkenazi

e

¹e \ā\ see ¹AY
²e \ē\ see ¹EE
é \ā\ see ¹AY
¹ea \ā\ see ¹AY
²ea \ā-ə\ see ¹AIA
³ea \ē\ see ¹EE
⁴ea \ē-ə\ see ¹IA
eabee \ē-bē\ see ¹EBE
eace \ēs\ see IECE
eaceable \ē-sə-bəl\ see ¹EASABLE
each \ēch\ beach, beech, bleach, breach, breech, each, fleech, leach, leech, peach, pleach, preach, reach, screech, speech, teach, beseech, forereach, impeach, outreach, unteach, overreach, practice-teach
eachable \ē-chə-bəl\

bleachable, leachable, reachable, teachable, impeachable, unimpeachable
eacher \ē-chər\ bleacher, creature, feature, leacher, preacher, reacher, screecher, teacher, defeature, disfeature, schoolteacher
eacherous \ech-rəs\ see ECHEROUS
eachery \ech-rē\ see ECHERY
eaching \ē-chiŋ\ see EECHING
eachment \ēch-mənt\ preachment, impeachment
eachy \ē-chē\ beachy, chichi, peachy, preachy, screechy, caliche, seviche
eacle \ē-kəl\ see ¹ECAL
eacly \ē-klē\ see EEKLY
eacon \ē-kən\ beacon, deacon,

sleeken, weaken, archdeacon,
Mohican, subdeacon,
Neorican

¹**ead** \ed\ bed, bled, bread,
bred, dead, dread, fed, fled,
head, lead, led, med, ped,
pled, read, red, redd, said,
shed, shred, sled, sped,
spread, stead, ted, thread,
tread, wed, zed, abed, afraid,
ahead, airhead, baldhead,
beachhead, bedspread,
bedstead, beebread, behead,
bestead, bighead, biped,
blackhead, blockhead,
bloodred, bloodshed, bobsled,
bonehead, bridgehead, brown
bread, bulkhead, bullhead,
cathead, childbed, coed, corn-
fed, crossbred, crosshead,
daybed, deadhead, death's-
head, deathbed, dispread,
dogsled, drophead, drumhead,
dumbhead, egghead, embed,
far-red, farmstead, fathead,
flatbed, forehead, foresaid,
gainsaid, godhead, half-bred,
hardhead, highbred,
hogshead, homebred,
homestead, hophead, hotbed,
hothead, ill-bred, inbred,
instead, juicehead, lamed,
light bread, longhead,
lowbred, lunkhead, masthead,
misled, misread, moped,
naled, nonsked, outsped,

outspread, packthread, phys
ed, pinhead, pithead, premed,
purebred, railhead, re-tread,
redhead, retread, riverbed,
roadbed, roadstead,
Roundhead, saphead,
scarehead, seabed, seedbed,
sheep ked, sheepshead,
sheetfed, shewbread,
shortbread, sickbed, skinhead,
snowshed, softhead,
sorehead, spearhead,
springhead, steelhead,
straightbred, streambed,
subhead, sweetbread,
swellhead, thickhead,
thunderhead, toolhead,
toolshed, towhead, trailhead,
unbred, unread, unsaid,
unthread, untread, warhead,
webfed, well-bred, well-read,
wellhead, whitehead,
widespread, wingspread,
woodshed, woolshed,
acidhead, aforesaid,
arrowhead, bubblehead,
bufflehead, chowderhead,
chucklehead, colorbred,
copperhead, dragonhead,
dunderhead, featherbed,
featherhead, fiddlehead,
figurehead, fountainhead,
gingerbread, go-ahead,
hammerhead, infrared,
interbred, knucklehead,
letterhead, loggerhead,

lowlihead, maidenhead, newlywed, overhead, overspread, pinniped, pointy-head, poppyhead, quadruped, Saint John's bread, Samoyed, sleepyhead, slugabed, standardbred, timberhead, thoroughbred, underbred, underfed, watershed, woodenhead, parallelepiped

²ead \ēd\ see EED

³ead \əd\ see ¹UD

¹eadable \ēd-ə-bəl\ kneadable, pleadable, readable

²eadable \ed-ə-bəl\ see EDIBLE

eaded \ed-əd\ bedded, headed, bareheaded, bigheaded, bullheaded, clearheaded, coolheaded, eggheaded, fatheaded, hardheaded, hotheaded, light-headed, longheaded, lunkheaded, pigheaded, pinheaded, roundheaded, sapheaded, softheaded, soreheaded, swelled-headed, swellheaded, thickheaded, towheaded, bubbleheaded, chowderheaded, chuckleheaded, dunderheaded, featherheaded, unleaded, white-headed, empty-headed, hydra-headed, knuckleheaded, levelheaded, muddleheaded, pointy-headed, puzzleheaded,

woodenheaded, woolly-headed

eaden \ed-ᵊn\ deaden, leaden, redden, steading, Armageddon

¹eader \ēd-ər\ cedar, ceder, feeder, kneader, leader, pleader, reader, seeder, speeder, weeder, bandleader, cheerleader, conceder, lip-reader, newsreader, nonreader, proofreader, repleader, ringleader, seceder, stampeder, stockbreeder, succeeder, copyreader, interpleader

²eader \ed-ər\ bedder, cheddar, chedar, header, shedder, shredder, sledder, spreader, tedder, threader, wedder, homesteader, doubleheader, triple-header

eadily \ed-ᵊl-ē\ headily, readily, unsteadily

¹eading \ed-iŋ\ bedding, heading, steading, wedding, bobsledding, farmsteading, subheading, wide-spreading

²eading \ed-ᵊn\ see EADEN

³eading \ēd-ᵊn\ see EDON

⁴eading \ēd-iŋ\ see ¹EEDING

¹eadle \ed-ᵊl\ see ¹EDAL

²eadle \ēd-ᵊl\ see EEDLE

eadly \ed-lē\ see EDLEY

ead of \ed-ə\ see EDDA

eadow \ed-ə\ see EDDA

¹**eadsman** \edz-mən\ headsman, leadsman

²**eadsman** \ēdz-mən\ see EEDSMAN

¹**eady** \ed-ē\ eddy, heady, leady, ready, steady, teddy, thready, already, makeready, unsteady, gingerbready, rough-and-ready

²**eady** \ēd-ē\ see EEDY

¹**eaf** \ef\ see ¹EF

²**eaf** \ēf\ see ¹IEF

eafless \ē-fləs\ see IEFLESS

eafy \ē-fē\ see EEFY

eag \ēg\ see IGUE

eager \ē-gər\ eager, leaguer, meager, beleaguer, intriguer

eagle \ē-gəl\ see EGAL

eague \ēg\ see IGUE

eaguer \ē-gər\ see EAGER

¹**eak** \ēk\ beak, bleak, cheek, chic, cleek, clique, creak, creek, Creek, eke, flic, freak, geek, gleek, Greek, keek, leak, leek, meek, peak, peek, peke, pic, pique, reek, screak, seek, sheik, sheikh, shriek, sic, Sikh, sleek, sneak, speak, squeak, steek, streak, streek, teak, tweak, weak, week, wreak, antique, apeak, batik, Belleek, bespeak, bezique, boutique, cacique, caique, critique, forepeak, forespeak, grosbeak, hairstreak, houseleek, muzhik, mystique, newspeak, nonpeak, oblique, off-peak, outspeak, perique, physique, pip-squeak, pratique, relique, technic, technique, Tajik, unique, unspeak, workweek, biunique, Bolshevik, dominique, doublespeak, ecofreak, fenugreek, hide-and-seek, Menshevik, semi-antique, verd antique, Veronique, opéra comique, realpolitik

²**eak** \āk\ see ¹AKE

³**eak** \ek\ see ECK

eakable \ā-kə-bəl\ see AKABLE

¹**eaked** \ē-kəd\ peaked, streaked

²**eaked** \ēkt\ beaked, freaked, peaked, streaked—*also pasts of verbs listed at* ¹EAK

³**eaked** \ik-əd\ see ¹ICKED

eaken \ē-kən\ see EACON

¹**eaker** \ē-kər\ beaker, leaker, reeker, seeker, sneaker, speaker, squeaker, loudspeaker, self-seeker, sunseeker, doublespeaker— *also comparatives of adjectives listed at* ¹EAK

²**eaker** \ā-kər\ see ¹AKER

¹**eaking** \ē-kiŋ\ sneaking, speaking, streaking, self-seeking

²**eaking** \ā-kiŋ\ see ¹AKING

eakish\ē-kish\bleakish, cliquish, freakish, weakish

eakly\ē-klē\see EEKLY

eaky\ē-kē\cheeky, cliquey, creaky, freaky, leaky, reeky, sneaky, screaky, squeaky, streaky, tiki, daishiki, dashiki, Tajiki, cock-a-leekie

¹eal\ē-əl\empyreal, hymeneal, laryngeal, apophyseal, pharmacopeial

²eal\ēl\ceil, chiel, creel, deal, deil, eel, feel, heal, heel, he'll, keel, kneel, leal, meal. peal, peel, real, reel, seal, seel, she'll, shiel, speel, spiel, squeal, steal, steel, teal, tuille, veal, weal, we'll, wheal, wheel, zeal, aiguille, allheal, anneal, appeal, bastille, bonemeal, bonspiel, cartwheel, chainwheel, chenille, cogwheel, conceal, congeal, cornmeal, enwheel, flywheel, forefeel, four- wheel, freewheel, genteel, handwheel, ideal, inchmeal, irreal, misdeal, mobile, newsreel, nosewheel, oatmeal, ordeal, pastille, piecemeal, pinwheel, repeal, reveal, schlemiel, self-heal, side-wheel, singspiel, somedeal, stabile, surreal, tahsil, Tarheel, unreal, unreel, unseal, acetyl, airmobile, bidonville, beau ideal, blastocoel, bloodmobile, Bogomil, bookmobile, campanile, chamomile, cochineal, cockatiel, commonweal, difficile, dishabille, down-at- heel, glockenspiel, goldenseal, manchineel, mercantile, pimpmobile, skimobile, snowmobile, thunderpeal, waterwheel, automobile, Solomon's seal, varicocele

³eal\āl\see AIL

⁴eal\il\see ILL

ealable\ē-lə-bəl\peelable, reelable, stealable, appealable, concealable, revealable, repealable, irrepealable, unappealable

eald\ēld\see IELD

ealed\ēld\see IELD

ealer\ē-lər\dealer, feeler, healer, heeler, kneeler, peeler, reeler, sealer, spieler, squealer, stealer, stelar, vealer, velar, wheeler, appealer, concealer, four- wheeler, freewheeler, newsdealer, repealer, revealer, scene-stealer, side- wheeler, stern-wheeler, two- wheeler, double-dealer, snowmobiler, wheeler-dealer

ealie\ē-lē\see EELY

ealing \ē-liŋ\ see EELING

¹**eally** \ē-ə-lē\ leally, ideally, hymeneally, industrially

²**eally** \il-ē\ see ¹ILLY

³**eally** \ē-lē\ see EELY

ealm \elm\ see ELM

ealment \ēl-mənt\ concealment, congealment, revealment

ealot \el-ət\ see ELLATE

ealotry \el-ə-trē\ see ELOTRY

ealous \el-əs\ jealous, trellis, zealous, cancellous, ocellus

ealousy \el-ə-sē\ see ELACY

ealth \elth\ health, stealth, wealth, commonwealth

ealthy \el-thē\ healthy, stealthy, wealthy, unhealthy

ealty \ēl-tē\ fealty, realty

¹**eam** \ēm\ beam, bream, cream, deem, deme, dream, gleam, mime, neem, ream, scheme, scream, seam, seem, steam, stream, team, teem, theme, abeam, agleam, airstream, berseem, beseem, bireme, blaspheme, bloodstream, centime, daydream, downstream, esteem, extreme, grapheme, hakim, headstream, hornbeam, ice cream, inseam, kilim, lexeme, mainstream, midstream, millime, millstream, moonbeam, morpheme, phoneme, redeem, regime, slipstream,

sunbeam, supreme, taxeme, toneme, trireme, unseam, upstream, academe, disesteem, double-team, enthymeme, misesteem, monotreme, self-esteem, succès d'estime, treponeme

²**eam** \im\ see ¹IM

eaman \ē-mən\ see ¹EMON

eamed \emt\ see EMPT

eamer \ē-mər\ creamer, dreamer, femur, lemur, reamer, schemer, screamer, seamer, steamer, streamer, blasphemer, daydreamer, redeemer

eaming \ē-miŋ\ see EEMING

eamish \ē-mish\ beamish, squeamish

eamster \ēm-stər\ seamster, teamster

eamy \ē-mē\ beamy, creamy, dreamy, gleamy, preemie, seamy, steamy, polysemy

¹**ean** \ē-ən\ aeon, eon, paean, peon, paeon, zein, Achaean, Actaeon, Aegean, Antaean, Archean, Augean, Chaldean, Cytherean, Fijian, Korean, Kuchean, Linnaean, Mandaean, Matthean, pampean, plebeian, protean, pygmaean, Tupi-Guaranian, Tupian, apogean, Aramaean, Atlantean, Caribbean, Cerberean, circadian,

cyclopean, Damoclean, empyrean, epigean, European, Galilean, Hasmonaean, Herculean, Jacobean, kallikrein, Maccabean, Manichaean, Mycenaean, Odyssean, panacean, perigean, Sadducean, Sisyphean, Typhoean, Tyrolean, antipodean, epicurean, Laodicean, proboscidean, Pythagorean, terpsichorean, un-European, epithalamion, Indo-European

²**ean** \ēn\ see ³INE

eaner \ē-nər\ cleaner, gleaner, keener, meaner, preener, teener, weaner, weiner, wiener, congener, demeanor, fourteener, carabiner, intervenor, misdemeanor, submariner, trampoliner

eanery \ēn-rē\ beanery, deanery, greenery, scenery, machinery

eanid \ē-ə-nəd\ Leonid, Oceanid

eanie \ē-nē\ see ¹INI

eaning \ē-niŋ\ greening, leaning, meaning, screening, housecleaning, spring-cleaning, sunscreening, unmeaning, well-meaning, overweening—*also present*

participles of verbs listed at ³INE

eanist \ē-nəst\ see ²INIST

eanliness \en-lē-nəs\ see ENDLINESS

eanling \ēn-liŋ\ greenling, weanling, yeanling

¹**eanly** \ēn-lē\ cleanly, greenly, leanly, meanly, queenly, pristinely, routinely, serpentinely, uncleanly

²**eanly** \en-lē\ see ENDLY

eanness \ēn-nəs\ cleanness, greenness, meanness, betweenness, uncleanness

eano \ē-nō\ see ²INO

eanor \ē-nər\ see EANER

eanse \enz\ see ¹ENS

eant \ent\ see ¹ENT

eanut \ē-nət\ peanut, tenet

eap \ēp\ see EEP

eapen \ē-pən\ see EEPEN

eaper \ē-pər\ see EEPER

eapie \ē-pē\ see EEPY

eapish \ē-pish\ see EEPISH

¹**ear** \er\ see ⁴ARE

²**ear** \ir\ see ²EER

¹**earable** \er-ə-bəl\ bearable, shareable, terrible, wearable, unbearable

²**earable** \ar-ə-bəl\ see ARABLE

earage \ir-ij\ see EERAGE

¹**earance** \ir-əns\ see ¹ERENCE

²**earance** \er-əns\ see ARENCE

earch \ərch\ see URCH

earchist \ər-chəst\ see IRCHIST

earchless \ ərch-ləs \ see
URCHLESS

¹**eard** \ ird \ beard, eared, tiered,
weird, afeard, bluebeard,
crop-eared, dog-eared,
graybeard, lop-eared,
misleared, whitebeard,
chandeliered, pre-
engineered—*also pasts of
verbs listed at* ²EER

²**eard** \ ərd \ see IRD

earean \ ir-ē-ən \ see ¹ERIAN

¹**eared** \ erd \ see AIRED

²**eared** \ ird \ see ¹EARD

¹**earer** \ er-ər \ airer, bearer,
carer, error, sharer, terror,
casebearer, crossbearer,
cupbearer, declarer, furbearer,
pallbearer, seafarer,
talebearer, torchbearer,
trainbearer, wayfarer, color-
bearer, standard-bearer,
stretcher-bearer—*also
comparatives of adjectives
listed at* ⁴ARE

²**earer** \ ir-ər \ cheerer, clearer,
fearer, hearer, mirror,
shearer, smearer, coherer,
sheepshearer, veneerer,
electioneerer—*also
comparatives of adjectives
listed at* ²EER

³**earer** \ ar-ər \ airer, bearer,
casebearer, crossbearer,
cupbearer, declarer, furbearer,
live-bearer, pallbearer,

seafarer, talebearer,
torchbearer, trainbearer,
wayfarer, color-bearer,
standard-bearer, stretcher-
bearer

earful \ ir-fəl \ cheerful, fearful,
tearful

earies \ ir-ēz \ see ERIES

¹**earing** \ ir-iŋ \ clearing, earing,
earring, gearing, God-fearing,
sheepshearing, fictioneering,
hard-of-hearing,
orienteering—*also present
participles of verbs listed at*
²EER

²**earing** \ er-iŋ \ see ¹ARING

earish \ er-ish \ see ¹ARISH

earl \ ərl \ see ¹IRL

earler \ ər-lər \ see IRLER

earless \ ir-ləs \ cheerless,
fearless, gearless, peerless,
tearless

¹**earling** \ ir-liŋ \ shearling,
yearling

²**earling** \ ər-lən \ see ERLIN

¹**early** \ ir-lē \ dearly, merely,
nearly, queerly, yearly,
austerely, biyearly, severely,
sincerely, cavalierly,
semiyearly, insincerely

²**early** \ ər-lē \ see URLY

earn \ ərn \ see URN

earned \ ərnd \ see URNED

earner \ ər-nər \ see URNER

earnist \ ər-nəst \ see ERNIST

earnt \ ərnt \ burnt, learnt,
   weren't

earring \ ir-iŋ \ see ¹EARING

earsal \ ər-səl \ see ¹ERSAL

earse \ ərs \ see ERSE

earser \ ər-sər \ see URSOR

eart \ ärt \ see ¹ART

earted \ ärt-əd \ hearted, parted,
   bighearted, coldhearted,
   downhearted, fainthearted,
   freehearted, good-hearted,
   greathearted, halfhearted,
   hard-hearted, kindhearted,
   largehearted, lighthearted,
   proudhearted, softhearted,
   stouthearted, truehearted,
   uncharted, warmhearted,
   weakhearted, wholehearted,
   brokenhearted,
   chickenhearted, heavyhearted,
   ironhearted, lionhearted,
   openhearted, single-hearted,
   stonyhearted, tenderhearted—
   also pasts of verbs listed at
   ¹ART

¹earth \ ärth \ see ARTH

²earth \ ərth \ see IRTH

earthen \ ər-thən \ see URTHEN

earthy \ ər-thē \ see ORTHY

eartily \ ärt-ᵊl-ē \ see ARTILY

eartless \ ärt-ləs \ see ARTLESS

earty \ ärt-ē \ see ¹ARTY

eary \ ir-ē \ aerie, beery, bleary,
   cheery, dreary, eerie, Erie,
   leery, peri, quaere, query,
   smeary, sphery, teary, veery,
   weary, aweary, Kashmiri,
   Valkyrie, world-weary, hara-
   kiri, miserere, overweary,
   whigmaleerie—*may also
   rhyme with words at* EIRIE

eas \ ē-əs \ see ¹EUS

¹easable \ ē-sə-bəl \ peaceable,
   increasable

²easable \ ē-zə-bəl \ see EASIBLE

¹easand \ iz-ᵊn \ see ²ISON

²easand \ ēz-ᵊnd \ see EASONED

¹ease \ ēs \ see IECE

²ease \ ēz \ see EZE

¹eased \ ēzd \ pleased,
   diseased—*also pasts of verbs
   listed at* EZE

²eased \ ēst \ see ¹EAST

easel \ ē-zəl \ bezel, deasil,
   diesel, easel, measle, teasel,
   weasel

easeless \ ē-sləs \ ceaseless,
   creaseless, greaseless

easement \ ēz-mənt \ easement,
   appeasement

¹easer \ ē-sər \ creaser, greaser,
   piecer, increaser, one-piecer,
   releaser, two-piecer

²easer \ ē-zər \ Caesar, freezer,
   geezer, greaser, pleaser,
   sneezer, squeezer, tweezer,
   appeaser, brainteaser,
   misfeasor, stripteaser,
   timepleaser

eash \ ēsh \ see ²ICHE

easible \ ē-zə-bəl \ feasible,
   squeezable, appeasable,

defeasible, infeasible,
inappeasable, indefeasible,
unappeasable

easil \ē-zəl\ *see* EASEL

easily \ēz-lē\ *see* EASLY

¹easing \ē-siŋ\ leasing,
unceasing—*also present
participles of verbs listed at*
IECE

²easing \ē-ziŋ\ pleasing,
subfreezing—*also present
participles of verbs listed at*
EZE

easingly \ē-siŋ-lē\ decreasingly,
increasingly, unceasingly

easle \ē-zəl\ *see* EASEL

easly \ēz-lē\ easily, measly

eason \ēz-ᵊn\ reason, season,
seisin, treason, disseisin, off-
season, unreason, diocesan

easonable \ēz-nə-bəl\
reasonable, seasonable,
treasonable, unreasonable,
unseasonable

easoned \ēz-ᵊnd\ weasand,
unreasoned—*also pasts of
verbs listed at* EASON

easoning \ēz-niŋ\ seasoning,
unreasoning

easonless \ēz-ᵊn-ləs\ reasonless,
seasonless

easor \ē-zər\ *see* ²EASER

¹east \ēst\ beast, east, feast,
fleeced, geest, least, piste,
priest, reest, triste, yeast,
archpriest, artiste, batiste,

deceased, hartebeest, modiste,
northeast, southeast, tachiste,
arriviste, hartebeest, north-
northeast, pointillist,
wildebeest—*also pasts of
verbs listed at* IECE

²east \est\ *see* EST

easted \es-təd\ *see* ESTED

easter \ē-stər\ Easter, leister,
quaestor, down-easter,
northeaster, southeaster

eastie \ē-stē\ *see* EASTY

eastly \ēst-lē\ beastly, priestly

easty \ē-stē\ beastie, yeasty

easurable \ezh-rə-bəl\
pleasurable, treasurable,
immeasurable

¹easure \ezh-ər\ leisure,
measure, pleasure, treasure,
admeasure, displeasure

²easure \ā-zhər\ *see* AZIER

easurer \ezh-ər-ər\ measurer,
treasurer

¹easy \ē-zē\ breezy, cheesy,
easy, greasy, queasy, sleazy,
sneezy, wheezy, pachisi,
Parcheesi, speakeasy, uneasy

²easy \ē-sē\ *see* EECY

¹eat \ēt\ beat, beet, bleat, cheat,
cleat, deet, eat, feat, fleet,
Geat, gleet, greet, heat, keet,
lied, meat, meet, mete, neat,
peat, pleat, seat, sheet, skeet,
sleet, street, suite, sweet,
teat, treat, tweet, weet,
wheat, accrete, aesthete,

afreet, athlete, backbeat,
backseat, broadsheet,
browbeat, buckwheat,
bystreet, clipsheet, compete,
compleat, complete, conceit,
concrete, crabmeat, deadbeat,
deceit, defeat, delete, deplete,
discreet, discrete, disseat,
downbeat, drumbeat, effete,
elite, en suite, entreat,
escheat, esthete, excrete,
facete, forcemeat, foresheet,
groundsheet, heartbeat, heat-
treat, helpmeet, hoofbeat, ill-
treat, mainsheet, maltreat,
mesquite, mincemeat,
mistreat, offbeat, petite,
preheat, receipt, recheat,
regreet, repeat, replete,
retreat, secrete, slip-sheet,
sweetmeat, terete, unmeet,
unseat, upbeat, vegete,
volkslied, zizith, aquavit,
bittersweet, cellulite, corps
d'elite, countryseat,
decathlete, exegete,
incomplete, indiscreet,
indiscrete, lorikeet,
marguerite, Masorete,
meadowsweet, obsolete,
overeat, overheat, Paraclete,
parakeet, pentathlete,
plebiscite, polychaete,
progamete, self-conceit,
semisweet, tête-à-tête,

superheat, triathlete, winding-
sheet
²**eat** \ āt \ see ¹ATE
³**eat** \ et \ see ¹ET
⁴**eat** \ it \ see ¹IT
eatable \ ēt-ə-bəl \ eatable,
heatable, treatable,
depletable, escheatable,
repeatable, unbeatable
¹**eated** \ ēt-əd \ heated, pleated,
conceited, deep-seated,
repeated—*also pasts of verbs
listed at* ¹EAT
²**eated** \ et-əd \ see ETID
³**eated** \ it-əd \ see ITTED
¹**eaten** \ ēt-ᵊn \ eaten, beaten,
cretin, neaten, sweeten,
wheaten, browbeaten, moth-
eaten, unbeaten, worm-eaten,
weather-beaten
²**eaten** \ āt-ᵊn \ see ¹ATEN
¹**eater** \ ēt-ər \ beater, bleater,
cheater, eater, fetor, greeter,
heater, liter, meter, peter,
Peter, pleater, praetor, rhetor,
seater, sheeter, skeeter,
teeter, treater, tweeter,
anteater, beefeater, blue
peter, Demeter, drumbeater,
eggbeater, excreter, fire-eater,
man-eater, Main Streeter,
maltreater, preheater,
propraetor, repeater, saltpeter,
secretor, seedeater, toadeater,
Wall Streeter, windcheater,
world-beater, altimeter,

centimeter, drunkometer,
lotus-eater, milliliter,
millimeter, overeater,
taximeter—*also comparatives
of adjectives listed at* ¹EAT

²**eater** \et-ər\ *see* ETTER

eatery \ēt-ə-rē\ *see* ETORY

¹**eath** \ēth\ eath, heath, neath,
sheath, wreath, beneath,
bequeath, monteith,
underneath

²**eath** \ēth\ *see* EATHE

eathe \ēth\ breathe, seethe,
sheathe, teethe, wreathe,
bequeath, ensheathe,
enwreathe, inbreathe,
unsheathe, unwreathe

eathean \ē-thē-ən\ lethean,
Promethean

¹**eather** \eth-ər\ *see* ¹ETHER

²**eather** \ē-thər\ *see* EITHER

eathern \eth-ərn\ *see* ETHERN

eathery \eth-rē\ feathery,
heathery, leathery

eathing \ē-thiŋ\ breathing,
sheathing, teething

eathless \eth-ləs\ breathless,
deathless

eathy \ē-thē\ heathy, lethe,
wreathy

eating \ēt-iŋ\ beating, eating,
meeting, seating, sheeting,
sweeting, breast-beating,
drumbeating, fire-eating,
man-eating, unweeting,
Sunday-go-to-meeting

eatise \ēt-əs\ *see* ETUS

¹**eatly** \āt-lē\ *see* ¹ATELY

²**eatly** \ēt-lē\ *see* EETLY

eature \ē-chər\ *see* EACHER

eaty \ēt-ē\ meaty, peaty, sleety,
sweetie, treaty, ziti, entreaty,
spermaceti

eau \ō\ *see* ¹OW

eaucracy \äk-rə-sē\ *see* OCRACY

eauteous \üt-ē-əs\ *see* UTEOUS

eautiful \üt-i-fəl\ *see* UTIFUL

eauty \üt-ē\ *see* ¹OOTY

eaux \ō\ *see* ¹OW

eavable \ē-və-bəl\ *see* EIVABLE

eaval \ē-vəl\ *see* IEVAL

¹**eave** \ēv\ breve, cleave, eve,
Eve, greave, grieve, heave,
leave, lief, peeve, reave,
reeve, reive, scrieve, sheave,
shrieve, sleave, sleeve,
steeve, thieve, weave, weve,
Abib, achieve, aggrieve,
believe, bereave, conceive,
deceive, inweave, khedive,
motive, naive, perceive, qui
vive, receive, relieve,
reprieve, retrieve, shirtsleeve,
unreeve, unweave, upheave,
apperceive, disbelieve,
interleave, interweave, make-
believe, misbelieve,
misconceive, preconceive,
semibreve, undeceive, adam-
and-eve, recitative, ticket-of-
leave, underachieve, Saint
Agnes' Eve

²**eave** \iv\ see ²IVE

eaved \ēvd\ leaved, sleeved, aggrieved, bereaved, relieved—*also pasts of verbs listed at* ¹EAVE

eavement \ēv-mənt\ see EVEMENT

eaven \ev-ən\ devon, heaven, leaven, levin, seven, Sevin, sweven, eleven, replevin

eaver \ē-vər\ see IEVER

eavers \ē-vərz\ cleavers, vivers

eaves \ēvz\ eaves, shirtsleeves

eavey \ē-vē\ peavey, divi-divi

eaward \ē-wərd\ see EEWARD

¹**eaze** \ēz\ see EZE

²**eaze** \āz\ see ¹AZE

eazy \ē-zē\ see ¹EASY

eb \eb\ bleb, deb, ebb, neb, pleb, reb, Reb, web, ardeb, celeb, cobweb, cubeb, Deneb, subdeb, cause célèbre, Johnny Reb, spiderweb

eba \ē-bə\ amoeba, zareba, copaiba

ebate \ab-ət\ see ABIT

ebb \eb\ see EB

ebble \eb-əl\ pebble, rebel, treble

ebbuck \ek-ək\ kebbuck, rebec

ebby \eb-ē\ blebby, maybe, webby, cobwebby

¹**ebe** \ē-bē\ BB, freebie, Hebe, phoebe, Phoebe, Seabee, caribe, Galibi

²**ebe** \ēb\ glebe, grebe, hebe, plebe, ephebe, sahib

ebec \eb-ək\ see EBBUCK

ebel \eb-əl\ see EBBLE

eber \ā-bər\ see ABOR

eble \eb-əl\ see EBBLE

ebo \ē-bō\ see IBO

ebral \ē-brəl\ cerebral, palpebral, vertebral

ebrity \eb-rət-ē\ celebrity, muliebrity

ebs \eps\ see EPS

ebt \et\ see ¹ET

ebted \et-əd\ see ETID

ebtor \et-ər\ see ETTER

ebus \ē-bəs\ Phoebus, rebus, ephebus

ec \ek\ see ECK

eca \ē-kə\ see ¹IKA

ecal \ē-kəl\ cecal, fecal, meikle, treacle, bibliothecal

ecan \ek-ən\ see ECKON

ecant \ē-kənt\ piquant, secant

ecca \ek-ə\ Decca, mecca, weka, Rebekah

eccable \ek-ə-bəl\ see ECKABLE

eccant \ek-ənt\ peccant, second

ecco \ek-ō\ see ECHO

ecency \ēs-ᵊn-sē\ decency, recency, indecency

ecent \ēs-ᵊnt\ decent, recent, indecent, obeisant

eces \ē-sēz\ see ECIES

¹**ech** \ek\ see ECK

²**ech** \ək\ see UCK

¹**eche** \āsh\ crèche, flèche, resh, seiche, bobeche, tête-bêche

²**eche** \esh\ see ¹ESH

èche \esh\ see ¹ESH

èche \esh\ see ¹ESH

eched \echt\ see ETCHED

echerous \ech-rəs\ lecherous, treacherous

echery \ech-rē\ lechery, treachery

echin \ek-ən\ see ECKON

echo \ek-ō\ deco, echo, gecko, secco, reecho

ecia \ē-shə\ see ¹ESIA

ecially \esh-lē\ see ESHLY

ecian \ē-shən\ see ¹ETION

ecibel \es-ə-bəl\ see ESSIBLE

¹**ecie** \ē-sē\ see EECY

²**ecie** \ē-shē\ see ISHI

ecies \ē-sēz\ feces, species, theses, prostheses, subspecies, exegeses

ecile \es-əl\ see ¹ESTLE

ecimal \es-ə-məl\ see ESIMAL

eciman \es-mən\ see ESSMAN

ecious \ē-shəs\ specious, capricious, facetious

eck \ek\ beck, check, cheque, Czech, deck, dreck, fleck, heck, lek, neck, peck, reck, sec, sneck, spec, speck, trek, wreak, wreck, Aztec, backcheck, bedeck, breakneck, cromlech, crookneck, cross-check, cusec, ewe-neck, exec,
flyspeck, fore-check, foredeck, gooseneck, haček, hatcheck, henpeck, high tech, kopeck, limbeck, Mixtec, paycheck, pinchbeck, Quebec, rebec, redneck, ringneck, roughneck, samekh, shipwreck, spot-check, tenrec, Toltec, Uzbek, wryneck, xebec, afterdeck, à la grecque, bodycheck, bottleneck, countercheck, demi-sec, discotheque, double-check, double-deck, hunt-and-peck, leatherneck, littleneck, Pont l'Évêque, quarterdeck, rubberneck, turtleneck, Yucatec, Zapotec, cinematheque, Melchizedek

eckable \ek-ə-bəl\ checkable, impeccable

ecked \ekt\ see ECT

ecker \ek-ər\ checker, chequer, decker, pecker, trekker, wrecker, exchequer, three-decker, woodpecker, dominicker, double-decker, rubbernecker

ecking \ek-iŋ\ decking, necking

ecklace \ek-ləs\ see ECKLESS

eckle \ek-əl\ deckle, freckle, heckle, shekel, speckle, kenspeckle

eckless \ek-ləs\ feckless, checkless, necklace, reckless, affectless

eckon \ek-ən\ beckon, reckon,
zechin, Aztecan, misreckon,
Toltecan, Yucatecan

¹**econd** \ek-ənd\ see ECUND

²**econd** \ek-ənt\ see ECCANT

ecque \ek\ see ECK

ecs \eks\ see EX

ect \ekt\ necked, sect, specked,
abject, affect, aspect, bisect,
cathect, collect, confect,
connect, convect, correct,
defect, deflect, deject, detect,
direct, dissect, effect, eject,
elect, erect, ewe-necked,
expect, goosenecked, infect,
inflect, inject, insect, inspect,
neglect, object, pandect,
perfect, porrect, prefect,
prelect, project, prospect,
protect, rednecked, refect,
reflect, reject, resect, respect,
ring-necked, select, stiff-
necked, subject, suspect,
traject, transect, trisect, V-
necked, architect,
circumspect, deselect, dialect,
disaffect, disconnect,
disinfect, disrespect, double-
decked, genuflect, incorrect,
indirect, intellect, interject,
intersect, introject, introspect,
misdirect, preselect, re-
collect, recollect, redirect,
reelect, resurrect, retrospect,
self-respect, turtlenecked,
vivisect, aftereffect,

hypercorrect, idiolect,
interconnect, semierect, semi-
indirect—*also pasts of verbs
listed at* ECK

ecta \ek-tə\ dejecta, ejecta,
perfecta, trifecta

ectable \ek-tə-bəl\ affectable,
collectible, correctable,
deflectable, delectable,
detectable, ejectable,
erectable, expectable,
inflectable, injectable,
electable, indefectible,
perfectible, projectable,
respectable, disrespectable,
indefectible

ectacle \ek-ti-kəl\ see ECTICAL

ectal \ek-tᵊl\ see ECTILE

ectance \ek-təns\ expectance,
reflectance

ectant \ek-tənt\ expectant,
humectant, injectant,
protectant, disinfectant

ectar \ek-tər\ see ECTOR

ectarous \ek-trəs\ see ECTRESS

ectary \ek-tə-rē\ sectary,
insectary

ected \ek-təd\ affected,
collected, complected,
dejected, recollected, self-
affected, self-collected, self-
elected, self-selected,
unaffected, undirected,
unexpected, unselected, inner-
directed, other-directed—*also
pasts of verbs listed at* ECT

directed, other-directed—*also
pasts of verbs listed at* ECT

ecten \ek-tən\ nekton, pecten,
pectin

ecter \ek-tər\ see ECTOR

ectible \ek-tə-bəl\ see ECTABLE

ectic \ek-tik\ hectic, pectic,
cathectic, eclectic, synectic,
anorectic, apoplectic,
catalectic, dialectic

ectical \ek-ti-kəl\ spectacle,
dialectical

ectile \ek-tᵊl\ sectile, erectile,
projectile, dialectal

ectin \ek-tən\ see ECTEN

ecting \ek-tiŋ\ affecting, self-
respecting, self-correcting

ection \ek-shən\ flexion,
lection, section, abjection,
advection, affection,
bisection, collection,
complexion, confection,
connection, connexion,
convection, correction,
defection, deflection,
dejection, detection,
direction, dissection, ejection,
election, erection, evection,
infection, inflection,
injection, inspection,
midsection, objection,
perfection, prelection,
projection, protection,
refection, reflection,
rejection, resection, selection,
subjection, subsection,

trajection, transection,
trisection, by-election,
circumspection, disaffection,
disconnection, disinfection,
genuflection, imperfection,
indirection, introjection,
introspection, insurrection,
intellection, interjection,
intersection, misdirection,
predilection, preselection,
recollection, redirection,
reelection, reinfection,
resurrection, retroflexion,
retrospection, vivisection,
hypercorrection,
interconnection

ectional \ek-shnəl\ sectional,
affectional, bisectional,
complexional, connectional,
convectional, correctional,
cross-sectional, directional,
inflectional, projectional,
reflectional, bidirectional,
introspectional, interjectional,
resurrectional, vivisectional,
omnidirectional,
unidirectional

ectionist \ek-shnəst\
perfectionist, projectionist,
protectionist, introspectionist,
resurrectionist, vivisectionist

ective \ek-tiv\ advective,
affective, bijective, collective,
connective, convective,
corrective, defective,
deflective, detective,

directive, effective, elective, ejective, infective, inflective, injective, invective, objective, perfective, perspective, projective, prospective, reflective, respective, selective, subjective, cost-effective, imperfective, ineffective, intellective, introspective, nondirective, nonobjective, retrospective, cryoprotective, intersubjective

ectless \ek-ləs\ see ECKLESS

ectly \ekt-lē\ abjectly, correctly, directly, erectly, incorrectly

ectness \ekt-nəs\ abjectness, correctness, directness, erectness, selectness, incorrectness, indirectness, hypercorrectness

ecto \ek-tō\ recto, perfecto

ectomy \ek-tə-mē\ mastectomy, vasectomy, appendectomy, tonsillectomy

ector \ek-tər\ hector, lector, nectar, rector, sector, specter, vector, bisector, collector, convector, corrector, defector, deflector, detector, director, dissector, effector, ejector, elector, erector, infector, injector, inspector, neglecter, objector, perfecter, projector, prospector, protector, reflector, selector, trisector, vivisector

ectoral \ek-trəl\ spectral, pectoral, electoral, protectoral

ectorate \ek-trət\ rectorate, directorate, electorate, inspectorate, protectorate

ectory \ek-trē\ rectory, directory, protectory, refectory, trajectory, ex-directory

ectral \ek-trəl\ see ECTORAL

ectress \ek-trəs\ nectarous, directress, electress, protectress

ectrix \ek-triks\ rectrix, directrix

ectrum \ek-trəm\ plectrum, spectrum, electrum

¹ectual \ek-chəl\ effectual, ineffectual, intellectual, anti-intellectual

²ectual \eksh-wəl\ see EXUAL

ectually \ek-chə-lē\ effectually, ineffectually, intellectually

¹ectural \ek-chə-rəl\ conjectural, prefectural, architectural

²ectural \ek-shrəl\ flexural, conjectural, architectural

ecture \ek-chər\ lecture, conjecture, prefecture, architecture

ectus \ek-təs\ conspectus, prospectus

ecular \ek-yə-lər\ secular, specular, molecular

ecum \ē-kəm\ vade mecum, subpoena duces tecum

ecund \ek-ənd\ fecund, second—*also pasts of verbs listed at* ECKON

ecutive \ek-ət-iv\ consecutive, executive, inconsecutive

ed \ed\ see ¹EAD

e'd \ēd\ see EED

¹eda \ēd-ə\ Leda, torpedo, alameda, olla podrida

²eda \äd-ə\ see ³ADA

¹edal \ed-ᵊl\ heddle, medal, meddle, pedal, peddle, treadle, backpedal, bipedal, soft-pedal, intermeddle

²edal \ēd-ᵊl\ see EEDLE

edance \ēd-ᵊns\ see EDENCE

¹edar \ed-ər\ see ²EADER

²edar \ēd-ər\ see ¹EADER

edator \ed-ət-ər\ see EDITOR

edd \ed\ see ¹EAD

edda \ed-ə\ meadow, Vedda, instead of

eddar \ed-ər\ see ²EADER

edded \ed-əd\ see EADED

edden \ed-ᵊn\ see EADEN

edder \ed-ər\ see ²EADER

edding \ed-iŋ\ see ¹EADING

eddle \ed-ᵊl\ see ¹EDAL

eddler \ed-lər\ meddler, medlar, peddler

eddon \ed-ᵊn\ see EADEN

eddy \ed-ē\ see ¹EADY

¹ede \äd\ see ¹ADE

²ede \ēd\ see EED

edeas \ēd-ē-əs\ see ¹EDIOUS

edel \äd-ᵊl\ see ADLE

edence \ēd-ᵊns\ credence, impedance, precedence, antecedence

edent \ēd-ᵊnt\ credent, needn't, decedent, precedent, succedent, antecedent

¹eder \äd-ər\ see ADER

²eder \ēd-ər\ see ¹EADER

edge \ej\ dredge, edge, fledge, hedge, kedge, ledge, pledge, sedge, sledge, veg, wedge, allege, frankpledge, gilt-edge, hard-edge, knife-edge, nutsedge, straightedge, featheredge, sortilege

edged \ejd\ edged, wedged, alleged, full-fledged, gilt-edged, unfledged, deckle-edged, double-edged—*also pasts of verbs listed at* EDGE

edger \ej-ər\ dredger, edger, hedger, ledger, leger, pledger

edgie \ej-ē\ see EDGY

edgy \ej-ē\ edgy, ledgy, sedgy, veggie, wedgie, wedgy

edi \äd-ē\ see ADY

edia \ēd-ē-ə\ media, acedia, cyclopedia, via media, encyclopedia

edial \ēd-ē-əl\ medial, predial, remedial

edian \ēd-ē-ən\ median, comedian, tragedian

ediant \ēd-ē-ənt\ see EDIENT

edible\ed-ə-bəl\credible, edible, spreadable, incredible, inedible

¹edic\ēd-ik\comedic, cyclopedic, logaoedic, orthopedic, encyclopedic

²edic\ed-ik\Eddic, medic, comedic, paramedic, samoyedic

³edic\ād-ik\see ¹ADIC

edicable\ed-i-kə-bəl\medicable, predicable, immedicable

edical\ed-i-kəl\medical, pedicle, premedical, biomedical, paramedical

edicate\ed-i-kət\dedicate, predicate

edicle\ed-i-kəl\see EDICAL

edience\ēd-ē-əns\expedience, obedience, disobedience, inexpedience

edient\ēd-ē-ənt\mediant, expedient, ingredient, obedient, submediant, disobedient, inexpedient

ediment\ed-ə-mənt\pediment, sediment, impediment

eding\ēd-iŋ\see ¹EEDING

¹edious\ēd-ē-əs\tedious, supersedeas

²edious\ē-jəs\see EGIS

edist\ēd-əst\orthopedist, encyclopedist

edit\ed-ət\credit, edit, accredit, coedit, discredit,

noncredit, reedit, subedit, copyedit

editor\ed-ət-ər\creditor, editor, predator, coeditor, subeditor

edium\ēd-ē-əm\medium, tedium, cypripedium

edlar\ed-lər\see EDDLER

edley\ed-lē\deadly, medley, redly, chance-medley

edly\ed-lē\see EDLEY

¹edo\ēd-ō\credo, lido, speedo, aikido, libido, Toledo, torpedo, tuxedo

²edo\ād-ō\see ²ADO

³edo\ēd-ə\see ¹EDA

edon\ēd-ᵊn\bleeding, Eden, steading, Sarpedon, boustrophedon

edouin\ed-wən\see EDWIN

edra\ē-drə\Phaedra, cathedra

edral\ē-drəl\cathedral, dihedral, trihedral, hemihedral, holohedral, octahedral, pentahedral, polyhedral, procathedral, tetrahedral, dodecahedral, icosahedral, tetartohedral

edulous\ej-ə-ləs\credulous, sedulous, incredulous

edum\ēd-əm\Edam, freedom, sedum

edure\ē-jər\besieger, procedure, supersedure

edwin\ed-wən\Edwin, bedouin

¹ee\ē\b, be, bee, Brie, c,

cay, cee, Cree, d, dee, dree,
e, fee, flea, flee, free, g,
gee, ghee, gie, glee, gree,
he, key, knee, lea, lee, li,
me, mi, p, pea, pee, plea,
pree, quay, re, scree, sea,
see, she, shri, si, ski,
spree, sri, t, tea, tee, the,
thee, three, ti, tree, Tshi,
twee, Twi, v, vee, we, wee,
whee, ye, z, zee, agley,
aiguille, agree, alee, alienee,
ani, Bacchae, bailee,
banshee, bargee, bawbee,
Belgae, bohea, bootee,
bougie, buckshee, burgee,
carefree, CB, Chablis,
Chaldee, chick-pea,
cowpea, croquis, curie,
debris, decree, deep-sea,
degree, donee, DP, draftee,
drawee, emcee, ennui, esprit,
etui, farci, feoffee, foresee,
fusee, GB, germfree, glacis,
goatee, grand prix, grandee,
grantee, GT, heart-free,
Horae, IC, Jaycee, jaygee,
jayvee, knock-knee, KP,
latchkey, lessee, low-key,
LP, maquis, marquee, MC,
métis, muggee, ngwee, OD,
off-key, ogee, Osee, Parcae,
pardie, passkey, Pawnee,
payee, perdie, per se, PG,
pledgee, pongee, post-free,
précis, puree, puttee, qt, rani,

razee, rooftree, rupee, rushee,
sati, scotfree, settee,
Shawnee, sightsee, signee,
sirree, spadille, spahi,
spondee, squeegee, squilgee,
standee, strophe, suttee,
sycee, TB, testee, 3-D, titi,
to-be, topee, towhee, townee,
trainee, trustee, trusty, Tupi,
turfski, turnkey, tutee, tutti,
TV, unbe, vendee, vestee,
Volsci, vouchee, whangee,
whoopee, would-be, yen-
shee, abatis, ABC, ABD,
absentee, addressee, adoptee,
advisee, allottee, ambergris,
AMP, amputee, appellee,
appointee, après-ski, arrestee,
assignee, attendee, B.V.D.,
Bahai, barley-bree, batterie,
billi-bi, bonhomie, booboisie,
bourgeoisie, brasserie,
brusquerie, bumblebee,
camporee, cap-a-pie,
causerie, CCD, charivari,
chickaree, chimpanzee, coati,
Coligny, committee,
conferee, consignee,
counselee, counterplea,
Danae, DDD, DDT,
debauchee, deportee, dernier
cri, deshabille, designee,
detainee, devisee, devotee,
diploe, disagree, discharge,
dishabille, divorce, divorcee,
DMT, dungaree, eau-de-vie,

employee, endorsee, enlistee, enrollee, epopee, escadrille, escapee, ESP, evictee, expellee, FAD, fancy-free, fedayee, filigree, fleur-de-lis, formulae, franchisee, fricassee, galilee, garnishee, gaucherie, Gemini, GTP, guarani, guarantee, honeybee, honoree, humble-bee, hydro-ski, inductee, internee, invitee, IUD, jacquerie, jamboree, jus soli, kidnappee, LCD, LED, legatee, libelee, licensee, LSD, maître d', manatee, millidegree, murderee, NAD, nominee, obligee, oversea, oversee, parolee, parti pris, patentee, pedigree, peppertree, picotee, piroshki, point d'appui, potpourri, praecipe, presentee, promisee, rapparee, referee, refugee, rejectee, renminbi, repartee, retiree, retrainee, returnee, saddletree, Sadducee, sangaree, selectee, Semele, shivaree, snickersnee, SOB, SST, Tenebrae, thirty-three, TNT, toile de Jouy, torii, transferee, undersea, vaccinee, verdigris, VIP, vis-à-vis, warrantee, Adar Sheni, alienee, biographee, bouquet garni, casus belli, charcuterie,

chincherinchee, chinoiserie, covenantee, dedicatee, delegatee, distributee, ESOP, evacuee, examinee, exuviae, facetiae, fait accompli, felo-de-se, interrogee, interviewee, jaborandi, minutiae, Pasiphae, prima facie, reliquiae, relocatee, Simon Legree, communicatee, taedium vitae, Tupi-Guarani, ignoratio elenchi, petitio principii

²ee \ ā \ see ¹AY

ée \ ā \ see ¹AY

eeable \ ē-ə-bəl \ seeable, skiable, agreeable, foreseeable, disagreeable

eebie \ ē-bē \ see ¹EBE

eece \ ēs \ see IECE

eeced \ ēst \ see ¹EAST

eech \ ēch \ see EACH

eecher \ ē-chər \ see EACHER

eeches \ ich-əz \ see ITCHES

eeching \ ē-chiŋ \ breeching, far-reaching—*also present participles of verbs listed at* EACH

eechy \ ē-chē \ see EACHY

eecy \ ē-sē \ fleecy, greasy, specie, AC/DC

eed \ ēd \ bead, bleed, brede, breed, cede, creed, deed, feed, glede, gleed, greed, he'd, heed, keyed, knead, kneed, lead, mead, Mede, meed, need, plead, read,

rede, reed, screed, seed,
she'd, speed, steed, swede,
treed, tweed, we'd, weed,
accede, airspeed, allseed,
bindweed, birdseed,
blueweed, bourride, breast-
feed, bugseed, burweed,
cheerlead, chickweed,
concede, crossbreed,
cudweed, debride, degreed,
duckweed, exceed, fairlead,
fireweed, flaxseed, Godspeed,
gulfweed, half-breed, hand-
feed, hawkweed, hayseed,
high-speed, horseweed,
impede, implead, inbreed,
indeed, ironweed, Jamshid,
jetbead, knapweed, knotweed,
linseed, lip-read, milkweed,
misdeed, mislead, misread,
moonseed, nosebleed, off-
speed, oilseed, pigweed,
pinweed, pokeweed,
pondweed, precede, proceed,
proofread, ragweed, rapeseed,
recede, reseed, rockweed,
seaweed, secede, self-feed,
Siegfried, sight-read,
silkweed, smartweed,
snakeweed, sneezeweed,
speed-read, spoon-feed, stall-
feed, stampede, stickseed,
stickweed, stinkweed,
succeed, ten-speed, tickseed,
weak-kneed, witchweed,
wormseed, aniseed, antecede,

beggarweed, bitterweed,
bottle-feed, bugleweed,
butterweed, carpetweed,
centipede, copyread,
cottonseed, cottonweed,
crazyweed, Ganymede,
interbreed, intercede,
interplead, jewelweed,
jimsonweed, locoweed,
millipede, overfeed,
pedigreed, pickerelweed,
pumpkinseed, retrocede,
riverweed, rosinweed,
silverweed, supersede,
thimbleweed, tumbleweed,
underfeed, waterweed,
velocipede

eedal \ēd-ᵊl\ see EEDLE
eeder \ēd-ər\ see ¹EADER
eedful \ēd-fəl\ heedful, needful
¹eeding \ēd-iŋ\ bleeding,
leading, reading, reeding,
inbreeding, linebreeding,
lipreading, outbreeding,
preceding, speed-reading
²eeding \ēd-ᵊn\ see EDON
eedle \ēd-ᵊl\ aedile, beadle,
credal, creedal, daedal,
needle, wheedle
eedless \ēd-ləs\ deedless,
heedless, needless, seedless
eedn't \ēd-ᵊnt\ see EDENT
eedo \ēd-ō\ see ¹EDO
eedom \ēd-əm\ see EDUM
eeds \ēdz\ needs, proceeds—
also plurals and possessives

*of nouns and third singular
presents of verbs listed at* EED

eedsman \ ēdz-mən \ beadsman,
seedsman

eedy \ ēd-ē \ beady, deedy,
greedy, needy, reedy, sayyid,
seedy, speedy, tweedy,
weedy

eef \ ēf \ see ¹IEF

eefy \ ē-fē \ beefy, leafy, reefy

eeing \ ē-iŋ \ seeing, skiing,
farseeing, ill-being, sight-
seeing, turfskiing, well-being,
waterskiing

¹**eek** \ ik \ see ICK

²**eek** \ ēk \ see ¹EAK

eeken \ ē-kən \ see EACON

eeker \ ē-kər \ see ¹EAKER

eekie \ ē-kē \ see EAKY

eeking \ ē-kiŋ \ see ¹EAKING

eekly \ ē-klē \ bleakly, chicly,
sleekly, weakly, weekly,
treacly, biweekly, midweekly,
newsweekly, triweekly,
semiweekly

eeks \ ēks \ see ¹IXE

eeky \ ē-kē \ see EAKY

eel \ ēl \ see ²EAL

eelable \ ē-lə-bəl \ see EALABLE

eeled \ ēld \ see IELD

eeler \ ē-lər \ see EALER

eelie \ ē-lē \ see EELY

eelin \ ē-lən \ see ELIN

eeling \ ē-liŋ \ ceiling, dealing,
feeling, peeling, shieling,
wheeling, appealing,

Darjeeling, freewheeling,
self-dealing, self-feeling, self-
sealing, unfeeling, double-
dealing, self-revealing,
snowmobiling, unappealing—
*also present participles of
verbs listed at* ²EAL

eelson \ el-sən \ see ELSON

eely \ ē-lē \ dele, eely, freely,
mealie, mealy, really, seely,
steelie, steely, stele,
surreally, syli, vealy,
wheelie, Swahili, campanile,
contumely, monostele

eem \ ēm \ see ¹EAM

eeman \ ē-mən \ see ¹EMON

eemer \ ē-mər \ see EAMER

eemie \ ē-mē \ see EAMY

eeming \ ē-miŋ \ seeming,
streaming, unbeseeming—
*also present participles of
verbs listed at* ¹EAM

eemly \ ēm-lē \ seemly,
supremely, unseemly

¹**een** \ in \ see ¹IN

²**een** \ ēn \ see ³INE

e'en \ ēn \ see ³INE

eener \ ē-nər \ see EANER

eenery \ ēn-rē \ see EANERY

eening \ ē-niŋ \ see EANING

eenling \ ēn-liŋ \ see EANLING

eenly \ ēn-lē \ see ¹EANLY

eenness \ ēn-nəs \ see EANNESS

eens \ ēnz \ teens, smithereens

eeny \ ē-nē \ see ¹INI

eep \ ēp \ beep, bleep, cheap,

cheep, clepe, creep, deep,
heap, jeep, keep, leap, neap,
peep, reap, seep, sheep,
sleep, sneap, steep, sweep,
threap, veep, weep, asleep,
barkeep, dustheap,
housekeep, knee-deep, skin-
deep, upkeep, upsweep,
overleap, oversleep

eepage \ē-pij\ creepage,
seepage

eepen \ē-pən\ cheapen, deepen,
steepen

eepence \əp-əns\ see UPPANCE

eepenny \əp-nē\ see OPENNY

eeper \ē-pər\ beeper, creeper,
keeper, leaper, peeper,
reaper, sleeper, sweeper,
weeper, barkeeper,
beekeeper, bookkeeper,
crowkeeper, doorkeeper,
gamekeeper, gatekeeper,
goalkeeper, housekeeper,
innkeeper, lockkeeper,
minesweeper, peacekeeper,
scorekeeper, shopkeeper,
stockkeeper, storekeeper,
timekeeper, zookeeper,
honeycreeper—*also
comparatives of adjectives
listed at* EEP

eeping \ē-piŋ\ creeping,
keeping, weeping,
beekeeping, bookkeeping,
gatekeeping, housekeeping,

minesweeping, peacekeeping,
safekeeping, timekeeping

eepish \ē-pish\ cheapish,
sheepish

eeple \ē-pəl\ see EOPLE

eepy \ē-pē\ cheapie, creepy,
seepy, sleepy, sweepy, tepee,
tipi, weepy

¹eer \ē-ər\ freer, seer, skier,
we're, CBer, decreer,
foreseer, sightseer, overseer,
water-skier

²eer \ir\ beer, bier, blear, cere,
cheer, clear, dear, deer,
drear, ear, fear, fere, fleer,
gear, hear, here, jeer, Lear,
leer, mere, mir, near, peer,
pier, queer, rear, schmear,
sear, seer, sere, shear, sheer,
skirr, smear, sneer, spear,
speer, sphere, spier, steer,
tear, tier, Tyr, veer, were,
year, adhere, Aesir, ambeer,
appear, arrear, austere,
Ayrshire, Berkshire, besmear,
brassiere, career, cashier,
cashmere, chimere, clavier,
cohere, compeer, destrier,
dog-ear, emir, Empire,
endear, ensphere, eyrir,
Fafnir, footgear, frontier,
gambier, haltere, Hampshire,
headgear, inhere, kefir,
killdeer, laveer, light-year,
man-year, menhir, mishear,
monsieur, mouse-ear, nadir,

pickeer, portiere, premier,
premiere, redear, rehear,
reindeer, revere, revers,
santir, severe, Shropshire,
sincere, slick-ear, tapir,
uprear, Vanir, veneer, vizier,
voir dire, wheatear, Ymir,
Yorkshire, zaire, atmosphere,
auctioneer, balladeer,
bandolier, bayadere,
Bedivere, belvedere,
biosphere, black-tailed deer,
bombardier, boutonniere,
brigadier, buccaneer,
budgeteer, cameleer,
cannoneer, cassimere,
cavalier, chandelier,
chanticleer, chevalier,
chiffonier, commandeer,
corsetiere, cuirassier, diapir,
disappear, domineer,
ecosphere, Elzevir, engineer,
fictioneer, financier,
fourdrinier, fusilier,
gadgeteer, gasolier, gazetteer,
gondolier, grenadier,
Guinevere, halberdier,
hemisphere, insincere,
interfere, jardiniere,
junketeer, kerseymere,
Lancashire, lavaliere,
leafleteer, missileer,
mountaineer, muleteer,
musketeer, mutineer,
overhear, overseer, oversteer,
pamphleteer, persevere,

pioneer, pistoleer, pontonier,
privateer, profiteer,
puppeteer, racketeer,
rocketeer, scrutineer,
sloganeer, sonneteer,
souvenir, stratosphere,
summiteer, understeer,
volunteer, white-tailed deer,
yesteryear, black marketeer,
carabineer, charioteer,
conventioneer, electioneer,
harquebusier

e'er \er\ see ⁴ARE

eerage \ir-ij\ peerage, steerage,
  arrearage

eered \ird\ see ¹EARD

eerer \ir-ər\ see ²EARER

eeress \ir-əs\ see EROUS

eerful \ir-fəl\ see EARFUL

¹eerie \ir-ē\ see EARY

²eerie \ē-rē\ see EIRIE

eering \ir-iŋ\ see ¹EARING

eerist \ir-əst\ see ¹ERIST

eerless \ir-ləs\ see EARLESS

eerly \ir-lē\ see ¹EARLY

eersman \irz-mən\ steersman,
  frontiersman

eery \ir-ē\ see EARY

ees \ēz\ see EZE

eese \ēz\ see EZE

eesh \ēsh\ see ²ICHE

eesi \ē-zē\ see ¹EASY

eesia \ē-zhə\ see ²ESIA

eesome \ē-səm\ gleesome,
  threesome

¹eest \āst\ see ACED

²eest \ēst\ see ¹EAST
eesy \ē-zē\ see ¹EASY
eet \ēt\ see ¹EAT
eetah \ēt-ə\ see ²ITA
eeten \ēt-ⁿn\ see ²EATEN
eeter \ēt-ər\ see ¹EATER
eethe \ēth\ see EATHE
eether \ē-thər\ see EITHER
eething \ē-thiŋ\ see EATHING
eetie \ēt-ē\ see EATY
eeting \ēt-iŋ\ see EATING
eetle \ēt-ᵊl\ see ETAL
eetly \ēt-lē\ featly, fleetly, neatly, sweetly, completely, concretely, discreetly, discretely, effetely, bittersweetly, incompletely, indiscreetly
eety \ēt-ē\ see EATY
ee-um \ē-əm\ see ¹EUM
eeve \ēv\ see ¹EAVE
eeved \ēvd\ see EAVED
eeves \ēvz\ see EAVES
eevil \ē-vəl\ see IEVAL
eevish \ē-vish\ peevish, thievish
eeward \ē-wərd\ leeward, seaward
eewee \ē-wē\ kiwi, peewee, pewee
eewit \ü-ət\ see UET
eez \ēz\ see EZE
eezable \ē-zə-bəl\ see EASIBLE
eeze \ēz\ see EZE
eezer \ē-zər\ see ²EASER
eezing \ē-ziŋ\ see ²EASING
eezy \ē-zē\ see ¹EASY

¹ef \ef\ chef, clef, deaf, ef, f, lev, ref, teff, aleph, enfeoff, stone-deaf, tone-deaf
²ef \ā\ see ¹AY
³ef \ēf\ see ¹IEF
eferable \ef-rə-bəl\ preferable, referable
eference \ef-rəns\ deference, preference, reference, cross-reference
eferent \ef-rənt\ deferent, referent
eff \ef\ see ¹EF
effer \ef-ər\ see EPHOR
efic \ef-ik\ benefic, malefic
eficence \ef-ə-səns\ beneficence, maleficence
eft \eft\ cleft, deft, eft, heft, klepht, left, theft, weft, bereft
efty \ef-tē\ hefty, lefty
¹eg \āg\ leg, plague, vague, yegg, blackleg, bootleg, bowleg, dogleg, foreleg, muskeg, nutmeg, redleg, renege, roughleg, stravage
²eg \eg\ beg, dreg, egg, gleg, keg, leg, peg, reg, skeg, squeg, yegg, blackleg, bootleg, bowleg, dogleg, foreleg, jackleg, jake leg, muskeg, nutmeg, redleg, renege, roughleg, Tuareg, unpeg, mumblety-peg
³eg \ej\ see EDGE
¹ega \eg-ə\ omega, rutabaga
²ega \ā-gə\ see ²AGA

³**ega** \ē-gə\ see ¹IGA

egal \ē-gəl\ beagle, eagle, egal, legal, regal, illegal, porbeagle, spread-eagle, viceregal, extralegal, paralegal, medicolegal

egan \ē-gən\ vegan, Mohegan

¹**ege** \ezh\ barege, cortege, manege, solfege

²**ege** \eg\ see ²EG

³**ege** \ej\ see EDGE

⁴**ege** \ēg\ see IGUE

⁵**ege** \ig\ see IG

eged \ejd\ see EDGED

egent \ē-jənt\ regent, sejant, allegiant, vice-regent

eger \ej-ər\ see EDGER

egg \eg\ see ²EG

eggar \eg-ər\ see EGGER

egger \eg-ər\ beggar, bootlegger, thousand-legger

eggie \ej-ē\ see EDGY

eggio \ej-ō\ arpeggio, solfeggio

eggs \egz\ see EGS

eggy \eg-ē\ dreggy, eggy, leggy, plaguey

egia \ē-jə\ Ouija, aqua regia, aquilegia, paraplegia

egian \ē-jən\ see EGION

egiant \ē-jənt\ see EGENT

egiate \ē-jət\ collegiate, elegit, intercollegiate

egic \ē-jik\ strategic, paraplegic, quadriplegic

egion \ē-jən\ legion, region,

Norwegian, subregion, collegian

egious \ē-jəs\ see EGIS

egis \ē-jəs\ aegis, egis, tedious, egregious

egit \ē-jət\ see EGIATE

egler \eg-lər\ kegler, regular

egm \em\ see ¹EM

egn \ān\ see ¹ANE

egnant \eg-nənt\ pregnant, regnant, impregnant, unpregnant

egnly \ān-lē\ see AINLY

egno \ān-yō\ see ¹ENO

ego \ē-gō\ chigoe, ego, amigo, alter ego, impetigo, superego

egs \egz\ sheerlegs, yellowlegs, butter-and-eggs, daddy longlegs—*also plurals and possessives of nouns and third singular presents of verbs listed at* ²EG

egular \eg-lər\ see EGLER

¹**eh** \ā\ see ¹AY

²**eh** \a\ see ³AH

ehen \ān\ see ¹ANE

¹**ei** \ēk\ dreich, skeigh

²**ei** \ā\ see ¹AY

³**ei** \ī\ see ¹Y

¹**eia** \ē-ə\ see ¹IA

²**eia** \ī-ə\ see ¹IAH

eial \ē-əl\ see ¹EAL

eic \ē-ik\ oleic, epigeic, logorrheic, mythopoeic, onomatopoeic

eich \ēk̲\ see ¹EI

eiche \ āsh \ see ¹ECHE

¹**eid** \ āt \ see ATE

²**eid** \ īt \ see ¹ITE

¹**eidel** \ ād-əl \ see ADLE

²**eidel** \ īd-ᵊl \ see IDAL

eidon \ īd-ᵊn \ see IDEN

eier \ īr \ see IRE

eifer \ ef-ər \ see EPHOR

¹**eige** \ āzh \ beige, assuage

²**eige** \ ā \ see ¹AY

eiger \ ī-gər \ see IGER

eigh \ ā \ see ¹AY

eighbor \ ā-bər \ see ABOR

¹**eight** \ āt \ see ATE

²**eight** \ īt \ see ¹ITE

eighter \ āt-ər \ see ATOR

eightless \ āt-ləs \ see ATELESS

eighty \ āt-ē \ see ATY

eign \ ān \ see ¹ANE

eigner \ ā-nər \ see AINER

eiji \ ā-jē \ see AGY

eik \ ēk \ see ¹EAK

eikh \ ēk \ see ¹EAK

eikle \ ē-kəl \ see ECAL

¹**eil** \ āl \ see AIL

²**eil** \ el \ see ¹EL

³**eil** \ ēl \ see ²EAL

eiled \ āld \ see AILED

eiler \ ī-lər \ see ILAR

¹**eiling** \ ā-liŋ \ see AILING

²**eiling** \ ē-liŋ \ see EELING

eillance \ ā-ləns \ see ALENCE

eillant \ ā-lənt \ see ALANT

eilles \ ālz \ see ALES

¹**eim** \ ām \ see ¹AME

²**eim** \ īm \ see ¹IME

eimer \ ī-mər \ see ¹IMER

¹**ein** \ ān \ see ¹ANE

²**ein** \ ē-ən \ see ¹EAN

³**ein** \ ēn \ see ³INE

⁴**ein** \ īn \ see ¹INE

¹**eine** \ ān \ see ¹ANE

²**eine** \ ēn \ see ³INE

eined \ ānd \ see AINED

¹**einer** \ ā-nər \ see AINER

²**einer** \ ē-nər \ see EANER

eing \ ē-iŋ \ see EEING

einie \ ī-nē \ see ¹INY

eining \ ā-niŋ \ see AINING

einous \ ā-nəs \ see AYNESS

eins \ ānz \ see AINS

einsman \ ānz-mən \ see
AINSMAN

eint \ ānt \ see AINT

einte \ ant \ see ⁵ANT

einture \ an-chər \ see ²ANCHER

einy \ ā-nē \ see AINY

eipt \ ēt \ see ¹EAT

eir \ er \ see ⁴ARE

eira \ ir-ə \ see ²ERA

eird \ ird \ see ¹EARD

eiress \ ar-əs \ see ²ARIS

eiric \ ī-rik \ see YRIC

eirie \ ē-rē \ feirie, tapsal-
teerie—*may also rhyme with
words at* EARY

eiro \ er-ō \ see ²ERO

eirs \ erz \ see AIRS

¹**eis** \ ās \ see ¹ACE

²**eis** \ ē-əs \ see ¹EUS

eisant \ ēs-ᵊnt \ see ECENT

eise \ ēz \ see EZE

eisen \ īz-ᵊn \ see ¹IZEN
¹eisha \ ā-shə \ see ACIA
²eisha \ ē-shə \ see ¹ESIA
eisin \ ēz-ᵊn \ see EASON
eiss \ īs \ see ¹ICE
eissen \ īs-ᵊn \ see ¹ISON
¹eist \ ā-əst \ see AYEST
²eist \ īst \ see ¹IST
¹eister \ ī-stər \ shyster, concertmeister, kapellmeister
²eister \ ē-stər \ see EASTER
eisty \ ī-stē \ feisty, nicety
eisure \ ē-zhər \ see EIZURE
¹eit \ ē-ət \ fiat, albeit, howbeit
²eit \ it \ see ¹IT
³eit \ ēt \ see ¹EAT
⁴eit \ īt \ see ¹ITE
eited \ ēt-əd \ see ¹EATED
eiter \ it-ər \ see ITTER
eith \ ēth \ see ¹EATH
either \ ē-thər \ breather, cither, neither, teether
eitus \ īt-əs \ see ITIS
eity \ ē-ət-ē \ deity, velleity, corporeity, spontaneity, synchroneity, diaphaneity, homogeneity, incorporeity, instantaneity, contemporaneity, extemporaneity, heterogeneity
eivable \ ē-və-bəl \ cleavable, achievable, believable, conceivable, deceivable, perceivable, receivable, relievable, retrievable, unbelievable, imperceivable, inconceivable, irretrievable, unbelievable, unconceivable
eive \ ēv \ see ¹EAVE
eiver \ ē-vər \ see IEVER
¹eize \ āz \ see ¹AZE
²eize \ ēz \ see EZE
eizure \ ē-zhər \ leisure, seizure
ejant \ ē-jənt \ see EGENT
ejo \ ā-ō \ see ¹EO
ek \ ek \ see ECK
¹eka \ ek-ə \ see ECCA
²eka \ ē-kə \ see ¹IKA
ekah \ ek-ə \ see ECCA
eke \ ēk \ see ¹EAK
ekel \ ek-əl \ see ECKLE
ekh \ ek \ see ECK
ekker \ ek-ər \ see ECKER
ekoe \ ē-kō \ see ICOT
ekton \ ek-tən \ see ECTEN
¹el \ el \ bel, bell, belle, cell, dell, dwell, el, ell, fell, gel, Hel, hell, jell, knell, l, mell, quell, sel, sell, shell, smell, snell, spell, swell, tell, they'll, well, yell, artel, barbell, befell, bluebell, boatel, bombshell, Boswell, botel, bridewell, cadelle, cartel, carvel, chandelle, clamshell, compel, cormel, cornel, corral, cowbell, cupel, diel, dispel, doorbell, dumbbell, eggshell, excel, expel, farewell, fjeld, foretell, gabelle, gazelle, gromwell, hard-shell, harebell, hotel,

impel, indwell, inkwell, jurel, lampshell, lapel, marcel, maxwell, micelle, misspell, morel, Moselle, motel, nacelle, noel, nutshell, outsell, pall-mall, pastel, pell-mell, pixel, presell, propel, quenelle, rakehell, rappel, rebel, refel, repel, respell, retell, riel, rondel, saurel, scalpel, seashell, sequel, softshell, solgel, speedwell, spinel, stairwell, unsell, until, unwell, upwell, wind-bell, APL, aquarelle, asphodel, Azazel, bagatelle, BAL, barbicel, bechamel, brocatelle, caramel, caravel, carousel, cascabel, chanterelle, chaparral, citadel, clientele, cockleshell, damozel, decibel, demoiselle, fare-thee-well, fontanel, immortelle, Jezebel, lenticel, mangonel, muscatel, ne'er-do-well, Neufchatel, nonpareil, organelle, oversell, parallel, pedicel, pennoncel, personnel, petronel, Philomel, pimpernel, show-and-tell, tortoiseshell, undersell, villanelle, William Tell, zinfandel, au naturel, mademoiselle, maître d'hôtel, matériel, spirituel,

antiparallel, antipersonnel, AWOL

²**el** \ āl \ see AIL

¹**ela** \ ē-lə \ selah, stela, candela, tequila, weigela, Philomela

²**ela** \ ā-lə \ see ³ALA

³**ela** \ el-ə \ see ELLA

elable \ el-ə-bəl \ see ELLABLE

elacy \ el-ə-sē \ jealousy, prelacy

elagh \ ä-lē \ see AILY

elah \ ē-lə \ see ¹ELA

elar \ ē-lər \ see EALER

elate \ el-ət \ see ELLATE

elatin \ el-ət-ᵊn \ see ELETON

elative \ el-ət-iv \ relative, appellative, correlative, irrelative

elch \ elch \ belch, squelch, welch, Welch, Welsh

¹**eld** \ eld \ eld, geld, held, meld, shelled, weld, beheld, danegeld, hard-shelled, upheld, withheld, jet-propelled, self-propelled, unparalleled—*also pasts of verbs listed at* ¹EL

²**eld** \ el \ see ¹EL

³**eld** \ elt \ see ELT

eldam \ el-dəm \ see ELDOM

elder \ el-dər \ elder, welder

eldom \ el-dəm \ beldam, seldom, hoteldom

¹**ele** \ ä-lē \ see AILY

²**ele** \ el \ see ¹EL

³**ele** \ el-ē \ see ELLY

⁴**ele** \ ē-lē \ see EELY

¹**eled** \eld\ see ¹ELD

²**eled** \ēld\ see IELD

eleon \ēl-yən\ see ²ELIAN

eletal \el-ət-ᵊl\ pelletal, skeletal

eleton \el-ət-ᵊn\ gelatin, skeleton

eleus \ē-lē-əs\ see ELIOUS

elf \elf\ elf, Guelf, pelf, self, shelf, bookshelf, herself, himself, itself, myself, nonself, oneself, ourself, thyself, yourself, mantelshelf, do-it-yourself

elfer \el-fər\ telpher, do-it-yourselfer

elfish \el-fish\ elfish, selfish, unselfish

eli \el-ē\ see ELLY

elia \ēl-yə\ camellia, lobelia, obelia, Ophelia, sedilia, stapelia, psychedelia, seguidilla

elial \ē-lē-əl\ Belial, epithelial

¹**elian** \ē-lē-ən\ abelian, Karelian, Mendelian

²**elian** \ēl-yən\ anthelion, aphelion, carnelian, chameleon, cornelian, Mendelian, parhelion, perihelion, Aristotelian, Mephistophelian

³**elian** \el-ē-ən\ see ELLIAN

elible \el-ə-bəl\ see ELLABLE

¹**elic** \ē-lik\ parhelic, autotelic

²**elic** \el-ik\ melic, relic, telic, angelic, Goidelic, smart aleck, archangelic, autotelic, philatelic, psychedelic

elical \el-i-kəl\ helical, pellicle, angelical, double-helical, evangelical

elier \el-yer\ see ELURE

elin \el-ən\ shieling, theelin

¹**elion** \el-ē-ən\ see ELLIAN

²**elion** \ēl-yən\ see ²ELIAN

elios \ē-lē-əs\ see ELIOUS

elious \ē-lē-əs\ Helios, Peleus, contumelious

elish \el-ish\ see ELLISH

elist \el-əst\ trellised, cellist, Nobelist, pastelist

¹**elk** \elk\ elk, whelk, yolk

²**elk** \ilk\ see ILK

ell \el\ see ¹EL

e'll \ēl\ see ²EAL

ella \el-ə\ bellow, fella, fellah, fellow, mellow, stella, yellow, bedfellow, candela, Capella, glabella, hail-fellow, lamella, novella, paella, patella, playfellow, prunella, quiniela, rubella, schoolfellow, sequela, umbrella, vanilla, yokefellow, a cappella, Cinderella, citronella, columella, fraxinella, mortadella, mozzarella, panatela, salmonella, sarsaparilla, subumbrella, tarantella, villanella, valpolicella

ellable \el-ə-bəl\ fellable,

gelable, compellable, expellable, indelible

ellah \el-ə\ see ELLA

ellan \el-ən\ see ELON

ellant \el-ənt\ gellant, appellant, flagellant, propellant, repellent, water-repellent

ellar \el-ər\ see ELLER

ellate \el-ət\ helot, pellet, prelate, zealot, appellate, flagellate, haustellate, lamellate, scutellate

ellative \el-ət-iv\ see ELATIVE

elle \el\ see ¹EL

ellean \el-ē-ən\ see ELLIAN

elled \eld\ see ¹ELD

ellent \el-ənt\ see ELLANT

eller \el-ər\ cellar, dweller, feller, heller, seller, sheller, smeller, speller, stellar, teller, yeller, best-seller, bookseller, compeller, expeller, foreteller, glabellar, impeller, indweller, lamellar, ocellar, patellar, propeller, rathskeller, repeller, rostellar, saltcellar, tale-teller, cereballar, circumstellar, columellar, fortune-teller, interstellar, storyteller

ellet \el-ət\ see ELLATE

elletal \el-ət-ᵊl\ see ELETAL

elli \el-ē\ see ELLY

ellia \ēl-yə\ see ELIA

ellian \el-ē-ən\ Chellean,

Boswellian, pre-Chellean, Sabellian, triskelion, Pantagruelian, Machiavellian

ellicle \el-i-kəl\ see ELICAL

ellie \el-ē\ see ELLY

elline \el-ən\ see ELON

elling \el-iŋ\ spelling, swelling, telling, bookselling, compelling, indwelling, misspelling, tale-telling, upwelling, fortune-telling, self-propelling

ellion \el-yən\ hellion, rebellion

ellis \el-əs\ see EALOUS

ellised \el-əst\ see ELIST

ellish \el-ish\ hellish, relish, disrelish, embellish

ellist \el-əst\ see ELIST

ello \el-ō\ cello, fellow, Jell-O, mellow, yellow, bargello, bedfellow, bordello, duello, hail-fellow, marshmallow, morello, niello, Othello, playfellow, schoolfellow, yokefellow, punchinello, ritornello, saltarello, Robin Goodfellow, violoncello

ell-o \el-ō\ see ELLO

ellous \el-əs\ see EALOUS

¹ellow \el-ə\ see ELLA

²ellow \el-ō\ see ELLO

ellum \el-əm\ blellum, skellum, vellum, postbellum, rostellum, antebellum, cerebellum

ellus \el-əs\ see EALOUS

elly\el-ē\belly, deli, felly, jelly, shelly, smelly, tele, telly, nice-nelly, potbelly, rakehelly, sowbelly, nervous Nellie, underbelly, vermicelli

elm\elm\elm, helm, realm, whelm, overwhelm, underwhelm

elon\el-ən\felon, melon, avellan, muskmelon, vitelline, watermelon

elop\el-əp\develop, envelop, redevelop, overdevelop

elopment\el-əp-mənt\development, envelopment, redevelopment, overdevelopment

elot\el-ət\see ELLATE

elotry\el-ə-trē\helotry, zealotry

elp\elp\help, kelp, skelp, whelp, yelp

elpher\el-fər\see ELFER

elsh\elch\see ELCH

elson\el-sən\keelson, nelson

elt\elt\belt, celt, Celt, dealt, dwelt, felt, gelt, melt, pelt, smelt, spelt, svelte, veld, welt, black belt, flybelt, forefelt, greenbelt, heartfelt, jacksmelt, self-belt, snowbelt, snowmelt, Sunbelt, shelterbelt

elte\elt\see ELT

elter\el-tər\melter, pelter, shelter, skelter, smelter,

spelter, swelter, welter, helter-skelter

elting\el-tiŋ\belting, felting, melting, pelting

elure\el-yər\velure, hotelier

elve\elv\delve, helve, shelve, twelve

ely\ē-lē\see EELY

¹em\em\crème, em, femme, gem, hem, m, mem, phlegm, REM, Shem, stem, them, ad rem, ahem, AM, bluestem, condemn, contemn, FM, idem, in rem, item, mayhem, millieme, modem, poem, problem, pro tem, proem, ABM, anadem, apothegm, apothem, diadem, exanthem, ibidem, meristem, OEM, SAM, stratagem, ad hominem, carpe diem, crème de la crème, ICBM, post meridiem, star-of-Bethlehem, terminus ad quem

²em\əm\see ¹UM

ema\ē-mə\bema, Lima, schema, eczema, edema, diastema, emphysema, terza rima, ottava rima

emacist\em-ə-səst\see EMICIST

eman\em-ən\see ²EMON

emane\em-ə-nē\see EMONY

emanence\em-ə-nəns\see EMINENCE

emanent\em-ə-nənt\see EMINENT

ematis \em-ət-əs\ see EMITUS
ematist \em-ət-əst\ see EMITIST
ematous \em-ət-əs\ see EMITUS
ember \em-bər\ ember,
member, December,
dismember, November,
remember, September,
disremember
¹**emble** \äm-bəl\ wamble,
ensemble
²**emble** \em-bəl\ tremble,
assemble, atremble,
dissemble, resemble,
disassemble
embler \em-blər\ temblor,
trembler, assembler,
dissembler
emblor \em-blər\ see EMBLER
embly \em-blē\ trembly,
assembly, disassembly, self-
assembly, subassembly
¹**eme** \em\ see ¹EM
²**eme** \ēm\ see ¹EAM
emely \ēm-lē\ see EEMLY
emen \ē-mən\ see ¹EMON
emer \ē-mər\ see EAMER
emeral \em-rəl\ femoral,
ephemeral
emery \em-rē\ emery, memory
emesis \em-ə-səs\ emesis,
nemesis
emi \em-ē\ see EMMY
emia \ē-mē-ə\ anemia,
bohemia, leukemia, toxemia,
academia, septicemia,
hypoglycemia

emian \ē-mē-ən\ anthemion,
Bohemian
¹**emic** \ē-mik\ emic, anemic,
graphemic, morphemic,
lexemic, phonemic, taxemic,
tonemic, epistemic
²**emic** \em-ik\ chemic,
alchemic, endemic,
pandemic, polemic, sachemic,
systemic, totemic, academic,
epidemic, epistemic
emical \em-i-kəl\ chemical,
alchemical, polemical,
academical, biochemical,
epidemical, petrochemical
emicist \em-ə-səst\ polemicist,
supremacist
emics \ē-miks\ graphemics,
morphemics, phonemics,
proxemics
eminal \em-ən-ᵊl\ geminal,
seminal
eminate \em-ə-nət\ geminate,
effeminate
eminence \em-ə-nəns\
eminence, remanence,
preeminence
eminent \em-ə-nənt\ eminent,
remanent, preeminent
eming \em-iŋ\ Fleming,
Heminge, lemming
eminge \em-iŋ\ see EMING
emini \em-ə-nē\ see EMONY
eminy \em-ə-nē\ see EMONY
emion \ē-mē-ən\ see EMIAN
emis \ē-məs\ see EMUS

emish \em-ish\ blemish, Flemish

emist \em-əst\ chemist, polemist, biochemist

emitist \em-ət-əst\ Semitist, systematist

emitus \em-ət-əs\ clematis, fremitus, edematous

emlin \em-lən\ gremlin, kremlin

emma \em-ə\ gemma, lemma, stemma, dilemma

emme \em\ see ¹EM

emmer \em-ər\ emmer, hemmer, stemmer, tremor, condemner, contemner

emming \em-iŋ\ see EMING

emmy \em-ē\ Emmy, gemmy, phlegmy, semi, stemmy

emn \em\ see ¹EM

emner \em-ər\ see EMMER

emnity \em-nət-ē\ indemnity, solemnity

emo \em-ō\ demo, memo

¹emon \ē-mən\ demon, freeman, gleeman, Piman, seaman, semen, pentstemon, Philemon, cacodemon

²emon \em-ən\ leman, lemon

emone \em-ə-nē\ see EMONY

emony \em-ə-nē\ Gemini, lemony, anemone, bigeminy, Gethsemane, hegemony

emor \em-ər\ see EMMER

emoral \em-rəl\ see EMERAL

emory \em-rē\ see EMERY

emous \ē-məs\ see EMUS

emp \emp\ hemp, temp

emperer \em-pər-ər\ emperor, temperer

emperor \em-pər-ər\ see EMPERER

emplar \em-plər\ Templar, exemplar

emple \em-pəl\ scmple, temple

emps \äⁿ\ see ¹ANT

empt \emt\ dreamt, kempt, tempt, attempt, contempt, exempt, preempt, undreamed, unkempt, tax-exempt

emptable \em-tə-bəl\ attemptable, contemptible

emptible \em-tə-bəl\ see EMPTABLE

emption \em-shən\ exemption, preemption, redemption

emptive \em-tiv\ preemptive, redemptive

emptor \em-tər\ tempter, preemptor, caveat emptor

emptory \em-trē\ peremptory, redemptory

emulous \em-yə-ləs\ emulous, tremulous

emur \ē-mər\ see EAMER

emus \ē-məs\ Remus, in extremis, Polyphemus, polysemous

emy \ē-mē\ see EAMY

¹en \en\ ben, den, en, fen, glen, hen, ken, n , pen, sen, Sten, ten, then, wen, when, wren, yen, Zen, again, amen, Big Ben, doyen, doyenne, hapten, Karen, La Tène, moorhen, peahen, pigpen, playpen, somewhen, Cheyenne, DPN, five-and-ten, FMN, julienne, LPN, madrilene, mise-en-scène, samisen, TPN, carcinogen, comedienne, equestrienne, tragedienne, Valenciennes

²en \ēn\ see ³INE

³en \aⁿ\ see ⁴IN

⁴en \ən\ see UN

¹ena \ā-nä\ see ¹AENA

²ena \ā-nə\ see ²ANA

³ena \än-yə\ see ³ANIA

⁴ena \ē-nə\ see ²INA

enable \en-ə-bəl\ tenable, amenable, untenable

enace \en-əs\ see ¹ENIS

enacle \en-i-kəl\ see ENICAL

enal \ēn-ᵊl\ penal, renal, venal, adrenal, vaccinal, duodenal

enancy \en-ən-sē\ tenancy, lieutenancy, subtenancy

enant \en-ənt\ pennant, tenant, lieutenant, se tenant, subtenant, sublieutenant, undertenant

¹enary \ē-nə-rē\ plenary, bicentenary, quatercentenary, semicentenary, sesquicentenary

²enary \en-ə-rē\ hennery, plenary, senary, venery, centenary, millenary, bicentenary, bimillenary, tercentenary, quatercentenary, semicentenary, sesquicentenary

enas \ē-nəs\ see ¹ENUS

enate \en-ət\ see ENNET

enator \en-ət-ər\ see ENITOR

ençal \en-səl\ see ENCIL

¹ence \ens\ see ENSE

²ence \äⁿs\ see ¹ANCE

³ence \äns\ see ²ANCE

encel \en-səl\ see ENCIL

enceless \en-sləs\ see ENSELESS

encer \en-sər\ see ENSOR

ench \ench\ bench, blench, clench, drench, french, French, mensch, quench, stench, tench, trench, wench, wrench, entrench, retrench, unclench, workbench, Anglo-French

enchant \en-chənt\ see ENTIENT

enched \encht\ trenched, unblenched—*also pasts of verbs listed at* ENCH

encher \en-chər\ see ENTURE

enchman \ench-mən\ Frenchman, henchman

encil \en-səl\ mensal, pencel, pencil, stencil, tensile, blue-pencil, commensal, extensile, Provençal, prehensile, red-pencil, utensil, intercensal

ençon \en-sən\ see ENSIGN

ency\en-sē\Montmorency,
residency, nonresidency

end\end\bend, blend, blende,
end, fend, friend, lend,
mend, rend, scend, send,
shend, spend, tend, trend,
vend, wend, Wend, addend,
amend, append, ascend,
attend, augend, befriend,
bookend, boyfriend, closed-
end, commend, compend,
contend, dead end, dead-end,
defend, depend, descend,
distend, downtrend, emend,
expend, extend, forfend,
girlfriend, godsend,
hornblende, impend, intend,
low-end, missend, misspend,
offend, outspend, perpend,
pitchblende, portend, pretend,
propend, protend, resend,
stipend, subtend, suspend,
transcend, unbend, unkenned,
upend, uptrend, weekend,
adherend, apprehend, bitter
end, comprehend,
condescend, discommend,
dividend, minuend,
overspend, recommend,
repetend, reprehend,
subtrahend, vilipend,
hyperextend, misapprehend,
overextend, superintend—*also
pasts of verbs listed at* ¹EN

enda\en-də\Venda, agenda,
hacienda—*also plurals of
nouns listed at* ENDUM

endable\en-də-bəl\lendable,
mendable, spendable,
vendible, amendable,
ascendable, commendable,
defendable, dependable,
descendible, expendable,
extendable, unbendable,
comprehendable,
recommendable

endal\en-dᵊl\Grendel,
prebendal, pudendal

endance\en-dəns\see ENDENCE

endancy\en-dən-sē\see
ENDENCY

endant\en-dənt\see ENDENT

ende\end\see END

ended\en-dəd\ended,
splendid, unfriended, double-
ended, open-ended,
undescended—*also pasts of
verbs listed at* END

endel\en-dᵊl\see ENDAL

endence\en-dəns\tendance,
ascendance, attendance,
intendance, resplendence,
transcendence,
condescendence,
independence,
superintendence

endency\en-dən-sē\pendency,
tendency, ascendancy,
dependency, resplendency,
transcendency,

superintendency, independency

endent \en-dənt\ pendant,
pendent, splendent,
appendant, ascendant,
attendant, defendant,
dependent, descendant,
impendent, intendant,
respendent, transcendent,
independent, superintendant,
semi-independent

ender \en-dər\ bender, blender,
fender, gender, lender,
render, mender, slender,
spender, sender, splendor,
tender, vendor, amender,
ascender, attender, auslander,
bartender, commender,
contender, defender,
descender, emender,
engender, expender, extender,
goaltender, hellbender,
intender, offender, pretender,
surrender, suspender,
weekender, double-ender,
moneylender, over-spender,
self-surrender

endi \en-dē\ trendy, effendi,
modus vivendi

endible \en-də-bəl\ see
ENDABLE

endid \en-dəd\ see ENDED

ending \en-diŋ\ ending,
pending, ascending,
attending, fence-mending,
goaltending, heartrending,
mind-bending, unbending,

unending, uncomprehending,
unpretending,
uncomprehending

endium \en-dē-əm\
compendium, antependium

endless \end-ləs\ endless,
friendless

endliness \en-lē-nəs\
friendliness, uncleanliness,
unfriendliness

endly \en-lē\ cleanly, friendly,
loop of Henle, uncleanly,
unfriendly

endment \en-mənt\ amendment,
intendment

endo \en-dō\ kendo, crescendo,
stringendo, decrescendo,
innuendo, diminuendo

endor \en-dər\ see ENDER

endous \en-dəs\ horrendous,
stupendous, tremendous

endron \en-drən\ philodendron,
rhododendron

ends \enz\ see ¹ENS

endum \en-dəm\ addendum,
agendum, pudendum,
corrigendum, referendum,
definiendum

endy \en-dē\ see ENDI

¹ene \ā-nā\ nene, sene

²ene \en\ see ¹EN

³ene \en-ē\ see ENNY

⁴ene \ē-nē\ see ¹INI

⁵ene \ēn\ see ¹INE

enel \en-ᵊl\ see ENNEL

eneous\ē-nē-əs\genius, homogeneous, heterogeneous

ener\ē-nər\see EANER

enerable\en-rə-bəl\generable, venerable, regenerable

eneracy\en-rə-sē\degeneracy, regeneracy

enerate\en-rət\degenerate, regenerate, unregenerate

enerative\en-rət-iv\generative, degenerative, regenerative

eneris\en-ə-rəs\mons veneris, sui generis

¹**enery**\en-ə-rē\see ²ENARY

²**enery**\ēn-rē\see EANERY

¹**enet**\en-ət\see ENNET

²**enet**\ē-nət\see EANUT

eng\aŋ\see ²ANG

enge\enj\venge, avenge, revenge

engi\eŋ-gē\dengue, sengi

engo\eŋ-gō\marengo, camerlengo

¹**ength**\eŋth\length, strength, full-length, half-length, wavelength, understrength

²**ength**\enth\see ENTH

engthen\eŋ-thən\lengthen, strengthen

engue\eŋ-gē\see ENGI

¹**enia**\ē-nē-ə\taenia, sarracenia, schizophrenia

²**enia**\ē-nyə\Encaenia, gardenia, Tigrinya

enial\ē-nē-əl\genial, menial, venial, congenial

enian\ē-nē-ən\Fenian, Armenian, Essenian, Icenian, sirenian, Slovenian, Achaemenian, Magdalenian

¹**enic**\ēn-ik\genic, scenic, photogenic, telegenic

²**enic**\en-ik\genic, fennec, pfennig, phrenic, scenic, splenic, sthenic, arsenic, asthenic, Edenic, Essenic, eugenic, Hellenic, hygienic, irenic, allergenic, androgenic, autogenic, calisthenic, cryogenic, cryptogenic, hygienic, mutagenic, Panhellenic, pathogenic, photogenic, Saracenic, schizophrenic, telegenic, carcinogenic, hallucinogenic

enical\en-i-kəl\cenacle, arsenical, galenical, ecumenical

enicist\en-ə-səst\eugenicist, ecumenicist

enics\en-iks\eugenics, euphenics, euthenics, hygienics, calisthenics, cryogenics—*also plurals and possessives of nouns listed at* ²ENIC

¹**enie**\en-ē\see ENNY

²**enie**\ē-nē\see ¹INI

enience\ē-nyəns\lenience, provenience, inconvenience

enient\ēn-yənt\convenient, prevenient

enim \en-əm\ see ENOM

enin \en-ən\ see ENNON

enior \ē-nyər\ senior, monsignor

¹**enis** \en-əs\ Denis, genus, menace, tenace, tennis, frontenis, summum genus

²**enis** \ē-nəs\ see ¹ENUS

¹**enison** \en-ə-sən\ benison, venison

²**enison** \en-ə-zən\ benison, denizen, venison

enist \en-əst\ tennist, euthenist

enitive \en-ət-iv\ genitive, lenitive, philoprogenitive

enitor \en-ət-ər\ senator, progenitor, primogenitor

enity \en-ət-ē\ see ENTITY

enium \ē-nē-əm\ hymenium, proscenium

enius \ē-nē-əs\ see ENEOUS

enizen \en-ə-zən\ see ²ENISON

enna \en-ə\ henna, senna, antenna, duenna, Gehenna, sienna

ennae \en-ē\ see ENNY

ennant \en-ənt\ see ENANT

¹**enne** \en\ see ¹EN

²**enne** \en-ē\ see ENNY

³**enne** \an\ see ⁵AN

ennec \en-ik\ see ²ENIC

enned \end\ see END

ennel \en-ᵊl\ crenel, fennel, kennel, unkennel

enner \en-ər\ see ¹ENOR

ennery \en-ə-rē\ see ²ENARY

ennet \en-ət\ genet, jennet, rennet, senate, sennet, sennit, tenet

enney \en-ē\ see ENNY

enni \en-ē\ see ENNY

ennial \en-ē-əl\ biennial, centennial, decennial, millennial, perennial, quadrennial, quinquennial, septennial, triennial, vicennial, bicentennial, bimillennial, postmillennial, premillennial, tercentennial, semicentennial, sesquicentennial, quadricentennial

ennig \en-ik\ see ²ENIC

ennin \en-ən\ see ENNON

ennis \en-əs\ see ¹ENIS

ennist \en-əst\ see ENIST

ennit \en-ət\ see ENNET

ennium \en-ē-əm\ biennium, decennium, millennium, quadrennium, quinquennium, triennium

ennon \en-ən\ pennon, rennin, tenon, antivenin

enny \en-ē\ any, benne, benny, blenney, Dene, fenny, genie, jenny, many, penni, penny, antennae, catchpenny, halfpenny, Na-dene, sixpenny, tenpenny, threepenny, truepenny, twopenny, lilangeni, spinning jenny

¹eno \ ān-yō \ segno, dal segno, jalapeño

²eno \ en-ō \ steno, ripieno

³eno \ ā-nō \ see ²ANO

enoch \ ē-nik \ see ¹INIC

enom \ en-əm \ dcnim, plenum, venom, envenom

enon \ en-ən \ see ENNON

¹**enor** \ en-ər \ tenner, tenor, tenour, countertenor

²**enor** \ ē-nər \ see EANER

enour \ en-ər \ see ¹ENOR

enous \ ē-nəs \ see ¹ENUS

¹**ens** \ enz \ cleanse, gens, lens, amends, beam-ends, weekends, sapiens, definiens, locum tenens—*also plurals and possessives of nouns and third singular presents of verbs listed at* ¹EN

²**ens** \ ens \ see ENSE

ensable \ en-sə-bəl \ see ENSIBLE

ensal \ en-səl \ see ENCIL

ensary \ ens-rē \ see ENSORY

ensch \ ench \ see ENCH

ense \ ens \ cense, dense, fence, flense, gens, hence, mense, pence, sense, spence, tense, thence, whence, commence, condense, defense, dispense, expense, immense, incense, intense, missense, nonsense, offense, prepense, pretense, propense, sequence, sixpence, subsequence, suspense, twopence, accidence, commonsense, confidence, consequence, diffidence, evidence, frankincense, multisense, nondefense, providence, recompense, residence, self-defense, subsequence, coincidence, ego-defense, inconsequence, nonresidence, self-confidence, self-evidence

enseful \ ens-fəl \ menseful, senseful, suspenseful

enseless \ en-sləs \ fenceless, senseless, defenseless, offenseless

ensem \ en-səm \ see ENSUM

enser \ en-sər \ see ENSOR

ensian \ en-chən \ see ENSION

ensible \ en-sə-bəl \ sensible, compensable, condensable, defensible, dispensable, distensible, extensible, insensible, ostensible, apprehensible, commonsensible, comprehensible, incondensable, indefensible, indispensable, reprehensible, supersensible, incomprehensible

ensign \ en-sən \ ensign, alençon

ensil \ en-səl \ see ENCIL

ensile \ en-səl \ see ENCIL

ension \ en-chən \ gentian, mention, pension, roentgen, tension, abstention,

ascension, attention,
contention, convention,
declension, descension,
detention, dimension,
dissension, distension,
extension, indention,
intension, intention,
invention, low-tension,
posttension, prehension,
pretension, prevention,
recension, retention,
subvention, suspension,
sustention, Vincentian,
Waldensian, Albigensian,
apprehension, circumvention,
comprehension,
condescension, contravention,
hypertension, hypotension,
inattention, reinvention,
reprehension, salientian,
incomprehension,
misapprehension,
nonintervention,
overextension,
Premonstratensian

ensional \ench-nəl\ tensional,
ascensional, attentional,
conventional, declensional,
dimensional, extensional,
intensional, intentional,
unconventional,
tridimensional,
unidimensional

ensioner \ench-nər\ see
ENTIONER

ensis \en-səs\ see ENSUS

ensitive \en-sət-iv\ sensitive,
insensitive, photosensitive,
hypersensitive, oversensitive,
photosensitive, supersensitive

ensity \en-sət-ē\ density,
tensity, extensity, immensity,
intensity, propensity

ensive \en-siv\ pensive, tensive,
ascensive, defensive,
expensive, extensive,
intensive, offensive,
ostensive, protensive,
suspensive, apprehensive,
coextensive, comprehensive,
hypertensive, hypotensive,
inexpensive, inoffensive,
reprehensive, self-defensive,
counteroffensive, labor-
intensive

ensor \en-sər\ censer, censor,
fencer, sensor, spencer,
tensor, commencer,
condenser, dispenser,
extensor, precensor,
sequencer, suspensor—*also
comparatives of adjectives
listed at* ENSE

ensory \ens-rē\ sensory,
dispensary, suspensory,
extrasensory, multisensory,
supersensory

¹ensual \en-chəl\ see ENTIAL

²ensual \ench-wəl\ see ¹ENTUAL

ensum \en-səm\ sensum, per
mensem

ensurable \ens-rə-bəl\

censurable, mensurable,
commensurable,
immensurable,
incommensurable
ensure\en-chər\see ENTURE
ensus\en-səs\census,
consensus, amanuensis
¹ent\ent\bent, cent, dent, gent,
hent, leant, lent, Lent, meant,
pent, rent, scent, sent, sklent,
spent, sprent, tent, vent,
went, absent, accent, Advent,
anent, ascent, assent,
augment, besprent, cement,
comment, concent, consent,
content, convent, descent,
detent, dissent, docent, event,
extent, ferment, foment,
forewent, forspent, fragment,
frequent, hell-bent, indent,
intent, invent, lament,
loment, mordent, outspent,
outwent, percent, pigment,
portent, present, prevent,
quitrent, relent, repent,
resent, segment, torment,
unbent, wisent, accident,
aliment, argument,
circumvent, compartment,
complement, compliment,
confident, devilment,
diffident, discontent,
document, evident, heaven-
sent, implement, instrument,
Jack-a-Lent, malcontent,
nonevent, Occident,

ornament, orient, president,
provident, regiment, reinvent,
represent, re-present, resident,
sediment, self-content,
subsequent, underwent,
supplement, coincident,
disorient, experiment,
inconsequent, misrepresent,
nonresident, privatdocent,
self-evident
²ent\änt\see ²ANT
³ent\äⁿ\see ¹ANT
enta\ent-ə\menta, yenta,
magenta, momenta, placenta,
polenta, tegmenta, tomenta,
irredenta, impedimenta
entable\ent-ə-bəl\presentable,
documentable, fermentable,
preventable, representable,
sedimentable
entacle\ent-i-kəl\see ENTICAL
entage\ent-ij\tentage, ventage,
percentage
ental\ent-ᵊl\cental, dental,
dentil, gentle, lentil, mental,
rental, cliental, fragmental,
parental, placental,
segmental, accidental,
adjustmental, apartmental,
biparental, compartmental,
complemental, condimental,
continental, departmental,
deterimental, developmental,
documental, excremental,
elemental, environmental,
firmamental, fundamental,

governmental, grandparental,
incidental, incremental,
instrumental, managemental,
monumental, nonjudgmental,
occidental, oriental,
ornamental, regimental,
rudimental, sacramental,
sentimental, supplemental,
temperamental,
transcendental, vestamental,
coincidental, experimental,
presentimental,
subcontinental,
transcontinental, uniparental,
intercontinental,
interdepartmental,
intergovernmental,
semigovernmental

entalist \ent-ᵊl-əst\ gentlest,
mentalist, documentalist,
fundamentalist,
governmentalist,
incrementalist,
instrumentalist, orientalist,
sacramentalist, sentimentalist,
transcendentalist,
environmentalist,
experimentalist

entalness \ent-ᵊl-nəs\ see
ENTLENESS

entance \ent-ᵊns\ see ENTENCE

entary \en-trē\ gentry, sentry,
passementerie, reentry,
subentry, alimentary,
complementary,
complimentary, documentary,

elementary, filamentary,
integumentary, parliamentary,
rudimentary, sedimentary,
supplementary, tenementary,
testamentary,
uncomplimentary,
unparliamentary,
semidocumentary

entative \ent-ət-iv\ tentative,
augmentative, fermentative,
frequentative, presentative,
preventative, argumentative,
representative,
misrepresentative

¹ente \en-tā\ al dente,
lentamente

²ente \ent-ē\ see ENTY

³ente \änt\ see ²ANT

ented \ent-əd\ tented,
augmented, contented,
demented, lamented,
segmented, untented,
battlemented, malcontented,
oriented, self-contented,
unfrequented, unprecedented,
overrepresented,
underrepresented—*also pasts
of verbs listed at* ¹ENT

enten \ent-ᵊn\ dentin, Lenten

entence \ent-ᵊns\ sentence,
repentance

enter \ent-ər\ center, enter,
mentor, renter, stentor, tenter,
venter, assenter, augmentor,
cementer, concenter,
consentor, dissenter, indenter,

fermenter, frequenter,
inventor, precentor,
preventer, rack-renter,
reenter, repenter, subcenter,
tormentor, documenter,
epicenter, representer,
supplementer, hypocenter,
metacenter, experimenter,
hundred-percenter

centerie \ en-trē \ see ENTARY

entful \ ent-fəl \ eventful,
resentful, uneventful

enth \ enth \ nth, strength, tenth,
crème de menthe

enthe \ enth \ see ENTH

enthesis \ en-thə-səs \ epenthesis,
parenthesis

enti \ ent-ē \ see ENTY

entia \ en-chə \ dementia,
sententia, differentia, in
absentia

ential \ en-chəl \ cadential,
consensual, credential,
demential, essential, eventual,
potential, prudential,
sciential, sentential,
sequential, tangential,
torrential, componential,
conferential, confidential,
consequential, deferential,
differential, evidential,
existential, expedential,
exponential, inessential,
inferential, influential,
intelligential, penitential,
pestilential, preferential,

presidential, providential,
referential, residential,
reverential, transferential,
unessential, circumferential,
equipotential, experiential,
inconsequential, interferential,
jurisprudential, multipotential,
reminiscential

entialist \ en-chə-ləst \
essentialist, existentialist

entian \ en-chən \ see ENSION

entiary \ ench-rē \ century,
penitentiary, plenipotentiary

entic \ ent-ik \ lentic, argentic,
authentic, crescentic, identic,
inauthentic

entical \ ent-i-kəl \ denticle,
pentacle, tentacle,
conventicle, identical,
nonidentical, self-identical

entice \ ent-əs \ see ENTOUS

enticle \ ent-i-kəl \ see ENTICAL

entient \ en-chənt \ penchant,
sentient, trenchant,
dissentient, insentient,
presentient

entil \ ent-ᵊl \ see ENTAL

entin \ ent-ᵊn \ see ENTEN

enting \ ent-iŋ \ dissenting,
unrelenting

ention \ en-chən \ see ENSION

entionable \ ench-nə-bəl \
mentionable, pensionable,
unmentionable

entional \ ench-nəl \ see
ENSIONAL

entioned \en-chənd\
aforementioned, well-
intentioned—*also pasts of
verbs listed at* ENSION

entioner \ench-nər\ mentioner,
pensioner, tensioner

entious \en-chəs\ abstentious,
contentious, licentious,
pretentious, sententious,
tendentious, conscientious,
unpretentious

entis \ent-əs\ see ENTOUS

entist \ent-əst\ dentist,
cinquecentist, irredentist

entity \en-ət-ē\ entity, lenity,
amenity, identity, nonentity,
obscenity, serenity,
coidentity, self-identity

entium \ent-ē-əm\ jus gentium,
unnilpentium

entive \ent-iv\ adventive,
attentive, incentive, inventive,
pendentive, preventive,
retentive, argumentive,
disincentive, inattentive

entle \ent-ᵊl\ see ENTAL

entleness \ent-ᵊl-nəs\
gentleness, accidentalness

entment \ent-mənt\
contentment, presentment,
resentment, discontentment,
self-contentment

ento \en-tō\ cento, lento,
memento, pimento, pimiento,
seicento, trecento,
cinquecento, papiamento,

portamento, quatrocento,
aggiornamento, divertimento,
pronunciamento, risorgimento

entor \ent-ər\ see ENTER

entous \ent-əs\ prentice,
apprentice, argentous,
momentous, portentous,
compos mentis, filamentous,
ligamentous, non compos
mentis, in loco parentis

entral \en-trəl\ central, ventral,
subcentral, dorsiventral

entress \en-trəs\ gentrice,
inventress

entric \en-trik\ centric, acentric,
concentric, dicentric,
eccentric, theocentric,
acrocentric, Christocentric,
egocentric, ethnocentric,
Eurocentric, geocentric,
polycentric, topocentric,
anthropocentric, areocentric,
Europocentric, heliocentric,
selenocentric

entrice \en-trəs\ see ENTRESS

entry \en-trē\ see ENTARY

¹entual \ench-wəl\ sensual,
accentual, consensual,
conventual, eventual

²entual \en-chəl\ see ENTIAL

entum \ent-əm\ centum,
mentum, cementum,
momentum, per centum,
tegmentum, tomentum,
argumentum

enture \en-chər\ bencher,

censure, denture, drencher, trencher, venture, wencher, adventure, backbencher, debenture, front-bencher, indenture, misventure, misadventure, peradventure

enturer \ench-rər \ venturer, adventurer

enturess \ench-rəs \ see ENTUROUS

enturous \ench-rəs \ venturous, adventuress, adventurous

entury \ench-rē \ see ENTIARY

enty \ent-ē \ plenty, senti, tenty, twenty, aplenty, licente, cognoscente, twenty-twenty, Deo volente, dolce far niente

enuis \en-yə-wəs \ see ENUOUS

enum \en-əm \ see ENOM

enuous \en-yə-wəs \ strenuous, tenuis, tenuous, ingenuous, disingenuous

¹enus \ē-nəs \ genus, lenis, penis, venous, Venus, Delphinus, Maecenas, Quirinus, silenus, intravenous

²enus \en-əs \ see ¹ENIS

enza \en-zə \ cadenza, credenza, influenza

¹eo \ā-ō \ cacao, paseo, rodeo, aparejo, cicisbeo, zapateo

²eo \ē-ō \ see ²IO

¹eoff \ef \ see ¹EF

²eoff \ēf \ see ¹IEF

eoffor \ef-ər \ see EPHOR

eolate \ē-ə-lət \ triolet, alveolate, areolate, urceolate

eoman \ō-mən \ see OMAN

eon \ē-ən \ see ¹EAN

eonid \ē-ə-nəd \ see EANID

eopard \ep-ərd \ jeopard, leopard, peppered, shepherd

eopardess \ep-ərd-əs \ shepherdess, leopardess

eople \ē-pəl \ people, pipal, steeple, dispeople, newspeople, salespeople, townspeople, tradespeople, unpeople, workpeople, anchorpeople, businesspeople, congresspeople

eordie \òrd-ē \ see ¹ORDY

eorem \ir-əm \ see ERUM

eorge \òrj \ see ORGE

eorgian \òr-jən \ see ORGIAN

eorist \ir-əst \ see ¹ERIST

eous \ē-əs \ see ¹EUS

ep \ep \ hep, pep, prep, rep, schlepp, skep, step, steppe, strep, yep, crowstep, doorstep, footstep, goose-step, instep, lockstep, misstep, one-step, quickstep, salep, sidestep, two-step, unstep, corbiestep, demirep, overstep, step-by-step

eparable \ep-rə-bəl \ reparable, separable, inseparable, irreparable

epe \āp \ see ¹APE

epee \ē-pē \ see EEPY

eper \ep-ər\ see EPPER

eperous \ep-rəs\ leprous, obstreperous

epey \ā-pē\ see APEY

eph \ef\ see ¹EF

epha \ē-fə\ ephah, synalepha, synaloepha

ephalin \ef-ə-lən\ cephalin, encephalon, enkephalin, acanthocephalan

ephaly \ef-ə-lē\ anencephaly, brachycephaly, microcephaly

epherd \ep-ərd\ see EOPARD

epherdess \ep-ərd-əs\ see EOPARDESS

ephone \ef-ə-nē\ see EPHONY

ephony \ef-ə-nē\ Persephone, telephony

ephor \ef-ər\ deafer, ephor, feoffor, heifer, zephyr, hasenpfeffer

ephrine \ef-rən\ epinephrine, norepinephrine

epht \eft\ see EFT

ephyr \ef-ər\ see EPHOR

epi \ā-pē\ see APEY

epid \ep-əd\ tepid, trepid, intrepid

epo \ēp-ō\ see EPOT

epot \ēp-ō\ depot, pepo

epp \ep\ see EP

eppe \ep\ see EP

epped \ept\ see EPT

epper \ep-ər\ hepper, leper, pepper, stepper, Colepeper, sidestepper

eppy \ep-ē\ peppy, preppy, orthoepy

eprous \ep-rəs\ see EPEROUS

eps \eps\ plebs, biceps, forceps, triceps, quadriceps, editio princeps—*also plurals and possessives of nouns and third singular presents of verbs listed at* EP

epsis \ep-səs\ skepsis, prolepsis, syllepsis

epsy \ep-sē\ catalepsy, epilepsy, narcolepsy, nympholepsy

ept \ept\ crept, kept, sept, slept, stepped, swept, wept, accept, adept, backswept, concept, except, incept, inept, percept, precept, transept, upswept, windswept, yclept, intercept, nympholept, overslept, self-concept—*also pasts of verbs listed at* EP

eptable \ep-tə-bəl\ see EPTIBLE

eptacle \ep-ti-kəl\ skeptical, conceptacle, receptacle

eptal \ep-tᵊl\ reptile, septal

epter \ep-tər\ see EPTOR

eptible \ep-tə-bəl\ acceptable, perceptible, susceptible, imperceptible, insusceptible, unacceptable

eptic \ep-tik\ peptic, septic, skeptic, aseptic, dyspeptic, eupeptic, proleptic, sylleptic, antiseptic, cataleptic, epileptic, narcoleptic, nympholeptic

eptical \ep-ti-kəl\ see EPTACLE

eptile \ep-t²l\ see EPTAL

eption \ep-shən\ conception, deception, exception, inception, perception, reception, subreption, apperception, contraception, interception, misconception, preconception, self-conception, self-perception

eptional \ep-shnəl\ conceptional, deceptional, exceptional, unexceptional

eptive \ep-tiv\ acceptive, conceptive, deceptive, exceptive, inceptive, perceptive, preceptive, receptive, susceptive, apperceptive, contraceptive, imperceptive

eptor \ep-tər\ scepter, accepter, acceptor, inceptor, preceptor, receptor, intercepter, interceptor

eptual \ep-chəl\ conceptual, perceptual

eptus \ep-təs\ conceptus, textus receptus

epy \ep-ē\ see EPPY

equal \ē-kwəl\ equal, sequel, coequal, unequal

eque \ek\ see ECK

equel \ē-kwəl\ see EQUAL

equence \ē-kwəns\ frequence, sequence, infrequence, subsequence

equency \ē-kwən-sē\ frequency, sequency, infrequency

equent \ē-kwənt\ frequent, sequent, infrequent

equer \ek-ər\ see ECKER

¹er \ā\ see ¹AY

²er \er\ see ⁴ARE

³er \ər\ see ¹EUR

¹era \er-ə\ era, Sarah, sclera, terra, caldera, sierra, tiara, cordillera, habanera, riviera

²era \ir-ə\ era, gerah, Hera, lira, Pyrrha, sera, sirrah, wirra, chimaera, chimera, hetaera, lempira, Madeira, mbira

erable \ər-ə-bəl\ thurible, conferrable, deferrable, deterrable, inferable, preferable, transferable

erah \ir-ə\ see ²ERA

¹eral \ir-əl\ feral, seral, spheral, virile

²eral \er-əl\ see ERIL

³eral \ər-əl\ see ERRAL

eraph \er-əf\ see ERIF

eratin \er-ət-²n\ keratin, Sheraton, Samaritan

erative \er-ət-iv\ see ¹ARATIVE

eraton \er-ət-²n\ see ERATIN

erb \ərb\ blurb, curb, herb, kerb, Serb, verb, acerb, adverb, disturb, exurb, perturb, potherb, pro-verb, proverb, reverb, suburb, superb

erbal \ ər-bəl \ burble, gerbil, herbal, verbal, deverbal, nonverbal, preverbal

erbalist \ ər-bə-ləst \ herbalist, verbalist, hyperbolist

erbally \ ər-bə-lē \ verbally, hyperbole, nonverbally

erber \ ər-bər \ see URBER

erbet \ ər-bət \ see URBIT

erbial \ ər-bē-əl \ adverbial, proverbial

erbid \ ər-bəd \ see URBID

erbil \ ər-bəl \ see ERBAL

erbium \ ər-bē-əm \ erbium, terbium, ytterbium

erbole \ ər-bə-lē \ see ERBALLY

erbolist \ ər-bə-ləst \ see ERBALIST

erby \ ər-bē \ derby, herby

ercal \ ər-kəl \ see IRCLE

erce \ ərs \ see ERSE

ercé \ ers \ see ¹ARCE

ercel \ ər-səl \ see ¹ERSAL

ercement \ ər-smənt \ amercement, disbursement

ercer \ ər-sər \ see URSOR

ercery \ ərs-rē \ see URSARY

erch \ ərch \ see URCH

ercha \ ər-chə \ virtue, gutta-percha

ercial \ ər-shəl \ commercial, inertial, controversial, uncommercial, semicommercial

ercian \ ər-shən \ see ERTIAN

ercible \ ər-sə-bəl \ see ERSIBLE

ercion \ ər-zhən \ see ¹ERSION

ercis \ ər-səs \ see ERSUS

ercive \ ər-siv \ see ERSIVE

ercular \ ər-kyə-lər \ see IRCULAR

ercy \ ər-sē \ Circe, mercy, pursy, gramercy, controversy

erde \ erd \ see AIRED

erder \ ərd-ər \ birder, girder, herder, murder, self-murder, sheepherder

erderer \ ərd-ər-ər \ see URDERER

erdin \ ərd-ᵊn \ see URDEN

erding \ ərd-iŋ \ wording, sheepherding

erdu \ ər-dü \ perdu, Urdu

erdure \ ər-jər \ see ERGER

¹ere \ er \ see ⁴ARE

²ere \ er-ē \ see ¹ARY

³ere \ ir \ see ²EER

⁴ere \ ir-ē \ see EARY

⁵ere \ ər \ see ¹EUR

e're \ ē-ər \ see ¹EER

ère \ er \ see ⁴ARE

ereal \ ir-ē-əl \ see ERIAL

ereid \ ir-ē-əd \ see ERIOD

erely \ ir-lē \ see ¹EARLY

erement \ er-ə-mənt \ see ERIMENT

¹erence \ ir-əns \ clearance, adherence, appearance, coherence, inherence, incoherence, interference, perseverance

²**erence** \ ər-əns \ see URRENCE

¹**erency** \ ir-ən-sē \ coherency, vicegerency

²**erency** \ er-ən-sē \ see ERRANCY

¹**erent** \ ir-ənt \ gerent, adherent, coherent, inherent, sederunt, vicegerent, incoherent

²**erent** \ er-ənt \ see ¹ARENT

¹**eren't** \ ərnt \ see EARNT

²**eren't** \ ər-ənt \ see URRENT

ereous \ ir-ē-əs \ see ERIOUS

erer \ ir-ər \ see ²EARER

¹**eres** \ erz \ see AIRS

²**eres** \ ir-ēz \ see ERIES

³**eres** \ ərs \ see ERS

eresy \ er-ə-sē \ clerisy, heresy

ereth \ er-ət \ see ERIT

ereus \ ir-ē-əs \ see ERIOUS

erf \ ərf \ see URF

erg \ ərg \ berg, burg, erg, exergue, hamburg, Hapsburg, homburg, iceberg, Newburg, svedberg, Venusberg, Rube Goldberg

erge \ ərj \ see URGE

ergeant \ är-jənt \ see ARGENT

ergence \ ər-jəns \ convergence, divergence, emergence, immergence, insurgence, resurgence, submergence

ergency \ ər-jən-sē \ urgency, convergency, detergency, divergency, emergency, insurgency, counterinsurgency

ergent \ ər-jənt \ see URGENT

ergeon \ ər-jin \ see URGEON

erger \ ər-jər \ merger, perjure, purger, scourger, urger, verdure, verger, deterger

ergic \ ər-jik \ allergic, synergic, theurgic, demiurgic, dramaturgic, thaumaturgic, alpha-adrenergic, beta-adrenergic

ergid \ ər-jid \ see URGID

ergne \ ərn \ see URN

ergo \ ər-gō \ ergo, Virgo

ergue \ ərg \ see ERG

ergy \ ər-jē \ see URGY

¹**eri** \ er-ē \ see ¹ARY

²**eri** \ ir-ē \ see EARY

¹**eria** \ ir-ē-ə \ feria, asteria, bacteria, collyria, criteria, diphtheria, Egeria, franseria, porphyria, wisteria, cafeteria, cryptomeria, latimeria, sansevieria, washateria, opera seria

²**eria** \ er-ē-ə \ see ARIA

erial \ ir-ē-əl \ aerial, cereal, ferial, serial, arterial, bacterial, empyreal, ethereal, funereal, imperial, material, sidereal, venereal, vizierial, immaterial, magisterial, managerial, ministerial, presbyterial

¹**erian** \ ir-ē-ən \ Adlerian, Assyrian, Aterian, Cimmerian, criterion, Hesperian, Hutterian, Hyperion, Iberian, Illyrian,

Mousterian, Mullerian,
Pierian, Shakespearean,
Spencerian, Spenglerian,
Sumerian, valerian,
Wagnerian, Hanoverian,
Presbyterian, Thraco-Illyrian

²**erian** \er-ē-ən\ see ¹ARIAN

¹**eric** \er-ik\ cleric, derrick,
ferric, xeric, aspheric,
chimeric, choleric,
cholesteric, entheric, generic,
Homeric, mesmeric, numeric,
alphanumeric, atmospheric,
climacteric, congeneric,
dysenteric, esoteric

²**eric** \ir-ik\ lyric, pyric,
pyrrhic, spheric, xeric,
aspheric, chimeric, empiric,
satiric, satyric, atmospheric,
hemispheric, stratospheric,
panegyric

erica \er-i-kə\ erica, America,
esoterica

¹**erical** \er-i-kəl\ clerical,
chimerical, numerical,
anticlerical

²**erical** \ir-i-kəl\ lyrical,
miracle, spherical, spiracle,
empirical, hemispherical

erics \er-iks\ sferics,
hysterics—*also plurals and
possessives of nouns listed at*
¹ERIC

eries \ir-ēz\ Ceres, series,
dundrearies, miniseries—*also
plurals and possessives of*

*nouns and third singular
presents of verbs listed at*
EARY

erif \er-əf\ seraph, serif,
sheriff, teraph, sans serif

eriff \er-əf\ see ERIF

eril \er-əl\ beryl, feral, ferrule,
ferule, peril, sterile, imperil,
chrysoberyl

erilant \er-ə-lənt\ see ERULENT

erile \er-əl\ see ERIL

erilous \er-ə-ləs\ perilous,
querulous, glomerulus

eriment \er-ə-mənt\ cerement,
experiment

eriod \ir-ē-əd\ myriad, Nereid,
period, photoperiod

erion \ir-ē-ən\ see ¹ERIAN

erior \ir-ē-ər\ anterior, exterior,
inferior, interior, posterior,
superior, ulterior—*also
comparatives of adjectives
listed at* EARY

eriot \er-ē-ət\ see ¹ARIAT

erious \ir-ē-əs\ cereus, Nereus,
serious, Sirius, cinereous,
delirious, Guarnerius,
imperious, mysterious,
deleterious

¹**erist** \ir-əst\ querist, theorist,
verist, careerist, panegyrist—
*also superlatives of adjectives
listed at* ²EER

²**erist** \er-əst\ see ARIST

erisy \er-ə-sē\ see ERESY

erit \er-ət\ ferret, merit, terret,

demerit, inherit, disinherit, Shemini Atzereth

eritable \ er-ət-ə-bəl \ heritable, veritable, inheritable

eritor \ er-ət-ər \ ferreter, heritor, inheritor

erity \ er-ət-ē \ ferity, ferrety, rarity, verity, asperity, celerity, dexterity, legerity, posterity, prosperity, severity, sincerity, temerity, insincerity, ambidexterity

erium \ ir-ē-əm \ bacterium, collyrium, delirium, imperium, psalterium, atmospherium, magisterium

¹erius \ er-ē-əs \ see ARIOUS

²erius \ ir-ē-əs \ see ERIOUS

erjure \ ər-jər \ see ERGER

erjury \ ərj-rē \ perjury, surgery

erk \ ərk \ see ¹ORK

erker \ ər-kər \ see ¹ORKER

erkin \ ər-kən \ see IRKIN

erking \ ər-kiŋ \ see ORKING

erkly \ ər-klē \ clerkly, berserkly

erky \ ər-kē \ birkie, jerky, murky, perky, smirky, turkey, Turki, herky-jerky

erle \ ərl \ see ¹IRL

erlie \ er-lē \ see AIRLY

erlin \ ər-lən \ merlin, Merlin, merlon, purlin, yearling

erling \ ər-liŋ \ see URLING

erlon \ ər-lən \ see ERLIN

erm \ ərm \ see ¹ORM

erma \ ər-mə \ dharma, herma, scleroderma, terra firma

ermal \ ər-məl \ dermal, thermal, ectodermal, endothermal, epidermal, exothermal, hydrothermal, hypodermal, hypothermal

erman \ ər-mən \ ermine, german, German, germen, merman, sermon, vermin, determine, extermine, predetermine, cousin-german, Tibeto-Burman

ermanent \ ərm-nənt \ permanent, determinant, impermanent, semipermanent

ermary \ ərm-rē \ see IRMARY

erment \ ər-mənt \ averment, conferment, deferment, determent, interment, preferment, disinterment

ermer \ ər-mər \ see URMUR

ermes \ ər-mēz \ Hermes, kermes

ermi \ ər-mē \ see ERMY

ermic \ ər-mik \ dharmic, thermic, geothermic, hypodermic, taxidermic, electrothermic

ermin \ ər-mən \ see ERMAN

erminable \ ərm-nə-bəl \ terminable, determinable, interminable, indeterminable

erminal \ ərm-nəl \ germinal, terminal, preterminal, subterminal

erminant \ərm-nənt\ see
ERMANENT

ermine \ər-mən\ see ERMAN

ermined \ər-mənd\ ermined,
determined, self-determined,
overdetermined

erminous \ər-mə-nəs\ terminus,
verminous, conterminous,
coterminous

erminus \ər-mə-nəs\ see
ERMINOUS

ermis \ər-məs\ dermis, kermis,
kirmess, thermos,
endodermis, epidermis,
exodermis

ermit \ər-mət\ hermit, Thermit

ermon \ər-mən\ see ERMAN

ermos \ər-məs\ see ERMIS

ermy \ər-mē\ fermi, germy,
squirmy, wormy, diathermy,
endothermy, taxidermy

¹ern \ern\ bairn, cairn, hern,
Sauternes, Ygerne

²ern \ərn\ see URN

erna \ər-nə\ dharna, sterna,
cisterna

ernal \ərn-ᵊl\ colonel, journal,
kernel, sternal, vernal,
diurnal, eternal, external,
fraternal, hibernal, infernal,
internal, maternal, nocturnal,
paternal, supernal, coeternal,
sempiternal, semidiurnal

ernary \ər-nə-rē\ fernery,
ternary, turnery, quaternary

¹erne \ern\ see ¹ERN

²erne \ərn\ see URN

erned \ərnd\ see URNED

ernel \ərn-ᵊl\ see ERNAL

erner \ər-nər\ see URNER

¹ernes \ern\ see ¹ERN

²ernes \ərn\ see URN

ernian \ər-nē-ən\ Hibernian,
quaternion, Saturnian

ernible \ər-nə-bəl\ see URNABLE

ernier \ər-nē-ər\ see OURNEYER

ernion \ər-nē-ən\ see ERNIAN

ernist \ər-nəst\ earnest, internist

ernity \ər-nət-ē\ eternity,
fraternity, maternity,
modernity, paternity,
quaternity, coeternity,
confraternity, sempiternity

ernment \ərn-mənt\
adjournment, attornment,
concernment, discernment,
internment

ernum \ər-nəm\ see URNUM

erny \ər-nē\ see ¹OURNEY

¹ero \ē-rō\ giro, hero, zero,
antihero

²ero \er-ō\ aero, cero, faro,
pharaoh, taro, bolero,
bracero, cruzeiro, Herero,
montero, pampero, primero,
ranchero, sombrero, torero,
vaquero, burladero, caballero,
Mescalero, novillero,
banderillero, carabinero,
embarcadero

³ero \ir-ō\ giro, guiro, gyro,
hero, zero, primero

erod \er-əd\ out-Herod, viverrid

eron \er-ən\ see ¹ARON

erous \ir-əs\ cerous, cirrous, cirrus, peeress, Pyrrhus, scirrhous, scirrhus, seeress, serous

erp \ərp\ see URP

erpe \ər-pē\ see IRPY

¹err \er\ see ⁴ARE

²err \ər\ see ¹EUR

erra \er-ə\ see ¹ERA

errable \ər-ə-bəl\ see ERABLE

errace \er-əs\ see ERROUS

erral \ər-əl\ scurrile, squirrel, conferral, deferral, demurral, referral, transferal

errancy \er-ən-sē\ errancy, aberrancy, coherency, inerrancy

errand \er-ənd\ errand, gerund

errant \er-ənt\ see ¹ARENT

erre \er\ see ⁴ARE

errence \ər-əns\ see URRENCE

errent \ər-ənt\ see URRENT

errer \ər-ər\ burrer, stirrer, conferrer, deferrer, demurer, demurrer, deterrer, inferrer, preferrer, referrer, transferrer

erret \er-ət\ see ERIT

erreter \er-ət-ər\ see ERITOR

erria \er-ē-ə\ see ARIA

errible \er-ə-bəl\ see ¹EARABLE

erric \er-ik\ see ¹ERIC

errick \er-ik\ see ¹ERIC

errid \er-əd\ see EROD

errie \er-ē\ see ¹ARY

erried \er-ēd\ berried, serried, varied—*also pasts of verbs listed at* ¹ARY

errier \er-ē-ər\ burier, terrier, varier, bullterrier—*also comparatives of adjectives listed at* ¹ARY

errily \er-ə-lē\ see ARILY

¹erring \er-iŋ\ see ¹ARING

²erring \ər-iŋ\ see URRING

erris \er-əs\ see ERROUS

erron \er-ən\ see ¹ARON

error \er-ər\ see ¹EARER

errous \er-əs\ derris, ferrous, parous, terrace, nonferrous, millionairess

errule \er-əl\ see ERIL

erry \er-ē\ see ¹ARY

ers \ərz\ furze, hers, somewheres—*also plurals and possessives of nouns and third singular presents of verbs listed at* ¹EUR

ersa \ər-sə\ bursa, vice versa

ersable \ər-sə-bəl\ see ERSIBLE

¹ersal \ər-səl\ bursal, tercel, versal, dispersal, rehearsal, reversal, transversal, traversal, universal

²ersal \är-səl\ see ARSAL

ersant \ərs-ᵊnt\ versant, conversant

ersary \ərs-rē\ see URSARY

erse \ərs\ birse, burse, curse, Erse, hearse, nurse, perse, purse, terce, terse, thyrse,

verse, worse, adverse,
amerce, asperse, averse,
coerce, commerce, converse,
cutpurse, disburse, disperse,
diverse, immerse, inverse,
Nez Perce, obverse, perverse,
rehearse, reverse, sesterce,
stress-verse, submerse,
transverse, traverse,
intersperse, reimburse,
universe

ersed \ ərst \ see URST

erser \ ər-sər \ see URSOR

ersey \ ər-zē \ furzy, jersey,
kersey

ersial \ ər-shəl \ see ERCIAL

ersian \ ər-zhən \ see ¹ERSION

ersible \ ər-sə-bəl \ coercible,
conversable, dispersible,
eversible, immersible,
reversible, submersible,
traversable, incoercible,
irreversible

¹ersion \ ər-zhən \ Persian,
version, aspersion, aversion,
coercion, conversion,
dispersion, diversion,
emersion, eversion,
excursion, immersion,
incursion, inversion,
perversion, recursion,
reversion, submersion,
subversion, ambiversion,
extroversion, interspersion,
introversion, reconversion,
retroversion, animadversion

²ersion \ ər-shən \ see ERTIAN

ersional \ ərzh-nəl \ versional,
conversional, reversional

ersionist \ ərzh-nəst \
diversionist, excursionist

¹ersity \ ər-sət-ē \ adversity,
diversity, multiversity,
university

²ersity \ ər-stē \ see IRSTY

ersive \ ər-siv \ cursive,
ambersive, aversive, coercive,
detersive, discursive,
dispersive, excursive,
inversive, perversive,
recursive, subversive,
extroversive, introversive

erson \ ərs-ᵊn \ person, worsen,
chairperson, houseperson,
newsperson, nonperson,
salesperson, spokesperson,
unperson, anchorperson,
businessperson, gentleperson

erst \ ərst \ see URST

ersted \ ər-stəd \ oersted,
worsted, kilooersted

ersus \ ər-səs \ cercis, thyrsus,
versus, excursus

ersy \ ər-sē \ see ERCY

¹ert \ ərt \ blurt, chert, curt, dirt,
flirt, girt, hurt, pert, quirt,
shirt, skirt, spurt, squirt,
sturt, vert, wert, wort, advert,
alert, assert, avert, bellwort,
birthwort, Blackshirt,
brownshirt, colewort, concert,
convert, covert, desert,

dessert, dissert, divert, evert, exert, expert, exsert, figwort, fleawort, frankfurt, glasswort, hoopskirt, hornwort, inert, insert, invert, lousewort, lungwort, madwort, milkwort, nightshirt, outskirt, overt, pervert, pilewort, ragwort, redshirt, revert, ribwort, saltwort, sandwort, seagirt, soapwort, spearwort, spleenwort, stitchwort, stonewort, subvert, sweatshirt, toothwort, T-shirt, ungirt, ambivert, bladderwort, butterwort, controvert, disconcert, extrovert, feverwort, inexpert, introvert, liverwort, malapert, miniskirt, mitrewort, moneywort, overshirt, overskirt, pennywort, pettiskirt, preconcert, reconvert, Saint-John's-wort, spiderwort, swallowwort, thoroughwort, undershirt, underskirt, animadvert, interconvert

²**ert** \ er \ see ⁴ARE

³**ert** \ at \ see ⁵AT

ertain \ ərt-ᵊn \ burton, certain, curtain, uncertain

ertant \ ərt-ᵊnt \ see ERTENT

erted \ ərt-əd \ skirted, concerted, perverted, T-shirted, extroverted, miniskirted, undershirted—

also pasts of verbs listed at ¹ERT

ertedly \ ərt-əd-lē \ assertedly, concertedly, pervertedly

ertence \ ərt-ᵊns \ advertence, inadvertence

ertent \ ərt-ᵊnt \ advertent, revertant, inadvertent

erter \ ərt-ər \ blurter, skirter, squirter, stertor, converter, inverter, subverter, controverter—*also comparatives of adjectives listed at* ¹ERT

¹**ertes** \ ərt-ēz \ certes, Laertes

²**ertes** \ ərts \ see ERTS

erth \ ərth \ see IRTH

ertial \ ər-shəl \ see ERCIAL

ertian \ ər-shən \ tertian, assertion, Cistercian, desertion, exertion, insertion, Mercian, self-assertion—*also words ending in* ersion *at* ¹ERSION

ertible \ ərt-ə-bəl \ convertible, invertible, controvertible, inconvertible, incontrovertible, interconvertible

ertile \ ərt-ᵊl \ curtal, fertile, hurtle, kirtle, myrtle, spurtle, turtle, cross-fertile, exsertile, infertile, interfertile

ertinence \ ərt-ᵊn-əns \ pertinence, purtenance, appurtenance, impertinence

¹**ertinent** \ərt-ᵊn-ənt\ pertinent, appurtenant, impertinent

²**ertinent** \ərt-nənt\ see IRTINENT

erting \ərt-iŋ\ shirting, skirting, disconcerting, self-asserting

ertion \ər-shən\ see ERTIAN

ertisement \ərt-əs-mənt\ advertisement, divertissement

ertium \ər-shəm\ see URTIUM

ertive \ərt-iv\ furtive, assertive, self-assertive, unassertive

ertor \ərt-ər\ see ERTER

erts \ərts\ certes, nerts, gigahertz, kilohertz, megahertz—*also plurals and possessives of nouns and third singular presents of verbs listed at* ¹ERT

¹**ertz** \erts\ hertz, weltschmerz

²**ertz** \ərts\ see ERTS

erule \er-əl\ see ERIL

erulent \er-ə-lənt\ sterilant, puberulent, pulverulent

erulous \er-ə-ləs\ see ERILOUS

erum \ir-əm\ theorem, serum

erund \er-ənd\ see ERRAND

erunt \er-ənt\ see ¹ARENT

erval \ər-vəl\ see ERVIL

ervancy \ər-vən-sē\ see ERVENCY

ervant \ər-vənt\ fervent, servant, maidservant, manservant, observant

ervative \ər-vət-iv\ conservative, preservative, neoconservative, semiconservative

ervator \ər-vət-ər\ see ERVITOR

erve \ərv\ curve, MIRV, nerve, serve, swerve, verve, conserve, deserve, disserve, hors d'oeuvre, incurve, innerve, observe, preserve, reserve, self-serve, subserve, unnerve, unreserve

erved \ərvd\ nerved, decurved, deserved, recurved, reserved, underserved, unreserved— *also pasts of verbs listed at* ERVE

ervency \ər-vən-sē\ fervency, conservancy

ervent \ər-vənt\ see ERVANT

erver \ər-vər\ fervor, server, deserver, observer, timeserver

ervice \ər-vəs\ nervous, service, disservice, full-service, in-service, self-service, interservice

ervil \ər-vəl\ chervil, serval, servile

ervile \ər-vəl\ see ERVIL

erviness \ər-vē-nəs\ nerviness, topsy-turviness

erving \ər-viŋ\ serving, deserving, self-serving, timeserving, unswerving

ervitor \ər-vət-ər\ servitor, conservator

ervor \ər-vər\ see ERVER

ervous \ər-vəs\ see ERVICE

ervy \ ər-vē \ see URVY
¹ery \ er-ē \ see ¹ARY
²ery \ ir-ē \ see EARY
eryl \ er-əl \ see ERIL
erz \ erts \ see ¹ERTZ
¹es \ ā \ see ¹AY
²es \ ās \ see ¹ACE
³es \ āz \ see ¹AZE
⁴es \ es \ see ESS
⁵es \ ēz \ see EZE
e's \ ēz \ see EZE
¹esa \ ā-sə \ mesa, presa, omasa
²esa \ ā-zə \ presa, impresa,
    marchesa, Bel Paese
esage \ es-ij \ see ESSAGE
¹esan \ āz-ᵊn \ see AZON
²esan \ ēz-ᵊn \ see EASON
esant \ ez-ᵊnt \ bezant, peasant,
    pheasant, pleasant, present,
    unpleasant, omnipresent
esce \ es \ see ESS
escence \ es-ᵊns \ essence,
    candescence, concrescence,
    excrescence, florescence,
    fluorescence, pearlescence,
    pubescence, putrescence,
    quiescence, quintessence,
    senescence, tumescence,
    turgescence, virescence,
    acquiescence, adolescence,
    arborescence, coalescence,
    convalescence, decalescence,
    defervescence, deliquescence,
    detumescence, effervescence,
    efflorescence, evanescence,
    incandescence, inflorescence,

    iridescence, juvenescence,
    luminescence, obsolescence,
    opalescence, prepubescence,
    preadolescence
escency \ es-ᵊn-sē \ excrescency,
    incessancy
escent \ es-ᵊnt \ crescent,
    candescent, canescent,
    concrescent, decrescent,
    depressant, excrescent,
    fluorescent, frutescent,
    incessant, increscent,
    liquescent, pearlescent,
    pubescent, putrescent,
    quiescent, rufescent,
    senescent, suppressant,
    tumescent, turgescent,
    virescent, acaulescent,
    acquiescent, adolescent,
    coalescent, convalescent,
    detumescent, effervescent,
    efflorescent, arborescent,
    evanescent, incandescent,
    inflorescent, intumescent,
    irridescent, juvenescent,
    luminescent, opalescent,
    phosphorescent, prepubescent,
    recrudescent, viridescent,
    antidepressant, preadolescent
escible \ es-ə-bəl \ see ESSIBLE
escience \ ēsh-əns \ nescience,
    prescience
escive \ es-iv \ see ESSIVE
escue \ es-kyü \ fescue, rescue
¹ese \ ēs \ see IECE
²ese \ ēz \ see EZE

esence \ez-ᵊns\ pleasance, presence, omnipresence

eseus \ē-sē-əs\ Theseus, Tiresias

¹esh \esh\ crèche, flèche, flesh, fresh, mesh, thresh, afresh, bobeche, calèche, enmesh, gooseflesh, horseflesh, immesh, parfleche, refresh, tête-bêche, Gilgamesh

²esh \āsh\ see ¹ECHE

³esh \ash\ see ³ASH

eshed \esht\ fleshed, meshed— *also pasts of verbs listed at* ¹ESH

eshen \esh-ən\ see ESSION

eshener \esh-nər\ see ESSIONER

esher \esh-ər\ see ESSURE

eshly \esh-lē\ fleshly, freshly, specially, especially

eshment \esh-mənt\ fleshment, enmeshment, refreshment

esi \ā-zē\ see AZY

¹esia \ē-shə\ geisha, magnesia, alopecia

²esia \ē-zhə\ freesia, amnesia, esthesia, frambesia, magnesia, rafflesia, analgesia, anesthesia, Indonesia, synesthesia

esial \ē-zē-əl\ mesial, ecclesial

¹esian \ē-zhən\ Friesian, Frisian, lesion, adhesion, Cartesian, cohesion, etesian, Salesian, Austronesian, holstein-friesian, Indonesian, Melanesian, Micronesian, Polynesian

²esian \ē-shən\ see ¹ETION

esias \ē-sē-əs\ see ESEUS

esicant \es-i-kənt\ see ESICCANT

esiccant \es-i-kənt\ desiccant, vesicant

esidency \ez-əd-ən-sē\ presidency, residency, nonresidency

esident \ez-əd-ənt\ president, resident, nonresident

esima \es-ə-mə\ Quinquagesima, Sexagesima, Septuagesima

esimal \es-ə-məl\ centesimal, millesimal, vigesimal, duodecimal, planetesimal, sexagesimal, infinitesimal

esin \ez-ᵊn\ resin, muezzin, oleoresin

esion \ē-zhən\ see ¹ESIAN

esis \ē-səs\ Croesus, thesis, tmesis, ascesis, askesis, esthesis, mimesis, prosthesis, anamnesis, catachresis, catechesis, Dionysus, exegesis, hyperkinesis, psychokinesis, telekinesis, amniocentesis

esium \ē-zē-əm\ see EZIUM

esive \ē-siv\ adhesive, cohesive

esk \esk\ see ESQUE

esling \ēz-liŋ\ Riesling, dieseling

esne \ēn\ see ³INE

¹**eso** \ā-sō\ peso, say-so

²**eso** \es-ō\ see ESSO

espite \es-pət\ see ESPOT

espot \es-pət\ despot, respite

esque \esk\ desk, burlesque, grotesque, moresque, arabesque, Bunyanesque, copydesk, gigantesque, humoresque, Junoesque, picaresque, picturesque, plateresque, Romanesque, sculpturesque, statuesque, churrigueresque

ess \es\ bless, cess, chess, cress, dress, ess, fess, guess, jess, less, loess, mess, ness, press, s, stress, tress, yes, abscess, access, address, aggress, assess, caress, clothespress, coatdress, compress, confess, depress, digress, distress, duress, egress, excess, express, finesse, handpress, headdress, housedress, impress, ingress, largess, nightdress, noblesse, obsess, oppress, outguess, pantdress, possess, precess, prestress, princess, process, profess, progress, re-press, recess, redress, regress, repress, shirtdress, sidedress, SS, success, sundress, suppress, Tebet, top-dress, transgress, undress, unless, winepress, ABS, acquiesce,

baroness, coalesce, convalesce, decompress, deliquesce, derepress, dispossess, effervesce, effloresce, evanesce, gentilesse, GR-S, IHS, in-process, incandesce, intumesce, inverness, letterpress, luminesce, Lyonnesse, nonetheless, obsolesce, otherguess, overdress, pennycress, phosphoresce, politesse, prepossess, preprocess, recrudesce, repossess, reprocess, retrogress, second-guess, SOS, unsuccess, watercress, window-dress, another-guess, nevertheless

essable \es-ə-bəl\ see ESSIBLE

essage \es-ij\ message, presage, expressage

essamine \es-mən\ see ESSMAN

essan \es-ᵊn\ see ESSEN

essancy \es-ᵊn-sē\ see ESCENCY

essant \es-ᵊnt\ see ESCENT

¹**esse** \es\ see ESS

²**esse** \es-ē\ see ESSY

essed \est\ see EST

essedly \es-əd-lē\ blessedly, confessedly, professedly, possessedly, self-possessedly

essel \es-əl\ see ¹ESTLE

essen \es-ᵊn\ lessen, lesson, messan, delicatessen

essence \es-ᵊns\ see ESCENCE

esser \es-ər\ see ESSOR

essful \es-fəl\ stressful, distressful, successful, unsuccessful

essian \esh-ən\ see ESSION

essible \es-ə-bəl\ decibel, accessible, addressable, compressible, confessable, depressible, expressible, impressible, processible, putrescible, suppressible, inaccessible, incompressible, inexpressible, insuppressible, irrepressible

essile \es-əl\ see ¹ESTLE

ession \esh-ən\ cession, freshen, hessian, session, accession, aggression, compression, concession, confession, depression, digression, discretion, egression, expression, impression, ingression, obsession, oppression, possession, precession, procession, profession, progression, recession, refreshen, regression, repression, secession, succession, suppression, transgression, decompression, dispossession, indiscretion, intercession, intersession, introgression, misimpression, prepossession, reimpression, repossession, retrogression, self-confession, self-expression, self-possession, supersession

essional \esh-nəl\ sessional, acessional, concessional, congressional, diagressional, expressional, obsessional, possessional, precessional, processional, professional, progressional, recessional, successional, paraprofessional, preprofessional, subprofessional, paraprofessional, semiprofessional

essioner \esh-nər\ freshener, concessioner

essionist \esh-nəst\ expressionist, repressionist, impressionist, secessionist

essity \es-tē\ see ESTY

essive \es-iv\ crescive, aggressive, caressive, compressive, concessive, degressive, depressive, digressive, excessive, expressive, impressive, ingressive, obsessive, oppressive, possessive, progressive, recessive, regressive, successive, suppressive, transgressive, inexpressive, retrogressive, unexpressive, manic-depressive

essman \es-mən\ pressman, expressman, jessamine, specimen

essment \es-mənt\ see ESTMENT

esso \es-ō\ gesso, peso, espresso

esson \es-ʾn\ see ESSEN

essor \es-ər\ dresser, guesser, lesser, pressor, stressor, addresser, aggressor, assessor, caresser, compressor, confessor, depressor, expressor, hairdresser, oppressor, processor, professor, regressor, repressor, successor, suppresssor, transgressor, vinedresser, antecessor, dispossessor, intercessor, predecessor, repossessor, second-guesser, microprocessor, multiprocessor

essory \es-ə-rē\ pessary, accessory, possessory, intercessory

essure \esh-ər\ pressure, impressure, low-pressure, refresher, acupressure, overpressure

essy \es-ē\ dressy, Jesse, messy

est \est\ best, breast, chest, crest, gest, geste, guest, hest, jessed, jest, lest, nest, pest, prest, quest, rest, test, tressed, vest, west, wrest, zest, abreast, appressed, armrest, arrest, attest, backrest, beau geste, behest, bequest, celeste, compressed, congest, conquest, contest, detest, devest, digest, divest, egest, field-test, flight-test, footrest, gabfest, hard-pressed, headrest, hillcrest, houseguest, imprest, incest, infest, ingest, inquest, interest, invest, low-test, Mae West, molest, northwest, posttest, pretest, professed, protest, redbreast, repressed, request, retest, revest, slugfest, southwest, suggest, trapnest, t-test, unblessed, undressed, unrest, unstressed, almagest, anapest, decongest, disinfest, disinterest, galley-west, manifest, north-northwest, palimpsest, predigest, reinvest, rinderpest, second-best, self-addressed, self-confessed, self-interest, self-possessed, supraprotest, uninterest, unprofessed, autosuggest, robin redbreast, thirty-second rest—*also pasts of verbs listed at* ESS

esta \es-tə\ cesta, cuesta, testa, vesta, Avesta, celesta, egesta, fiesta, ingesta, siesta, Zend-Avesta

estable \es-tə-bəl\ see ESTIBLE

estae \es-tē \see ESTY

estal \es-t³l \crestal, pestle, vestal

estan \es-tən \see ESTINE

estant \es-tənt \arrestant, contestant, infestant, protestant, decongestant, disinfestant, manifestant

este \est \see EST

ested \es-təd \crested, nested, tested, vested, time-tested, double-breasted, indigested, single-breasted—*also pasts of verbs listed at* EST

ester \es-tər \ester, Esther, fester, jester, Leicester, nester, Nestor, pester, quaestor, quester, questor, nester, tester, wester, yester, ancestor, arrester, contester, detester, digester, infester, investor, molester, northwester, semester, sequester, southwester, sou'wester, suggester, trimester, Winchester, arbalester, empty-nester, monoester, polyester

estial \es-tē-əl \bestial, celestial, forestial

estible \es-tə-bəl \testable, comestible, detestable, digestible, ingestible, investable, suggestible, incontestable, indigestible

estic \es-tik \gestic, domestic

majestic, anapestic, catachrestic

estical \es-ti-kəl \see ESTICLE

esticle \es-ti-kəl \testicle, catachrestical

estimate \es-tə-mət \estimate, guesstimate

estinate \es-tə-nət \festinate, predestinate

estine \es-tən \destine, Avestan, clandestine, intestine, predestine

esting \es-tiŋ \cresting, vesting, westing, arresting

estion \es-chən \question, congestion, cross-question, digestion, egestion, ingestion, self-question, suggestion, decongestion, indigestion, self-suggestion, autosuggestion

estis \es-təs \cestus, testis, Alcestis, asbestos, Hephaestus

estival \es-tə-vəl \estival, festival

estive \es-tiv \festive, restive, congestive, digestive, egestive, ingestive, suggestive, decongestive

¹estle \es-əl \decile, nestle, pestle, sessile, trestle, vessel, wrestle, Indian-wrestle

²estle \as-əl \see ²ASSEL

³estle \əs-əl \see USTLE

estless \est-ləs \crestless, restless

estment \es-mənt\ vestment,
    arrestment, assessment,
    divestment, impressment,
    investment, disinvestment,
    reinvestment
esto \es-tō\ pesto, presto,
    manifesto
estor \es-tər\ see ESTER
estos \es-təs\ see ESTIS
estra \es-trə\ fenestra,
    orchestra, palaestra,
    Clytemnestra
estral \es-trəl\ estral, kestrel,
    ancestral, campestral,
    fenestral, semestral, orchestral
estrel \es-trəl\ see ESTRAL
estress \es-trəs\ see ESTRUS
estrial \es-trē-əl\ semestrial,
    terrestrial, extraterrestrial
estrian \es-trē-ən\ equestrian,
    pedestrian
estrous \es-trəs\ see ESTRUS
estrum \es-trəm\ estrum,
    sequestrum
estrus \es-trəs\ estrous, estrus,
    ancestress
estry \es-trē\ vestry, ancestry
estuous \es-chə-wəs\
    incestuous, tempestuous
esture \es-chər\ gesture, vesture
estus \es-təs\ see ESTIS
esty \es-tē\ chesty, testae, testy,
    pesty, zesty, res gestae,
    necessity
¹**et** \et\ bet, debt, et, fret, get,
    jet, let, Lett, met, net, pet,

ret, set, stet, sweat, Tet,
threat, vet, wet, whet, yet,
abet, aigrette, asset, backset,
baguette, banquette, barbette,
barrette, beget, beset,
boneset, brevet, briquette,
brochette, brunet, burette,
burnet, cadet, cassette,
cermet, coquet, coquette,
cornet, corselet, corvette,
coset, courgette, croquette,
curette, curvet, cuvette,
daleth, dinette, diskette,
dragnet, duet, egret, fan-jet,
fishnet, flechette, forget,
frisette, gazette, georgette,
gillnet, grisette, handset,
hard-set, headset, inlet, inset,
kismet, layette, lorgnette,
lunette, maquette, mind-set,
moonset, moquette, motet,
musette, noisette, nonet,
nymphet, octet, offset, onset,
Osset, outlet, outset, paillette,
palet, pallette, paupiette,
pipette, piquet, planchette,
poussette, preset, quartet,
quickset, quintet, raclette,
ramet, regret, reset, revet,
rocket, roomette, rosette,
roulette, saw-whet, septet,
sestet, sextet, sharp-set,
soubrette, spinet,
stylet, sublet, subset, sunset,
Syrette, tacet, thickset,
toilette, tonette, trijet,

typeset, unset, upset, vedette, vignette, well-set, aiguillette, alphabet, anchoret, anisette, avocet, banneret, basinet, bassinet, bayonet, bobbinet, briolette, burgonet, calumet, canzonet, castanet, cellarette, chemisette, cigarette, clarinet, consolette, coronet, corselet, crepe suzette, dragonet, electret, en brochette, epaulet, epithet, etiquette, falconet, farmerette, flageolet, flannelette, heavyset, jaconet, Juliett, kitchenette, landaulet, lanneret, launderette, Leatherette, luncheonette, maisonette, majorette, marmoset, marquisette, martinet, mignonette, minaret, minuet, miquelet, novelette, oubliette, parapet, photoset, pirouette, quodlibet, rondelet, satinet, scilicet, sermonette, serviette, silhouette, sobriquet, solleret, somerset, soviet, spinneret, statuette, stockinette, suffragette, superjet, swimmeret, taboret, thermoset, towelette, trebuchet, tricolette, underlet, usherette, vinaigrette, wagonette, analphabet, bachelorette, drum majorette, electrojet, marionette,

micropipette, musique concrète, photo-offset, videlicet, audiocassette, caulifloweret, hail-fellow-well-met, videocassette

²**et** \ā\ see ¹AY

³**et** \āt\ see ¹ATE

⁴**et** \es\ see ESS

¹**eta** \āt-ə\ see ²ATA

²**eta** \et-ə\ see ETTA

³**eta** \ēt-ə\ see ²ITA

¹**etable** \et-ə-bəl\ see ETTABLE

²**etable** \ēt-ə-bəl\ see EATABLE

etal \ēt-ᵊl\ beetle, betel, fetal, decretal, excretal

etan \et-ᵊn\ Breton, threaten, Tibetan

etch \ech\ catch, etch, fetch, fletch, ketch, lech, letch, retch, sketch, stretch, vetch, wretch, backstretch, homestretch, outstretch

etched \echt\ teched, farfetched

etcher \ech-ər\ etcher, catcher, fetcher, fletcher, lecher, sketcher, stretcher, cowcatcher, dogcatcher, eye-catcher, flycatcher, gnatcatcher

etchy \ech-ē\ sketchy, stretchy, tetchy

¹**ete** \āt\ see ¹ATE

²**ete** \et\ see ¹ET

³**ete** \ēt\ see ¹EAT

ête \āt\ see ¹ATE

eted \ād\ see ¹ADE

etel \ēt-ᵊl\ see ETAL

etely \ēt-lē\ see EETLY

eteor \ēt-ē-ər\ meteor,
confiteor—*also comparatives
of adjectives listed at* EATY

eter \ēt-ər\ see ¹EATER

etera \e-trə\ see ETRA

eterate \et-ə-rət\ see ETERIT

eterit \et-ə-rət\ pretcrit,
inveterate

etes \ēt-əs\ see ETUS

etful \et-fəl\ fretful, forgetful

¹eth \eth\ breath, breadth,
death, saith, Seth, snath,
daleth, handbreadth,
hairbreadth, Macbeth,
Ashtoreth, isopleth,
megadeath, shibboleth

²eth \ās\ see ¹ACE

³eth \āt\ see ¹ATE

⁴eth \et\ see ¹ET

ethe \ē-thē\ see EATHY

¹ether \eth-ər\ blether, feather,
heather, leather, nether,
tether, weather, wether,
whether, aweather,
bellwether, pinfeather,
together, untether, altogether,
get-together

²ether \ᵺh-ər\ see ¹OTHER

ethern \eth-ərn\ brethren,
leathern

ethic \eth-ik\ ethic, erethic

ethyl \eth-əl\ bethel, ethyl,
methyl, triethyl

¹eti \ēt-ē\ see EATY

²eti \āt-ē\ see ATY

etian \ē-shən\ see ¹ETION

¹etic \ēt-ik\ thetic, acetic,
docetic

etic \et-ik\ etic, thetic,
aesthetic, ascetic, athletic,
balletic, bathetic, cosmetic,
docetic, eidetic, emetic,
frenetic, gametic, genetic,
hermetic, kinetic, limnetic,
magnetic, mimetic, noetic,
Ossetic, paretic, pathetic,
phenetic, phonetic, phrenetic,
phyletic, poetic, prophetic,
prosthetic, pyretic, splenetic,
syncretic, syndetic, synthetic,
tonetic, Venetic, alphabetic,
analgetic, anesthetic,
antithetic, apathetic,
asyndetic, copacetic,
cybernetic, diabetic, dietetic,
digenetic, diphyletic, diuretic,
empathetic, energetic,
epithetic, geodetic, homiletic,
Masoretic, nomothetic,
parenthetic, sympathetic,
synergetic, synesthetic,
aeromagnetic, antimagnetic,
antipathetic, antipoetic,
antipyretic, apologetic,
epexigetic, epigenetic,
ferrimagnetic, ferromagnetic,
geomagnetic, gyromagnetic,
homogametic, hydrokinetic,
hydromagnetic, hyperkinetic,
isomagnetic, monophyletic,

morphogenetic, ontogenetic, optokinetic, palingenetic, paramagnetic, pathogenetic, peripatetic, phylogenetic, polyphyletic, psychokinetic, telekinetic, thermomagnetic, aposiopetic, cyanogenetic, electrokinetic, electromagnetic, heterogametic, parasympathetic, parthenogenetic, psychotomimetic, unapologetic, onomatopoetic

etical \et-i-kəl\ metical, reticle, aesthetical, genetical, heretical, phonetical, antithetical, arithmetical, catechetical, cybernetical, epithetical, exegetical, geodetical, hypothetical, parenthetical, theoretical, atheoretical, epexegetical

eticist \et-ə-səst\ geneticist, kineticist, cyberneticist

etics \et-iks\ aesthetics, athletics, genetics, homiletics, kinetics, phonetics, poetics, tonetics, cybernetics, dietetics, apologetics, cytogenetics, immunogenetics—*also plurals and possessives of nouns listed at* ETIC

etid \et-əd\ fetid, fretted, sweated, indebted,

parapeted—*also pasts of verbs listed at* ¹ET

etin \ēt-ⁿn\ see ¹EATEN

¹etion \ē-shən\ Grecian, accretion, Capetian, completion, concretion, deletion, depletion, excretion, Ossetian, Phoenician, repletion, secretion, suppletion, Tahitian, Austronesian, Melanesian, Polynesian, Taracahitian

²etion \esh-ən\ see ESSION

etious \ē-shəs\ see ECIOUS

etis \ēt-əs\ see ETUS

etist \et-əst\ cornetist, librettist, vignettist, clarinetist, exegetist, operettist—*also superlatives of adjectives listed at* ¹ET

etitive \et-ət-iv\ competitive, repetitive, uncompetitive, anticompetitive

etive \ēt-iv\ accretive, completive, decretive, depletive, secretive, suppletive

¹etl \ät-ⁿl\ see ATAL

²etl \et-ⁿl\ see ETTLE

etland \et-lənd\ Shetland, wetland

etment \et-mənt\ abetment, besetment, curettement, revetment

¹eto \āt-ō\ see ²ATO

²eto \ēt-ō\ see ¹ITO

¹**etor** \et-ər\ see ETTER

²**etor** \ēt-ər\ see ¹EATER

etory \ēt-ə-rē\ eatery, decretory, secretory, suppletory

etous \ēt-əs\ see ETUS

etra \e-trə\ tetra, etcetera

¹**etral** \ē-trəl\ petrel, retral

²**etral** \e-trəl\ see ¹ETREL

être \etr³\ fête champêtre, raison d'être

¹**etrel** \e-trəl\ petrel, petrol, retral

²**etrel** \ē-trəl\ see ¹ETRAL

etric \e-trik\ metric, obstetric, symmetric, asymmetric, barometric, decametric, dekametric, diametric, geometric, isometric, optometric, psychometric, telemetric, volumetric, sociometric

etrical \e-tri-kəl\ metrical, obstetrical, symmetrical, asymmetrical, barometrical, diametrical, geometrical, unsymmetrical

etrics \e-triks\ obstetrics, isometrics

etrist \e-trəst\ metrist, belletrist

etrol \e-trəl\ see ¹ETREL

ets \ets\ let's, pantalets, solonetz—*also plurals and possessives of nouns and third singular presents of verbs listed at* ¹ET

ett \et\ see ¹ET

etta \et-ə\ betta, feta, geta, biretta, cabretta, galleta, mozzetta, poinsettia, vendetta, anchoveta, arietta, cabaletta, operetta, sinfonietta

ettable \et-ə-bəl\ retable, wettable, forgettable, regrettable, unforgettable

ette \et\ see ¹ET

etter \et-ər\ better, bettor, debtor, fetter, getter, letter, netter, rhetor, setter, sweater, tetter, wetter, whetter, abettor, begetter, bonesetter, enfetter, gill-netter, go-getter, jet-setter, newsletter, pacesetter, pinsetter, red-letter, regretter, trendsetter, typesetter, unfetter, vignetter, carburetter—*also comparatives of adjectives listed at* ¹ET

ettered \et-ərd\ lettered, unfettered, unlettered

ettia \et-ə\ see ETTA

ettiness \it-ē-nəs\ see ITTINESS

etting \et-iŋ\ netting, setting, bed-wetting, bloodletting, go-getting, onsetting, thermosetting, phototypesetting

ettish \et-ish\ fetish, Lettish, pettish, wettish, coquettish, novelettish

ettle \et-³l\ fettle, kettle, metal,

mettle, nettle, petal, settle,
shtetl, bimetal, gunmetal,
nonmetal, teakettle, unsettle

ettlesome \et-ᵊl-səm\
mettlesome, nettlesome

ettling \et-liŋ\ fettling, settling

etto \et-ō\ ghetto, stretto,
cavetto, falsetto, in petto,
larghetto, libretto, palmetto,
stiletto, zucchetto, allegretto,
amaretto, amoretto,
fianchetto, lazaretto,
vaporetto

ettor \et-ər\ see ETTER

¹etty \et-ē\ jetty, netty, petit,
petty, sweaty, yeti, brown
Betty, cavetti, confetti,
libretti, machete, spaghetti,
amoretti, spermacetti,
cappelletti, cavalletti,
vaporetti

²etty \it-ē\ see ITTY

etum \ēt-əm\ pinetum,
arboretum, equisetum

etus \ēt-əs\ Cetus, fetus, Thetis,
treatise, acetous, Admetus,
boletus, coitus, quietus,
diabetes

euce \üs\ see ¹USE

euced \ü-səd\ see UCID

eucey \ü-sē\ see UICY

euch \ük\ see UKE

euchre \ü-kər\ see UCRE

eud \üd\ see UDE

eudal \üd-ᵊl\ see OODLE

eudist \üd-əst\ see ¹UDIST

eudo \üd-ō\ see UDO

eue \ü\ see ¹EW

euer \ü-ər\ see ¹EWER

euk \ük\ see UKE

¹eul \əl\ see ¹ULL

²eul \ərl\ see IRL

eulah \ü-lə\ see ULA

eulean \ü-lē-ən\ see ULEAN

¹eum \ē-əm\ geum, lyceum,
museum, no-see-um, odeum,
per diem, Te Deum,
athenaeum, coliseum,
colosseum, hypogeum,
mausoleum

²eum \ā-əm\ see AHUM

³eum \üm\ see ¹OOM

euma \ü-mə\ see UMA

eume \üm\ see ¹OOM

eumon \ü-mən\ see UMAN

eumy \ü-mē\ see OOMY

eunt \ənt\ see ¹UNT

eunuch \ü-nik\ see UNIC

¹eur \ər\ birr, blur, buhr, burr,
chirr, churr, cur, curr, err,
fir, for, fur, her, knur, murre,
myrrh, per, purr, shirr, sir,
skirr, slur, spur, stir, thir,
'twere, were, whir, your,
you're, à deux, astir, aver,
bestir, chasseur, chauffeur,
claqueur, coiffeur, concur,
confer, danseur, defer,
demur, deter, douceur,
farceur, flaneur, friseur,
frondeur, hauteur, incur,
infer, inter, jongleur,

larkspur, liqueur, longspur,
masseur, occur, poseur,
prefer, recur, refer, sandbur,
sandspur, seigneur, transfer,
voyeur, accoucheur, amateur,
cocklebur, colporteur,
connoisseur, cri de coeur,
cross-refer, cubature,
curvature, de rigueur,
disinter, force majeure, franc-
tireur, monseigneur,
nonconcur, pasticheur,
prosateur, raconteur,
rapporteur, regisseur,
saboteur, secateur, underfur,
voyageur, arbitrageur,
carillonneur, entrepreneur,
litterateur, provacateur,
restaurateur, agent
provocateur
²**eur** \ úr \ see ¹URE
eure \ ər \ see ¹EUR
eurial \ úr-ē-əl \ see ¹URIAL
eurish \ ər-ish \ see OURISH
eury \ úr-ē \ see ¹URY
¹**eus** \ ē-əs \ Aeneas, Aggeus,
Alpheus, Chryseis, Micheas,
uraeus, coryphaeus, epigeous,
scarabaeus, prelate nullius
²**eus** \ üs \ see ¹USE
¹**euse** \ əz \ buzz, 'cause, coz,
does, fuzz, 'twas, was,
abuzz, berceuse, chanteuse,
coiffeuse, danseuse, diseuse,
masseuse, outdoes, undoes,

vendeuse, Betelgeuse,
mitrailleuse, overdoes
²**euse** \ üs \ see ¹USE
³**euse** \ üz \ see ²USE
¹**eusel** \ ü-səl \ see ¹USAL
²**eusel** \ ü-zəl \ see ²USAL
eut \ üt \ see UTE
euter \ üt-ər \ see UTER
euth \ üth \ see ³OUTH
eutic \ üt-ik \ see UTIC
eutical \ üt-i-kəl \ see UTICAL
eutics \ üt-iks \ toreutics,
hermeneutics, therapeutics
eutist \ üt-əst \ see UTIST
euton \ üt-ᵊn \ see UTAN
eutonist \ üt-ᵊn-əst \ see UTENIST
euve \ əv \ see ¹OVE
euver \ ü-vər \ see ³OVER
¹**eux** \ ü \ see ¹EW
²**eux** \ ər \ see ¹EUR
ev \ ef \ see ¹EF
eva \ ē-və \ see ²IVA
eval \ ē-vəl \ see IEVAL
evalent \ ev-ə-lənt \ see EVOLENT
evan \ ē-vən \ see EVEN
¹**eve** \ ev \ breve, rev, Sevres,
alla breve
²**eve** \ ēv \ see ¹EAVE
evel \ ev-əl \ bevel, devil, level,
revel, baselevel, bedevil, bi-
level, daredevil, dishevel, go-
devil, split-level
eveler \ ev-lər \ leveler, reveler
evelly \ ev-ə-lē \ heavily, levelly,
reveille
evement \ ēv-mənt \

achievement, aggrievement,
bereavement,
underachievement

even \ē-vən\ even, break-even,
Genevan, uneven

eventh \ev-ənth\ seventh,
eleventh

¹**ever** \ev-ər\ clever, ever,
lever, never, sever, dissever,
endeavor, forever, however,
soever, whatever, whenever,
wherever, whichever,
whoever, whomever,
cantilever, howsoever, live-
forever, whatsoever,
whencesoever, whensoever,
wheresoever, whichsoever,
whomsoever, whosesoever,
whosoever, whithersoever

²**ever** \ē-vər\ see IEVER

everage \ev-rij\ beverage,
leverage

everence \ev-rəns\ reverence,
severance, disseverance,
irreverence

every \ev-rē\ every, reverie

eviate \ē-vē-ət\ deviate, qiviut

evice \ev-əs\ clevis, crevice

evil \ē-vəl\ see IEVAL

evilry \ev-əl-rē\ devilry, revelry

evious \ē-vē-əs\ devious,
previous

evity \ev-ət-ē\ brevity, levity,
longevity

evo \ē-vō\ in vivo, relievo,
ring-a-lievo, alto-relievo,

basso-relievo, mezzo-relievo,
recitativo

evocable \ev-ə-kə-bəl\
evocable, revocable,
irrevocable

evolence \ev-ə-ləns\ prevalence,
benevolence, malevolence

evolent \ev-ə-lənt\ prevalent,
benevolent, malevolent

evous \ē-vəs\ grievous, nevus,
longevous, redivivus

evus \ē-vəs\ see EVOUS

evy \ev-ē\ bevy, heavy, levee,
levy, replevy, top-heavy

¹**ew** \ü\ blue, boo, brew,
chew, clew, clue, coo, coup,
crew, cue, dew, do, doux,
drew, due, ewe, few, flew,
flu, flue, fou, glue, gnu, goo,
hew, hue, Jew, knew, lieu,
loo, mew, moo, moue, mu,
new, nu, ooh, pew, phew,
piu, pooh, prau, q, queue,
roux, rue, screw, shoe, shoo,
shrew, Sioux, skew, slew,
slough, slue, smew, sou,
sous, spew, sprue, stew,
strew, sue, thew, threw, thro,
through, to, too, true, two,
u, view, whew, who, woo,
Wu, xu, yew, you, zoo,
accrue, adieu, ado, aircrew,
airscrew, anew, askew, au
jus, bamboo, battu, battue,
bedew, beshrew, bestrew,
bijou, boubou, brand-new,

breakthrough, burgoo,
cachou, canoe, caoutchouc,
construe, corkscrew, coypu,
CQ, debut, ecu, endue,
ensue, eschew, floor-through,
fondue, fordo, foreknew,
gumshoe, guru, hairdo,
hereto, horseshoe, how-to,
imbrue, imbue, IQ,
jackscrew, karoo, kazoo,
kung fu, lean-to, make-do,
me-too, mildew, milieu,
miscue, misdo, misknew,
muumuu, non-U, one-two,
outdo, outgrew, perdu, poilu,
preview, pursue, purview,
ragout, redo, renew, review,
revue, rough-hew, run-
through, see-through, set-to,
setscrew, shampoo, Shih Tzu,
skiddoo, snafu, snowshoe,
soft-shoe, span-new, subdue,
surtout, taboo, tattoo, thank-
you, thereto, thumbscrew, to-
do, too-too, undo, undue,
unglue, unscrew, untrue,
vatu, vendue, venue, vertu,
virtu, wahoo, walk-through,
wherethrough, whereto,
who's who, withdrew,
worldview, aperçu, avenue,
babassu, ballyhoo, barbecue,
barley-broo, billet-doux,
black-and-blue, buckaroo,
bugaboo, callaloo, caribou,
catechu, clerihew, cockatoo,
counterview, déjà vu, derring-
do, detinue, feverfew, follow-
through, gardyloo, hitherto,
honeydew, ingenue,
interview, IOU, jabiru,
kangaroo, kinkajou, loup-
garou, manitou, marabou,
Montague, ormolu, overdo,
overdue, overflew, overgrew,
overshoe, overstrew,
overthrough, overview,
parvenu, parvenue, pas de
deux, passe-partout, PDQ,
peekaboo, Port Salut,
rendezvous, residue, retinue,
revenue, seppuku, succès fou,
switcheroo, talking-to,
teleview, Telugu, thereunto,
thirty-two, thitherto, tinamou,
trou-de-loup, twenty-two,
view halloo, wallaroo,
waterloo, well-to-do, whoop-
de-do, Xanadu, didgeridoo,
hullabaloo, pirarucu, Port du
Salut, tu-whit tu-whoo
²ew \ō\ see ¹OW
¹ewable \ō-ə-bəl\ see ¹OWABLE
²ewable \ü-ə-bəl\ see UABLE
ewage \ü-ij\ brewage, sewage
ewal \ü-əl\ see ¹UEL
ewar \ü-ər\ see ¹EWER
eward \ûrd\ see ¹URED
ewd \üd\ see UDE
ewdness \üd-nəs\ see UDINOUS
¹ewe \ō\ see ¹OW
²ewe \ü\ see ¹EW

ewed \üd\ see UDE

ewee \ē-wē\ see EEWEE

ewel \ü-əl\ see ¹UEL

eweled \üld\ see OOLED

¹ewer \ü-ər\ brewer, chewer, dewar, doer, ewer, fewer, hewer, queuer, screwer, sewer, skewer, spewer, suer, viewer, wooer, you're, horseshoer, me-tooer, misdoer, previewer, renewer, reviewer, shampooer, snowshoer, tattooer, undoer, wrongdoer, barbecuer, evildoer, interviewer, revenuer, televiewer—*also comparatives of adjectives listed at ¹*EW

²ewer \ōr\ see ¹ORE

³ewer \ur\ see ¹URE

ewerage \ur-ij\ see ¹OORAGE

ewery \ur-ē\ see ¹URY

ewess \ü-əs\ Jewess, lewis, Shabuoth

ewie \ü-ē\ see EWY

ewing \ō-iŋ\ see ¹OING

ewis \ü-əs\ see EWESS

ewish \ü-ish\ bluish, Jewish, newish, shrewish, aguish

ewl \ül\ see ¹OOL

ewless \ü-ləs\ crewless, dewless, shoeless, viewless

ewly \ü-lē\ see ULY

ewman \ü-mən\ see UMAN

ewment \ü-mənt\ strewment, accruement

ewn \ün\ see ¹OON

ewness \ü-nəs\ blueness, dueness, newness, skewness, askewness

ewpie \ü-pē\ see OOPY

ewry \ur-ē\ see ¹URY

ews \üz\ see ²USE

ewsman \üz-mən\ bluesman, newsman

ewsy \ü-zē\ see OOZY

ewt \üt\ see UTE

ewter \üt-ər\ see UTER

ewterer \üt-ər-ər\ see UITERER

ewy \ü-ē\ bluey, buoy, chewy, dewy, flooey, gluey, gooey, hooey, newie, phooey, rouille, screwy, sloughy, viewy, chop suey, mildewy, ratatouille, waterzooi

ex \eks\ dex, ex, flex, hex, lex, rex, sex, specs, vex, x, annex, apex, carex, codex, complex, convex, cortex, culex, desex, duplex, DX, ibex, ilex, index, Kleenex, Lastex, latex, mirex, murex, MX, narthex, perplex, pollex, Pyrex, reflex, remex, Rx, scolex, silex, silvex, simplex, spandex, telex, Tex-Mex, triplex, unsex, vertex, videotex, vortex, analects, biconvex, circumflex, cross-index, googolplex, haruspex, intersex, multiplex, pontifex, retroflex, spinifex, subindex, unisex—*also plurals and possessives of nouns and third singular presents of verbs listed at* ECK

exas \ek-səs\ *see* EXUS

exed \ekst\ *see* EXT

exedly \ek-səd-lē\ vexedly, perplexedly

exer \ek-sər\ flexor, hexer, duplexer, indexer, multiplexer

exia \ek-sē-ə\ dyslexia, anorexia

exic \ek-sik\ dyslexic, anorexic

exical \ek-si-kəl\ lexical, indexical

exion \ek-shən\ *see* ECTION

exis \ek-səs\ *see* EXUS

exity \ek-sət-ē\ complexity, convexity, perplexity

exive \ek-siv\ reflexive, irreflexive

exor \ek-sər\ *see* EXER

ext \ekst\ next, sexed, sext, text, vexed, context, deflexed, inflexed, perplexed, plaintext, pretext, reflexed, subtext, urtext, ciphertext, oversexed, teletext, undersexed—*also pasts of verbs listed at* EX

extant \ek-stənt\ extant, sextant

exterous \ek-strəs\ dexterous, ambidextrous

extrous \ek-strəs\ *see* EXTEROUS

extual \eks-chəl\ textual, contextual, subtextual

exual \eksh-wəl\ sexual, asexual, bisexual, effectual, pansexual, transsexual, ambisexual, homosexual, hypersexual, intersexual, parasexual, psychosexual, unisexual, heterosexual, sociosexual, anti-intellectual

exural \ek-shrəl\ *see* ²ECTURAL

exus \ek-səs\ lexis, nexus, plexus, texas, apoplexy

exy \ek-sē\ prexy, sexy, apoplexy

¹ey \ā\ *see* ¹AY

²ey \ē\ *see* ¹EE

³ey \ī\ *see* ¹Y

¹eya \ā-ə\ *see* ¹AIA

²eya \ē-ə\ *see* ¹IA

eyance \ā-əns\ abeyance, conveyance, purveyance, surveillance, reconveyance

eyant \ā-ənt\ mayn't, abeyant, surveillant

eyas \ī-əs\ *see* IAS

ey'd \ād\ *see* ¹ADE

eye \ī\ *see* ¹Y

¹eyed \ēd\ *see* EED

²eyed \īd\ *see* ¹IDE

eyedness \īd-nəs\ eyedness, snideness, cockeyedness

eyeless \ī-ləs\ *see* ILUS

eyelet \ī-lət\ *see* ILOT

eyen \īn\ *see* ¹INE

eyer \ā-ər\ *see* ¹AYER

eyes \īz\ see IZE
eying \ā-iŋ\ see AYING
¹ey'll \āl\ see AIL
²ey'll \el\ see ¹EL
eyness \ā-nəs\ see AYNESS
eyor \ā-ər\ see ¹AYER
ey're \er\ see ⁴ARE
eyre \er\ see ⁴ARE
eyrie \īr-ē\ see ¹IRY
eyser \ī-zər\ see IZER
ey've \āv\ see ²AVE
ez \ā\ see ¹AY
eza \ē-zə\ visa, mestiza, lespedeza
eze \ēz\ bise, breeze, cheese, ease, feaze, feeze, freeze, frieze, he's, jeez, lees, please, res, seize, she's, sleaze, sneeze, squeeze, tease, tweeze, wheeze, appease, Aries, betise, Burmese, camise, cerise, chemise, Chinese, deep-freeze, degrease, disease, displease, disseise, d.t.'s, fasces, fauces, headcheese, heartsease, Kirghiz, Maltese, marquise, menses, nates, Pisces, quick-freeze, reprise, sharp-freeze, soubise, striptease, Tabriz, trapeze, unease, unfreeze, Amboinese, Androcles,

Annamese, antifreeze, Assamese, Balinese, Brooklynese, Cantonese, Damocles, diocese, expertise, Faeroese, Heracles, Hercules, Hyades, Japanese, Javanese, Johnsonese, journalese, Kanarese, legalese, litotes, manganese, Nipponese, overseas, Pekinese, Pekingese, Pleiades, Portuguese, Siamese, Silures, Sinhalese, Albigenses, antipodes, archdiocese, Averroës, bona fides, cheval-de-frise, computerese, Eumenides, Great Pyrenees, Hesperides, Hippomenes, Indo-Chinese, nephritides, officialese, Philoctetes, superficies, telegraphese, Vietnamese, educationese, Mephistopheles, sociologese, sword of Damocles, muscae volitantes—*also plurals and possessives of nouns and third singular presents of verbs listed at* ¹EE
ezel \ē-zəl\ see EASEL
ezium \ē-zē-əm\ magnesium, trapezium
ezzle \ez-əl\ bezel, embezzle

i

¹i \ē\ see ¹EE

²i \ī\ see ¹Y

¹ia \ē-ə\ Gaea, kea, rhea, rya, via, althaea, buddleia, cabrilla, cattleya, fantasia, Hygeia, idea, mantilla, Medea, mens rea, ohia, Oriya, ouguiya, rupiah, sangria, spirea, tortilla, barathea, bougainvillea, camarilla, cascarilla, Cytherea, dulcinea, Galatea, gonorrhea, granadilla, hamartia, latakia, logorrhea, Manzanilla, mausolea, mythopoeia, panacea, Parousia, pharmacopoeia, pizzeria, ratafia, sabadilla, sapodilla, seguidilla, sinfonia, trattoria, alfilaria, Ave Maria, Cassiopeia, echeveria, peripeteia, prosopopoeia, onomatopoeia

²ia \ī-ə\ see ¹IAH

¹iable \ī-ə-bəl\ dryable, dyeable, flyable, friable, liable, pliable, triable, viable, deniable, inviable, reliable, certifiable, classifiable, justifiable, liquefiable, notifiable, pacifiable, qualifiable, quantifiable, rectifiable, satisfiable, specifiable, undeniable, unifiable, verifiable, emulsifiable, identifiable, unfalsifiable

²iable \ē-ə-bəl\ see EEABLE

iacal \ī-ə-kəl\ dandiacal, heliacal, maniacal, theriacal, zodiacal, ammoniacal, elegiacal, simoniacal, dipsomaniacal, egomaniacal, hypochondriacal, monomaniacal, nympomaniacal, pyromaniacal, paradisiacal, bibliomaniacal, megalomaniacal

iad \ī-əd\ see YAD

¹iah \ī-ə\ ayah, bayou, maya, Maya, playa, stria, via, Aglaia, messiah, papaya, pariah, Thalia, Black Maria, Hezekiah, jambalaya, Jeremiah, Nehemiah, Obadiah, Zechariah, Zephaniah, Iphigenia, peripeteia

²iah \ē-ə\ see ¹IA

¹ial \ī-əl\ diel, pial

²ial \īl\ see ¹ILE

ialer \ī-lər\ see ILAR

ially \ē-ə-lē\ see ¹EALLY

iam \ī-əm\ Priam, perd diem

¹ian \ē-ən\ see ¹EAN

²**ian** \ī-ən\ see ¹ION

iance \ī-əns\ science, affiance, alliance, appliance, compliance, defiance, nonscience, reliance, mesalliance, misalliance

iancy \ī-ən-sē\ pliancy, compliancy

iant \ī-ənt\ client, giant, pliant, riant, affiant, compliant, defiant, reliant, incompliant, self-reliant, supergiant

iao \aú\ see ²OW

iaour \aúr\ see ²OWER

iaper \ī-pər\ see IPER

iar \īr\ see ¹IRE

¹**iary** \ī-rē\ diary, fiery, miry, priory, Valkyrie, venire

²**iary** \īr-ē\ see ¹IRY

ias \ī-əs\ Aias, bias, dais, eyas, Lias, pious, Abdias, Elias, Messias, Nehemias, Tobias, Ananias, Jeremias, Malachias, Sophonias, Zacharias

iasis \ī-ə-səs\ diesis, diocese, archdiocese, psoriasis, acariasis, amebiasis, ascariasis, bilharziasis, helminthiasis, leishmaniasis, satyriasis, elephantiasis, hypochondriasis, schistosomiasis

¹**iat** \ē-ət\ see ¹EIT

²**iat** \ī-ət\ see IET

iate \ī-ət\ see IET

iatry \ī-ə-trē\ podiatry, psychiatry

iaus \aús\ see ²OUSE

¹**ib** \ib\ bib, bibb, crib, drib, fib, gib, glib, jib, lib, nib, rib, sib, squib, ad-lib, corncrib, midrib, sahib, memsahib

²**ib** \ēb\ see ²EBE

³**ib** \ēv\ see ¹EAVE

iba \ē-bə\ see EBA

ibable \ī-bə-bəl\ bribable, ascribable, describable, indescribable

ibal \ī-bəl\ bible, libel, scribal, tribal

ibb \ib\ see ¹IB

ibband \ib-ən\ see IBBON

ibbed \ibd\ bibbed, rock-ribbed—*also pasts of verbs listed at* ¹IB

ibber \ib-ər\ bibber, cribber, dibber, fibber, gibber, glibber, jibber, ribber

ibbet \ib-ət\ gibbet, contribute, exhibit, inhibit, prohibit, flibbertigibbet

ibbing \ib-iŋ\ cribbing, ribbing

ibble \ib-əl\ dibble, dribble, fribble, gribble, kibble, nibble, quibble, scribble, sibyl

ibbler \ib-lər\ dribbler, nibbler, quibbler, scribbler

ibbly \ib-lē\ dribbly, ghibli, glibly

ibbon\ib-ən\gibbon, ribband, ribbon

¹**ibe**\īb\bribe, gibe, gybe, jibe, kibe, scribe, tribe, vibe, ascribe, conscribe, describe, imbibe, inscribe, prescribe, proscribe, subscribe, transcribe, circumscribe, diatribe, redescribe, superscribe, oversubscribe

²**ibe**\ē-bē\see ¹EBE

ibel\ī-bəl\see IBAL

iber\ī-bər\briber, fiber, giber, scriber, describer, inscriber, prescriber, proscriber, subscriber, transcriber

ibi\ē-bē\see ¹EBE

ibit\ib-ət\see IBBET

ibitive\ib-ət-iv\exhibitive, prohibitive

ibitor\ib-ət-ər\contributor, exhibitor, inhibitor

ible\ī-bəl\see IBAL

iblet\ib-lət\driblet, riblet

ibli\ib-lē\see IBBLY

ibly\ib-lē\see IBBLY

ibo\ē-bō\Ibo, gazebo

ibrous\ī-brəs\fibrous, hybris

ibs\ibz\dibs, nibs, spareribs—
*also plurals and possessives
of nouns and third singular
presents of verbs listed at* ¹IB

ibular\ib-yə-lər\fibular, mandibular, vestibular, infundibular

¹**ibute**\ib-yət\tribute, attribute,
contribute, distribute, redistribute

²**ibute**\ib-ət\see IBBET

ibutive\ib-yət-iv\attributive, contributive, distributive, retributive, redistributive

ibutor\ib-ət-ər\see IBITOR

ibyl\ib-əl\see IBBLE

¹**ic**\ik\see ICK

²**ic**\ēk\see ¹EAK

¹**ica**\ī-kə\mica, Micah, pica, pika, plica, spica, Spica, Formica, lorica, balalaika

²**ica**\ē-kə\see ¹IKA

icable\ik-ə-bəl\despicable, explicable, extricable, inexplicable, inextricable

icah\ī-kə\see ¹ICA

ical\ik-əl\see ICKLE

icament\ik-ə-mənt\
medicament, predicament

ican\ē-kən\see EACON

icar\ik-ər\see ¹ICKER

icative\ik-ət-iv\fricative, siccative, affricative, explicative, indicative, vindicative, multiplicative

iccative\ik-ət-iv\see ICATIVE

iccio\ē-chō\capriccio, pasticcio

¹**ice**\īs\dice, fice, fyce, gneiss, ice, lice, lyse, mice, nice, pice, price, rice, rise, slice, spice, splice, syce, thrice, trice, twice, vice, vise, advice, allspice, bride-price, concise, deice, device, entice,

excise, precise, suffice,
beggars-lice, cockatrice,
edelweiss, imprecise,
merchandise, overprice,
paradise, point-device,
sacrifice, underprice,
imparadise, self-sacrifice

²**ice** \ē-chä\ see ¹ICHE

³**ice** \ēs\ see IECE

⁴**ice** \ī-sē\ see ICY

⁵**ice** \īz\ see IZE

iceless \ī-sləs\ iceless, priceless

icely \is-lē\ see ISTLY

iceous \ish-əs\ see ¹ICIOUS

icer \ī-sər\ dicer, nicer, pricer,
ricer, slicer, splicer, deicer,
sufficer, sacrificer, self-
sacrificer

ices \ī-sēz\ Pisces, Anchises,
Polynices, Coma Berenices

icety \ī-stē\ see EISTY

icey \ī-sē\ see ICY

¹**ich** \ich\ see ITCH

²**ich** \ik\ see ICK

ichael \ī-kəl\ see ¹YCLE

¹**iche** \ē-chä\ ceviche, seviche,
Beatrice, cantatrice

²**iche** \ēsh\ fiche, leash, quiche,
sneesh, baksheesh, corniche,
hashish, maxixe, pastiche,
schottische, unleash,
microfiche, nouveau riche

³**iche** \ish\ see ¹ISH

⁴**iche** \ich\ see ITCH

⁵**iche** \ē-chē\ see EACHY

¹**ichen** \ī-kən\ lichen, liken

²**ichen** \ich-ən\ see ITCHEN

icher \ich-ər\ see ITCHER

iches \ich-əz\ see ITCHES

¹**ichi** \ē-chē\ see EACHY

²**ichi** \ē-shē\ see ISHI

ichment \ich-mənt\ see
ITCHMENT

ichu \ish-ü\ see ¹ISSUE

icia \ish-ə\ see ITIA

icial \ish-əl\ altricial, comitial,
initial, judicial, official,
simplicial, solstitial, surficial,
artificial, beneficial,
cicatricial, interstitial,
prejudicial, sacrificial,
superficial

ician \ē-shən\ see ¹ETION

icience \ish-əns\ omniscience,
insufficience

iciency \ish-ən-sē\ deficiency,
efficiency, proficiency,
sufficiency, inefficiency,
immunodeficiency

icient \ish-ənt\ deficient,
efficient, omniscient,
proficient, sufficient,
coefficient, inefficient,
insufficient, self-sufficient

icinable \is-nə-bəl\ see
ISTENABLE

¹**icinal** \is-ᵊn-əl\ vicinal,
officinal, vaticinal

²**icinal** \is-nəl\ medicinal,
vicinal

¹**icing** \ī-siŋ\ icing, splicing,
self-sufficing

²**icing** \ ī-ziŋ \ see IZING

¹**icious** \ ish-əs \ vicious,
ambitious, auspicious,
capricious, delicious,
factitious, fictitious,
flagitious, judicious,
lubricious, malicious,
nutritious, Odysseus,
officious, pernicious,
propitious, pumiceous,
seditious, sericeous,
suspicious, adscititious,
adventitious, avaricious,
expeditious, inauspicious,
injudicious, meretricious,
prejudicious, subreptitious,
superstitious, suppositious,
surreptitious, excrementitious,
supposititious

²**icious** \ ē-shəs \ see ECIOUS

icipal \ is-ə-bəl \ see ISSIBLE

icipant \ is-ə-pənt \ anticipant,
participant

icit \ is-ət \ licit, complicit,
elicit, explicit, illicit,
implicit, solicit, inexplicit

¹**icitor** \ is-ət-ər \ elicitor,
solicitor

²**icitor** \ is-tər \ see ISTER

icitous \ is-ət-əs \ complicitous,
duplicitous, felicitous,
solicitous, infelicitous

¹**icity** \ is-ət-ē \ basicity,
causticity, centricity,
chronicity, complicity,
conicity, cyclicity, duplicity,
ethnicity, felicity, lubricity,
mendicity, plasticity,
publicity, rhythmicity,
seismicity, simplicity,
spasticity, sphericity, tonicity,
toxicity, triplicity, atomicity,
authenticity, canonicity,
catholicity, concentricity,
domesticity, eccentricity,
elasticity, electricity,
ellipticity, endemicity,
ergodicity, historicity,
iconicity, impudicity,
infelicity, multiplicity,
organicity, pneumaticity,
quadruplicity, specificity,
volcanicity, aperiodicity,
aromaticity, automaticity,
ecumenicity, egocentricity,
epidemicity, ethnocentricity,
hydrophilicity,
hydrophobicity,
inauthenticity, inelasticity,
pathogenicity, periodicity,
theocentricity,
anthropocentricity,
carcinogenicity

²**icity** \ is-tē \ christie, misty,
twisty, wristy, publicity,
simplicity, Corpus Christi,
elasticity, electricity,
sacahuiste

ick \ ik \ brick, chick, click,
crick, creek, dick, flick, hick,
kick, KWIC, lick, mick,
nick, pic, pick, prick, quick,

rick, shtick, sic, sick, slick,
snick, spick, stick, strick,
thick, tic, tick, trick, wick,
airsick, alsike, bootlick,
brainsick, broomstick,
carsick, chopstick, cowlick,
crabstick, dabchick, detick,
dik-dik, dipstick, drop-kick,
drumstick, firebrick,
flagstick, goldbrick,
greensick, handpick, hayrick,
heartsick, homesick, joystick,
lipstick, lovesick, matchstick,
moujik, muzhik, nightstick,
nitpick, nonstick, nutpick,
pigstick, pinprick, placekick,
redbrick, rubric, seasick, self-
stick, shashlik, sidekick,
slapstick, slipstick, Tajik,
toothpick, topkick, unpick,
unstick, uptick, yardstick,
bailiwick, Bolshevik,
candlestick, candlewick,
dominick, double-quick,
EBCDIC, fiddlestick,
hemistich, heretic, lunatic,
Menshevik, meterstick,
overtrick, politic, politick,
polyptych, singlestick,
taperstick, undertrick,
Watson-Crick, arithmetic,
carrot-and-stick, computernik,
impolitic, kinnikinnick

¹icked \ik-əd\ peaked, picked,
wicked

²icked \ikt\ see ¹ICT

ickel \ik-əl\ see ICKLE

icken \ik-ən\ chicken, quicken,
sicken, stricken, thicken,
awestricken, panic-stricken,
planet-stricken, poverty-
stricken

ickens \ik-ənz\ dickens,
pickings—*also plurals and
possessives of nouns and third
singular presents of verbs
listed at* ICKEN

¹icker \ik-ər\ bicker, dicker,
flicker, icker, liquor, nicker,
picker, pricker, sicker,
slicker, snicker, sticker,
ticker, tricker, vicar, whicker,
wicker, billsticker, bootlicker,
dropkicker, nitpicker,
pigsticker, placekicker,
ragpicker, dominicker,
politicker—*also comparatives
of adjectives listed at* ICK

²icker \ek-ər\ see ECKER

ickery \ik-rē\ chicory, flickery,
hickory, snickery, trickery

icket \ik-ət\ cricket, picket,
pricket, spigot, stickit,
thicket, ticket, wicket, big-
ticket

ickety \ik-ət-ē\ rickety,
thickety, pernickety,
persnickety

ickey \ik-ē\ see ICKY

ickie \ik-ē\ see ICKY

icking \ik-iŋ\ ticking, wicking,

brain-picking, high-sticking,
nit-picking, cotton-picking

ickings \ ik-ənz \ see ICKENS

ickish \ ik-ish \ hickish, sickish,
trickish

ickit \ ik-ət \ see ICKET

ickle \ ik-əl \ brickle, chicle,
cycle, fickle, mickle, nickel,
pickle, picul, prickle, sickle,
stickle, strickle, tical, tickle,
trickle, bicycle, icicle,
obstacle, Popsicle, spectacle,
tricycle, vehicle,
pumpernickel

ickler \ ik-lər \ stickler, tickler,
bicycler, particular

ickly \ ik-lē \ fickly, prickly,
quickly, sickly, slickly,
particularly, impoliticly

ickness \ ik-nəs \ lychnis,
quickness, sickness,
slickness, thickness,
airsickness, heartsickness,
homesickness, lovesickness,
seasickness

icksy \ ik-sē \ see IXIE

icky \ ik-ē \ hickey, icky, kicky,
picky, quickie, rickey, sickie,
sticky, tricky, doohickey,
Tajiki

icle \ ik-əl \ see ICKLE

¹icly \ ik-lē \ see ICKLY

²icly \ ē-klē \ see EEKLY

ico \ ē-kō \ see ICOT

icope \ ik-ə-pē \ see ICOPY

icopy \ ik-ə-pē \ wicopy,
pericope

icory \ ik-rē \ see ICKERY

icot \ ē-kō \ fico, pekoe, picot,
tricot

ics \ iks \ see ¹IX

¹ict \ ikt \ picked, Pict, strict,
ticked, addict, afflict,
conflict, constrict, convict,
delict, depict, edict, evict,
inflict, lipsticked, predict,
restrict, unlicked, benedict,
contradict, derelict, interdict,
maledict, eggs Benedict—*also
pasts of verbs listed at* ICK

²ict \ īt \ see ¹ITE

ictable \ īt-ə-bəl \ see ¹ITABLE

ictal \ ik-t³l \ fictile, rictal,
edictal

icter \ ik-tər \ see ICTOR

ictic \ ik-tik \ deictic, panmictic,
amphimictic, apodictic

ictile \ ik-t³l \ see ICTAL

ictim \ ik-təm \ see ICTUM

iction \ ik-shən \ diction, fiction,
friction, stiction, addiction,
affliction, confliction,
constriction, conviction,
depiction, eviction, indiction,
infliction, nonfiction,
prediction, reliction,
restriction, transfixion,
benediction, contradiction,
crucifixion, dereliction,
jurisdiction, malediction,
valediction

ictional \ik-shnəl\ fictional, frictional, nonfictional, jurisdictional

ictionist \ik-shnəst\ fictionist, restrictionist

ictive \ik-tiv\ fictive, addictive, afflictive, conflictive, constrictive, inflictive, restrictive, vindictive, nonrestrictive

ictment \īt-mənt\ see ITEMENT

ictor \ik-tər\ lictor, stricter, victor, constrictor, depicter, evictor, inflicter, contradictor

ictory \ik-trē\ victory, benedictory, contradictory, maledictory, valedictory

ictual \it-ʾl\ see ITTLE

ictualler \it-ʾl-ər\ see ITALER

ictum \ik-təm\ dictum, victim, obiter dictum

icture \ik-chər\ picture, stricture

ictus \ik-təs\ ictus, rictus, Benedictus

icul \ik-əl\ see ICKLE

icula \ik-yə-lə\ auricula, Canicula

iculant \ik-yə-lənt\ gesticulant, matriculant

¹icular \ik-yə-lər\ spicular, acicular, articular, auricular, canicular, clavicular, curricular, cuticular, fascicular, follicular, funicular, lenticular, navicular, orbicular, ossicular, particular, radicular, reticular, testicular, vehicular, ventricular, vermicular, versicular, vesicular, appendicular, perpendicular, extracurricular, extravehicular

²icular \ik-lər\ see ICKLER

icularly \ik-lē\ see ICKLY

iculate \ik-yə-lət\ articulate, denticulate, geniculate, particulate, reticulate, straticulate, vermiculate, inarticulate

iculous \ik-yə-ləs\ meticulous, pediculous, ridiculous

iculum \ik-yə-ləm\ curriculum, reticulum, diverticulum

icuous \ik-yə-wəs\ conspicuous, perspicuous, transpicuous, inconspicuous

icus \ī-kəs\ ficus, umbilicus

icy \ī-sē\ dicey, icy, pricey, spicy, vice

¹id \id\ bid, chid, did, fid, gid, grid, hid, id, kid, lid, mid, quid, rid, skid, slid, squid, whid, amid, backslid, bifid, eyelid, forbid, nonskid, outdid, resid, trifid, undid, katydid, ootid, overbid, overdid, pyramid, underbid, tertium quid

²id \ēd\ see EED

I'd \īd\ see ¹IDE

ida\ēd-ə\see ¹EDA

¹idable\īd-ə-bəl\guidable, decidable, dividable, subdividable

²idable\id-ə-bəl\see IDDABLE

idal\īd-ᵊl\bridal, bridle, idle, idol, idyll, seidel, sidle, tidal, unbridle, Barmecidal, fratricidal, fungicidal, genocidal, germicidal, herbicidal, homicidal, intertidal, lunitidal, matricidal, parricidal, patricidal, septicidal, spermicidal, suicidal, viricidal, virucidal, bactericidal, infanticidal, insecticidal

idance\īd-ᵊns\guidance, stridence, abidance, misguidance

idas\īd-əs\Midas, nidus

iday\īd-ē\Friday, tidy, vide, alcaide, man Friday, untidy, mala fide

idays\īd-ēz\see ¹IDES

iddable\id-ə-bəl\biddable, formidable

iddance\id-ᵊns\riddance, forbiddance

idden\id-ᵊn\bidden, chiden, hidden, midden, ridden, stridden, swidden, backslidden, bedridden, bestridden, forbidden, outbidden, unbidden, overridden

idder\id-ər\bidder, kidder, siddur, skidder, consider, forbidder, reconsider, underbidder

iddie\id-ē\see IDDY

iddish\id-ish\kiddish, Yiddish

iddity\id-ət-ē\see IDITY

iddle\id-ᵊl\diddle, fiddle, griddle, middle, piddle, riddle, twiddle, unriddle, paradiddle, taradiddle

iddler\id-lər\diddler, fiddler, middler, riddler

iddling\id-liŋ\fiddling, middling, piddling, riddling

iddock\id-ik\see IDIC

iddur\id-ər\see IDDER

iddy\id-ē\biddy, giddy, kiddie, middy, midi, skiddy, widdy

¹ide\īd\bide, bride, chide, eyed, glide, guide, hide, I'd, pied, pride, ride, side, slide, snide, stride, thighed, tide, tried, wide, abide, allied, applied, aside, astride, backside, backslide, bankside, beachside, bedside, beside, bestride, betide, blear-eyed, blindside, broadside, bromide, bug-eyed, clear-eyed, cockeyed, cold-eyed, collide, confide, courtside, cowhide, cross-eyed,

curbside, dayside, decide,
deride, divide, dockside,
downside, dry-eyed, elide,
fireside, foreside, freeze-
dried, glass-eyed, green-eyed,
hagride, hayride, hillside,
horsehide, inside, ironside,
joyride, kingside, lakeside,
landslide, lynx-eyed,
misguide, moon-eyed,
nightside, noontide, offside,
onside, outride, outside, pie-
eyed, poolside, pop-eyed,
preside, provide, quayside,
queenside, rawhide, reside,
ringside, riptide, roadside,
seaside, sharp-eyed, shipside,
shoreside, Shrovetide, sloe-
eyed, snowslide, springtide,
squint-eyed, stateside,
statewide, storewide,
streamside, subside, tongue-
tied, topside, trackside,
trailside, untried, vat-dyed,
walleyed, waveguide,
wayside, wide-eyed, wild-
eyed, worldwide, yuletide,
almond-eyed, alongside,
Argus-eyed, Barmecide,
bleary-eyed, bona fide,
Christmastide, citified,
citywide, classified, coincide,
countrified, countryside, cut-
and-dried, cyanide, deicide,
dewy-eyed, dignified,
Eastertide, eventide, feticide,

fluoride, fratricide, fungicide,
genocide, germicide, gimlet-
eyed, goggle-eyed, herbicide,
homicide, humified,
matricide, misty-eyed,
miticide, monoxide,
mountainside, nationwide,
Naugahyde, open-eyed,
override, overstride,
parricide, Passiontide,
patricide, pesticide, qualified,
rarefied, raticide, regicide,
riverside, set-aside, silverside,
sissified, slickenside, starry-
eyed, subdivide, suicide,
supply-side, underside,
verbicide, vermicide, viricide,
waterside, Whitsuntide,
wintertide, dissatisfied,
formaldehyde, infanticide, ·
insecticide, interallied, Jekyll
and Hyde, preoccupied,
rodenticide, self-satisfied,
thalidomide, Trinitytide,
tyrannicide, uxoricide,
overqualified, parasiticide—
also pasts of verbs listed at ¹Y

²**ide** \ēd\ see EED

idean \id-ē-ən\ see IDIAN

ided \īd-əd\ sided, lopsided,
one-sided, slab-sided, two-
sided, many-sided,
sobersided—*also pasts of
verbs listed at* ¹IDE

ideless \īd-ləs\ idlesse, tideless

iden \īd-ᵊn\ guidon, widen, Poseidon

idence \īd-ᵊns\ see IDANCE

ideness \īd-nəs\ see EYEDNESS

ident \īd-ᵊnt\ strident, trident

ideon \id-ē-ən\ see IDIAN

ideous \id-ē-əs\ see IDIOUS

¹ider \īd-ər\ bider, cider, eider, glider, guider, hider, rider, slider, spider, strider, stridor, abider, backslider, confider, decider, derider, divider, insider, joyrider, misguider, outrider, outsider, presider, provider, resider, rough rider, subdivider, supply-sider—*also comparatives of adjectives listed at* ¹IDE

²ider \id-ər\ see IDDER

¹ides \īd-ēz\ Fridays, Aristides—*also plurals and possessives of nouns and third singular presents of verbs listed at* IDAY

²ides \īdz\ ides, besides, burnsides, silversides, sobersides—*also plurals and possessives of nouns and third singular presents of verbs listed at* ¹IDE

idge \ij\ bridge, fidge, fridge, midge, ridge, abridge, browridge, drawbridge, footbridge, teethridge

idged \ijd\ ridged, unabridged—*also pasts of verbs listed at* IDGE

idgen \ij-ən\ see YGIAN

idget \ij-ət\ digit, fidget, midget, widget, double-digit

idgin \ij-ən\ see YGIAN

idi \id-ē\ see IDDY

idian \id-ē-ən\ Gideon, Lydian, ascidian, Dravidian, euclidean, meridian, obsidian, ophidian, quotidian, viridian, enchiridion, non-euclidean

idic \id-ik\ piddock, acidic, bromidic, Davidic, druidic, fatidic, fluidic, Hasidic, nuclidic

idical \id-i-kəl\ druidical, fatidical, juridical, veridical, pyramidical

idiem \id-ē-əm\ idiom, iridium, presidium, rubidium, post meridiem, ante meridiem

iding \īd-iŋ\ riding, siding, tiding, abiding, confiding, joyriding, law-abiding, nondividing

idiom \id-ē-əm\ see IDIEM

idious \id-ē-əs\ hideous, fastidious, insidious, invidious, perfidious

idity \id-ət-ē\ quiddity, acidity, aridity, avidity, cupidity, fluidity, flaccidity, floridity, frigidity, gelidity, gravidity, hispidity, humidity, hybridity, limpidity, liquidity, lividity,

lucidity, morbidity, rabidity,
rapidity, rigidity, sapidity,
solidity, stupidity, tepidity,
timidity, torridity, turbidity,
turgidity, validity, vapidity,
viridity, viscidity, illiquidity,
insipidity, intrepidity,
invalidity

idium \id-ē-əm\ see IDIEM

idle \īd-ᵊl\ see IDAL

idlesse \īd-ləs\ see IDELESS

¹**ido** \īd-ō\ dido, Dido, fido

²**ido** \ēd-ō\ see ¹EDO

idol \īd-ᵊl\ see IDAL

idst \idst\ didst, midst, amidst

¹**idual** \ij-wəl\ residual,
individual

²**idual** \ij-əl\ see IGIL

idulent \ij-ə-lənt\ see IGILANT

idulous \ij-ə-ləs\ stridulous,
acidulous

idus \īd-əs\ see IDAS

iduum \ij-ə-wəm\ triduum,
residuum

idy \īd-ē\ see IDAY

idyll \īd-ᵊl\ see IDAL

¹**ie** \ā\ see ¹AY

²**ie** \ē\ see ¹EE

³**ie** \ī\ see ¹Y

iece \ēs\ cease, crease, fleece,
grease, kris, lease, niece,
peace, piece, apiece,
Burmese, camise, caprice,
cerise, chemise, Chinese,
codpiece, coulisse,
crosspiece, decease, decrease,

degrease, earpiece, eyepiece,
fieldpiece, grandniece,
hairpiece, headpiece,
heelpiece, increase, lend-
lease, mouthpiece, nosepiece,
obese, pelisse, police, release, release, seapiece,
shankpiece, showpiece,
sidepiece, stringpiece,
sublease, surcease, tailpiece,
timepiece, toepiece, two-
piece, valise, workpiece,
afterpiece, altarpiece,
Amboinese, Annamese,
Assamese, Balinese,
Brooklynese, Cantonese,
centerpiece, chimneypiece,
diocese, directrice, ex libris,
expertise, Faeroese,
frontispiece, mantelpiece,
masterpiece, Nipponese,
Pekinese, Pekingese,
Portugese, predecease,
rerelease, Siamese, Sinhalese,
verdigris, archdiocese,
computerese, officialese,
telegraphese, Vietnamese,
educationese

iecer \ē-sər\ see ¹EASER

¹**ied** \ēd\ see EED

²**ied** \ēt\ see ¹EAT

³**ied** \īd\ see ¹IDE

¹**ief** \ēf\ beef, brief, chief, fief,
grief, kef, leaf, lief, reef,
sheaf, thief, belief, debrief,
endleaf, enfeoff, flyleaf,

loose-leaf, massif, motif, naif, relief, sharif, sherif, shinleaf, bas-relief, cloverleaf, disbelief, handkerchief, leatherleaf, neckerchief, leitmotiv, misbelief, overleaf, unbelief, waterleaf, aperitif

²**ief** \ēv\ see ¹EAVE

iefless \ē-fləs\ briefless, leafless

iefly \ē-flē\ briefly, chiefly

ieg \ēg\ see IGUE

¹**iege** \ēj\ liege, siege, besiege, prestige

²**iege** \ēzh\ see ¹IGE

ieger \ē-jər\ see EDURE

iek \ēk\ see ¹EAK

¹**iel** \ēl\ see ²EAL

²**iel** \ī-əl\ see ¹IAL

iela \el-ə\ see ELLA

ield \ēld\ bield, field, keeled, shield, weald, wheeled, wield, yield, afield, airfield, backfield, brickfield, coalfield, cornfield, downfield, four-wheeled, goldfield, grainfield, infield, midfield, outfield, playfield, snowfield, subfield, unsealed, upfield, well-heeled, windshield, battlefield, broken-field, chesterfield, color-field, track-and-field, unaneled—*also pasts of verbs listed at* ²EAL

ielder \ēl-dər\ fielder, shielder,

wielder, yielder, infielder, outfielder

ieler \ē-lər\ see EALER

ieless \ī-ləs\ see ILUS

¹**ieling** \ē-lən\ see ELIN

²**ieling** \ē-liŋ\ see EELING

¹**iem** \ē-əm\ see ¹EUM

²**iem** \ī-əm\ see IAM

ien \ēn\ see ³INE

ience \ī-əns\ see IANCE

iend \end\ see END

iendless \en-ləs\ see ENDLESS

iendliness \en-lē-nəs\ see ENDLINESS

iendly \en-lē\ see ENDLY

iene \ēn\ see ³INE

¹**iener** \ē-nər\ see EANER

²**iener** \ē-nē\ see ¹INI

ienic \en-ik\ see ²ENIC

ienics \en-iks\ see ENICS

ienie \ē-nē\ see ¹INI

ienist \ē-nəst\ see ²INIST

iennes \en\ see ¹EN

ient \ī-ənt\ see IANT

¹**ier** \ir\ see ²EER

²**ier** \ē-ər\ see ¹EER

³**ier** \īr\ see ¹IRE

ierate \ir-ət\ see IRIT

ierce \irs\ birse, fierce, pierce, tierce, transpierce

¹**iere** \er\ see ⁴ARE

²**iere** \ir\ see ²EER

iered \ird\ see ¹EARD

ieria \ir-ē-ə\ see ¹ERIA

ierial \ir-ē-əl\ see ERIAL

ierian \ir-ē-ən\ see ¹ERIAN

ierly \ir-lē\ see ¹EARLY
iersman \irz-mən\ see EERSMAN
iery \ī-rē\ see ¹IARY
ies \ēz\ see EZE
iesel \ē-zəl\ see EASEL
ieseling \ēz-liŋ\ see ESLING
iesian \ē-zhən\ see ¹ESIAN
iesis \ī-ə-səs\ see IASIS
iesling \ēz-liŋ\ see ESLING
iest \ēst\ see ¹EAST
iestly \ēst-lē\ see EASTLY
iet \ī-ət\ diet, fiat, quiet, riot,
   striate, disquiet, unquiet
ietal \ī-ət-ᵊl\ parietal, societal,
   varietal
ieter \ī-ət-ər\ dieter, quieter,
   rioter, proprietor
ietor \ī-ət-ər\ see IETER
iety \ī-ət-ē\ piety, anxiety,
   dubiety, impiety, nimiety,
   propriety, satiety, sobriety,
   society, variety, contrariety,
   impropriety, inebriety,
   insobriety, notoriety
ieu \ü\ see ¹EW
ieur \ir\ see ²EER
ievable \ē-və-bəl\ see EIVABLE
ieval \ē-vəl\ evil, shrieval,
   weevil, coeval, khedival,
   primeval, reprieval, retrieval,
   upheaval, medieval
¹ieve \iv\ see ²IVE
²ieve \ēv\ see ¹EAVE
ieved \ēvd\ see EAVED
ievement \ēv-mənt\ see
   EVEMENT

iever \ē-vər\ beaver, cleaver,
   fever, griever, leaver, reaver,
   reiver, weaver, achiever,
   believer, conceiver, deceiver,
   enfever, perceiver, receiver,
   reliever, retriever, upheaver,
   school-leaver, transceiver,
   cantilever, disbeliever,
   misbeliever, misconceiver,
   unbeliever, overachiever,
   underachiever
ievish \ē-vish\ see EEVISH
¹ievo \ē-vō\ see EVO
²ievo \ä-vō\ see AVO
ievous \ē-vəs\ see EVOUS
ieze \ēz\ see EZE
¹if \if\ see IFF
²if \ēf\ see ¹IEF
ife \īf\ fife, knife, life, rife,
   strife, wife, alewife,
   drawknife, fishwife,
   goodwife, half-life,
   housewife, jackknife,
   loosestrife, lowlife, mid-life,
   nightlife, oldwife, penknife,
   pro-life, true-life, wakerife,
   wildlife, afterlife, antilife,
   Duncan Phyfe, pocketknife
ifeless \ī-fləs\ lifeless,
   strifeless, wifeless
ifer \ī-fər\ see IPHER
iferous \if-rəs\ coniferous,
   floriferous, lactiferous,
   luciferous, pestiferous,
   somniferous, splendiferous,
   vociferous, carboniferous,

luminiferous, odoriferous,
salutiferous, seminiferous,
soporiferous, sudoriferous

ifery \ if-rē \ midwifery,
periphery

iff \ if \ biff, cliff, glyph, if, jiff,
kif, miff, quiff, riff, Riff,
skiff, sniff, spliff, stiff, tiff,
whiff, midriff, triglyph,
anaglyph, bindle stiff,
hieroglyph, hippogriff,
logograph, petroglyph

iffany \ if-ə-nē \ see IPHONY

iffed \ ift \ see IFT

iffen \ if-ən \ see IFFIN

iffian \ if-ē-ən \ Riffian,
Pecksniffian

iffin \ if-ən \ griffin, griffon,
stiffen, tiffin

iffish \ if-ish \ sniffish, stiffish

iffle \ if-əl \ piffle, riffle, skiffle,
sniffle, whiffle

iffler \ if-lər \ riffler, sniffler,
whiffler

iffness \ if-nəs \ stiffness,
swiftness

iffon \ if-ən \ see IFFIN

iffy \ if-ē \ iffy, cliffy, jiffy,
sniffy, spiffy

ific \ if-ik \ glyphic, calcific,
febrific, horrific, magnific,
pacific, prolific, salvific,
specific, terrific, vivific,
anaglyphic, beatific, calorific,
colorific, felicific, frigorific,
hieroglyphic, honorific,

scientific, soporific, sudorific,
tenebrific, prescientific

ifical \ if-i-kəl \ magnifical,
pontifical

ificate \ if-i-kət \ certificate,
pontificate

ificent \ if-ə-sənt \ magnificent,
omnificent

ifle \ ī-fəl \ rifle, stifle, trifle

ifling \ ī-fliŋ \ rifling, stifling,
trifling

ift \ ift \ drift, gift, grift, lift, rift,
shift, shrift, sift, squiffed,
swift, thrift, adrift, airlift,
blueshift, downshift, face-lift,
festschrift, forklift,
frameshift, gearshift,
makeshift, redshift, shoplift,
snowdrift, spendthrift,
spindrift, spoondrift, unshift,
uplift, upshift—*also pasts of
verbs listed at* IFF

ifter \ if-tər \ drifter, snifter,
swifter, sceneshifter,
shoplifter

ifth \ ith \ see ²ITH

iftness \ if-nəs \ see IFFNESS

ifty \ if-tē \ drifty, fifty, nifty,
shifty, thrifty, fifty-fifty

ig \ ig \ big, brig, dig, fig, frig,
gig, grig, jig, pig, prig, rig,
sprig, swig, trig, twig, vig,
Whig, wig, zig, bagwig,
bigwig, earwig, hedgepig,
lime-twig, renege, shindig,
unrig, caprifig, infra dig,

jury-rig, periwig, thimblerig, whirligig, thingamajig

¹**iga** \ē-gə\ Vega, viga, omega, quadriga

²**iga** \ī-gə\ see AIGA

igamous \ig-ə-məs\ bigamous, polygamous

igamy \ig-ə-mē\ bigamy, digamy, polygamy

¹**igan** \ī-gən\ ligan, tigon

²**igan** \ig-ən\ see IGGIN

igand \ig-ənd\ brigand, ligand

igas \ī-gəs\ see YGOUS

igate \ig-ət\ see ¹IGOT

¹**ige** \ēzh\ siege, prestige, noblesse oblige

²**ige** \ēj\ see ¹IEGE

igel \ij-əl\ see IGIL

igenous \ij-ə-nəs\ see IGINOUS

igeon \ij-ən\ see YGIAN

iger \ī-gər\ tiger, braunschweiger

igerent \ij-rənt\ belligerent, refrigerant, cobelligerent

iggan \ig-ən\ see IGGIN

iggard \ig-ərd\ figured, niggard, triggered—*also pasts of verbs listed at* IGGER

igged \igd\ twigged, wigged, bewigged, cat-rigged, square-rigged, periwigged—*also pasts of verbs listed at* IG

igger \ig-ər\ bigger, chigger, digger, jigger, nigger, rigger, rigor, snigger, swigger, trigger, vigor, vigour,

ditchdigger, outrigger, rejigger, reneger, square-rigger, thimblerigger

iggered \ig-ərd\ see IGGARD

iggery \ig-ə-rē\ piggery, priggery, Whiggery

iggie \ig-ē\ see IGGY

iggin \ig-ən\ biggin, piggin, wigan, balbriggan

iggish \ig-ish\ biggish, piggish, priggish, Whiggish

iggle \ig-əl\ giggle, higgle, jiggle, niggle, sniggle, squiggle, wiggle, wriggle

iggler \ig-lər\ giggler, higgler, niggler, wiggler, wriggler

iggy \ig-ē\ biggie, twiggy

igh \ī\ see ¹Y

ighed \īd\ see ¹IDE

ighland \ī-lənd\ highland, island

ighlander \ī-lən-dər\ highlander, islander

ighly \ī-lē\ see YLY

ighness \ī-nəs\ see ¹INUS

ight \īt\ see ¹ITE

ightable \īt-ə-bəl\ see ¹ITABLE

ighted \īt-əd\ sighted, whited, attrited, benighted, clear-sighted, farsighted, foresighted, longsighted, nearsighted, sharp-sighted, shortsighted, skylighted, united—*also pasts of verbs listed at* ¹ITE

ighten \īt-ᵊn\ brighten, chitin,

chiton, frighten, heighten, lighten, tighten, titan, triton, whiten, enlighten

ightener\īt-nər\brightener, lightener, tightener, whitener

ightening\īt-niŋ\see IGHTNING

ighter\īt-ər\see ¹ITER

ightful\īt-fəl\frightful, rightful, spiteful, sprightful, delightful, despiteful, foresightful, insightful

ightie\īt-ē\see ²ITE

ightily\īt-ᵊl-ē\flightily, mightily

ightiness\īt-ē-nəs\flightiness, mightiness, almightiness

ighting\īt-iŋ\see ITING

ightless\īt-ləs\flightless, lightless, sightless

ightly\īt-lē\knightly, lightly, nightly, rightly, sightly, sprightly, whitely, fortnightly, midnightly, unsightly—*also adverbs formed by adding -ly to adjectives listed at* ¹ITE

ightment\īt-mənt\see ITEMENT

ightning\īt-niŋ\lightning, belt-tightening

ightn't\īt-ᵊnt\see ITANT

ights\īts\lights, nights, tights, footlights, houselights, weeknights—*also plurals and possessives of nouns and third singular presents of verbs listed at* ¹ITE

ightsome\īt-səm\lightsome, delightsome

ighty\īt-ē\see ²ITE

igian\ij-ən\see YGIAN

igid\ij-əd\frigid, rigid

igil\ij-əl\Rigel, sigil, strigil, vigil, residual

igilant\ij-ə-lənt\vigilant, acidulent

igine\ij-ə-nē\polygyny, aborigine

iginous\ij-ə-nəs\caliginous, fuliginous, indigenous, polygynous, vertiginous

igion\ij-ən\see YGIAN

igious\ij-əs\litigious, prestigious, prodigious, religious, irreligious

igit\ij-ət\see IDGET

iglet\ig-lət\piglet, wiglet

¹igm\im\see ¹IM

²igm\īm\see ¹IME

igma\ig-mə\sigma, stigma, enigma, kerygma

igment\ig-mənt\figment, pigment

ign\īn\see ¹INE

ignable\ī-nə-bəl\see INABLE

ignancy\ig-nən-sē\benignancy, malignancy

ignant\ig-nənt\benignant, indignant, malignant

igned\īnd\see ¹IND

igneous\ig-nē-əs\igneous, ligneous

igner\ī-nər\see ¹INER

igness \ig-nəs\ bigness, Cygnus

ignet \ig-nət\ see YGNET

igning \ī-niŋ\ see INING

ignity \ig-nət-ē\ dignity, indignity, malignity

ignly \īn-lē\ see ¹INELY

ignment \īn-mənt\ alignment, assignment, confinement, consignment, enshrinement, refinement, nonalignment, realignment

ignon \in-yən\ see INION

ignor \ē-nyər\ see ENIOR

¹igo \ī-gō\ prurigo, vitiligo

²igo \ē-gō\ see EGO

igoe \ē-gō\ see EGO

igon \ī-gən\ see ¹IGAN

igor \ig-ər\ see IGGER

igorous \ig-rəs\ rigorous, vigorous

¹igot \ig-ət\ bigot, frigate, gigot, spigot

²igot \ik-ət\ see ICKET

igour \ig-ər\ see IGGER

igrapher \ig-rə-fər\ calligrapher, epigrapher, polygrapher, serigrapher

igraphist \ig-rə-fəst\ calligraphist, epigraphist, polygraphist

igraphy \ig-rə-fē\ calligraphy, epigraphy, pseudepigraphy

igue \ēg\ gigue, league, blitzkrieg, colleague, fatigue, garigue, intrigue, renege, sitzkrieg, squeteague, wampumpeag

iguer \ē-gər\ see EAGER

iguous \ig-yə-wəs\ ambiguous, contiguous, exiguous, unambiguous

igured \ig-ərd\ see IGGARD

ii \ī\ see ¹Y

iing \ē-iŋ\ see EEING

ija \ē-jə\ see EGIA

ijah \ī-jə\ Elijah, steatopygia

ijl \īl\ see ¹ILE

¹ik \ik\ see ICK

²ik \ēk\ see ¹EAK

¹ika \ē-kə\ pika, theca, areca, eureka, paprika, oiticica, bibliotheca

²ika \ī-kə\ see ¹ICA

¹ike \ī-kē\ Nike, Psyche, crikey, spiky

²ike \īk\ bike, caique, dike, fyke, haik, hike, kike, like, mike, Mike, pike, psych, shrike, sike, spike, strike, tyke, alike, belike, catlike, childlike, clocklike, dislike, fly-strike, garpike, godlike, handspike, hitchhike, homelike, lifelike, mislike, pealike, prooflike, push-bike, rampike, restrike, scalelike, sheaflike, shunpike, suchlike, ten-strike, turnpike, unlike, Vandyke, warlike, wifelike, winglike, berrylike, businesslike, fatherlike,

ladylike, look-alike,
machinelike, marlinespike,
minibike, motorbike,
rubberlike, soundalike,
thunderstrike, womanlike,
workmanlike,
unsportsmanlike
³**ike**\ik\see ICK
¹**iked**\īkt\liked, piked, spiked,
vandyked—*also pasts of
verbs listed at* ²IKE
²**iked**\ī-kəd\see YCAD
iken\ī-kən\see ¹ICHEN
iker\ī-kər\biker, diker, duiker,
hiker, piker, spiker, striker,
disliker, hitchhiker,
shunpiker, minibiker
ikey\ī-kē\see ¹IKE
ikh\ēk\see ¹EAK
¹**iki**\ik-ē\see ICKY
²**iki**\ē-kē\see EAKY
iking\ī-kiŋ\liking, striking,
Viking, shunpiking
iky\ī-kē\see ¹IKE
il\il\see ILL
¹**ila**\il-ə\see ²ILLA
²**ila**\ē-lə\see ELA
ilage\ī-lij\mileage, silage
ilament\il-ə-mənt\filament,
habiliment, monofilament
ilar\ī-lər\dialer, filar, hilar,
miler, smiler, stylar, styler,
tiler, beguiler, bifilar,
compiler, defiler, freestyler,
profiler, rottweiler, stockpiler,
unifilar

ilbert\il-bərt\filbert, gilbert
¹**ilch**\ilk\see ILK
²**ilch**\ilch\filch, milch, zilch
¹**ild**\īld\mild, piled, wild,
brainchild, godchild,
grandchild, hog-wild, man-
child, pantiled, schoolchild,
self-styled, stepchild—*also
pasts of verbs listed at* ¹ILE
²**ild**\il\see ILL
³**ild**\ilt\see ILT
⁴**ild**\ild\see ILLED
ilder\il-dər\builder, gilder,
guilder, wilder, bewilder,
shipbuilder, upbuilder,
bodybuilder, jerry-builder
ilding\il-diŋ\building, gilding,
hilding, abuilding,
outbuilding, shipbuilding,
bodybuilding—*also present
participles of verbs listed at*
ILLED
ildish\īl-dish\childish, wildish
ildly\īl-lē\childly, mildly,
wildly
¹**ile**\īl\aisle, bile, dial, faille,
file, guile, I'll, isle, lisle,
mile, phial, pile, rile, roil,
smile, spile, stile, style, tile,
trial, vial, vile, viol, while,
wile, aedile, agile, anile,
argyle, audile, awhile, axile,
beguile, compile, condyle,
cross-file, de Stijl, decile,
defile, denial, docile, ductile,
enisle, ensile, erewhile,

erstwhile, espial, exile,
febrile, fictile, fissile, flexile,
fragile, freestyle, futile,
genial, gentile, gracile,
habile, hairstyle, Kabyle,
labile, life-style, meanwhile,
mistral, mobile, motile,
nubile, pantile, penile,
pensile, profile, puerile,
quartile, quintile, reptile,
resile, retrial, revile, sandpile,
scissile, sectile, senile,
servile, sessile, stabile,
stockpile, sundial, tactile,
tensile, textile, turnstile,
unpile, utile, vagile, virile,
woodpile, worthwhile,
afebrile, airmobile,
Anglophile, chamomile,
contractile, crocodile,
discophile, domicile,
endostyle, epistyle, erectile,
extensile, Francophile,
Gallophile, halophile,
homophile, hypostyle,
infantile, interfile, juvenile,
low-profile, mercantile,
negrophile, oenophile,
otherwhile, pedophile,
pennyroyal, percentile,
peristyle, prehensile,
projectile, protractile,
pulsatile, reconcile, refractile,
retractile, self-denial,
Slavophile, spermophile,
thermopile, turophile,

urostyle, versatile, vibratile,
xenophile, ailurophile,
amphiprostyle, audiophile,
bibliophile, fluviatile,
Germanophile, heterophile,
Italophile, nucleophile
²ile \il\ see ILL
³ile \ē-lē\ see EELY
⁴ile \ēl\ see ²EAL
ilead \il-ē-əd\ see ILIAD
ileage \ī-lij\ see ILAGE
ileal \il-ē-əl\ see ¹ILIAL
ileless \īl-ləs\ guileless,
  pileless, smileless
¹iler \ē-lər\ see EALER
²iler \ī-lər\ see ILAR
ileum \il-ē-əm\ see ILIUM
iley \ī-lē\ see YLY
¹ili \il-ē\ see ¹ILLY
²ili \ē-lē\ see EELY
¹ilia \il-ē-ə\ Anglophilia,
  basophilia, coprophilia,
  hemophilia, juvenilia,
  necrophilia, neophilia,
  pedophilia, sensibilia,
  memorabilia
²ilia \il-yə\ sedilia,
  bougainvillea, sensibilia,
  memorabilia
³ilia \ēl-yə\ see ELIA
iliad \il-ē-əd\ Iliad, balm of
  Gilead
¹ilial \il-ē-əl\ filial, ileal,
  familial, unfilial
²ilial \il-yəl\ filial, familial,
  unfilial

¹**ilian** \ il-ē-ən \ Basilian, reptilian, Abbevillian, crocodilian, preexilian, vespertilian

²**ilian** \ il-yən \ see ILLION

ilias \ il-ē-əs \ see ¹ILIOUS

iliate \ il-ē-ət \ ciliate, affiliate

ilic \ il-ik \ killick, acrylic, Cyrillic, dactylic, exilic, hemophilic, idyllic, sibylic, Anglophilic, necrophilic, pedophilic, postexilic, zoophilic, bibliophilic

ilica \ il-i-kə \ silica, basilica

ilican \ il-i-kən \ see ILICON

ilicon \ il-i-kən \ silicon, spillikin, basilican

ilience \ il-yəns \ see ILLIANCE

iliency \ il-yən-sē \ see ILLIANCY

ilient \ il-yənt \ brilliant, resilient

iliment \ il-ə-mənt \ see ILAMENT

¹**iling** \ ī-liŋ \ filing, piling, spiling, styling, tiling, hairstyling

²**iling** \ ē-liŋ \ see EELING

ilion \ il-yən \ see ILLION

¹**ilious** \ il-ē-əs \ punctilious, supercilious, materfamilias, paterfamilias

²**ilious** \ il-yəs \ bilious, atrabilious, supercilious

ilitant \ il-ə-tənt \ militant, rehabilitant

ility \ il-ət-ē \ ability, agility, anility, civility, debility, docility, ductility, facility,

fertility, fragility, futility, gentility, gracility, hostility, humility, lability, mobility, motility, nobility, nubility, scurrility, sectility, senility, stability, sterility, suability, tactility, tranquility, utility, vagility, virility, actability, affability, arability, audibility, bearability, biddability, breathability, brushability, capability, changeability, coilability, contractility, countability, credibility, crossability, culpability, curability, cutability, disability, disutility, drapability, drillability, drinkability, durability, dyeability, edibility, equability, erectility, fallibility, feasibility, fishability, flammability, flexibility, forgeability, formability, frangibility, friability, gullibility, imbecility, immobility, inability, incivility, indocility, infantility, infertility, instability, inutility, juvenility, laudability, leachability, legibility, liability, likability, livability, mailability, meltability, miscibility, movability, mutability, notability,

packability, placability,
plausibility, playability,
portability, possibility,
potability, pregnability,
prehensility, printability,
probability, puerility,
readability, risibility,
roadability, salability,
sensibility, sewability,
shareability, sociability,
solubility, solvability,
spreadability, squeezability,
stainability, stretchability,
tenability, testability,
traceability, treatability,
tunability, usability,
vendability, versatility,
viability, visibility, volatility,
washability, wearability,
wettability, workability,
absorbability, acceptability,
accessibility, accountability,
adaptability, adjustability,
admirability, admissibility,
adoptability, adorability,
advisability, affectability,
agreeability, alterability,
amenability, amiability,
amicability, appealability,
applicability, approachability,
assumability, attainability,
availability, believability,
collapsibility, combustability,
comparability, compatibility,
compensability,
compressability,

computability, conceivability,
conductability, confirmability,
contemptibility,
contractibility, controllability,
convertibility, corrigibility,
corruptibility, cultivability,
damageability, decidability,
deductibility, defeasibility,
defensibility, delectability,
demonstrability, deniability,
dependability, desirability,
destructibility, detachability,
detectability, deterrability,
detonability, digestibility,
dilatability, dispensability,
disposability, dissociability,
dissolubility, distensibility,
distractibility, divisibility,
educability, electability,
eligibility, employability,
enforceability, equitability,
erasability, erodability,
exchangeability, excitability,
excludability, exhaustibility,
expansibility, expendability,
explosibility, exportability,
extensibility, extractibility,
extrudability, fashionability,
fatigability, filterability,
fissionability, formidability,
habitability, heritability,
illegibility, immiscibility,
immovability, immutability,
impalpability, impassability,
impassibility, impeccability,
implacability, implausibility,

impossibility, impregnability,
impressibility, improbability,
improvability, inaudibility,
incapability, incredibility,
indelibility, inductibility,
ineffability, infallibility,
infeasibility, inflammability,
inflexibility, infrangibility,
infusibility, insensibility,
insolubility, insurability,
intangibility, invincibility,
invisibility, irascibility,
irritability, knowledgeability,
machinability,
maintainability,
manageability, marketability,
merchantability,
measurability, modulability,
navigability, negligibility,
nonflammability, openability,
operability, opposability,
palatability, penetrability,
perceptibility, perdurability,
perfectibility, performability,
perishability, permeability,
permissibility, pleasurability,
practicability, preferability,
presentability, preservability,
preventability, processibility,
programmability,
punishability, reasonability,
refundability, reliability,
renewability, repeatability,
reputability, resistibility,
respectability, responsibility,
retrievability, reusability,

reversability, salvageability,
separability, severability,
serviceability, suggestability,
supportability, suppressibility,
survivability, susceptibility,
tolerability, trafficability,
transferability, translatability,
transmissibility,
transplantability,
transportability,
unflappability, unthinkability,
untouchability, variability,
violability, vulnerability,
weatherability, alienability,
analyzability, assimilability,
codifiability,
commensurability,
communicability,
comprehensibility,
decomposability,
deliverability,
discriminability,
disrespectability,
distinguishability,
enumerability,
exceptionability,
hypnotizability, illimitability,
impenetrability,
imperishability,
impermeability,
impermissibility,
imponderability,
impracticability,
impressionability,
inaccessibility,
inadmissibility, inadvisability,

inalterability, inapplicability,
incalculability,
incombustibility,
incomparability,
incompatibility,
incompressibility,
inconceivability,
incontestability,
inconvertibility,
incorrigibility,
incorruptibility,
indefeasibility, indefensibility,
indefinability,
indestructibility,
indigestibility,
indispensability,
indissolubility, indivisibility,
indomitability, indubitability,
ineducability, ineffaceability,
ineligibility, ineluctability,
inevitability, inexhaustibility,
inexplicability,
inexpressibility,
inextricability, inheritability,
insatiability, inseparability,
insociability, insusceptibility,
intelligibility,
interchangeability,
intolerability, invariability,
invulnerability, irreducibility,
irreformability, irrefutability,
irremovability, irrepealability,
irreplaceability,
irrepressibility,
irreproachability,
irresistibility, irresponsibility,

irretrievability, irreversibility,
irrevocability,
maneuverability,
manipulability, negotiability,
polarizability, recognizability,
recoverability, rectifiability,
reprehensibility,
reproducibility,
substitutability,
unacceptability,
unaccountability,
understandability,
undesirability, verifiability,
biodegradability,
differentiability,
inalienability,
incommensurability,
incommunicability,
incomprehensibility,
indefatigability,
indistinguishability,
ineradicability,
incontrovertibility,
irreconcilability,
irreproducibility

ilium \il-ē-əm\ cilium, ileum,
ilium, milium, trillium,
beryllium, penicillium

ilk \ilk\ bilk, ilk, milch, milk,
silk, whelk, buttermilk,
liebfraumilch

ilky \il-kē\ milky, silky

ill \il\ bill, brill, chill, dill,
drill, fill, frill, gill, grill,
grille, hill, ill, kill, krill, mil,
mill, mille, nil, nill, pill,

prill, quill, real, rill, shill,
shrill, sild, sill, skill, spill,
squill, still, swill, thill, thrill,
til, till, trill, twill, vill, will,
anthill, backfill, bluegill,
cranesbill, crossbill, dentil,
distill, doorsill, downhill,
duckbill, dullsville, dunghill,
fiberfill, foothill, freewill,
fulfill, goodwill, gristmill,
handbill, hawksbill, hornbill,
instill, lambkill, landfill,
limekiln, manille, molehill,
mudsill, no-till, playbill,
quadrille, refill, sawmill, self-
will, sheathbill, shoebill,
sidehill, sigil, spadille,
spoonbill, stabile, standstill,
stockstill, storksbill, T-bill,
treadmill, unreal, until,
uphill, vaudeville, waxbill,
waybill, windchill, windmill,
chlorophyll, daffodil,
deshabille, dishabille,
escadrille, espadrille,
Francophil, Hooverville,
overfill, overkill, overspill,
razorbill, rototill, tormentil,
verticil, windowsill,
whippoorwill, winter-kill,
Yggdrasil, acidophil,
ivorybill, run-of-the-mill

I'll \ īl \ see ¹ILE

¹**illa** \ ē-yə \ barilla, cuadrilla,
banderilla, quesadilla,

²**illa** \ il-ə \ pillow, scilla, Scylla,
squilla, villa, willow, ancilla,
axilla, cedilla, chinchilla,
flotilla, gorilla, guerrilla,
manila, megillah, papilla,
perilla, scintilla, vanilla,
camarilla, cascarilla,
granadilla, potentilla,
sabadilla, sapodilla,
sarsaparilla

³**illa** \ ē-ə \ see ¹IA

⁴**illa** \ ēl-yə \ see ELIA

illable \ il-ə-bəl \ billable,
drillable, fillable, spillable,
syllable, tillable, disyllable,
refillable, trisyllable,
decasyllable, monosyllable,
octosyllable, polysyllable,
hendecasyllable

illage \ il-ij \ grillage, millage,
pillage, spillage, tillage,
village, no-tillage, permillage

illah \ il-ə \ see ²ILLA

illain \ il-ən \ see ILLON

illar \ il-ər \ see ILLER

illary \ il-ə-rē \ phyllary,
codicillary

illate \ il-ət \ see ILLET

¹**ille** \ il \ see ILL

²**ille** \ ē \ see ¹EE

³**ille** \ ēl \ see ²EAL

illea \ il-yə \ see ²ILIA

illed \ ild \ build, dilled, gild,
gilled, guild, skilled, twilled,
willed, Brynhild, engild,
gold-filled, goodwilled,
rebuild, self-willed,

spoonbilled, unbuild, unskilled, upbuild, wergild, jerry-build, overbuild, semiskilled—*also pasts of verbs listed at* ILL

illedness \il-nəs\ see ILLNESS

illein \il-ən\ see ILLON

iller \il-ər\ biller, chiller, driller, filler, giller, griller, hiller, killer, miller, pillar, schiller, spiller, swiller, thriller, tiller, triller, axillar, distiller, fulfiller, painkiller, pralltriller, caterpillar, lady-killer, Rototiller—*also comparatives of adjectives listed at* ILL

illery \il-rē\ pillory, artillery, distillery

illes \il-ēz\ see ILLIES

illet \il-ət\ billet, fillet, millet, rillet, skillet, willet, distillate

illful \il-fəl\ skillful, willful, unskillful

illi \il-ē\ see ¹ILLY

¹**illian** \il-ē-ən\ see ¹ILIAN

²**illian** \il-yən\ see ILLION

illiance \il-yəns\ brilliance, resilience

illiancy \il-yən-sē\ brilliancy, resiliency

illiant \il-yənt\ see ILIENT

illick \il-ik\ see ILIC

illie \il-ē\ see ¹ILLY

illies \il-ēz\ willies, Achilles—

also plurals and possessives of nouns listed at ¹ILLY

illikin \il-i-kən\ see ILICON

¹**illin** \il-əm\ see ILLUM

²**illin** \il-ən\ see ILLON

illing \il-iŋ\ billing, drilling, filling, killing, milling, schilling, shilling, skilling, twilling, willing, fulfilling, unwilling

illion \il-yən\ billion, jillion, million, pillion, trillion, zillion, caecilian, Castilian, centillion, civilian, cotillion, decillion, modillion, nonillion, octillion, pavilion, postilion, quadrillion, quintillion, reptilian, septillion, sextillion, toubillion, vaudevillian, vermilion, crocodilian, preexilian, quindecillion, sexdecillion, tredecillion, undecillion, vespertilian, vigintillion, duodecillion, novemdecillion, octodecillion, septendecillion, quattuordecillion

illium \il-ē-əm\ see ILIUM

illness \il-nəs\ chillness, illness, shrillness, stillness, self-willedness

¹**illo** \il-ō\ billow, pillow, willow, Negrillo, tornillo, armadillo, cigarillo, coyotillo, peccadillo

²**illo** \ē-ō\ see ²IO

illon \il-ən\ billon, villain, villein, tefillin

illory \il-rē\ see ILLERY

illous \il-əs\ see ILLUS

¹**illow** \il-ə\ see ²ILLA

²**illow** \il-ō\ see ¹ILLO

illowy \il-ə-wē\ billowy, pillowy, willowy

illum \il-əm\ chillum, tefillin, vexillum

illus \il-əs\ villous, bacillus, lapillus, amaryllis, toga virilis

¹**illy** \il-ē\ billy, chili, chilly, dilly, filly, frilly, gillie, hilly, illy, lily, really, silly, stilly, bacilli, Caerphilly, daylily, guidwillie, hillbilly, piccalilli, rockabilly, willy-nilly

²**illy** \il-lē\ shrilly, stilly

iln \il\ see ILL

¹**ilo** \ī-lō\ milo, phyllo, silo

²**ilo** \ē-lō\ kilo, phyllo

ilom \ī-ləm\ see ILUM

iloquence \il-ə-kwəns\ grandiloquence, magniloquence

iloquent \il-ə-kwənt\ grandiloquent, magniloquent

iloquist \il-ə-kwəst\ soliloquist, ventriloquist

iloquy \il-ə-kwē\ soliloquy, ventriloquy

ilot \ī-lət\ eyelet, islet, pilot, stylet, copilot, autopilot

ils \ils\ fils, grilse

ilse \ils\ see ILS

ilt \ilt\ built, gilt, guilt, hilt, jilt, kilt, lilt, milt, quilt, silt, stilt, tilt, wilt, atilt, bloodguilt, Brunhild, homebuilt, inbuilt, rebuilt, unbuilt, uptilt, carvel-built, clinker-built, custom-built

ilter \il-tər\ filter, kilter, milter, philter

ilth \ilth\ filth, spilth, tilth

iltie \il-tē\ see ILTY

ilton \ilt-ᵊn\ Stilton, Wilton

ilty \il-tē\ guilty, kiltie, milty, silty, bloodguilty

ilum \ī-ləm\ filum, hilum, phylum, whilom, xylem, asylum

ilus \ī-ləs\ eyeless, pilus, stylus, tieless

ily \il-ē\ see ¹ILLY

¹**im** \im\ bream, brim, dim, glim, grim, gym, him, hymn, limb, limn, mim, nim, prim, rim, scrim, shim, skim, slim, swim, trim, vim, whim, bedim, dislimn, forelimb, passim, prelim, Purim, slim-jim, snap-brim, acronym, anonym, antonym, eponym, homonym, metonym, paradigm, paronym, pseudonym, seraphim, synonym, tautonym, toponym, underbrim, ad interim

²im \ēm\ *see* ¹EAM

I'm \īm\ *see* ¹IME

ima \ē-mə\ *see* EMA

imable \ī-mə-bəl\ climable, sublimable, unclimbable

imace \im-əs\ grimace, tzimmes

image \im-ij\ image, scrimmage, self-image, afterimage

iman \ē-mən\ *see* ¹EMON

imate \ī-mət\ climate, primate, acclimate

¹imb \im\ *see* ¹IM

²imb \īm\ *see* ¹IME

imba \im-bə\ limba, kalimba, marimba

imbable \ī-mə-bəl\ *see* IMABLE

imbal \im-bəl\ *see* IMBLE

imbale \im-bəl\ *see* IMBLE

imbed \imd\ limbed, rimmed, clean-limbed—*also pasts of verbs listed at* ¹IM

¹imber \im-bər\ limber, timber, sawtimber, unlimber

²imber \ī-mər\ *see* ¹IMER

imble \im-bəl\ cymbal, gimbal, nimble, symbol, thimble, timbal, timbale, wimble

imbo \im-bō\ bimbo, limbo, akimbo, gumbo-limbo

imbral \am-brəl\ *see* AMBREL

imbre \am-bər\ *see* ²AMBAR

imbrel \im-brəl\ timbrel, whimbrel

imbus \im-bəs\ limbus, nimbus

¹ime \īm\ chime, climb, clime, crime, dime, disme, grime, I'm, lime, mime, prime, rhyme, rime, slime, stime, thyme, time, airtime, all-time, bedtime, begrime, big time, birdlime, daytime, downtime, enzyme, flextime, foretime, halftime, lifetime, longtime, lunchtime, Maytime, mealtime, meantime, nighttime, noontime, old-time, onetime, part-time, pastime, peacetime, playtime, quicklime, ragtime, schooltime, seedtime, small-time, sometime, space-time, springtime, sublime, teatime, two-time, uptime, wartime, aftertime, anytime, beforetime, Christmastime, dinnertime, double-time, harvesttime, Jotunheim, lysozyme, maritime, monorhyme, overtime, pantomime, paradigm, summertime, wintertime, nickel-and-dime

²ime \ēm\ *see* ¹EAM

imel \im-əl\ gimel, gimmal, kümmel

imeless \īm-ləs\ rhymeless, timeless

imely \īm-lē\ primely, timely, untimely

imen \ī-mən\ flyman, hymen, limen, Simon

imeon \ im-ē-ən \ see IMIAN
imeous \ ī-məs \ see IMIS
¹imer \ ī-mər \ chimer, climber,
dimer, mimer, primer,
rhymer, timer, trimer, old-
timer, small-timer, sublimer,
two-timer, wisenheimer
²imer \ im-ər \ see IMMER
imerick \ im-rik \ see YMRIC
imes \ īmz \ times, betimes,
daytimes, sometimes,
betweentimes, oftentimes—
*also plurals and possessives
of nouns and third singular
presents of verbs listed at*
¹IME
imeter \ im-ət-ər \ dimeter,
limiter, scimitar, trimeter,
altimeter, delimiter,
perimeter, tachymeter
imetry \ im-ə-trē \ symmetry,
gravimetry, polarimetry
imian \ im-ē-ən \ Simeon,
simian, Endymion
imic \ im-ik \ see ²YMIC
imical \ im-i-kəl \ inimical,
metonymical, synonymical,
toponymical
imicry \ im-i-krē \ gimmickry,
mimicry
imile \ im-ə-lē \ simile,
swimmily, facsimile
¹iminal \ im-ən-ᵊl \ criminal,
liminal, subliminal,
supraliminal
²iminal \ im-nəl \ see YMNAL

iminy \ im-ə-nē \ see IMONY
imis \ ī-məs \ primus, thymus,
timeous, imprimis, untimeous
imitable \ im-ət-ə-bəl \ imitable,
illimitable, inimitable
imitar \ im-ət-ər \ see IMETER
imiter \ im-ət-ər \ see IMETER
imity \ im-ət-ē \ dimity,
proximity, sublimity,
anonymity, equanimity,
longanimity, magnanimity,
pseudonymity, synonymity,
unanimity, pusillanimity
immable \ im-ə-bəl \ dimmable,
swimmable
immage \ im-ij \ see IMAGE
immal \ im-əl \ see IMEL
immed \ imd \ see IMBED
immer \ im-ər \ brimmer,
dimmer, glimmer, krimmer,
limmer, limner, primer,
shimmer, simmer, skimmer,
swimmer, trimmer—*also
comparatives of adjectives
listed at* ¹IM
immes \ im-əs \ see IMACE
immick \ im-ik \ see ²YMIC
immickry \ im-i-krē \ see IMICRY
immily \ im-ə-lē \ see IMILE
immy \ im-ē \ jimmy, limby,
shimmy, swimmy
imn \ im \ see ¹IM
imner \ im-ər \ see IMMER
imo \ ē-mō \ primo, sentimo
imon \ ī-mən \ see IMEN

imony \im-ə-nē\ simony,
  niminy-piminy
imothy \im-ə-thē\ timothy,
  Timothy, polymathy
imp \imp\ blimp, chimp, crimp,
  gimp, guimpe, imp, limp,
  pimp, primp, scrimp, shrimp,
  simp, skimp, wimp,
  comsymp
impe \imp\ see IMP
imper \im-pər\ limper,
  shrimper, simper, whimper
imping \im-pən\ see YMPAN
impish \im-pish\ blimpish,
  impish
imple \im-pəl\ dimple, pimple,
  simple, wimple, oversimple
imply \im-plē\ dimply, limply,
  pimply, simply
impy \im-pē\ crimpy, gimpy,
  scrimpy, shrimpy, skimpy,
  wimpy
imsy \im-zē\ flimsy, slimsy,
  whimsy
imulus \im-yə-ləs\ limulus,
  stimulus
imus \ī-məs\ see IMIS
imy \ī-mē\ grimy, limey, limy,
  rimy, slimy, stymie, thymy
¹in \in\ been, bin, blin, chin,
  din, fin, Finn, gin, grin,
  Gwyn, hin, in, inn, kin, linn,
  pin, shin, Shin, sin, skin,
  spin, thin, tin, twin, whin,
  win, wyn, yin, again, agin,
  akin, all-in, backspin,

bearskin, begin, bowfin,
break-in, buckskin, built-in,
calfskin, capeskin, cave-in,
chagrin, close in, clothespin,
coonskin, crankpin, cut-in,
deerskin, doeskin, drive-in,
drop-in, duckpin, dustbin,
fill-in, foreskin, goatskin,
hairpin, has-been, headpin,
herein, kidskin, kingpin,
lambskin, lead-in, lie-in,
linchpin, live-in, lived-in,
lobe-fin, locked-in, look-in,
love-in, moleskin, Nankin,
ninepin, no-win, oilskin,
Pekin, pigskin, pinyin, plug-
in, pushpin, redskin, ruin,
run-in, saimin, scarfpin,
scarfskin, sealskin, set-in,
sharkskin, sheepskin, shoo-in,
shut-in, sidespin, sit-in, sleep-
in, snakeskin, stand-in, step-
in, stickpin, swanskin,
tailspin, take-in, teach-in,
tenpin, therein, tholepin,
threadfin, throw-in, tie-in,
tiepin, tip-in, toe-in, trade-in,
tuned-in, turn-in, unpin,
walk-in, weigh-in, wherein,
wineskin, within, woolskin,
write-in, candlepin, catechin,
Lohengrin, lying-in,
mandolin, maximin, Mickey
Finn, onionskin, palanquin,
underpin, underspin,
Vietminh, violin, whipper-in

²**in** \ēn\ see ³INE
³**in** \an\ see ⁵AN
⁴**in** \aⁿ\ coup de main, doyen, moulin, serin, coq au vin, fleur de coin
¹**ina** \ī-nə\ china, mina, mynah, angina, Lucina, piscina, salina, shechinah, vagina, Cochin China, kamaaina, Poland China
²**ina** \ē-nə\ kina, Shina, plena, vena, vina, arena, Athena, cantina, catena, coquina, euglena, farina, fontina, hyena, kachina, marina, novena, patina, piscina, platina, retsina, salina, sestina, Shechinah, subpoena, verbena, ballerina, casuarina, catilena, cavatina, concertina, javelina, ocarina, palomino, semolina, signorina, sonatina
inable \ī-nə-bəl\ minable, consignable, declinable, definable, inclinable, indeclinable, indefinable
¹**inah** \ē-nə\ see ²INA
²**inah** \ī-nə\ see ¹INA
¹**inal** \īn-ᵊl\ clinal, final, rhinal, spinal, trinal, vinyl, matutinal, officinal, quarterfinal, semifinal, serotinal
²**inal** \ēn-ᵊl\ see ENAL

inally \īn-ᵊl-ē\ clinally, finally, spinally, matutinally
inary \ī-nə-rē\ binary, trinary
inative \in-ət-iv\ see INITIVE
inc \iŋk\ see INK
inca \iŋ-kə\ Inca, vinca
incal \iŋ-kəl\ see INKLE
incan \iŋ-kən\ Incan, Lincoln
ince \ins\ blintz, chintz, mince, prince, quince, rinse, since, wince, convince, evince, shinsplints
incely \in-slē\ princely, tinselly
incer \in-chər\ see INCHER
inch \inch\ chinch, cinch, clinch, finch, flinch, inch, lynch, pinch, squinch, winch, bullfinch, goldfinch, greenfinch, hawfinch, unclinch
incher \in-chər\ clincher, flincher, lyncher, pincer, pincher, wincher, affenpinscher, penny-pincher, Doberman pinscher
inching \in-chiŋ\ unflinching, penny-pinching
incible \in-sə-bəl\ principal, principle, vincible, evincible, invincible, inconvincible
incing \in-siŋ\ ginseng, mincing, convincing, unconvincing
incipal \in-sə-bəl\ see INCIBLE
inciple \in-sə-bəl\ see INCIBLE
incky \iŋ-kē\ see INKY

incoln \ in-kən \ see INCAN

inct \ iŋt \ linked, tinct, distinct, extinct, instinct, precinct, succinct, unlinked, indistinct

inction \ iŋ-shən \ distinction, extinction, contradistinction

inctive \ iŋ-tiv \ distinctive, extinctive, instinctive, indistinctive

incture \ iŋ-chər \ cincture, tincture

¹ind \ īnd \ bind, blind, find, grind, hind, kind, mind, rind, signed, spined, tined, wind, wynd, affined, behind, confined, inclined, night-blind, purblind, refined, remind, rewind, sand-blind, snow-blind, spellbind, stone-blind, streamlined, unbind, unkind, unwind, color-blind, double-blind, gavelkind, gravel-blind, hoodman-blind, humankind, mastermind, nonaligned, single-blind, unaligned, undersigned, well-defined, womankind—*also pasts of verbs listed at* ¹INE

²ind \ ind \ finned, Ind, skinned, wind, crosswind, downwind, exscind, prescind, rescind, soft-finned, thick-skinned, thin-skinned, upwind, whirlwind, woodwind, Amerind, spiny-finned, tamarind—*also pasts of verbs listed at* ¹IN

³ind \ int \ see INT

¹inded \ īn-dəd \ minded, rinded, broad-minded, fair-minded, high-minded, large-minded, like-minded, low-minded, right-minded, small-minded, strong-minded, tough-minded, weak-minded, absentminded, bloody-minded, civic-minded, evil-minded, feebleminded, narrow-minded, open-minded, simpleminded, single-minded, social-minded, tender-minded—*also regular pasts of verbs listed at* ¹IND

²inded \ in-dəd \ brinded, windowed, long-winded, short-winded, broken-winded—*also pasts of verbs listed at* ²IND

¹inder \ īn-dər \ binder, blinder, finder, grinder, hinder, minder, winder, bookbinder, faultfinder, highbinder, pathfinder, self-binder, sidewinder, spellbinder, stem-winder, viewfinder, organ-grinder—*also comparatives of adjectives listed at* ¹IND

²inder \ in-dər \ cinder, hinder, tinder

indful \ īn-fəl \ mindful, remindful, unmindful

indhi \ in-dē \ see INDY

indi \in-dē\ see INDY
indic \in-dik\ Indic, syndic
inding \īn-diŋ\ binding, finding, winding, bookbinding, fact-finding, faultfinding, pathfinding, self-winding, stem-winding
indlass \in-ləs\ see INLESS
indle \in-dᵊl\ brindle, dwindle, kindle, spindle, swindle, enkindle
indless \īn-ləs\ kindless, mindless, spineless
¹indling \in-lən\ pindling, spindling
²indling \in-liŋ\ dwindling, kindling, pindling, spindling
¹indly \in-lē\ see INLY
²indly \īn-lē\ see ¹INELY
indness \īn-nəs\ blindness, fineness, kindness, purblindness, unkindness, loving-kindness
indowed \in-dəd\ see ²INDED
indy \in-dē\ Hindi, lindy, shindy, Sindhi, windy
¹ine \īn\ bine, brine, chine, cline, dine, dyne, eyen, fine, Jain, kine, line, mine, nine, pine, rind, shine, shrine, sign, spine, spline, stein, swine, syne, thine, tine, trine, twine, vine, whine, wine, A-line, affine, airline, align, alkyne, alpine, assign, balkline, baseline, beeline,

benign, bloodline, bovine, bowline, breadline, buntline, byline, canine, caprine, carbine, carmine, cervine, clothesline, coastline, combine, compline, condign, confine, consign, corvine, cutline, dateline, deadline, decline, define, design, divine, dragline, driveline, earthshine, enshrine, ensign, entwine, equine, feline, ferine, fraulein, frontline, gantline, grapevine, guideline, hairline, hard-line, headline, hemline, hipline, incline, indign, intertwine, jawline, lang syne, lifeline, longline, lupine, mainline, malign, midline, moline, moonshine, off-line, old-line, opine, outline, outshine, ovine, Pauline, Petrine, pipeline, piscine, pontine, porcine, potline, propine, quinine, rapine, recline, redline, refine, reline, repine, resign, roofline, Sabine, saline, setline, shoreline, sideline, Sixtine, skyline, straight-line, strandline, streamline, strychnine, subline, sunshine, supine, syncline, taurine, touchline, towline, tramline, trephine, trotline, truckline, tumpline,

turbine, untwine, ursine,
vespine, vulpine, waistline,
woodbine, zayin, zebrine,
aerodyne, alkaline,
androgyne, anodyne,
anserine, anticline, aquiline,
argentine, asinine, auld lang
syne, borderline, bottom-line,
Byzantine, calamine,
calcimine, Caroline,
catarrhine, celandine,
centerline, cisalpine,
clandestine, colubrine,
columbine, Columbine,
concubine, countermine,
countersign, crystalline,
disincline, eglantine,
endocrine, exocrine,
falconine, fescennine,
Frankenstein, gregarine,
infantine, interline, iodine,
Johannine, leonine,
monkeyshine, muscadine,
opaline, palatine, passerine,
porcupine, psittacine, realign,
redefine, redesign, riverine,
saccharine, sapphirine,
saturnine, serpentine,
sibylline, sixty-nine,
subalpine, Theatine,
timberline, turnverein,
turpentine, underline,
undermine, Ursuline, uterine,
valentine, vespertine,
viperine, vulturine, waterline,
zibeline, accipitrine,

adamantine, adulterine,
alexandrine, amaranthine,
Capitoline, elephantine
²**ine** \ē-nā\ fine, wahine
³**ine** \ēn\ bean, clean, dean,
dene, e'en, gene, glean,
green, jean, keen, lean, lien,
mean, mesne, mien, peen,
preen, quean, queen, scene,
screen, seen, sheen, shin, sin,
skean, skene, spean, spleen,
teen, tween, wean, ween,
wheen, yean, baleen,
beguine, Beguine, between,
boreen, bovine, buckbean,
caffeine, canteen, carbine,
careen, chlorine, chopine,
chorine, citrine, codeine,
colleen, convene, cotquean,
cuisine, dasheen, dauphine,
demean, demesne, dentine,
dry-clean, dudeen, eighteen,
Essene, fanzine, fascine,
fifteen, fourteen, gamine,
gangrene, glassine, gyrene,
Hellene, hoatzin, holstein,
horsebean, houseclean,
hygiene, khamsin, Ladin,
lateen, latrine, machine,
malines, marine, moline,
moreen, morphine, nankeen,
Nicene, nineteen, nongreen,
obscene, offscreen, on-screen,
patine, piscine, poteen,
praline, preteen, pristine,
propine, protein, quinine,

ratteen, ravine, routine,
saline, saltine, sardine,
sateen, scalene, serene,
shagreen, shebeen, siren,
Sistine, sixteen, Slovene,
soybean, spalpeen,
strychnine, subteen,
sunscreen, takin, taurine,
terrene, terrine, thirteen,
tontine, tureen, umpteen,
unclean, undine, unseen,
vaccine, vitrine, windscreen,
yestreen, zechin, almandine,
argentine, barkentine,
bengaline, bombazine,
brigandine, brigantine,
brilliantine, Byzantine,
carotene, carrageen,
celandine, clandestine,
columbine, contravene, crepe
de chine, crystalline,
damascene, Dexedrine,
Dramamine, duvetyn,
eglantine, endocrine, Eocene,
epicene, estaurine, evergreen,
fescennine, figurine, fluorine,
gabardine, gaberdine,
gadarene, galantine, gasoline,
Ghibelline, go-between,
grenadine, Gretna Green,
guillotine, Halloween, haute
cuisine, Hippocrene,
histamine, Holocene, in-
between, indigene, intervene,
kerosene, langoustine,
legatine, libertine, limousine,

M16, magazine, mangosteen,
margravine, melamine,
messaline, Methedrine,
mezzanine, Miocene,
mousseline, Nazarene,
nectarine, nicotine, overseen,
opaline, organzine, palanquin,
palatine, pelerine, percaline,
peregrine, philhellene,
Philistine, Pleistocene,
Pliocene, riverine, quarantine,
reserpine, saccharine,
sapphirine, schizophrene,
serpentine, seventeen,
silkaline, Stelazine,
submarine, subroutine,
supervene, tambourine,
tangerine, Theatine,
tourmaline, trampoline,
transmarine, travertine,
Tridentine, Vaseline,
velveteen, wintergreen,
wolverine, Ursuline,
adamantine, alexandrine,
amphetamine, aquamarine,
Benedictine, elephantine,
internecine, nouvelle cuisine,
Oligocene, Paleocene,
ultramarine, antihistamine,
oleomargarine
⁴ine \ in-ē \ see INNY
⁵ine \ ē-nē \ see ¹INI
⁶ine \ ən \ see UN
inea \ in-ē \ see INNY
ineal \ in-ē-əl \ finial, lineal,

matrilineal, patrilineal,
unilineal

ined \īnd\ see ¹IND

ineless \īn-ləs\ see INDLESS

¹**inely** \īn-lē\ blindly, finely,
kindly, affinely, condignly,
equinely, felinely, purblindly,
unkindly

²**inely** \ēn-lē\ see ¹EANLY

inement \īn-mənt\ see IGNMENT

ineness \īn-nəs\ see INDNESS

ineous \in-ē-əs\ gramineous,
sanguineous, consanguineous,
ignominious

¹**iner** \ī-nər\ briner, diner, finer,
liner, miner, minor, shiner,
Shriner, signer, twiner,
whiner, airliner, aligner,
byliner, combiner, confiner,
cosigner, definer, designer,
diviner, eyeliner, hardliner,
headliner, incliner, jetliner,
long-liner, moonshiner, one-
liner, recliner, refiner,
repiner, sideliner, soft-liner,
streamliner, Canis Minor,
forty-niner, party-liner, Ursa
Minor, superliner

²**iner** \ē-nər\ see EANER

¹**inery** \īn-rē\ finery, pinery,
vinery, winery, refinery

²**inery** \ēn-rē\ see EANERY

ines \ēn\ see ³INE

inest \ī-nəst\ see ¹INIST

inet \in-ət\ see INNET

inew \in-yü\ see INUE

ing \iŋ\ bring, Ching, cling,
ding, fling, king, ling, Ming,
ping, ring, sing, sling, spring,
sting, string, swing, thing,
wing, wring, zing,
backswing, bedspring, bi-
swing, bitewing, bowstring,
bullring, clearwing,
downswing, drawstring,
earring, first-string, forewing,
G-string, greenwing,
hairspring, hamstring,
handspring, headspring,
heartstring, lacewing,
lapwing, latchstring,
mainspring, O-ring, offspring,
plaything, redwing,
shoestring, unsling, unstring,
upspring, upswing,
wellspring, whitewing, wind-
wing, wingding, à la king,
anything, buck-and-wing,
ding-a-ling, double-ring,
everything, innerspring,
pigeonwing, underwing

inga \iŋ-gə\ anhinga, syringa

inge \inj\ binge, cringe, dinge,
fringe, hinge, singe, springe,
swinge, tinge, twinge,
impinge, infringe, syringe,
unhinge

inged \iŋd\ ringed, stringed,
winged, net-winged—*also
regular pasts of verbs listed
at* ING

ingement \ inj-mənt \
　impingement, infringement
ingency \ in-jən-sē \ stringency,
　astringency, contingency
ingent \ in-jənt \ stringent,
　astringent, constringent,
　contingent, refringent
¹inger \ iŋ-ər \ bringer, clinger,
　flinger, pinger, ringer, singer,
　springer, stinger, stringer,
　swinger, winger, wringer,
　zinger, folksinger, gunslinger,
　humdinger, left-winger,
　mudslinger, right-winger,
　mastersinger, Meistersinger,
　minnesinger
²inger \ iŋ-gər \ finger, linger,
　five-finger, forefinger,
　malinger, ladyfinger
³inger \ in-jər \ ginger, injure,
　singer, swinger
ingery \ inj-rē \ gingery, injury
inghy \ iŋ-ē \ see ¹INGY
ingi \ iŋ-ē \ see ¹INGY
ingian \ in-jən \ Thuringian,
　Carlovingian, Carolingian,
　Merovingian
inging \ iŋ-iŋ \ ringing,
　springing, stringing,
　swinging, folksinging, free-
　swinging, gunslinging,
　handwringing, mudslinging,
　upbringing
ingit \ iŋ-kət \ see INKET
ingle \ iŋ-gəl \ cringle, dingle,
　jingle, mingle, shingle,

single, tingle, atingle,
　commingle, immingle, Kriss
　Kringle, surcingle,
　intermingle
ingler \ iŋ-glər \ jingler, shingler
inglet \ iŋ-lət \ kinglet, ringlet,
　winglet
ingletree \ iŋ-gəl-trē \ singletree,
　swingletree
ingly \ iŋ-glē \ jingly, shingly,
　singly, tingly
ingo \ iŋ-gō \ bingo, dingo,
　gringo, jingo, lingo, pingo,
　flamingo, Mandingo
ings \ iŋz \ Kings, eyestrings—
　also plurals and possessives
　of nouns and third singular
　presents of verbs listed at ING
ingue \ aŋ \ see ²ANG
inguish \ iŋ-wish \ distinguish,
　extinguish
¹ingy \ iŋ-ē \ clingy, dinghy,
　springy, stringy, swingy,
　zingy, shilingi
²ingy \ in-jē \ dingy, mingy,
　stingy
inh \ in \ see ¹IN
¹ini \ ē-nē \ beanie, djinni, genie,
　greeny, jinni, sheeny,
　spleeny, teeny, weeny,
　wienie, Alcmene, Athene,
　bikini, linguine, martini,
　rappini, Selene, tahini,
　wahine, zucchini, fantoccini,
　fettucine, malihini, nota bene,

scaloppine, spaghettini, teeny-
weeny, tetrazzini, tortellini
²**ini**\in-ē\see INNY
inia\in-ē-ə\zinnia, gloxinia,
Lavinia
inial\in-ē-əl\see INEAL
¹**inian**\in-ē-ən\Arminian,
Darwinian, Latinian,
Sardinian, Socinian,
Apollinian, Augustinian
²**inian**\in-yən\see INION
¹**inic**\ē-nik\Enoch, nicotinic
²**inic**\in-ik\clinic, cynic,
Finnic, platinic, rabbinic,
Jacobinic, mandarinic,
misogynic, nicotinic,
parafinic
inical\in-i-kəl\binnacle,
clinical, cynical, finical,
pinnacle, dominical,
Jacobinical
inican\in-i-kən\see INIKIN
inikin\in-i-kən\minikin,
Dominican
inim\in-əm\minim,
Houyhnhnm
ining\ī-niŋ\lining, mining,
shining, designing, inclining,
long-lining, interlining,
undesigning
inion\in-yən\minion, minyan,
pinion, piñon, champignon,
dominion, opinion, Sardinian,
Abyssinian
¹**inis**\in-əs\finis, pinnace,
Erinys

²**inis**\ī-nəs\see ¹INUS
inish\in-ish\finish, Finnish,
thinnish, diminish, refinish
¹**inist**\ī-nəst\dynast, finest,
Plotinist, Byzantinist
²**inist**\ē-nəst\hygienist,
machinist, Orleanist,
Byzantinist, magazinist,
trampolinist
initive\in-ət-iv\carminative,
definitive, infinitive
inity\in-ət-ē\Trinity, affinity,
bovinity, concinnity, divinity,
felinity, feminity, infinity,
latinity, salinity, sanguinity,
vicinity, virginity, alkalinity,
aquitinity, clandestinity,
consanguinity, crystallinity,
femininity, inconcinnity,
masculinity, saccharinity
inium\in-ē-əm\delphinium,
triclinium, aluminium,
condominium
injure\in-jər\see ³INGER
injury\inj-rē\see INGERY
ink\iŋk\blink, brink, chink,
clink, dink, drink, fink, gink,
ink, jink, kink, link, mink,
pink, plink, prink, rink,
shrink, sink, skink, slink,
stink, swink, sync, think,
wink, zinc, bethink, chewink,
cross-link, eyewink,
groupthink, hoodwink,
iceblink, lip-synch, misthink,
outthink, rethink, snowblink,

unkink, bobolink,
countersink, doublethink,
interlink, kitchen-sink, rinky-
dink

inka \ iŋ-kə \ see INCA

inkable \ iŋ-kə-bəl \ drinkable,
sinkable, thinkable,
unthinkable

inkage \ iŋ kij \ linkage,
shrinkage, sinkage

inke \ iŋ-kē \ see INKY

inked \ iŋt \ see INCT

inker \ iŋ-kər \ blinker, clinker,
drinker, pinker, sinker,
skinker, stinker, tinker,
winker, diesinker, freethinker,
headshrinker

inket \ iŋ-kət \ Tlingit, trinket

inkey \ iŋ-kē \ see INKY

inkgo \ iŋ-kō \ see INKO

inkie \ iŋ-kē \ see INKY

inking \ iŋ-kiŋ \ freethinking,
unblinking, unthinking

inkle \ iŋ-kəl \ crinkle, inkle,
sprinkle, tinkle, twinkle,
winkle, wrinkle, besprinkle,
periwinkle, Rip van Winkle

inkling \ iŋ-kliŋ \ inkling,
sprinkling, twinkling

inkly \ iŋ-klē \ crinkly, pinkly,
tinkly, twinkly, wrinkly

inko \ iŋ-kō \ ginkgo, pinko

inks \ iŋs \ see INX

inky \ iŋ-kē \ dinkey, dinky,
inky, kinky, pinkie, pinky,

slinky, stinky, zincky,
Malinke

inless \ in-ləs \ chinless, sinless,
skinless, spinless, windlass

inly \ in-lē \ inly, spindly, thinly

inn \ in \ see ¹IN

innace \ in-əs \ see ¹INIS

innacle \ in-i-kəl \ see INICAL

inned \ ind \ see ²IND

inner \ in-ər \ dinner, ginner,
grinner, inner, pinner, sinner,
skinner, spinner, spinor,
thinner, tinner, winner,
beginner, breadwinner,
prizewinner, money-spinner

innet \ in-ət \ linnet, minute,
spinet

inney \ in-ē \ see INNY

inni \ ē-nē \ see ¹INI

innia \ in-e-ə \ see INIA

innic \ in-ik \ see ²INIC

innie \ in-ē \ see INNY

inning \ in-iŋ \ ginning, inning,
spinning, winning, beginning,
breadwinning, prizewinning,
underpinning

innish \ in-ish \ see INISH

innity \ in-ət-ē \ see INITY

¹**innow** \ in-ə \ pinna, minnow,
winnow, topminnow

²**innow** \ in-ō \ minnow, winnow,
topminnow

inny \ in-ē \ cine, finny, ginny,
guinea, hinny, mini, ninny,
shinny, skinny, spinney,
squinny, tinny, whinny,

Winnie, ignominy,
pickaninny

¹ino \ī-nō\ lino, rhino, Taino,
wino, albino

²ino \ē-nō\ beano, chino, keno,
leno, Pinot, vino, bambino,
casino, cioppino, ladino,
merino, sordino, zecchino,
andantino, Angeleno,
Bardolino, campesino,
cappuccino, concertino,
Filipino, maraschino,
palomino, Pilipino, sopranino

³ino \ē-nə\ see ²INA

iñon \in-yən\ see INION

¹inor \in-ər\ see INNER

²inor \ī-nər\ see ¹INER

inot \ē-nō\ see ²INO

inous \ī-nəs\ see ¹INUS

inscher \in-chər\ see INCHER

inse \ins\ see INCE

inselly \in-slē\ see INCELY

inseng \in-siŋ\ see INCING

insky \in-skē\ buttinsky,
kolinsky

inster \in-stər\ minster,
spinster, Axminster,
Kidderminster

int \int\ bint, dint, flint, glint,
hint, lint, mint, print, quint,
skint, splint, sprint, squint,
stint, suint, tint, blueprint,
catmint, footprint, forint,
gunflint, handprint, hoofprint,
horsemint, imprint, in-print,
large-print, newsprint,

offprint, preprint, remint,
reprint, skinflint, spearmint,
thumbprint, voiceprint,
aquatint, calamint,
cuckoopint, fingerprint,
mezzotint, monotint,
overprint, peppermint,
photoprint, wunderkind,
Septuagint

intage \int-ij\ mintage, vintage

intager \int-i-jər\ see INTEGER

intain \int-ᵊn\ see INTON

¹intal \int-ᵊl\ lintel, pintle,
quintal, Septuagintal

²intal \ant-ᵊl\ see ANTLE

integer \int-i-jər\ integer,
vintager

intel \int-ᵊl\ see ¹INTAL

inter \int-ər\ hinter, linter,
minter, printer, sinter,
splinter, sprinter, squinter,
tinter, winter, imprinter,
midwinter, reprinter,
overwinter, teleprinter

intery \int-ə-rē\ printery,
splintery

inth \inth\ plinth, helminth,
colocynth, labyrinth, terebinth

inthian \in-thē-ən\ Corinthian,
labyrinthian

inthine \in-thən\ hyacinthine,
labyrinthine

inting \int-iŋ\ imprinting,
unstinting

intle \int-ᵊl\ see ¹INTAL

¹into\in-tō\pinto, Shinto, spinto

²into\in-tü\thereinto, whereinto

inton\int-ᵊn\quintain, badminton

ints\ins\see INCE

inty\int-ē\flinty, linty, minty, squinty, pepperminty

intz\ins\see INCE

inue\in-yü\sinew, continue, discontinue

inuous\in-yə-wəs\sinuous, continuous, discontinuous

¹inus\ī-nəs\dryness, finis, highness, Minos, minus, shyness, sinus, slyness, spinous, vinous, wryness, Delphinus, echinus, Quirinus

²inus\ē-nəs\see ¹ENUS

lnute\in-ət\see INNET

inx\iŋs\jinx, links, lynx, minx, sphinx, methinks, tiddledywinks

¹iny\ī-nē\briny, heinie, liny, piny, shiny, spiny, tiny, twiny, viny, whiny, winy, sunshiny

²iny\in-ē\see INNY

inya\ē-nyə\see ²ENIA

inyan\in-yən\see INION

inyl\īn-ᵊl\see ¹INAL

inys\in-əs\see ¹INIS

¹io\ī-ō\bayou, bio, Clio, Io, Lucayo

²io\ē-ō\brio, clio, guyot, Leo, trio, caudillo, con brio, Negrillo, tornillo, cigarillo, ocotillo

iocese\ī-ə-səs\see IASIS

iolate\ī-ə-lət\see ¹IOLET

¹iolet\ī-ə-lət\triolet, violate, violet, inviolate, ultraviolet

²iolet\ē-ə-lət\see EOLATE

¹ion\ī-ən\ayin, cyan, ion, lion, Mayan, scion, Sion, Zion, Amphion, anion, Bisayan, Ixion, Orion, Visayan, circadian, dandelion, zwitterion

²ion\ē-ən\see ¹EAN

ior\īr\see ¹IRE

iory\ī-rē\see ¹IARY

iot\ī-ət\see IET

ioter\ī-ət-ər\see IETER

iouan\ü-ən\see UAN

ious\ī-əs\see IAS

ioux\ü\see ¹EW

ip\ip\blip, chip, clip, dip, drip, flip, grip, grippe, gyp, hip, kip, lip, nip, pip, quip, rip, scrip, ship, sip, skip, slip, snip, strip, tip, trip, whip, yip, zip, airship, airstrip, atrip, bullwhip, catnip, chiefship, clerkship, courtship, cowslip, deanship, equip, fieldstrip, filmstrip, flagship, friendship, guildship, gunship, half-slip, handgrip, hardship, harelip, headship, horsewhip, inclip, judgeship, kingship, kinship, landslip, lightship, lordship, nonslip, outstrip, oxlip, pip-pip, princeship, Q-ship, queenship, reship, round-trip, saintship, sheep-dip, sideslip, spaceship, steamship, thaneship, township, transship, troopship, unship, unzip, wardship, warship, airmanship, authorship, battleship, brinkmanship, censorship, chairmanship, chaplainship, chieftainship, churchmanship, coverslip, dealership, draftsmanship, ego-trip, externship, fellowship, fingertip, gamesmanship, grantsmanship, helmsmanship, horsemanship, internship, ladyship, leadership, lectureship, listenership, marksmanship, membership, microchip, oarsmanship, overslip, partnership, penmanship, pogonip, premiership, readership, ridership, rulership, scholarship, seamanship, showmanship, skinny-dip, speakership, sponsorship, sportsmanship, statesmanship, stewardship, studentship, swordsmanship, trusteeship, underlip,

upmanship, viewership, workmanship, assistantship, attorneyship, championship, chancellorship, citizenship, companionship, containership, dictatorship, directorship, good-fellowship, guardianship, instructorship, landownership, laureateship, governorship, musicianship, one-upmanship, outdoorsmanship, professorship, protectorship, receivership, relationship, survivorship, treasurership, ambassadorship, associateship, bipartisanship, entrepreneurship, librarianship, nonpartisanship, proprietorship, secretaryship, solicitorship, interrelationship

ipal \ē-pəl \ see EOPLE

ipatus \ip-ət-əs \ see IPITOUS

ipe \īp \ Cuyp, gripe, hype, pipe, ripe, slype, snipe, stipe, stripe, swipe, tripe, type, wipe, bagpipe, blowpipe, drainpipe, hornpipe, lead-pipe, panpipe, pinstripe, rareripe, sideswipe, standpipe, stovepipe, tintype, touch-type, unripe, windpipe, archetype, Dutchman's-pipe, guttersnipe, Linotype, liripipe, logotype, monotype, overripe, prototype,

stenotype, Teletype,
electrotype, stereotype,
daguerreotype

¹iped \ī-ped\ biped,
parallelepiped

²iped \īpt\ stiped, striped, pin-
striped—*also pasts of verbs
listed at* IPE

ipend \ī-pənd\ ripened, stipend

iper \ī-pər\ diaper, griper,
hyper, piper, riper, sniper,
striper, viper, wiper,
bagpiper, sandpiper, candy-
striper, stereotyper

iperous \ī-prəs\ see YPRESS

ipetal \ip-ət-ᵊl\ basipetal,
bicipital, centripetal, occipital

ipety \ip-ət-ē\ snippety,
peripety, serendipity

iph \if\ see IFF

iphany \if-ə-nē\ see IPHONY

ipher \ī-fər\ cipher, lifer, rifer,
decipher, encipher, pro-lifer,
right-to-lifer

iphery \if-rē\ see IFERY

iphon \ī-fən\ see YPHEN

iphony \if-ə-nē\ tiffany,
antiphony, epiphany,
polyphony

ipi \ē-pē\ see EEPY

ipid \ip-əd\ lipid, insipid

ipience \ip-ē-əns\ incipience,
percipience, impercipience

ipient \ip-ē-ənt\ excipient,
incipient, percipient,
recipient, impercipient

iping \ī-piŋ\ piping, striping,
blood-typing

ipit \ip-ət\ see IPPET

ipital \ip-ət-əl\ see IPETAL

ipitance \ip-ət-əns\ see
IPOTENCE

ipitant \ip-ət-ənt\ see IPOTENT

ipitous \ip-ət-əs\ peripatus,
precipitous, serendipitous

ipity \ip-ət-ē\ see IPETY

¹iple \ip-əl\ see IPPLE

²iple \ī-pəl\ see YPAL

ipless \ip-ləs\ dripless, lipless,
zipless

ipment \ip-mənt\ shipment,
equipment, transshipment

ipoli \ip-ə-lē\ see IPPILY

ipotence \ip-ət-əns\
omnipotence, precipitance

ipotent \ip-ət-ənt\ omnipotent,
plenipotent, pluripotent,
precipitant

¹ippe \ip\ see IP

²ippe \ip-ē\ see IPPY

ipped \ipt\ see IPT

ippee \ip-ē\ see IPPY

ippen \ip-ən\ lippen, pippin

ipper \ip-ər\ chipper, clipper,
dipper, dripper, flipper,
gripper, hipper, kipper,
nipper, ripper, shipper,
sipper, skipper, slipper,
snipper, stripper, tipper,
tripper, whipper, zipper, day-
tripper, Yom-Kippur, double-

dipper, gallinipper, lady's
slipper, skinny-dipper

ippery \ip-rē\ frippery, slippery

ippet \ip-ət\ pipit, sippet,
snippet, tippet, trippet,
whippet

ippety \ip-ət-ē\ see IPETY

ippie \ip-ē\ see IPPY

ippily \ip-ə-lē\ nippily, tripoli

ippin \ip-ən\ see IPPEN

ipping \ip-iŋ\ clipping,
dripping, lipping, nipping,
ripping, shipping, double-
dipping, skinny-dipping

ippingly \ip-iŋ-lē\ grippingly,
nippingly, trippingly

ipple \ip-əl\ cripple, nipple,
ripple, stipple, tipple, triple,
participle

ippur \ip-ər\ see IPPER

ippy \ip-ē\ dippy, drippy,
grippy, hippie, lippy, nippy,
slippy, snippy, tippy, whippy,
yippee, zippy, Xanthippe

ips \ips\ snips, thrips, eclipse,
ellipse, midships, amidships,
athwartships, fish-and-chips,
tidytips, apocalypse—*also
plurals and possessives of
nouns and third singular
presents of verbs listed at* IP

ipse \ips\ see IPS

ipso \ip-sō\ dipso, calypso

ipster \ip-stər\ hipster, tipster

ipsy \ip-sē\ see YPSY

ipt \ipt\ crypt, hipped, lipped,

ripped, script, tipped,
conscript, decrypt, encrypt,
harelipped, postscript,
prescript, rescript, subscript,
tight-lipped, transcript,
typescript, eucalypt, filter-
tipped, manuscript,
nondescript, superscript,
swivel-hipped—*also pasts of
verbs listed at* IP

iptic \ip-tik\ see YPTIC

iption \ip-shən\ ascription,
conniption, conscription,
decryption, description,
Egyptian, encryption,
inscription, prescription,
proscription, subscription,
transcription, circumscription,
nonprescription

iptive \ip-tiv\ ascriptive,
descriptive, inscriptive,
prescriptive, proscriptive

iptych \ip-tik\ see YPTIC

ipular \ip-yə-lər\ stipular,
manipular

ipy \ī-pē\ stripy, typey,
stenotypy, daguerrotypy,
stereotypy

iquant \ē-kənt\ see ECANT

ique \ēk\ see ¹EAK

iquey \ē-kē\ see EAKY

iquish \ē-kish\ see EAKISH

iquitous \ik-wət-əs\ iniquitous,
ubiquitous

iquity \ik-wət-ē\ antiquity,
iniquity, obliquity, ubiquity

iquor \ik-ər\ see ¹ICKER

¹ir \ir\ see ²EER

²ir \ər\ see ¹EUR

¹ira \ir-ə\ see ²ERA

²ira \ī-rə\ see YRA

irable \ī-rə-bəl\ wirable, acquirable, desirable, respirable, undesirable

iracle \ir-i-kəl\ see ²ERICAL

irae \īr-ē\ see ¹IRY

iral \ī-rəl\ gyral, spiral, viral

irant \ī-rənt\ spirant, tyrant, aspirant, retirant

irate \ir-ət\ see IRIT

irca \ər-kə\ see ¹URKA

irce \ər-sē\ see ERCY

irch \ərch\ see URCH

irchen \ər-chən\ see URCHIN

ircher \ər-chər\ Bircher, lurcher, nurture

irchist \ər-chəst\ Birchist, researchist

ircon \ər-kən\ see IRKIN

ircuit \ər-kət\ circuit, trifurcate, microcircuit

ircular \ər-kyə-lər\ circular, opercular, tubercular, semicircular

ird \ərd\ bird, burred, curd, furred, gird, heard, herd, nerd, spurred, surd, third, turd, word, absurd, begird, bellbird, blackbird, bluebird, buzzword, byword, catbird, catchword, cowbird, cowherd, crossword, cussword, engird, goatherd, headword, jailbird, jaybird, kingbird, loanword, lovebird, lyrebird, oilbird, password, potsherd, railbird, rainbird, redbird, reword, ricebird, seabird, shorebird, snakebird, snowbird, songbird, sunbird, surfbird, swearword, swineherd, textured, ungird, unheard, watchword, yardbird, afterword, bowerbird, butcher-bird, cedarbird, dollybird, hummingbird, ladybird, mockingbird, ovenbird, overheard, riflebird, tailorbird, thunderbird, undergird, wattlebird, weaverbird, wirlybird—*also pasts of verbs listed at* ¹EUR

irder \ərd-ər\ see ERDER

irdie \ərd-ē\ see URDY

irdle \ərd-ᵊl\ see URDLE

irdum \ərd-əm\ dirdum, reductio ad absurdum

¹ire \īr\ briar, brier, byre, choir, dire, drier, fire, flier, friar, fryer, gyre, hire, ire, liar, lyre, mire, prier, prior, pyre, quire, shire, sire, spier, spire, squire, tier, tire, trier, wire, zaire, acquire, admire, afire, Altair, aspire, attire, backfire, balefire, barbed wire, barbwire, bemire, bonfire, brushfire, bushfire, catbrier, cease-fire, complier, conspire, defier, denier, desire, drumfire, empire, Empire, entire, esquire, expire, flytier, grandsire, greenbrier, gunfire, haywire, hellfire, highflier, hot-wire, inquire, inspire, misfire, outlier, perspire, pismire, prior, quagmire, require, respire, retire, rimfire, samphire, sapphire, satire, Shropshire, spitfire, surefire, suspire, sweetbrier, tightwire, transpire, umpire, vampire, wildfire, amplifier, Biedermeier, butterflyer, classifier, fortifier, lammergeier, magnifier, modifier, multiplier, nullifier, pacifier, qualifier, quantifier, rapid-fire, rectifier, retrofire, sanctifier, testifier, versifier, identifier, intensifier, Second Empire—*also nouns formed by adding* -er *to verbs listed at* ¹Y

²**ire** \ir\ *see* ²EER

³**ire** \ī-rē\ *see* ¹IARY

⁴**ire** \īr-ē\ *see* ¹IRY

ired \īrd\ spired, tired, wired, retired—*also pasts of verbs listed at* ¹IRE

ireless \īr-ləs\ tireless, wireless

ireman \īr-mən\ fireman, wireman

irement \īr-mənt\ environment, requirement, retirement

iren \ī-rən\ gyron, siren, environ, sapphirine

irge \ərj\ *see* URGE

irgin \ər-jən\ *see* URGEON

irgo \ər-gō\ *see* ERGO

iri \ir-ē\ *see* EARY

iric \ir-ik\ *see* ²ERIC

irile \ir-əl\ *see* ¹ERAL

irine \ī-rən\ *see* IREN

iring \īr-iŋ\ firing, wiring, retiring

irious \ir-ē-əs\ *see* ERIOUS

iris \ī-rəs\ *see* IRUS

irish \īr-ish\ Irish, squirish

irit \ir-ət\ spirit, dispirit, emirate, inspirit, vizierate

irium \ir-ē-əm\ *see* ERIUM

irius \ir-ē-əs\ *see* ERIOUS

¹**irk** \irk\ birk, kirk

²**irk** \ərk\ *see* ¹ORK

irker \ər-kər\ *see* ¹ORKER

irkie \ər-kē\ *see* ERKY

irkin \ər-kən\ firkin, gherkin, jerkin, zircon

irky \ər-kē\ *see* ERKY

¹**irl** \ərl\ birl, burl, churl, curl, dirl, earl, furl, girl, hurl, knurl, merle, pearl, purl, skirl, squirrel, swirl, thirl, thurl, tirl, twirl, virl, whirl, whorl, aswirl, awhirl, cowgirl, impearl, pas seul,

playgirl, salesgirl, schoolgirl, uncurl, unfurl, mother-of-pearl

²**irl** \irl\ dirl, skirl

irler \ər-lər\ birler, curler, pearler, twirler, whirler

irlie \ər-lē\ see URLY

irlish \ər-lish\ see URLISH

irly \ər-lē\ see URLY

irm \ərm\ see ¹ORM

irma \ər-mə\ see ERMA

irmary \ərm-rē\ spermary, infirmary

irmess \ər-məs\ see ERMIS

irmity \ər-mət-ē\ furmity, infirmity

irmy \ər-mē\ see ERMY

¹**irn** \irn\ firn, girn, pirn

²**irn** \ərn\ see URN

¹**iro** \ir-ō\ see ³ERO

²**iro** \ē-rō\ see ¹ERO

³**iro** \ī-rō\ see ¹YRO

¹**iron** \īrn\ iron, andiron, environ, flatiron, gridiron

²**iron** \ī-rən\ see IREN

ironment \īr-mənt\ see IREMENT

irp \ərp\ see URP

irps \ərps\ stirps, turps—*also plurals and possessives of nouns and third singular presents of verbs listed at* URP

irpy \ər-pē\ chirpy, Euterpe

irque \ərk\ see ¹ORK

¹**irr** \ir\ see ²EER

²**irr** \ər\ see ¹EUR

irra \ir-ə\ see ²ERA

irrah \ir-ə\ see ²ERA

¹**irrel** \ərl\ see ¹IRL

²**irrel** \ər-əl\ see ERRAL

irrely \ər-lē\ see URLY

irrer \ər-ər\ see ERRER

irrhous \ir-əs\ see EROUS

irrhus \ir-əs\ see EROUS

irring \ər-iŋ\ see URRING

irror \ir-ər\ see ²EARER

irrous \ir-əs\ see EROUS

irrup \ər-əp\ chirrup, stirrup, syrup

irrupy \ər-ə-pē\ chirrupy, syrupy

irrus \ir-əs\ see EROUS

irry \ər-ē\ see URRY

irsch \irsh\ see IRSH

¹**irse** \irs\ see IERCE

²**irse** \ərs\ see ERSE

irsh \irsh\ girsh, kirsch

irst \ərst\ see URST

irsty \ər-stē\ thirsty, bloodthirsty, multiversity, university

irt \ərt\ see ¹ERT

irted \ərt-əd\ see ERTED

irter \ərt-ər\ see ERTER

irth \ərth\ berth, birth, dearth, earth, firth, girth, mirth, worth, childbirth, rebirth, self-worth, stillbirth, unearth, afterbirth, down-to-earth, pennyworth

irthful \ərth-fəl\ mirthful, worthful

irthless\ ərth-ləs\ mirthless, worthless

irtinent\ ərt-nənt\ pertinent, appurtenant, impertinent

irting\ ərt-iŋ\ see ERTING

irtle\ ərt-ᵊl\ see ERTILE

irtually\ ərch-lē\ see URCHLY

irtue\ ər-chə\ see ERCHA

irty\ ərt-ē\ dirty, shirty, thirty

irus\ ī-rəs\ iris, virus, desirous, Osiris, papyrus

irv\ ərv\ see ERVE

¹**iry**\ īr-ē\ eyrie, friary, miry, spiry, wiry, expiry, inquiry, praemunire, anno hegirae

²**iry**\ ī-rē\ see ¹IARY

i's\ īz\ see IZE

¹**is**\ is\ see ¹ISS

²**is**\ iz\ see ¹IZ

³**is**\ ē\ see ¹EE

⁴**is**\ ēs\ see IECE

isa\ ē-zə\ see EZA

isable\ ī-zə-bəl\ see IZABLE

¹**isal**\ ī-səl\ Faisal, sisal, skysail, trysail, paradisal

²**isal**\ ī-zəl\ incisal, reprisal, revisal, surprisal, paradisal

isan\ is-ᵊn\ see ISTEN

isbe\ iz-bē\ Frisbee, Thisbe

isbee\ iz-bē\ see ISBE

isc\ isk\ see ISK

iscable\ is-kə-bəl\ confiscable, episcopal

iscan\ is-kən\ see ISKIN

iscate\ is-kət\ see ISKET

isce\ is\ see ¹ISS

¹**iscean**\ ī-sē-ən\ Piscean, Dionysian

²**iscean**\ is-kē-ən\ Piscean, ornithischian

³**iscean**\ is-ē-ən\ see ¹YSIAN

iscence\ is-ᵊns\ puissance, dehiscence, impuissance, indehiscence, reminiscence, reviviscence

iscent\ is-ᵊnt\ puissant, dehiscent, impuissant, indehiscent, reminiscent, reviviscent

isces\ ī-sēz\ see ICES

ische\ ēsh\ see ²ICHE

ischian\ is-kē-ən\ see ²ISCEAN

iscia\ ish-ə\ see ITIA

iscible\ is-ə-bəl\ see ISSIBLE

iscience\ ish-əns\ see ICIENCE

iscient\ ish-ənt\ see ICIENT

isco\ is-kō\ cisco, disco, Morisco

iscopal\ is-kə-bəl\ see ISCABLE

iscous\ is-kəs\ see ISCUS

iscuit\ is-kət\ see ISKET

iscus\ is-kəs\ discus, viscous, viscus, hibiscus, meniscus

¹**ise**\ ēs\ see IECE

²**ise**\ ēz\ see EZE

³**ise**\ īs\ see ¹ICE

⁴**ise**\ īz\ see IZE

¹**ised**\ īst\ see ¹IST

²**ised**\ īzd\ see IZED

isel\ iz-əl\ see IZZLE

iseled\ iz-əld\ see IZZLED

iseler\ iz-lər\ see IZZLER

isement \īz-mənt\ advisement, chastisement, despisement, disguisement, advertisement, disfranchisement, enfranchisement, disenfranchisement

iser \ī-zər\ see IZER

ises \ī-sēz\ see ICES

¹ish \ish\ dish, fiche, fish, flysch, pish, squish, swish, whish, wish, blackfish, blowfish, bluefish, bonefish, catfish, codfish, crawfish, crayfish, dogfish, filefish, finfish, flatfish, garfish, globefish, goldfish, kingfish, knish, lungfish, monkfish, pigfish, pipefish, ratfish, redfish, rockfish, sailfish, sawfish, shellfish, spearfish, starfish, stonefish, sunfish, swordfish, tilefish, unwish, weakfish, whitefish, angelfish, anglerfish, archerfish, butterfish, candlefish, cuttlefish, damselfish, devilfish, jellyfish, John Bullish, ladyfish, lionfish, microfiche, muttonfish, needlefish, overfish, paddlefish, ribbonfish, silverfish, triggerfish

²ish \ēsh\ see ²ICHE

isha \ish-ə\ see ITIA

ishable \ish-ə-bəl\ fishable, justiciable

ished \isht\ dished, whisht— *also pasts of verbs listed at* ¹ISH

isher \ish-ər\ fisher, fissure, swisher, ill-wisher, kingfisher, well-wisher

ishery \ish-rē\ fishery, Tishri, shellfishery

ishi \ē-shē\ chichi, specie, maharishi

ishing \ish-iŋ\ bonefishing, fly-fishing, sportfishing, well-wishing

ishioner \ish-nər\ see ITIONER

ishna \ish-nə\ Krishna, Mishnah

ishnah \ish-nə\ see ISHNA

isht \isht\ see ISHED

ishy \ish-ē\ dishy, fishy, squishy, swishy

isi \ē-zē\ see ¹EASY

isia \izh-ə\ baptisia, Dionysia, artemisia

¹isian \izh-ən\ see ISION

²isian \ē-zhən\ see ¹ESIAN

isible \iz-ə-bəl\ risible, visible, divisible, invisible, indivisible

ising \ī-ziŋ\ see IZING

ision \izh-ən\ fission, Frisian, scission, vision, abscission, collision, concision, decision, derision, division, elision, elysian, envision, excision, incision, misprision,

precisian, precision,
prevision, provision, recision,
rescission, revision,
circumcision, Dionysian,
imprecision, indecision,
subdivision, supervision,
television

isional \izh-nəl\ visional,
collisional, decisional,
divisional, excisional,
previsional, provisional

isis \ī-səs\ crisis, Isis, lysis,
nisus, Dionysus, stare decisis

isit \iz-ət\ visit, exquisite,
revisit

isite \iz-ət\ see ISIT

isitive \iz-ət-iv\ acquisitive,
inquisitive

isitor \iz-ət-ər\ visitor,
acquisitor, inquisitor

¹isive \ī-siv\ visive, decisive,
derisive, divisive, incisive,
indecisive

²isive \iz-iv\ visive, derisive,
divisive

isk \isk\ bisque, brisk, disk,
fisc, frisk, risk, whisk,
asterisk, basilisk, blastodisc,
obelisk, odalisque, tamarisk,
videodisc

isker \is-kər\ brisker, frisker,
risker, whisker

isket \is-kət\ biscuit, brisket,
confiscate

iskey \is-kē\ see ISKY

iskie \is-kē\ see ISKY

iskin \is-kən\ siskin, Franciscan

isky \is-kē\ frisky, pliskie,
risky, whiskey

islander \ī-lən-dər\ see
IGHLANDER

isle \īl\ see ¹ILE

islet \ī-lət\ see ILOT

isling \iz-liŋ\ brisling, quisling

isly \iz-lē\ see IZZLY

ism \iz-əm\ chrism, chrisom,
ism, prism, schism, abysm,
autism, baalism, baptism,
Birchism, bossism,
Buddhism, casteism,
centrism, charism, Chartism,
chemism, classism, cubism,
cultism, czarism, deism,
dwarfism, faddism, fascism,
fauvism, Gaullism, Grecism,
Hobbism, holism, Jainism,
Klanism, leftism, lyrism,
Mahdism, Maoism, Marxism,
monism, mutism, Nazism,
nudism, Orphism, priggism,
purism, racism, Ramism,
rightism, sadism, Saivism,
sapphism, Scotism, sexism,
Shaktism, Shiism, Sikhism,
simplism, snobbism, sophism,
statism, Sufism, tachism,
Tantrism, Taoism, theism,
Thomism, tourism, tropism,
truism, Turkism, verism,
Whiggism, Yahwism,
absurdism, activism,
Adventism, alarmism,

albinism, alpinism, altruism, amorphism, anarchism, aneurysm, anglicism, animism, aphorism, archaism, asterism, atavism, atheism, atomism, atticism, Bahaism, barbarism, Benthamism, biblicism, blackguardism, bolshevism, boosterism, botulism, bourbonism, Brahmanism, Briticism, Byronism, cabalism, Caesarism, Calvinism, careerism, Castroism, cataclysm, catechism, Catharism, centralism, chauvinism, chimerism, classicism, colorism, communism, concretism, conformism, cretinism, criticism, cronyism, cynicism, dadaism, dandyism, Darwinism, defeatism, de Gaullism, despotism, die-hardism, dimorphism, Docetism, do-goodism, dogmatism, Donatism, Don Juanism, druidism, dualism, dynamism, egoism, egotism, elitism, embolism, endemism, erethism, ergotism, erotism, escapism, Essenism, etatism, eunuchism, euphemism, euphuism, exorcism, expertism, extremism, fairyism, familism, fatalism,

feminism, feudalism, fideism, Fidelism, fogyism, foreignism, formalism, futurism, Galenism, gallicism, galvanism, gangsterism, genteelism, Germanism, giantism, gigantism, globalism, gnosticism, Gongorism, Gothicism, gourmandism, gradualism, grangerism, greenbackism, Hasidism, heathenism, Hebraism, hedonism, Hellenism, helotism, hermetism, hermitism, heroism, highbrowism, Hinduism, hipsterism, hirsutism, hispanism, Hitlerism, hoodlumism, hoodooism, hucksterism, humanism, Hussitism, hybridism, hypnotism, Ibsenism, idealism, imagism, Irishism, Islamism, Jansenism, jingoism, journalism, John Bullism, Judaism, Junkerism, kaiserism, Krishnaism, Ku Kluxism, laconism, laicism, Lamaism, Lamarckism, landlordism, Latinism, legalism, Leninism, lobbyism, localism, locoism, Lollardism, lyricism, magnetism, mammonism, mannerism, Marcionism,

masochism, mechanism,
melanism, meliorism,
Menshevism, Mendelism,
mentalism, mesmerism,
methodism, me-tooism,
modernism, Mohockism,
monachism, monadism,
monarchism, mongolism,
Montanism, moralism,
Mormonism, morphinism,
mullahism, mysticism,
narcissism, nationalism,
nativism, nepotism,
neutralism, new dealism,
nihilism, nomadism,
occultism, onanism,
optimism, oralism,
Orangeism, organism,
ostracism, pacifism,
paganism, Pan-Slavism,
pantheism, paroxysm,
Parsiism, passivism,
pauperism, pessimism,
phallicism, pianism, pietism,
plagiarism, Platonism,
pleinairism, Plotinism,
pluralism, pointillism,
populism, pragmatism,
presentism, privatism,
prosaism, Prussianism,
puerilism, pugilism,
Puseyism, Pyrrhonism,
Quakerism, quietism,
rabbinism, racialism,
rationalism, realism,
reformism, rheumatism,

rigorism, robotism,
Romanism, Rousseauism,
rowdyism, royalism,
satanism, savagism,
scapegoatism, schematism,
scientism, sciolism,
Scotticism, Semitism,
Shakerism, Shamanism,
Shintoism, skepticism,
socialism, solecism,
solipsism, Southernism,
specialism, speciesism,
Spartanism, Spinozism,
spiritism, spoonerism,
Stalinism, standpattism,
stoicism, syllogism,
symbolism, synchronism,
syncretism, synergism,
talmudism, tarantism,
tectonism, tenebrism,
terrorism, Teutonism,
titanism, Titoism, tokenism,
Toryism, totalism, totemism,
transvestism, traumatism,
tribalism, tritheism,
Trotskyism, ultraism,
unionism, urbanism, utopism,
Vaishnavism, vampirism,
vandalism, vanguardism,
Vedantism, veganism,
verbalism, virilism, vitalism,
vocalism, volcanism,
voodooism, vorticism,
voyeurism, vulcanism,
vulgarism, Wahhabism,
warlordism, welfarism,

Wellerism, witticism,
yahooism, Yankeeism,
Yiddishism, Zionism,
zombiism, absenteeism,
absolutism, abstractionism,
adoptionism, adventurism,
aestheticism, Africanism,
agnosticism, alcoholism,
alienism, amateurism,
amoralism, anabaptism,
anachronism, Anglicanism,
animalism, antagonism,
Arianism, astigmatism,
athleticism, asynchronism,
Atlanticism, atonalism,
automatism, avant-gardism,
behaviorism, Big Brotherism,
bilingualism, biologism,
bipedalism, biracialism,
Bonapartism, bureaucratism,
cannibalism, capitalism,
Cartesianism, Catholicism,
cavalierism, charlatanism,
clericalism, collectivism,
Colonel Blimpism,
commensalism,
commercialism,
communalism, Confucianism,
conservatism, constructivism,
consumerism, corporatism,
creationism, credentialism,
determinism, diabolism,
didacticism, diffusionism,
dilettantism, doctrinairism,
do-nothingism, eclecticism,
ecumenism, egocentrism,

Eleatism, empiricism,
epicenism, epicurism,
epigonism, eremitism,
eroticism, erraticism,
essentialism, ethnocentrism,
eudaemonism, euhemerism,
evangelism, exclusivism,
exoticism, expansionism,
expressionism, externalism,
Fabianism, factionalism,
factualism, fanaticism,
favoritism, federalism,
Fenianism, feuilletonism, fifth
columnism, flagellantism,
Fourierism, fraternalism,
freneticism, Freudianism,
funambulism, functionalism,
gallicanism, gutturalism,
henotheism, hermeticism,
Hispanicism, historicism,
hooliganism, Hugenotism,
hypocorism, idiotism,
illiberalism, illuminism,
illusionism, immanentism,
impressionism, indifferentism,
Indianism, infantilism,
inflationism, initialism,
insularism, invalidism,
iotacism, irredentism,
Ishmaelitism, Italianism,
Jacobinism, Jacobitism,
jesuitism, Keynesianism,
know-nothingism, legitimism,
lesbianism, liberalism,
libertinism, literalism,
Lutheranism, Lysenkoism,

Magianism, malapropism, mandarinism, McCarthyism, medievalism, mercantilism, messianism, metabolism, metamorphism, militarism, minimalism, misoneism, monasticism, monetarism, monotheism, mosaicism, mutualism, naturalism, Naziritism, necrophilism, negativism, neologism, neo-Nazism, neuroticism, nicenellyism, nominalism, nonconformism, objectivism, obscurantism, obstructionism, officialism, opportunism, organicism, pacificism, Pantagruelism, parallelism, parasitism, pastoralism, paternalism, patriotism, Peeping Tomism, perfectionism, personalism, pharisaism, physicalism, plebeianism, poeticism, polyglotism, polytheism, positivism, postmodernism, pragmaticism, primitivism, probabilism, progressivism, proselytism, protectionism, Protestantism, provincialism, pseudomorphism, psychologism, puritanism, radicalism, rationalism, recidivism, reductionism, refugeeism, regionalism, relativism, restrictionism,

revisionism, revivalism, ritualism, romanticism, ruffianism, Sadduceeism, salvationism, sansculottism, sardonicism, scholasticism, secessionism, sectarianism, sectionalism, secularism, sensualism, separatism, serialism, Slavophilism, solidarism, somnambulism, sovietism, Stakhanovism, structuralism, subjectivism, surrealism, Sybaritism, sycophantism, systematism, Tammanyism, teetotalism, theocentrism, triumphalism, Uncle Tomism, vagabondism, ventriloquism, vigilantism, voluntarism, volunteerism, Wesleyanism, workaholism, Zwinglianism, abolitionism, academicism, agrarianism, Americanism, analphabetism, anthropomorphism, anthropopathism, anti-Semitism, Arminianism, autoerotism, barbarianism, bibliophilism, bicameralism, biculturalism, biloquialism, bipartisanism, bohemianism, colloquialism, colonialism, conceptualism, confessionalism, constitutionalism, conventionalism, corporativism, cosmopolitism,

deviationism, ecumenicism,
emotionalism, esotericism,
Europocentrism,
evolutionism, exhibitionism,
existentialism, expatriatism,
fundamentalism,
governmentalism,
Hegelianism,
hermaphroditism,
hypercriticism, imperialism,
incendiarism, incrementalism,
indeterminism, industrialism,
instrumentalism,
interventionism,
introspectionism,
irrationalism, isolationism,
Malthusianism,
Manichaeanism, manorialism,
materialism, millennialism,
Monarchianism,
mongolianism,
Monophysitism,
Muhammadanism,
multilingualism,
neoclassicism, Neoplatonism,
neorealism, Nestorianism,
Occidentalism, operationism,
orientalism, Palladianism,
parajournalism, parochialism,
particularism, pedestrianism,
Pelagianism, Pentecostalism,
phenomenalism,
photojournalism, pictorialism,
pococurantism,
Postimpressionism,
professionalism,

pseudoclassicism,
reconstructionism,
republicanism,
Rosicrucianism,
sacerdotalism,
sacramentalism, self-
determinism, sadomasochism,
sectarianism, sensationalism,
sentimentalism, socinianism,
spiritualism, theatricalism,
Tractarianism, traditionalism,
transcendentalism,
transsexualism, trilateralism,
ultramontanism, universalism,
utopianism, vernacularism,
Victorianism, vocationalism,
voluntaryism,
Albigensianism,
anticlericalism,
antiquarianism,
apocalypticism,
assimilationism,
associationism,
Augustinianism,
autoeroticism, ceremonialism,
collaborationism,
congregationalism,
cosmopolitanism,
ecclesiasticism,
ecumenicalism,
environmentalism,
Evangelicalism,
Hamiltonianism,
homoeroticism, epicureanism,
experimentalism,
immaterialism, individualism,

institutionalism,
intellectualism,
internationalism,
libertarianism, middle-of-the-
roadism, millenarianism, neo-
conservatism, neo-
impressionism,
operationalism, Pan-
Americanism, Peripateticism,
Pre-Raphaelitism,
Presbyterianism,
Pythegoreanism,
Rastafarianism,
reactionaryism,
Sabbatarianism,
supernaturalism,
Swedenborgianism,
territorialism, Trinitarianism,
unitarianism, vegetarianism,
Zoroastrianism,
Aristotelianism,
authoritarianism,
egalitarianism,
Episcopalianism,
humanitarianism,
Machiavellianism,
neocolonialism,
predestinarianism,
representationalism,
utilitarianism,
establishmentarianism,
latitudinarianism

isma \iz-mə\ charisma, melisma
ismal \iz-məl\ see YSMAL
isme \īm\ see ¹IME

ismo \ēz-mō\ machismo,
verismo, caudillismo
iso \ē-sō\ miso, chorizo
isom \iz-əm\ see ISM
¹ison \īs-ᵊn\ bison, hyson,
Meissen, streptomycin,
Aureomycin, erythromycin
²ison \iz-ᵊn\ dizen, mizzen,
prison, risen, weasand,
wizen, arisen, imprison,
uprisen
isor \ī-zər\ see IZER
isored \ī-zərd\ guisard, visored
isory \īz-rē\ advisory,
provisory, revisory,
supervisory
isp \isp\ crisp, lisp, wisp, will-
o-the-wisp
isper \is-pər\ crisper, lisper,
whisper
ispy \is-pē\ crispy, wispy
isque \isk\ see ISK
iss \is\ bis, bliss, cis, cuisse,
Dis, hiss, kiss, miss, piss,
sis, Swiss, this, vis, wis,
abyss, amiss, coulisse,
dehisce, dismiss, iwis,
koumiss, remiss, submiss,
ambergris, hit-and-miss, hit-
or-miss, reminisce, verdigris
issa \is-ə\ abscissa, mantissa,
vibrissa
issable \is-ə-bəl\ see ISSIBLE
issal \is-əl\ see ISTLE
issance \is-ᵊns\ see ISCENCE
issant \is-ᵊnt\ see ISCENT

¹**isse**\is\see ISS

²**isse**\ēs\see IECE

issed\ist\see ²IST

issel\is-əl\see ISTLE

isser\is-ər\hisser, kisser

issible\is-ə-bəl\kissable,
miscible, admissible,
immiscible, municipal,
omissible, permissible,
remissible, transmissible,
impermissible, inadmissible

issile\is-əl\see ISTLE

¹**ission**\ish-ən\see ITION

²**ission**\izh-ən\see ISION

issionable\ish-nə-bəl\
fissionable, conditionable

issioner\ish-nər\see ITIONER

issive\is-iv\missive,
admissive, derisive,
dismissive, emissive,
permissive, submissive,
transmissive

issome\is-əm\lissome,
alyssum

issor\iz-ər\scissor, whizzer

¹**issue**\ish-ü\fichu, issue,
tissue, reissue, overissue

²**issue**\ish-ə\see ITIA

issure\ish-ər\see ISHER

issus\is-əs\byssus, missus,
Mrs., narcissus

issy\is-ē\missy, prissy, sissy

¹**ist**\īst\Christ, feist, heist,
hist, tryst, zeitgeist,
Antichrist, black-a-vised,

poltergeist—*also pasts of
verbs listed at* ¹ICE

²**ist**\ist\cist, cyst, fist, gist,
grist, kist, list, mist, pissed,
schist, tryst, twist, whist,
wist, wrist, assist, blacklist,
checklist, consist, delist,
desist, encyst, enlist, entwist,
exist, handlist, insist, persist,
playlist, protist, resist,
shortlist, subsist, untwist,
catechist, coexist, dadaist,
exorcist, intertwist, preexist,
love-in-a-mist—*also pasts of
verbs listed at* ISS

³**ist**\ēst\see ¹EAST

¹**ista**\ē-stə\turista, camorrista,
Fidelista

²**ista**\is-tə\crista, vista, arista,
ballista, sacahuiste

istaed\is-təd\see ISTED

istal\is-tᵊl\crystal, distal,
listel, pistil, pistol

istan\is-tən\see ISTON

istance\is-təns\see ISTENCE

istant\is-tənt\see ISTENT

¹**iste**\is-tē\see ²ICITY

²**iste**\ēst\see ¹EAST

isted\is-təd\vistaed,
closefisted, enlisted, ham-
fisted, hardfisted, limp-
wristed, tightfisted, two-
fisted, unlisted, untwisted,
white-listed, ironfisted,
unassisted—*also pasts of
verbs listed at* ²IST

istel \is-t³l\ see ISTAL

isten \is-³n\ christen, glisten,
  listen, Nisan

istenable \is-nə-bəl\ listenable,
  medicinable

istence \is-təns\ distance,
  assistance, consistence,
  existence, insistence,
  outdistance, persistence,
  resistance, subsistence,
  coexistence, inconsistence,
  inexistence, nonexistence,
  nonresistance, preexistence

istency \is-tən-sē\ consistency,
  insistency, persistency,
  inconsistency

istent \is-tənt\ distant, assistant,
  consistent, existent, insistent,
  persistent, resistant,
  subsistent, coexistent,
  equidistant, inconsistent,
  inexistent, nonexistent,
  nonpersistent, nonresistant,
  preexistent

ister \is-tər\ bister, blister,
  clyster, glister, klister, lister,
  mister, sister, twister,
  resister, resistor, solicitor,
  stepsister, transistor

istery \is-trē\ see ISTORY

istful \ist-fəl\ tristful, wistful

isthmus \is-məs\ see ISTMAS

isti \is-tē\ see ²ICITY

istic \is-tik\ cystic, distich,
  fistic, mystic, artistic,
  autistic, ballistic, cladistic,

cubistic, eristic, fascistic,
faunistic, floristic, heuristic,
holistic, hubristic, juristic,
linguistic, logistic, meristic,
monistic, patristic, phlogistic,
puristic, sadistic, simplistic,
sophistic, statistic, stylistic,
Taoistic, theistic, Thomistic,
touristic, truistic, veristic,
wholistic, Yahwistic,
activistic, agonistic,
alchemistic, altruistic,
amoristic, anarchistic,
animistic, aphoristic,
archaistic, atavistic, atheistic,
atomistic, belletristic,
cabalistic, Calvinistic,
casuistic, catechistic,
Catharistic, centralistic,
chauvinistic, communistic,
dadaistic, dualistic,
dyslogistic, egoistic, egotistic,
essayistic, eucharistic,
eulogistic, euphemistic,
euphuistic, exorcistic,
fabulistic, familistic,
fatalistic, feministic,
fetishistic, feudalistic,
fideistic, formalistic,
futuristic, gongoristic,
haggadistic, Hebraistic,
hedonistic, Hellenistic,
humanistic, humoristic,
idealistic, imagistic, inartistic,
Jansenistic, jingoistic,
journalistic, Judaistic,

Lamaistic, legalistic, masochistic, mechanistic, melanistic, mentalistic, methodistic, modernistic, moralistic, narcissistic, nationalistic, nativistic, nepotistic, nihilistic, novelistic, onanistic, optimistic, pantheistic, pessimistic, pianistic, pietistic, plagiaristic, Platonistic, pluralistic, pointillistic, populistic, pugilistic, quietistic, realistic, Romanistic, sciolistic, shamanistic, shintoistic, socialistic, solecistic, solipsistic, specialistic, surrealistic, syllogistic, symbolistic, synchronistic, syncretistic, synergistic, terroristic, totalistic, totemistic, ultraistic, unrealistic, urbanistic, utopistic, vandalistic, verbalistic, vitalistic, voodooistic, voyeuristic, Zionistic, absolutistic, adventuristic, anachronistic, animalistic, anomalistic, antagonistic, behavioristic, cannibalistic, capitalistic, characteristic, collectivistic, contortionistic, deterministic, evangelistic, eudaemonistic, euhemeristic, expansionistic,

expressionistic, extralinguistic, functionalistic, Hinayanistic, hypocoristic, immanentistic, impressionistic, liberalistic, literalistic, Mahayanistic, melioristic, mercantilistic, militaristic, mediumistic, metalinguistic, misogynistic, monopolistic, monotheistic, naturalistic, negativistic, neologistic, opportunistic, paternalistic, physicalistic, polytheistic, probabilistic, propagandistic, rationalistic, recidivistic, reductionistic, relativistic, revivalistic, ritualistic, secularistic, sensualistic, separatistic, somnambulistic, ventriloquistic, violinistic, voluntaristic, colonialistic, commercialistic, Deuteronomistic, emotionalistic, exhibitionistic, fundamentalistic, existentalistic, imperialistic, indeterministic, introspectionistic, irrationalistic, materialistic, oligopolistic, Postimpressionistic, sadomasochistic, sensationalistic, sociolinguistic, spiritualistic, traditionalistic, individualistic

istical \is-ti-kəl\ mystical,
deistical, eristical,
linguistical, logistical,
monistical, patristical,
sophistical, statistical,
theistical, alchemistical,
atheistical, casuistical,
egoistical, egotistical,
exorcistical, pantheistical,
anomalistical, hypocoristical,
monotheistical, polytheistical

istich \is-tik\ see ISTIC

istics \is-tiks\ ballistics,
ekistics, linguistics, logistics,
patristics, statistics, stylistics,
futuristics, criminalistics—
*also plurals and possessives
of nouns listed at* ISTIC

istie \is-tē\ see ²ICITY

istil \is-tᵊl\ see ISTAL

istine \is-tən\ see ISTON

istle \is-əl\ bristle, fissile,
gristle, missal, missile,
scissile, thistle, whistle,
abyssal, dickcissel, dismissal,
epistle

istler \is-lər\ whistler, epistler

istless \ist-ləs\ listless, resistless

istly \is-lē\ bristly, gristly,
thistly, sweet cicely

istmas \is-məs\ Christmas,
isthmus

isto \is-tō\ aristo, Callisto

istol \is-tᵊl\ see ISTAL

iston \is-tən\ piston, Tristan,

Philistine, phlogiston,
amethystine

istor \is-tər\ see ISTER

istory \is-trē\ blistery, history,
mystery, consistory,
prehistory

istral \is-trəl\ mistral, sinistral

istress \is-trəs\ mistress,
headmistress, postmistress,
schoolmistress, sinistrous,
taskmistress, toastmistress

istrophe \is-trə-fē\ antistrophe,
epistrophe

istrous \is-trəs\ see ISTRESS

isty \is-tē\ see ²ICITY

isus \ī-səs\ see ISIS

¹it \it\ bit, bitt, brit, Brit, chit,
dit, fit, flit, frit, grit, hit, it,
kit, knit, lit, mitt, nit, pit,
quit, shit, sit, skit, slit, snit,
spit, split, sprit, teat, tit, twit,
whit, wit, writ, zit, acquit,
admit, armpit, backbit, befit,
bowsprit, bullshit, bushtit,
cesspit, close-knit, cockpit,
commit, culprit, demit,
dimwit, emit, fleapit, gaslit,
godwit, half-wit, horseshit,
house-sit, legit, misfit,
mishit, moonlit, nitwit, obit,
omit, outfit, outwit, peewit,
permit, pinch-hit, Prakrit,
pulpit, refit, remit, Sanskrit,
starlit, submit, sunlit, switch-
hit, tidbit, titbit, tomtit,
transmit, turnspit, twilit, two-

bit, unfit, unknit, well-knit,
baby-sit, benefit, counterfeit,
hypocrite, intermit, intromit,
manumit, recommit, retrofit,
cost-benefit, lickety-split,
overcommit, jack-in-the-pulpit

²**it** \ē\ see ¹EE

³**it** \ēt\ see ¹EAT

¹**ita** \īt-ə\ vita, baryta, amanita

²**ita** \ēt-ə\ cheetah, eta, pita,
theta, vita, zeta, Akita,
bonito, casita, excreta, Lolita,
mosquito, partita, amanita,
arboreta, feterita, incognita,
manzanita, margarita,
senhorita, senorita, Bhagavad
Gita

¹**itable** \īt-ə-bəl\ citable,
writable, excitable, indictable,
copyrightable, extraditable

²**itable** \it-ə-bəl\ see ITTABLE

itae \īt-ē\ see ²ITE

¹**ital** \īt-ᵊl\ title, vital, detrital,
entitle, nontitle, recital,
requital, subtitle, intravital,
supravital

²**ital** \it-ᵊl\ see ITTLE

italer \īt-ᵊl-ər\ victualler,
belittler, Hospitaler

italist \īt-ᵊl-əst\ titlist, vitalist,
recitalist

itan \īt-ᵊn\ see IGHTEN

itant \īt-ᵊnt\ mightn't, excitant,
incitant, renitent

itany \it-ᵊn-ē\ dittany, litany

itch \ich\ bitch, ditch, fitch,

flitch, glitch, hitch, itch,
kitsch, niche, pitch, quitch,
rich, snitch, stitch, such,
switch, twitch, which, witch,
backstitch, bewitch, cross-
stitch, enrich, hemstitch,
lockstitch, slow-pitch,
topstitch, unhitch, whipstitch,
czarevitch, featherstitch, son
of a bitch

itchen \ich-ən\ kitchen, richen

itcher \ich-ər\ hitcher, pitcher,
richer, snitcher, stitcher,
switcher, enricher,
hemstitcher, Lubavitcher,
water witcher

¹**itchery** \ich-ə-rē\ bitchery,
obituary

²**itchery** \ich-rē\ stitchery,
witchery, bewitchery

itches \ich-əz\ britches, riches,
Dutchman's-breeches—*also
plurals and possessives of
nouns and third singular
presents of verbs listed at*
ITCH

itchman \ich-mən\ pitchman,
switchman

itchment \ich-mənt\
bewitchment, enrichment

itchy \ich-ē\ bitchy, itchy,
kitschy, pitchy, twitchy,
witchy

it'd \it-əd\ see ITTED

¹**ite** \īt\ bight, bite, blight,
bright, byte, cite, dight, dite,

fight, flight, fright, height, hight, kite, knight, krait, kyte, light, might, mite, night, plight, quite, right, rite, sight, site, sleight, slight, smite, spite, sprite, tight, trite, white, wight, wite, wright, write, affright, airtight, albite, alight, all right, all-night, aright, backbite, backlight, bedight, Birchite, birthright, bobwhite, bombsight, bullfight, campsite, cockfight, contrite, daylight, deadlight, delight, despite, dogfight, downright, droplight, earthlight, excite, eyebright, eyesight, fanlight, finite, firefight, firelight, fistfight, flashlight, fleabite, floodlight, foresight, forthright, fortnight, frostbite, Gadite, gaslight, gastight, ghostwrite, graphite, gunfight, Gunite, half-light, Hamite, handwrite, headlight, highlight, hindsight, Hittite, homesite, hoplite, Hussite, ignite, illite, infight, in-flight, incite, indict, indite, insight, invite, jacklight, jadeite, lamplight, Levite, lighttight, lignite, limelight, lintwhite, Lucite, Luddite, lyddite, Melchite, midnight, millwright, miswrite,

moonlight, night-light, off-white, on-site, outright, outsight, partite, penlight, playwright, polite, prizefight, pyrite, recite, requite, respite, rushlight, safelight, searchlight, Semite, Servite, Shemite, Shiite, shipwright, sidelight, skintight, skylight, skywrite, snakebite, snow-white, spaceflight, speedlight, spotlight, starlight, sticktight, stoplight, streetlight, sunlight, Sunnite, taillight, termite, tonight, torchlight, trothplight, twilight, twi-night, typewrite, unite, unsight, upright, uptight, wainwright, weeknight, wheelwright, acolyte, aconite, Ammonite, Amorite, anchorite, anthracite, antiwhite, apartheid, appetite, Bakelite, Benthamite, bipartite, black-and-white, blatherskite, bleacherite, Canaanite, Carmelite, castroite, catamite, cellulite, copyright, disunite, dynamite, erudite, expedite, extradite, Fahrenheit, fly-by-night, gelignite, gesundheit, Hashemite, Hepplewhite, Himyarite, Hitlerite, hug-me-tight, impolite, Ishmaelite, Israelite, Jacobite, Josephite,

laborite, Leninite, lily-white,
localite, malachite,
manganite, Marcionite,
Masonite, Mennonite,
Minorite, Moabite,
muscovite, Nazirite, overbite,
overflight, overnight,
oversight, overwrite, parasite,
plebiscite, proselyte,
Puseyite, pyrrhotite,
recondite, reunite, satellite,
socialite, sodalite, sodomite,
Stagirite, stalactite,
stalagmite, Sybarite,
transfinite, transvestite,
tripartite, troglodyte,
Trotskyite, underwrite,
urbanite, Wahhabite,
watertight, Wycliffite,
cosmopolite, exurbanite,
gemütlichkeit, hermaphrodite,
Indo-Hittite, McCarthyite,
multipartite, quadripartite,
suburbanite, theodolite,
Areopagite, Pre-Raphaelite

²**ite** \ īt-ē \ flighty, mighty,
nightie, whitey, whity,
almighty, Venite, Aphrodite,
aqua vitae, arborvitae, lignum
vitae

³**ite** \ it \ see ¹IT

⁴**ite** \ ēt \ see ¹EAT

ited \ īt-əd \ see IGHTED

iteful \ īt-fəl \ see IGHTFUL

itely \ īt-lē \ see IGHTLY

item \ īt-əm \ item, ad infinitum

itement \ īt-mənt \ alightment,
excitement, incitement,
indictment

iten \ īt-ᵊn \ see IGHTEN

itener \ īt-nər \ see IGHTENER

itent \ īt-ᵊnt \ see ITANT

iteor \ ēt-ē-ər \ see ETEOR

¹**iter** \ īt-ər \ blighter, fighter,
lighter, miter, niter, titer,
writer, braillewriter, exciter,
first-nighter, lamplighter, one-
nighter, prizefighter,
screenwriter, scriptwriter,
songwriter, sportswriter,
states righter, typewriter,
copywriter, expediter, fly-by-
nighter, underwriter,
teletypewriter—*also nouns
and comparatives of
adjectives formed by adding
-er to verbs listed at* ¹ITE

²**iter** \ it-ər \ see ITTER

³**iter** \ ēt-ər \ see ¹EATER

iteral \ it-ə-rəl \ clitoral, literal,
littoral, sublittoral, triliteral

iterally \ it-ər-lē \ see ITTERLY

iterate \ it-ə-rət \ literate,
illiterate, nonliterate,
preliterate, presbyterate,
subliterate, semiliterate

ites \ īt-ēz \ barytes, sorites,
Thersites—*also plurals and
possessives of nouns listed at*
²ITE

itey \ īt-ē \ see ²ITE

¹**ith** \ ith \ with, withe, forthwith,
herewith, forthwith,

herewith, therewith,
wherewith

²**ith** \ ith \ fifth, frith, grith, kith,
myth, pith, sith, smith, swith,
with, withe, blacksmith,
forthwith, goldsmith,
gunsmith, locksmith,
songsmith, therewith,
tinsmith, tunesmith,
whitesmith, wordsmith,
coppersmith, eolith, megalith,
microlith, monolith, neolith,
silversmith, paleolith

³**ith** \ ēt \ see ¹EAT

¹**ithe** \ īth \ blithe, kithe, lithe,
scythe, tithe, withe, writhe

²**ithe** \ ith \ see ²ITH

³**ithe** \ ith \ see ¹ITH

¹**ithee** \ ith-ē \ see ²ITHY

²**ithee** \ ith-ē \ see ¹ITHY

ither \ ith-ər \ blither, cither,
dither, hither, slither, swither,
thither, whither, wither,
zither, come-hither,
nowhither, somewhither

itherward \ ith-ər-wərd \
thitherward, whitherward

ithesome \ īth-səm \ blithesome,
lithesome

ithia \ ith-ē-ə \ see YTHIA

ithic \ ith-ik \ lithic, ornithic,
batholithic, Eolithic,
megalithic, Mesolithic,
monolithic, neolithic,
Paleolithic

ithing \ ī-thiŋ \ tithing, trithing

ithmic \ ith-mik \ see YTHMIC

¹**ithy** \ ith-ē \ prithee, smithy,
stithy, withy

²**ithy** \ ith-ē \ pithy, prithee,
smithy, withy

iti \ ēt-ē \ see EATY

itia \ ish-ə \ issue, tissue, wisha,
comitia, episcia, indicia,
militia, reissue, Dionysia

itial \ ish-əl \ see ICIAL

¹**itian** \ ish-ən \ see ITION

²**itian** \ ē-shən \ see ¹ETION

itiate \ ish-ət \ initiate, novitiate,
uninitiate

itic \ it-ik \ critic, arthritic,
bronchitic, dendritic, enclitic,
granitic, graphitic, Hamitic,
jaditic, mephitic, pruritic,
rachitic, Sanskritic, Semitic,
Shemitic, Sinitic, anaclitic,
analytic, anchoritic, catalytic,
cenobitic, copralitic,
crystallitic, diacritic, dialytic,
dynamitic, eremitic,
Himyaritic, hypercritic,
jesuitic, paralytic, parasitic,
sodomitic, stalactitic,
stalagmitic, sybaritic,
thallophytic, troglodytic,
cryptanalytic, electrolytic,
hermaphroditic, meteoritic,
Monophysitic, psychoanalytic

itical \ it-i-kəl \ critical,
Levitical, political, analytical,
apolitical, cenobitical,
diacritical, eremitical,

hypercritical, hypocritical, impolitical, Jacobitical, jesuitical, parasitical, sodomitical, geopolitical, meteoritical, sociopolitical

itics \ it-iks \ Semitics, analytics, meteoritics—*also plurals and possessives of nouns listed at* ITIC

itid \ it-əd \ see ITTED

itin \ it-ᵊn \ see IGHTEN

iting \ īt-iŋ \ biting, flyting, lighting, whiting, writing, bullfighting, cockfighting, exciting, frostbiting, handwriting, infighting, inviting, newswriting, prewriting, prizefighting, skywriting, songwriting, sportswriting, typewriting

ition \ ish-ən \ fission, hycian, mission, titian, addition, admission, ambition, attrition, audition, beautician, clinician, cognition, coition, commission, condition, contrition, demission, dentition, dismission, edition, emission, ethician, fruition, ignition, logician, magician, monition, mortician, munition, musician, nutrition, omission, optician, partition, patrician, perdition, petition, Phoenician, physician, position, punition, remission, rendition, sedition, submission, suspicion, tactician, technician, tradition, transition, transmission, tuition, volition, abolition, acquisition, admonition, aesthetician, air-condition, ammunition, apparition, apposition, coalition, competition, composition, cosmetician, decommission, decondition, definition, demolition, deposition, dietitian, Dionysian, disposition, disquisition, electrician, erudition, exhibition, expedition, exposition, extradition, imposition, inhibition, inquisition, intermission, intromission, intuition, linguistician, logistician, malnutrition, malposition, manumission, mathematician, mechanician, micturition, obstetrician, opposition, Ordovician, parturition, phonetician, politician, precognition, precondition, premonition, preposition, prohibition, proposition, recognition, recondition, repetition, requisition, rhetorician, statistician, superstition,

supposition, transposition,
academician, arithmetician,
decomposition, diagnostician,
dialectician, disinhibition,
geometrician, geriatrician,
indisposition, interposition,
juxtaposition, metaphysician,
onomastician, pediatrician,
presupposition, redefinition,
semiotician, theoretician,
superimposition

itionable\ish-nə-bəl\see
ISSIONABLE

itional\ish-nəl\additional,
attritional, cognitional,
coitional, conditional,
nutritional, positional,
traditional, transitional,
tuitional, volitional,
apparitional, appositional,
compositional, definitional,
depositional, expositional,
inquisitional, oppositional,
prepositional, propositional,
repetitional, suppositional,
transpositional, unconditional,
juxtapositional,
presuppositional

itioner\ish-nər\missioner,
commissioner, conditioner,
parishioner, partitioner,
petitioner, practitioner,
exhibitioner, malpractitioner

itionist\ish-nəst\nutritionist,
partitionist, abolitionist,
coalitionist, demolitionist,

exhibitionist, intuitionist,
oppositionist, prohibitionist

itious\ish-əs\see ¹ICIOUS

itis\īt-əs\situs, Titus, arthritis,
bronchitis, bursitis, colitis,
cystitis, detritus, gastritis,
iritis, mastitis, nephritis,
neuritis, phlebitis, dermatitis,
enteritis, gingivitis, hepatitis,
Heracleitus, ileitis, laryngitis,
meningitis, pharyngitis,
prostatitis, retinitis, sinusitis,
tonsillitis, spondylitis,
tendinitis, urethritis, vaginitis,
appendicitis, conjunctivitis,
encephalitis, endocarditis,
peritonitis, analysis situs,
diverticulitis, gastroenteritis,
poliomyelitis

itish\it-ish\British, skittish

itle\īt-ᵊl\see ¹ITAL

itless\it-ləs\hitless, witless

it'll\it-ᵊl\see ITTLE

itment\it-mənt\fitment,
commitment, remitment,
recommitment,
overcommitment

itness\it-nəs\fitness, witness,
earwitness, eyewitness,
unfitness

¹ito\ēt-ō\keto, veto, bonito,
burrito, graffito, magneto,
Miskito, mosquito, Negrito,
incognito, sanbenito

²ito\ēt-ə\see ²ITA

¹iton\it-ᵊn\see ITTEN

²iton \īt-ᵊn\ see IGHTEN

itoral \it-ə-rəl\ see ITERAL

itral \ī-trəl\ mitral, nitrile

itrile \ī-trəl\ see ITRAL

it's \its\ see ITS

its \its\ blitz, glitz, grits, it's,
its, quits, spitz, slivovitz—
*also plurals and possessives
of nouns and third singular
presents of verbs listed at* ¹IT

itsail \it-səl\ see ITZEL

itsch \ich\ see ITCH

itschy \ich-ē\ see ITCHY

itsy \it-sē\ see ITZY

itt \it\ see ¹IT

itta \it-ə\ shittah, vitta

ittable \it-ə-bəl\ committable,
habitable, hospitable,
remittable, transmittable,
inhospitable

ittah \it-ə\ see ITTA

ittal \it-ᵊl\ see ITTLE

ittance \it-ᵊns\ pittance,
quittance, acquittance,
admittance, emittance,
immittance, remittance,
transmittance, intermittence

ittany \it-ᵊn-ē\ see ITANY

itted \it-əd\ it'd, nitid, pitted,
teated, witted, committed,
dim-witted, half-witted,
quick-witted, sharp-witted,
slow-witted, thick-witted,
unbitted, unfitted,
uncommitted—*also pasts of
verbs listed at* ¹IT

ittee \it-ē\ see ITTY

itten \it-ᵊn\ bitten, Briton,
kitten, litten, mitten, smitten,
witting, written, backbitten,
flea-bitten, hard-bitten,
rewritten, unwritten

ittence \it-ᵊns\ see ITTANCE

ittent \it-ᵊnt\ remittent,
intermittent, intromittent

itter \it-ər\ bitter, chitter,
critter, fitter, flitter, fritter,
glitter, hitter, jitter, knitter,
litter, quitter, quittor, sitter,
skitter, slitter, spitter, titter,
twitter, aglitter, atwitter, bed-
sitter, embitter, emitter,
hairsplitter, no-hitter,
outfitter, rail-splitter, remitter,
shipfitter, steamfitter, switch-
hitter, transmitter, benefiter,
counterfeiter, intromitter

itterer \it-ər-ər\ fritterer,
litterer, twitterer

itterly \it-ər-lē\ bitterly, literally

ittern \it-ərn\ bittern, cittern,
gittern

ittery \it-ə-rē\ glittery, jittery,
littery, skittery, twittery

ittie \it-ē\ see ITTY

ittiness \it-ē-nəs\ grittiness,
prettiness, wittiness

¹itting \it-iŋ\ fitting, sitting,
splitting, witting, befitting,
earsplitting, fence-sitting,
formfitting, hairsplitting,
hard-hitting, house-sitting,

resitting, sidesplitting,
unfitting, unwitting,
unremitting

²itting \it-ᵊn\ see ITTEN

ittish \it-ish\ see ITISH

ittle \it-ᵊl\ brittle, it'll, kittle,
little, skittle, spital, spittle,
tittle, victual, whittle, wittol,
acquittal, belittle, committal,
embrittle, hospital, lickspittle,
remittal, transmittal,
noncommittal, recommittal

ittler \it-ᵊl-ər\ see ITALER

ittol \it-ᵊl\ see ITTLE

ittor \it-ər\ see ITTER

ittoral \it-ə-rəl\ see ITERAL

itty \it-ē\ bitty, city, ditty,
gritty, kitty, pity, pretty,
tittie, witty, committee, self-
pity, itty-bitty, nitty-gritty,
subcommittee, supercity,
Walter Mitty

itual \ich-wəl\ ritual, habitual

ituary \ich-ə-rē\ see ¹ITCHERY

itum \īt-əm\ see ITEM

itus \īt-əs\ see ITIS

¹ity \it-ē\ see ITTY

²ity \īt-ē\ see ²ITE

itz \its\ see ITS

¹itza \ēt-sə\ pizza, czaritza

²itza \it-sə\ czaritza, tamburitza

itzel \it-səl\ schnitzel, spritsail,
Wiener schnitzel

itzy \it-sē\ bitsy, glitzy,
ritzy, schizy

ius \ē-əs\ see ¹EUS

¹iv \iv\ see ²IVE

²iv \ēf\ see ¹IEF

¹iva \ī-və\ Saiva, gingiva,
Godiva, saliva

²iva \ē-və\ diva, kiva, siva,
viva, geneva, yeshiva

³iva \iv-ə\ Shiva, Siva

¹ivable \ī-və-bəl\ drivable,
derivable, revivable,
survivable

²ivable \iv-ə-bəl\ livable,
forgivable

ival \ī-vəl\ rival, archival,
arrival, revival, survival,
adjectival, conjunctival,
genitival, substantival,
infinitival

ivalent \iv-ə-lənt\ ambivalent,
equivalent, unambivalent

ivan \iv-ən\ see IVEN

ivance \ī-vəns\ connivance,
contrivance, survivance

ivative \iv-ət-iv\ privative,
derivative

¹ive \īv\ chive, dive, drive,
five, gyve, hive, I've, jive,
live, rive, shrive, skive,
strive, thrive, wive, alive,
archive, Argive, arrive,
beehive, connive, contrive,
deprive, derive, endive,
nosedive, ogive, revive,
self-drive, skin-dive, survive,
test-drive, forty-five,
overdrive, power-dive

²ive \iv\ give, live, sheave,

shiv, sieve, spiv, forgive,
misgive, outlive, relive,
unlive, underactive

³ive \ ēv \ see ¹EAVE

ivel \ iv-əl \ civil, drivel, frivol,
shrivel, snivel, swivel

iven \ iv-ən \ given, riven,
Sivan, striven, thriven,
forgiven

¹iver \ ī-vər \ diver, driver, fiver,
arriver, cabdriver, conniver,
contriver, deriver, reviver,
screwdriver, survivor

²iver \ iv-ər \ flivver, giver,
liver, quiver, river, shiver,
sliver, almsgiver, aquiver,
deliver, downriver, forgiver,
lawgiver, upriver

¹ivers \ ī-vərz \ divers, vivers—
also plurals and possessives
of nouns listed at ¹IVER

²ivers \ ē-vərz \ see EAVERS

ivery \ iv-rē \ livery, shivery,
delivery

ives \ īvz \ fives, hives—also
plurals and possessives of
nouns and third singular
presents of verbs listed at ¹IVE

ivet \ iv-ət \ civet, divot, pivot,
privet, rivet, swivet, trivet

¹ivi \ iv-ē \ see IVVY

²ivi \ ē-vē \ see EAVEY

ivial \ iv-ē-əl \ trivial, convivial,
quadrivial

ivid \ iv-əd \ livid, vivid

ivil \ iv-əl \ see IVEL

ivilly \ iv-ə-lē \ civilly, privily,
uncivilly

ivily \ iv-ə-lē \ see IVILLY

iving \ iv-iŋ \ giving, living,
almsgiving, forgiving, free-
living, misgiving,
thanksgiving

ivion \ iv-ē-ən \ Vivian, oblivion

ivious \ iv-ē-əs \ lascivious,
oblivious

ivity \ iv-ət-ē \ privity, acclivity,
activity, captivity, declivity,
festivity, motivity, nativity,
proclivity, absorptivity,
adaptivity, additivity,
affectivity, aggressivity,
coercivity, cognitivity,
collectivity, compulsivity,
conductivity, connectivity,
creativity, destructivity,
diffusivity, directivity,
effectivity, emissivity,
emotivity, exclusivity,
exhaustivity, expansivity,
expressivity, impassivity,
inactivity, infectivity,
negativity, perceptivity,
perfectivity, permittivity,
positivity, primitivity,
productivity, reactivity,
receptivity, reflexivity,
relativity, resistivity,
retentivity, selectivity,
sensitivity, subjectivity,
susceptivity, transitivity,
distributivity, hyperactivity,

insensitivity, overactivity,
retroactivity, radioactivity,
hypersensitivity

ivium \ iv-ē-əm \ trivium,
quadrivium

iviut \ ē-vē-ət \ see EVIATE

ivo \ ē-vō \ see EVO

ivocal \ iv-ə-kəl \ equivocal,
univocal, unequivocal

ivol \ iv-əl \ see IVEL

ivor \ ī-vər \ see ¹IVER

ivorous \ iv-rəs \ carnivorous,
granivorous, omnivorous,
insectivorous

ivot \ iv-ət \ see IVET

ivus \ ē-vəs \ see EVOUS

ivver \ iv-ər \ see ²IVER

ivvy \ iv-ē \ chivy, civvy, divvy,
privy, skivvy, tantivy, divi-
divi

ivy \ iv-ē \ see IVVY

iwi \ ē-wē \ see EEWEE

¹ix \ iks \ Brix, fix, mix, nix,
pyx, six, Styx, admix, affix,
blanc fixe, commix, deep-six,
immix, infix, prefix, prix
fixe, prolix, subfix, suffix,
transfix, unfix, antefix,
cicatrix, crucifix, eighty-six,
intermix, politics, six-o-six,
superfix, geopolitics—*also
plurals and possessives of
nouns and third singular
presents of verbs listed at* ICK

²ix \ ē \ see ¹EE

ixal \ ik-səl \ pixel, affixal,
prefixal, suffixal

¹ixe \ ēks \ breeks, prix fixe, idée
fixe—*also plurals and
possessives of nouns and third
singular presents of verbs
listed at* ¹EAK

²ixe \ iks \ see ¹IX

³ixe \ ēsh \ see ²ICHE

ixed \ ikst \ fixed, mixed, twixt,
betwixt, well-fixed—*also
pasts of verbs listed at* ¹IX

ixel \ ik-səl \ see IXAL

ixer \ ik-sər \ fixer, mixer, elixir

ixia \ ik-sē-ə \ asphyxia,
panmixia

ixie \ ik-sē \ Dixie, nixie, Nixie,
pixie, pyxie, tricksy

ixion \ ik-shən \ see ICTION

ixir \ ik-sər \ see IXER

ixit \ ik-sət \ quixote, ipse dixit

ixote \ ik-sət \ see IXIT

ixt \ ikst \ see IXED

ixture \ iks-chər \ fixture,
mixture, admixture,
commixture, intermixture

iya \ ē-ə \ see ¹IA

¹iz \ iz \ biz, fizz, frizz, his, is,
Ms., quiz, 'tis, whiz, wiz,
gee-whiz, show biz

²iz \ ēz \ see EZE

iza \ ē-zə \ see EZA

izable \ ī-zə-bəl \ sizable,
advisable, cognizable,
devisable, excisable,
amortizable, analyzable,

criticizable, dramatizable,
exercisable, fertilizable,
hypnotizable, inadvisable,
localizable, magnetizable,
mechanizable, memorizable,
pulverizable, recognizable,
vaporizable, computerizable,
generalizable,
uncompromisable

izar \ i-zər \ see IZER

izard \ iz-ərd \ blizzard, gizzard,
izzard, lizard, vizard, wizard

ize \ īz \ guise, prise, prize, rise,
size, wise, abscise, advise,
apprise, apprize, arise, assize,
baptize, breadthwise, capsize,
chastise, clockwise, cognize,
comprise, crabwise,
crosswise, demise, despise,
devise, disguise, disprize,
downsize, earthrise,
edgewise, emprise, endwise,
excise, fanwise, franchise,
full-size, grecize, high-rise,
incise, king-size, leastwise,
lengthwise, Levi's, life-size,
likewise, low-rise, man-size,
midsize, misprize, moonrise,
nowise, outsize, piecewise,
pint-size, premise, quantize,
remise, reprise, revise,
slantwise, streetwise, stylize,
suffice, sunrise, surmise,
surprise, twin-size, uprise,
advertise, aggrandize,
agonize, alchemize, amortize,

analyze, anglicize, anywise,
aphorize, arabize, atomize,
authorize, balkanize,
barbarize, bastardize,
bestialize, bolshevize,
botanize, bowdlerize,
brutalize, burglarize, canalize,
canonize, capsulize,
caramelize, carbonize,
catalyze, catechize, cauterize,
centralize, channelize,
Christianize, cicatrize,
circumcise, civilize,
classicize, colonize,
communize, compromise,
concertize, concretize,
criticize, crystalize,
customize, demonize,
deputize, dialyze, digitize,
disfranchise, dogmatize,
dramatize, elegize,
empathize, emphasize,
energize, enfranchise,
enterprise, equalize, erotize,
eternize, etherize, eulogize,
exercise, exorcise, factorize,
fantasize, fascistize, feminize,
fertilize, feudalize, fictionize,
finalize, formalize, formulize,
fossilize, fragmentize,
fraternize, gallicize,
galvanize, germanize,
ghettoize, glamorize,
globalize, gormandize,
gothicize, gourmandize,
grecianize, harmonize,

heathenize, hebraize,
hellenize, humanize,
hybridize, hypnotize, idolize,
immunize, improvise, ionize,
Islamize, itemize, jeopardize,
journalize, Judaize, laicize,
latinize, legalize, lionize,
liquidize, localize, magnetize,
marbleize, martyrize,
maximize, mechanize,
melanize, melodize,
memorize, merchandise,
mesmerize, methodize,
metricize, minimize,
mobilize, modernize,
moisturize, monetize,
mongrelize, moralize,
motorize, mythicize,
narcotize, nasalize, neutralize,
normalize, notarize, novelize,
obelize, odorize, optimize,
organize, ostracize,
otherwise, oversize, oxidize,
paganize, paradise, paralyze,
pasteurize, patronize,
pauperize, penalize, penny-
wise, pidginize, plagiarize,
plasticize, Platonize,
pluralize, pocket-size,
poetize, polarize, polemize,
pressurize, privatize,
prussianize, publicize,
pulverize, randomize, realize,
recognize, rhapsodize,
robotize, romanize, rubberize,
sanitize, satirize, scandalize,

schematize, schismatize,
scrutinize, sensitize,
sermonize, signalize,
simonize, sinicize, slenderize,
sloganize, socialize,
sodomize, solarize, sonnetize,
specialize, stabilize, Stalinize,
standardize, sterilize,
stigmatize, subsidize,
summarize, supervise,
syllogize, symbolize,
sympathize, synchronize,
syncretize, synopsize,
synthesize, systemize,
tantalize, televise, temporize,
tenderize, terrorize, tetanize,
teutonize, texturize, theorize,
thermalize, totalize,
tranquilize, traumatize,
tyrannize, unionize, unitize,
urbanize, utilize, valorize,
vandalize, vaporize,
verbalize, vernalize,
victimize, vitalize, vocalize,
vulcanize, vulgarize, weather-
wise, weatherize, westernize,
winterize, womanize,
worldly-wise, accessorize,
acclimatize, actualize,
allegorize, alphabetize,
analogize, anatomize,
anesthetize, animalize,
annualize, antagonize,
anthologize, anticlockwise,
apologize, apostatize,
apostrophize, arabicize,

aromatize, baby blue-eyes,
bureaucratize, cannibalize,
capitalize, categorize,
catholicize, characterize,
commercialize, communalize,
computerize, conservatize,
containerize, contrariwise,
conveyorize, cosmeticize,
counterclockwise, criminalize,
cryptanalize, de-emphasize,
decentralize, decolonize,
dehumanize, deionize,
demagnetize, demobilize,
democratize, demoralize,
deodorize, depersonalize,
depolarize, desalinize,
desensitize, destabilize,
digitalize, disenfranchise,
disorganize, economize,
emotionalize, epitomize,
eroticize, eternalize,
euthanatize, evangelize,
extemporize, externalize,
familiarize, fanaticize,
federalize, fictionalize,
formularize, gelatinize,
generalize, geologize,
Hispanicize, homogenize,
hospitalize, hypothesize,
idealize, illegalize,
immobilize, immortalize,
impersonalize, initialize,
internalize, italicize,
legitimize, liberalize,
literalize, lobotomize,
lysogenize, macadamize,

metabolize, metastasize,
militarize, mineralize,
monopolize, mythologize,
nationalize, naturalize,
parenthesize, philosophize,
politicize, popularize,
proselytize, regularize,
reorganize, revitalize,
romanticize, secularize,
sexualize, sovietize,
subjectivize, suburbanize,
subvocalize, systematize,
temporalize, theologize,
traditionalize, transistorize,
trivialize, ventriloquize,
visualize, Americanize,
apotheosize, colonialize,
compartmentalize,
conceptualize, decriminalize,
demilitarize, denaturalize,
departmentalize, depoliticize,
desexualize, Europeanize,
exteriorize, immaterialize,
individualize, industrialize,
internationalize, legitimatize,
materialize, miniaturize,
particularize, politicalize,
phychoanalyze, self-actualize,
sentimentalize, spiritualize,
underutilize, universalize,
constitutionalize,
dematerialize, editorialize,
intellectualize,
deinstitutionalize—*also
plurals and possessives of*

nouns and third singular presents of verbs listed at ¹Y

ized \īzd\ sized, advised, outsized, ergotized, ill-advised, pearlized, Sanforized, unadvised, undersized, varisized, well-advised, elasticized, modularized—*also pasts of verbs listed at* IZE

¹**izen** \īz-³n\ bison, dizen, greisen, bedizen, horizon, spiegeleisen

²**izen** \iz-³n\ see ²ISON

izer \ī-zər\ geyser, kaiser, miser, prizer, riser, sizar, visor, wiser, adviser, divisor, incisor, appetizer, atomizer, energizer, enterpriser, equalizer, exerciser, fertilizer, organizer, oxidizer, stabilizer, supervisor, synthesizer, totalizer, tranquilizer, tyrannizer, vaporizer, deodorizer—*also nouns formed by adding* -er *to verbs listed at* IZE

izing \ī-ziŋ\ rising, sizing, uprising, appetizing, enterprising, merchandising, self-sufficing, self-sacrificing, uncompromising

¹**izo** \ē-zō\ chorizo, mestizo

²**izo** \ē-sō\ see ISO

izon \īz-³n\ see ¹IZEN

izy \it-sē\ see ITZY

izz \iz\ see ¹IZ

izza \ēt-sə\ see ¹ITZA

izzard \iz-ərd\ see IZARD

izzen \iz-³n\ see ²ISON

izzer \iz-ər\ see ISSOR

izzical \iz-i-kəl\ see YSICAL

izzle \iz-əl\ chisel, drizzle, fizzle, frizzle, grizzle, mizzle, pizzle, sizzle, swizzle

izzled \iz-əld\ chiseled, grizzled—*also pasts of verbs listed at* IZZLE

izzler \iz-lər\ chiseler, sizzler, swizzler

izzly \iz-lē\ drizzly, grisly, grizzly, mizzly

izzy \iz-ē\ busy, dizzy, fizzy, frizzy, tizzy

O

o \ü\ see ¹EW

¹**oa** \ō-ə\ boa, koa, moa, Noah, proa, stoa, aloha, balboa, jerboa, quinoa

²**oa** \ō\ see ¹OW

oable \ü-ə-bəl\ see UABLE

oach \ōch\ broach, brooch, coach, loach, poach, roach,

abroach, approach, caroche, cockroach, encroach, reproach, stagecoach

oachable \ō-chə-bəl\ coachable, approachable, inapproachable, irreproachable, unapproachable

oacher \ō-chər\ broacher, coacher, cloture, poacher, encroacher

¹oad \ōd\ see ODE

²oad \òd\ see ¹AUD

oader \ōd-ər\ see ODER

oadie \ōd-ē\ see ²ODY

oady \ōd-ē\ see ²ODY

oaf \ōf\ loaf, oaf, qoph, witloof, sugarloaf

oafer \ō-fər\ see OFER

oagie \ō-gē\ see OGIE

oah \ō-ə\ see ¹OA

oak \ōk\ see OKE

oaken \ō-kən\ see OKEN

oaker \ō-kər\ see OKER

oakum \ō-kəm\ see OKUM

oaky \ō-kē\ see OKY

oal \ōl\ see ¹OLE

oalie \ō-lē\ see ¹OLY

¹oam \ō-əm\ see ¹OEM

²oam \ōm\ see ¹OME

oamer \ō-mər\ see ¹OMER

oaming \ō-miŋ\ coaming, combing, gloaming—*also present participles of verbs listed at* ¹OME

oamy \ō-mē\ foamy, homey, loamy, show-me, Naomi, Salome

¹oan \ō-ən\ roan, rowan, Minoan, Samoan, waygoing, Eskimoan, protozoan

²oan \ōn\ see ¹ONE

oaner \ō-nər\ see ¹ONER

oaning \ō-niŋ\ see ²ONING

oap \ōp\ see OPE

oaper \ō-pər\ see OPER

oapy \ō-pē\ see OPI

¹oar \ōr\ see ¹ORE

²oar \òr\ see ¹OR

¹oard \ōrd\ board, floored, ford, gourd, hoard, horde, oared, pored, sword, toward, aboard, afford, backboard, backsword, baseboard, billboard, blackboard, breadboard, broadsword, buckboard, cardboard, chalkboard, chipboard, clapboard, clipboard, corkboard, dashboard, duckboard, flashboard, floorboard, footboard, freeboard, garboard, hardboard, headboard, inboard, keyboard, lapboard, leeboard, matchboard, moldboard, outboard, packboard, pasteboard, patchboard, pegboard, pressboard, punchboard, sailboard, scoreboard, seaboard, shipboard,

sideboard, signboard,
skateboard, smallsword,
soundboard, splashboard,
springboard, storyboard,
surfboard, switchboard,
tailboard, wallboard,
washboard, word-hoard,
aboveboard, centerboard,
checkerboard, fiberboard,
fingerboard, mortarboard,
overboard, paddleboard,
paperboard, pinafored,
plasterboard, pompadoured,
shuffleboard, smorgasbord,
teeterboard, untoward,
weatherboard, particleboard—
also pasts of verbs listed at
¹ORE

²**oard** \ ȯrd \ board, chord, cord,
ford, gourd, lord, sward,
sword, toward, ward, aboard,
accord, award, backboard,
backsword, baseboard,
billboard, blackboard,
breadboard, broadsword,
buckboard, cardboard,
chalkboard, chipboard,
clapboard, clipboard,
concord, corkboard,
dashboard, duckboard,
discord, fjord, flashboard,
floorboard, footboard,
freeboard, garboard,
greensward, landlord,
matchboard, moldboard,
outboard, packboard,

pasteboard, patchboard,
pegboard, pressboard,
punchboard, rearward, record,
reward, sailboard, scoreboard,
seaboard, shipboard,
sideboard, signboard,
skateboard, slumlord,
smallsword, soundboard,
splashboard, springboard,
surfboard, switchboard,
tailboard, untoward,
wallboard, washboard, word-
hoard, warlord, whipcord,
aboveboard, centerboard,
checkerboard, clavichord,
disaccord, fingerboard,
harpsichord, mortarboard,
overboard, overlord,
paddleboard, paperboard,
plasterboard, shuffleboard,
smorgasbord, storyboard,
teeterboard, tetrachord,
weatherboard, misericord,
particleboard—*also pasts of
verbs listed at* ¹OR

oarder \ ȯrd-ər \ boarder,
hoarder, keyboarder,
skateboarder, surfboarder

oarding \ ȯrd-iŋ \ hoarding,
skateboarding,
weatherboarding

oared \ ȯrd \ see ¹OARD

¹**oarer** \ ȯr-ər \ see ¹ORER

²**oarer** \ ȯr-ər \ see ¹ORRER

oaring \ ȯr-iŋ \ see ORING

oarious \ ȯr-ē-əs \ see ORIOUS

oarish \ȯr-ish\ see ¹ORISH

¹**oarse** \ȯrs\ see ¹OURSE

²**oarse** \ȯrs\ see ¹ORSE

oarsen \ȯrs-ᵊn\ coarsen, hoarsen, whoreson

oarsman \ȯrz-mən\ oarsman, outdoorsman

oart \ȯrt\ see ¹ORT

oary \ȯr-ē\ see ORY

oast \ōst\ see ²OST

oastal \ōs-tᵊl\ see ¹OSTAL

oaster \ō-stər\ coaster, poster, roaster, throwster, toaster, billposter, four-poster, roller coaster

oasty \ō-stē\ see OSTY

oat \ōt\ bloat, boat, coat, cote, cote, Croat, dote, float, gloat, goat, groat, haute, moat, mote, mote, note, oat, phot, quote, rote, shoat, smote, stoat, throat, tote, vote, wrote, afloat, airboat, bluecoat, bumboat, capote, catboat, compote, connote, coyote, cutthroat, demote, denote, devote, dovecote, emote, endnote, fireboat, fistnote, flatboat, footnote, greatcoat, gunboat, headnote, houseboat, housecoat, iceboat, keelboat, keynote, lifeboat, longboat, pigboat, promote, Q-boat, raincoat, redcoat, remote, rewrote, rowboat, sailboat, scapegoat, sheepcote, showboat, speedboat, steamboat, Sukkoth, surfboat, tailcoat, topcoat, towboat, tugboat, turncoat, U-boat, unquote, wainscot, whaleboat, whitethroat, woodnote, workboat, anecdote, antidote, asymptote, creosote, entrecote, ferryboat, motorboat, overcoat, paddleboat, papillote, petticoat, powerboat, redingote, riverboat, rubythroat, Shabuoth, sugarcoat, symbiote, table d'hôte, undercoat, yellowthroat, thirty-second note

oate \ō-ət\ see ¹OET

oated \ōt-əd\ coated, noted, throated, devoted, tailcoated, petticoated—*also pasts of verbs listed at* OAT

oaten \ōt-ᵊn\ see OTON

oater \ōt-ər\ bloater, boater, coater, doter, floater, gloater, motor, noter, oater, rotor, scoter, toter, voter, houseboater, iceboater, keynoter, promoter, pulmotor, sailboater, trimotor, locomotor, motorboater

oath \ōth\ see OWTH

oathe \ōth\ see OTHE

oathing \ō-thiŋ\ see OTHING

oating \ōt-iŋ\ coating, free-
floating, iceboating,
sailboating, scapegoating,
speedboating, wainscoting,
motorboating, undercoating

oatswain \ōs-ᵊn\ see OSIN

oaty \ōt-ē\ see ¹OTE

oax \ōks\ coax, hoax—*also
plurals and possessives of
nouns and third singular
presents of verbs listed at* OKE

¹**ob** \äb\ Ab, blob, bob, cob,
fob, glob, gob, hob, job,
knob, lob, mob, nob, rob,
slob, snob, sob, squab, stob,
swab, throb, yob, bedaub,
corncob, demob, doorknob,
heartthrob, hobnob, kabob,
macabre, nabob, nawab,
skibob, memsahib, shish
kebab, thingamabob

²**ob** \ōb\ see ¹OBE

oba \ō-bə\ arroba, jojoba,
algaroba

obably \äb-lē\ see OBBLY

obal \ō-bəl\ see OBLE

obally \ō-bə-lē\ globally,
primum mobile

obar \ō-bər\ see OBER

obber \äb-ər\ bobber, caber,
clobber, cobber, jobber,
robber, slobber, swabber,
throbber, hobnobber,
Micawber, Skibobber,
stockjobber

obbery \äb-rē\ bobbery,
jobbery, robbery, slobbery,
snobbery, corroboree

obbet \äb-ət\ gobbet, probit

obbin \äb-ən\ see OBIN

obbing \äb-iŋ\ skibobbing,
stockjobbing

obbish \äb-ish\ slobbish,
snobbish

obbler \äb-lər\ cobbler,
gobbler, hobbler, nobbler,
squabbler, wobbler

obbly \äb-lē\ knobbly,
probably, wobbly, Wobbly

obby \äb-ē\ bobby, cobby,
dobby, globby, hobby,
knobby, lobby, nobby,
snobby, swabbie, Punjabi,
Wahhabi

¹**obe** \ōb\ daube, globe, Job,
lobe, probe, robe, strobe,
bathrobe, conglobe, disrobe,
earlobe, enrobe, microbe,
wardrobe, Anglophobe,
claustrophobe, Francophobe,
negrophobe, xenophobe,
ailurophobe

²**obe** \ō-bē\ see OBY

obeah \ō-bē-ə\ see OBIA

obelus \äb-ə-ləs\ see ABILIS

ober \ō-bər\ lobar, sober,
October

obi \ō-bē\ see OBY

obia \ō-bē-ə\ cobia, obeah,
phobia, acrophobia,
algophobia, Anglophobia,
claustrophobia, homophobia,

hydrophobia, negrophobia,
photophobia, xenophobia,
agoraphobia,
triskaidekaphobia

obic \ō-bik \phobic, aerobic,
anaerobic, claustrophobic,
homophobic, hydrophobic,
photophobic, xenophobic

¹obile \ō-bə-lē \see OBALLY

²obile \ō-bəl \see OBLE

obin \äb-ən \bobbin, dobbin,
graben, robin, round-robin

¹obit \ō-bət \obit, robot, Tobit,
post-obit

²obit \äb-ət \see OBBET

oble \ō-bəl \coble, global,
mobile, noble, airmobile,
ennoble, ignoble, immobile

obo \ō-bō \gobo, hobo, kobo,
lobo, oboe, adobo

oboe \ō-bō \see OBO

obol \äb-əl \see ¹ABBLE

oboree \äb-ə-rē \see OBBERY

obot \ō-bət \see ¹OBIT

obra \ō-brə \cobra, dobra

obster \äb-stər \lobster, mobster

obular \äb-yə-lər \globular,
lobular

obule \äb-yül \globule, lobule

oby \ō-bē \goby, obi, Obie,
toby, adobe

¹oc \ōk \see OKE

²oc \äk \see ¹OCK

³oc \ók \see ALK

oca \ō-kə \coca, mocha, oca,

Asoka, carioca, mandioca,
tapioca

ocable \ō-kə-bəl \smokable,
vocable, evocable

ocage \äk-ij \see OCKAGE

ocal \ō-kəl \focal, local, socle,
vocal, yokel, bifocal,
subvocal, trifocal, unvocal

ocative \äk-ət-iv \locative,
vocative, evocative,
provocative

occa \äk-ə \see ¹AKA

occer \äk-ər \see OCKER

occie \äch-ē \see OTCHY

occo \äk-ō \mako, shako,
socko, taco, cheechako,
guanaco, morocco, scirocco,
sirocco

occule \äk-yül \floccule, locule

occulent \äk-yə-lənt \flocculent,
inoculant

occulus \äk-yə-ləs \flocculus,
loculus

oce \ō-chē \see ¹OCHE

ocean \ō-shən \see OTION

ocent \ōs-ᵊnt \docent, nocent

ocess \äs-əs \process, colossus,
proboscis

¹och \ōk \see OKE

²och \äk \see ¹OCK

ocha \ō-kə \see OCA

ochal \äk-əl \see OCKLE

¹oche \ō-chē \penoche, sotto
voce, veloce, mezza voce

²oche \ōsh \cloche, gauche,
brioche, caroche, guilloche

³**oche** \ō-kē\ see OKY

⁴**oche** \ōch\ see OACH

⁵**oche** \osh\ see ²ASH

ochee \ō-kē\ see OKY

ocher \ō-kər\ see OKER

ochle \ək-əl\ see UCKLE

ochs \äks\ see OX

ociable \ō-shə-bəl\ sociable, associable, dissociable, insociable, negotiable, unsociable, indissociable, renegotiable

ocial \ō-shəl\ social, asocial, dissocial, precocial, unsocial, antisocial

ocially \ōsh-lē\ gauchely, socially

ocile \äs-əl\ see OSSAL

ocious \ō-shəs\ atrocious, ferocious, precocious

¹**ock** \äk\ bloc, block, bock, brock, chock, clock, cock, croc, crock, doc, dock, floc, flock, frock, hock, jock, knock, lakh, loch, lock, lough, Mach, mock, nock, pock, roc, rock, schlock, shock, smock, sock, stock, wok, yak, yock, acock, ad hoc, aftershock, amok, backblock, bangkok, baroque, bawcock, bedrock, bemock, bibcock, bitstock, blackcock, blesbok, bloodstock, bois d'arc, breechblock, burdock, buttstock, caprock, coldcock, deadlock, debacle, defrock, dry dock, duroc, earlock, en bloc, epoch, fatstock, feedstock, fetlock, firelock, flintlock, forelock, gamecock, gemsbok, gridlock, gunlock, hammerlock, havelock, haycock, headlock, headstock, hemlock, kapok, livestock, lovelock, matchlock, Mohock, Nisroch, nostoc, o'clock, oarlock, padlock, peacock, penstock, petcock, pibroch, picklock, pinchcock, Polack, post hoc, rhebok, rimrock, roadblock, rootstock, Rorschach, rowlock, shamrock, Sheetrock, sherlock, shylock, Slovak, springbok, steenbok, stopcock, tarok, ticktock, traprock, warlock, wedlock, woodcock, wristlock, zwieback, alpenstock, antiknock, Arawak, billycock, chockablock, hollyhock, interlock, John Hancock, lady's-smock, laughingstock, manioc, mantlerock, monadnock, Otomac, poppycock, Ragnarok, shuttlecock, spatterdock, turkey-cock, weathercock, electroshock

²**ock** \ok\ see ALK

ockage \äk-ij\ blockage,

brockage, dockage, lockage, socage

ocked \äkt\ crocked, concoct, decoct, entr'acte, half-cocked, landlocked, periproct, entoproct—*also pasts of verbs listed at* ¹OCK

ocker \äk-ər\ blocker, clocker, cocker, docker, hocker, knocker, locker, makar, mocker, rocker, shocker, soccer, stocker, footlocker, appleknocker, knickerbocker

ockery \äk-rē\ crockery, mockery, rockery

ocket \äk-ət\ brocket, crocket, docket, locket, pocket, rocket, socket, sprocket, pickpocket, skyrocket, out-of-pocket, retro-rocket

ockey \äk-ē\ see OCKY

ockian \äk-ē-ən\ Comstockian, Slovakian

ockiness \äk-ē-nəs\ cockiness, rockiness, stockiness

ocking \äk-iŋ\ flocking, shocking, smocking, stocking, bluestocking, silk-stocking

ockish \äk-ish\ blockish, stockish

ockle \äk-əl\ coccal, cockle, socle, debacle, epochal

ockney \äk-nē\ cockney, Procne

ocko \äk-ō\ see OCCO

ocks \äks\ see OX

ocky \äk-ē\ blocky, cocky, hockey, jockey, pocky, rocky, sake, schlocky, stocky, Yaqui, Abnaki, Iraqi, pea cocky, rumaki, sukiyaki, jabberwocky, teriyaki

ocle \ō-kəl\ see OCAL

ocne \äk-nē\ see OCKNEY

ocu \ō-kō\ coco, cocoa, loco, poco, rococo, crème de cacao, locofoco, poco a poco

ocoa \ō-kō\ see OCO

ocracy \äk-rə-sē\ autocracy, bureaucracy, democracy, hypocrisy, mobocracy, plutocracy, slavocracy, technocracy, theocracy, aristocracy, gerontocracy, gynecocracy, meritocracy, thalassocracy

ocre \ō-kər\ see OKER

ocrisy \äk-rə-sē\ see OCRACY

ocsin \äk-sən\ see OXIN

oct \äkt\ see OCKED

oction \äk-shən\ concoction, decoction

octor \äk-tər\ doctor, proctor, concocter

oculant \äk-yə-lənt\ see OCCULENT

ocular \äk-yə-lər\ jocular, locular, ocular, binocular, monocular, intraocular

ocule \äk-yül\ see OCCULE

oculus \äk-yə-ləs\ see OCCULUS

ocum \ō-kəm\ see OKUM

ocus\ō-kəs\crocus, focus, hocus, locus, prefocus, refocus, soft-focus, hocus-pocus

ocused\ō-kəst\see OCUST

ocust\ō-kəst\locust, unfocused

ocutor\äk-yət-ər\prolocutor, interlocutor

¹od\äd\bod, clod, cod, fade, gaud, god, hod, mod, nod, od, odd, plod, pod, prod, quad, quod, rod, scrod, shod, sod, squad, tod, trod, wad, amphipod, aubade, ballade, bipod, couvade, croustade, dry-shod, ephod, facade, fantod, glissade, hot-rod, jihad, lingcod, Nimrod, oeillade, pomade, peasecod, ramrod, roughshod, roulade, saccade, scalade, seedpod, slipshod, synod, tie-rod, tightwad, tomcod, torsade, tripod, accolade, arthropod, bigarade, carbonnade, defilade, demigod, enfilade, esculade, esplanade, fulsillade, gallopade, gastropod, goldenrod, hexapod, lycopod, monkeypod, octopod, promenade, cephalopod, rodomontade, dégringolade, fanfaronade, Upanishad, Scheherazade

²od\ō\see ¹OW

³od\ōd\see ODE

⁴od\ùd\see ¹OOD

⁵od\ȯd\see ¹AUD

oda\ōd-ə\coda, soda, pagoda, sal soda

odal\ōd-ᵊl\modal, nodal, yodel, cathodal

odden\äd-ᵊn\sodden, trodden, downtrodden

odder\äd-ər\dodder, fodder, khaddar, modder, nodder, odder, plodder, prodder, solder, wadder, glissader, hot-rodder—*also comparatives of adjectives listed at* ¹OD

oddery\äd-rē\see AWDRY

oddess\äd-əs\bodice, goddess

oddish\äd-ish\cloddish, kaddish

oddle\äd-ᵊl\coddle, model, noddle, swaddle, toddle, twaddle, waddle, remodel, mollycoddle

oddler\äd-lər\coddler, modeler, toddler, twaddler, waddler, mollycoddler

oddy\äd-ē\see ¹ODY

ode\ōd\bode, bowed, code, goad, load, lode, mode, node, ode, road, rode, Spode, strode, toad, toed, woad, wood, abode, bestrode, boatload, byroad, carload, cartload, caseload, commode, corrode, crossroad, decode, displode, embowed, encode, epode, erode, explode, forebode, freeload, geode, highroad, implode, inroad, no-load, off-load, outmode, payload, planeload, railroad, sarod, shipload, square-toed, threnode, trainload, truckload, unload, à la mode, antipode, discommode, electrode, episode, impastoed, incommode, Nesselrode, overrode, palinode, pigeon-toed—*also pasts of verbs listed at* ¹OW

odeine \ōd-ē-ən\ see ODIAN
odel \ōd-ᵊl\ see ODAL
odeler \äd-lər\ see ODDLER
oden \ōd-ᵊn\ loden, Odin, Woden
odeon \ōd-ē-ən\ see ODIAN
oder \ōd-ər\ coder, loader, odor, breechloader, decoder, freeloader, malodor, railroader, unloader, middle-of-the-roader
oderate \äd-rət\ quadrate, moderate, immoderate
odest \äd-əst\ Mahdist, modest, haggadist, immodest—*also superlatives of adjectives listed at* ¹OD
odesy \äd-ə-sē\ geodesy, theodicy
odeum \ōd-ē-əm\ see ODIUM
odge \äj\ see ¹AGE

odger \äj-ər\ codger, dodger, lodger, roger, Jolly Roger, stinking roger
odgy \äj-ē\ dodgy, podgy, stodgy, mistagogy, pedagogy
odian \ōd-ē-ən\ codeine, Cambodian, custodian, melodeon, nickelodeon
odic \äd-ik\ zaddik, cathodic, ergodic, melodic, methodic, monodic, periodic, prosodic, rhapsodic, spasmodic, synodic, threnodic, episodic, periodic, antismasmodic, aperiodic, upanishadic
odical \äd-i-kəl\ methodical, monodical, prosodical, synodical, episodical, immethodical, periodical
odice \äd əs\ see ODDESS
odicy \äd-ə-sē\ see ODESY
odin \ōd-ᵊn\ see ODEN
odious \ōd-ē-əs\ odious, commodious, melodious, incommodious
odity \äd-ət-ē\ oddity, commodity, incommodity
odium \ōd-ē-əm\ odeum, odium, podium, rhodium, sodium
odless \äd-ləs\ godless, rodless
odling \äd-liŋ\ codling, godling
odo \ōd-ō\ dodo, Quasimodo
odom \äd-əm\ shahdom, Sodom
odor \ōd-ər\ see ODER

odular \ äj-ə-lər \ modular, nodular

odule \ äj-ül \ module, nodule

¹**ody** \ äd-ē \ body, cloddy, gaudy, Mahdi, noddy, sadhe, shoddy, toddy, waddy, wadi, anybody, blackbody, dogsbody, embody, homebody, nobody, somebody, antibody, busybody, disembody, everybody, underbody

²**ody** \ ōd-ē \ roadie, toady, polypody

¹**oe** \ ō \ see ¹OW

²**oe** \ ō-ē \ see OWY

³**oe** \ ē \ see ¹EE

oea \ ȯi-ə \ see OIA

oeba \ ē-bə \ see EBA

oebe \ ē-bē \ see ¹EBE

oebel \ ā-bəl \ see ABLE

oebus \ ē-bəs \ see EBUS

oed \ ōd \ see ODE

oehn \ ən \ see UN

oeia \ ē-ə \ see ¹IA

oeic \ ē-ik \ see EIC

oel \ ō-əl \ Joel, bestowal, protozoal

¹**oeless** \ ō-ləs \ see OLUS

²**oeless** \ ü-ləs \ see EWLESS

¹**oem** \ ō-əm \ poem, proem, jeroboam

²**oem** \ ōm \ see ¹OME

³**oem** \ ȯm \ see ¹AUM

oeman \ ō-mən \ see OMAN

oena \ ē-nə \ see ²INA

¹**oentgen** \ en-chən \ see ENSION

²**oentgen** \ ən-chən \ see UNCHEON

oepha \ ē-fə \ see EPHA

¹**o'er** \ ȯr \ see ¹ORE

²**o'er** \ ȯr \ see ¹OR

oer \ ȯr \ see ¹ORE

²**oer** \ ü-ər \ see ¹EWER

³**oer** \ u̇r \ see ¹URE

⁴**oer** \ ȯr \ see ¹OR

¹**oes** \ əz \ see ¹EUSE

²**oes** \ ōz \ see ²OSE

oesn't \ əz-ᵊnt \ see ASN'T

oest \ ü-əst \ see OOIST

oesus \ ē-səs \ see ESIS

¹**oet** \ ō-ət \ poet, inchoate, introit

²**oet** \ ȯit \ see ¹OIT

oetess \ ō-ət-əs \ coitus, poetess

oeuf \ əf \ see UFF

oeur \ ər \ see ¹EUR

oeuvre \ ərv \ see ERVE

oey \ ō-ē \ see OWY

¹**of** \ äv \ see ²OLVE

²**of** \ əv \ see ¹OVE

³**of** \ ȯf \ see ²OFF

ofar \ ō-fər \ see OFER

ofer \ ō-fər \ chauffeur, gofer, gopher, loafer, Ophir, shofar

¹**off** \ äf \ boff, coif, doff, goif, kaph, prof, quaff, scoff, shroff, taw, toff, carafe, pilaf

²**off** \ ȯf \ cough, doff, off, scoff, taw, trough, blast-off, brush-off, cast-off, castoff, checkoff, Chekhov, cutoff,

die-off, drop-off, face-off,
falloff, far-off, goof-off,
hands-off, jump-off, kickoff,
knockoff, layoff, leadoff, lift-
off, one-off, payoff, pick-off,
pickoff, play-off, rake-off,
rip-off, roll-off, runoff,
sawed-off, sell-off, send-off,
setoff, show-off, shutoff,
spin-off, standoff, takeoff,
tap-off, tip-off, trade-off,
turnoff, well-off, Wolof,
write-off, better-off, cooling-
off, damping-off, philosophe,
beef Stroganoff

¹**offal** \ äf-əl \ see AFEL

²**offal** \ ȯ-fəl \ see AWFUL

offee \ ȯ-fē \ coffee, toffee

¹**offer** \ äf-ər \ coffer, gauffer,
goffer, offer, proffer, quaffer,
scoffer, troffer, reoffer

²**offer** \ ȯf-ər \ goffer, offer,
troffer, reoffer

offin \ ȯ-fən \ coffin, dauphin,
soften, uncoffin

offing \ ȯf-iŋ \ offing, rolfing

offit \ äf-ət \ see OFIT

offle \ ȯ-fəl \ see AWFUL

ofit \ äf-ət \ profit, prophet,
soffit, nonprofit, not-for-profit

ofle \ ü-fəl \ see UEFUL

¹**oft** \ ȯft \ croft, loft, oft, soft,
toft, aloft, hayloft,
undercroft—*also pasts of
verbs listed at* ²OFF

²**oft** \ äft \ see ¹AFT

often \ ȯ-fən \ see OFFIN

ofty \ ȯf-tē \ lofty, softy, toplofty

¹**og** \ äg \ bog, clog, cog, flog,
fog, frog, grog, hog, jog,
log, nog, prog, quag, shog,
slog, smog, tog, wog, agog,
backlog, bullfrog, defog,
eclogue, eggnog, footslog,
groundhog, gulag, photog,
prologue, putlog, quahog,
sandhog, stalag, warthog,
analog, analogue, antilog,
apalogue, catalog, decalogue,
demagogue, dialogue,
golliwog, monologue,
mummichog, mystagogue,
nouvelle vague, pedagogue,
pollywog, semilog, sinologue,
synagogue, theologue,
waterlog

²**og** \ ȯg \ bog, clog, dog, fog,
frog, hog, jog, log, smog,
wog, backlog, bandog, befog,
bird-dog, bulldog, bullfrog,
coydog, defog, eclogue,
firedog, groundhog, hangdog,
hedgehog, hotdog, lapdog,
leapfrog, prologue, quahog,
sandhog, seadog, sheepdog,
warthog, watchdog, analog,
analogue, apologue, catalog,
decalogue, dialogue, dog-eat-
dog, duologue, epilogue,
homologue, monologue,
mummichog, pettifog,
pollywog, sinologue,

theologue, Tagalog,
travelogue, underdog,
waterlog, yellow-dog,
ideologue
³og \ ȯg \ see ¹OGUE
oga \ ō-gə \ toga, yoga,
Conestoga
ogamous \ äg-ə-məs \
endogamous, exogamous,
monogamous, heterogamous
ogamy \ äg-ə-mē \ endogamy,
exogamy, homogamy,
monogamy
ogan \ ō-gən \ brogan, shogun,
slogan
ogany \ äg-ə-nē \ see OGONY
ogative \ äg-ət-iv \ derogative,
prerogative, interrogative
¹oge \ ōj \ doge, gamboge,
horologe
²oge \ ōzh \ loge, Limoges
³oge \ ō-jē \ see OJI
⁴oge \ üzh \ see ²UGE
ogenous \ äj-ə-nəs \
androgynous, erogenous,
homogenous, monogynous,
heterogenous
ogeny \ äj-ə-nē \ progeny,
androgeny, autogeny,
homogeny, monogyny,
ontogeny, phylogeny,
heterogeny
¹oger \ äj-ər \ see ODGER
²oger \ ȯg-ər \ see ²OGGER
oges \ ōzh \ see ²OGE
¹ogey \ ō-gē \ see OGIE

²ogey \ ủg-ē \ see OOGIE
oggan \ äg-ən \ see OGGIN
¹ogger \ äg-ər \ agar, flogger,
jogger, laager, lager, logger,
slogger, defogger,
footslogger, agar-agar,
cataloger, pettifogger
²ogger \ ȯg-ər \ auger, augur,
jogger, logger, maugre,
sauger, defogger, hotdogger,
cataloger, pettifogger
¹oggery \ äg-rē \ toggery,
demagoguery
²oggery \ ȯ-gə-rē \ augury,
doggery
oggin \ äg-ən \ noggin, toboggan
oggle \ äg-əl \ boggle, goggle,
joggle, ogle, toggle,
boondoggle, hornswoggle,
synagogal
¹oggy \ äg-ē \ boggy, foggy,
groggy, quaggy, smoggy,
soggy, yagi, demagogy
²oggy \ ȯg-ē \ foggy, soggy
¹ogh \ ōg \ see ¹OGUE
²ogh \ ōk \ see OKE
ogi \ ō-gē \ see OGIE
ogian \ ō-jən \ see OJAN
ogic \ äj-ik \ logic, choplogic,
illogic, anagogic, analogic,
biologic, chronologic,
cryptologic, cytologic,
demagogic, dendrologic,
dialogic, ecologic, ethnologic,
geologic, histologic,
horologic, hydrologic,

mythologic, neurologic,
nosologic, oncologic,
pathologic, pedagogic,
pedologic, petrologic,
phonologic, proctologic,
psychologic, serologic,
technologic, theologic,
virologic, zoologic,
dermatologic, etiologic,
gerontologic, gynecologic,
hagiologic, hematologic,
ideologic, immunologic,
ophthalmologic, ornithologic,
pharmacologic, physiologic,
roentgenologic, sociologic,
teleologic, teratologic,
toxicologic, volcanologic,
bacteriologic, endocrinologic,
meteorologic, paleontologic,
parasitologic, sedimentologic,
symptomologic,
epidemiologic

ogical \ äj-i-kəl \ logical,
alogical, illogical, anagogical,
analogical, biological,
Christological, chronological,
cosmological, cryptological,
cytological, dendrological,
ecological, enological,
ethnological, ethological,
gemological, geological,
graphological, histological,
horological, hydrological,
limnological, morphological,
mycological, mythological,
necrological, neurological,

nomological, oncological,
pathological, pedagogical,
pedological, penological,
petrological, philological,
phonological, phrenological,
phycological, proctological,
psephological, psychological,
scatological, seismological,
serological, sinological,
tautological, technological,
theological, topological,
typological, ufological,
virological, zoological,
abiological, anthropological,
archaeological, cardiological,
climatological,
criminological,
demonological,
dermatological,
embryological, entomological,
eschatological, etiological,
etymological, futurological,
genealogical, gerontological,
gynecological, hagiological,
hematological, herpetological,
ichthyological, iconological,
ideological, immunological,
Mariological, methodological,
mineralogical, musicological,
numerological,
ophthalmological,
ornithological,
pharmacological,
phraseological, physiological,
primatological,
roentgenological,

selenological, semiological,
sociological, teleological,
teratological, terminological,
thanatological, toxicological,
volcanological,
bacteriological,
characterological,
dialectological,
ecclesiological,
endocrinological,
epistemological,
meteorological,
paleontological,
parasitological,
phenomenological,
sedimentological,
symptomatological,
epidemiological,
gastroenterological

ogie \ō-gē\ bogey, bogie, dogie,
fogy, hoagie, logy, pogy,
stogie, vogie, yogi, pirogi

ogle \äg-əl\ see OGGLE

oglio \ōl-yō\ see ¹OLLO

¹ogna \ō-nə\ see ONA

²ogna \ō-nē\ see ¹ONY

ogne \ōn\ see ¹ONE

ogned \ōnd\ see ¹ONED

ogo \ō-gō\ go-go, logo, a-go-go

ogony \äg-ə-nē\ cosmogony,
mahogany, theogony

ographer \äg-rə-fər\
biographer, cartographer,
chorographer, cryptographer,
demographer, discographer,
ethnographer, geographer,

lithographer, mythographer,
phonographer, photographer,
pornographer, stenographer,
typographer, bibliographer,
choreographer, hagiographer,
heliographer, iconographer,
lexicographer, oceanographer,
paleographer, autobiographer,
biogeographer,
chromatographer,
cinematographer,
historiographer

ography \äg-rə-fē\ aerography,
autography, biography,
cacography, cartography,
chorography, chronography,
cosmography, cryptography,
demography, discography,
ethnography, filmography,
geography, holography,
hydrography, hypsography,
lithography, lymphography,
mammography, mythography,
nomography, orthography,
phonography, photography,
pictography, planography,
pornography, reprography,
stenography, thermography,
tomography, topography,
typography, venography,
xerography, xylography,
angiography, aortography,
bibliography, cardiography,
choreography,
chromatography,
crystallography, hagiography,

heliography, iconography, lexicography, metallography, oceanography, paleography, physiography, radiography, roentgenography, arteriography, autobiography, cinematography, encephalography, historiography, psychobiography, electroencephalography

ogrom \äg-rəm\ grogram, pogrom

¹ogue \ōg\ brogue, drogue, rogue, togue, vogue, yogh, collogue, crannog, pirogue, prorogue, disembogue

²ogue \äg\ see ¹OG

³ogue \óg\ see ²OG

oguery \äg-rē\ see ¹OGGERY

oguish \ō-gish\ roguish, voguish

ogun \ō-gən\ see OGAN

ogynous \äj-ə-nəs\ see OGENOUS

ogyny \äj-ə-nē\ see OGENY

oh \ō\ see ¹OW

oha \ō-ə\ see ¹OA

ohl \ōl\ see ¹OLE

ohm \ōm\ see ¹OME

ohn \än\ see ¹ON

ohns \änz\ see ONZE

¹oi \ä\ see ¹A

²oi \ói\ see OY

oia \ói-ə\ cholla, olla, toea, arroyo, sequoia, cherimoya, paranoia

oian \ói-ən\ see OYEN

oic \ō-ik\ stoic, azoic, bistroic, echoic, heroic, anechoic, Cenozoic, Mesozoic, mock-heroic, antiheroic, Paleozoic

oice \óis\ choice, voice, devoice, invoice, pro-choice, rejoice, unvoice, sailor's-choice

oiced \óist\ see OIST

oicer \ói-sər\ choicer, voicer, pro-choicer, rejoicer

¹oid \óid\ void, android, avoid, chancroid, colloid, conoid, cuboid, cycloid, deltoid, dendroid, devoid, discoid, fungoid, globoid, hydroid, hypnoid, keloid, mucoid, Negroid, ovoid, percoid, prismoid, pygmoid, rhizoid, rhomboid, schizoid, scombroid, sigmoid, spheroid, steroid, styloid, tabloid, thalloid, thyroid, toroid, toxoid, trochoid, typhoid, Veddoid, viroid, adenoid, alkaloid, amoeboid, aneroid, anthropoid, arachnoid, asteroid, Australoid, carcinoid, Caucasoid, celluloid, crystalloid, ellipsoid, embryoid, eunuchoid, helicoid, hemorrhoid, hominoid, humanoid, hysteroid, metalloid,

Mongoloid, myeloid,
nautiloid, nucleoid, obovoid,
opioid, osteoid, paranoid,
planetoid, Polaroid,
rheumatoid, solenoid,
Stalinoid, trapezoid,
unalloyed, unemployed,
cannabinoid, carotenoid,
meteoroid, tuberculoid,
underemployed,
Neanderthaloid—*also pasts of
verbs listed at* OY

²**oid** \ä\ *see* ¹A

oidal \ȯid-ᵊl\ chancroidal,
choroidal, colloidal,
conchoidal, cuboidal,
cycloidal, discoidal,
spheroidal, toroidal,
adenoidal, asteroidal,
ellipsoidal, emulsoidal,
hemorrhoidal, metalloidal,
planetoidal, saccharoidal,
trapezoidal, paraboloidal

oider \ȯid-ər\ broider, voider,
avoider, embroider,
reembroider

oie \ä\ ¹A

oif \äf\ *see* ¹OFF

oign \ȯin\ *see* ¹OIN

oil \ȯil\ boil, broil, coil, foil,
hoyle, moil, loyal, noil, oil,
roil, royal, soil, spoil, toil,
voile, aboil, airfoil, assoil,
charbroil, cinquefoil, despoil,
embroil, entoil, garboil,
gargoyle, gumboil, hard-boil,

langue d'oïl, milfoil, non-oil,
parboil, recoil, subsoil,
supercoil, tinfoil, topsoil,
trefoil, turmoil, counterfoil,
disloyal, hydrofoil, quatrefoil,
rhyme royal, surroyal,
pennyroyal

oilage \ȯi-lij\ soilage, spoilage

¹**oile** \äl\ *see* ¹AL

²**oile** \ȯil\ *see* OIL

oiled \ȯild\ foiled, oiled, hard-
boiled, soft-boiled,
uncoiled—*also pasts of verbs
listed at* OIL

oiler \ȯi-lər\ boiler, broiler,
moiler, oiler, spoiler, toiler,
charbroiler, despoiler, Free-
Soiler, subsoiler, potboiler

oiling \ȯi-liŋ\ boiling, moiling

oilless \ȯil-ləs\ soilless,
recoilless

oilsman \ȯilz-mən\ foilsman,
spoilsman

oilus \ȯi-ləs\ *see* OYLESS

oily \ȯi-lē\ doily, oily, roily

¹**oin** \ȯin\ coin, foin, groin,
groyne, join, loin, quoin,
adjoin, conjoin, disjoin,
eloign, enjoin, essoin,
purloin, recoin, rejoin,
sainfoin, sirloin, subjoin,
tenderloin, Assiniboin

²**oin** \aⁿ\ *see* ⁴IN

oine \än\ *see* ¹ON

oined \ȯind\ conjoined,

uncoined—*also pasts of verbs listed at* ¹OIN

oiner \ ȯi-nər \ coiner, joiner

o-ing \ ō-iŋ \ see ¹OING

¹**oing** \ ō-iŋ \ bowing, going, knowing, rowing, sewing, showing, churchgoing, deep-going, foregoing, glassblowing, ingrowing, mind-blowing, ongoing, outgoing, seagoing, waygoing, concertgoing, easygoing, moviegoing, oceangoing, operagoing, theatergoing, thoroughgoing, whistle-blowing, to-ing and fro-ing—*also present participles of verbs listed at* ¹OW

²**oing** \ ü-iŋ \ bluing, doing, misdoing, undoing, wrongdoing, evildoing—*also present participles of verbs listed at* ¹EW

³**oing** \ ō-ən \ see ¹OAN

¹**oint** \ ȯint \ joint, point, adjoint, anoint, appoint, aroint, ballpoint, bluepoint, checkpoint, conjoint, disjoint, drypoint, eyepoint, gunpoint, midpoint, outpoint, pinpoint, pourpoint, standpoint, tuck-point, viewpoint, counterpoint, disappoint, needlepoint, petit point

²**oint** \ ant \ see ⁵ANT

ointed \ ȯint-əd \ jointed, pointed, lap-jointed, loose-jointed, double-jointed, well-appointed—*also pasts of verbs listed at* ¹OINT

ointer \ ȯint-ər \ jointer, pointer, anointer

ointment \ ȯint-mənt \ ointment, anointment, appointment, disappointment

¹**oir** \ īr \ see ¹IRE

²**oir** \ är \ see ³AR

³**oir** \ ȯir \ see OYER

⁴**oir** \ ȯr \ see ¹OR

¹**oire** \ är \ see ³AR

²**oire** \ ȯir \ see OYER

³**oire** \ ȯr \ see ¹OR

¹**ois** \ ä \ see ¹A

²**ois** \ ȯi \ see OY

³**ois** \ ȯiz \ see ²OISE

¹**oise** \ äz \ poise, 'twas, vase, was, bourgeoise, Lamaze, ukase, vichyssoise—*also plurals and possessives of nouns and third singular presents of verbs listed at* ¹A

²**oise** \ ȯiz \ hoise, noise, poise, turquoise, counterpoise, equipoise, avoirdupois—*also plurals and possessives of nouns and third singular presents of verbs listed at* OY

oison \ ȯiz-ᵊn \ foison, poison, empoison

oist \ ȯist \ foist, hoist, joist, moist, voiced, unvoiced,

semimoist—*also pasts of
verbs listed at* OICE

oister \ȯi-stər \ cloister, moister,
oyster, roister

oisterous \ȯi-strəs \ see OISTRESS

oistral \ȯi-strəl \ cloistral,
coistrel

oistrel \ȯi-strəl \ see OISTRAL

oistress \ȯi-strəs \ cloistress,
boisterous, roisterous

oisy \ȯi-zē \ noisy, cramoisie

¹**oit** \ȯit \ doit, droit, poet, quoit,
adroit, exploit, maladroit

²**oit** \āt \ see ¹ATE

³**oit** \ō-ət \ see ¹OET

⁴**oit** \ä \ see ¹A

oite \ät \ see ¹OT

oiter \ȯit-ər \ goiter, loiter,
exploiter, reconnoiter

oitus \ō-ət-əs \ see OETESS

ojan \ō-jən \ Trojan, theologian

oji \ō-jē \ shoji, anagoge

¹**ok** \äk \ see ¹OCK

²**ok** \ək \ see UCK

oka \ō-kə \ see OCA

okable \ō-kə-bəl \ see OCABLE

oke \ōk \ bloke, broke, choke,
cloak, coke, Coke, croak,
folk, hoke, joke, moke, oak,
oke, poke, roque, smoke,
soak, soke, spoke, stoke,
stroke, toke, toque, woke,
yogh, yoke, yolk, ad hoc,
awoke, backstroke, baroque,
bespoke, breaststroke, chain-
smoke, convoke, cowpoke,

downstroke, evoke,
heatstroke, housebroke, in-
joke, invoke, keystroke,
kinfolk, kinsfolk, menfolk,
Nisroch, outspoke, presoak,
provoke, revoke, she-oak,
sidestroke, slowpoke,
sunstroke, townsfolk,
uncloak, unyoke, upstroke,
workfolk, artichoke,
equivoque, gentlefolk,
herrenvolk, masterstroke,
okeydoke, thunderstroke,
womenfolk

oked \ōkt \ stoked, yolked

okel \ō-kəl \ see OCAL

oken \ō-kən \ broken, oaken,
spoken, token, woken,
awoken, bespoken, betoken,
fair-spoken, foretoken, free-
spoken, heartbroken,
housebroken, outspoken,
plainspoken, short-spoken,
soft-spoken, unbroken, well-
spoken, wind-broken

oker \ō-kər \ broker, choker,
croaker, joker, ocher, poker,
soaker, smoker, stoker,
stroker, chain-smoker,
invoker, pawnbroker,
provoker, revoker,
stockbroker, mediocre

okey \ō-kē \ see OKY

oki \ō-kē \ see OKY

okie \ō-kē \ see OKY

okum \ō-kəm\ hokum, locum, oakum

oky \ō-kē\ choky, croaky, folkie, hokey, Loki, Okie, pokey, poky, smoky, troche, trochee, yolky, hokeypokey

¹ol \ōl\ see ¹OLE

²ol \äl\ see ¹AL

³ol \ol\ see ALL

ola \ō-lə\ bola, cola, tola, boffola, braciola, gondola, granola, mandola, payola, pergola, scagliola, viola, acerola, ayatollah, gladiola, Gorgonzola, hemiola, moviola, roseola

olable \ō-lə-bəl\ see OLLABLE

olace \äl-əs\ see OLIS

oland \ō-lənd\ see OWLAND

¹olar \ō-lər\ see OLLER

²olar \äl-ər\ see OLLAR

olas \ō-ləs\ see OLUS

olater \äl-ət-ər\ bardolater, idolater, bibliolater, Mariolater

olatrous \äl-ə-trəs\ idolatrous, bibliolatrous, heliolatrous

olatry \äl-ə-trē\ bardolatry, idolatry, statolatry, zoolatry, bibliolatry, heliolatry, iconolatry, Mariolatry

¹old \ōld\ bold, bowled, cold, fold, gold, hold, mold, mould, old, polled, scold, sold, soled, souled, told, wold, acold, age-old, ahold,

behold, billfold, blindfold, controlled, Cotswold, enfold, fanfold, foothold, foretold, freehold, gatefold, handhold, household, ice-cold, infold, leasehold, pinfold, potholed, roothold, scaffold, sheepfold, stone-cold, stronghold, threshold, toehold, twice-told, unfold, untold, uphold, whole-souled, withhold, centerfold, copyhold, manifold, manyfold, marigold, multifold, oversold, petioled, severalfold, stranglehold, throttlehold— *also pasts of verbs listed at* ¹OLE \

²old \old\ see ALD

oldan \ōl-dən\ see OLDEN

olden \ōl-dən\ golden, holden, olden, soldan, beholden, embolden

¹older \ōl-dər\ boulder, folder, holder, molder, polder, shoulder, smolder, bondholder, cardholder, householder, jobholder, landholder, placeholder, shareholder, slaveholder, stadtholder, stakeholder, stockholder, toolholder, officeholder, titleholder, policyholder—*also comparatives of adjectives listed at* ¹OLD

²**older**\äd-ər\see ODDER

oldie\ōl-dē\see OLDY

olding\ōl-diŋ\holding,
 molding, hand-holding,
 landholding, slaveholding

oldster\ōl-stər\see OLSTER

oldy\ōl-dē\moldy, oldie

¹**ole**\ōl\bole, boll, bowl, coal,
 cole, dhole, dole, droll, foal,
 goal, hole, knoll, kohl, mole,
 pole, Pole, poll, prole, role,
 roll, scroll, shoal, skoal, sol,
 sole, soul, stole, stroll, thole,
 tole, toll, troll, vole, whole,
 armhole, atoll, bankroll,
 bedroll, blowhole, borehole,
 bunghole, cajole, catchpole,
 charcoal, chuckhole, condole,
 console, control, creole,
 Creole, drumroll, enroll,
 ensoul, extol, eyehole,
 fishbowl, flagpole, foxhole,
 frijol, hellhole, inscroll,
 insole, keyhole, kneehole,
 knothole, logroll, loophole,
 manhole, maypole, Mongol,
 outsole, parole, patrol,
 payroll, peephole, pesthole,
 pinhole, pistole, porthole,
 posthole, pothole, redpoll,
 resole, ridgepole, Sheol,
 sinkhole, sotol, stokehole,
 tadpole, taphole, thumbhole,
 top-hole, touchhole, turnsole,
 unroll, washbowl, wormhole,
 amatol, aureole, banderole,
 bannerol, barcarole,
 buttonhole, cabriole,
 camisole, capriole, caracole,
 carmagnole, casserole,
 croquignole, cubbyhole,
 decontrol, Demerol, escarole,
 farandole, fumarole,
 girandole, grand guignol,
 innersole, methanol, oriole,
 oversoul, petiole, pigeonhole,
 protocol, rigmarole,
 Seminole, cholesterol

²**ole**\ō-lē\see ¹OLY

³**ole**\òl\see ALL

olean\ō-lē-ən\see ¹OLIAN

oled\ōld\see ¹OLD

oleful\ōl-fəl\doleful, soulful

olely\ō-lē\see ¹OLY

olem\ō-ləm\golem, solum

olemn\äl-əm\see OLUMN

¹**oleon**\ō-lē-ən\see ¹OLIAN

²**oleon**\ōl-yən\see ²OLIAN

¹**oler**\ō-lər\see OLLER

²**oler**\äl-ər\see OLLAR

olery\ōl-rē\see OLLERY

olesome\ōl-səm\dolesome,
 Folsom, wholesome

oless\ō-ləs\see OLUS

oleum\ō-lē-əm\see OLIUM

oleus\ō-lē-əs\coleus, soleus

oley\ō-lē\see ¹OLY

olf\əlf\see ULF

olfing\óf-iŋ\see OFFING

oli\ō-lē\see ¹OLY

olia\ō-lē-ə\pignolia,
 melancholia

¹**olian** \ō-lē-ən\ aeolian,
Aeolian, eolian, Mongolian,
napoleon, simoleon,
Tyrolean, Anatolian

²**olian** \ōl-yən\ Aeolian, eolian,
Mongolian, napoleon,
Anatolian

¹**olic** \äl-ik\ colic, frolic, Gaelic,
rollick, Aeolic, bucolic,
carbolic, embolic, Mongolic,
symbolic, systolic, alcoholic,
anabolic, apostolic, catabolic,
diabolic, hyperbolic,
melancholic, metabolic,
parabolic, vitriolic,
workaholic

²**olic** \ō-lik\ colic, fumarolic,
bibliopolic

olid \äl-əd\ solid, squalid,
stolid—*also pasts of verbs
listed at* ¹ALA

olis \äl-əs\ braless, polis,
solace, tallith, torticollis

olish \äl-ish\ polish, abolish,
demolish, apple-polish

olitan \äl-ət-ᵊn\ cosmopolitan,
megapolitan, metropolitan,
Neapolitan, megalopolitan

olity \äl-ət-ē\ see ¹ALITY

olium \ō-lē-əm\ scholium,
linoleum, petroleum, trifolium

olivar \äl-ə-vər\ see OLIVER

oliver \äl-ə-vər\ bolivar, Oliver

¹**olk** \elk\ see ¹ELK

²**olk** \ōk\ see OKE

³**olk** \əlk\ see ULK

⁴**olk** \ȯk\ see ALK

olked \ōkt\ see OKED

olkie \ō-kē\ see OKY

olky \ō-kē\ see OKY

¹**oll** \ōl\ see OLE

²**oll** \äl\ see ¹AL

³**oll** \ȯl\ see ALL

¹**olla** \äl-ə\ see ²ALA

²**olla** \ȯi-ə\ see OIA

ollable \ō-lə-bəl\ controllable,
inconsolable, uncontrollable

ollack \äl-ək\ see OLOCH

¹**ollah** \ō-lə\ see OLA

²**ollah** \äl-ə\ see ²ALA

³**ollah** \əl-ə\ see ¹ULLAH

ollands \äl-ənz\ see OLLINS

ollar \äl-ər\ choler, collar,
dollar, dolor, haler, holler,
scholar, squalor, taler, thaler,
blue-collar, brass-collar, half-
dollar, white-collar,
Emmentaler, Eurodollar,
petrodollar

ollard \äl-ərd\ bollard, collard,
collered, hollered, Lollard,
pollard

olled \ōld\ see ¹OLD

ollee \ō-lē\ see ¹OLY

ollege \äl-ij\ see OWLEDGE

¹**ollen** \ō-lən\ see OLON

²**ollen** \əl-ə\ see ¹ULLAH

³**ollen** \əl-ən\ see ULLEN

⁴**ollen** \ȯ-lən\ see ALLEN

oller \ō-lər\ bowler, choler,
dolor, droller, molar, polar,
poler, poller, roller, solar,

stroller, troller, bankroller, cajoler, comptroller, controller, extoller, patroller, premolar, steamroller, buttonholer, logroller, Maryknoller, pigeonholer

ollery \ōl-rē\ drollery, cajolery

ollet \äl-ət\ collet, tallith, wallet

olley \äl-ē\ see ¹OLLY

ollick \äl-ik\ see ¹OLIC

ollie \äl-ē\ see ¹OLLY

olling \ō-liŋ\ bowling, logrolling—*also present participles of verbs listed at* ¹OLE

ollins \äl-ənz\ collins, Hollands

ollis \äl-əs\ see OLIS

ollity \äl-ət-ē\ see ¹ALITY

¹ollo \ōl-yō\ imbroglio, arroz con pollo

²ollo \ō-yō\ see O-YO

³ollo \äl-ō\ see ¹OLLOW

ollop \äl-əp\ collop, dollop, lollop, polyp, scallop, scollop, trollop, wallop, codswallop, escallop

¹ollow \äl-ō\ follow, hollo, hollow, swallow, wallow, Apollo, robalo

²ollow \äl-ə\ see ²ALA

ollower \äl-ə-wər\ follower, swallower, wallower

ollster \ōl-stər\ see OLSTER

¹olly \äl-ē\ brolly, collie, colly, dolly, folly, golly, holly, jolly, Lally, lolly, molly,

Pali, poly, quale, trolley, volley, finale, loblolly, Nepali, Somali, Svengali, tamale, melancholy, pastorale, teocalli

²olly \ò-lē\ see AWLY

olm \ōm\ see ¹OME

olman \ōl-mən\ dolman, dolmen, patrolman

olmen \ōl-mən\ see OLMAN

olo \ō-lō\ bolo, kolo, nolo, polo, solo, Barolo

oloch \äl-ək\ Moloch, pollack, rowlock

ologer \äl-ə-jər\ astrologer, chronologer, horologer, mythologer

ologist \äl-ə-jəst\ anthologist, biologist, cetologist, conchologist, cosmologist, cryptologist, cytologist, dendrologist, ecologist, enologist, ethnologist, ethologist, fetologist, gemologist, geologist, graphologist, histologist, horologist, hydrologist, Indologist, limnologist, mixologist, morphologist, mycologist, mythologist, necrologist, nephrologist, neurologist, oncologist, ontologist, oologist, pathologist, pedologist, penologist, petrologist, philologist, phonologist,

phrenologist, phycologist,
psychologist, seismologist,
serologist, sexologist,
sinologist, technologist,
topologist, typologist,
ufologist, virologist,
zoologist, anthropologist,
archaeologist, audiologist,
cardiologist, climatologist,
cosmetologist, criminologist,
dermatologist, Egyptologist,
embryologist, entomologist,
enzymologist, escapologist,
etymologist, futurologist,
genealogist, gerontologist,
gynecologist, hematologist,
herpetologist, ichthyologist,
ideologist, immunologist,
kremlinologist, lexicologist,
martyrologist, methodologist,
mineralogist, musicologist,
nematalogist, numerologist,
oceanologist,
ophthalmologist,
ornithologist, osteologist,
papyrologist, pharmacologist,
phraseologist, physiologist,
planetologist, primatologist,
rheumatologist,
roentgenologist, semiologist,
sociologist, speleologist,
teleologist, teratologist,
thanatologist, toxicologist,
urbanologist, volcanologist,
bacteriologist, dialectologist,
endocrinologist,

epistemologist, liturgiologist,
meteorologist, neonatologist,
paleontologist, parasitologist,
phenomenologist,
sedimentologist,
anesthesiologist,
epidemiologist,
gastroenterologist

ologous \äl-ə-gəs\ heterologous,
homologous, tautologous

ology \äl-ə-jē\ anthology,
apology, astrology, biology,
bryology, cetology,
Christology, chronology,
conchology, cosmology,
cryptology, cytology,
dendrology, doxology,
ecology, enology, ethnology,
ethology, fetology, gemology,
geology, graphology,
histology, homology,
horology, hydrology,
hymnology, Indology,
limnology, lithology,
mixology, morphology,
mycology, myology,
mythology, necrology,
nephrology, neurology,
nosology, oncology,
ontology, oology, pathology,
pedology, penology,
petrology, philology,
phlebology, phonology,
phrenology, phycology,
proctology, psychology,
scatology, seismology,

serology, sexology, sinology,
symbology, tautology,
technology, tetralogy,
theology, topology,
trichology, typology, ufology,
urology, virology, zoology,
angelology, anthropology,
archaeology, audiology,
axiology, cardiology,
climatology, codicology,
cosmetology, craniology,
criminology, dactylology,
demonology, deontology,
dermatology, Egyptology,
embryology, entomology,
enzymology, escapology,
eschatology, etiology,
etymology, futurology,
genealogy, gerontology,
gynecology, hematology,
herpetology, ichthyology,
iconology, ideology,
immunology, kremlinology,
laryngology, lexicology,
Mariology, martyrology,
methodology, mineralogy,
musicology, nematology,
numerology, oceanology,
opthalmology, ornithology,
osteology, pharmacology,
phraseology, physiology,
planetology, primatology,
radiology, reflexology,
rheumatology, roentgenology,
semiology, sociology,
speleology, teleology,
teratology, terminology,
thanatology, toxicology,
urbanology, volcanology,
vulcanology, bacteriology,
dialectology, ecclesiology,
endocrinology, epistemology,
liturgiology, metapsychology,
meteorology, microbiology,
neonatology, onomatology,
paleontology,
parapsychology, parasitology,
phenomenology,
sedimentology,
symptomatology,
anesthesiology, epidemiology,
ethnomusicology,
gastroenterology,
periodontology,
otorhinolaryngology

olon \ ō-lən \ bowline, colon,
solon, stolen, stollen, stolon,
swollen, eidolon, semicolon

olonel \ ərn-ᵊl \ see ERNAL

olonist \ äl-ə-nəst \ colonist,
Stalinist

¹**olor** \ əl-ər \ color, cruller,
culler, muller, sculler,
bicolor, discolor, off-color,
three-color, tricolor,
Technicolor, watercolor

²**olor** \ ō-lər \ see OLLER

³**olor** \ äl-ər \ see OLLAR

olored \ əl-ərd \ colored, dullard,
bicolored, rose-colored,
varicolored

olp \ ōp \ see OPE

olpen \ō-pən\ see OPEN
olsom \ōl-səm\ see OLESOME
olster \ōl-stər\ bolster, holster, oldster, pollster, upholster
¹olt \ōlt\ bolt, colt, dolt, holt, jolt, molt, poult, smolt, volt, eyebolt, kingbolt, revolt, ringbolt, unbolt, thunderbolt
²olt \ōlt\ see ALT
olter \ōl-tər\ bolter, coulter
oltish \ōl-tish\ coltish, doltish
oluble \äl-yə-bəl\ soluble, voluble, dissoluble, insoluble, irresoluble, resoluble, indissoluble
olum \ō-ləm\ see OLEM
olumn \äl-əm\ column, slalom, solemn, Malayalam
olus \ō-ləs\ bolas, bolus, solus, snowless, toeless, electroless, gladiolus, holus-bolus
olvable \äl-və-bəl\ solvable, dissolvable, evolvable, insolvable, resolvable, revolvable, irresolvable
¹olve \älv\ salve, solve, absolve, convolve, devolve, dissolve, evolve, coevolve, involve, resolve, revolve
²olve \äv\ grave, of, salve, Slav, suave, taw, waw, convolve, devolve, dissolve, evolve, exclave, moshav, resolve, thereof, whereof, Zouave, Tishah-b'Ab, unheard-of, well-thought-of

olvement \älv-mənt\ evolvement, involvement, noninvolvement
olver \äl-vər\ solver, absolver, dissolver, involver, revolver
¹oly \ō-lē\ goalie, holey, holy, lowly, mole, moly, pollee, slowly, solely, aioli, amole, cannoli, frijole, pinole, unholy, guacamole, ravioli, roly-poly
²oly \äl-ē\ see ¹OLLY
olyp \äl-əp\ see OLLOP
¹om \äm\ balm, bomb, bombe, calm, from, gaum, glom, malm, mom, palm, pram, prom, psalm, qualm, rhomb, tom, A-bomb, aplomb, ashram, becalm, cheongsam, coulomb, dive-bomb, embalm, firebomb, grande dame, H-bomb, imam, Islam, Long Tom, napalm, nizam, noncom, phenom, pogrom, pom-pom, reclame, rhabdom, salaam, schoolmarm, sitcom, tam-tam, therefrom, tom-tom, wherefrom, wigwam, cardamom, diatom, intercom, Peeping Tom, Uncle Tom
²om \ōm\ see ¹OME
³om \üm\ see OOM
⁴om \əm\ see ¹UM
oma \ō-mə\ chroma, coma, soma, aroma, diploma, glaucoma, sarcoma,

carcinoma, granuloma,
melanoma

¹**omace** \äm-əs\ see OMISE

²**omace** \əm-əs\ see UMMOUS

omach \ō-ək\ see UMMOCK

omache \äm-ə-kē\ see OMACHY

omachy \äm-ə-kē\
Andromache, logomachy

omal \ō-məl\ domal, stomal,
prodromal, chromosomal

omaly \äm-ə-lē\ balmily,
homily, anomaly

oman \ō-mən\ bowman,
foeman, gnomon, nomen,
omen, Roman, showman,
snowman, yeoman, abdomen,
agnomen, cognomen,
crossbowman, longbowman,
praenomen, Sertoman

omany \äm-ə-nē\ see OMINY

omas \äm-əs\ see OMISE

omathy \äm-ə-thē\
chrestomathy, stichomythy

¹**omb** \ōm\ see ¹OME

²**omb** \üm\ see ¹OOM

³**omb** \äm\ see ¹OM

⁴**omb** \əm\ see ¹UM

¹**ombe** \ōm\ see ¹OME

²**ombe** \üm\ see ¹OOM

³**ombe** \äm\ see ¹OM

ombed \ümd\ see OOMED

¹**omber** \äm-ər\ bomber,
calmer, palmar, palmer, dive-
bomber, embalmer

²**omber** \äm-bər\ ombre,
sambar, somber

³**omber** \ō-mər\ see ¹OMER

ombic \ō-mik\ see ²OMIC

ombical \ō-mi-kəl\ see ²OMICAL

ombie \äm-bē\ zombie,
Abercrombie

ombing \ō-miŋ\ see OAMING

ombo \äm-bō\ combo, mambo,
sambo

¹**ombre** \äm-brē\ hombre,
ombre

²**ombre** \äm-bər\ see ²OMBER

³**ombre** \əm-brē\ see UMBERY

ombus \äm-bəs\ rhombus,
thrombus

¹**ome** \ōm\ brougham, chrome,
comb, combe, dome, foam,
gloam, gnome, holm, home,
loam, mome, nome, ohm,
om, poem, pome, roam,
Rom, tome, airdrome, at-
home, bichrome, cockscomb,
coulomb, coxcomb, defoam,
down-home, ogham,
seadrome, shalom, sholom,
syndrome, aerodrome,
astrodome, catacomb,
chromosome, currycomb,
double-dome, gastronome,
halidrome, hecatomb,
hippodrome, honeycomb,
metronome, monochrome,
motordrome, palindrome,
ribosome, stay-at-home,
Styrofoam

²**ome** \ō-mē\ see OAMY

³**ome** \əm\ see ¹UM

omedy \äm-əd-ē\ comedy, psalmody, tragicomedy

¹omely \əm-lē\ see ²UMBLY

²omely \ōm-lē\ comely, homely

omen \ō-mən\ see OMAN

omenal \äm-ən-ᵊl\ see OMINAL

omene \äm-ə-nē\ see OMINY

¹omer \ō-mər\ comber, foamer, homer, omer, roamer, vomer, beachcomber, Reaumur, Lag b'Omer, misnomer

²omer \əm-ər\ see UMMER

omet \äm-ət\ comet, grommet, vomit

ometer \äm-ət-ər\ barometer, chronometer, cyclometer, drunkometer, ergometer, gasometer, geometer, hydrometer, hygrometer, kilometer, manometer, micrometer, odometer, pedometer, photometer, pulsometer, pyrometer, rheometer, seismometer, spectrometer, speedometer, tachometer, thermometer, anemometer, audiometer, electrometer, magnetometer, alcoholometer

ometry \äm-ə-trē\ barometry, chronometry, geometry, isometry, micrometry, optometry, photometry, psychometry, seismometry, thermometry, craniometry, sociometry, trigonometry

omey \ō-mē\ see OAMY

omi \ō-mē\ see OAMY

¹omic \äm-ik\ comic, anomic, atomic, coelomic, Islamic, tsunamic, agronomic, anatomic, antinomic, autonomic, economic, ergonomic, gastronomic, metronomic, subatomic, taxonomic, tragicomic, Deuteronomic, heroicomic, physiognomic, seriocomic, macroeconomic, microeconomic, socioeconomic

²omic \ō-mik\ gnomic, oghamic, rhizomic, catacombic, monochromic, palindromic

¹omical \äm-i-kəl\ comical, domical, agronomical, anatomical, astronomical, economical, gastronomical, metronomical, tragicomical, heroicomical, physiognomical

²omical \ō-mi-kəl\ domical, coxcombical

omics \äm-iks\ atomics, Islamics, tectonics, bionomics, economics, ergonomics, macroeconomics, microeconomics—*also plurals and possessives of nouns listed at* ¹OMIC

omily \äm-ə-lē\ see OMALY

ominal \äm-ən-ᵊl\ nominal,

abdominal, cognominal,
phenomenal, epiphenomenal

ominance \ äm-nəns \
dominance, prominence,
predominance

ominant \ äm-nənt \ dominant,
prominent, predominant,
semidominant, subdominant,
superdominant

ominate \ äm-ə-nət \ innominate,
prenominate

omine \ äm-ə-nē \ see OMINY

ominence \ äm-nəns \ see
OMINANCE

ominent \ äm-nənt \ see OMINANT

oming \ əm-iŋ \ coming,
plumbing, becoming,
forthcoming, homecoming,
incoming, oncoming,
shortcoming, upcoming,
unbecoming, up-and-
coming—*also present
participles of verbs listed at*
¹UM

omini \ äm-ə-nē \ see OMINY

ominous \ äm-ə-nəs \ ominous,
prolegomenous

ominy \ äm-ə-nē \ hominy,
Romany, Melpomene, anno
Domini, eo nomine

omise \ äm-əs \ pomace,
promise, shammes, shamus,
Thomas, doubting Thomas

omish \ ō-mish \ gnomish,
Romish

omit \ äm-ət \ see OMET

omium \ ō-mē-əm \ chromium,
holmium, encomium,
prostomium

¹**omma** \ äm-ə \ see ²AMA

²**omma** \ əm-ə \ see UMMA

¹**ommel** \ äm-əl \ pommel, Jamil,
trommel

²**ommel** \ əm-əl \ pommel,
pummel, Beau Brummell

ommet \ äm-ət \ see OMET

ommie \ äm-ē \ see ¹AMI

ommon \ äm-ən \ Brahman,
common, shaman, yamen

ommoner \ äm-ə-nər \ almoner,
commoner, gewürztraminer

¹**ommy** \ äm-ē \ see ¹AMI

²**ommy** \ əm-ē \ see UMMY

omo \ ō-mō \ bromo, homo,
majordomo

omon \ ō-mən \ see OMAN

¹**omp** \ ämp \ champ, chomp,
clomp, comp, pomp, romp,
stamp, stomp, swamp, tramp,
tromp, whomp

²**omp** \ əmp \ see UMP

ompany \ əmp-nē \ company,
accompany

¹**ompass** \ äm-pəs \ compass,
pompous, encompass,
gyrocompass

²**ompass** \ əm-pəs \ compass,
rumpus, encompass,
gyrocompass

omper \ äm-pər \ romper,
stamper, swamper,
wafflestomper

omplement \ äm-plə-mənt \
  complement, compliment
ompliment \ äm-plə-mənt \ see
  OMPLEMENT
ompo \ äm-pō \ campo, compo
ompous \ äm-pəs \ see ¹OMPASS
ompt \ aůnt \ see ²OUNT
ompy \ äm-pē \ scampi, swampy
omythy \ äm-ə-thē \ see OMATHY
¹on \ än \ ban, chon, con, conn,
  dawn, don, faun, fawn, gone,
  guan, Han, John, khan,
  maun, mon, on, pan, pawn,
  phon, prawn, Shan, spawn,
  swan, wan, yawn, yon, yuan,
  aeon, add-on, agon, agone,
  Akan, alençon, ancon, anon,
  archon, argon, atman, axon,
  baton, blouson, bon ton,
  bonbon, boron, boson,
  bouillon, Brython, bygone,
  caisson, Calgon, canton,
  capon, chaconne, chiffon,
  chignon, chiton, chrismon,
  cistron, clip-on, codon, come-
  on, cordon, coupon,
  crampon, crayon, crepon,
  cretonne, crouton, Dacron,
  dead-on, Dear John, dewan,
  doggone, doggoned, Don
  Juan, eon, exon, far-gone,
  flacon, foregone, Freon,
  fronton, Gibran, gluon,
  gnomon, Gosplan, guidon,
  hadron, hazan, hogan, icon,
  intron, kaon, Kerman,

Khoisan, Kirman, koan,
krypton, kurgan, lauan,
lepton, liman, macron,
Memnon, meson, micron,
moron, mouton, muon,
natron, neon, nephron,
neuron, neutron, ninon,
nylon, odds-on, Orlon,
outgone, pacon, parton,
Pathan, pavane, pecan, peon,
Phaethon, photon, phyton,
pion, pinon, piton, plankton,
pluton, pompon, proton, put-
on, pylon, python, Qur'an,
radon, rayon, recon, rhyton,
run-on, salon, Shaban,
shaman, shaitan, Shingon,
slip-on, snap-on, solon,
soupçon, soutane, stolon,
Szechuan, taipan, tampon,
taxon, Teflon, teston,
thereon, tisane, torchon,
toucan, toyon, trigon, Tristan,
triton, trogon, Typhon,
tzigane, uhlan, upon, walk-
on, witan, whereon, wonton,
xenon, yaupon, zircon,
Acheron, Ahriman, aileron,
amazon, amnion, autobahn,
Avalon, Babylon, balmacaan,
Bantustan, baryon, betatron,
biathlon, cabochon, carillon,
carryon, celadon, chorion,
colophon, cyclotron, decagon,
decathlon, demijohn,
deuteron, dipteron, echelon,

electron, elevon, epsilon, etymon, fermion, follow-on, goings-on, gonfalon, graviton, harijan, helicon, heptagon, hexagon, hopping John, leprechaun, lexicon, liaison, logion, macédoine, marathon, marzipan, mastodon, Mellotron, morion, myrmidon, negatron, nonagon, noumenon, nucleon, Oberon, octagon, omicron, organon, ostracon, pantheon, paragon, Parmesan, parmigiana, Parthenon, pentagon, Percheron, Phlegethon, polygon, positron, Procyon, put-upon, Ramadan, Rubicon, silicon, tachyon, talkathon, telamon, telethon, thereupon, undergone, upsilon, virion, walkathon, whereupon, woebegone, abutilon, Agamemnon, archenteron, arrière-ban, asyndeton, automaton, Bellerophon, bildungsroman, carrying-on, dodecagon, encephalon, ephemeron, himation, interferon, Laocoön, mesenteron, millimicron, oxymoron, phenomenon, protozoon, septentrion, sine qua non, t'ai chi ch'uan, anacoluthon, diencephalon,

mesencephalon, metencephalon, prolegomenon, prothalamion, prosencephalon, spermatozoon, telencephalon, epiphenomenon, myelencephalon, kyrie eleison

²**on** \ō\n\ fond, ton, ballon, baton, bouillon, flacon, fourgon, frisson, garçon, lorgnon, maçon, marron, Marron, mouflon, soupçon, Aubusson, bourguignon, feuilleton, Ganelon, limaçon, papillon, filet mignon, Saint Emilion

³**on** \ȯn\ awn, bonne, brawn, dawn, drawn, faun, fawn, gone, lawn, maun, on, pawn, prawn, spawn, won, yawn, add-on, agon, agone, begone, bygone, chaconne, clip-on, come-on, dead-on, doggone, far-gone, foregone, hands-on, hard-on, head-on, hereon, impawn, indrawn, odds-on, outgone, put-on, run-on, slip-on, snap-on, thereon, turned-on, upon, walk-on, whereon, wiredrawn, withdrawn, bourguignonne, carryon, follow-on, goings-on, hanger-on, hereupon, looker-on, put-upon, thereupon, undergone, whereupon, woebegone, carrying-on

⁴on \ōn\ see ¹ONE

⁵on \ən\ see UN

ona \ō-nə\ dona, Jonah, krone, trona, Bellona, bologna, cinchona, corona, kimono, madrona, persona, Desdemona, Rosh Hashanah, in propria persona

ona \on-yə\ see ³ONIA

onachal \än-i-kəl\ see ONICAL

onae \ō-nē\ see ¹ONY

onah \ō-nə\ see ONA

onal \ōn-ᵊl\ clonal, tonal, zonal, atonal, coronal, hormonal, baritonal, microtonal, polytonal, semitonal

onant \ō-nənt\ see ONENT

onas \ō-nəs\ see ²ONUS

onative \ō-nət-iv\ conative, donative

onc \äŋk\ see ¹ONK

¹once \äns\ see ²ANCE

²once \əns\ see UNCE

¹onch \äŋk\ see ¹ONK

²onch \änch\ see ¹AUNCH

oncha \äŋ-kə\ see ANKA

oncho \än-chō\ honcho, poncho, rancho

onchus \äŋ-kəs\ bronchus, rhonchus

¹ond \änd\ blond, bond, fond, frond, Gond, pond, rand, sonde, wand, yond, abscond, beau monde, beyond, despond, gourmand, haut monde, millpond, neoned,

pair-bond, respond, allemande, towmond, correspond, demimonde, Eurobond, vagabond, radiosonde, slough of despond—*also pasts of verbs listed at* ¹ON

²ond \ōⁿ\ see ²ON

³ond \ȯnt\ see ¹AUNT

onda \än-də\ Lahnda, Golconda, anaconda

ondage \än-dij\ bondage, vagabondage

ondam \än-dəm\ see ¹ONDOM

ondant \än-dənt\ see ONDENT

onday \ən-dē\ see UNDI

ondays \ən-dēz\ see UNDAYS

onde \änd\ see ¹OND

ondeau \än-dō\ see ONDO

ondel \än-dᵊl\ condyle, fondle, rondel

ondence \än-dəns\ correspondence, despondence

ondency \än-dən-sē\ despondency, correspondency

ondent \än-dənt\ fondant, despondent, respondent, corespondent, correspondent

¹onder \än-dər\ bonder, condor, maunder, ponder, squander, wander, yonder, zander, absconder, responder, transponder—*also comparatives of adjectives listed at* ¹OND

²onder \ən-dər\ see UNDER

ondly \än-lē \ see ¹ANLY

ondness \än-nəs \ see ANNESS

ondo \än-dō \ condo, rondeau,
rondo, secondo, tondo,
forzando, glissando, lentando,
parlando, scherzando,
sforzando, allargando,
rallentando, ritardando,
accelerando

¹**ondom** \än-dəm \ condom,
quondam

²**ondom** \ən-dəm \ see UNDUM

ondor \än-dər \ see ¹ONDER

ondrous \ən-drəs \ see
UNDEROUS

ondyle \än-dᵊl \ see ONDEL

¹**one** \ōn \ blown, bone, clone,
cone, crone, drone, flown,
groan, grown, hone, known,
loan, lone, moan, Mon,
mown, none, own, phone,
pone, prone, roan, scone,
sewn, shone, shoon, shown,
sone, sown, stone, throne,
thrown, tone, trone, won,
zone, agon, aitchbone, alone,
atone, backbone, bemoan,
birthstone, breastbone,
brimstone, brownstone,
capstone, cheekbone,
chinbone, cogon, cologne,
colon, condone, curbstone,
cyclone, daimon, debone,
depone, dethrone, disown,
earphone, enthrone,
fieldstone, flagstone,
flyblown, freestone, full-
blown, gallstone, gemstone,
gravestone, grindstone,
hailstone, halftone,
headphone, headstone, high-
flown, hipbone, homegrown,
hormone, impone, ingrown,
intone, jawbone, keystone,
leone, limestone, lodestone,
milestone, millstone,
misknown, moonstone,
oilstone, outgrown,
outshown, ozone, peon,
pinbone, pinecone, pinon,
pinyon, postpone, propone,
rezone, rhinestone, sandstone,
shade-grown, shinbone,
Shoshone, soapstone, T-bone,
tailbone, thighbone,
tombstone, touchstone,
tritone, trombone, turnstone,
twelve-tone, two-tone,
unknown, unthrone, well-
known, whalebone,
whetstone, windblown,
wishbone, allophone,
anglophone, anklebone,
barbitone, barytone,
bombardon, chaperon,
cherrystone, cobblestone,
collarbone, cornerstone,
cortisone, cuttlebone,
diaphone, Dictaphone,
epigone, francophone,
gramophone, herringbone,
homophone, ironstone,

knucklebone, marrowbone, megaphone, mellophone, methadone, microphone, microtone, minestrone, monotone, overblown, overflown, overgrown, overthrown, overtone, Picturephone, polyphone, rottenstone, sacaton, saxophone, semitone, shacklebone, silicone, sousaphone, speakerphone, stepping-stone, telephone, undertone, vibraphone, xylophone, anticyclone, bred-in-the-bone, eau de cologne, radiophone, sine qua non, testosterone, videophone, Darby and Joan, radiotelephone

²**one** \ō-nē\ see ¹ONY

³**one** \än\ see ¹ON

⁴**one** \ən\ see UN

⁵**one** \ón\ see ³ON

onean \ō-nē-ən\ see ¹ONIAN

¹**oned** \ōnd\ boned, stoned, toned, cologned, high-toned, pre-owned, rawboned, rhinestoned, two-toned, cobblestoned—*also pasts of verbs listed at* ¹ONE

²**oned** \än\ see ¹ON

oneless \ōn-ləs\ boneless, toneless

onely \ōn-lē\ lonely, only, pronely

onement \ōn-mənt\ atonement, cantonment, dethronement, disownment, enthronement

oneness \ən-nəs\ dunness, doneness, oneness, rotundness

onent \ō-nənt\ sonant, component, deponent, exponent, opponent, proponent

oneous \ō-nē-əs\ see ONIOUS

¹**oner** \ō-nər\ boner, donor, droner, groaner, honer, loaner, loner, stoner, toner, zoner, condoner, dethroner, intoner, landowner, shipowner, telephoner

²**oner** \ón-ər\ see ¹AWNER

onerous \än-ə-rəs\ onerous, sonorous

ones \ōnz\ nones, sawbones, Davy Jones, lazybones, skull and crossbones—*also plurals and possessives of nouns and third singular presents of verbs listed at* ¹ONE

onest \än-əst\ honest, dishonest, Hinayanist, Mahayanist

¹**oney** \ō-nē\ see ¹ONY

²**oney** \ən-ē\ see UNNY

¹**ong** \äŋ\ bong, gong, hong, prong, Tang, tong, yang, barong, biltong, dingdong, dugong, kiang, liang, Mah-Jongg, Ping-Pong, sarong, satang, billabong,

scuppernong, Sturm und
Drang, Vietcong, ylang-ylang

²**ong** \ȯŋ \ bong, dong, gong,
long, prong, song, strong,
thong, throng, tong, wrong,
agelong, along, barong,
belong, biltong, chaise
longue, daylong, dingdong,
diphthong, dugong, endlong,
erelong, furlong, headlong,
headstrong, kampong,
lifelong, livelong, monthlong,
nightlong, oblong, oolong,
part-song, Ping-Pong,
plainsong, prolong, sarong,
sidelong, singsong, so long,
souchong, yearlong,
billabong, cradlesong,
evensong, scuppernong, sing-
along, tagalong, Vietcong

³**ong** \əŋ \ see ¹UNG

onga \äŋ-gə \ conga, tonga,
mridanga

onge \ənj \ see UNGE

onged \ȯŋd \ pronged, thonged,
multipronged—*also pasts of
verbs listed at* ²ONG

¹**onger** \əŋ-gər \ hunger,
monger, younger, fellmonger,
fishmonger, ironmonger,
newsmonger, prasemonger,
scaremonger, warmonger,
whoremonger, wordmonger,
costermonger, fashionmonger,
rumormonger, scandalmonger

²**onger** \ən-jər \ see ¹UNGER

ongery \əŋ-grē \ hungry,
fellmongery, ironmongery

ongful \ȯŋ-fəl \ wrongful,
songful

ongin \ən-jən \ see UNGEON

ongish \ȯŋ-ish \ longish,
strongish

ongo \äŋ-gō \ bongo, congou,
Kongo, mongo, Niger-Congo

ongous \əŋ-gəs \ see UNGOUS

¹**ongue** \əŋ \ see ¹UNG

²**ongue** \ȯŋ \ see ²ONG

ongued \ənd \ lunged, tongued

ongy \ən-jē \ see UNGY

onhomous \än-ə-məs \ see
ONYMOUS

oni \ō-nē \ see ¹ONY

¹**onia** \ō-nē-ə \ bignonia,
clintonia, mahonia,
paulownia, Polonia, tithonia,
valonia, zirconia

²**onia** \ō-nyə \ ammonia,
pneumonia, Polonia, tithonia,
valonia

³**onia** \ōn-yə \ doña, begonia

onial \ō-nē-əl \ baronial,
colonial, ceremonial,
matrimonial, testimonial

¹**onian** \ō-nē-ən \ chthonian,
aeonian, Antonian, Baconian,
Clactonian, demonian,
Devonian, draconian,
Estonian, favonian,
gorgonian, Ionian,
Jacksonian, Oxonian,
plutonian, Samsonian,

Shoshonean, Slavonian,
Amazonian, Apollonian,
Babylonian, calypsonian,
Chalcedonian, Hamiltonian,
parkinsonian

²**onlan** \ō-nyən \ Zonian,
Amazonian, Babylonian,
Estonian, Macedonian

onic \än-ik \ chronic, chthonic,
conic, dornick, phonic, sonic,
tonic, Aaronic, agonic,
atonic, benthonic, bionic,
Brittonic, Brythonic, bubonic,
Byronic, canonic, carbonic,
cryonic, cyclonic, daimonic,
demonic, draconic, euphonic,
gnomonic, harmonic,
hedonic, ionic, Ionic, ironic,
laconic, Masonic, mnemonic,
planktonic, platonic, plutonic,
pneumonic, Puranic,
Pythonic, sardonic, sermonic,
Slavonic, symphonic,
synchronic, tectonic,
Teutonic, ultrasonic, zirconic,
catatonic, diachronic,
diatonic, disharmonic,
electronic, embryonic,
hegemonic, histrionic,
homophonic, hydroponic,
inharmonic, isotonic,
macaronic, megaphonic,
microphonic, monophonic,
monotonic, nonionic,
Philharmonic, polyphonic,
quadraphonic, semitonic,

Solomonic, supersonic,
supertonic, telephonic,
architectonic, chameleonic,
cardiotonic, electrotonic,
geotectonic, Neoplatonic,
stereophonic

onica \än-i-kə \ harmonica,
japonica, veronica

onical \än-i-kəl \ chronicle,
conical, monachal, monocle,
canonical, demonical,
ironical, deuterocanonical

onicals \än-i-kəlz \ Chronicles,
canonicals

onicle \än-i-kəl \ see ONICAL

onicles \än-i-kəlz \ see ONICALS

onics \än-iks \ onyx, phonics,
bionics, cryonics,
mnemonics, Ovonics,
sardonyx, tectonics, avionics,
electronics, histrionics,
hydroponics, microphonics,
nucleonics, quadriphonics,
radionics, supersonics,
thermionics, architectonics—
*also plurals and possessives
of nouns listed at* ONIC

¹**oning** \än-iŋ \ awning,
couponing

²**oning** \ō-niŋ \ loaning,
jawboning, landowning

onion \ən-yən \ see UNION

onious \ō-nē-əs \ erroneous,
euphonious, felonious,
harmonious, Polonius,
symphonious, acrimonious,

ceremonious, disharmonious,
inharmonious, parsimonious,
sanctimonious,
unceremonious

¹**onis** \ō-nəs\ see ²ONUS

²**onis** \än-əs\ see ¹ONUS

onish \än-ish\ donnish, monish,
admonish, astonish,
premonish, leprechaunish

onishment \än-ish-mənt\
admonishment, astonishment

onium \ō-nē-əm\ euphonium,
harmonium, plutonium,
pandemonium

onius \ō-nē-əs\ see ONIOUS

onjon \än-jən\ see UNGEON

onjure \än-jər\ conjure, rondure

¹**onk** \äŋk\ ankh, bronc, clonk,
conch, conk, honk, plonk,
zonk, honkytonk

²**onk** \əŋk\ see UNK

onker \äŋ-kər\ conker,
conquer, honker

¹**onkey** \äŋ-kē\ see ONKY

²**onkey** \əŋ-kē\ see UNKY

onkian \äŋ-kē-ən\ conquian,
Algonkian

onky \äŋ-kē\ conkey, donkey,
honkie, wonky, yanqui

onless \ən-ləs\ see UNLESS

only \ōn-lē\ see ONELY

onment \ōn-mənt\ see ONEMENT

onn \än\ see ¹ON

¹**onna** \ón-ə\ donna, fauna

²**onna** \än-ə\ see ¹ANA

onnage \ən-ij\ see UNNAGE

¹**onne** \än\ see ¹ON

²**onne** \ən\ see UN

³**onne** \ón\ see ³ON

onner \än-ər\ see ¹ONOR

onnet \än-ət\ bonnet, sonnet,
bluebonnet, sunbonnet,
warbonnet

onnish \än-ish\ see ONISH

¹**onny** \än-ē\ see ¹ANI

²**onny** \ən-ē\ see UNNY

¹**ono** \ō-nō\ phono, cui bono,
kimono, kakemono,
makimono

²**ono** \ō-nə\ see ONA

³**ono** \än-ō\ see ¹ANO

onocle \än-i-kəl\ see ONICAL

onomer \än-ə-mər\ monomer,
astronomer, comonomer

onomist \än-ə-məst\
agronomist, autonomist,
economist, ergonomist,
gastronomist, synonymist,
taxonomist, Deuteronomist

onomous \än-ə-məs\ see
ONYMOUS

onomy \än-ə-mē\ agronomy,
antonymy, astronomy,
autonomy, economy,
eponymy, gastronomy,
homonomy, metonymy,
synonymy, taxonomy,
toponymy, Deuteronomy,
diseconomy, heteronomy

¹**onor** \än-ər\ Bonner, fawner,
goner, honor, dishonor,

marathoner, Afrikaner, weimaraner

²**onor** \ ō-nər \ see ¹ONER

onorous \ än-ə-rəs \ see ONEROUS

onquer \ äŋ-kər \ see ONKER

onquian \ äŋ-kē-ən \ see ONKIAN

ons \ änz \ see ONZE

onsil \ än-səl \ see ONSUL

onsor \ än-sər \ panzer, sponsor

onsul \ än-səl \ consul, tonsil

on't \ ōnt \ don't, won't

¹**ont** \ ənt \ blunt, brunt, bunt, front, grunt, hunt, lunt, punt, runt, shunt, strunt, stunt, want, wont, affront, beachfront, bowfront, breakfront, confront, forefront, housefront, lakefront, manhunt, out-front, seafront, shirtfront, shorefront, storefront, swell-front, up-front, witch-hunt, battlefront, oceanfront, riverfront, waterfront

²**ont** \ änt \ see ²ANT

³**ont** \ ȯnt \ see ¹AUNT

¹**ontal** \ änt-ᵊl \ pontil, fontal, quantal, horizontal, periodontal

²**ontal** \ ənt-ᵊl \ see UNTLE

onte \ änt-ē \ see ¹ANTI

onted \ ȯnt-əd \ wonted, undaunted—*also pasts of verbs listed at* ¹AUNT

onter \ ənt-ər \ see UNTER

onth \ ənth \ month, billionth, millionth, trillionth, twelvemonth

ontian \ änt-ē-ən \ Zontian, post-Kantian

ontic \ änt-ik \ ontic, Vedantic, orthodontic, anacreontic

ontil \ änt-ᵊl \ see ¹ONTAL

ontinent \ änt-ᵊn-ənt \ continent, incontinent, subcontinent, supercontinent

ontist \ änt-əst \ Vedantist, orthodontist, prosthodontist

onton \ änt-ᵊn \ ponton, wanton

ontra \ än-trə \ contra, mantra, tantra, per contra

ontre \ änt-ər \ see ¹AUNTER

¹**onus** \ än-əs \ Cronus, Faunus, Adonis

²**onus** \ ō-nəs \ bonus, Cronus, Jonas, onus, slowness, Adonis, colonus

¹**ony** \ ō-nē \ bony, coney, crony, phony, pony, stony, tony, Tony, yoni, baloney, bologna, canzone, Oenone, padrone, spumoni, tortoni, abalone, acrimony, agrimony, alimony, antimony, cannelloni, ceremony, chalcedony, colophony, macaroni, matrimony, minestrone, palimony, parsimony, patrimony, pepperoni, provolone, rigatoni, sanctimony, telephony, testimony,

zabaglione, con espressione,
conversazione, dramatis
personae

²**ony** \än-ē\ see ¹ANI

onymist \än-ə-məst\ see
ONOMIST

onymous \än-ə-məs\
bonhomous, anonymous,
antonymous, autonomous,
eponymous, homonymous,
pseudonymous, synonymous,
heteronomous

onymy \än-ə-mē\ see ONOMY

¹**onyon** \än-yən\ ronyon,
wanion

²**onyon** \ən-yən\ see UNION

onyx \än-iks\ see ONICS

onze \änz\ bonze, bronze, pons,
long johns, Afrikaans,
solitons, islet of
Langerhans—*also plurals and
possessives of nouns and third
singular presents of verbs
listed at* ¹ON

onzi \än-zē\ see ONZY

onzy \än-zē\ bronzy, Ponzi

oo \ü\ see ¹EW

oob \üb\ see UBE

oober \ü-bər\ see UBER

ooby \ü-bē\ booby, looby, ruby

¹**ooch** \üch\ brooch, hooch,
mooch, pooch, smooch,
capuche, scaramouch

²**ooch** \ōch\ see OACH

oocher \ü-chər\ see UTURE

oochy \ü-chē\ smoochy,
Baluchi, penuche

¹**ood** \ud\ good, hood, pud,
rudd, should, stood, wood,
would, yod, basswood,
bentwood, boxwood,
brushwood, childhood,
cordwood, deadwood, do-
good, dogwood, driftwood,
falsehood, firewood,
girlhood, godhood,
greasewood, greenwood,
groundwood, gumwood,
hardwood, ironwood,
knighthood, maidhood,
manhood, monkhood,
monkshood, no-good,
pinewood, plywood,
priesthood, pulpwood,
redwood, rosewood,
sainthood, selfhood,
softwood, sonhood,
statehood, stinkwood,
Talmud, teakwood, unhood,
Wedgwood, wifehood,
withstood, wormwood,
arrowwood, bachelorhood,
brotherhood, buttonwood,
candlewood, cedarwood,
cottonwood, fatherhood,
hardihood, Hollywood,
likelihood, livelihood,
maidenhood, motherhood,
nationhood, neighborhood,
parenthood, peckerwood,
personhood, Robin Hood,

sandalwood, scattergood,
servanthood, sisterhood,
spinsterhood, toddlerhood,
tulipwood, understood,
widowhood, womanhood,
misunderstood, unlikelihood,
widowerhood

²**ood** \ ōd \ see ODE

³**ood** \ üd \ see UDE

⁴**ood** \ əd \ see ¹UD

¹**ooded** \ əd-əd \ blooded, cold-
blooded, full-blooded, half-
blooded, hot-blooded, pure-
blooded, red-blooded, star-
studded, warm-blooded—*also
pasts of verbs listed at* ¹UD

²**ooded** \ ùd-əd \ hooded,
wooded, hard-wooded, soft-
wooded

¹**ooder** \ üd-ər \ see UDER

²**ooder** \ əd-ər \ see UDDER

ooding \ ùd-iŋ \ pudding, do-
gooding

oodle \ üd-ᵊl \ boodle, doodle,
feudal, noodle, poodle,
strudel, caboodle, flapdoodle,
paludal, Yankee-Doodle

oodman \ ùd-mən \ goodman,
woodman

oodoo \ üd-ü \ hoodoo, kudu,
voodoo

oods \ ùdz \ backwoods, dry
goods, piney woods—*also
plurals and possessives of
nouns and third singular*

presents of verbs listed at
¹OOD

oodsman \ ùdz-mən \ woodsman,
ombudsman

¹**oody** \ üd-ē \ broody, moody

²**oody** \ ùd-ē \ cuddy, goody,
hoody, woody, goody-goody

³**oody** \ əd-ē \ see ¹UDDY

ooer \ ü-ər \ see ¹EWER

ooey \ ü-ē \ see EWY

¹**oof** \ üf \ goof, kloof, poof,
pouf, proof, roof, spoof,
woof, aloof, behoof,
disproof, fireproof, foolproof,
forehoof, rustproof, shadoof,
soundproof, sunroof,
Tartuffe, unroof, bulletproof,
opera bouffe, shatterproof,
waterproof, weatherproof

²**oof** \ ùf \ hoof, poof, roof,
woof, forehoof, Tartuffe

³**oof** \ ōf \ see OAF

⁴**oof** \ üv \ see ³OVE

oofah \ ü-fə \ see UFA

¹**oofer** \ ü-fər \ proofer, roofer,
twofer, waterproofer

²**oofer** \ ùf-ər \ hoofer, woofer

oofy \ ü-fē \ goofy, spoofy, Sufi

ooge \ üj \ see ¹UGE

ooger \ ùg-ər \ see UGUR

oogie \ ùg-ē \ bogey, boogie,
boogie-woogie

oo-goo \ ü-gü \ see UGU

ooh \ ü \ see ¹EW

ooh-pooh \ ü-pü \ hoopoe, pooh-
pooh

ooi \ ü-ē \ see EWY

ooist \ ü-əst \ doest, tattooist, voodooist—*also superlatives of adjectives listed at* ¹EW

¹ook \ ùk \ book, brook, cook, crook, gook, hook, look, nook, rook, schnook, shook, snook, took, bankbook, betook, billhook, caoutchouc, chapbook, checkbook, Chinook, cookbook, forsook, fishhook, guidebook, handbook, hornbook, hymnbook, logbook, matchbook, mistook, notebook, outlook, partook, passbook, playbook, pothook, promptbook, psalmbook, retook, schoolbook, scrapbook, sketchbook, skyhook, songbook, studbook, textbook, unhook, workbook, yearbook, buttonhook, copybook, donnybrook, gerenuk, inglenook, overbook, overlook, overtook, pocketbook, storybook, tenterhook, undertook, Volapuk, gobbledygook

²ook \ ük \ see UKE

ooka \ ü-kə \ bazooka, felucca, palooka, verruca

ookah \ ùk-ə \ hookah, sukkah

ooker \ ùk-ər \ booker, cooker,

hooker, looker, snooker, good-looker, onlooker

ookery \ ùk-ə-rē \ crookery, rookery

ookie \ ùk-ē \ bookie, cookie, hooky, nooky, rookie, rooky, walkie-lookie

ooking \ ùk-iŋ \ booking, good-looking, onlooking

ooklet \ ùk-lət \ booklet, brooklet, hooklet

¹ooks \ ùks \ deluxe, gadzooks—*also plurals and possessives of nouns and third singular presents of verbs listed at* UKE

²ooks \ üks \ crux, luxe, zooks, deluxe, gadzooks—*also plurals and possessives of nouns and third singular presents of verbs listed at* ¹OOK

¹ooky \ ü-kē \ kooky, spooky, bouzouki, Kabuki, saluki

²ooky \ ùk-ē \ see OOKIE

¹ool \ ül \ boule, boulle, buhl, cool, drool, fool, fuel, ghoul, gul, joule, mewl, mule, pool, pul, pule, rule, school, spool, stool, tool, tulle, you'll, yule, air-cool, ampoule, babul, befool, carpool, cesspool, curule, Elul, faldstool, footstool, misrule, preschool, retool, self-rule, synfuel, toadstool, tomfool, uncool, vanpool, whirlpool, fascicule, gallinule, graticule, lenticule, majuscule, minuscule, molecule, monticule, overrule, reticule, ridicule, vestibule, water-cool

²ool \ùl\ see ¹UL

oola \ü-lə\ see ULA

oolean \ü-lē-ən\ see ULEAN

ooled \üld\ bejeweled, unschooled, vestibuled—*also pasts of verbs listed at* ¹OOL

ooler \ü-lər\ cooler, gular, puler, ruler, carpooler, grade-schooler, high schooler, preschooler, ridiculer, watercooler

oolie \ü-lē\ see ULY

oolish \ü-lish\ coolish, foolish, ghoulish, mulish, pound-foolish

¹oolly \ü-lē\ see ULY

²oolly \ùl-ē\ see ²ULLY

¹oom \üm\ bloom, boom, broom, brougham, brume, combe, cwm, doom, flume, fume, gloom, glume, groom, khoum, loom, neume, plume, rheum, room, spume, tomb, toom, vroom, whom, womb, zoom, abloom, assume, ballroom, barroom, bathroom, bedroom, boardroom, bridegroom, broadloom, checkroom, classroom, cloakroom, coatroom, consume, costume,

courtroom, darkroom, dayroom, entomb, enwomb, exhume, foredoom, greenroom, guardroom, headroom, heirloom, homeroom, houseroom, illume, inhume, jibboom, legroom, legume, lunchroom, mudroom, mushroom, newsroom, perfume, playroom, poolroom, pressroom, presume, proofroom, relume, resume, salesroom, schoolroom, showroom, sickroom, simoom, stateroom, stockroom, storeroom, subsume, taproom, Targum, tearoom, toolroom, wardroom, washroom, workroom, anteroom, checkerbloom, dyer's broom, elbowroom, impostume, locker-room, nom de plume, smoke-filled room, witches'-broom

²oom \ùm\ see ²UM

oomed \ümd\ groomed, plumed, wombed, well-groomed—*also pasts of verbs listed at* ¹OOM

oomer \ü-mər\ see UMER

oomily \ü-mə-lē\ gloomily, contumely

¹ooming \ü-mən\ see UMAN

²ooming \ü-miŋ\ see UMING

oomlet \üm-lət\ boomlet,
plumelet

oomy \ü-mē\ bloomy, boomy,
fumy, gloomy, plumy,
rheumy, roomy, spumy,
costumey

¹oon \ün\ boon, coon, croon,
dune, goon, hewn, June,
loon, lune, moon, noon,
prune, rune, shoon, soon,
spoon, swoon, strewn, toon,
tune, aswoon, attune, baboon,
balloon, bassoon, buffoon,
cardoon, cartoon, cocoon,
commune, doubloon,
dragoon, festoon, fine-tune,
forenoon, gaboon, gadroon,
galloon, Gudrun, half-moon,
harpoon, immune, impugn,
jargoon, jejune, lagoon,
lampoon, lardoon, maroon,
monsoon, Neptune, oppugn,
patroon, platoon, poltroon,
pontoon, premune, puccoon,
quadroon, raccoon, ratoon,
repugn, rockoon, rough-
hewn, saloon, shalloon,
soupspoon, spittoon,
spontoon, teaspoon, tribune,
triune, tuchun, tycoon,
typhoon, untune, Walloon,
afternoon, barracoon,
dessertspoon, honeymoon,
importune, macaroon,
octoroon, opportune,
pantaloon, picaroon,

picayune, rigadoon,
saskatoon, tablespoon,
contrabassoon, inopportune

²oon \ōn\ see ¹ONE

oonal \ün-ᵊl\ see UNAL

ooner \ü-nər\ crooner, crowner,
lunar, pruner, schooner,
sooner, swooner, tuner,
harpooner, lacunar,
lampooner, oppugner,
honeymooner, semilunar

¹oonery \ün-rē\ buffoonery,
lampoonery, poltroonery

²oonery \ü-nə-rē\ see UNARY

ooney \ü-nē\ see OONY

oonie \ü-nē\ see OONY

ooning \ü-niŋ\ nooning,
ballooning, cartooning,
gadrooning

oonish \ü-nish\ moonish,
buffoonish, cartoonish,
picayunish

oonless \ün-ləs\ moonless,
tuneless, woundless

oons \ünz\ lunes, zounds,
eftsoons, afternoons—*also
plurals and possessives of
nouns and third singular
presents of verbs listed at*
¹OON

oony \ü-nē\ gooney, loony,
luny, Moonie, moony,
puisne, puny, spoony, Zuni

o-op \üp\ see ¹OOP

¹oop \üp\ bloop, coop, co-op,
croup, droop, drupe, dupe,

goop, group, loop, loupe,
poop, roup, scoop, sloop,
snoop, soup, stoop, stoup,
stupe, swoop, troop, troupe,
whoop, age-group, in-group,
out-group, recoup, regroup,
subgroup, T-group, cock-a-
hoop, nincompoop,
paratroop

²**oop** \ úp \ hoop, whoop,
cock-a-hoop

oopee \ ü-pē \ see OOPY

ooper \ ü-pər \ blooper, cooper,
duper, grouper, looper,
scooper, snooper, stupor,
swooper, super, trooper,
trouper, party pooper,
paratrooper, super-duper

ooping \ ü-piŋ \ grouping,
trooping

oopoe \ ü-pü \ see OOH-POOH

oops \ úps \ hoops, oops,
whoops, woops

oopy \ ü-pē \ croupy, droopy,
groupie, Kewpie, loopy,
snoopy, soupy, Tupi,
whoopee

¹**oor** \ ōr \ see ¹ORE

²**oor** \ úr \ see ¹URE

³**oor** \ ȯr \ see ¹OR

¹**oorage** \ úr-ij \ moorage,
sewerage

²**oorage** \ ōr-ij \ see ²ORAGE

³**oorage** \ ȯr-ij \ see ³ORAGE

oored \ ōrd \ see ¹OARD

oorer \ ōr-ər \ see ¹ORER

oori \ úr-ē \ see ¹URY

¹**ooring** \ ōr-iŋ \ see ¹ORING

²**ooring** \ úr-iŋ \ see URING

¹**oorish** \ úr-ish \ boorish,
Moorish, poorish, whorish

²**oorish** \ ȯr-ish \ see ¹ORISH

oorly \ úr-lē \ see URELY

oorman \ ōr-mən \ see OREMAN

¹**oors** \ ōrz \ yours, indoors,
outdoors, withindoors,
withoutdoors—*also plurals
and possessives of nouns and
third singular presents of
verbs listed at* ¹ORE

²**oors** \ ȯrz \ Bors, yours,
outdoors, underdrawers,
withindoors, Louis
Quatorze—*also plurals and
possessives of nouns and third
singular presents of verbs
listed at* ¹OR

oorsman \ ōrz-mən \ see
OARSMAN

oosa \ ü-sə \ see ¹USA

¹**oose** \ üs \ see ¹USE

²**oose** \ üz \ see ²USE

¹**ooser** \ ü-sər \ see UCER

²**ooser** \ ü-zər \ see USER

oosey \ ü-sē \ see UICY

¹**oosh** \ üsh \ see OUCHE

²**oosh** \ ush \ see ²USH

oost \ üst \ boost, juiced, roost,
langouste, produced, self-
induced—*also pasts of verbs
listed at* ¹USE

ooster \ us-tər \ rooster,
Worcester

oosy \ ü-zē \ see OOZY

¹oot \ ut \ foot, put, root, soot,
afoot, barefoot, bigfoot,
bird's-foot, Blackfoot,
clubfoot, crow's-foot, enroot,
flatfoot, forefoot, hotfoot,
input, kaput, outfoot, output,
Rajput, snakeroot, splayfoot,
taproot, throughput, uproot,
acre-foot, arrowroot,
bitterroot, cajeput, candle-
foot, gingerroot, orrisroot,
pussyfoot, tenderfoot,
underfoot

²oot \ üt \ see UTE

³oot \ ət \ see ¹UT

¹ootage \ üt-ij \ fruitage, rootage,
scutage

²ootage \ ut-ij \ footage, rootage

¹ooted \ üt-əd \ booted, fruited,
muted, suited, abluted, deep-
rooted, jackbooted,
pantsuited, voluted—*also
pasts of verbs listed at* UTE

²ooted \ ut-əd \ footed,
barefooted, clubfooted, deep-
rooted, duckfooted, fleet-
footed, four-footed, light-
footed, slow-footed,
splayfooted, surefooted, web-
footed, wing-footed, cloven-
footed—*also pasts of verbs
listed at* ¹OOT

¹ooter \ ut-ər \ footer, putter,
shot-putter, pussyfooter

²ooter \ üt-ər \ see UTER

¹ooth \ üth \ smooth, soothe,
tooth

²ooth \ üth \ booth, couth, crwth,
routh, ruth, Ruth, scouth,
sleuth, sooth, tooth, truth,
youth, bucktooth, eyetooth,
forsooth, half-truth, sawtooth,
selcouth, tollbooth, uncouth,
untruth, vermouth,
snaggletooth

oothe \ üth \ see ¹OOTH

oothless \ üth-ləs \ see UTHLESS

oothly \ üth-lē \ soothly,
uncouthly

oothy \ ü-thē \ couthie, toothy

ootie \ üt-ē \ see ¹OOTY

¹ooting \ ut-iŋ \ footing, off-
putting

²ooting \ üt-iŋ \ see UTING

ootle \ üt-ᵊl \ see UTILE

ootless \ üt-ləs \ bootless,
fruitless

ootlet \ üt-lət \ fruitlet, rootlet

oots \ üts \ boots, firstfruits,
slyboots, shoot-the-chutes—
*also plurals and possessives
of nouns and third singular
presents of verbs listed at* UTE

¹ooty \ üt-ē \ beauty, booty,
Clootie, cootie, cutie, duty,
footy, fluty, fruity, hooty,
rooty, snooty, sooty, tutti,

agouti, heavy-duty,
persecutee, tutti-frutti
²ooty \üt-ē \rooty, sooty, tutti
³ooty \ət-ē \see UTTY
oove \üv \see ³OVE
oover \ü-vər \see ³OVER
oovy \ü-vē \groovy, movie
ooze \üz \see ²USE
oozer \ü-zər \see USER
oozle \ü-zəl \see ²USAL
oozy \ü-zē \bluesy, boozy,
choosy, floozy, newsy, oozy,
woozy, Jacuzzi
¹op \äp \bop, chap, chop, clop,
cop, crop, drop, flop, fop,
glop, hop, knop, lop, mop,
op, plop, pop, prop, scop,
shop, slop, sop, stop, strop,
swap, top, whop, wop,
airdrop, atop, backdrop,
backstop, bakeshop, barhop,
bebop, bellhop, blacktop,
bookshop, carhop, cartop,
chop-chop, clip-clop, clop-
clop, coin-op, co-op,
countertop, desktop,
dewdrop, doorstop,
dramshop, Dunlop, eardrop,
eavesdrop, ESOP, estop, f-
stop, fire-stop, flattop, flip-
flop, foretop, grogshop,
gumdrop, hardtop, hedgehop,
hilltop, hockshop, housetop,
joypop, maintop, milksop,
nonstop, outcrop, pawnshop,
ragtop, raindrop, redtop,

ripstop, rooftop, sharecrop,
shortstop, skin-pop, slipslop,
snowdrop, soursop,
stonecrop, sweatshop,
sweetshop, teardrop, tip-top,
treetop, unstop, workshop,
agitprop, barbershop, Ethiop,
island-hop, lollipop,
malaprop, mom-and-pop,
mountaintop, overtop, table-
hop, tabletop, teenybop,
turboprop, whistle-stop,
window-shop
²op \ō \see ¹OW
opa \ō-pə \opah, Europa
opah \ō-pə \see OPA
opal \ō-pəl \copal, nopal, opal
ope \ōp \cope, coup, dope,
grope, holp, hope, lope,
mope, nope, ope, pope, rope,
scop, scope, slope, soap,
stope, taupe, tope, trope,
aslope, elope, gantlope,
gantelope, myope, pyrope,
sandsoap, soft-soap,
tightrope, towrope, antelope,
antipope, calliope,
cantaloupe, chronoscope,
envelope, Ethiope, gyroscope,
horoscope, interlope, isotope,
kinescope, microscope,
misanthrope, periscope,
phalarope, radarscope,
sniperscope, snooperscope,
stethoscope, telescope,

heliotrope, kaleidoscope,
stereoscope

opean \ō-pē-ən\ see OPIAN

opee \ō-pē\ see OPI

open \ō-pən\ holpen, open,
reopen

opence \əp-əns\ see UPPANCE

openny \əp-nē\ threepenny,
twopenny

oper \ō-pər\ coper, doper,
groper, loper, moper, roper,
soaper, toper, eloper, soft-
soaper, interloper

opera \äp-rə\ see OPRA

opery \ō-prē\ popery, ropery

opey \ō-pē\ see OPI

oph \ōf\ see OAF

ophagous \äf-ə-gəs\
coprophagous, esophagus,
necrophagous, sarcophagus,
zoophagous, anthropophagous

ophagy \äf-ə-jē\ geophagy,
coprophagy, anthropophagy

¹ophe \ō-fē\ see OPHY

²ophe \ōf\ see ²OFF

opher \ō-fər\ see OFER

ophet \äf-ət\ see OFIT

¹ophic \äf-ik\ strophic,
antistrophic, apostrophic,
catastrophic

²ophic \ō-fik\ strophic, trophic,
atrophic

ophical \äf-i-kəl\ philosophical,
theosophical

ophir \ō-fər\ see OFER

ophonous \äf-ə-nəs\
cacophonous, homophonous

ophony \äf-ə-nē\ cacophony,
colophony, homophony,
monophony, theophany,
heterophony, stereophony

ophy \ō-fē\ sophy, strophe,
trophy

opi \ō-pē\ dopey, Hopi, mopey,
ropy, soapy, topee, topi

opia \ō-pē-ə\ dystopia, myopia,
sinopia, utopia, cornucopia

opian \ō-pē-ən\ Aesopian,
cyclopean, dystopian,
utopian, Ethiopian,
cornucopian

¹opic \äp-ik\ topic, tropic,
Aesopic, anthropic, ectopic,
Ethiopic, subtropic,
gyroscopic, hygroscopic,
macroscopic, microscopic,
misanthropic, periscopic,
philanthropic, semitropic,
stethoscopic, telescopic,
kaleidoscopic, stereoscopic

²opic \ō-pik\ tropic, myopic,
Ethiopic, psychotropic

opical \äp-i-kəl\ topical,
tropical, anthropical,
subtropical, microscopical,
philanthropical, semitropical,
Neotropical

oplar \äp-lər\ see OPPLER

opless \äp-ləs\ topless,
metropolis

¹opolis \äp-ə-ləs\ propolis,

acropolis, cosmopolis,
necropolis, megalopolis,
metropolis

²opolis \äp-ləs\ see OPLESS

opolist \äp-ə-ləst\ monopolist,
bibliopolist

opoly \äp-ə-lē\ choppily,
floppily, sloppily, duopoly,
vox populi, oligopoly

oppa \äp-ə\ see ¹APA

opped \äpt\ see OPT

oppel \äp-əl\ see OPPLE

opper \äp-ər\ bopper, chopper,
copper, cropper, dropper,
flopper, hopper, lopper,
mopper, popper, proper,
shopper, stopper, swapper,
topper, whopper, yapper,
clodhopper, eavesdropper,
eyedropper, eyepopper,
grasshopper, hedgehopper,
improper, job-hopper,
joypopper, leafhopper,
namedropper, sharecropper,
showstopper, skin-popper,
table-hopper, teenybopper,
treehopper, woodchopper,
window-shopper

oppery \äp-rē\ coppery, foppery

oppet \äp-ət\ moppet, poppet

oppily \äp-ə-lē\ see OPOLY

oppiness \äp-ē-nəs\ choppiness,
floppiness, sloppiness

opping \äp-iŋ\ hopping,
sopping, topping, whopping,

clodhopping, eye-popping,
job-hopping, name-dropping

opple \äp-əl\ popple, stopple,
topple, estoppel

oppler \äp-lər\ Doppler, poplar

oppy \äp-ē\ choppy, copy,
crappie, floppy, gloppy,
kopje, poppy, sloppy, soppy,
stroppy, jalopy, okapi,
serape, microcopy, photocopy

opra \äp-rə\ copra, opera

ops \äps\ chops, copse, Ops,
tops, beechdrops, cyclops,
Pelops, pinedrops, sundrops,
muttonchops, triceratops—
*also plurals and possessives
of nouns and third singular
presents of verbs listed at* ¹OP

opse \äps\ see OPS

opsy \äp-sē\ dropsy, autopsy,
biopsy, necropsy

opt \äpt\ Copt, knopped, opt,
topped, adopt, close-cropped,
co-opt, end-stopped—*also
pasts of verbs listed at* ¹OP

opter \äp-tər\ copter, adopter,
helicopter, ornithopter

optic \äp-tik\ Coptic, optic,
synoptic

optimist \äp-tə-məst\ optimist,
Optimist, Soroptimist

option \äp-shən\ option,
adoption, co-option

optric \äp-trik\ catoptric,
dioptric

opula \äp-yə-lə\ copula,
 scopula
opulace \äp-yə-ləs\ populace,
 populous
opuli \äp-ə-lē\ see OPOLY
opulous \äp-yə-ləs\ see
 OPULACE
opus \ō-pəs\ opus, Canopus,
 magnum opus,
 pithecanthropus
¹opy \ō-pē\ see OPI
²opy \äp-ē\ see OPPY
¹oque \ōk\ see OKE
²oque \äk\ see ¹OCK
³oque \ōk\ see ALK
oquial \ō-kwē-əl\ colloquial,
 ventriloquial
¹or \ȯr\ boar, Boer, bore,
 chore, core, corps, crore,
 door, drawer, floor, for, fore,
 four, frore, gnawer, gore,
 kor, moire, mor, more, nor,
 oar, o'er, or, ore, pore, pour,
 roar, sawer, score, shore,
 snore, soar, sore, splore,
 spoor, spore, store, swore,
 Thor, tor, tore, torr, war,
 whore, wore, yore, your,
 you're, abhor, actor, adore,
 afore, and/or, ashore,
 backdoor, bailor, bandore,
 bedsore, before, bezoar,
 bookstore, candor, captor,
 centaur, claymore, closed-
 door, condor, decor, deplore,
 donor, downpour, drugstore,
 encore, ephor, explore,
 eyesore, feoffor, fetor,
 folklore, footsore, forswore,
 fourscore, furor, ichor,
 galore, lessor, memoir,
 mentor, milord, Nestor,
 offshore, onshore, outdoor,
 outpour, outsoar, outwore,
 pastor, rancor, rapport,
 raptor, Realtor, restore,
 rhetor, savior, seafloor,
 seashore, sector, seignior,
 senhor, señor, sensor, settlor,
 signor, smoothbore,
 sophomore, stentor, stertor,
 stressor, stridor, temblor,
 tensor, therefor, therefore,
 threescore, trapdoor, turgor,
 uproar, vendor, wherefore,
 woodlore, abattoir, albacore,
 alongshore, anymore,
 brontosaur, carnivore,
 commodore, comprador,
 confessor, consignor,
 corridor, cuspidor, devisor,
 dinosaur, door-to-door, either-
 or, elector, evermore,
 franchisor, guarantor,
 hackamore, humidor, louis
 d'or, man-of-war, matador,
 metaphor, meteor, Minotaur,
 mirador, nevermore,
 omnivore, out-of-door,
 picador, pinafore,
 pompadour, predator,
 promisor, pterosaur,

reservoir, sagamore,
semaphore, stegosaur,
troubadour, stevedore,
sycamore, theretofore, tug-of-
war, two-by-four, uncalled-
for, underscore, vavasor,
warrantor, alienor,
ambassador, conquistador,
conservator, forevermore,
heldentenor, ichthyosaur,
legislator, plesiosaur,
toreador, tyrannosaur,
administrator, lobster
thermidor

²**or** \ör\ see ¹ORE

³**or** \ər\ see ¹EUR

¹**ora** \ōr-ə\ bora, flora, hora,
mora, sora, Torah, angora,
aurora, fedora, Masora,
menorah, pandora, remora,
senhora, señora, signora,
grandiflora, Simchas Torah,
Tuscarora

²**ora** \òr-ə\ aura, bora, flora,
mora, sora, Torah, angora,
aurora, begorra, camorra,
fedora, gemara, menorah,
pandora, senhora, señora,
signora, grandiflora, Simchas
Torah, Tuscarora

¹**orable** \ōr-ə-bəl\ pourable,
storable, adorable, deplorable,
restorable

²**orable** \òr-ə-bəl\ horrible,
adorable, deplorable,
restorable

oracle \òr-ə-kəl\ coracle, oracle

¹**orage** \är-ij\ barrage, borage,
forage, porridge

²**orage** \ōr-ij\ floorage, storage

³**orage** \òr-ij\ borage, floorage,
forage, porridge, storage

¹**orah** \ōr-ə\ see ¹ORA

²**orah** \òr-ə\ see ²ORA

¹**oral** \ōr-əl\ choral, floral, oral,
aboral, auroral, peroral,
restoral, sororal

²**oral** \òr-əl\ aural, choral,
coral, floral, laurel, moral,
oral, sorrel, aboral, amoral,
balmoral, binaural, immoral,
monaural, peroral, sororal

³**oral** \òrl\ quarrel, schorl,
whorl, ceorl

oram \òr-əm\ see ORUM

orate \òr-ət\ see ORET

¹**orative** \ōr-ət-iv\ explorative,
restorative

²**orative** \òr-ət-iv\ explorative,
pejorative, restorative

orb \òrb\ forb, orb, sorb, Sorb,
absorb, adsorb, desorb, resorb

orbate \òr-bət\ see ORBIT

orbeil \òr-bəl\ see ORBEL

orbel \òr-bəl\ corbeil, corbel,
warble

orbet \òr-bət\ see ORBIT

orbit \òr-bət\ orbit, sorbet,
adsorbate

orc \òrk\ see ²ORK

orcas \òr-kəs\ Dorcas, orchis

¹**orce** \ōrs\ see ¹OURSE

²**orce** \órs\ see ¹ORSE

orced \órst\ see ¹ORST

¹**orceful** \órs-fəl\ forceful, resourceful

²**orceful** \órs-fəl\ see ORSEFUL

¹**orcement** \ōr-smənt\ deforcement, divorcement, enforcement, reinforcement

²**orcement** \òr-smənt\ see ORSEMENT

orcer \ōr-sər\ courser, reinforcer—*also comparatives of adjectives listed at* ¹OURSE

orch \órch\ porch, scorch, torch, blowtorch

orcher \òr-chər\ courtier, scorcher, torture

orchid \òr-kəd\ forked, orchid, cryptorchid, monorchid

orchis \òr-kəs\ see ORCAS

¹**ord** \ōrd\ see ¹OARD

²**ord** \ərd\ see IRD

³**ord** \òr\ see ¹OR

⁴**ord** \órd\ see ²OARD

ordancy \órd-ⁿn-sē\ mordancy, discordancy

ordant \órd-ⁿnt\ mordant, mordent, accordant, concordant, discordant

orde \órd\ see ¹OARD

orded \órd-əd\ see ²ARDED

ordent \órd-ⁿnt\ see ORDANT

order \órd-ər\ boarder, border, corder, order, warder, awarder, disorder, recorder, reorder, rewarder, made-to-order

ordered \órd-ərd\ bordered, ordered—*also pasts of verbs listed at* ORDER

ordial \órd-ē-əl\ exordial, primordial

ordid \órd-əd\ see ²ARDED

¹**ording** \órd-iŋ\ lording, recording, rewarding—*also present participles of verbs listed at* ²OARD

²**ording** \ərd-iŋ\ see ERDING

ordingly \órd-iŋ-lē\ accordingly, rewardingly

ordion \órd-ē-ən\ accordion, Edwardian

ordist \órd-əst\ recordist, clavichordist, harpsichordist

ordon \órd-ⁿn\ see ²ARDEN

ordure \òr-jər\ see ORGER

¹**ordy** \órd-ē\ Geordie, Lordy, awardee

²**ordy** \ərd-ē\ see URDY

¹**ore** \ōr\ blower, boar, Boer, bore, chore, core, corps, crore, door, floor, fore, four, frore, goer, grower, gore, hoar, hoer, lore, knower, more, mower, o'er, oar, ore, poor, pore, pour, roar, rower, score, sewer, shore, shower, snore, soar, sore, sower, splore, spoor, spore, store, swore, thrower, tore, whore, wore, yore, your, you're,

adore, afore, ashore, backdoor, bandore, bedsore, before, bezoar, bookstore, churchgoer, claymore, closed-door, deplore, downpour, drugstore, encore, explore, Exmoor, eyesore, flamethrower, folklore, footsore, forebore, foregoer, forgoer, forswore, fourscore, furor, galore, glassblower, hard-core, ignore, implore, indoor, inpour, inshore, lakeshore, mindblower, mohur, offshore, onshore, outdoor, outpour, outsoar, outwore, playgoer, rapport, restore, seafloor, seashore, senhor, signor, smoothbore, snowblower, sophomore, temblor, therefore, threescore, trapdoor, uproar, vetoer, wherefore, winegrower, woodlore, albacore, alongshore, anymore, commodore, concertgoer, cuspidor, door-to-door, en rapport, evermore, furthermore, hackamore, hellebore, herbivore, heretofore, manticore, moviegoer, millepore, nevermore, omnivore, operagoer, out-of-door, petit four, pinafore, pompadour, sagamore, semaphore, stevedore, sycamore, theatergoer, theretofore, troubadour, two-by-four, underscore, vavasor, whistle-blower, cinemagoer, esprit de corps, forevermore, hereinbefore, insectivore

²ore \ ȯr-ē \ see ORY

³ore \ u̇r \ see ¹URE

⁴ore \ ər-ə \ see ¹OROUGH

oreal \ ȯr-ē-əl \ see ORIAL

orean \ ȯr-ē-ən \ see ORIAN

oreas \ ȯr-ē-əs \ see ORIOUS

ored \ ȯrd \ see ¹OARD

oredom \ ȯrd-əm \ boredom, whoredom

orehead \ ȯr-əd \ see ORRID

¹oreign \ är-ən \ see ¹ORIN

²oreign \ ȯr-ən \ see ²ORIN

oreigner \ ȯr-ə-nər \ see ORONER

orem \ ōr-əm \ see ORUM

oreman \ ȯr-mən \ corpsman, doorman, foreman, longshoreman

oreous \ ȯr-ē-əs \ see ORIOUS

¹orer \ ōr-ər \ borer, corer, floorer, pourer, roarer, scorer, schnorrer, snorer, soarer, adorer, deplorer, explorer— *also comparatives of adjectives listed at* ¹ORE

²orer \ ȯr-ər \ see ¹ORRER

oreson \ ōrs-ᵊn \ see OARSEN

orest \ ȯr-əst \ see ORIST

orester \ ȯr-ə-stər \ see ORISTER

oret \ ōr-ət \ floret, sororate

oreum \ȯr-ē-əm\ see ORIUM

oreward \ȯr-wərd\ see
OREWORD

oreword \ȯr-wərd\ foreword,
shoreward

orf \ȯrf\ see ORPH

org \ȯrg\ morgue, cyborg

organ \ȯr-gən\ gorgon,
Morgan, organ, Demogorgon

orge \ȯrj\ forge, George, gorge,
scourge, disgorge, drop-forge,
engorge, reforge

orger \ȯr-jər\ bordure, forger,
gorger, ordure

orgi \ȯr-gē\ see ORGY

orgian \ȯr-jən\ Georgian,
Swedenborgian

orgon \ȯr-gən\ see ORGAN

orgue \ȯrg\ see ORG

orgy \ȯr-gē\ corgi, porgy

ori \ȯr-ē\ see ORY

oria \ȯr-ē-ə\ gloria, noria,
scoria, centaurea, euphoria,
victoria, phantasmagoria

orial \ȯr-ē-əl\ boreal, oriel,
oriole, arboreal, armorial,
auctorial, authorial, cantorial,
censorial, corporeal,
cursorial, factorial, fossorial,
manorial, marmoreal,
memorial, pictorial,
praetorial, proctorial,
raptorial, rectorial, sartorial,
seignorial, sensorial,
sponsorial, tonsorial, tutorial,
uxorial, vectorial,

conductorial, consistorial,
curatorial, dictatorial,
directorial, editorial,
equatorial, immemorial,
incorporeal, janitorial,
monitorial, monsignorial,
natatorial, piscatorial,
preceptorial, professorial,
purgatorial, reportorial,
senatorial, territorial,
ambassadorial, conservatorial,
combinatorial, conspiratorial,
extracorporeal, gladiatorial,
gubernatorial, imperatorial,
inquisitorial, legislatorial,
procuratorial, prosecutorial,
extraterritorial,
improvisatorial

oriam \ȯr-ē-əm\ see ORIUM

orian \ȯr-ē-ən\ Dorian, saurian,
Taurean, aurorean, Gregorian,
historian, Nestorian,
praetorian, stentorian,
victorian, dinosaurian,
hyperborean, Oratorian,
prehistorian, senatorian,
terpsichorean, salutatorian,
valedictorian

oriant \ȯr-ē-ənt\ see ORIENT

oriat \ȯr-ē-ət\ see ²AUREATE

oric \ȯr-ik\ auric, choric, Doric,
toric, Armoric, caloric,
clitoric, dysphoric, euphoric,
folkloric, historic,
phosphoric, plethoric, pyloric,
anaphoric, metaphoric,

meteoric, paregoric,
prehistoric, sophomoric,
aleatoric, phantasmagoric

orical \ȯr-i-kəl \ auricle,
historical, rhetorical,
ahistorical, allegorical,
categorical, metaphorical,
oratorical

orics \ȯr-iks \ see ORYX

¹orid \ȯr-əd \ see ORRID

²orid \är-əd \ florid, forehead,
horrid, torrid—*also pasts of
verbs listed at* ¹ARA

oriel \ȯr-ē-əl \ see ORIAL

orient \ȯr-ē-ənt \ orient,
euphoriant

¹orin \är-ən \ florin, foreign,
sarin, sporran, warren

²orin \ȯr-ən \ florin, foreign,
sporran, warren

³orin \ȯr-ən \ see ORINE

orine \ȯr-ən \ chlorine, florin,
cephalosporin

oring \ȯr-iŋ \ boring, flooring,
roaring, shoring, longshoring,
outpouring, rip-roaring

öring \ər-iŋ \ see URRING

oriole \ȯr-ē-əl \ see ORIAL

orious \ȯr-ē-əs \ aureus, Boreas,
glorious, arboreous,
censorious, inglorious,
laborious, notorious,
sartorius, uproarious,
uxorious, vainglorious,
victorious, meritorious

¹oris \ōr-əs \ see ¹ORUS

²oris \ȯr-əs \ see AURUS

¹orish \ȯr-ish \ boarish, poorish,
whorish, folklorish

²orish \u̇r-ish \ see ¹OORISH

¹orist \ȯr-əst \ florist, forest,
sorest, afforest, deforest,
folklorist, reforest, allegorist

²orist \ōr-əst \ florist, folklorist,
allegorist—*also superlatives
of adjectives listed at* ¹ORE

orister \ȯr-ə-stər \ chorister,
forester

ority \ȯr-ət-ər \ authority,
majority, minority, priority,
seniority, sonority, apriority,
exteriority, inferiority,
interiority, posteriority,
superiority

orium \ōr-ē-əm \ castoreum,
ciborium, emporium,
pastorium, scriptorium,
sensorium, auditorium,
crematorium, in memoriam,
moratorium, natatorium,
sanitorium, sudatorium

¹ork \ərk \ burke, chirk, cirque,
clerk, dirk, irk, jerk, lurk,
murk, perk, quirk, shirk,
smirk, stirk, Turk, work,
yerk, artwork, berserk,
breastwork, brickwork,
bridgework, brightwork,
brushwork, capework,
casework, clockwork,
Dunkirk, earthwork,
fieldwork, firework, flatwork,

footwork, framework,
groundwork, guesswork,
hackwork, handwork,
headwork, homework,
housework, ironwork, knee-
jerk, legwork, lifework,
make-work, meshwork,
network, outwork, patchwork,
piecework, presswork,
rework, roadwork, salesclerk,
schoolwork, spadework,
steelwork, stickwork,
stonework, teamwork,
timework, topwork,
waxwork, woodwork,
basketwork, busywork,
crewelwork, donkeywork,
fancywork, handiwork,
journeywork, masterwork,
needlework, openwork,
overwork, paperwork,
plasterwork, soda jerk,
wonderwork, cabinetwork

²**ork**\órk\cork, fork, pork,
quark, stork, torque, bulwark,
futhorc, hayfork, pitchfork,
uncork

¹**orked**\órkt\corked, forked,
uncorked

²**orked**\ór-kəd\see ORCHID

¹**orker**\ər-kər\jerker, lurker,
shirker, worker, berserker,
caseworker, dockworker,
field-worker, handworker,
ironworker, pieceworker,
steelworker, tearjerker,

wageworker, woodworker,
autoworker, metalworker,
needleworker, wonderworker

²**orker**\ór-kər\corker, forker,
porker, torquer

orking\ər-kiŋ\hardworking,
tear-jerking, woodworking,
wonder-working

orky\ór-kē\corky, forky,
porky

¹**orl**\ərl\see ¹IRL

²**orl**\órl\see ³ORAL

orld\ərld\burled, knurled,
whorled, world, dreamworld,
old-world, demiworld,
netherworld, otherworld,
underworld—*also pasts of
verbs listed at* ¹IRL

orled\ərld\see ORLD

¹**orm**\ərm\berm, firm, germ,
herm, perm, sperm, squirm,
term, therm, worm, affirm,
bookworm, confirm,
cutworm, deperm, deworm,
earthworm, flatworm,
glowworm, heartworm,
hookworm, hornworm,
inchworm, infirm, long-term,
lugworm, lungworm,
midterm, pinworm,
ringworm, roundworm,
sandworm, screwworm, short-
term, silkworm, tapeworm,
angleworm, armyworm,
caddis worm, disaffirm,
disconfirm, gymnosperm,

pachyderm, reconfirm,
angiosperm, echinoderm

²**orm** \ órm \ corm, dorm, form,
norm, storm, swarm, warm,
aswarm, barnstorm,
brainstorm, conform, deform,
Delorme, free-form,
hailstorm, inform, L-form,
landform, life-form,
lukewarm, perform,
planform, platform, postform,
preform, rainstorm, re-form,
reform, sandstorm,
snowstorm, transform,
triform, windstorm,
chloroform, cruciform,
dendriform, dentiform,
disciform, fungiform,
funnelform, fusiform,
letterform, microform,
multiform, nonconform,
thunderstorm, uniform,
vermiform

ormable \ ór-mə-bəl \ formable,
conformable, performable,
transformable

ormal \ ór-məl \ formal, normal,
abnormal, conformal,
informal, subnormal,
paranormal, semiformal,
supernormal

ormally \ ór-mə-lē \ formally,
formerly, normally, stormily,
abnormally, informally,
subnormally, paranormally,
supernormally

orman \ ór-mən \ corpsman,
Mormon, Norman, Anglo-
Norman

ormance \ ór-məns \
conformance, performance,
nonconformance

ormant \ ór-mənt \ dormant,
formant, informant

ormative \ ór-mət-iv \ formative,
normative, informative,
performative, reformative,
transformative

orme \ órm \ see ²ORM

ormed \ órmd \ formed, normed,
informed, malformed,
unformed—*also pasts of
verbs listed at* ²ORM

¹**ormer** \ ór-mər \ dormer,
former, swarmer, warmer,
barnstormer, brainstormer,
conformer, heart-warmer,
informer, performer,
reformer, transformer,
performer

²**ormer** \ ər-mər \ see URMUR

ormerly \ ór-mə-lē \ see
ORMALLY

ormie \ ór-mē \ see ¹ORMY

ormily \ ór-mə-lē \ see ORMALLY

orming \ ór-miŋ \ brainstorming,
heartwarming, housewarming,
habit-forming

ormist \ ór-məst \ warmest,
conformist, reformist,
nonconformist

ormity \ ór-mət-ē \ conformity,

deformity, enormity,
nonconformity, uniformity
ormless \ òrm-ləs \ formless,
gormless
ormon \ òr-mən \ see ORMAN
¹**ormy** \ òr-mē \ stormy, dormie
²**ormy** \ ər-mē \ see ERMY
¹**orn** \ ōrn \ borne, bourn,
mourn, shorn, sworn, torn,
worn, airborne, careworn,
foreborn, forsworn, forworn,
outworn, seaborne, shipborne,
shopworn, skyborne,
timeworn, well-worn,
waterborne, waterworn,
weatherworn
²**orn** \ òrn \ born, bourn, corn,
horn, lorn, morn, mourn,
Norn, porn, scorn, shorn,
sworn, thorn, torn, warn,
worn, acorn, adorn, airborne,
alphorn, althorn, baseborn,
bicorne, bighorn, blackthorn,
boxthorn, broomcorn,
buckthorn, bullhorn,
careworn, Christ's-thorn,
dehorn, earthborn, einkorn,
firstborn, foghorn, foresworn,
forewarn, forlorn, forworn,
freeborn, greenhorn,
hartshorn, hawthorn,
highborn, inborn, inkhorn,
krummhorn, leghorn,
longhorn, lovelorn, lowborn,
newborn, outworn, popcorn,
pronghorn, reborn, seaborne,

shipborne, shoehorn,
shopworn, shorthorn,
skyborne, soilborne, stillborn,
stinkhorn, suborn, timeworn,
tinhorn, tricorne, trueborn,
twice-born, unborn, unworn,
wayworn, wellborn, well-
worn, wind-borne, alpenhorn,
barleycorn, Capricorn,
flügelhorn, foreign-born,
peppercorn, unicorn,
waterborne, waterworn,
weatherworn, winterbourne
³**orn** \ ərn \ see URN
ornament \ òr-nə-mənt \
ornament, tournament
¹**orne** \ ōrn \ see ¹ORN
²**orne** \ òrn \ see ²ORN
orned \ òrnd \ horned, thorned,
unadorned—*also pasts of
verbs listed at* ²ORN
orner \ òr-nər \ warner, Cape
Horner, dehorner, suborner
ornery \ än-rē \ see ¹ANNERY
orney \ ər-nē \ see ¹OURNEY
ornful \ òrn-fəl \ mournful,
scornful
ornice \ òr-nəs \ cornice, ornice,
notornis
orning \ òr-niŋ \ morning,
mourning, warning, aborning
ornis \ òr-nəs \ see ORNICE
ornment \ ərn-mənt \ see
ERNMENT
orny \ òr-nē \ corny, horny,
thorny, tourney

oroner\ȯr-ə-nər\coroner, foreigner, warrener

¹orough\ər-ə\borough, burgh, burro, burrow, curragh, furrow, ore, thorough, Yarborough, kookaburra

²orough\ər-ō\see ¹URROW

¹orous\ōr-əs\see ¹ORUS

²orous\ȯr-əs\see AURUS

orp\ȯrp\dorp, gorp, thorp, warp, Australorp

orper\ȯr-pər\dorper, torpor

orph\ȯrf\corf, dwarf, morph, swarf, wharf, ectomorph, endomorph, lagomorph, mesomorph

orpheus\ȯr-fē-əs\Morpheus, Orpheus

orphic\ȯr-fik\orphic, ectomorphic, endomorphic, mesomorphic, pseudomorphic, metamorphic, anthropomorphic

orphrey\ȯr-frē\orphrey, porphyry

orphyry\ȯr-frē\see ORPHREY

orpoise\ȯr-pəs\see ORPUS

orpor\ȯr-pər\see ORPER

¹orps\ōr\see ¹ORE

²orps\ȯr\see ¹OR

¹orpsman\ōr-mən\see OREMAN

²orpsman\ȯr-mən\see ORMAN

orpus\ȯr-pəs\corpus, porpoise, habeas corpus

orque\ȯrk\see ²ORK

orquer\ȯr-kər\see ²ORKER

¹orra\är-ə\see ¹ARA

²orra\ȯr-ə\see ²ORA

orrader\är-əd-ər\see ORRIDOR

¹orran\är-ən\see ¹ORIN

²orran\ȯr-ən\see ²ORIN

orrel\ȯr-əl\see ²ORAL

orrent\ȯr-ənt\horrent, torrent, warrant, abhorrent

¹orrer\ȯr-ər\borer, horror, roarer, schnorrer, sorer, abhorrer, explorer

²orrer\ōr-ər\see ¹ORER

orrible\ȯr-ə-bəl\see ²ORABLE

orrid\ȯr-əd\florid, forehead, horrid, torrid

¹orridge\är-ij\see ¹ORAGE

²orridge\ȯr-ij\see ³ORAGE

orridor\är-əd-ər\corridor, forrader

¹orrie\är-ē\see ¹ARI

²orrie\ȯr-ē\see ORY

orrier\ȯr-ē-ər\see ARRIOR

¹orris\är-əs\charas, morris, orris, Polaris

²orris\ōr-əs\see ¹ORUS

³orris\ȯr-əs\see AURUS

orror\ȯr-ər\see ¹ORRER

¹orrow\är-ō\borrow, claro, morrow, sorrow, taro, saguaro, tomorrow

²orrow\är-ə\see ¹ARA

¹orry\är-ē\see ¹ARI

²orry\ər-ē\see URRY

ors\ȯrz\see ²OORS

orsal\ȯr-səl\see ORSEL

¹orse\ȯrs\coarse, corse,

course, force, gorse, hoarse, horse, Norse, source, clotheshorse, concourse, deforce, discourse, divorce, endorse, enforce, extrorse, introrse, packhorse, perforce, post-horse, racecourse, racehorse, recourse, remorse, retrorse, sawhorse, stringcourse, unhorse, war-horse, workhorse, charley horse, hobbyhorse, stalking-horse, reinforce, watercourse

²**orse** \ərs\ see ERSE

orseful \órs-fəl\ forceful, remorseful, resourceful

orsel \ór-səl\ dorsal, morsel

orseman \ór-smən\ horseman, Norseman

orsement \ór-smənt\ endorsement, reinforcement

orsen \ərs-ᵊn\ see ERSON

orser \ər-sər\ see URSOR

orsey \ór-sē\ see ORSY

orsion \ór-shən\ see ²ORTION

¹**orst** \órst\ forced, horst—*also pasts of verbs listed at* ¹ORSE

²**orst** \ərst\ see URST

orsted \ər-stəd\ see ERSTED

orsum \ór-səm\ dorsum, foursome

orsy \ór-sē\ gorsy, horsey

¹**ort** \órt\ boart, bort, court, fort, forte, mort, ort, port, Porte, quart, short, snort, sort, sport, swart, thwart, tort, torte, wart, wort, abort, airport, amort, aport, assort, athwart, backcourt, bellwort, birthwort, bistort, cavort, cohort, colewort, comport, consort, contort, crosscourt, deport, disport, distort, downcourt, effort, escort, exhort, export, extort, frontcourt, glasswort, gosport, milkwort, outport, passport, purport, ragwort, report, re-sort, resort, retort, seaport, spaceport, spoilsport, support, transport, bladderwort, davenport, nonsupport, pennywort, Saint-John's wort, ultrashort, worrywart, pianoforte, underreport

²**ort** \ōr\ see ¹ORE

³**ort** \ərt\ see ¹ERT

⁴**ort** \ór\ see ¹OR

orta \órt-ə\ sort of, torte, aorta

ortable \órt-ə-bəl\ portable, deportable, exportable, importable, reportable, supportable, transportable, insupportable

ortage \órt-ij\ portage, shortage, colportage

ortal \órt-ᵊl\ chortle, mortal, portal, quartile, immortal

ortar \órt-ər\ see ORTER

ortative \órt-ət-iv\ hortative, portative, assortative, exhortative

¹**orte** \ ȯrt \ see ¹ORT

²**orte** \ ȯrt-ē \ see ORTY

orted \ ȯrt-əd \ warted, assorted, ill-sorted—*also pasts of verbs listed at* ¹ORT

ortedly \ ȯrt-əd-lē \ purportedly, reportedly

orten \ ȯrt-ᵊn \ quartan, shorten, foreshorten

orter \ ȯrt-ər \ mortar, porter, snorter, sorter, colporteur, distorter, exhorter, exporter, extorter, importer, reporter, resorter, ripsnorter, transporter—*also comparatives of adjectives listed at* ¹ORT

orteur \ ȯrt-ər \ see ORTER

¹**orth** \ ȯrth \ forth, fourth, north, thenceforth

²**orth** \ ərth \ see IRTH

orthful \ ərth-fəl \ see IRTHFUL

orthless \ ərth-ləs \ see IRTHLESS

orthy \ ər-thē \ earthy, worthy, airworthy, blameworthy, newsworthy, noteworthy, praiseworthy, seaworthy, trustworthy, creditworthy

ortic \ ȯrt-ik \ see ²ARTIC

ortical \ ȯrt-i-kəl \ cortical, vortical

ortie \ ȯrt-ē \ see ORTY

orting \ ȯrt-iŋ \ sporting, self-supporting

¹**ortion** \ ōr-shən \ portion, apportion, proportion, disproportion, reapportion

²**ortion** \ ȯr-shən \ portion, torsion, abortion, apportion, contortion, distortion, extorsion, extortion, proportion, retortion, disproportion, reapportion, antiabortion

ortionate \ ȯr-shnət \ extortionate, proportionate, disproportionate

ortionist \ ȯr-shnəst \ abortionist, contortionist, extortionist

ortis \ ȯrt-əs \ fortis, mortise, tortoise, aquafortis, rigor mortis

ortise \ ȯrt-əs \ see ORTIS

ortive \ ȯrt-iv \ sportive, abortive, contortive, extortive

ortle \ ȯrt-ᵊl \ see ORTAL

¹**ortly** \ ȯrt-lē \ courtly, portly

²**ortly** \ ȯrt-lē \ courtly, portly, shortly, thwartly

ortment \ ȯrt-mənt \ assortment, comportment, deportment, disportment

ortoise \ ȯrt-əs \ see ORTIS

orts \ ȯrts \ quartz, shorts, sports, undershorts—*also plurals and possessives of nouns and third singular presents of verbs listed at* ¹ORT

ortunate \ ȯrch-nət \ fortunate, importunate

orture\ȯr-chər\see ORCHER

orty\ȯrt-ē\forty, shorty, sortie,
sporty, warty, mezzo forte,
pianoforte

orum\ōr-əm\foram, forum,
jorum, quorum, decorum, ad
valorem, cockalorum,
indecorum, variorum, pons
asinorum, sanctum
sanctorum, schola cantorum

¹orus\ōr-əs\chorus, Horus,
loris, porous, sorus, torus,
canorous, decorous, pelorus,
phosphorus, sonorous, doch-
an-dorris

²orus\ōr-əs\see AURUS

orward\ȯr-wərd\forward,
shoreward, flash-forward,
henceforward, carryforward

ory\ȯr-ē\corrie, dory, glory,
gory, hoary, lorry, lory,
quarry, saury, sorry, story,
Tory, zori, centaury,
clerestory, John Dory,
outlawry, satori, vainglory, a
priori, allegory, amatory,
auditory, cacciatore,
castratory, category, con
amore, crematory, damnatory,
decretory, desultory, dilatory,
dormitory, expletory,
feudatory, fumitory,
gustatory, gyratory, hortatory,
hunky-dory, inventory,
laudatory, lavatory,
mandatory, migratory,

minatory, monitory, nugatory,
offertory, oratory, overstory,
predatory, prefatory,
probatory, promissory,
promontory, purgatory,
repertory, signatory,
statutory, sudatory, territory,
transitory, understory,
vibratory, vomitory, yakitori,
accusatory, admonitory,
adulatory, a fortiori, aleatory,
ambulatory, amendatory,
applicatory, approbatory,
celebratory, circulatory,
combinatory, commendatory,
compensatory, condemnatory,
confirmatory, confiscatory,
conservatory, consolatory,
contributory, copulatory,
cosignatory, declamatory,
declaratory, dedicatory,
defamatory, denigratory,
depilatory, depository,
derogatory, designatory,
dispensatory, divinatory,
escalatory, excitatory,
exclamatory, exculpatory,
excusatory, exhibitory,
exhortatory, expiatory,
expiratory, explanatory,
explicatory, exploratory,
expository, expurgatory,
incantatory, incubatory,
indicatory, inflammatory,
informatory, innovatory,
inspiratory, inundatory,

invitatory, judicatory,
laboratory, masticatory,
masturbatory, memento mori,
millefiori, modulatory,
obfuscatory, obligatory,
observatory, performatory,
persecutory, predicatory,
premonitory, preparatory,
prohibitory, reformatory,
regulatory, repository,
retributory, revelatory,
respiratory, salutatory,
stipulatory, supplicatory,
transmigratory, undulatory,
adjudicatory, a posteriori,
annihilatory, annunciatory,
anticipatory, appreciatory,
assimilatory, circumlocutory,
classificatory, concilliatory,
confabulatory, congratulatory,
de-escalatory, denunciatory,
depreciatory, discriminatory,
ejaculatory, hallucinatory,
improvisatore, improvisatory,
interrogatory, intimidatory,
investigatory, participatory,
propitiatory, recommendatory,
recriminatory, renunciatory,
reverberatory, viola d'amore,
amelioratory,
overcompensatory,
reconciliatory, supererogatory
oryx \ òr-iks \ oryx, Armorics,
combinatorics
orze \ órz \ see ²OORS
¹os \ äs \ boss, doss, dross, floss,

fosse, gloss, joss, os, pross,
stoss, toss, bathos, benthos,
bugloss, chaos, cosmos,
demos, emboss, Eos, epos,
Eros, ethos, Hyksos, kaross,
kudos, kvass, Logos, mythos,
nol-pros, nonpros, pathos,
peplos, pharos, ringtoss,
telos, topos, tripos, coup de
grace, demitasse, extrados,
intrados, isogloss, reredos,
semigloss, Thanatos, volte-
face
²os \ ō \ see ¹OW
³os \ ōs \ see ¹OSE
⁴os \ ós \ see ¹OSS
¹osa \ ō-sə \ mimosa, curiosa,
virtuosa, anorexia nervosa
²osa \ ō-zə \ mimosa, mucosa,
serosa, sub rosa, curiosa,
virtuosa
¹osable \ ō-zə-bəl \ closable,
disposable, erosible,
explosible, opposable,
reclosable, supposable,
decomposable, superposable,
indecomposable,
superimposable
²osable \ ü-zə-bəl \ see USABLE
osal \ ō-zəl \ hosel, losel,
deposal, disposal, proposal,
reposal, supposal
osan \ ōs-ᵊn \ see OSIN
¹oschen \ ō-shən \ see OTION
²oschen \ ó-shən \ see AUTION
oscible \ äs-ə-bəl \ see OSSIBLE

oscoe \äs-kō\ roscoe, fiasco

oscopy \äs-kə-pē\ arthroscopy, microscopy, spectroscopy

¹**ose** \ōs\ close, dose, gross, os, cosmos, crustose, cymose, dextrose, engross, erose, fructose, globose, glucose, jocose, lactose, maltose, mannose, megadose, morose, mythos, nodose, pappose, pathos, pentose, pilose, plumose, ramose, rhamnose, ribose, rugose, scapose, schistose, setose, spinose, strigose, sucrose, Sukkoth, triose, vadose, ventricose, verbose, viscose, adios, adipose, bellicose, calvados, cellulose, comatose, diagnose, grandiose, granulose, inter alios, lachrymose, otiose, overdose, racemose, Shabuoth, tuberose, varicose, inter vivos, metamorphose, religiose

²**ose** \ōz\ brose, chose, close, clothes, cloze, doze, froze, gloze, hose, nose, pose, prose, rose, appose, aros, bedclothes, bluenose, brownnose, bulldoze, compose, depose, dextrose, disclose, dispose, enclose, expose, foreclose, fructose, glucose, impose, nightclothes, oppose, plainclothes, primrose, propose, quickfroze, repose, rockrose, shovelnose, suppose, transpose, tuberose, unclose, uprose, viscose, wind rose, counterpose, decompose, diagnose, discompose, indispose, interpose, juxtapose, pettitoes, predispose, presuppose, pussytoes, recompose, shovelnose, superpose, underclothes, anastomose, metamorphose, overexpose, superimpose, underexpose— *also plurals and possessives of nouns and third singular presents of verbs listed at* ¹OW

³**ose** \üz\ see ²USE

osed \ōzd\ closed, nosed, composed, exposed, hard-nosed, opposed, pug-nosed, snub-nosed, stenosed, supposed, unclosed, indisposed, shovel-nosed, toffee-nosed, well-disposed— *also pasts of verbs listed at* ²OSE

osel \ō-zəl\ see OSAL

osen \ōz-ᵊn\ chosen, frozen, quickfrozen, lederhosen

¹**oser** \ō-zər\ closer, dozer, poser, proser, brownnoser, bulldozer, composer, discloser, disposer, exposer,

imposer, opposer, proposer,
decomposer, interposer,
photocomposer

²**oser** \ü-zər\ see USER

¹**oset** \ō-zət\ see ²OSIT

²**oset** \äz-ət\ see ¹OSIT

osey \ō-zē\ see OSY

osh \òsh\ see ²ASH

¹**oshed** \äsht\ sloshed,
galoshed—*also pasts of verbs
listed at* ¹ASH

²**oshed** \òsht\ see ¹ASHED

osher \äsh-ər\ see ¹ASHER

osia \ō-shə\ see ¹OTIA

osible \ō-zə-bəl\ see ¹OSABLE

osier \ō-zhər\ see OSURE

osily \ō-zə-lē\ cozily, nosily,
rosily

osin \ōs-ⁿn\ boatswain, Mosan,
pocosin

using \ō-ziŋ\ closing, nosing,
disclosing, imposing,
supposing

osion \ō-zhən\ plosion,
corrosion, displosion, erosion,
explosion, implosion

osis \ō-səs\ gnosis, hypnosis,
narcosis, necrosis, neurosis,
osmosis, prognosis,
psychosis, sclerosis,
thrombosis, brucellosis,
cyanosis, dermatosis,
diagnosis, halitosis, heterosis,
psittacosis, scoliosis, silicosis,
symbiosis, autohypnosis,
coccidiosis, mononucleosis,

pediculosis, psychoneurosis,
tuberculosis

¹**osit** \äz-ət\ closet, posit,
composite, deposit, exposit

²**osit** \ō-zət\ prosit, roset

osite \äz-ət\ see ¹OSIT

ositive \äz-ət-iv\ positive,
appositive

ositor \äz-ət-ər\ compositor,
depositor, expositor

osive \ō-siv\ plosive, corrosive,
erosive, explosive, implosive,
purposive

osk \äsk\ mosque, kiosk,
abelmosk

¹**oso** \ō-sō\ proso, maestoso,
rebozo, arioso, furioso,
gracioso, grandioso, mafioso,
spiritoso, vigoroso, virtuoso,
concerto grosso

²**oso** \ō-zō\ bozo, rebozo,
furioso, gracioso, grandioso,
spiritoso, vigoroso

³**oso** \ü-sō\ see USOE

osophy \äs-ə-fē\ philosophy,
theosophy, anthroposophy

osque \äsk\ see OSK

¹**oss** \òs\ boss, cross, crosse,
floss, gloss, loss, moss,
sauce, toss, across, bugloss,
crisscross, emboss, lacrosse,
outcross, pathos, ringtoss,
topcross, uncross, albatross,
applesauce, autocross,
double-cross, intercross,
motocross, semigloss

²**oss** \ ōs \ see ¹OSE

³**oss** \ äs \ see ¹OS

ossa \ äs-ə \ see ¹ASA

ossable \ äs-ə-bəl \ see OSSIBLE

ossal \ äs-əl \ docile, dossal, fossil, glossal, jostle, tassel, throstle, warsle, wassail, apostle, colossal, indocile, isoglossal

¹**osse** \ äs \ see ¹OS

²**osse** \ äs-ē \ see ¹OSSY

³**osse** \ òs \ see ¹OSS

ossed \ òst \ see ³OST

osser \ ò-sər \ crosser, saucer, double-crosser

osset \ äs-ət \ cosset, faucet, Osset, posset

ossible \ äs-ə-bəl \ possible, cognoscible, embossable, impossible

ossic \ äs-ik \ see OSSICK

ossick \ äs-ik \ fossick, isoglossic

ossil \ äs-əl \ see OSSAL

ossity \ äs-ət-ē \ adiposity, atrocity, callosity, ferocity, gibbosity, monstrosity, pomposity, porosity, precocity, velocity, viscosity, zygosity, animosity, bellicosity, curiosity, generosity, grandiosity, hideosity, luminosity, nebulosity, preciosity, reciprocity, scrupulosity, sensuosity, sinuosity, strenuosity, tortuosity,

tuberosity, varicosity, virtuosity, impetuosity, religiosity, voluminosity, impecuniosity

ossly \ òs-lē \ costly, crossly

osso \ ō-sō \ see ¹OSO

ossular \ äs-ə-lər \ grossular, wassailer

ossum \ äs-əm \ blossom, passim, possum, opossum

ossus \ äs-əs \ see OCESS

¹**ossy** \ äs-ē \ Aussie, bossy, dassie, drossy, flossy, glossy, posse, quasi, dalasi, sannyasi

²**ossy** \ ò-sē \ Aussie, bossy, lossy, mossy

¹**ost** \ äst \ sol-faist, Pentecost, teleost—*also pasts of verbs listed at* ¹OS

²**ost** \ ōst \ boast, coast, ghost, host, most, oast, post, roast, toast, almost, bedpost, compost, doorpost, endmost, foremost, gatepost, goalpost, guidepost, headmost, hindmost, impost, inmost, midmost, milepost, Milquetoast, outmost, outpost, provost, rearmost, riposte, seacoast, signpost, sternmost, sternpost, topmost, upmost, utmost, aftermost, ante-post, bottommost, coast-to-coast, easternmost, farthermost, fingerpost, furthermost, headforemost,

hithermost, innermost,
lowermost, nethermost,
northernmost, outermost,
rudderpost, southernmost,
sternforemost, undermost,
uppermost, uttermost,
westernmost

³**ost** \óst \cost, frost, lost,
accost, defrost, exhaust,
hoarfrost, star-crossed,
holocaust, Pentecost,
permafrost—*also pasts of
verbs listed at* ¹OSS

⁴**ost** \əst \see ¹UST

osta \äs-tə \costa, pasta

¹**ostal** \ōs-t'l \coastal, postal

²**ostal** \äs-t'l \see OSTEL

ostasy \äs-tə-sē \apostasy,
isostasy

oste \ōst \see ²OST

ostel \äs-t'l \hostel, hostile,
Pentecostal

¹**oster** \äs-tər \coster, foster,
roster, Double Gloucester,
impostor, piaster, paternoster
snollygoster

²**oster** \ós-tər \foster, roster,
Double Gloucester

³**oster** \ō-stər \see OASTER

ostic \äs-tik \Gnostic, acrostic,
agnostic, prognostic,
diagnostic

ostile \äs-t'l \see OSTEL

ostle \äs-əl \see OSSAL

¹**ostly** \ōst-lē \ghostly, hostly,
mostly

²**ostly** \ós-lē \see OSSLY

ostomy \äs-tə-mē \ostomy,
colostomy, enterostomy

ostor \äs-tər \see ¹OSTER

¹**ostral** \ós-trəl \austral, rostral

²**ostral** \äs-trəl \see OSTREL

ostrel \äs-trəl \austral, costrel,
nostril, rostral, wastrel,
colostral

ostril \äs-trəl \see OSTREL

ostrum \äs-trəm \nostrum,
rostrum, colostrum

osty \ō-stē \ghosty, toasty

osure \ō-zhər \closure, crosier,
osier, composure, disclosure,
disposure, enclosure,
exclosure, exposure,
foreclosure, discomposure,
overexposure, underexposure

osy \ō-zē \cozy, dozy, mosey,
nosy, posy, prosy, rosy, ring-
around-a-rosy

osyne \äs-ᵊn-ē \Euphrosyne,
Mnemosyne

osz \ósh \see ²ASH

¹**ot** \ät \at, aught, baht, blot,
boite, bot, chott, clot, cot,
dot, ghat, got, grot, hot, jat,
jot, khat, knot, kyat, lot, Lot,
motte, naught, not, pâte, plot,
pot, rot, scot, Scot, shot,
skat, slot, snot, sot, spot,
squat, swat, swot, tot, trot,
twat, watt, what, wot, yacht,
allot, ascot, begot, besot, big
shot, bloodshot, bowknot,

boycott, buckshot, bullshot,
cachepot, calotte, cannot,
crackpot, Crockpot, culotte,
dashpot, despot, dreadnought,
earshot, ergot, escot, eyeshot,
eyespot, feedlot, fiat,
fleshpot, forgot, fox-trot,
fusspot, fylfot, garrote,
gavotte, grapeshot, gunshot,
half-knot, have-not, hotchpot,
hotshot, jackpot, Korat,
kumquat, long shot, loquat,
marplot, mascot, motmot,
one-shot, Pequot, potshot,
red-hot, robot, sandlot,
sexpot, Shabbat, shallot,
Shebat, sheepcote, slingshot,
slipknot, slungshot, snapshot,
somewhat, stinkpot, stockpot,
subplot, sunspot, teapot,
topknot, tosspot, try-pot,
upshot, wainscot, whatnot,
white-hot, woodlot, aeronaut,
aliquot, apparat, apricot,
aquanaut, argonaut, astronaut,
bergamot, cachalot, Camelot,
caveat, coffeepot, cosmonaut,
counterplot, flowerpot,
gallipot, guillemot, Hottentot,
Hugenot, kilowatt, Lancelot,
megawatt, microdot, ocelot,
overshot, paraquat, patriot,
Penobscot, peridot, polka dot,
polyglot, samizdat,
sansculotte, scattershot,
tommyrot, touch-me-not,

underplot, undershot,
Wyandot, wyandotte,
compatriot, forget-me-not,
requiescat, Johnny-on-the-spot
²ot\ō\see ¹OW
³ot\ōt\see OAT
⁴ot\ȯt\see ¹OUGHT
ôt\ō\see ¹OW
ota\ōt-ə\bota, flota, lota,
    quota, rota, biota, Dakota,
    iota, pelota
otable\ōt-ə-bəl\notable,
    potable, quotable
otage\ōt-ij\dotage, flotage,
    anecdotage
otal\ōt-ᵊl\dotal, motile,
    scrotal, total, immotile,
    subtotal, teetotal, anecdotal,
    antidotal, sacerdotal
otalist\ōt-ᵊl-əst\teetotalist,
    anecdotalist, sacerdotalist
otamus\ät-ə-məs\see OTOMOUS
otany\ät-ᵊn-ē\botany, cottony,
    monotony
otarist\ōt-ə-rəst\motorist,
    votarist
otary\ōt-ə-rē\coterie, rotary,
    votary, locomotory,
    prothonotary
otch\äch\blotch, botch,
    crotch, hotch, notch, scotch,
    Scotch, splotch, swatch,
    watch, bird-watch,
    deathwatch, debauch,
    dogwatch, hopscotch,
    hotchpotch, Sasquatch,

stopwatch, top-notch,
wristwatch, butterscotch
otchet \äch-ət\ crotchet, rochet
otchman \äch-mən\ Scotchman,
watchman
otchy \äch-ē\ blotchy, boccie,
botchy, splotchy, hibachi,
huarache, vivace, mariachi
¹ote \ōt-ē\ dhoti, floaty, loti,
throaty, cenote, coyote,
chayote, peyote, quixote
²ote \ōt\ see OAT
³ote \ät\ see ¹OT
otea \ōt-ē-ə\ protea, scotia
oted \ōt-əd\ see OATED
otem \ōt-əm\ see OTUM
oten \ōt-ᵊn\ see OTON
oter \ōt-ər\ see OATER
oterie \ōt-ə-rē\ see OTARY
¹oth \äth\ Goth, swath, troth,
betroth, Naboth, Alioth,
behemoth, Ustrogoth,
Visigoth
²oth \óth\ broth, cloth, froth,
moth, sloth, swath, troth,
wroth, betroth, breechcloth,
broadcloth, cheesecloth,
dishcloth, facecloth,
loincloth, oilcloth, sackcloth,
sailcloth, washcloth, Alioth,
behemoth, tablecloth
³oth \ōs\ see ¹OSE
⁴oth \ōt\ see OAT
⁵oth \ōth\ see OWTH
othal \óth-əl\ see OTHEL

othe \ōth\ clothe, loathe,
betroth, unclothe
othel \óth-əl\ brothel, betrothal
¹other \əth-ər\ brother, mother,
other, rather, smother, tother,
whether, another, foremother,
godmother, grandmother,
housemother, stepbrother,
stepmother
²other \äth-ər\ see ¹ATHER
otherly \əth-ər-lē\ brotherly,
motherly, southerly,
grandmotherly
othes \ōz\ see ²OSE
othesis \äth-ə-səs\ prothesis,
hypothesis
othic \äth-ik\ gothic,
Ostrogothic, Visigothic
othing \ō-thin\ clothing,
loathing, underclothing
oti \ōt-ē\ see ¹OTE
¹otia \ō-shə\ scotia, agnosia
²otia \ōt-ē-ə\ see OTEA
otiable \ō-shə-bəl\ see OCIABLE
otiant \ō-shənt\ see OTIENT
¹otic \ät-ik\ Scotic, aquatic,
biotic, chaotic, demotic,
despotic, erotic, exotic,
hypnotic, narcotic, necrotic,
neurotic, Nilotic, osmotic,
psychotic, quixotic, robotic,
sclerotic, semiotic, abiotic,
anecdotic, asymptotic,
bibliotic, embryotic,
epiglottic, Hugenotic, idiotic,
macrobiotic, melanotic,

patriotic, posthypnotic, sansculottic, symbiotic, antibiotic, autoerotic, compatriotic, homoerotic

²**otic** \ōt-ik\ lotic, photic, aphotic, dichotic

³**otic** \ot-ik\ see AUTIC

otica \ät-i-kə\ erotica, exotica

otice \ōt-əs\ see OTUS

otics \ät-iks\ robotics, astronautics, bibliotics—*also plurals and possessives of nouns listed at* ¹OTIC

otid \ät-əd\ see OTTED

otient \ō-shənt\ quotient, negotiant

otile \ōt-ᵊl\ see OTAL

¹**oting** \ōt-iŋ\ see OATING

²**oting** \ät-iŋ\ see OTTING

¹**otinous** \ät-nəs\ see OTNESS

²**otinous** \ät-ᵊn-əs\ see ¹OTONOUS

otion \ō-shən\ groschen, lotion, motion, notion, ocean, potion, commotion, demotion, devotion, emotion, Laotian, promotion, slow-motion, locomotion

otional \ō-shnəl\ motional, notional, devotional, emotional, promotional, unemotional

otist \ōt-əst\ protist, Scotist, anecdotist

otive \ōt-iv\ motive, votive, emotive, promotive, automotive, locomotive

otl \ät-ᵊl\ see OTTLE

otley \ät-lē\ see OTLY

otly \ät-lē\ Atli, hotly, motley

otment \ät-mənt\ allotment, ballottement

otness \ät-nəs\ hotness, squatness, monotonous, serotinous

¹**oto** \ō-tō\ Sotho, con moto

²**oto** \ōt-ō\ koto, photo, roto, ex-voto, in toto, telephoto

otomous \ät-ə-məs\ dichotomous, hippopotamus

otomy \ät-ə-mē\ dichotomy, lobotomy, tracheotomy, episiotomy

oton \ōt-ᵊn\ croton, Jotun, oaten, verboten

¹**otonous** \ät-ᵊn-əs\ rottenness, monotonous, serotinous

²**otonous** \ät-nəs\ see OTNESS

otor \ōt-ər\ see OATER

otorist \ōt-ə-rəst\ see OTARIST

otory \ōt-ə-rē\ see OTARY

ots \äts\ hots, lots, Scots, swats, ersatz—*also plurals and possessives of nouns and third singular presents of verbs listed at* ¹OT

otsman \ät-smən\ Scotsman, yachtsman

ott \ät\ see ¹OT

otta \ät-ə\ see ¹ATA

ottage \ät-ij\ cottage, plottage, pottage, wattage

ottal \ät-ᵊl\ see OTTLE

otte\ät\see ¹OT

otted\ät-əd\knotted, potted, spotted, carotid, proglottid, polka-dotted—*also pasts of verbs listed at* ¹OT

ottement\ät-mənt\see OTMENT

otten\ät-ⁿn\cotton, gotten, gratin, ratton, rotten, shotten, au gratin, begotten, forgotten, guncotton, ill-gotten, misbegotten, sauerbraten

ottenness\ät-ⁿn-əs\see ¹OTONOUS

otter\ät-ər\blotter, cotter, dotter, knotter, otter, plotter, potter, rotter, spotter, squatter, swatter, Tatar, totter, trotter, water, alotter, boycotter, flyswatter, garroter, globe-trotter, pinspotter, sandlotter, alma mater, imperator, teeter-totter—*also comparatives of adjectives listed at* ¹OT *and words ending in* -water *listed at* ¹ATER

ottery\ät-ə-rē\lottery, pottery, tottery, watery

ottic\ät-ik\see ¹OTIC

ottid\ät-əd\see OTTED

ottie\ät-ē\see ATI

otting\ät-iŋ\jotting, wainscoting

ottis\ät-əs\glottis, clematis, epiglottis, literatus

ottische\ät-ish\see OTTISH

ottish\ät-ish\hottish, schottische, Scottish, sottish, sansculottish

ottle\ät-ⁿl\bottle, dottle, glottal, mottle, pottle, ratel, rotl, throttle, wattle, atlatl, bluebottle, monocotyl, Nahuatl, epiglottal, Quetzalcoatl

¹otto\ät-ō\see ¹ATO

²otto\ȯt-ō\see ¹AUTO

ottom\ät-əm\see ¹ATUM

otty\ät-ē\see ATI

otum\ōt-əm\notum, scrotum, totem, factotum, teetotum

otun\ōt-ⁿn\see OTON

oture\ō-chər\see OACHER

otus\ōt-əs\lotus, notice

oty\ȯt-ē\see ¹AUGHTY

otyl\ät-ⁿl\see OTTLE

¹ou\ō\see ¹OW

²ou\ü\see ¹EW

³ou\au̇\see ²OW

ouble\əb-əl\see UBBLE

oubler\əb-lər\doubler, bubbler, troubler

oubly\əb-lē\see UBBLY

oubt\au̇t\see ³OUT

oubted\au̇t-əd\see OUTED

oubter\au̇t-ər\see ²OUTER

¹ouc\ü\see ¹EW

²ouc\ük\see UKE

³ouc\u̇k\see ¹OOK

ouce\üs\see ¹USE

¹oucester\äs-tər\see ¹OSTER

²oucester\ȯs-tər\see ²OSTER

¹**ouch** \üch\ see ¹OOCH

²**ouch** \üsh\ see OUCHE

³**ouch** \əch\ see ¹UTCH

⁴**ouch** \au̇ch\ couch, crouch, grouch, ouch, pouch, slouch, vouch, avouch, debouch, scaramouch

ouche \üsh\ douche, louche, ruche, squoosh, swoosh, whoosh, barouche, capuche, cartouche, debouch, farouche, kurus, tarboosh, scaramouch

¹**ouchy** \əch-ē\ see UCHY

²**ouchy** \au̇-chē\ grouchy, pouchy, slouchy

ou'd \üd\ see UDE

¹**oud** \üd\ see UDE

²**oud** \au̇d\ boughed, bowed, cloud, crowd, loud, proud, shroud, stroud, aloud, becloud, enshroud, highbrowed, house-proud, purse-proud, thundercloud, unbowed, overcrowd, thundercloud—*also pasts of verbs listed at* ²OW

ouda \üd-ə\ see UDA

oudy \au̇d-ē\ see OWDY

oue \ü\ see ¹EW

ouf \üf\ see ¹OOF

ouffe \üf\ see ¹OOF

¹**ouge** \üj\ see ¹UGE

²**ouge** \üzh\ see ²UGE

³**ouge** \au̇j\ gouge, scrouge

¹**ough** \ō\ see ¹OW

²**ough** \ü\ see ¹EW

³**ough** \au̇\ see ²OW

⁴**ough** \äk\ see ¹OCK

⁵**ough** \əf\ see UFF

⁶**ough** \ȯf\ see ²OFF

¹**ougham** \ōm\ see ¹OME

²**ougham** \üm\ see ¹OOM

oughed \au̇d\ see ²OUD

oughen \əf-ən\ see UFFIN

ougher \əf-ər\ see UFFER

oughie \əf-ē\ see UFFY

oughish \əf-ish\ see UFFISH

oughly \əf-lē\ see UFFLY

¹**ought** \ȯt\ aught, bought, brought, caught, dot, fought, fraught, ghat, naught, nought, ought, sought, taught, taut, thought, wrought, besought, distraught, dreadnought, forethought, handwrought, high-wrought, onslaught, self-taught, store-bought, unthought, aeronaut, aforethought, afterthought, aquanaut, argonaut, astronaut, cosmonaut, juggernaut, overbought, overwrought

²**ought** \au̇t\ see ³OUT

oughten \ȯt-ᵊn\ see AUTEN

oughty \au̇t-ē\ doughty, droughty, gouty, pouty, snouty, trouty

¹**oughy** \ō-ē\ see OWY

²**oughy** \ü-ē\ see EWY

ouille \ü-ē\ see EWY

ouk \ük\ see UKE

ouki \ü-kē\ see ¹OOKY

¹oul \ōl\ see ¹OLE
²oul \ül\ see ¹OOL
³oul \aúl\ see ²OWL
¹ould \ōld\ see ¹OLD
²ould \úd\ see ¹OOD
oulder \ōl-dər\ see ¹OLDER
ouldered \ōl-dərd\ bouldered,
  shouldered, round-shouldered,
  square-shouldered—*also pasts
  of verbs listed at* ¹OLDER
ouldest \úd-əst\ couldest,
  shouldest, wouldest,
  Talmudist
ouldn't \úd-ᵊnt\ shouldn't,
  wouldn't
¹oule \ü-lē\ see ULY
²oule \ül\ see ¹OOL
ouled \ōld\ see ¹OLD
oulee \ü-lē\ see ULY
¹ouleh \ü-lə\ see ULA
²ouleh \ü-lē\ see ULY
ouli \ü-lē\ see ULY
ouling \aú-liŋ\ see ²OWLING
oulish \ü-lish\ see OOLISH
¹ou'll \ül\ see ¹OOL
²ou'll \úl\ see ¹UL
oulle \ül\ see ¹OOL
oully \aú-lē\ see ²OWLY
oult \ōlt\ see ¹OLT
oulter \ōl-tər\ see OLTER
oum \üm\ see ¹OOM
oumenal \ü-mən-ᵊl\ see UMINAL
oun \aún\ see ²OWN
ounce \aúns\ bounce, flounce,
  jounce, ounce, pounce,
  trounce, announce, denounce,

enounce, pronounce,
  renounce, mispronounce
ouncement \aún-smənt\
  announcement,
  denouncement,
  pronouncement
ouncer \aún-sər\ bouncer,
  announcer
ouncil \aún-səl\ see OUNSEL
ouncy \aún-sē\ bouncy,
  flouncy, jouncy, viscountcy
¹ound \ünd\ stound, swound,
  wound—*also pasts of verbs
  listed at* ¹OON
²ound \aúnd\ bound, crowned,
  found, ground, hound,
  mound, pound, round, sound,
  stound, swound, wound,
  abound, aground, all-round,
  around, astound, background,
  bloodhound, campground,
  chowhound, compound,
  confound, coonhound,
  dachshund, deerhound,
  earthbound, eastbound,
  elkhound, expound,
  fairground, fogbound, foot-
  pound, foreground, foxhound,
  go-round, greyhound,
  hardbound, hellhound,
  hidebound, homebound,
  horehound, housebound,
  icebound, impound, inbound,
  newfound, northbound,
  outbound, playground,
  profound, propound, rebound,

redound, resound, rockbound, snowbound, softbound, southbound, spellbound, stone-ground, stormbound, strikebound, surround, unbound, well-found, westbound, wolfhound, year-round, aboveground, all-around, battleground, decompound, go-around, muscle-bound, outward-bound, paperbound, runaround, turnaround, ultrasound, underground, weather-bound, wraparound, merry-go-round, superabound—*also pasts of verbs listed at* ²OWN

oundal \ aùn-d³l \ poundal, roundel

oundary \ aùn-drē \ see OUNDRY

ounded \ aùn-dəd \ drownded, rounded, confounded, unbounded, unfounded, well-founded, well-grounded

oundel \ aùn-d³l \ see OUNDAL

ounder \ aùn-dər \ bounder, flounder, founder, grounder, pounder, rounder, sounder, all-rounder, dumbfounder, tenpounder

ounding \ aùn-diŋ \ drownding, grounding, sounding, astounding, high-sounding, rockhounding

¹oundless \ ün-ləs \ see OONLESS

²oundless \ aùn-ləs \ groundless, soundless

oundlet \ aùn-lət \ see OWNLET

oundling \ aùn-liŋ \ foundling, groundling

oundness \ aùn-nəs \ roundness, unsoundness

oundry \ aùn-drē \ boundary, foundry

¹ounds \ ünz \ see OONS

²ounds \ aùnz \ hounds, zounds, inbounds, out-of-bounds— *also plurals and possessives of nouns and third singular presents of verbs listed at* ²OUND

oundsel \ aùn-səl \ see OUNSEL

oundsman \ aùnz-mən \ see OWNSMAN

ounge \ aùnj \ lounge, scrounge, chaise lounge

ounger \ əŋ-gər \ see ¹ONGER

ounker \ əŋ-kər \ see UNKER

ounsel \ aùn-səl \ council, counsel, groundsel

¹ount \ änt \ see ²ANT

²ount \ aùnt \ compt, count, fount, mount, account, amount, demount, discount, dismount, high-count, miscount, recount, remount, seamount, surmount, viscount, catamount, paramount, rediscount, tantamount, undercount

ountable \ aùnt-ə-bəl \

countable, accountable, demountable, discountable, surmountable, insurmountable, unaccountable

ountain \ aunt-ᵊn \ fountain, mountain, transmountain, cat-a-mountain

ountcy \ aun-sē \ see OUNCY

ounter \ aunt-ər \ counter, discounter, encounter, recounter, rencounter

ountess \ aunt-əs \ countess, viscountess

ountie \ aunt-ē \ see OUNTY

ounting \ aunt-iŋ \ mounting, accounting

ounty \ aunt-ē \ bounty, county, Mountie, viscounty

¹**oup** \ ōp \ see OPE

²**oup** \ ü \ see ¹EW

³**oup** \ üp \ see ¹OOP

¹**oupe** \ ōp \ see OPE

²**oupe** \ üp \ see ¹OOP

ouper \ ü-pər \ see OOPER

oupie \ ü-pē \ see OOPY

ouping \ ü-piŋ \ see OOPING

ouple \ əp-əl \ see UPLE

ouplet \ əp-lət \ see ¹UPLET

oupous \ ü-pəs \ see UPUS

oupy \ ü-pē \ see OOPY

¹**our** \ ōr \ see ¹ORE

²**our** \ ür \ see ¹URE

³**our** \ aur \ see ²OWER

⁴**our** \ är \ see ³AR

⁵**our** \ ər \ see ¹EUR

⁶**our** \ ȯr \ see ¹OR

oura \ ur-ə \ see URA

ourable \ ōr-ə-bəl \ see ¹ORABLE

ourage \ ər-ij \ courage, demurrage, discourage, encourage

¹**ourbon** \ ər-bən \ see ¹URBAN

²**ourbon** \ ür-bən \ see ²URBAN

¹**ource** \ ōrs \ see ¹OURSE

²**ource** \ ȯrs \ see ¹ORSE

¹**ourceful** \ ōrs-fəl \ see ¹ORCEFUL

²**ourceful** \ ȯrs-fəl \ see ORSEFUL

¹**ourd** \ ōrd \ see ¹OARD

²**ourd** \ ȯrd \ see ²OARD

ourde \ urd \ see ¹URED

¹**ou're** \ ōr \ see ¹ORE

²**ou're** \ ü-ər \ see ¹EWER

³**ou're** \ ur \ see ¹URE

⁴**ou're** \ ər \ see ¹EUR

⁵**ou're** \ ȯr \ see ¹OR

oured \ ōrd \ see ¹OARD

¹**ourer** \ ōr-ər \ see ¹ORER

²**ourer** \ ür-ər \ see ¹URER

³**ourer** \ aur-ər \ flowerer, scourer, deflowerer, devourer—*also comparatives of adjectives listed at* ²OWER

ourg \ ur \ see ¹URE

¹**ourge** \ ərj \ see URGE

²**ourge** \ ȯrj \ see ORGE

ourger \ ər-jər \ see ERGER

ouri \ ur-ē \ see ¹URY

¹**ourier** \ ur-ē-ər \ courier, couturier, couturiere, vaunt-courier

²**ourier** \ ər-ē-ər \ see URRIER

¹**ouring** \ōr-iŋ\ see ORING
²**ouring** \ur-iŋ\ see URING
ourish \ər-ish\ currish, flourish, nourish, amateurish
ourist \ur-əst\ see URIST
ourly \aur-lē\ dourly, hourly, sourly
¹**ourn** \ōrn\ see ¹ORN
²**ourn** \ərn\ see URN
³**ourn** \ȯrn\ see ²ORN
ournal \ərn-°l\ see ERNAL
ournament \ȯr-nə-mənt\ see ORNAMENT
ourne \ōrn\ see ¹ORN
¹**ourney** \ər-nē\ ferny, gurney, journey, tourney, attorney
²**ourney** \ȯr-nē\ see ORNY
ourneyer \ər-nē-ər\ journeyer, vernier
ournful \ȯrn-fəl\ see ORNFUL
ourning \ȯr-niŋ\ see ORNING
ournment \ərn-mənt\ see ERNMENT
¹**ours** \ōrz\ see ¹OORS
²**ours** \ärz\ see ARS
³**ours** \ȯrz\ see ²OORS
⁴**ours** \aurz\ ours, after-hours— *also plurals and possessives of nouns and third singular presents of verbs listed at* ²OWER
¹**ourse** \ōrs\ coarse, course, force, hoarse, source, concourse, deforce, discourse, divorce, enforce, perforce, racecourse, recourse,

resource, intercourse, reinforce, telecourse, tour de force, watercourse
²**ourse** \ȯrs\ see ¹ORSE
oursome \ȯr-səm\ see ORSUM
ourt \ȯrt\ see ¹ORT
ourtesy \ərt-ə-sē\ courtesy, curtesy, discourtesy
ourth \ȯrth\ see ¹ORTH
ourtier \ȯr-chər\ see ORCHER
¹**ourtly** \ōrt-lē\ see ¹ORTLY
²**ourtly** \ȯrt-lē\ see ²ORTLY
oury \aur-ē\ see OWERY
¹**ous** \ü\ see ¹EW
²**ous** \üs\ see ¹USE
ousal \au-zəl\ housel, spousal, tousle, arousal, carousal
ousand \auz-°n\ see OWSON
¹**ouse** \üs\ see ¹USE
²**ouse** \aus\ blouse, chiaus, chouse, douse, grouse, house, louse, mouse, scouse, souse, spouse, bathhouse, Bauhaus, birdhouse, blockhouse, bughouse, bunkhouse, cathouse, chophouse, clubhouse, courthouse, deckhouse, degauss, delouse, doghouse, dollhouse, dormouse, espouse, farmhouse, firehouse, flophouse, gashouse, glasshouse, greenhouse, guardhouse, henhouse, hothouse, icehouse, in-house, lighthouse, lobscouse,

longhouse, madhouse,
nuthouse, outhouse,
penthouse, playhouse,
poorhouse, roadhouse,
roughhouse, roundhouse,
schoolhouse, smokehouse,
springhouse, statehouse,
storehouse, teahouse,
titmouse, tollhouse,
warehouse, washhouse,
wheelhouse, White House,
whorehouse, workhouse,
boardinghouse, clearinghouse,
coffeehouse, countinghouse,
customhouse, house-to-house,
meetinghouse, Mickey
Mouse, pilothouse,
porterhouse, powerhouse,
slaughterhouse, sugarhouse,
summerhouse

³**ouse** \ aüz \ blouse, bouse,
bowse, browse, douse,
dowse, drowse, house,
mouse, rouse, spouse, touse,
arouse, carouse, delouse,
espouse, rehouse,
roughhouse, warehouse—*also
plurals and possessives of
nouns and third singular
presents of verbs listed at* ²OW

ousel \ aü-zəl \ see OUSAL

ouser \ aü-zər \ dowser, houser,
mouser, schnauzer, trouser,
wowser, warehouser, rabble-
rouser

ousin \ əz-ᵊn \ see ¹OZEN

ousinage \ əz-ᵊn-ij \ cousinage,
cozenage

ousing \ aü-ziŋ \ housing,
rousing, rabble-rousing

¹**ousle** \ ü-zəl \ see ²USAL

²**ousle** \ aü-zəl \ see OUSAL

ousse \ üs \ see ¹USE

ousseau \ ü-sō \ see USOE

oust \ aüst \ Faust, joust, oust,
roust—*also pasts of verbs
listed at* ²OUSE

ouste \ üst \ see OOST

¹**ousy** \ aü-zē \ see OWSY

²**ousy** \ aü-sē \ mousy, Firdawsi

¹**out** \ ü \ see ¹EW

²**out** \ üt \ see UTE

³**out** \ aüt \ bout, clout, doubt,
drought, flout, glout, gout,
grout, knout, kraut, lout, out,
pout, rout, route, scout,
shout, snout, spout, sprout,
stout, tout, trout, ablaut,
about, all-out, bailout,
blackout, blowout, breakout,
breechclout, brownout,
burned-out, burnout,
checkout, clapped-out,
closeout, cookout, cop-out,
cutout, devout, dishclout,
downspout, dropout, dugout,
eelpout, fade-out, fallout, far-
out, flameout, flat-out,
foldout, force-out, freak-out,
full-out, groundout, handout,
hangout, hideout, holdout,
knockout, layout, lights-out,

lockout, lookout, misdoubt,
payout, phaseout, pitchout,
printout, pullout, punch-out,
putout, rainspout, readout,
redoubt, rollout, sellout,
setout, shakeout, shoot-out,
shutout, sick-out, sold-out,
spaced-out, spinout, stakeout,
standout, straight-out, stretch-
out, strikeout, takeout,
thought-out, throughout,
throw out, time-out, tryout,
turnout, umlaut, walkout,
washed-out, washout, way-
out, whacked-out, whiteout,
wipeout, without, workout,
worn-out, all get-out,
carryout, diner-out, down-
and-out, falling-out,
gadabout, hereabout,
knockabout, layabout, out-
and-out, roundabout,
rouseabout, roustabout,
runabout, sauerkraut,
stirabout, thereabout,
turnabout, walkabout,
waterspout

¹oute \üt\ see UTE

²oute \aut\ see ³OUT

outed \aut-əd\ snouted,
spouted, undoubted—*also
pasts of verbs listed at* ³OUT

¹outer \üt-ər\ see UTER

²outer \aut-ər\ doubter, flouter,
grouter, outer, pouter, router,
scouter, shouter, spouter,

touter, come-outer, down-
and-outer, out-and-outer

¹outh \üth\ see ²OOTH

²outh \auth\ mouth, routh,
scouth, south, bad-mouth,
goalmouth, loudmouth, poor-
mouth, blabbermouth,
cottonmouth, hand-to-mouth,
word-of-mouth

outherly \ath-ər-lē\ see
OTHERLY

outhful \üth-fəl\ see UTHFUL

outhie \ü-thē\ see OOTHY

outhly \üth-lē\ see OOTHLY

outi \üt-ē\ see ¹OOTY

outing \aut-iŋ\ outing, scouting

outish \aut-ish\ loutish, snoutish

outre \üt-ər\ see UTER

outrement \ü-trə-mənt\ see
UTRIMENT

outs \auts\ hereabouts, ins and
outs, thereabouts,
whereabouts

outy \aut-ē\ see OUGHTY

ou've \üv\ see ³OVE

ouver \ü-vər\ see ³OVER

oux \ü\ see ¹EW

ouy \ē\ see ¹EE

ouyhnhnm \in-əm\ see INIM

ouzel \ü-zəl\ see ²USAL

ov \of\ see ²OFF

ova \ō-və\ nova, Jehovah,
bossa nova, Casanova,
supernova

ovable \ü-və-bəl\ movable,
provable, approvable,

disprovable, immovable,
improvable, removable,
irremovable

ovah \ō-və\ see OVA

oval \ü-vəl\ approval, removal,
disapproval

ovat \əv-ət\ see OVET

¹**ove** \əv\ dove, glove, love, of,
shove, above, foxglove,
hereof, ringdove, thereof,
truelove, whereof, ladylove,
light-o'-love, roman-fleuve,
turtledove, unheard of, well-
thought-of, hereinabove

²**ove** \ōv\ clove, cove, dove,
drove, grove, hove, Jove,
mauve, rove, stove, strove,
throve, trove, wove, alcove,
cookstove, mangrove,
interwove, treasure trove

³**ove** \üv\ groove, move, poof,
poove, prove, you've,
approve, behoove, commove,
disprove, improve, remove,
reprove, disapprove

¹**ovel** \äv-əl\ grovel, novel,
antinovel

²**ovel** \əv-əl\ grovel, hovel,
shovel

ovement \üv-mənt\ movement,
improvement

¹**oven** \əv-ən\ coven, oven,
sloven

²**oven** \ō-vən\ cloven, coven,
woven, handwoven,
interwoven

¹**over** \əv-ər\ cover, glover,
hover, lover, plover,
discover, dustcover,
hardcover, re-cover, recover,
slipcover, softcover, uncover,
windhover, undercover

²**over** \ō-vər\ clover, drover,
over, plover, rover, stover,
trover, allover, changeover,
crossover, cutover, flashover,
flopover, flyover, hangover,
holdover, layover, leftover,
moreover, once-over,
Passover, popover, pullover,
pushover, rollover, runover,
slipover, spillover, stopover,
strikeover, takeover, turnover,
voice-over, walkover,
warmed-over, carryover,
crossing-over, going-over

³**over** \ü-vər\ groover, louver,
mover, prover, improver,
maneuver, remover, reprover,
disapprover

⁴**over** \äv-ər\ see ¹AVER

overable \əv-rə-bəl\
discoverable, recoverable,
irrecoverable

overly \əv-ər-lē\ loverly, Sir
Roger de Coverley

overt \ō-vərt\ covert, overt

overy \əv-rē\ discovery,
recovery

ovet \əv-ət\ covet, lovat

ovian \ō-vē-ən\ Jovian,
Markovian, Pavlovian

ovie \ ü-vē \ see OOVY

ovo \ ō-vō \ Provo, ab ovo, de novo

ovost \ äv-əst \ see AVIST

¹**ow** \ ō \ beau, blow, bow, Chou, crow, do, doe, dough, ewe, floe, flow, foe, fro, froe, frow, glow, go, grow, ho, hoe, jo, know, lo, low, mho, mot, mow, no, No, O, oh, owe, pow, pro, rho, roe, row, schmo, sew, shew, show, sloe, slow, snow, so, sow, stow, strow, though, throe, throw, toe, tow, trow, whoa, woe, aglow, ago, airflow, airglow, alow, although, backhoe, bandeau, barlow, bateau, below, bestow, bon mot, Bordeaux, bravo, by-blow, cachepot, chapeau, chateau, Chi-Rho, cockcrow, cornrow, crossbow, Day-Glo, dayglow, de trop, deathblow, deco, down-bow, elbow, escrow, fencerow, flambeau, flyblow, fogbow, forego, foreknow, forgo, galop, genro, gigot, gung ho, hallo, heave-ho, hedgerow, heigh-ho, hello, hollo, hullo, inflow, jabot, Jane Doe, jim crow, John Doe, kayo, KO, longbow, low-low, macho, mahoe, maillot, manteau, merlot, misknow, Moho, morceau, mucro, mudflow, nightglow, no-no, no-show, nouveau, outflow, outgo, outgrow, oxbow, Pernod, picot, Pinot, plateau, pronto, rainbow, reflow, regrow, repo, reseau, rondeau, rondo, rouleau, sabot, scarecrow, self-sow, serow, shadblow, sideshow, skid row, so-so, sourdough, sunbow, tableau, tiptoe, tonneau, trousseau, unsew, up-bow, upthrow, Watteau, windrow, afterglow, aikido, alpenglow, apropos, art deco, art nouveau, audio, barrio, bibelot, bordereau, buffalo, bungalow, Bushido, buteo, calico, cameo, cachalot, cembalo, centimo, chassepot, cheerio, cogito, comedo, comme il faut, counterflow, curaçao, curassow, curio, daimyo, danio, do-si-do, domino, dynamo, embryo, entrepôt, Erato, escargot, Eskimo, extrados, fabliau, folio, fricandeau, furbelow, gigolo, go-no-go, guacharo, hammertoe, haricot, heel-and-toe, hetero, HMO, Holy Joe, indigo, kakapo, latigo, long-ago, massicot, medico, mistletoe, modulo, Navaho, Navajo, NCO, nuncio, oleo,

olio, overflow, overgrow,
overthrow, ovolo, patio,
peridot, picaro, piccolo,
Pierrot, polio, pomelo,
pompano, portico, Prospero,
proximo, quid pro quo, radio,
raree-show, ratio, Richard
Roe, rococo, rodeo, Romeo,
saddlebow, sapsago, Scorpio,
semipro, sloppy joe, so-and-
so, status quo, stereo, stop-
and-go, studio, subito,
tallyho, tangelo, ticktacktoe,
tit-tat-toe, TKO, to-and-fro,
tombolo, touraco, tournedos,
tremolo, tuckahoe, tupelo,
UFO, ultimo, undergo,
undertow, vertigo, vibrio,
virago, vireo, Arapaho,
centesimo, con spirito,
continuo, DMSO, ex nihilo,
fantastico, fellatio, fortissimo,
get-up-and-go, hereinbelow,
in utero, in vacuo, lentissimo,
lothario, magnifico,
malapropos, milesimo,
oregano, politico, portfolio,
presidio, prestissimo,
punctilio, quo warranto,
scenario, simpatico, ab initio,
archipelago, braggadocio,
duodecimo, ex officio,
generalissimo, impresario,
internuncio, oratorio,
pianissimo, rose of Jericho

²**ow**\aù\bough, bow, brow,
chiao, chow, ciao, cow,
dhow, Dou, dow, Dow, Frau,
hao, how, howe, jow, Lao,
mow, now, ow, plow, pow,
prau, prow, row, scow,
slough, sough, sow, Tao, tau,
thou, vow, wow, allow,
avow, bowwow, cacao,
cahow, chowchow, chow
chow, endow, enow, erenow,
eyebrow, gangplow, hausfrau,
haymow, highbrow,
hoosegow, know-how,
kowtow, landau, lowbrow,
luau, meow, miaow, nohow,
powwow, snowplow,
somehow, anyhow, curaçao,
disallow, disavow, disendow,
middlebrow, holier-than-thou

¹**owable**\ō-ə-bəl\knowable,
sewable, unknowable

²**owable**\aù-ə-bəl\plowable,
allowable, disavowable

owage\ō-ij\flowage, stowage,
towage

¹**owal**\ō-əl\see OEL

²**owal**\aùl\see ²OWL

¹**owan**\ō-ən\see ¹OAN

²**owan**\aù-ən\Gawain, gowan,
rowan, rowen

¹**oward**\ōrd\see ¹OARD

²**oward**\aùrd\see OWERED

³**oward**\ord\see ²OARD

¹**owd**\üd\see UDE

²**owd**\aùd\see ²OUD

owdah\aùd-ə\see ³AUDE

owder \aud-ər\ chowder, powder, gunpowder—*also comparatives of adjectives listed at* ²OUD

owdy \aud-ē\ cloudy, dowdy, howdy, rowdy, cum laude, pandowdy, magna cum laude, summa cum laude

owe \ō\ see ¹OW

¹**owed** \ōd\ see ODE

²**owed** \aud\ see ²OUD

owedly \au-əd-lē\ allowedly, avowedly

owel \aul\ see ²OWL

oweling \au-liŋ\ see ²OWLING

owen \au-ən\ see ²OWAN

¹**ower** \ōr\ see ¹ORE

²**ower** \aur\ bower, cower, dour, dower, flour, flower, gaur, giaour, glower, hour, lower, our, plower, power, scour, shower, sour, tour, tower, vower, avower, cornflower, deflower, devour, embower, empower, firepower, high-power, man-hour, mayflower, moonflower, off-hour, pasqueflower, repower, safflower, sunflower, wallflower, watchtower, wildflower, willpower, candlepower, cauliflower, disendower, overpower, passionflower, superpower, sweet-and-sour, thundershower, waterpower, womanpower

owered \aurd\ coward, flowered, powered, towered, high-powered, ivory-towered, superpowered, underpowered—*also pasts of verbs listed at* ²OWER

owerer \aur-ər\ see ³OURER

owerful \aur-fəl\ flowerful, powerful

owering \au-riŋ\ lowering, nonflowering

owery \aur-ē\ bowery, cauri, dowry, floury, flowery, kauri, Maori, showery

owff \auf\ howff, langlauf

owhee \ō-ē\ see OWY

owing \ō-iŋ\ see ¹OING

¹**owl** \ōl\ see ¹OLE

²**owl** \aul\ bowel, cowl, dowel, foul, fowl, growl, howl, jowl, owl, prowl, rowel, scowl, towel, trowel, vowel, yowl, avowal, batfowl, befoul, embowel, peafowl, seafowl, wildfowl, disavowal, disembowel, waterfowl

owland \ō-lənd\ lowland, Roland

owledge \äl-ij\ college, knowledge, acknowledge, foreknowledge

¹**owler** \ō-lər\ see OLLER

²**owler** \au-lər\ growler, howler, waterfowler

owless \ō-ləs\ see OLUS

owline \ō-lən\ see OLON

¹owling \ō-liŋ\ see OLLING

²owling \aù-liŋ\ cowling, growling, howling, toweling, antifouling, waterfowling

owlock \äl-ək\ see OLOCH

¹owly \ō-lē\ see ¹OLY

²owly \aù-lē\ foully, growly, haole, jowly

¹owman \ō-mən\ see OMAN

²owman \aù-mən\ bowman, cowman, plowman

ow-me \ō-mē\ see OAMY

¹own \ōn\ see ¹ONE

²own \aùn\ brown, clown, crown, down, drown, frown, gown, lown, noun, town, boomtown, breakdown, bringdown, clampdown, closedown, comedown, countdown, crackdown, crosstown, downtown, drawdown, embrown, facedown, godown, hoedown, hometown, knockdown, letdown, lookdown, lowdown, markdown, meltdown, nightgown, pastedown, phasedown, pronoun, pushdown, putdown, renown, rubdown, rundown, scale-down, shakedown, showdown, shutdown, sit-down, slowdown, Southdown,

splashdown, step-down, stripped-down, sundown, thumbs-down, top-down, touchdown, turndown, uncrown, uptown, write-down, broken-down, buttondown, Chinatown, dressing-down, eiderdown, hand-me-down, reach-me-down, shantytown, tumbledown, upside down, watered-down, man-about-town

ownded \aùn-dəd\ see OUNDED

ownding \aùn-diŋ\ see OUNDING

¹owned \ōnd\ see ¹ONED

²owned \aùnd\ see ²OUND

¹owner \ō-nər\ see ¹ONER

²owner \ü-nər\ see OONER

³owner \aù-nər\ browner, crowner, downer, sundowner

owness \ō-nəs\ see ²ONUS

ownia \ō-nē-ə\ see ¹ONIA

ownie \aù-nē\ see OWNY

owning \ō-niŋ\ see ²ONING

ownish \aù-nish\ brownish, clownish

ownlet \aùn-lət\ roundlet, townlet

ownsman \aùnz-mən\ gownsman, roundsman, townsman

owny \aù-nē\ brownie, browny, downy, townie

owry \aùr-ē\ see OWERY

owse \aùz\ see ²OUSE

owser \aů-zər\ see OUSER

owson \aůz-ᵊn\ thousand, advowson

owster \ō-stər\ see OASTER

owsy \aů-zē\ blowsy, drowsy, lousy

owth \ōth\ both, growth, loath, loth, oath, quoth, sloth, troth, wroth, betroth, outgrowth, upgrowth, Alioth, intergrowth, overgrowth, undergrowth

owy \ō-ē\ blowy, Chloe, doughy, joey, showy, snowy, towhee, echoey, kalanchoe

ox \äks\ box, cox, fox, gox, lox, ox, pax, phlox, pox, aurochs, bandbox, boondocks, cowpox, dreadlocks, firebox, gearbox, hatbox, hotbox, icebox, jukebox, lockbox, mailbox, matchbox, musk-ox, outfox, pillbox, postbox, redox, saltbox, sandbox, smallpox, snuffbox, soapbox, strongbox, sweatbox, toolbox, unbox, volvox, witness-box, workbox, Xerox, chatterbox, equinox, orthodox, paradox, pillar-box, shadowbox, Skinner box, tinderbox, heterodox, jack-in-the-box, unorthodox, neoorthodox, dementia praecox—*also plurals and possessives of*

nouns and third singular presents of verbs listed at ¹OCK

oxer \äk-sər\ boxer, Boxer, bobby-soxer

oxie \äk-sē\ see OXY

oxin \äk-sən\ coxswain, tocsin, toxin, dioxin, aflatoxin, mycotoxin

oxswain \äk-sən\ see OXIN

oxy \äk-sē\ boxy, doxy, foxy, moxie, oxy, proxy, epoxy, orthodoxy, heterodoxy, neoorthodoxy

oy \ȯi\ boy, buoy, cloy, coy, foy, goy, hoy, joy, ploy, poi, soy, strawy, toy, troy, ahoy, alloy, Amoy, annoy, batboy, bellboy, bok choy, borzoi, busboy, callboy, carboy, charpoy, choirboy, convoy, cowboy, decoy, deploy, destroy, doughboy, employ, enjoy, envoy, fly-boy, footboy, hautbois, highboy, houseboy, killjoy, linkboy, lowboy, McCoy, newsboy, playboy, plowboy, po'boy, postboy, potboy, Rob Roy, schoolboy, sepoy, tallboy, teapoy, tomboy, travois, viceroy, Adonai, bullyboy, copyboy, corduroy, hoi polloi, Illinois, Iroquois, maccaboy, overjoy, paperboy,

redeploy, reemploy,
Tinkertoy, Helen of Troy
oya \ ȯi-ə \ see OIA
oyable \ ȯi-ə-bəl \ deployable,
employable
¹oyal \ īl \ see ¹ILE
²oyal \ ȯil \ see OIL
oyalist \ ȯi-ə-ləst \ loyalist,
royalist
oyalty \ ȯil-tē \ loyalty, royalty,
disloyalty, viceroyalty
oyance \ ȯi-əns \ joyance,
annoyance, chatoyance,
clairvoyance, flamboyance
oyancy \ ȯi-ən-sē \ buoyancy,
chatoyancy, flamboyancy
oyant \ ȯi-ənt \ buoyant,
chatoyant, clairvoyant,
flamboyant
oyed \ ȯid \ see ¹OID
oyen \ ȯi-ən \ doyen, Guyen,
Iroquoian
oyer \ ȯir \ coir, foyer, moire,
caloyer, destroyer
oying \ ȯiŋ \ see AWING

oyle \ ȯil \ see OIL
oyless \ ȯi-ləs \ joyless, Troilus
oyment \ ȯi-mənt \ deployment,
employment, enjoyment,
unemployment
oyne \ ȯin \ see ¹OIN
¹oyo \ ȯi-ō \ boyo, arroyo
²oyo \ ȯi-ə \ see OIA
o-yo \ ō-yō \ yo-yo, criollo
oyster \ ȯi-stər \ see OISTER
¹oz \ əz \ see ¹EUSE
²oz \ ȯz \ see ¹AUSE
oze \ ōz \ see ²OSE
¹ozen \ əz-ᵊn \ cousin, cozen,
dozen, cater-cousin
²ozen \ ōz-ᵊn \ see OSEN
ozenage \ əz-ᵊn-ij \ see OUSINAGE
ozer \ ō-zər \ see ¹OSER
ozily \ ō-zə-lē \ see OSILY
¹ozo \ ō-sō \ see ¹OSO
²ozo \ ō-zō \ see ²OSO
ozy \ ō-zē \ see OSY
ozzer \ äz-ər \ rozzer, alcazar
ozzle \ äz-əl \ nozzle, schnozzle

u

²u \ ü \ see ¹EW
ua \ ü-ə \ skua, lehua, Quechua,
Timucua
uable \ ü-ə-bəl \ chewable,

doable, suable, viewable,
accruable, construable,
renewable
ual \ ü-əl \ see ¹UEL

uan\ü-ən\bruin, ruin, Siouan, yuan

uancy\ü-ən-sē\see UENCY

uant\ü-ənt\see UENT

uart\see ¹URT

ub\əb\chub, club, cub, drub, dub, flub, grub, hub, nub, pub, rub, scrub, shrub, slub, snub, stub, sub, tub, bathtub, flubdub, hubbub, nightclub, washtub, overdub, Beelzebub

uba\ü-bə\juba, scuba, tuba

ubal\ü-bəl\Jubal, nubile, ruble, tubal

ubbard\əb-ərd\cupboard, Mother Hubbard

ubber\əb-ər\blubber, clubber, drubber, dubber, grubber, lubber, rubber, scrubber, slubber, snubber, tubber, landlubber, nightclubber

ubbery\əb-rē\blubbery, rubbery, shrubbery

ubbily\əb-ə-lē\chubbily, grubbily

ubbin\əb-ən\dubbin, nubbin

ubbing\əb-iŋ\drubbing, rubbing, slubbing, landlubbing

ubble\əb-əl\bubble, double, nubble, rubble, stubble, trouble, abubble, redouble, undouble, hubble-bubble

ubbler\əb-lər\see OUBLER

ubbly\əb-lē\bubbly, doubly, nubbly, stubbly

ubby\əb-ē\chubby, clubby, cubby, grubby, hubby, nubby, Rabi, scrubby, shrubby, snubby, stubby, tubby

ube\üb\boob, cube, lube, rube, tube, blowtube, flashcube, haboob, jujube

uber\ü-bər\cuber, goober, tuber

uberance\ü-brəns\exuberance, protuberance

uberant\ü-brənt\exuberant, protuberant

uberous\ü-brəs\see UBRIS

ubic\ü-bik\cubic, pubic, cherubic

ubile\ü-bəl\see UBAL

ubious\ü-bē-əs\dubious, rubious

ubis\ü-bəs\pubis, rubus

uble\ü-bəl\see UBAL

ublic\əb-lik\public, republic

ublican\əb-li-kən\publican, republican

ubric\ü-brik\lubric, rubric

ubrious\ü-brē-əs\lugubrious, salubrious, insalubrious

ubris\ü-brəs\hubris, tuberous

ubtile\ət-ᵊl\see UTTLE

ubus\ü-bəs\see UBIS

uby\ü-bē\see OOBY

uca\ü-kə\see OOKA

ucal\ü-kəl\ducal, nuchal, archducal

ucan\ü-kən\kuchen, Lucan

ucat \ək-ət\ see UCKET
¹ucca \ü-kə\ see OOKA
²ucca \ək-ə\ see UKKA
uccal \ək-əl\ see UCKLE
ucco \ək-ō\ see UCKO
uccor \ək-ər\ see UCKER
uccory \ək-rē\ see UCKERY
ucculence \ək-yə-ləns\ see UCULENCE
uce \üs\ see ¹USE
uced \üst\ see OOST
ucement \ü-smənt\ inducement, seducement
ucence \üs-³ns\ nuisance, translucence
ucer \ü-sər\ juicer, looser, adducer, Bull Mooser, inducer, lime-juicer, producer, transducer, introducer, reproducer
¹uch \ich\ see ITCH
²uch \ük\ see UKE
³uch \əch\ see ¹UTCH
uchal \ü-kəl\ see UCAL
¹uche \ü-chē\ see OOCHY
²uche \üch\ see ¹OOCH
³uche \üsh\ see OUCHE
uchen \ü-kən\ see UCAN
ucher \ü-chər\ see UTURE
uchin \ü-shən\ see UTION
uchsia \ü-shə\ see UTIA
uchy \əch-ē\ duchy, smutchy, touchy, archduchy
ucial \ü-shəl\ crucial, fiducial
ucian \ü-shən\ see UTION
ucible \ü-sə-bəl\ crucible,

deducible, educible, inducible, producible, protrusible, irreducible, reproducible, irreproducible
ucid \ü-səd\ deuced, lucid, pellucid
ucifer \ü-sə-fər\ crucifer, Lucifer
ucity \ü-sət-ē\ abstrusity, caducity
ucive \ü-siv\ see USIVE
uck \ək\ buck, chuck, cluck, cruck, duck, guck, huck, luck, muck, pluck, puck, ruck, schmuck, shuck, snuck, struck, stuck, suck, truck, tuck, yech, yuck, amok, awestruck, bushbuck, Canuck, dumbstruck, Kalmuck, lame-duck, light-struck, moonstruck, mukluk, muktuk, potluck, reedbuck, roebuck, sawbuck, shelduck, stagestruck, sunstruck, upchuck, woodchuck, geoduck, Habakkuk, megabuck, muckamuck, nip and tuck, high-muck-a-muck
ucker \ək-ər\ bucker, chukker, ducker, mucker, plucker, pucker, shucker, succor, sucker, trucker, tucker, bloodsucker, sapsucker, seersucker
uckery \ək-rē\ puckery, succory

ucket \ək-ət\ bucket, ducat,
tucket, gutbucket

uckle \ək-əl\ buccal, buckle,
chuckle, knuckle, suckle,
truckle, bare-knuckle,
parbuckle, pinochle,
swashbuckle, turnbuckle,
unbuckle, honeysuckle

uckled \ək-əld\ cuckold,
knuckled, bare-knuckled—
also pasts of verbs listed at
UCKLE

uckler \ək-lər\ buckler,
knuckler, swashbuckler

uckling \ək-liŋ\ duckling,
suckling, swashbuckling

ucko \ək-ō\ bucko, stucco

uckold \ək-əld\ see UCKLED

ucks \əks\ see ¹UX

uckus \ùk-əs\ ruckus, Sukkoth

ucky \ək-ē\ ducky, lucky,
mucky, plucky, yucky,
unlucky, happy-go-lucky

uco \ü-kō\ pachuco, osso buco

ucre \ü-kər\ euchre, lucre

uct \əkt\ duct, abduct, adduct,
conduct, construct, deduct,
destruct, eruct, induct,
instruct, obstruct, aqueduct,
reconstruct, usufruct,
viaduct—*also pasts of verbs
listed at* UCK

uctable \ək-tə-bəl\ see UCTIBLE

uctal \ək-tᵊl\ ductal, ductile

uctance \ək-təns\ conductance,
inductance, reluctance

uctible \ək-tə-bəl\ conductible,
constructible, deductible,
destructible, indestructible,
ineluctable, reconstructible

uctile \ək-tᵊl\ see UCTAL

ucting \ək-tiŋ\ ducting,
semiconducting

uction \ək-shən\ fluxion,
ruction, suction, abduction,
adduction, conduction,
construction, deduction,
destruction, eduction,
effluxion, induction,
instruction, obstruction,
production, reduction,
seduction, introduction,
reconstruction, reproduction

uctive \ək-tiv\ adductive,
conductive, constructive,
deductive, destructive,
inductive, instructive,
productive, reductive,
seductive, reconstructive,
reproductive, self-destructive,
counterproductive

uctor \ək-tər\ abductor,
adductor, conductor,
constructor, destructor,
eductor, inductor, instructor,
reconstructor, semiconductor

uctress \ək-trəs\ conductress,
instructress, seductress

uculence \ək-yə-ləns\
succulence, truculence

ucy \ü-sē\ see UICY

¹ud \əd\ blood, bud, crud, cud,

dud, flood, fud, mud, rudd, scud, spud, stud, sudd, thud, coldblood, disbud, half-blood, hotblood, lifeblood, oxblood, redbud, rosebud, stick-in-the-mud

²ud \ üd \ see UDE

³ud \ ùd \ see ¹OOD

uda \ üd-ə \ Buddha, Gouda, Judah, remuda, barracuda

udable \ üd-ə-bəl \ excludable, extrudable, includable, ineludible

udah \ üd-ə \ see UDA

udal \ üd-ᵊl \ see OODLE

udas \ üd-əs \ Judas, Santa Gertrudis

¹udd \ üd \ see ¹OOD

²udd \ əd \ see ¹UD

udded \ əd-əd \ see ¹OODED

udder \ əd-ər \ budder, flooder, judder, rudder, shudder, udder

uddha \ üd-ə \ see UDA

uddhist \ üd-əst \ see ¹UDIST

uddie \ əd-ē \ see ¹UDDY

¹udding \ əd-iŋ \ budding, studding

²udding \ ùd-iŋ \ see OODING

uddle \ əd-ᵊl \ buddle, cuddle, fuddle, huddle, muddle, puddle, ruddle, befuddle

uddly \ əd-lē \ cuddly, muddly

¹uddy \ əd-ē \ bloody, buddy, cruddy, cuddy, duddie, muddy, ruddy, study, fuddy-duddy, understudy

²uddy \ üd-ē \ see ²OODY

ude \ üd \ brood, crowd, crude, dude, feud, food, hued, Jude, lewd, mood, nude, oud, pood, prude, pseud, rood, rude, shrewd, snood, stewed, wood, wud, you'd, allude, collude, conclude, delude, denude, elude, etude, exclude, extrude, exude, fast-food, include, intrude, obtrude, occlude, postlude, preclude, prelude, protrude, Quaalude, seafood, seclude, subdued, transude, unglued, altitude, amplitude, aptitude, attitude, certitude, consuetude, crassitude, desuetude, finitude, fortitude, gratitude, habitude, hebetude, interlude, lassitude, latitude, longitude, magnitude, mansuetude, multitude, negritude, platitude, plenitude, plentitude, promptitude, pulchritude, quietude, rectitude, seminude, servitude, solitude, turpitude, vastitude, beatitude, correctitude, decrepitude, exactitude, inaptitude, incertitude, infinitude, ingratitude, inquietude, similitude, solicitude, vicissitude, dissimilitude, inexactitude, verisimilitude

udel \üd-ᵊl\ see OODLE

udeness \üd-nəs\ see UDINOUS

udent \üd-ᵊnt\ prudent, imprudent, student, jurisprudent

uder \üd-ər\ brooder, Tudor, concluder, deluder, excluder, extruder, intruder, obtruder, preluder—*also comparatives of adjectives listed at* UDE

¹**udge** \əj\ budge, drudge, fudge, grudge, judge, nudge, sludge, smudge, trudge, adjudge, begrudge, forejudge, misjudge, prejudge

²**udge** \üj\ see ¹UGE

udgeon \əj-ən\ bludgeon, dudgeon, gudgeon, curmudgeon

udget \əj-ət\ budget, fussbudget

udgie \əj-ē\ see UDGY

udging \əj-iŋ\ drudging, grudging

udgy \əj-ē\ budgie, pudgy, sludgy, smudgy

udible \üd-ə-bəl\ see UDABLE

udinal \üd-nəl\ altitudinal, aptitudinal, attitudinal, latitudinal, longitudinal, platitudinal

udinous \üd-nəs\ crudeness, lewdness, rudeness, shrewdness, altitudinous,

multitudinous, platitudinous, plenitudinous, pulchritudinous

udis \üd-əs\ see UDAS

udish \üd-ish\ dudish, prudish

¹**udist** \üd-əst\ Buddhist, feudist, nudist—*also superlatives of adjectives listed at* UDE

²**udist** \úd-əst\ see OULDEST

udity \üd-ət-ē\ crudity, nudity

udo \üd-ō\ judo, kudo, pseudo, scudo, studo, testudo

udor \üd-ər\ see UDER

udsman \údz-mən\ see OODSMAN

udu \üd-ü\ see OODOO

udy \əd-ē\ see ¹UDDY

ue \ü\ see ¹EW

ued \üd\ see UDE

ueful \ü-fəl\ rueful, truffle, pantofle

ueghel \ü-gəl\ see UGAL

¹**uel** \ü-əl\ crewel, cruel, dual, duel, gruel, jewel, newel, accrual, eschewal, refuel, renewal, Pantagruel

²**uel** \ül\ see ¹OOL

uely \ü-lē\ see ULY

uement \ü-mənt\ see EWMENT

uence \ü-əns\ buoyance, affluence, confluence, congruence, effluence, influence, pursuance, refluence, incongruence

uency \ü-ən-sē\ fluency,

truancy, affluency,
congruency, nonfluency

ueness \ü-nəs\ see EWNESS

uenster \ən-stər\ see UNSTER

uent \ü-ənt\ fluent, suint,
truant, affluent, confluent,
congruent, effluent, influent,
incongruent

uer \ü-ər\ see ¹EWER

uerdon \ərd-²n\ see URDEN

uerile \uṙ-əl\ see URAL

ues \üz\ see ²USE

uesman \üz-mən\ see EWSMAN

uesome \ü-səm\ gruesome,
twosome

uesy \ü-zē\ see OOZY

uet \ü-ət\ bluet, cruet, peewit,
suet, conduit, intuit

uette \et\ see ¹ET

uey \ü-ē\ see EWY

ufa \ü-fə\ loofah, tufa, opera
buffa

uff \əf\ bluff, buff, chough,
chuff, cuff, duff, fluff, gruff,
guff, huff, luff, muff, puff,
rough, ruff, scruff, scuff,
slough, snuff, sough, stuff,
tough, tuff, dyestuff, earmuff,
enough, foodstuff, handcuff,
rebuff, oeil-de-boeuf,
overstuff

uffa \ü-fə\ see UFA

¹uffe \üf\ see ¹OOF

²uffe \üf\ see ²OOF

uffed \əft\ chuffed, ruffed, tuft,

candytuft—*also pasts of verbs
listed at* UFF

uffel \əf-əl\ see ¹UFFLE

uffer \əf-ər\ bluffer, buffer,
duffer, puffer, rougher,
snuffer, stuffer, suffer,
candlesnuffer—*also
comparatives of adjectives
listed at* UFF

uffet \əf-ət\ buffet, tuffet

uffin \əf-ən\ muffin, puffin,
roughen, toughen, ragamuffin

uffish \əf-ish\ huffish, roughish

¹uffle \əf-əl\ duffel, muffle,
ruffle, scuffle, shuffle,
snuffle, truffle, reshuffle,
unmuffle

²uffle \ü-fəl\ see UEFUL

uffled \əf-əld\ truffled,
unruffled—*also pasts of verbs
listed at* UFFLE

uffler \əf-lər\ muffler, shuffler,
snuffler

uffly \əf-lē\ bluffly, gruffly,
roughly, ruffly

uffy \əf-ē\ chuffy, fluffy, huffy,
puffy, scruffy, snuffy, stuffy,
toughie

ufi \ü-fē\ see OOFY

uft \əft\ see UFFED

ufti \əf-tē\ mufti, tufty

ufty \əf-tē\ see UFTI

ug \əg\ bug, chug, drug, dug,
fug, hug, jug, lug, mug,
plug, pug, rug, shrug, slug,
smug, snug, thug, tug, ugh,

vug, bedbug, billbug, debug,
earplug, firebug, fireplug,
goldbug, humbug, ladybug,
lovebug, stinkbug, unplug,
chugalug, doodlebug,
jitterbug, litterbug, mealybug,
shutterbug
uga\ü-gə\beluga, Cayuga
ugal\ü-gəl\Brueghel, bugle,
frugal, fugal, fugle, conjugal
ugar\úg-ər\see UGUR
ugary\úg-rē\buggery, sugary
¹uge\üj\huge, kludge, scrooge,
scrouge, stooge, deluge,
centrifuge, subterfuge
²uge\üzh\luge, rouge, deluge,
gamboge, refuge
uggaree\əg-rē\see ¹UGGERY
¹ugger\əg-ər\bugger, chugger,
lugger, mugger, plugger,
rugger, slugger, hugger-
mugger
²ugger\úg-ər\see UGUR
¹uggery\əg-rē\buggery,
puggaree, snuggery,
thuggery, skulduggery
²uggery\úg-rē\see UGARY
ugget\əg-ət\drugget, nugget
uggie\əg-ē\see UGGY
uggish\əg-ish\sluggish,
thuggish
uggle\əg-əl\guggle, juggle,
smuggle, snuggle, struggle
uggler\əg-lər\juggler,
smuggler, struggler

uggy\əg-ē\buggy, druggie,
druggy, fuggy, luggie, muggy
ugh\əg\see UG
ugle\ü-gəl\see UGAL
ugly\əg-lē\smugly, ugly, plug-
ugly
ugn\ün\see ¹OON
ugner\ü-nər\see OONER
ugric\ü-grik\tugrik, Ugric,
Finno-Ugric
ugrik\ü-grik\see UGRIC
ugu\ü-gü\fugu, goo-goo
ugur\úg-ər\booger, bugger,
sugar
uhl\ül\see ¹OOL
uhr\ər\see ¹EUR
ührer\úr-ər\see ¹URER
uice\üs\see ¹USE
uiced\üst\see OOST
uiceless\ü-sləs\see USELESS
uicer\ü-sər\see UCER
uicy\ü-sē\goosey, juicy,
sluicy, sprucy, acey-deucey
uid\ü-əd\druid, fluid
uidable\īd-ə-bəl\see ¹IDABLE
uidance\īd-ᵊns\see IDANCE
uide\īd\see ¹IDE
uider\īd-ər\see ¹IDER
uidon\īd-ᵊn\see IDEN
uiker\ī-kər\see IKER
uild\ild\see ILLED
uilder\il-dər\see ILDER
uilding\il-diŋ\see ILDING
uile\īl\see ¹ILE
uileless\īl-ləs\see ILELESS
uiler\ī-lər\see ILAR

uilt\ilt\ see ILT

uimpe\amp\ see ³AMP

¹**uin**\ü-ən\ see UAN

²**uin**\ən\ see UN

uing\ü-iŋ\ see ²OING

uint\ü-ənt\ see UENT

uirdly\ùr-lē\ see URELY

uisance\üs-²ns\ see UCENCE

uisard\ī-zərd\ see ISORED

¹**uisc**\üz\ see ²USE

²**uise**\īz\ see IZE

uiser\ü-zər\ see USER

uish\ü-ish\ see EWISH

uisne\ü-nē\ see OONY

uiste\is-tē\ see ²ICITY

¹**uit**\ü-ət\ see UET

²**uit**\üt\ see UTE

uitable\üt-ə-bəl\ see UTABLE

uitage\üt-ij\ see ¹OOTAGE

uite\üt\ see UTE

uited\üt-əd\ see ¹OOTED

uiter\üt-ər\ see UTER

uiterer\üt-ər-ər\ fruiterer, pewterer

uiting\üt-iŋ\ see UTING

uitless\üt-ləs\ see OOTLESS

uitlet\üt-lət\ see OOTLET

uitor\üt-ər\ see UTER

uitous\ü-ət-əs\ circuitous, fortuitous, gratuitous

uits\üts\ see OOTS

¹**uittle**\üt-²l\ see UTILE

²**uittle**\ət-²l\ see UTTLE

¹**uity**\ü-ət-ē\ acuity, annuity, circuity, congruity, fatuity, fortuity, gratuity, vacuity, ambiguity, assiduity, conspicuity, contiguity, continuity, incongruity, ingenuity, perpetuity, promiscuity, superfluity, discontinuity

²**uity**\üt-ē\ see ¹OOTY

¹**uk**\ük\ see UKE

²**uk**\ùk\ see ¹OOK

³**uk**\ək\ see UCK

uke\ük\ cuke, duke, fluke, gook, juke, kook, Luke, nuke, puke, souk, snook, spook, tuque, uke, yeuk, archduke, Baruch, caoutchouc, Chinook, Mamluk, rebuke, Heptateuch, Hexateuch, Pentateuch

uki\ü-kē\ see ¹OOKY

ukka\ək-ə\ chukka, pukka, yucca, felucca

ukkah\ùk-ə\ see OOKAH

ukker\ək-ər\ see UCKER

ukkoth\ùk-əs\ see UCKUS

¹**ul**\ùl\ bull, full, pull, shul, wool, you'll, armful, bagful, bellpull, brimful, bulbul, canful, capful, carful, cheekful, chestful, chock-full, cupful, drawerful, earful, eyeful, fistful, forkful, glassful, handful, houseful, jarful, John Bull, jugful, leg-pull, mouthful, outpull, pailful, panful, pipeful, plateful, potful, push-pull,

rackful, roomful, sackful, scoopful, shelfful, skinful, spoonful, stickful, tankful, tinful, topful, trainful, trayful, trunkful, tubful, barrelful, basketful, bellyful, teaspoonful, dyed-in-the-wool, tablespoonful

²**ul** \ül\ see ¹OOL

³**ul** \əl\ see ¹ULL

ula \ü-lə\ Beulah, Fula, hula, moola, pula, ampulla, tabbouleh

ular \ü-lər\ see OOLER

ulcent \əl-sənt\ see ULSANT

ulcer \əl-sər\ see ULSER

ulch \əlch\ cultch, gulch, mulch

¹**ule** \ü-lē\ see ULY

²**ule** \ül\ see ¹OOL

ulean \ü-lē-ən\ Boolean, Acheulean, cerulean

uled \üld\ see OOLED

ulep \ü-ləp\ see ULIP

uler \ü-lər\ see OOLER

ulet \əl-ət\ see ¹ULLET

¹**uley** \ü-lē\ see ULY

²**uley** \ül-ē\ see ²ULLY

ulf \əlf\ golf, gulf, engulf

ulgar \əl-gər\ see ULGUR

ulge \əlj\ bulge, divulge, indulge, overindulge

¹**ulgence** \əl-jəns\ divulgence, indulgence, refulgence

²**ulgence** \úl-jəns\ effulgence, refulgence

ulgent \əl-jənt\ fulgent, indulgent

ulgur \əl-gər\ bulgur, vulgar

uli \úl-ē\ see ²ULLY

ulip \ü-ləp\ julep, tulip

ulish \ü-lish\ see OOLISH

ulity \ü-lət-ē\ credulity, garrulity, sedulity, incredulity

ulk \əlk\ bulk, hulk, skulk, sulk, yolk

ulky \əl-kē\ bulky, sulky

¹**ull** \əl\ cull, dull, gull, hull, lull, mull, null, scull, skull, stull, trull, annul, mogul, numskull, pas seul

²**ull** \úl\ see ¹UL

¹**ulla** \úl-ə\ bulla, mullah, ampulla

²**ulla** \ü-lə\ see ULA

³**ulla** \əl-ə\ see ¹ULLAH

ullage \əl-ij\ sullage, ullage

¹**ullah** \əl-ə\ Gullah, mullah, nullah, stollen, medulla, ayatollah

²**ullah** \úl-ə\ see ¹ULLA

ullan \əl-ən\ see ULLEN

ullard \əl-ərd\ see OLORED

ullate \əl-ət\ see ¹ULLET

ulle \ül\ see ¹OOL

ullein \əl-ən\ see ULLEN

ullen \əl-ən\ mullein, stollen, sullen, Lucullan

¹**uller** \úl-ər\ fuller, puller

²**uller** \əl-ər\ see ¹OLOR

¹**ullet** \əl-ət\ culet, cullet, gullet, mullet, cucullate

²**ullet** \ùl-ət\ bullet, pullet
ulley \ùl-ē\ see ²ULLY
ullion \əl-yən\ cullion, mullion, scullion, slumgullion
ullman \ùl-mən\ fulmine, Pullman
¹**ully** \əl-ē\ cully, dully, gully, sully
²**ully** \ùl-ē\ bully, fully, gully, muley, puli, pulley, woolly
ulmine \ùl-mən\ see ULLMAN
ulp \əlp\ gulp, pulp, insculp
ulsant \əl-sənt\ pulsant, convulsant, demulcent
ulse \əls\ dulse, pulse, avulse, convulse, expulse, impulse, repulse
ulser \əl-sər\ pulser, ulcer
ulsion \əl-shən\ pulsion, avulsion, compulsion, convulsion, emulsion, evulsion, expulsion, impulsion, propulsion, repulsion, revulsion
ulsive \əl-siv\ compulsive, convulsive, emulsive, expulsive, impulsive, propulsive, repulsive
ult \əlt\ cult, adult, consult, exult, incult, indult, insult, occult, penult, result, tumult, catapult, antepenult
ultancy \əlt-ᵊn-sē\ consultancy, exultancy
ultant \əlt-ᵊnt\ consultant, exultant, resultant

ultch \əlch\ see ULCH
ulter \əl-tər\ consultor, insulter, occulter
ultery \əl-trē\ see ULTRY
ultor \əl-tər\ see ULTER
ultry \əl-trē\ sultry, adultery
ultural \əlch-rəl\ cultural, cross-cultural, subcultural, agricultural, countercultural, horticultural
ulture \əl-chər\ culture, multure, vulture, subculture, agriculture, apiculture, aquaculture, aviculture, counterculture, floriculture, horticulture, mariculture, monoculture, silviculture, viniculture
ulty \əl-tē\ see ¹ALTI
ulu \ü-lü\ lulu, Zulu
ulva \əl-və\ ulva, vulva
ulvar \əl-vər\ see ULVER
ulver \əl-vər\ culver, vulvar
uly \ü-lē\ bluely, boule, coolie, coolly, coulee, duly, muley, newly, puli, stoolie, Thule, truly, tule, guayule, patchouli, tabbouleh, unduly, unruly, ultima Thule
¹**um** \əm\ bum, chum, come, crumb, cum, drum, dumb, from, glum, gum, hum, lum, mum, numb, plum, plumb, rhumb, rum, scrum, scum, slum, some, strum, sum, swum, them, thrum, thumb,

alum, aplomb, become,
benumb, degum, dim sum,
dumdum, eardrum, ho-hum,
humdrum, income, outcome,
subgum, succumb, therefrom,
Tom Thumb, tom-tom,
wherefrom, yum-yum,
kettledrum, overcome,
sugarplum, hop-o'my-thumb

²**um** \ùm\ cum, groom,
Targum, mare librum—*also
words ending in* -room *listed
at* ¹OOM

³**um** \üm\ see ¹OOM

uma \ü-mə\ duma, pneuma,
puma, satsuma

umable \ü-mə-bəl\ assumable,
consumable, presumable,
subsumable, inconsumable

uman \ü-mən\ blooming,
crewman, human, lumen,
numen, Yuman, acumen,
albumen, albumin, bitumen,
ichneumon, illumine,
inhuman, panhuman,
subhuman, antihuman,
catechumen, protohuman,
superhuman

umanist \ü-mə-nəst\ see
UMENIST

umanous \ü-mə-nəs\ see
UMINOUS

umb \əm\ see ¹UM

umbar \əm-bər\ see ¹UMBER

umbed \əmd\ green-thumbed,
unplumbed

umbel \əm-bəl\ see UMBLE

umbency \əm-bən-sē\
incumbency, recumbency

umbent \əm-bənt\ decumbent,
incumbent, procumbent,
recumbent, superincumbent

¹**umber** \əm-bər\ cumber,
lumbar, lumber, number,
slumber, umber, cucumber,
encumber, outnumber,
renumber, disencumber

²**umber** \əm-ər\ see UMMER

umbered \əm-bərd\
unnumbered,
unencumbered—*also pasts of
verbs listed at* ¹UMBER

umberous \əm-brəs\ see
UMBROUS

umbery \əm-brē\ ombre,
slumbery

umbing \əm-iŋ\ see OMING

umble \əm-bəl\ bumble,
crumble, fumble, grumble,
humble, jumble, mumble,
rumble, scumble, stumble,
tumble, umbel, rough-and-
tumble

umbler \əm-blər\ bumbler,
fumbler, grumbler, mumbler,
rumbler, stumbler, tumbler

umbling \əm-bliŋ\ rumbling,
tumbling

¹**umbly** \əm-blē\ crumbly,
grumbly, humbly, mumbly,
rumbly

²**umbly** \ əm-lē \ comely, dumbly, dumly, numbly

umbness \ əm-nəs \ dumbness, glumness, numbness, alumnus

umbo \ əm-bō \ gumbo, jumbo, umbo, mumbo jumbo

umbra \ əm-brə \ umbra, penumbra

umbral \ əm-brəl \ see UMBRIL

umbril \ əm-brəl \ tumbril, umbral, pcnumbral

umbrous \ əm-brəs \ cumbrous, slumberous

ume \ üm \ see ¹OOM

umed \ ümd \ see OOMED

umedly \ ü-məd-lē \ consumedly, presumedly

umelet \ üm-lət \ see OOMLET

umely \ ü-mə-lē \ see OOMILY

umen \ ü-mən \ see UMAN

umenist \ ü-mə-nəst \ humanist, luminist, ecumenist, illuminist, phillumenist

umer \ ü-mər \ bloomer, groomer, humor, roomer, rumor, tumor, consumer, costumer, exhumer, perfumer, presumer, schussboomer

umeral \ üm-rəl \ humeral, humoral, numeral

umerous \ üm-rəs \ see UMOROUS

umerus \ üm-rəs \ see UMOROUS

umey \ ü-mē \ see OOMY

umf \ əmf \ see UMPH

umice \ əm-əs \ see UMMOUS

umid \ ü-məd \ humid, tumid

¹**umin** \ əm-ən \ cumin, summon

²**umin** \ ü-mən \ see UMAN

uminal \ ü-mən-ᵊl \ luminal, noumenal

uminate \ ü-mə-nət \ acuminate, illuminate

umine \ ü-mən \ see UMAN

uming \ ü-miŋ \ blooming, consuming, everblooming, time-consuming, unassuming—*also present participles of verbs listed at* ¹OOM

uminist \ ü-mə-nəst \ see UMENIST

uminous \ ü-mə-nəs \ luminous, numinous, albuminous, aluminous, bituminous, leguminous, quadrumanous, voluminous

umma \ əm-ə \ gumma, momma, summa

¹**ummary** \ əm-rē \ see ²UMMERY

²**ummary** \ əm-ə-rē \ see ¹UMMERY

ummate \ əm-ət \ see UMMET

ummel \ əm-əl \ see ²OMMEL

ummell \ əm-əl \ see ²OMMEL

ummer \ əm-ər \ bummer, comer, drummer, gummer, hummer, mummer, plumber, rummer, slummer, strummer, summer, latecomer, midsummer, newcomer, overcomer, up-and-comer—

*also comparatives of
adjectives listed at* ¹UM

¹**ummery** \əm-ə-rē\ flummery,
mummery, summary,
summery

²**ummery** \əm-rē\ cymry,
flummery, summary,
summery

ummet \əm-ət\ grummet,
plummet, summit,
consummate

ummie \əm-ē\ see UMMY

ummit \əm-ət\ see UMMET

ummock \əm-ək\ hummock,
stomach

ummon \əm-ən\ see ¹UMIN

ummoner \əm-nər\ see UMNAR

ummous \əm-əs\ gummous,
pomace, pumice

ummox \əm-əks\ flummox,
hummocks, lummox,
stomachs

ummy \əm-ē\ chummy,
crummie, crummy, dummy,
gummy, mommy, mummy,
plummy, rummy, scummy,
slummy, tummy, yummy

umnar \əm-nər\ summoner,
columnar

umness \əm-nəs\ see UMBNESS

umnus \əm-nəs\ see UMBNESS

umor \ü-mər\ see UMER

umoral \üm-rəl\ see UMERAL

umorous \üm-rəs\ humerus,
humorous, numerous,
tumorous, innumerous

umous \ü-məs\ brumous,
humus, spumous, posthumous

ump \əmp\ bump, chump,
clomp, clump, comp, crump,
dump, flump, frump, grump,
hump, jump, lump, mump,
plump, pump, rump, slump,
stump, sump, thump, trump,
tump, ump, whump,
mugwump, no-trump, tub-
thump, callithump, overtrump

umper \əm-pər\ bumper,
dumper, jumper, lumper,
plumper, pumper, stumper,
thumper, tub-thumper

umph \əmf\ bumf, humph,
galumph, harrumph

umpish \əm-pish\ dumpish,
frumpish, lumpish, plumpish

umpkin \əŋ-kən\ see UNKEN

umple \əm-pəl\ crumple,
rumple

umply \əm-plē\ crumply,
plumply, rumply

umps \əms\ dumps, mumps—
*also plurals and possessives
of nouns and third singular
presents of verbs listed at*
UMP

umption \əm-shən\ gumption,
assumption, consumption,
presumption, resumption,
subsumption

umptious \əm-shəs\ bumptious,
scrumptious, presumptuous

umptive \əm-tiv \assumptive, consumptive, presumptive

¹umptuous \əm-chəs \ sumptuous, presumptuous

²umptuous \əm-shəs \see UMPTIOUS

umpus \əm-pəs \see ²OMPASS

umpy \əm-pē \bumpy, clumpy, dumpy, frumpy, grumpy, humpy, jumpy, lumpy, stumpy

umulous \ü-myə-ləs \see UMULUS

umulus \ü-myə-ləs \cumulous, cumulus, tumulus

umus \ü-məs \see UMOUS

umy \ü-mē \see OOMY

un \ən \bun, can, done, dun, fen, foehn, fun, gun, Hun, jun, maun, none, nun, one, pun, run, shun, son, spun, stun, sun, sunn, ton, tonne, tun, when, won, A-1, begun, blowgun, chaconne, finespun, flashgun, forerun, godson, grandson, handgun, homespun, long run, outdone, outgun, outrun, popgun, pressrun, rerun, sea-run, shotgun, six-gun, stepson, undone, V-1, well-done, Acheron, Algonquin, allemande, all-or-none, hit-and-run, kiloton, machine-gun, megaton, one-on-one, one-to-one, overdone, overrun, PL/1, Sally Lunn, scattergun, tommy gun, twenty-one, underdone, underrun, alexandrine

una \ü-nə \Buna, puna, tuna, kahuna, lacuna, laguna, vicuña, Cunha

¹uña \ü-nə \see UNA

²uña \ün-yə \see UNIA

unal \ün-ᵊl \communal, jejunal, lagoonal, monsoonal, tribunal

unar \ü-nər \see OONER

unary \ü-nə-rē \unary, festoonery, sublunary, superlunary

unate \ü-nət \unit, lacunate, tribunate

unc \ənk \see UNK

unce \əns \dunce, once—*also plurals and possessives of nouns and third singular presents of verbs listed at* ¹ONT

unch \ənch \brunch, bunch, crunch, hunch, lunch, munch, punch, scrunch, keypunch

uncheon \ən-chən \luncheon, puncheon, roentgen, truncheon

uncher \ən-chər \cruncher, luncher, muncher, cowpuncher, keypuncher, counterpuncher

unchy \ən-chē \bunchy, crunchy, punchy

uncial \ ən-sē-əl \ uncial, internuncial

uncle \ əŋ-kəl \ nuncle, uncle, carbuncle, caruncle, furuncle, granduncle, peduncle

¹unco \ əŋ-kō \ bunco, junco, unco

²unco \ əŋ-kə \ see UNKAH

unct \ əŋt \ trunked, adjunct, conjunct, defunct, disjunct—*also pasts of verbs listed at* UNK

unction \ əŋ-shən \ function, junction, unction, compunction, conjunction, disjunction, dysfunction, injunction, malfunction, extreme unction

unctional \ əŋ-shnəl \ functional, junctional, dysfunctional

unctious \ əŋ-shəs \ compunctious, rambunctious

unctory \ əŋ-trē \ emunctory, perfunctory

uncture \ əŋ-chər \ juncture, puncture, acupuncture, conjuncture, disjuncture

uncular \ əŋ-kyə-lər \ avuncular, carbuncular, peduncular

unculus \ əŋ-kyə-ləs \ homunculus, ranunculus

¹und \ ənd \ bund, fund, gunned, obtund, refund, rotund, secund, cummerbund, orotund, pudibund, rubicund,

underfund—*also pasts of verbs listed at* UN

²und \ únd \ bund, dachshund

³und \ únt \ see ¹UNT

⁴und \ aúnd \ see ²OUND

unda \ ən-də \ osmunda, rotunda, barramunda, floribunda

undae \ ən-dē \ see UNDI

undant \ ən-dənt \ abundant, redundant, superabundant

unday \ ən-dē \ see UNDI

undays \ ən-dēz \ Mondays, Sundays, undies—*also plurals and possessives of nouns listed at* UNDI

undem \ ən-dəm \ see UNDUM

under \ ən-dər \ blunder, plunder, sunder, thunder, under, wonder, asunder, hereunder, thereunder

underous \ ən-drəs \ plunderous, wondrous, thunderous

undi \ ən-dē \ Monday, sundae, Sunday, Whitmonday, Whitsunday, barramundi, jaguarundi, Mrs. Grundy, salmagundi, coatimundi

undies \ ən-dēz \ see UNDAYS

undity \ ən-dət-ē \ fecundity, profundity, rotundity, moribundity, orotundity, rubicundity

undle \ ən-d³l \ bundle, rundle, trundle, unbundle

undness \ ən-nəs \ see ONENESS

undum\ən-dəm\condom,
corundum, ad eundem,
Carborundum

undy\ən-dē\see UNDI

une\ün\see ¹OON

uneless\ün-ləs\see OONLESS

uner\ü-nər\see OONER

unes\ünz\see OONS

¹ung\əŋ\bung, clung, dung,
flung, hung, lung, pung,
rung, slung, sprung, strung,
stung, sung, swung, tongue,
tung, wrung, young, among,
far-flung, high-strung,
unstrung, unsung, adder's-
tongue, double-tongue, triple-
tongue, overhung, overstrung,
underslung

²ung\ůŋ\Sung, Nibelung,
geländesprung,
Götterdämmerung

ungal\ən-gəl\see UNGLE

unge\ənj\lunge, plunge,
sponge, expunge

unged\ənd\see ONGUED

ungeon\ən-jən\donjon,
dungeon, spongin

¹unger\ən-jər\lunger, plunger,
sponger, expunger

²unger\əŋ-gər\see ¹ONGER

ungible\ən-jə-bəl\fungible,
inexpungible

ungle\əŋ-gəl\bungle, fungal,
jungle, pungle

ungo\əŋ-gō\fungo, mungo

ungous\əŋ-gəs\fungous,
fungus, humongous

ungry\ən-grē\see ONGERY

ungus\əŋ-gəs\see UNGOUS

ungy\ən-jē\grungy, spongy

unha\ü-nə\see UNA

uni\ü-nē\see OONY

unia\ün-yə\petunia, vicuña

unic\ü-nik\eunuch, Punic,
runic, tunic

unicate\ü-ni-kət\tunicate,
excommunicate

union\ən-yən\bunion,
grunion, onion, ronyon,
trunnion, Paul Bunyan

¹unish\ən-ish\Hunnish, punish

²unish\ü-nish\see OONISH

unit\ü-nət\see UNATE

unitive\ü-nət-iv\punitive,
unitive

unity\ü-nət-ē\unity,
community, disunity,
immunity, impunity,
importunity, opportunity

unk\əŋk\bunk, chunk, clunk,
drunk, dunk, flunk, funk,
gunk, hunk, junk, monk,
plunk, punk, shrunk, skunk,
slunk, spunk, stunk, sunk,
thunk, trunk, chipmunk,
debunk, Podunk, punch-
drunk, quidnunc

unkah\əŋ-kə\punkah, unco

unkard\əŋ-kərd\bunkered,
drunkard, Dunkard, hunkered

unked\əŋt\see UNCT

unken \əŋ-kən\ drunken, pumpkin, shrunken, sunken

unker \əŋ-kər\ bunker, clunker, Dunker, flunker, hunker, junker, lunker, plunker, younker, debunker, spelunker

unkie \əŋ-kē\ see UNKY

unks \əŋs\ hunks, quincunx—*also plurals and possessives of nouns and third singular presents of verbs listed at* UNK

unky \əŋ-kē\ chunky, clunky, donkey, flunky, funky, gunky, Hunky, junkie, junky, monkey, punkie, punky, spunkie, spunky

unless \ən-ləs\ runless, sonless, sunless

unn \ən\ see UN

unnage \ən-ij\ dunnage, tonnage

unned \ənd\ see ¹UND

unnel \ən-ᵊl\ funnel, gunnel, gunwale, runnel, trunnel, tunnel

unner \ən-ər\ cunner, gunner, runner, scunner, stunner, tonner, forerunner, front-runner, gunrunner, roadrunner, rumrunner

unnery \ən-rē\ gunnery, nunnery

unness \ən-nəs\ see ONENESS

unning \ən-iŋ\ cunning, running, stunning

unnion \ən-yən\ see UNION

unnish \ən-ish\ see ¹UNISH

unny \ən-ē\ bunny, funny, gunny, honey, money, runny, sonny, sunny, tunny

uno \ü-nō\ Juno, numero uno

unster \ən-stər\ Muenster, punster

¹unt \ünt\ dachshund, exeunt

²unt \ənt\ see ¹ONT

untal \ənt-ᵊl\ see UNTLE

unter \ənt-ər\ blunter, bunter, chunter, grunter, hunter, punter, shunter, confronter, headhunter, pothunter, witch-hunter

unting \ənt-iŋ\ bunting, wanting, head-hunting, witch-hunting—*also present participles of verbs listed at* ¹ONT

untle \ənt-ᵊl\ frontal, gruntle, confrontal, disgruntle, contrapuntal

unty \ənt-ē\ punty, runty

unwale \ən-ᵊl\ see UNNEL

unx \əŋs\ see UNKS

uny \ü-nē\ see OONY

unyan \ən-yən\ see UNION

uoth \ü-əs\ see EWESS

¹uoy \ü-ē\ see EWY

²uoy \ói\ see OY

uoyance \ü-əns\ see UENCE

uoyancy \ói-ən-sē\ see OYANCY

uoyant \ói-ənt\ see OYANT

up \əp\ cup, dup, hup, pup,

scup, sup, tup, up, yup,
backup, balls-up, bang-up,
beat-up, blowup, breakup,
brush up, buildup, built-up,
call-up, catch-up, change-up,
checkup, chin-up, cleanup,
close-up, cock-up, crack-up,
cutup, dried-up, dustup,
eggcup, eyecup, faceup,
flare-up, foul-up, frame-up,
getup, giddap, grown-up,
hang-up, heads-up, hepped
up, het up, holdup, hookup,
hopped-up, jam-up, kickup,
kingcup, lash-up, lay-up,
lead-up, letup, line up,
linkup, lockup, lookup, louse
up, made-up, makeup,
markup, matchup, mix-up,
mixed-up, mock-up, mop-up,
mug up, nip-up, one-up,
pasteup, pickup, pileup,
pinup, pop-up, pull-up,
punch-up, push-up, put-up,
re-up, roundup, run-up,
scaleup, screwup, send-up,
setup, shack up, shake-up,
shape-up, shook-up, shoot up,
sign up, sit-up, slap-up,
slipup, smashup, speedup,
stand-up, start-up, step up,
stepped-up, stickup, stuck-up,
sum-up, sunup, take-up,
teacup, thumbs-up, tie-up,
toss-up, touch-up, trumped-
up, tune-up, turnup, walk-up,
warm-up, washed-up,
washup, windup, workup,
wrap-up, write-up, belly up,
buttercup, cover-up, follow-
up, higher-up, hurry-up, pick-
me-up, pony up, runner-up,
seven-up, shoot-em-up,
summing-up, up-and-up,
wickiup, Johnny jump-up,
sunny-side up

upa \ ü-pə \ pupa, stupa
upas \ ü-pəs \ see UPUS
upboard \ əb-ərd \ see UBBARD
upe \ üp \ see ¹OOP
upel \ ü-pəl \ see ²UPLE
upelet \ ü-plət \ see ²UPLET
uper \ ü-pər \ see OOPER
upi \ ü-pē \ see OOPY
upid \ ü-pəd \ Cupid, stupid
upil \ ü-pəl \ see ²UPLE
¹**uple** \ əp-əl \ couple, supple,
  quadruple, quintuple,
  sextuple, uncouple
²**uple** \ ü-pəl \ cupel, duple,
  pupil, scruple
³**uple** \ üp-əl \ supple, quadruple,
  quintuple, sextuple
¹**uplet** \ əp-lət \ couplet,
  gradruplet, quintuplet,
  sextuplet
²**uplet** \ ü-plət \ drupelet,
  quadruplet
uplicate \ ü-pli-kət \ duplicate,
  quadruplicate, quintuplicate,
  sextuplicate
upor \ ü-pər \ see OOPER

uppance \ əp-əns \ threepence, twopence, comeuppance

upper \ əp-ər \ crupper, scupper, supper, upper, stand-upper

uppie \ əp-ē \ see UPPY

¹**upple** \ üp-əl \ see ³UPLE

²**upple** \ əp-əl \ see ¹UPLE

uppy \ əp-ē \ cuppy, guppy, puppy, yuppie

upt \ əpt \ abrupt, corrupt, disrupt, erupt, irrupt, incorrupt, interrupt—*also pasts of verbs listed at* UP

upter \ əp-tər \ corrupter, disrupter, interrupter

uptible \ əp-tə-bəl \ corruptible, eruptible, irruptible, incorruptible, interruptible

uption \ əp-shən \ abruption, corruption, disruption, eruption, irruption, interruption

uptive \ əp-tiv \ corruptive, disruptive, eruptive, irruptive, interruptive

upus \ ü-pəs \ croupous, lupus, upas

uque \ ük \ see UKE

¹**ur** \ ōr \ see ¹ORE

²**ur** \ ùr \ see ¹URE

³**ur** \ ər \ see ¹EUR

ura \ ùr-ə \ dura, durra, Jura, sura, surah, bravura, caesura, datura, tamboura, tempura, aqua pura, appoggiatura, coloratura, camera obscura

urable \ ùr-ə-bəl \ curable, durable, thurible, endurable, incurable, insurable, perdurable

uracy \ ùr-ə-sē \ curacy, obduracy

urae \ ùr-ē \ see ¹URY

urah \ ùr-ə \ see URA

ural \ ùr-əl \ crural, jural, mural, neural, plural, puerile, rural, caesural, commissural, extramural, intramural

uralist \ ùr-ə-ləst \ muralist, pluralist, ruralist

urance \ ùr-əns \ durance, assurance, endurance, insurance, coinsurance, reassurance, reinsurance

urate \ ùr-ət \ curate, turret, obdurate, barbiturate

urb \ ərb \ see ERB

¹**urban** \ ər-bən \ bourbon, rurban, turban, turbine, urban, exurban, suburban, interurban

²**urban** \ ùr-bən \ bourbon, rurban

urber \ ər-bər \ Berber, disturber

urbia \ ər-bē-ə \ exurbia, suburbia

urbid \ ər-bəd \ turbid, verbid

urbine \ ər-bən \ see ¹URBAN

urbit \ ər-bət \ burbot, sherbet, turbit, turbot

urble \ ər-bəl \ see ERBAL

urbot \ ər-bət \ see URBIT

urcate\ər-kət\see IRCUIT

urch\ərch\birch, church, curch, lurch, perch, search, smirch, besmirch, research, unchurch

urchin\ər-chən\birchen, urchin

urchly\ərch-lē\churchly, virtually

¹**urd**\ûrd\see ¹URED

²**urd**\ərd\see IRD

urdane\ərd-ᵊn\see URDEN

urden\ərd-ᵊn\burden, guerdon, lurdane, verdin, disburden, unburden, overburden

urder\ərd-ər\see ERDER

urderer\ərd-ər-ər\murderer, verderer

urdle\ərd-ᵊl\curdle, girdle, hurdle, engirdle

urdu\ər-dü\see ERDU

urdum\ərd-əm\see IRDUM

urdy\ərd-ē\birdie, sturdy, wordy, hurdy-gurdy

¹**ure**\ûr\Boer, boor, bourg, cure, dour, ewer, fewer, lure, moor, Moor, poor, pure, sewer, skewer, spoor, stour, sure, tour, whore, your, you're, abjure, adjure, allure, amour, Ashur, assure, brochure, ceinture, cocksure, coiffure, conjure, contour, couture, demure, detour, dirt-poor, endure, ensure,

Exmoor, faubourg, Fraktur, grandeur, gravure, guipure, hachure, immure, impure, insure, inure, kultur, land-poor, langur, ligure, manure, mature, mohur, obscure, parure, perdure, procure, secure, siddur, tambour, tandoor, tenure, Uighur, unmoor, velour, velure, amateur, aperture, armature, blackamoor, carrefour, carte du jour, coinsure, commissure, confiture, connoisseur, coverture, cubature, curvature, cynosure, debouchure, embouchure, epicure, filature, forfeiture, garniture, geniture, green-manure, haute couture, immature, insecure, ligature, manicure, overture, paramour, pedicure, plat du jour, portraiture, prelature, premature, quadrature, reassure, Reaumur, reinsure, saboteur, sepulture, sequitur, signature, simon-pure, sinecure, soup du jour, tablature, temperature, troubadour, white amur, vavasour, Yom Kippur, candidature, caricature, discomfiture, distemperature, divestiture, entablature, entrepreneur, expenditure,

imprimatur, investiture,
literature, miniature,
musculature, nomenclature,
nonsequitur, primogeniture,
ultraminiature

²**ure**\ùr-ē\see ¹URY

urean\ùr-ē-ən\see URIAN

ureau\ùr-ō\see URO

¹**ured**\ùrd\gourde, Kurd, urd,
assured, steward,
underinsured—*also pasts of
verbs listed at* ¹URE

²**ured**\ərd\see IRD

urely\ùr-lē\buirdly, poorly,
purely, surely, cocksurely,
demurely, impurely,
maturely, obscurely,
immaturely, insecurely,
prematurely

urement\ùr-mənt\allurement,
immurement, inurement,
procurement, securement

uren\ùr-ən\see ²URIN

ureous\ùr-ē-əs\see URIOUS

¹**urer**\ùr-ər\curer, führer,
furor, furore, juror, lurer,
tourer, abjurer, assurer,
insurer, manurer, procurer,
tambourer, coinsurer,
reinsurer—*also comparatives
of adjectives listed at* ¹URE

²**urer**\ər-ər\see ERRER

¹**urety**\ùr-ət-ē\see URITY

²**urety**\ùrt-ē\see URTI

urf\ərf\kerf, scurf, serf, surf,
turf, enserf, bodysurf

urfy\ər-fē\Murphy, scurfy,
turfy

urg\ərg\see ERG

urge\ərj\dirge, merge, purge,
scourge, serge, splurge,
spurge, surge, urge, verge,
converge, deterge, diverge,
emerge, immerge, resurge,
submerge, upsurge,
dramaturge

urgence\ər-jəns\see ERGENCE

urgency\ər-jən-sē\see
ERGENCY

urgent\ər-jənt\urgent,
assurgent, convergent,
detergent, divergent,
emergent, insurgent,
resurgent, preemergent

urgeon\ər-jən\burgeon,
sturgeon, surgeon, virgin

¹**urger**\ər-gər\burgher, turgor,
cheeseburger, hamburger,
Limburger

²**urger**\ər-jər\see ERGER

urgery\ərj-rē\see ERJURY

¹**urgh**\ər-ə\see ¹OROUGH

²**urgh**\ər-ō\see ¹URROW

urgher\ər-gər\see ¹URGER

urgic\ər-jik\see ERGIC

urgical\ər-ji-kəl\surgical,
liturgical, theurgical,
dramaturgical

urgid\ər-jəd\turgid, synergid

urgle\ər-gəl\burgle, gurgle

urgor\ər-gər\see ¹URGER

urgy \ ər-jē \ clergy, dramaturgy, metallurgy

uri \ ů-rē \ see ¹URY

¹**urial** \ ů-rē-əl \ curial, urial, Uriel, mercurial, seigneurial, tenurial, entrepreneurial

²**urial** \ er-ē-əl \ see ARIAL

urian \ ů-rē-ən \ durian, Hurrian, Arthurian, centurion, epicurean

uriance \ ů-rē-əns \ see URIENCE

uriant \ ů-rē-ənt \ see URIENT

¹**urible** \ ů-rə-bəl \ see URABLE

²**urible** \ ər-ə-bəl \ see ERABLE

uric \ ů-rik \ uric, mercuric, sulfuric

urid \ ů-rəd \ lurid, murid

urie \ ů-rē \ see ¹URY

uriel \ ů-rē-əl \ see ¹URIAL

urience \ ů-rē-əns \ prurience, luxuriance

urient \ ů-rē-ənt \ esurient, luxuriant, parturient

¹**urier** \ er-ē-ər \ see ERRIER

²**urier** \ ů-rē-ər \ see ¹OURIER

uriere \ ů-rē-ər \ see ¹OURIER

¹**urin** \ ər-ən \ burin, murrain

²**urin** \ ů-rən \ burin, Huron, urine, Belgian Tervuren

urine \ ů-rən \ see ²URIN

uring \ ů-riŋ \ during, mooring, touring

urion \ ů-rē-ən \ see URIAN

urious \ ů-rē-əs \ curious, furious, spurious, incurious, injurious, luxurious,

penurious, perjurious, sulfureous, usurious

uris \ ů-rəs \ see URUS

urist \ ů-rəst \ purist, tourist, manicurist, pedicurist, caricaturist, chiaroscurist, miniaturist—*also superlatives of adjectives listed at* ¹URE

urity \ ů-rət-ē \ purity, surety, futurity, impurity, maturity, obscurity, security, immaturity, insecurity, prematurity

urk \ ərk \ see ¹ORK

¹**urka** \ ər-kə \ charka, circa, Gurkha, mazurka

²**urka** \ ů-kə \ Gurkha, mazurka

urke \ ərk \ see ¹ORK

urker \ ər-kər \ see ¹ORKER

urkey \ ər-kē \ see ERKY

¹**urkha** \ ů-kə \ see ²URKA

²**urkha** \ ər-kə \ see ¹URKA

urki \ ər-kē \ see ERKY

urky \ ər-kē \ see ERKY

url \ ərl \ see ¹IRL

urled \ ərld \ see ORLD

urlew \ ərl-ü \ curlew, purlieu

urlieu \ ərl-ü \ see URLEW

urlin \ ər-lən \ see ERLIN

urling \ ər-liŋ \ curling, hurling, sterling—*also present participles of verbs listed at* ¹IRL

urlish \ ər-lish \ churlish, girlish

urly \ ər-lē \ burley, burly, curly, early, girlie, hurly, knurly,

pearly, squirrely, surly,
swirly, twirly, whirly, hurly-
burly

urman \ ər-mən \ see ERMAN

urmity \ ər-mət-ē \ see IRMITY

urmur \ ər-mər \ firmer,
infirmer, murmur, termer,
wormer

urn \ ərn \ burn, churn, curn,
earn, erne, fern, kern, learn,
pirn, quern, spurn, stern,
tern, terne, turn, urn, yearn,
adjourn, astern, attorn,
casern, concern, discern,
downturn, epergne, eterne,
extern, heartburn, intern,
lucerne, nocturn, nocturne,
outturn, return, sauternes,
secern, sojourn, sunburn,
unlearn, upturn, U-turn,
windburn, Comintern,
overturn, taciturn, unconcern

urnable \ ər-nə-bəl \ burnable,
discernible, returnable,
indiscernible

urnal \ ərn-ᵊl \ see ERNAL

urne \ ərn \ see URN

urned \ ərnd \ burned, durned,
concerned, unearned,
unlearned, well-turned,
windburned—*also pasts of
verbs listed at* URN

urner \ ər-nər \ burner, earner,
turner, discerner, returner,
afterburner

urnery \ ər-nə-rē \ see ERNARY

urney \ ər-nē \ see ¹OURNEY

urnian \ ər-nē-ən \ see ERNIAN

urnish \ ər-nish \ burnish,
furnish

urnt \ ərnt \ see EARNT

urnum \ ər-nəm \ sternum,
alburnum, laburnum,
viburnum

uro \ uṙ-ō \ bureau, duro, euro,
enduro, maduro, politburo,
chiaroscuro

uron \ uṙ-ən \ see ²URIN

uror \ uṙ-ər \ see ¹URER

urore \ uṙ-ər \ see ¹URER

urous \ uṙ-əs \ see URUS

urp \ ərp \ burp, chirp, slurp,
stirp, twerp, usurp

urphy \ ər-fē \ see URFY

urple \ ər-pəl \ purple, empurple

urplice \ ər-pləs \ see URPLUS

urplus \ ər-pləs \ surplice,
surplus

urps \ ərps \ see IRPS

urr \ ər \ see ¹EUR

¹urra \ uṙ-ə \ see URA

²urra \ ər-ə \ see ¹OROUGH

urrage \ ər-ij \ see OURAGE

urragh \ ər-ə \ see ¹OROUGH

urrain \ ər-ən \ see ¹URIN

urral \ ər-əl \ see ERRAL

urrant \ ər-ənt \ see URRENT

urre \ ər \ see ¹EUR

urred \ ərd \ see IRD

urrence \ ər-əns \ concurrence,
conference, deterrence,

incurrence, occurrence, transference

urrent \ ər-ənt \ currant, current, weren't, concurrent, crosscurrent, decurrent, deterrent, occurrent, recurrent, susurrant, countercurrent, undercurrent, supercurrent

urrer \ ər-ər \ see ERRER

urret \ ùr-ət \ see URATE

urrey \ ər-ē \ see URRY

urrian \ ùr-ē-ən \ see URIAN

urrie \ ər-ē \ see URRY

urrier \ ər-ē-ər \ courier, currier, furrier, hurrier, worrier—*also comparatives of adjectives listed at* URRY

urring \ ər-iŋ \ furring, shirring, stirring, skiöring, unerring— *also present participles of verbs listed at* ¹EUR

urrish \ ər-ish \ see OURISH

¹**urro** \ ər-ə \ see ¹OROUGH

²**urro** \ ər-ō \ see ¹URROW

¹**urrow** \ ər-ō \ borough, burgh, burro, burrow, furrow, thorough

²**urrow** \ ər-ə \ see ¹OROUGH

urry \ ər-ē \ blurry, burry, curry, flurry, furry, dhurrie, gurry, hurry, murrey, scurry, slurry, spurrey, surrey, whirry, worry, hurry-scurry

ursa \ ər-sə \ see ERSA

ursal \ ər-səl \ see ¹ERSAL

ursar \ ər-sər \ see URSOR

ursary \ ərs-rē \ bursary, cursory, mercery, nursery, anniversary

urse \ ərs \ see ERSE

ursed \ ərst \ see URST

ursement \ ər-smənt \ see ERCEMENT

urser \ ər-sər \ see URSOR

ursery \ ərs-rē \ see URSARY

ursion \ ər-zhən \ see ¹ERSION

ursionist \ ərzh-nəst \ see ERSIONIST

ursive \ ər-siv \ see ERSIVE

ursor \ ər-sər \ bursar, cursor, mercer, nurser, purser, worser, disburser, disperser, precursor, rehearser, reverser, traverser

ursory \ ərs-rē \ see URSARY

urst \ ərst \ burst, cursed, durst, erst, first, thirst, verst, worst, wurst, accursed, airburst, athirst, cloudburst, emersed, feetfirst, headfirst, outburst, sunburst, liverwurst—*also pasts of verbs listed at* ERSE

ursus \ ər-səs \ see ERSUS

¹**ursy** \ ər-sē \ see ERCY

²**ursy** \ əs-ē \ see USSY

¹**urt** \ ùrt \ Stuart, yurt

²**urt** \ ərt \ see ¹ERT

urtain \ ərt-ᵊn \ see ERTAIN

urtal \ ərt-ᵊl \ see ERTILE

urtenance \ ərt-ᵊn-əns \ see ERTINENCE

urtenant \ ərt-nənt \ see IRTINENT

urter \ ərt-ər \ see ERTER

urtesy \ ərt-ə-sē \ see OURTESY

urthen \ ər-<u>th</u>ən \ burthen,
  earthen

urther \ ər-<u>th</u>ər \ further,
  murther

urti \ ùrt-ē \ pretty, surety,
  Trimurti

urtium \ ər-shəm \ nasturtium,
  sestertium

urtive \ ərt-iv \ see ERTIVE

urtle \ ərt-ᵊl \ see ERTILE

urton \ ərt-ᵊn \ see ERTAIN

urture \ ər-chər \ see IRCHER

uru \ ùr-ü \ guru, kuru

urus \ ùr-əs \ urus, Arcturus,
  mercurous, sulfurous, sui
  juris, tinea cruris

urve \ ərv \ see ERVE

urved \ ərvd \ see ERVED

urviness \ ər-vē-nəs \ see
  ERVINESS

urvy \ ər-vē \ curvy, nervy,
  scurvy, topsy-turvy

¹ury \ ùr-ē \ brewery, curie,
  fleury, fury, houri, Jewry,
  jury, Bhojpuri, de jure,
  tandoori, lusus naturae

²ury \ er-ē \ see ¹ARY

urze \ ərz \ see ERS

urzy \ ər-zē \ see ERSEY

¹us \ əs \ bus, buss, crus, cuss,
  fuss, muss, must, plus, pus,
  Russ, thus, truss, us, airbus,
  concuss, cost-plus, discuss,

nonplus, percuss, railbus,
  untruss, autobus, blunderbuss,
  microbus, minibus

²us \ ü \ see ¹EW

³us \ üs \ see ¹USE

⁴us \ üsh \ see OUCHE

⁵us \ üz \ see ²USE

¹usa \ ü-sə \ Medusa, Appaloosa

²usa \ ü-zə \ Medusa, Arethusa

usable \ ü-zə-bəl \ fusible,
  losable, usable, abusable,
  diffusible, excusable,
  infusible, reusable,
  transfusible, inexcusable,
  irrecusable

¹usal \ ü-səl \ streusel, occlusal

²usal \ ü-zəl \ foozle, fusil,
  ouzel, snoozle, streusel,
  tousle, accusal, bamboozle,
  occlusal, perusal, refusal

usc \ əsk \ see USK

uscan \ əs-kən \ buskin, Tuscan,
  Etruscan, molluscan

uscat \ əs-kət \ see USKET

uscle \ əs-əl \ see USTLE

uscular \ əs-kyə-lər \ muscular,
  corpuscular, crepuscular,
  majuscular

uscule \ əs-kyül \ crepuscule,
  opuscule

¹use \ üs \ crouse, crus, cruse,
  deuce, douce, douse, goose,
  juice, loose, moose, mousse,
  noose, nous, puce, rhus, ruse,
  Russ, schuss, sluice, spruce,
  truce, use, Zeus, abstruse,

abuse, adduce, Atreus, burnoose, caboose, Cayuse, Cepheus, ceruse, conduce, couscous, deduce, diffuse, disuse, educe, effuse, excuse, footloose, induce, misuse, mongoose, Morpheus, negus, obtuse, Orpheus, papoose, Pelcus, Perseus, prepuce, produce, profuse, Proteus, recluse, reduce, refuse, retuse, reuse, Sanctus, seduce, Tereus, Theseus, traduce, transduce, unloose, vamoose, Betelgeuse, calaboose, charlotte russe, introduce, mass-produce, Odysseus, Prometheus, reproduce, self-abuse, Typhoeus, hypotenuse

²**use** \ üz \ blues, booze, bruise, choose, cruise, cruse, Druze, flews, fuse, lose, muse, news, ooze, roose, ruse, schmooze, snooze, trews, use, whose, abuse, accuse, amuse, bemuse, chanteuse, chartreuse, coiffeuse, confuse, contuse, danseuse, defuse, diffuse, disuse, effuse, enthuse, excuse, illuse, infuse, masseuse, misuse, perfuse, peruse, recluse, refuse, reuse, suffuse, transfuse, vendeuse,

Betelgeuse, disabuse, interfuse, p's and q's

used \ üzd \ used, confused, underused—*also pasts of verbs listedat* ²USE

useless \ ü-sləs \ juiceless, useless

user \ ü-zər \ boozer, bruiser, chooser, cruiser, doozer, loser, snoozer, user, abuser, accuser, amuser, diffuser, excuser, infuser, peruser

¹**ush** \ əsh \ blush, brush, crush, flush, gush, hush, lush, mush, plush, rush, shush, slush, squush, thrush, tush, airbrush, bulrush, hairbrush, hush-hush, inrush, nailbrush, onrush, paintbrush, sagebrush, toothbrush, uprush, bottlebrush, underbrush

²**ush** \ ush \ bush, mush, push, shush, squoosh, swoosh, tush, whoosh, ambush, rosebush, thornbush

¹**usher** \ əsh-ər \ blusher, brusher, crusher, gusher, musher, rusher, usher, fourflusher, goldrusher—*also comparatives of adjectives listed at* ¹USH

²**usher** \ ush-ər \ pusher, ambusher

ushi \ ush-ē \ see ²USHY

ushing \ əsh-iŋ \ onrushing,
toothbrushing, unblushing

¹**ushy** \ əsh-ē \ brushy, gushy,
mushy, plushy, rushy, slushy

²**ushy** \ üsh-ē \ bushy, cushy,
mushy, pushy, sushi

usian \ ü-zhən \ see USION

¹**usible** \ ü-sə-bəl \ see UCIBLE

²**usible** \ ü-zə-bəl \ see USABLE

usic \ ü-zik \ music, Tungusic

usil \ ü-zəl \ see ²USAL

using \ əs-iŋ \ busing, trussing,
antibusing

usion \ ü-zhən \ fusion, affusion,
allusion, Carthusian,
collusion, conclusion,
confusion, contusion,
delusion, diffusion, effusion,
elusion, exclusion, extrusion,
illusion, inclusion, infusion,
intrusion, Malthusian,
obtrusion, occlusion,
perfusion, prelusion,
profusion, prolusion,
protrusion, reclusion,
seclusion, transfusion,
Venusian, disillusion,
malocclusion

usionist \ üzh-nəst \ fusionist,
diffusionist, exclusionist,
illusionist

usity \ ü-sət-ē \ see UCITY

usive \ ü-siv \ abusive, allusive,
amusive, collusive,
conclusive, conducive,
delusive, diffusive, effusive,
elusive, exclusive, extrusive,
illusive, inclusive, intrusive,
obtrusive, occlusive,
prelusive, protrusive,
reclusive, inconclusive

usk \ əsk \ brusque, cusk, dusk,
husk, musk, rusk, tusk,
subfusc

usker \ əs-kər \ busker, husker,
tusker

usket \ əs-kət \ muscat, musket

uskie \ əs-kē \ see USKY

uskin \ əs-kən \ see USCAN

usky \ əs-kē \ dusky, husky,
muskie, musky

usly \ əs-lē \ pussley, thusly

usoe \ ü-sō \ trousseau, whoso,
Robinson Crusoe

usory \ üs-ə-rē \ delusory,
prolusory, illusory

usque \ əsk \ see USK

¹**uss** \ ús \ puss, Russ, schuss,
chartreuse, sea puss,
sourpuss, octopus, platypus

²**uss** \ üs \ see ¹USE

³**uss** \ əs \ see ¹US

ussant \ əs-ᵊnt \ mustn't,
discussant

ussate \ əs-ət \ see USSET

usse \ üs \ see ¹USE

ussel \ əs-əl \ see USTLE

usset \ əs-ət \ gusset, russet,
decussate

ussian \ əsh-ən \ see USSION

ussing \ əs-iŋ \ see USING

ussion \ əsh-ən \ Russian,

concussion, discussion,
percussion, repercussion

ussive \ əs-iv \ jussive, tussive,
concussive, percussive,
repercussive

ussle \ əs-əl \ see USTLE

ussley \ əs-lē \ see USLY

ussy \ əs-ē \ fussy, hussy,
mussy, pursy, pussy

¹ust \ əst \ bust, crust, dost, dust,
gust, just, lust, must, musth,
rust, thrust, trust, wast,
adjust, adust, august,
combust, degust, disgust,
distrust, encrust, entrust,
mistrust, piecrust, robust,
stardust, upthrust, antitrust,
dryasdust, unitrust,
wanderlust—*also pasts of
verbs listed at* ¹US

²ust \ əs \ see ¹US

ustable \ əs-tə-bəl \ see USTIBLE

ustard \ əs-tərd \ bustard,
custard, mustard—*also pasts
of verbs listed at* USTER

usted \ əs-təd \ disgusted,
maladjusted—*also pasts of
verbs listed at* ¹UST

uster \ əs-tər \ bluster, buster,
cluster, duster, fluster, luster,
muster, thruster, adjuster,
blockbuster, combustor,
deluster, gangbuster,
lackluster, sodbuster,
trustbuster, antitruster,
filibuster

ustful \ əst-fəl \ lustful, thrustful,
trustful, distrustful

usth \ əst \ see ¹UST

ustian \ əs-chən \ see USTION

ustible \ əs-tə-bəl \ adjustable,
combustible, incombustible

ustic \ əs-tik \ fustic, rustic

ustion \ əs-chən \ fustian,
combustion

ustious \ əs-chəs \ robustious,
rumbustious

ustive \ əs-tiv \ adjustive,
combustive, maladjustive

ustle \ əs-əl \ bustle, hustle,
muscle, mussel, rustle,
trestle, tussle, crepuscle

ustn't \ əs-ᵊnt \ see USSANT

ustom \ əs-təm \ custom,
frustum, accustom,
disaccustom

ustor \ əs-tər \ see USTER

ustrious \ əs-trē-əs \ illustrious,
industrious

ustrous \ əs-trəs \ blustrous,
lustrous

ustule \ əs-chül \ frustule,
pustule

ustum \ əs-təm \ see USTOM

usty \ əs-tē \ busty, crusty,
dusty, fusty, gusty, lusty,
musty, rusty, trusty

usy \ iz-ē \ see IZZY

¹ut \ ət \ but, butt, cut, glut, gut,
hut, jut, mutt, nut, putt, rut,
scut, shut, slut, smut, soot,
strut, tut, ut, what, abut,

beechnut, catgut, chestnut,
clean-cut, clear-cut, cobnut,
cockshut, crosscut,
groundnut, haircut, locknut,
peanut, pignut, rebut, rotgut,
shortcut, somewhat, tut-tut,
uncut, walnut, woodcut,
butternut, hazelnut,
scuttlebutt, undercut,
uppercut, open-and-shut

²ut \ ü \ see ¹EW

³ut \ üt \ see UTE

⁴ut \ ət \ see ¹OOT

uta \ üt-ə \ likuta, valuta

utable \ üt-ə-bəl \ mutable,
scrutable, suitable,
commutable, computable,
disputable, immutable,
inscrutable, permutable,
statutable, executable,
incommutable, incomputable,
indisputable, irrefutable,
prosecutable, substitutable

utage \ üt-ij \ see ¹OOTAGE

utal \ üt-ᵊl \ see UTILE

utan \ üt-ᵊn \ cutin, gluten,
mutine, Teuton, Laputan,
rambutan, highfalutin

utant \ üt-ᵊnt \ mutant, disputant,
pollutant

utative \ üt-ət-iv \ putative,
commutative, imputative

¹utch \ əch \ clutch, crutch,
cutch, dutch, Dutch, grutch,
hutch, much, scutch, smutch,

such, touch, nonesuch,
retouch, overmuch

²utch \ úch \ butch, putsch

utcher \ əch-ər \ scutcher,
retoucher

utchy \ əch-ē \ see UCHY

ute \ üt \ boot, bruit, brut, brute,
butte, chute, cloot, coot,
cute, flute, fruit, glout, hoot,
jute, Jute, loot, lute, moot,
mute, newt, pood, root, rout,
route, scoot, scute, shoot,
snoot, soot, suit, suite, toot,
tout, ut, Ute, acute, astute,
beetroot, birthroot, bloodroot,
breadfruit, butut, cahoot,
cheroot, clubroot, commute,
compute, confute, crapshoot,
deaf-mute, depute, dilute,
dispute, elute, en route,
enroot, folkmoot, freeboot,
galoot, grapefruit, hardboot,
hirsute, imbrute, impute,
jackboot, jackfruit, jumpsuit,
kashruth, lawsuit, minute,
nonsuit, offshoot, outshoot,
Paiute, pantsuit, permute,
playsuit, pollute, pursuit,
recruit, refute, repute, salute,
seaboot, snowsuit, solute,
sunsuit, swimsuit, taproot,
tracksuit, transmute, uproot,
volute, absolute, Aleut,
arrowroot, attribute,
bandicoot, bitterroot,
bodysuit, boilersuit,

bumbershoot, constitute,
convolute, destitute,
disrepute, dissolute, evolute,
execute, gingerroot, institute,
involute, kiwifruit, malamute,
overshoot, parachute,
persecute, prosecute,
prostitute, qiviut, resolute,
restitute, revolute, subacute,
substitute, troubleshoot,
undershoot, electrocute,
Hardecanute, irresolute,
reconstitute

uted\üt-əd\see ¹OOTED

utee\üt-ē\see ¹OOTY

utely\üt-lē\cutely, mutely,
accutely, astutely, minutely,
absolutely, dissolutely,
irresolutely

uten\üt-ᵊn\see UTAN

uteness\üt-nəs\cuteness,
glutenous, glutinous,
muteness, mutinous,
acuteness, diluteness,
hirsuteness, absoluteness,
destituteness, dissoluteness,
irresoluteness

utenist\üt-ᵊn-əst\lutenist,
Teutonist

utenous\üt-nəs\see UTENESS

uteous\üt-ē-əs\beauteous,
duteous, gluteus, luteous

uter\üt-ər\neuter, fluter,
hooter, looter, pewter, rooter,
router, scooter, shooter,
souter, suiter, suitor, tooter,

tutor, accoutre, commuter,
computer, confuter,
crapshooter, diluter, disputer,
freebooter, peashooter,
recruiter, saluter,
sharpshooter, six-shooter,
trapshooter, two-suiter, zoot-
suiter, coadjutor, executor,
instituter, persecutor,
prosecutor, prostitutor,
troubleshooter,
microcomputer,
minicomputer—*also
comparatives of adjectives
listed at* UTE

utes\üts\see OOTS

uteus\üt-ē-əs\see UTEOUS

¹uth\üt\see UTE

²uth\üth\see ²OOTH

uthful\üth-fəl\ruthful, truthful,
youthful, untruthful

uthless\üth-ləs\ruthless,
toothless

utia\ü-shə\fuchsia, minutia

utian\ü-shən\see UTION

utic\üt-ik\maieutic, scorbutic,
toreutic, hermeneutic,
parachutic, propaedeutic,
therapeutic

utical\üt-i-kəl\cuticle,
hermeneutical, pharmaceutical

uticle\üt-i-kəl\see UTICAL

utie\üt-ē\see ¹OOTY

utiful\üt-i-fəl\beautiful, dutiful

utile\üt-ᵊl\brutal, cuittle,

footle, futile, tootle, utile,
inutile

utin \üt-ᵊn\ see UTAN

utine \üt-ᵊn\ see UTAN

uting \üt-iŋ\ fluting, luting,
suiting, sharpshooting,
trapshooting

¹**utinous** \üt-ᵊn-əs\ glutinous,
mutinous

²**utinous** \üt-nəs\ see UTENESS

utiny \üt-ᵊn-ē\ mutiny, scrutiny

ution \ü-shən\ ablution,
capuchin, Confucian,
dilution, elution, locution,
pollution, solution,
absolution, allocution,
attribution, comminution,
consecution, constitution,
contribution, convolution,
destitution, devolution,
diminution, dissolution,
distribution, elocution,
evolution, execution,
institution, involution,
lilliputian, persecution,
prosecution, prostitution,
resolution, restitution,
retribution, revolution,
Rosicrucian, substitution,
antipollution, circumlocution,
electrocution, irresolution,
maldistribution,
reconstitution, redistribution

utionist \ü-shnəst\
devolutionist, elocutionist,

evolutionist, revolutionist,
redistributionist

utish \üt-ish\ brutish, Vutish

utist \üt-əst\ chutist, flutist,
absolutist, parachutist,
therapeutist—*also superlatives
of adjectives listed at* UTE

utive \üt-iv\ dilutive,
constitutive, persecutive,
substitutive

utlass \ət-ləs\ cutlass, gutless

utler \ət-lər\ butler, cutler,
sutler

utless \ət-ləs\ see UTLASS

utlet \ət-lət\ cutlet, nutlet

utment \ət-mənt\ hutment,
abutment

utney \ət-nē\ chutney, gluttony

uto \üt-ō\ Pluto, putto, Basuto,
cornuto, tenuto, sostenuto

utor \üt-ər\ see UTER

utriment \ü-trə-mənt\
nutriment, accoutrement

uts \əts\ see UTZ

utsch \ủch\ see ²UTCH

utsy \ət-sē\ gutsy, klutzy

utt \ət\ see ¹UT

uttal \ət-ᵊl\ see UTTLE

utte \üt\ see UTE

uttee \ət-ē\ see UTTY

¹**utter** \ət-ər\ butter, clutter,
cutter, flutter, gutter, mutter,
putter, scutter, shutter,
splutter, sputter, strutter,
stutter, utter, abutter, aflutter,
haircutter, price-cutter,

rebutter, stonecutter,
unclutter, woodcutter
²**utter** \út-ər\ see ¹OOTER
uttery \ət-ə-rē\ buttery,
fluttery, spluttery
¹**utti** \üt-ē\ see ¹OOTY
²**utti** \üt-ē\ see ²OOTY
utting \ùt-iŋ\ see ¹OOTING
uttish \ət-ish\ ruttish, sluttish
uttle \ət-ᵊl\ cuittle, scuttle,
shuttle, subtile, subtle,
rebuttal
utto \üt-ō\ see UTO
uttock \ət-ək\ buttock, futtock
utton \ət-ᵊn\ button, glutton,
mutton, keybutton, unbutton,
leg-of-mutton
uttony \ət-nē\ see UTNEY
utty \ət-ē\ butty, gutty, jutty,
nutty, puttee, putty, rutty,
smutty, sooty
utum \üt-əm\ scutum, sputum
uture \ü-chər\ blucher, future,
moocher, suture
uty \üt-ē\ see ¹OOTY
utz \əts\ futz, klutz, nuts—*also
plurals and possessives of
nouns and third singular
presents of verbs listed at* ¹UT
utzy \ət-sē\ see UTSY
uu \ü\ see ¹EW
uvial \ü-vē-əl\ fluvial, pluvial,

alluvial, colluvial, diluvial,
eluvial
uvian \ü-vē-ən\ alluvion,
diluvian, vesuvian, Vesuvian,
postdiluvian, antediluvian
uvion \ü-vē-ən\ see UVIAN
uvium \ü-vē-əm\ alluvium,
colluvium, effluvium,
eluvium
¹**ux** \əks\ crux, flux, lux, tux,
afflux, aw-shucks, conflux,
deluxe, efflux, influx, redux,
reflux—*also plurals and
possessives of nouns and third
singular presents of verbs
listed at* UCK
²**ux** \üks\ see ²OOKS
¹**uxe** \üks\ see ¹OOKS
²**uxe** \üks\ see ²OOKS
³**uxe** \əks\ see ¹UX
uxion \ək-shən\ see UCTION
uy \ī\ see ¹Y
uyot \ē-ō\ see ²IO
uyp \īp\ see IPE
uze \üz\ see ²USE
uzz \əz\ see ¹EUSE
uzzi \ü-zē\ see OOZY
uzzle \əz-əl\ guzzle, muzzle,
nuzzle, puzzle
uzzler \əz-lər\ guzzler, puzzler,
gas-guzzler
uzzy \əz-ē\ fuzzy, muzzy,
scuzzy

y

¹y\ī\ai, ay, aye, bi, buy, by,
bye, chi, cry, die, dry, dye,
eye, fie, fly, fry, guy, hi,
hie, high, i, I, lie, lye, my,
nigh, phi, pi, pie, ply, pry,
psi, rye, scythe, sei, shy,
sigh, sky, sly, spry, spy, sty,
Tai, Thai, thigh, thy, tie, try,
vie, why, wry, wye, xi, Y ,
aby, agley, air-dry, ally, anti,
apply, assai, awry, aye-aye,
Bacchae, Baha'i, banzai,
barfly, Belgae, belie, bigeye,
birds-eye, blackfly, blow-dry,
blowby, blowfly, blue-sky,
bone-dry, bonsai, botfly,
buckeye, bugeye, bulls-eye,
bye-bye, canaille, catchfly,
cat's-eye, cockeye, cockshy,
comply, cross-eye, deadeye,
decry, deep-fry, deerfly,
defy, deny, descry, drip-dry,
elhi, Eli, espy, firefly, fish-
eye, flyby, forby, freeze-dry,
frogeye, gadfly, gallfly, GI,
good-bye, greenfly, grisaille,
gun-shy, Hawkeye, hereby,
hi-fi, hog-tie, horsefly,
housefly, imply, jai alai,
July, knee-high, lanai, lay-by,
Levi, magpie, mao-tai,
Masai, medfly, Moirai,
mooneye, nearby, necktie,

nisi, outbye, outcry, oxeye,
panfry, Parcae, piece-dye,
pigsty, pinkeye, pop eye,
potpie, quasi, rabbi, re-try,
red-eye, rely, reply, rough-
dry, sci-fi, semi, serai,
shanghai, shoofly, shut-eye,
sky-high, small-fry, sockeye,
stand by, standby, stir-fry,
supply, swing-by, terai, test-
fly, thereby, tie-dye, titi,
tongue-tie, two-ply, untie,
walleye, watcheye, well-nigh,
whereby, whitefly, wise guy,
worms-eye, acidify, Adonai,
alibi, alkali, amplify, apple-
pie, argufy, basify, beautify,
butterfly, by-and-by, calcify,
certify, citify, clarify,
classify, cockneyfy, codify,
crucify, cut-and-dry, damnify,
damselfly, dandify, deify,
densify, dignify, dobsonfly,
do-or-die, dragonfly, edify,
falsify, fortify, frenchify,
fructify, gasify, Gemini,
gentrify, glorify, goggle-eye,
goldeneye, gratify, Haggai,
hexerei, horrify, Iceni,
justify, lignify, liquefy,
Lorelei, lullaby, magnify,
Malachi, modify, mollify,
Mordecai, mortify, multi-ply,

multiply, mummify, mystify,
nazify, nitrify, notify, nullify,
occupy, ossify, overbuy,
overfly, overlie, pacify,
passerby, peccavi, petrify,
PPI, preachify, prettify,
prophesy, purify, putrefy,
qualify, quantify, ramify,
rarefy, ratify, RBI, rectify,
reify, res gestae, resupply,
Russify, samurai, sanctify,
satisfy, scarify, semidry,
signify, simplify, sine die,
specify, speechify, stratify,
stultify, stupefy, Tenebrae,
terrify, testify, tigereye,
typify, uglify, ultrahigh,
underlie, unify, Veneti,
verify, versify, vilify, vinify,
vitrify, vivify, acetify, a
priori, beatify, decertify,
declassify, demystify,
denazify, detoxify, Dioscuri,
disqualify, dissatisfy,
diversify, electrify,
exemplify, facetiae, Helvetii,
humidify, identify,
indemnify, intensify,
objectify, personify,
preoccupy, reliquiae, reunify,
revivify, rigidify, saponify,
solemnify, solidify, syllabify,
transmogrify, undersupply,
vox populi, a fortiori,
caravanserai, corpus delicti,
deacidify, dehumidify, modus

vivendi, nolle prosequi,
oversimplify, amicus curiae,
curriculum vitae, modus
operandi
²y \ē\ see ¹EE
ya \ē-ə\ see ¹IA
yable \ī-ə-bəl\ see ¹IABLE
yad \ī-əd\ dryad, dyad, naiad,
    sayyid, triad, hamadryad,
    jeremiad
yan \ī-ən\ see ¹ION
ybe \īb\ see ¹IBE
ybris \ī-brəs\ see IBROUS
ycad \ī-kəd\ cycad, spiked
yce \īs\ see ¹ICE
¹ych \ik\ see ICK
²ych \īk\ see ²IKE
yche \ī-kē\ see ¹IKE
ychnis \ik-nəs\ see ICKNESS
ycian \ish-ən\ see ITION
ycin \īs-ᵊn\ see ¹ISON
¹ycle \ī-kəl\ cycle, Michael,
    recycle, epicycle, hemicycle,
    kilocycle, motorcycle,
    unicycle
²ycle \ik-əl\ see ICKLE
ycler \ik-lər\ see ICKLER
yde \īd\ see ¹IDE
ydian \id-ē-ən\ see IDIAN
ye \ī\ see ¹Y
yeable \ī-ə-bəl\ see ¹IABLE
yed \īd\ see ¹IDE
yer \īr\ see ¹IRE
yfe \īf\ see IFE
ygamous \ig-ə-məs\ see
    IGAMOUS

ygamy \ig-ə-mē\ see IGAMY
ygia \ī-jə\ see IJAH
ygian \ij-ən\ Phrygian, pidgin, pigeon, smidgen, stygian, wigeon, religion, Cantabrigian, irreligion, callipygian
ygma \ig-mə\ see IGMA
ygnet \ig-nət\ cygnet, signet
ygnus \ig-nəs\ see IGNESS
ygos \ī-gəs\ see YGOUS
ygous \ī-gəs\ gigas, azygos, callipygous, hemizygous, homozygous, steatopygous
ygrapher \ig-rə-fər\ see IGRAPHER
ygraphist \ig-rə-fəst\ see IGRAPHIST
ygyny \ij-ə-nē\ see IGINE
ying \ī-iŋ\ crying, flying, lying, trying, high-flying, low-lying, outlying, undying, terrifying, underlying
yke \īk\ see ²IKE
yked \īkt\ see ¹IKED
yl \ēl\ see ²EAL
ylar \ī-lər\ see ILAR
yle \īl\ see ¹ILE
ylem \ī-ləm\ see ILUM
yler \ī-lər\ see ILAR
ylet \ī-lət\ see ILOT
yli \ē-lē\ see EELY
ylic \il-ik\ see ILIC
yling \ī-liŋ\ see ¹ILING
ylla \il-ə\ see ²ILLA
yllable \il-ə-bəl\ see ILLABLE

yllary \il-ə-rē\ see ILLARY
yllic \il-ik\ see ILIC
yllis \il-əs\ see ILLUS
yllium \il-ē-əm\ see ILIUM
¹yllo \ē-lō\ see ²ILO
²yllo \ī-lō\ see ¹ILO
ylum \ī-ləm\ see ILUM
ylus \ī-ləs\ see ILUS
yly \ī-lē\ dryly, highly, maile, riley, shyly, slyly, smiley, wily, wryly, life of Riley
ym \im\ see ¹IM
yma \ī-mə\ Chaima, cyma
yman \ī-mən\ see IMEN
ymathy \im-ə-thē\ see IMOTHY
ymbal \im-bəl\ see IMBLE
ymbalist \im-bə-ləst\ cymbalist, symbolist
ymbol \im-bəl\ see IMBLE
ymbolist \im-bə-ləst\ see YMBALIST
yme \īm\ see ¹IME
ymeless \īm-ləs\ see IMELESS
ymen \ī-mən\ see IMEN
ymer \ī-mər\ see ¹IMER
¹ymic \ī-mik\ thymic, enzymic
²ymic \im-ik\ gimmick, mimic, bulimic, acronymic, antonymic, eponymic, homonymic, matronymic, metonymic, patronymic, synonymic, toponymic
ymical \im-i-kəl\ see IMICAL
ymie \ī-mē\ see IMY
ymion \im-ē-ən\ see IMIAN
ymity \im-ət-ē\ see IMITY

ymmetry \im-ə-trē\ see IMETRY

ymn \im\ see ¹IM

ymnal \im-nəl\ criminal, hymnal

ymp \imp\ see IMP

ympan \im-pən\ pimping, tympan

ymph \imf\ lymph, nymph

ymric \im-rik\ Cymric, limerick

ymry \əm-rē\ see ²UMMERY

ymus \ī-məs\ see IMIS

ymy \ī-mē\ see IMY

yn \in\ see ¹IN

ynah \ī-nə\ see ¹INA

ynast \ī-nəst\ see ¹INIST

¹ynch \inch\ see INCH

²ynch \iŋk\ see INK

yncher \in-chər\ see INCHER

ynd \īnd\ see ¹IND

yndic \in-dik\ see INDIC

yne \īn\ see ¹INE

yness \ī-nəs\ see ¹INUS

ynic \in-ik\ see ²INIC

ynical \in-i-kəl\ see INICAL

ynth \inth\ see INTH

ynx \iŋs\ see INX

yone \ī-ə-nē\ see YONY

yony \ī-ə-nē\ bryony, Alcyone

yp \ip\ see IP

ypal \ī-pəl\ typal, disciple, archetypal, prototypal

ype \īp\ see IPE

yper \ī-pər\ see IPER

ypey \ī-pē\ see IPY

yph \if\ see IFF

yphen \ī-fən\ hyphen, siphon

yphic \if-ik\ see IFIC

yphony \if-ə-nē\ see IPHONY

ypic \ip-ik\ typic, philippic, genotypic, holotypic, stereotypic

yping \ī-piŋ\ see IPING

ypo \ī-pō\ hypo, typo

ypress \ī-prəs\ cypress, viperous

ypse \ips\ see IPS

ypso \ip-sō\ see IPSO

ypsy \ip-sē\ gypsy, Gypsy, tipsy

ypt \ipt\ see IPT

yptian \ip-shən\ see IPTION

yptic \ip-tik\ cryptic, diptych, styptic, triptych, ecliptic, elliptic, apocalyptic

ypy \ī-pē\ see IPY

yr \ir\ see ²EER

yra \ī-rə\ Lyra, naira, bell-lyra, hegira, hetaira, palmyra, spirogyra

yral \ī-rəl\ see IRAL

yrant \ī-rənt\ see IRANT

yre \īr\ see ¹IRE

yreal \ir-ē-əl\ see ERIAL

yria \ir-ē-ə\ see ¹ERIA

yriad \ir-ē-əd\ see ERIOD

yrian \ir-ē-ən\ see ¹ERIAN

yric \ī-rik\ pyric, oneiric, panegyric, see ²ERIC

yrical \ir-i-kəl\ see ²ERICAL

¹yrie \ir-ē\ see EARY

²yrie \ī-rē\ see ¹IARY

yrist \ir-əst\ see ¹ERIST

yrium \ir-ē-əm\ see ERIUM

¹yro \ī-rō\biro, gyro, Gyro, tyro

²yro \ir-ō\ see ³ERO

yron \ir-ən\ see IREN

yrrh \ər\ see ¹EUR

yrrha \ir-ə\ see ²ERA

yrrhic \ir-ik\ see ²ERIC

yrrhus \ir-əs\ see EROUS

yrse \ərs\ see ERSE

yrsus \ər-səs\ see ERSUS

yrtle \ərt-ᵊl\ see ERTILE

yrup \ər-əp\ see IRRUP

yrupy \ər-ə-pē\ see IRRUPY

yrus \ī-rəs\ see IRUS

ysail \ī-səl\ see ¹ISAL

ysch \ish\ see ¹ISH

yse \īs\ see ¹ICE

¹ysia \ish-ə\ see ITIA

²ysia \izh-ə\ see ISIA

¹ysian \is-ē-ən\Piscean, Odyssean, Dionysian

²ysian \ish-ən\ see ITION

³ysian \izh-ən\ see ISION

⁴ysian \ī-sē-ən\ see ¹ISCEAN

ysical \iz-i-kəl\physical, quizzical, metaphysical

ysis \ī-səs\ see ISIS

ysm \iz-əm\ see ISM

ysmal \iz-məl\dismal, abysmal, baptismal, cataclysmal, catechismal

yson \is-ᵊn\ see ¹ISON

yss \is\ see ISS

yssal \is-əl\ see ISTLE

yssean \is-ē-ən\ see ¹YSIAN

ysseus \ish-əs\ see ¹ICIOUS

yssum \is-əm\ see ISSOME

yssus \is-əs\ see ISSUS

yst \ist\ see ²IST

ystal \is-tᵊl\ see ISTAL

¹yster \is-tər\ see ISTER

²yster \ī-stər\ see ¹EISTER

ystery \is-trē\ see ISTORY

ystic \is-tik\ see ISTIC

ystical \is-ti-kəl\ see ISTICAL

ystine \is-tən\ see ISTON

¹ysus \ē-səs\ see ESIS

²ysus \ī-səs\ see ISIS

yta \īt-ə\ see ¹ITA

yte \īt\ see ¹ITE

yterate \it-ə-rət\ see ITERATE

ytes \īt-ēz\ see ITES

¹ythe \ī\ see ¹Y

²ythe \ith̲\ see ¹ITHE

ythia \ith-ē-ə\lithia, forsythia, stichomythia

ythian \ith-ē-ən\Pythian, Scythian

ythmic \ith̲-mik\rhythmic, arrhythmic, eurythmic, logarithmic

ytic \it-ik\ see ITIC

ytical \it-i-kəl\ see ITICAL

ytics \it-iks\ see ITICS

yting \īt-iŋ\ see ITING

yve \īv\ see ¹IVE

yx \iks\ see ¹IX

yxia \ik-sē-ə\ see IXIA

yxie \ik-sē\ see IXIE

yze \īz\ see IZE